Georges Mandel
and the Third Republic

Georges Mandel
and the Third Republic.

John M. Sherwood

Stanford University Press, Stanford, California, 1970

Sources of photographs and illustrations: Nos. 1, 2, 4, 7, 8, 10, 19,
René Dazy; Nos. 11, 12, 14, 16, 22, Keystone Press Agency;
Nos. 5, 6, 9, 15, Société de la Propriété Artistique et des Dessins
et Modèles; Nos. 3, 17, H. Roger Viollet; No. 13, United
Press International, Inc.; No. 18, Association pour la Diffusion
des Arts Graphiques et Plastiques.

Stanford University Press, Stanford, California
© 1970 by the Board of Trustees of the Leland Stanford Junior University
Printed in the United States of America
ISBN 0-8047-0731-6 LC 74-97916

*To my wife Joan
and our children Michelle,
Barbara, and Jacqueline*

Preface

*Des personnalités politiques de l'entre-deux-guerres, Georges Mandel
était assurément l'une des plus curieuses et des plus puissantes. Il
avait su se faire haïr, il avait su se faire aimer. Personne ne pouvait
demeurer à son égard indifférent.*

Victor Bucaille

GEORGES MANDEL, one of the leading political figures of the Third
French Republic, is best remembered today for his opposition to Nazi
Germany during the 1930's and his refusal to accept defeat in 1940. After
Marshal Pétain assumed power, those in favor of continued resistance hoped
that Mandel might be able to keep France in the war by rallying the colonies. Instead, he was arrested and imprisoned by Pétain's government. Thus
the role of savior that had seemed destined for Mandel passed to the relatively unknown General de Gaulle, whereas Mandel, after four years in
prison, was to be assassinated by French Fascists in 1944.

Mandel began his career in 1903 as a young journalist on *L'Aurore*, the
Radical daily published by Georges Clemenceau, whom he was to serve in
various capacities for sixteen years. When Clemenceau became prime minister in 1917, Mandel became his chief personal assistant for internal affairs.
In this post he was responsible for the surveillance of the press, the repression of defeatist and pacifist movements, the prosecution of suspected traitors, and the control of strikes and demonstrations. His activities won for
him a reputation as a capable but Machiavellian leader, and earned for him
as well the hatred of many influential politicians. These men blocked his
return to power for nearly fifteen years after Clemenceau's retirement from
politics in 1920. During that time Mandel had two main aims: to force
Germany to abide by the Treaty of Versailles, and to establish a viable
two-party system in France. Tempering some of the most abrasive aspects
of his personality, he finally received a cabinet post in 1934, and won general acclaim because of the efficiency of his administration and because of
his astute use of the press. He frequently remarked how easy it was "to
shape opinion, to inspire in people reactions which they think are their
own, but which in reality we have suggested."

After 1934, except under the Popular Front, Mandel was a fixture in
every government. For many people, he became one of the hopes of the
country, which was threatened externally by Nazi Germany, and inter-

nally by the impact of the depression and by ideological cleavages that destroyed any semblance of national unity. After the German breakthrough
in May 1940, when Prime Minister Paul Reynaud made some dramatic
changes in his government, Léon Blum stated that the most striking of
these changes was "the installation at the Ministry of the Interior of M.
Georges Mandel, whose foresight, authority, and firmness are legendary
and almost mysterious." And the Royalist Charles Maurras declared that
"like all of his predecessors, he will be confronted with an impossible situation. But he is perhaps the only man who can handle it without hurting
the regime."

Mandel was an enigma in his own time. He remains an enigma today,
for he is remembered both as a courageous patriot and martyr and as a
consummate politician and manipulator who inspired fear, hatred, and
grudging respect, but rarely liking or friendship. Indeed, his entire life was
filled with such contrasts. He was first of all what Albert Memmi considers
an anomaly, a conservative and nationalist Jew. He was also a firm republican who had an authoritarian temperament and a committed parliamentarian who avoided debate in Parliament. Moreover, in the course of his
public life he was at one time or another either allied with or supported
by every group in French politics from the Action Française to the Communists. In short, he was one of the most elusive figures of the Third Republic, a constant embarrassment to friend and enemy alike, who would
have preferred to praise or damn without qualification, but were always
forced instead to explain away some portion of his career.

A biography of Georges Mandel presents special difficulties. There are
almost no letters, personal papers, or archival materials available. More than
thirty boxes of his books and papers were seized by the Germans in 1940
and never recovered. Presumably they were lost in the confusion and destruction of 1945. Because of this loss, because he seldom wrote personal
letters, and because few of those close to him wrote memoirs, the personal
side of Mandel's life seems beyond recapture. I have therefore concentrated
on his public life, describing both the major issues in which he was caught
up, and the minor intrigues and maneuvers to which he devoted so much
attention, for these not only show how he operated, but explain much of
the influence he exercised over his colleagues.

The sources for the public part of Mandel's career are numerous, if not
always satisfactory. There are Mandel's own speeches and articles, various
memoirs of the period, and many people who remember him. Most useful
of all are the newspapers of the time. They were frequently biased and
inaccurate, but their writers were well informed, and they contain infor-

mation available nowhere else. To use them profitably, one need only keep in mind both the bias of the individual newspaper and the bias of the specific writer.

There remain many aspects of Mandel's life about which one would like to know more: his early years; the source of his financial support in his later career; his relations with Clemenceau, Flandin, Herriot, Laval, Millerand, Poincaré, Reynaud, and Tardieu; and the role he played in various events, particularly as Clemenceau's assistant during World War I. But some of these areas seem likely to remain obscure, at least until new documents are found.

In the course of my research, I have become indebted to many people, especially to Fritz Stern and Philip Williams who first suggested the topic in a seminar at Columbia University, to Rudolph Binion and John Cairns for their careful reading and constructive criticism of the manuscript, to René Rémond for his aid and advice while I was in Paris, and to all of the men and women who kindly granted me interviews. I am also indebted to Louis Cadars, Maurice Duverger, François Goguel, Marc Granet, Henri Michel, Guy Raïssac, and Mlle Josée Lassalle and the staff of the *Sud-Ouest* in Bordeaux for aid, advice, and introductions; to Pierre Gaxotte and Emile Liquard for their letters; to Louis-Georges Planes for allowing me to quote from his unpublished memoirs; to one of Mandel's former assistants, who preferred to remain anonymous, for answering questions for several hours; and to one of Mandel's former associates, who also preferred to remain anonymous, for allowing me to see various notes and documents concerning Mandel.

I am grateful as well to Mrs. Autumn Simmons of the Stanford University Press for editorial assistance, to Peter Larmour, James A. Leith, and Michael R. Marrus for having taken the trouble to locate documents and pictures, or to check information for me in Paris, and to Mlle Francine Douchand for typing the manuscript. A special debt of gratitude is owed to Shepard Clough for many things, including his guidance of the later stages of research and the personal interest he showed in me as in all his students. Financial assistance enabling me to spend two years in Paris was provided by the Fulbright Commission and Columbia University. The Queen's University Research Committee helped pay for the typing and indexing and for the cost of reproducing the illustrations.

Finally, I would like to thank my family and friends for their help and encouragement over many years.

J.M.S.

Contents

Eight pages of pictures follow p. 194

Georges Mandel
and the Third Republic

1. Louis Rothschild

*On ne cloître plus les Israélites, on ne tend plus les chaînes aux
extrémités des rues qu'ils habitent, mais on crée autour d'eux
une atmosphère hostile, atmosphère de défiance, de haine latente, de
préjugés inavoués et d'autant plus puissante, un ghetto autrement
terrible que celui auquel on pourrait échapper par la révolte ou
par l'exil. Cette animosité se dissimule et cependant le juif
intelligent, et il n'est pas rare, la perçoit; il sent l'impression
d'un mur que les adversaires ont dressé entre lui et ceux au
milieu desquels il vit.*

Bernard Lazare

GEORGES MANDEL—or to call him by his real name, Louis Rothschild—
was born on June 5, 1885, in a small villa in Chatou, a town near Paris,
where his family was spending the summer months. His father Edmond ran
a clothing establishment in the Sentier district of Paris and made the
family comfortable, if not well-to-do. According to Mandel's friend Georges
Wormser, it was a petit bourgeois family "in moderately easy circumstances."[1] Little is known about them because they led normal, obscure
lives.

His grandfather Adolphe Abraham Rothschild was born in Sulzbach,
Bavaria, in 1814, moved to Paris before he was thirty years old, and there
married Nanette Nether, a native Parisian. At his death in 1864 he was
survived by at least one son, Edmond, born in Paris in 1843, who married
Hermine Mandel from Marmoutier in Alsace. There were three sons from
this marriage—Louis, Adrien, and Robert—of whom Louis was the eldest.

The facts about his birth and family are simple and easily verified,[2] but
they were the subject of serious controversy throughout his life. His enemies
sometimes claimed that he was the son of Clemenceau or of the banker
Rothschild.[3] In 1920, when passion against Germany was still heated, a
Socialist deputy seriously accused him of having been born in Frankfurt.[4]
The year before, the leftist weekly *Le Progrès Civique*, among whose con-
tributors were such respectable scholars as Alphonse Aulard, Charles Seig-
nobos, and Charles Gide, had defied Mandel to produce a copy of his birth
certificate.[5] One writer claims to have checked the archives of the city hall
at Chatou, and to have found no record of his birth.[6] When Xavier Vallat,
Vichy Commissioner of Jewish Affairs, was arrested in 1944, a copy of
Mandel's birth certificate was found among his papers.[7]

Some of this curiosity was only natural. In 1902, when he was seventeen, he began to write articles for left-wing journals for which the name Rothschild sounded far too affluent. He decided to adopt his mother's maiden name, Mandel, and changed his first name from Louis to Georges in order to avoid confusion with his uncle, Louis Mandel.[8] Clearly his motive was not to conceal his Jewish ancestry, and indeed in a few years his real name became widely known.

Something more sinister than curiosity, however, lay behind the constant attempt to prove he was not of French birth. Ever since the Revolution, the Jews had enjoyed full civil liberties, and although they still suffered from social discrimination, they had become progressively more integrated into French life. Most of them preferred to ignore the prejudice that still existed, and placed their faith in a process of gradual enlightenment. By and large, they were strongly patriotic and greatly attached to the Republic. Julien Benda has written of his parents, who were contemporaries of Mandel's mother and father:

From their Jewish families, without any formal teaching, they imbibed a respect for the Republic with the air that they breathed. They transmitted it to me in the same way that they had received it....

The patriotism of my parents was, I believe, that of many French Jews of the time, and perhaps also of today. My parents were profoundly attached to France ..., but that attachment was intellectual; it contained no instinctive, physical, or irrational element. What my father loved in France was its civilization, its moralists ..., the great liberal tradition, the Revolution....

My father's attachment to the Revolution was due in part to his gratitude that it had emancipated his race, and given the Jews civil and political liberties. ... About the use we should make of that liberty that had been granted to us, my father had a conception shared by an entire class of Jews at the time. Since the modern state had opened all doors to us, admitted us to all the competitive examinations, we should profit from the opportunity that had finally been given to us to prove by our ability to work and by our intellectual gifts that we were not the inferior race depicted by our detractors, but on the contrary a race of the first order....[9]

In the 1880's for the first time in nearly a century, the trust of French Jews in their country was seriously shaken. Early in the decade there had been sporadic anti-Semitic attacks in books and newspapers, but nothing had prepared them for Edouard Drumont's venomous *La France juive*, which appeared in 1886 and sold 100,000 copies within a year. In this and later books, Drumont blamed all of France's ills on the Jews. His ideas found a ready audience among the Catholics and Monarchists, who were at that time looking for someone to blame for the continued success of the Republic and their own progressive exclusion from participation in it.[10] Nevertheless,

Drumont might have been only a passing phenomenon had it not been for the Dreyfus Affair (1894–1906).

Opinion in France was inflamed by the case of this Jewish officer convicted of treason by a military court, and imprisoned on Devil's Island. The affair became one more episode in the struggle between republicans and Monarchists. The Catholics, who had gradually been evicted from public employment after the establishment of the Republic in 1875, regarded the army as their last bastion and strongly supported it throughout the case. In part at least, they attributed their continued decline in power and influence to Jewish plots, and launched an anti-Semitic campaign. During the elections of 1898, the Catholic daily *La Croix* declared, "We will vote only for candidates who will undertake to propose, support, and vote for a law forbidding Jews to vote, or to hold any military or civil office in the state."[11]

It is clear from Mandel's later career that he was strongly influenced both by this revival of anti-Semitism at the end of the century and by the type of Jewish upbringing described by Benda. From his family he seems to have inherited an unshakable devotion to France and an overwhelming personal ambition. This ambition was from the first directed toward politics. His brother Adrien recalls that by the age of twelve, Mandel was delivering speeches to his family on the issues of the day and commenting on what he would do when he became prime minister. For his thirteenth birthday, he asked his father for a subscription to the *Journal Officiel* as a reward for his work at school.[12] A frail constitution accentuated his early intellectual interests. A friend described him as a "sickly and puny" young man with an aversion to all physical exercise. The countryside held no interest for him. What he loved was reading and meditating alone in a library. His reading, like his ambition, was from the first directed toward politics, and history. The writers of the Restoration and the July Monarchy, Montalembert, Guizot, and Thiers, so influenced him that throughout his life they reappeared in his conversation and speeches. His favorite historical figures were all statesmen, among whom he considered Richelieu the greatest.[13]

But if his Jewish background helped to foster his patriotism and his desire to play a role in public affairs, it also made his playing that role much less likely. Many of his countrymen did not look on Jews as real Frenchmen. That he strongly felt this residual form of discrimination is clear from a number of things. In later years, unlike Léon Blum, Mandel was usually careful not to surround himself with assistants who were Jewish, and he never admitted that his grandfather had been born outside France. He always emphasized that his mother came from the Jewish community of Alsace, one of the oldest in France.[14] In his desire to provide himself with a more acceptable pedigree, he sometimes went to absurd lengths. During the 1919 election campaign, for instance, he claimed that his grandfather had fought in the Revolution of 1830 and had his name inscribed on the Colonne de Juillet in the Place de la Bastille. When opponents pointed out that there was neither a Mandel nor a Rothschild among the names engraved on the Colonne, Mandel ingeniously asserted that his grandfather's name had been inscribed *inside* the monument.[15] Moreover, he once said that thirty members of his family had fallen on the field of battle defending France, but on another occasion this became ten members of his family.[16] In a speech he stated that two of his brothers had been killed in World War I. Later he changed this to one brother. The truth was that neither of his brothers had been killed.[17]

If Mandel was worried that his family had not shed enough blood for the country, he was equally defensive about his mediocre scholastic record. He first attended a private school, the Ecole Springer, before transferring to the Lycée Condorcet, only a few minutes from the family's apartment at 17 rue Chateaudun. The Lycée Condorcet was one of the most famous of the Paris secondary schools. Many of the leading political and literary figures of modern France—François Guizot, Hippolyte Taine, Joseph Caillaux, André Tardieu, Marcel Proust, André Malraux, Henri Massis, and Jean Cocteau—were trained in its classrooms. At the turn of the century, it was predominantly bourgeois in tone. The sons of doctors, lawyers, and intellectuals who attended the school seem to have regarded the four or five Jewish students among them as interlopers.[18] In any case, Mandel made few friends among his classmates, who were put off by his solemn air, his impeccable dress and his haughty aloofness.[19] He refused to call his fellow students by their first names and coldly addressed them instead as "Monsieur."[20]

Mandel entered the Lycée in November 1901, weeks after the semester had started, and somewhat behind the other students in preparation. His inadequate background in philosophy was evident to his professors, as was his lack of interest in the sciences. He showed a natural aptitude only for history. At the beginning of the year his history instructor noted: "seems to be intelligent," and at the end awarded him the fourth prize. He made notable progress, particularly in philosophy, but not enough to pass the baccalaureate examination. Returning to the Lycée in the autumn of 1902 for another year of preparation, he studied first under the philosopher Léon Brunschvig, and then under Emile Chartier, better known as Alain, who replaced Brunschvig at mid-year. Chartier commented that Mandel had "a good mind"; "he speaks often and almost always to the point." He advised him to concentrate on improving his written work.[21]

After finishing at the Lycée in the spring of 1903, Mandel did not even consider going on for further studies, but immediately sought a position as a journalist. In later years, he became aware of his lack of the proper credentials in what Albert Thibaudet has called "la république des professeurs."[22] In 1923 he caused a furor in the Conseil Général de la Gironde when he tried to put his fellow councilors in their place by haughtily announcing that he knew what he was talking about, for he had once attended the Ecole Normale. When his opponents, who were tireless in checking his statements, revealed that they had been unable to find any record of his attendance at the school, Mandel disdainfully and untruthfully replied that he had been accepted with a special class but had resigned shortly afterward.[23]

There is no need to exaggerate the importance of these incidents, but they do indicate that Mandel was acutely, perhaps excessively, aware of anything in his background that might possibly be an impediment to his career. To compensate for his sense of social inferiority, his physical frailty, and his extremely youthful appearance, he adopted a formal mode of dress. What began as an affectation developed into a memorable style by which the French public was able to recognize him immediately. He was always faultlessly attired in the black suit, high stiff collar, and bowler hat fashionable in his youth. Mandel also tried to distinguish himself by an excessively polite manner of speaking that defied intimacy, by a scornful arrogance toward his colleagues, and particularly by a depth of knowledge of French politics and politicians that never failed to astonish. This knowledge was, in fact, so vast and detailed that he was frequently called the Fouché of the Third Republic. To Mandel as to Fouché, knowledge was more than the necessary prerequisite for the formulation of policy; it was power itself, power to manipulate men and ultimately to control events.

Unlike Fouché, however, Mandel never became a pure opportunist. Despite his complexes and his cynicism, which verged on misanthropy, he maintained his faith in France, which he once proudly said was his only religion,[24] and in the republican form of government, of which he became one of the outstanding defenders during the rising tide of authoritarianism in the 1930's. Mandel was equally determined to establish his own superiority and to preserve his country. It is part of his tragedy that his Jewish background, which seems to have inspired both ambitions, in the end helped prevent him from achieving either of them.

2. Georges Mandel

La politique, c'est l'art, la volonté, la passion de gouverner.

Louis Barthou

OF THE TWO ROADS to power under the Third Republic, law and journalism, Mandel decided very early that the latter was quicker and surer. In August 1902, shortly after his seventeenth birthday, he began to publish articles under the name of Georges Mandel in the republican daily *Le Siècle*. Mandel's father had been active in republican circles since the Second Empire,[1] and seems to have had some prominent friends, the most notable of whom was the Jewish politician and historian of the Dreyfus Affair, Joseph Reinach. It was through his intervention that Mandel was able to write for *Le Siècle*.[2]

Unlike many Jews of his class at the time, who, according to Léon Blum, "thought only of digging a hole in the ground to hide in,"[3] Mandel took this first opportunity to strike back at the French Catholics, the strongest supporters of the anti-Semitic movement. From August 1902 to June 1903, while still attending classes at the Lycée, Mandel contributed seven front-page articles to the paper. They reveal a naive and vehement anticlericalism: "Everywhere and always, it is the 'ministers of God,' monks of all sorts, who are engaged in the lowest sort of commerce and in the most vile practices, selling the bread of the soul as others sell the bread of the body."[4]

The articles were in no way remarkable, and after the paper changed hands in February 1903, only one of Mandel's contributions was accepted. Forced to turn to Joseph Reinach once again, Mandel this time received a recommendation to Georges Clemenceau, the Radical editor of *L'Aurore*.[5] Clemenceau had become the young man's idol. Mandel had carefully collected all of his articles and read all of his old speeches in the *Journal Officiel*.[6] He undoubtedly admired Clemenceau for the leading role he had played among the Dreyfusards. He was the one who, in 1898, had published Zola's famous letter "J'Accuse" in *L'Aurore*. Thereafter he attacked the government daily in its columns until Dreyfus won a retrial.

For the first twenty years of the Republic, Clemenceau had led the Radical republicans in the Chamber of Deputies, overthrowing cabinet after cabinet without ever coming to power himself. Because of a remote involvement in the Panama Canal scandal, his constituents had turned him out of Parliament in 1892. Thereafter, he turned to journalism to make a living, finally regaining national influence as a result of the Dreyfus Affair. In 1902 he won a seat in the Senate and reestablished himself as one of the leaders of the Radical Party.

Mandel had no difficulty obtaining a position on *L'Aurore*, for Clemenceau, like many editors of the time, casually recruited his staff on the basis of recommendations. Paid little or nothing, young journalists were expected to be satisfied with the opportunity to get their writing published and to make contacts in the political and literary world. Georges Gombault, François Albert, Emile Buré, and Paul Lévy all served apprenticeships with Mandel on *L'Aurore*. Through Albert, Mandel met other intellectuals, among whom were Robert de Jouvenel and Albert Bayet, and often dined with them in a café near Les Halles. Though changing political issues later pushed Albert and Bayet more to the left and Mandel more to the right, they maintained a sympathetic interest in each other's careers, more united by their common allegiance to the Republic than separated by their differences on policy.[7]

In the beginning, however, Mandel was a source of wonder and amusement to the rest of the staff. His first day at the paper was still remembered years later. "He was pale, slightly hunched, dressed entirely in black, and carried a heavy brief case under his arm...." He looked very strange to the other journalists, a rather Bohemian group, whose levity surprised him as much as his seriousness shocked them.[8] He was already dogmatic, peremptory and perfectly self-possessed.[9] Although his success at school had been limited, he had gained an extensive knowledge of political events that overflowed almost inexhaustibly in his conversation. Years later, Emile Buré remembered that "the history of the Third Republic had no secrets for him; there was never a factual or a chronological error in the speeches with which he willingly entertained us."[10] Even Clemenceau remarked sarcastically that Mandel "would know everything if he knew how to write."[11]

Mandel gave everyone he met the impression of being wealthy.[12] His mother provided him with the money to maintain the style of life he had adopted, as she would continue to finance his activities for some time to come.[13] Within a few years he would set himself up in a fashionable apartment, and, to the amusement of some of his friends, would even hire a personal secretary.[14]

Although he may have looked and occasionally acted like a young dandy, Mandel's very serious goal was to establish a foothold in the political world. He hoped to pursue this goal at *L'Aurore*, where Clemenceau was interested in little more than his daily editorial, and articles were assigned according to the inspiration of the moment. Anxious to prove himself, Mandel had only to wait for an older but less assiduous colleague to pass on an unwanted chore to him.[15] During the winter of 1903 he probably wrote brief news stories, but his name appeared only on occasional feature articles, most of which denounced the Church. There were also a few long, careful studies of Talleyrand and the Revolutionary period in which he showed a detailed knowledge of the literature.

His anticlericalism, of course, he shared with the rest of the staff. The back page of the paper advertised the "Bibliothèque anticléricale de *L'Aurore*," which sold such titles as *Les secrets des Jésuites, A bas le confessionnel*, and *Les crimes du cléricalisme*. Whatever the content of these books, Mandel matched them in ferocity. "Throughout fifteen centuries of power," he wrote, "the clergy have engaged in nothing but works of oppression and death."[16] His zeal was too much even for some of his colleagues. "We eat priests for breakfast every day around here," he was told, "so don't look so hungry."[17] By May 1904, his articles began to appear more frequently, and in June he was assigned to write a daily story on the Russo-Japanese War. Foreign and colonial affairs began to occupy his attention more and more, though he still occasionally wrote anticlerical articles. All of Mandel's articles, in contrast to those of his colleagues, were crammed with facts. After his summer vacations, which he seemed to spend in prolonged reading, he would write particularly detailed review articles analyzing political affairs in different countries throughout the world.

Mandel stayed at *L'Aurore* for three years, all the while aiming at much higher things. "For him," it was said, "*L'Aurore* was the antechamber of the Palais-Bourbon, of the Ministry of Foreign Affairs, or of the Ministry of the Interior. Through the sheer force of his will, his tenacity, and his patience, and despite his physical defects, of which he was well aware, he was determined to get into the Chamber of Deputies. After that, *quo non ascendam!*"[18]

His first opportunity to climb the political ladder came in March 1906 when Clemenceau accepted the ministry of the Interior in the Sarrien cabinet. Mandel was among the host of young journalists from *L'Aurore* who hoped to follow their editor into the government as secretaries, assistants, attachés or general factotums. Clemenceau took a number of his protégés with him, but refused to take Mandel, although Buré apparently interceded for him.[19] The story goes that he then simply installed himself as an assistant in Clemenceau's secretariat without so much as a nod of assent.[20] The truth is that he finally got a position on the recommendation of Albert Bayet's father-in-law, Alphonse Aulard, who was an old friend and associate of Clemenceau.[21]

He was assigned to the staff of Albert Sarraut, the young but influential director of the *Dépêche de Toulouse*, for whom Clemenceau had just created the office of under-secretary of the Interior. Sarraut remembers Mandel from their first meeting as a slender, almost frail, very correctly dressed young man with a striking face. His enormous forehead "seemed made to enclose a world of thought; under it shone deep-set direct eyes, which fixed on you with an acute intensity.... His voice was always calm, and he spoke with perfect elegance, yet without affectation." Sarraut said as well that Mandel had a brilliant mind and was a fountain of knowledge. "He had read everything, the philosophers, the moralists, the politicians and particularly the historians. He knew the history of France, especially that of the Third Republic, better than anyone else."[22]

Not expecting the cabinet to last for more than two months, Mandel applied himself to learning as much as he could about the business of government, in order, says a friend, "to become more quickly capable of conducting it himself one day."[23] His diligence was finally recognized and rewarded by Clemenceau, who attached Mandel to his own staff in June 1907, when Albert Sarraut resigned. Clemenceau, who was now prime minister, gave Mandel the very welcome duty of keeping him informed of what was taking place in the press and in Parliament. Mandel astonished the rest of the staff by his ability to give, without notes, the clearest, most precise, and most complete press résumés they had ever heard. By the end of such a summary, Clemenceau "had learned everything he needed to know to continue the political struggle of the day."[24]

In the afternoon, Mandel attended Parliament and talked to the representatives, trying to gather all the detailed information the government needed to avoid unexpected pitfalls. Clemenceau's grandson recalls that Mandel particularly enjoyed reporting what had taken place at the Chamber during the day. He seemed to know all about the deputies and senators and liked to add his own sarcastic comments to the day's political gossip.

Although he recognized Mandel's abilities, Clemenceau's grandson disliked him immediately without knowing why. "He was very nice to me, but I always felt like a rabbit in front of a serpent. I felt that he was so much superior to me, so much more intelligent, that I was never able to speak a word when he was there."[25]

There is no doubt that Mandel's personality aroused antagonism, as did his duties in Parliament, which left him open to the charge of spying. One day in the Chamber Emile Constant criticized the government. Two young assistants of ministers in Clemenceau's cabinet, Albert Favre and Jérôme Lévy, later congratulated him on his attack. The incident was reported to Clemenceau, and the two culprits, at first threatened with dismissal, were finally assigned to new tasks. Favre's previous chief, Emile Combes, and Maurice Berteaux, the popular and influential leader of the opposition to

Clemenceau within the Radical Party, had intervened with the Prime Minister to save them.

Shortly thereafter, seeing Mandel in the corridors of the Chamber, Berteaux accused him of having informed on Favre and Lévy. When Mandel denied the charge, Berteaux, a robust man with a violent temper, seized him by the ears and shoved him against a wall. With the upper portion of his body immobilized, Mandel responded in the only way possible—by kicking his antagonist. He then challenged Berteaux to a duel. The incident caused considerable comment. Although Clemenceau usually enjoyed duels and frequently gave duelling lessons to his young friends,[26] he forced Mandel to resign, not wanting to be even remotely involved in a fight with one of the most prominent deputies in the Chamber. The outcome of the incident was anticlimactic. Berteaux insisted that he had received satisfaction in striking Mandel and refused to fight. The duel was cancelled, and Mandel soon resumed his duties with the Prime Minister.[27]

If Clemenceau had once been reluctant to appoint Mandel, he would now have been reluctant to lose him, for he depended increasingly on his assistant's vast knowledge. Eventually, he "could no longer do without the living encyclopedia he had at his beck and call."[28] Yet the relationship between them was not so simple as this suggests. Clemenceau would often get so angry with Mandel that he would dismiss him, but the next day Mandel would return to work as if nothing had happened. He was, according to another of Clemenceau's assistants, the only one who was not afraid of Clemenceau and who often got the better of him.[29]

Mandel's chief rival for Clemenceau's favor was a young secretary named Alfred Roth, whom the Prime Minister had attached to his staff after observing his work in the prefectoral system. Their colleagues considered both of these young men to be "energetic, versatile, competent, extremely audacious, and capable of being brutal if necessary."[30] Their influence may be explained not only by their personal ability, but also by their willingness to concern themselves with the administrative details that Clemenceau gladly left to subordinates, provided their work caused no complaint in Parliament.

Roth soon won out in the competition, and ran the Ministry of the Interior within the limits set by Clemenceau.[31] Although he and Mandel had similar characters, their ambitions differed greatly. Having risen from the prefectoral system, Roth returned to it with a more important position after Clemenceau fell from power in 1909. Before he was thirty he had been named a prefect. Mandel, on the other hand, aimed at something higher than the administrative post that would have been his for the asking. He was not interested in moderate prestige, a good salary, and a safe pension. The road to success for him led through Parliament, and eventually to the government, to the seat of power, where he would be able to determine policy and not merely execute it. He was only twenty-four when Clemenceau's government was overthrown in July 1909, but having spent six years as a spectator of the political scene, he was eager to become a direct participant.

II

Undoubtedly Mandel had hoped that the Clemenceau cabinet would preside over the parliamentary elections scheduled for April 1910, but he was so impatient to enter the Chamber of Deputies that he decided to become a candidate even without the official backing he had anticipated. His chances were poor. He was two months short of the legal age for election and looked even younger. Also, he chose to run as a Radical in the predominantly working-class district of Levallois-Perret in Paris, where a small number of Radical and Republican voters were sandwiched between solid blocs of Catholics and Socialists. In 1902 the election had gone to the Catholics, and in 1906 to the Socialist lawyer Albert Willm.

To overcome these disadvantages, Mandel began his campaign in September 1909, seven months before the scheduled elections. The results of his opening moves were encouraging. He declared himself the standard-bearer of the Radical Party, and obtained the backing of the moderate Republicans, the local representatives of the Alliance Démocratique. He also received favorable notices from the rightist press, which called him a skillful speaker and declared: "If it were not for his Jewish origin, we might be among those who support his candidacy."[32]

By January, however, Mandel's hopes had vanished. The Right had nominated Lieutenant Colonel Rousset, a staunch Catholic. The Radicals rejected Mandel as their official candidate and supported Jean Brack. Even the moderate Republicans, as a result of disputes with Mandel, withdrew their support and backed the official Radical candidate.

As a member of the Radical Party, Mandel should have withdrawn in favor of Brack, but he stayed in the campaign and ran as "le candidat d'union républicaine anti-collectiviste." The local Radicals then expelled him from the party with the traditional anti-Semitic accusation that he was the agent of Jewish financial interests.

Levallois was famous for its heated campaigns and violent electoral meetings. By the beginning of April, posters were being plastered over one another for lack of bare walls. Mandel's posters predominated, entirely covering the front of one school. The café meetings were noisy and almost impossible to conduct. According to one paper, Mandel was the candidate most feared by his opponents—not because he had a chance of winning, but because he was tireless in holding daily meetings and attacking them.

Colonel Rousset's supporters admitted a grudging admiration for Mandel, but found the general tenor of his speeches intolerable. It was his sarcasm as well as his tendency to turn every speech into a lecture on the history of the Republic that annoyed them. Rousset said that he had known from incidents in the corridors of the Chamber that Mandel was self-assured, but he had not known that he was insolent. He was so antagonized by Mandel's attacks that he continued to counter-attack even after the elections. He accused Mandel of conducting "the most scandalous, shameful and cynical campaign I have ever seen," and gloated that "neither the flood of posters, nor the sickening deluge of insults, defamations and lies, nor even the torrent of gold from Jewish banks saved him from a disgraceful disaster."

On the face of it, the election was indeed a disaster. Willm was reelected on the first ballot with 10,567 votes, while Rousset received 4,282, Brack 2,511, and Mandel only 1,912. Nevertheless, for a young, unknown, bourgeois Jewish candidate to have received almost 2,000 votes in a working-class district was an excellent performance.

With that consolation, Mandel returned to his work with Clemenceau, whose difficult nature usually inspired his assistants with one desire: to obtain an appointment elsewhere and leave his service as quickly as they could. The only exception was Mandel, who remained tenaciously faithful in spite of the perverse pleasure Clemenceau took in insulting him and mocking the Jews.[33] After the defeat of the government in July 1909, Mandel called frequently at the former Prime Minister's home. At first he was repeatedly told that his services were no longer needed. However, in November Clemenceau decided to employ him as the Paris representative of a new daily he intended to found in his constituency in the Var.[34]

At the *Journal du Var*, which first appeared on April 16, 1910, Mandel quickly went beyond the administrative tasks assigned to him, submitting a weekly lead article and suggesting changes in the format and content of the paper. Clemenceau's departure on a lecture tour of South America from June to October 1910 left Mandel in virtual control of the paper almost from the start. In the spring of 1911 he wrote an article attacking Under-Secretary of the Interior Constant for affording legal protection to an unauthorized congregation of nuns in his own constituency in the Gironde, while belonging to a professedly anticlerical government. The accusation was brought to the floor of the Chamber by the Radical deputy Leo Bouyssou, and Mandel's name was mentioned in the debate. When Clemenceau learned of the incident, he was furious at Mandel's meddling and forbade him to publish articles in the *Journal du Var* without express authorization. It was eighteen months before the ban was lifted and he was again allowed to write for the paper.[35]

During this period, nevertheless, Mandel seems to have overcome Clemenceau's lingering doubts about him. In 1912, when the former Prime Minister decided to found a Paris daily, it was to Mandel that he confided the responsibility of arranging all the details involved: raising capital, contracting with a printer, choosing a site, hiring a staff, and concluding agreements with the various news, advertising, and distribution agencies. "Clemenceau, who could not handle these questions himself, was surprised to see with what authority and assurance his collaborator had dealt with them and began to have greater confidence in him."[36]

Mandel was undoubtedly an able and diligent assistant, but his sights were always set on the Chamber of Deputies. He used his position with Clemenceau to make friends, connections, and contacts in political circles.[37] One of Clemenceau's secretaries remarked that he

was not yet the all-powerful Père Joseph of our Richelieu, hated, feared and mocked. Caricature had not yet distorted his features. Clemenceau's political adversaries called him Georges, not Jéroboam, and his nose was pictured as it was in reality, i.e. almost straight and of average length. He was already well known in the parliamentary milieu, however, and was considered to be intelligent, able, capable of utilizing to his own advantage any opportunity which might occur, and, if necessary, of creating his own opportunities. Everyone who knew him predicted for him a successful political career.[38]

For the 1914 elections he planned to be a candidate in the Var, where he would be able to benefit from Clemenceau's prestige and use the *Journal du Var* in his campaign. Through his writings and visits he was already making his name known in the area. Then at the end of 1912, the former Prime Minister decided to stop publishing the *Journal du Var* and devote himself to his new Paris daily. Despite this loss of the local newspaper on whose backing Mandel had counted very heavily, he was unwilling to give up all hope. He finally succeeded in obtaining the reluctant support of Clemenceau, who was afraid that Mandel would not have sufficient appeal for voters in the south of France. Clemenceau withdrew his support, however, when the prefect, Louis Hudelo, advised him that Mandel's certain defeat would hurt him politically.[39] Forced to find another constituency, Mandel chose Castellane in the Basses-Alpes, one of the smallest and poorest districts in France and one of the few areas in which outright bribery was still practiced.[40] There it was possible to be elected with only 1,500 votes.

Mandel and a wealthy financier, Jacques Stern, both applied for the official investiture of the Radical Party and were both refused, the party preferring not to disappoint either of them. Mandel then ran as the "candidat d'union et de concentration républicaine," and Stern as an independent Radical. Stern was supported by the most important local daily because, as its editorial writer said, "his position, his record, his experience, and the powerful means of action at his disposal indicate that he is the only one who will be able to carry out his promises."[41]

Mandel had less money to spend on his campaign than Stern, but he was able to capitalize on his association with Clemenceau. The electoral journal he created for the campaign said that during his three years with the former Prime Minister, he had made influential friends in the government and in Parliament. Furthermore, there was a great community of interests between Clemenceau's constituency and Castellane, "which is the natural extension of the Var: the construction of roads and railways, the development of tourism, the expansion of agricultural credit, etc. The bond of friendship between M. Clemenceau and his former *chef de cabinet*, M. Mandel, will speed up these projects common to the two departments, which the famous Senator from the Var ... is certain to support with his talent and influence."[42]

Mandel asked his powerful friends in the administration to have a new sub-prefect, Paul Vacquier, appointed to Castellane shortly before the elections. Vacquier immediately began to visit the people and use all of his influence as the representative of the government to persuade them to vote for Mandel.[43] The opposition registered a subtle protest. They announced that they refused to believe the rumors of a "brutal, official and public intervention in favor of one republican candidate against another." They preferred to believe, they said, that "the sub-prefect ... has gone to the great expense of hiring an automobile for the sole purpose of getting to know his arrondissement more quickly."[44]

Mandel's backers protested in kind against the methods used by Stern. "Some people say," they wrote, "that the electors of Castellane can be bribed. We protest against that unjustified accusation. ... We do not want to insult the people of Castellane by comparing them to the Norman peasant of whom it was said that he put the money of the rich candidate in his pocket and the ballot of his opponent in the urn. We do not doubt that they will refuse the gifts of the corruptor, if there is one, and vote for the candidate of morality and principles."[45]

This campaign may have had an unfortunate effect on Mandel's conception of democratic procedures and provincial elections. In one small village, after talking for more than an hour about foreign and internal problems, Mandel asked the mayor to estimate the number of votes he could expect to receive. The mayor hesitated for a moment and then replied: "*Eh bien.* ... We are poor people. Our village is not rich and we need everyone's help. Not knowing who will be elected, we don't want to antagonize anyone. The twenty-four electors of the village held a meeting last night, and as there are three candidates, we have decided to give each candidate eight votes."[46]

Unfortunately, Mandel was unable to obtain such an equitable distribution throughout the arrondissement. On election day Stern received 1,551 votes to Mandel's 729. The remaining 1,000 votes were scattered among five other candidates. Since Stern had failed to receive an absolute majority, the system of election then in effect required that a run-off election be held in two weeks. The other candidates desisted in Mandel's favor, giving him a very slight chance of victory on the second ballot. But on May 5 Mandel himself withdrew from the election, sending a letter to the papers and to the voters informing them of his reasons. "I have tried to conduct an honest political campaign," he said, "but an unscrupulous adversary has resorted to bribery. He has been free with his gifts, promises and favors to the villages and to individuals. There is not a single means of corruption ... that he has not used."[47]

Although twice defeated, Mandel was still only twenty-nine years old and had no intention of giving up his ambition of becoming a deputy. The next general election was four years away, but vacancies due to death or illness were bound to occur in the meantime, and he was determined to get one of these chance openings. When the Radical deputy from Lesparre in the Gironde died on July 5, 1914, the parties in the area began seeking candidates for the forthcoming by-election. The Radicals, lacking a local candidate of sufficient stature, asked the advice of their Paris colleagues. The vice-president of the Chamber, Leo Bouyssou, a prominent Radical and the man who had aided Mandel in his attack on the Monis government in 1911, now recommended him to Lucien Teyssier, one of the leaders of the party in the Gironde.[48] After some visits and correspondence, Mandel was accepted as their candidate, but the war intervened and all elections were postponed until the end of hostilities. Nevertheless, Mandel did not forget Lesparre, and in the absence of a regular deputy, acted as its unofficial representative in Paris. Lesparre lost nothing by the bargain, for by the end of the war, through his association with Clemenceau, Mandel had become more powerful than any ordinary deputy.

3. The Tiger and the Fox

*A prince being thus obliged to know well how to act as a beast must imitate
the fox and the lion, for the lion cannot protect himself from traps,
and the fox cannot defend himself from wolves. One must therefore be a
fox to recognize traps, and a lion to frighten wolves. Those that wish to be
only lions do not understand this.*

Machiavelli

IN THE TEN YEARS after he joined Clemenceau on *L'Aurore,* Mandel's
ideas evolved considerably. Earlier, when clericalism was the prime enemy
of the republicans, he had been in the mainstream of the Radical Party,
denouncing the Catholics and advocating an alliance with the Socialists.
"Experience proves," he then wrote, "that in a free country there are no
enemies on the Left. Socialism is the vanguard of democracy. Whoever
opposes it is only helping the reactionary forces."[1]

In foreign affairs as well he had been on the Left. Despite France's treaty
with Russia, he criticized the Czarist regime and hoped for a democratic
revolution that would oust the Romanovs.[2] He also opposed the rampant
imperialism of the European nations that were dividing the world up
among themselves. "Foreign conquests," he said, "are outlets for social
bestiality ... and too often ... have served only the base aims of shady businessmen and corrupt financiers."[3]

His conception of France's role in the world was akin to General de
Gaulle's later vision of her as the princess in the fairy tales, "dedicated to
an exalted and exceptional destiny."[4] In the conflict between Greece and
Turkey over the island of Crete, he wanted France to take the lead in persuading Turkey to return the island to Greece before violence began.

It is not sufficient for the representatives of a great country like ours to have
adopted a policy similar to that of our neighbors, or even to have favored a more
moderate and humane policy towards this unfortunate people struggling for its
freedom and independence. Let other nations concern themselves solely with
their own interests ... ; we have no right to do so. It is said justly that *noblesse
oblige,* and our traditions, our past, the ideas and principles of which we are the
champions in the world, all require us to play a more active role.[5]

The changes in his thought were due both to his experience of power under Clemenceau and to changing political circumstances. After Clemenceau
took office in 1906, first as minister of the Interior and then as prime minister,
France experienced the greatest wave of strikes in her history. In comparison
with later years, the number of men involved in 1906—438,466—was not

extraordinary. But the movement coincided with the high tide of revolutionary agitation for a general strike to overthrow the entire capitalist regime. There was considerable fear that a revolution would break out on May 1, 1906. Many people crossed the Channel; others laid in stocks of food; and Clemenceau brought in more police than Paris had seen at any time since the Commune.

Within two years Clemenceau succeeded both in stopping the strikes and in breaking the revolutionary élan of the workers. In 1908 only 99,042 men struck, fewer than in any except a war year. But by pitting the army against the strikers, he also broke the ties between his own avowedly reformist government and the Socialists.

Clemenceau had come into power enjoying more sympathy on the Left than any previous prime minister. His Radical predecessor, Emile Combes, had settled the clerical question by separating church and state and disbanding most of the religious orders. Clemenceau had been expected to carry out the rest of the Radical program and bring about many long-delayed reforms. In the event, his ambitious program was sidetracked by the strike movement. When his government was overthrown in 1909, only two minor reforms had been enacted. He had entered office as a social reformer; he left it as a pillar of the social order, execrated by the Socialists and by many members of his own party.

Thereafter Clemenceau refused to cooperate with the Socialists on any level, resigning from the executive committee of the Radical Party in 1910 because of the support it had given to Socialist candidates in some local elections.[6] He opposed the Socialists not only because of what he considered to be their vague dreams and anarchic schemes, but also because he thought they were unpatriotic.

In the nineteenth century, patriotism had been a left-wing phenomenon. It dated from 1793 and the *levée en masse* when the people had been summoned to defend the country and the revolutionary gains against the foreign invaders threatening to restore the king. The tradition took deep root. In 1870 it inspired the continued resistance of the Parisian workers long after most of their compatriots were ready to surrender to the Germans. But when the republic that was established after the bloody repression of the Commune failed to bring about substantial social reforms, the workers gradually became alienated from the rest of the country and grew less susceptible to patriotic appeals. The Monarchists and Catholics eventually took up the banner of patriotism dropped by the Left and waved it in order to rally opinion against the republican form of government. In their view, only a monarchy would be strong enough to stand up against the Germans in a new conflict.

Clemenceau had no sympathy with the strident nationalists on the Right, but he was the heir of the old Jacobin patriots for whom the defense of the country was the highest good. He never forgot either the loss of Alsace-Lorraine or the continued threat represented by the great empire bridging the Rhine. Although fear and hatred of the Germans had subsided by the turn of the century, it revived after 1905 as a result of German sabre-rattling over being excluded from the division of spoils in Africa. In 1908 Clemenceau began to suspect that another war with Germany was inevitable. By 1912 he was convinced of it.[7] Thus he disliked the Socialists as much for their pacifism and antipatriotic propaganda, as for their support of the strike movement.

Clemenceau's fear of Germany and his restless energy led him out of semi-retirement in 1912 at the age of seventy-one. That year he helped to overthrow Prime Minister Caillaux, who was suspected of favoring concessions to Germany. The following year Clemenceau founded a new Paris daily, *L'Homme Libre*, which he immediately threw into the battle to raise the term of compulsory military service from two to three years. "One must be wilfully blind," he wrote, "not to see that [Germany's] rage for domination ... must lead to the extermination of France. If the catastrophe is inevitable, we must prepare ourselves to face it with all our energy."[8]

Clemenceau's one thought thereafter was to return to power, for he had no faith in anyone else's leadership.

Unfortunately, [he reflected,] the men in the highest offices (and I suspect neither their intentions nor their intelligence) incarnate all the weaknesses that have led us to the edge of the abyss. In the happy days of peace and progress they present a distinguished appearance, and are specially qualified to distribute prizes. But I am absolutely convinced that they are incapable of taking risks ... and of facing up to the simple and terrible dilemma: *vouloir ou mourir*.[9]

During this period Mandel's ideas followed the same evolution as Clemenceau's. By 1910 he too was convinced of the danger from Germany.[10] While he still expressed his sympathy with those nations struggling for liberty and justice, he now thought that France's foreign policy "should be determined solely on the basis of practical considerations."[11] He no longer criticized Russia for her internal regime, but instead praised her for supporting "the just ambitions of the Slavic world against the policy of *Drang Nach Osten*."[12] He now completely accepted the French occupation of Morocco, and criticized Germany for interfering with the "legitimate efforts of France and England to establish civilization and progress."[13] There was no more talk of colonialism as an outlet for "social bestiality."

By 1913 Mandel had definitely left the mainstream of the Radical Party. As early as 1910 he had told the Party's "so-called directors" that far from allying themselves with the Socialists in order to win elections, they should denounce their antipatriotic campaign.[14] For him, the Socialists had become "les ennemis de la Patrie."[15]

Moreover, whereas the Radicals were generally indifferent to foreign affairs, Mandel was intensely concerned about the subject.[16] He also believed firmly in the necessity of maintaining order and authority in the state, while his Radical colleagues still clung to the vision of a republic in which an eternally suspicious populace exercised vigilant control over the government through its representatives. This general mistrust he considered to be an anachronism, a relic of the past when "the nation and the state were constantly in conflict; today they are one and the same."[17]

It was all the easier for Mandel to break with the Left in that social reform had never been of more than incidental interest to him. He wanted to rule France, not reform it. Clemenceau had spent thirty years as spokesman for the cause of the workers, but Mandel was uninterested in this side of his career. What he learned from the old statesman, said a friend, was "a way of acting, ... a technique of governing. In watching the Tiger at his daily tasks, Georges Mandel soon realized that politics is essentially a problem of will power...."[18]

Mandel was basically a nineteenth-century individualist strongly imbued with Social Darwinian ideas. Whatever success he had known, he attributed to his own wit and determination. He believed that each man controls his own fate and saw no point in large-scale social reforms that left the individual unchanged. In a commencement address in 1927, he declared:

[In Nature] ... selection takes place at every level for the benefit of the strongest. Among the smallest creatures, as among men, there rages a merciless war. ... The conflicts between nations which we would all like to end ... are only the transposition to the military level of the conflicts of ambitions and interests that have always embroiled human beings. Trying to end war without ending its cause is futile. Undoubtedly it is easier to reform institutions than to change men. Yet, of what value are the best laws and the most magnificent institutions, if the people for whom they are created have not been morally prepared to live under them?[19]

In 1913 Mandel's ideas coincided remarkably well with Clemenceau's. Eventually his conception of internal politics would separate him from the old statesman, but they would always remain united by their fear of German hegemony and their determination to maintain France's independent position in the world.

II

Clemenceau's campaign to regain control of French policy faced many obstacles. The Right hated him for his anticlericalism, and the Left for his authoritarianism. His bitterest enemy was the President of France himself, Raymond Poincaré, whose election Clemenceau had tried to block in 1913.

Although Clemenceau's name was brought up at every cabinet crisis, Poincaré always managed to find some reason for not summoning him. He realized that Clemenceau wanted to become premier, not because of ambition, but "because he is convinced that he will save the country, and that no one else can do it." But the more Poincaré reflected, the more convinced he became that "so long as victory is possible, he is capable of ruining everything. A day will come perhaps when I will say: 'now that everything seems lost, he is capable of saving everything.'"[20]

The day did not come until 1917. In the spring of that year, for the first time since the Battle of the Marne, France seriously risked losing the war. Although the renewed German submarine campaign brought the United States into the war in April, it also threatened Allied supply lines. Over-all Allied capability for fighting the war had already been endangered by the March revolution in Russia. In the west, moreover, General Nivelle's disastrous spring offensive had broken the morale of the army. Thirty to forty thousand men mutinied, and some even spoke of marching on Paris.[21] While a new commander, General Pétain, tried to restore order in the army, many civilians gradually lost the will to fight on. The number of strikes mounted, and the spread of pacifism among the workers became a serious danger.

At about the same time, the public learned of cases of treason involving friends or acquaintances of two influential Radical leaders, former Prime Minister Joseph Caillaux and Interior Minister Jean-Louis Malvy. Caillaux was thought to favor a negotiated peace and was known to have maintained friendly relations with the director of the left-wing Parisian paper, the *Bonnet Rouge*, who, it was now revealed, had taken money from the Germans to spread defeatist propaganda. Caillaux had also been in correspondence with another traitor, Paul Bolo, commonly known as Bolo Pasha, a cosmopolitan adventurer of French origin who was in the pay of the German government. There was no evidence that Caillaux himself had committed treason, but as Poincaré later wrote to Clemenceau, "A terrible fate has placed Caillaux on every path where traitors are met."[22]

Suspicions of Malvy, an old friend of Caillaux, had even less foundation, but were equally disturbing because of his position in the government. Malvy had been minister of the Interior since 1914 and as such was responsible for governmental subsidies paid to the *Bonnet Rouge* early in the war. He had also taken the admittedly risky decision in 1914 not to arrest the left-wing leaders listed in the famous Carnet B as potential threats to national security. Until 1917 his leniency had been condoned as the necessary price of working-class support for the war, but with the revelations of treason, the increased number of strikes, and the spread of pacifist propaganda, his continued refusal to act seemed to some both dangerous and culpable.

Clemenceau, already the leading advocate of all-out war, publicly accused Malvy in the Senate of "betraying the interests of France" by not arresting the most influential defeatists. He revealed what his own policy would be if he took office. "There are six thousand names in the Carnet B," he said. "If we arrested or legally prosecuted fifteen of them, all the rest could be left alone. It is because of those fifteen men that the government hesitates."[23] It was clear that *he* would have no hesitations.

Widespread attacks on Malvy forced him to resign at the end of August, and brought down the government a few days later. By this time Poincaré was undoubtedly ready to summon Clemenceau, but fear of him on the Left was so great that the President was forced to delay still longer. He called the brilliant but indecisive Paul Painlevé, whose makeshift government managed to remain in power for as long as two months only because it was known that Clemenceau was waiting in the wings.[24]

At the end of October, Poincaré quietly advised Clemenceau to get ready to take power.[25] The President's friend Alfred Capus of the Académie Française wrote an article declaring that the policy advocated by Clemenceau for the treason cases was supported by the public without reservations. The only other possible policy was that of Caillaux. "We must choose between them, quickly and resolutely."[26] A few days later the Painlevé government fell, and Poincaré went through the motions of consulting the leaders of Parliament. But when one deputy objected that a Clemenceau government might cause the workers to revolt and bring about civil war, he replied, "I must choose between Caillaux and Clemenceau. My choice is made."[27]

On November 16, 1917, Clemenceau assumed power. The date can be considered the turning point of the war for France, for thereafter there was no doubt that the country would fight to the end. Determined to galvanize the will of the French people to resist, he set out to convince them that slackness and defeatism would not be tolerated. Clemenceau himself had accused Malvy of "betraying the interests of France." Léon Daudet accused him of delivering the plans for the ill-fated spring offensive to the Germans. These were wild charges, but the atmosphere generated by Clemenceau was such that, as one representative noted, if they had accused Malvy of putting the towers of Notre Dame in his suitcase, no one would have objected. No deputy could be sure he would not be the next to be accused.[28] In any case, on November 22 Malvy suddenly asked the Chamber to discuss Daudet's accusation. He seemed to think it prudent to have his case examined by a political rather than a military court. The deputies, including Malvy's friends, accordingly charged him with treason and sent him before the Senate sitting as a high court.

Throughout the winter and spring, public attention was kept focused on internal affairs by the successive accusation, arrest, and trial of various leaders.[29] In January Caillaux was imprisoned; the following month the trial of Bolo Pasha started; in March Ernest Judet, the right-wing editor of *L'Eclair*, suddenly decided he needed a long vacation in Switzerland. Rumors circulated about the identity of the next victims. Among those mentioned were General Sarrail, former commander-in-chief of the Balkan army, and former Prime Ministers René Viviani and Aristide Briand.[30]

The cases against Malvy and Caillaux were intended to symbolize Clemenceau's determination to continue the war. It was said that "he discovers traitors because he needs them."[31] Caillaux himself was later able to regard his plight philosophically: "I do not hold it against Clemenceau. At that time he had to find a traitor to strengthen the confidence of the anxious public. If I had been in power, I would perhaps have done the same thing, except that he would have played the role of traitor."[32]

Of those tried for treason, Bolo Pasha, Alphonse Lenoir, and Emile Duval were executed. Others, including Leymarie, Malvy's secretary, received prison sentences of up to ten years. Caillaux and Malvy, however, had been at most imprudent in their actions and words. Although Malvy had been charged with treason, he was found guilty only of having "betrayed the duties of his office," for which he was sentenced to five years' banishment from France.[33] Caillaux's trial, probably for want of convincing evidence, was delayed until after the war, when he was found guilty of the rather vague crime of having written letters resulting in the revelation to the enemy of information damaging to the political and military situation of France. Having spent more than two years in prison already, he was immediately released, but was banished from the major cities of France.

Of far more immediate importance to the government in 1917 were the activities of former Prime Minister Aristide Briand, whom Clemenceau called "the leading light of French defeatism."[34] In the summer of 1917, when France was at her weakest, the Germans had contacted Briand about the possibility of opening peace negotiations. Briand informed the government of the talks and to all appearances broke them off at its request. Clemenceau had no evidence until December 1919 that Briand had continued discussions without the government's approval, but in 1917 suspicions were almost as good as proof, and threats almost as valuable as action. Rumors that Clemenceau was preparing a case against him were sufficient to immoblize Briand for the rest of the war.[35]

The repeated accusations and trials created an atmosphere supercharged with fear, suspicion, and animosity, but they also succeeded in reinvigorating the country. Among those who recognized the importance of Clemenceau's contribution to France's war effort was Ludendorff, who commented that "his policy was a war policy; he suppressed every sign of peace agitation and strengthened the spirit of his country. His proceedings against Caillaux showed clearly what we were to expect of him."[36] The deputy Abel Ferry said that his actions against Caillaux, Bolo, and others exalted national feeling and prevented "the physical fatigue of the body of the nation from reaching the head as it did in Russia."[37] It mattered little that injustices were committed; the people required resolute action and the sense of being governed, which Clemenceau quickly supplied. Expressions of discontent had to be stifled for the moment. With Clemenceau exercising dictatorial powers and enjoying unprecedented popularity, his enemies could only attack Mandel, his so-called *éminence grise*.

III

For several years Mandel had been Clemenceau's closest collaborator. In the winter of 1910 he had moved from a luxurious apartment at 3 rue Hamelin to a more modest flat at 72 avenue Mozart in order to be near Clemenceau's home.[38] When the German advance of August 1914 forced the government to move to Bordeaux, Clemenceau followed it. Mandel, who was already credited with exercising extensive influence over the former Prime Minister, was the only member of his staff to accompany him.[39]

During the war Mandel spent all of his time either in the office of *L'Homme Libre*, which appeared as *L'Homme Enchaîné* after the censors suppressed an issue, or in the corridors of the Chamber of Deputies. He wrote a few articles for the paper, but his main task was the one he had assumed almost ten years earlier: to supply Clemenceau with the information he needed to carry on his campaign against the government. Mandel gave him a résumé of the press, reported what had occurred in the Chamber, and brought new deputies and potential ministers to him for conversations.[40] Clemenceau's grandson has said that "for every member of Parliament, he knew exactly the number of votes by which he had been elected, his program, and the measures he had supported or opposed. He knew everything about his private life and character; he knew his exact age and almost his entire life history. For this reason, he was very useful to Grandfather."[41]

Mandel's eagerness to learn extended not only to the personal lives of politicians but also to the smallest details of French domestic and foreign affairs. He believed that many of his contemporaries knew less about their country's recent history than they knew about Louis XIV or the Revolution, with the result that "many errors have been committed with the complicity of public opinion, which a little knowledge would have sufficed to avoid."[42]

Sometimes it seemed as if Mandel possessed not only knowledge, but foresight. Clemenceau's grandson recalls that one day when Clemenceau ecstatically praised the Russian "steamroller" for the great gains it had made against the Germans, Mandel interrupted him: "I don't agree with you at all. The 'steamroller' will be annihilated shortly; the Germans will crush it when they want to. Moreover, a revolution is going to sweep away Czarism, and the first act of the new government will be to betray us and sign a separate peace, leaving the Allies to fight Germany alone."[43]

Convinced from the beginning of the war that only Clemenceau could save France, Mandel had carried on a continuous campaign to return him to power. According to Georges Wormser, without the authorization or even the knowledge of Clemenceau, Mandel attacked the President of the Republic, stirred up opposition to the successive governments, arranged for various deputies, including the Socialist Pierre Laval, to intervene in Parliament, and promised posts in Clemenceau's future cabinet to others. When Poincaré still obstinately refused to summon Clemenceau, Mandel even began a campaign to force him to resign.[44] Mandel's campaign was unsuccessful, of course, but Poincaré was finally driven by the desperate situation to resort to Clemenceau, who chose Mandel as his chief personal assistant— his *chef de cabinet*.

Mandel was already well known in political circles. On the day the government was formed, the leftist daily *Le Pays* described him for its readers:

Georges Mandel, who is collaborating with Clemenceau in forming the "grand ministère," has a knife-like figure, steely eyes set in a beardless face, and thin, disdainful lips. Inexhaustibly eloquent in the anterooms of the Chamber, Mandel for several years has been the liaison between the editor of *L'Homme Enchaîné* and the deputies. Clemenceau . . . knew only a few of them and had no desire to meet the rest. Mandel, on the other hand, knows them better than anyone in France. He has analyzed the strengths and weaknesses of each one, and knows all the parties, groups, and subgroups. He likes to organize and thwart backstage maneuvers. . . . In the press gallery, he gave the speeches that the orators should have made on the floor of the Chamber. He frequently suggested grandiose political plans to those in power, and in crises was ready with his advice. He was undoubtedly preparing to play the role of mentor in the government—his government.[45]

Because Clemenceau was primarily preoccupied with the conduct of the war, he left internal affairs in the hands of Mandel. One day when Clemenceau and Poincaré were privately debating the action to be taken in a certain matter, Clemenceau told the President, "Mandel will arrange everything. He is amazing. *Avec son nez de juif, il fait des gens ce qu'il veut.* . . . He's really an encyclopedia. One couldn't ask for a better collaborator."[46] Mandel himself is supposed to have said, "I knew all his ideas. I identified myself with him to the point where we had only to exchange a gesture, a look, in order to understand one another. He gave me *carte blanche*."[47]

Mandel first set about consolidating support for the government in the Chamber.[48] The policies Clemenceau had been summoned to carry out— the repression of defeatism and the pursuit of the war until Allied victory— were enthusiastically supported only on the Right. Feelings on the Left ranged from the Radicals' cautious reserve to the Socialists' outright opposition. Assured of the support of the Right in any case, Mandel tried to get the Left to back the government by offering them most of the cabinet posts in the new government. Each leftist group received at least one, and the Socialists were offered several ministries, including the office of under-secretary of the Interior for Pierre Laval, the CGT (Confédération Générale du Travail) lawyer listed in the Carnet B. At a meeting of the Socialist deputies on November 15, Laval spoke forcefully and at length in favor of accepting Clemenceau's offer, but the party decided almost unanimously to oppose the government, obliging Laval and others to reject the bait.[49]

After the formation of the cabinet, Mandel's essential functions were to control the press and Parliament, and to maintain order in the country. His methods were not always the most refined. It is said that he used Pierre Laval to spy on his fellow Socialists and harass in Parliament those ministers who displeased Mandel.[50] Another Machiavellian scheme attributed to Mandel concerns Ernest Judet, condemned to death *in absentia* for treason and acquitted when he returned to France after the war. On meeting Mandel some years later, Judet refused to shake hands with him because of the part Mandel had played in his conviction. Mandel then explained: "What could I do? I needed a traitor from the Right in order to balance the traitor from the Left [Joseph Caillaux]. You were the one from the Right. You didn't risk anything as you were In Switzerland and besides, since you were really innocent, it didn't do you any harm."[51]

He is also held personally responsible for many other acts or plans of the government: the campaign blaming Socialist ex-minister Albert Thomas for the high cost of living and branding him *Père de la vie chère*;[52] letting President Poincaré read in the newspapers that his friend Senator Humbert had been arrested for complicity in the Bolo Pasha case;[53] arresting on charges of treason the prominent leftist deputy and director of *La Vérité*, Paul Meunier, and keeping him in jail for more than two years before his case was finally dismissed;[54] preparing the dossier against Caillaux;[55] planning to put Marshal Joffre under house arrest for thirty days;[56] transmitting information to the Royalist *Action Française* for use in campaigns against Clemenceau's opponents;[57] and investigating the administration of Senator Edouard Herriot as Mayor of Lyons. In the Senate, Herriot denounced Interior Minister Jules Pams for the action, but he had no doubt who was actually responsible for it, and in later years remarked that "Georges Mandel was one of my most determined political adversaries. After the last war he wanted to imprison me over some question of food supply."[58]

It is difficult to determine the role played by Mandel in these affairs, but years before, he had explained the principle that undoubtedly motivated most of them:

The prosecution of individuals always has more effect than general measures against a group. If the General Confederation of Labor were dissolved tomorrow, it would be impossible to prevent the immediate creation of a new confederation, probably headed by the same men. On the other hand, although less theatrical, the arrest and condemnation of any leaders guilty of an offense or a crime, would be more effective and would quickly throw their followers into confusion.[59]

Mandel took a particular interest in regulating the press. At the time, a deputy wrote about Mandel's methods: "For the publications, there are subsidies; for the men, changes in their military status, deferments, honors, and even threats; everything is used and—unfortunately—everything succeeds."[60]

The opposition press, of course, was most seriously affected. *Bonsoir* was seized seven times, and *L'Oeuvre* was threatened with daily seizure if it appeared, as it said it would, without prior approval of the censors. The more moderate and less independent papers were also subject to pressure when they stepped out of line. Threats, balanced by a bribe—the post of under-secretary of the Merchant Marine for the son of its director—were supposedly sufficient to bring the *Petit Parisien* back from its erring ways. Léon Bailby's *Intransigeant* was constantly harassed, and the entire administrative staff of *Le Matin* was threatened with prosecution for illegal traffic in newsprint. Those journals willing to cooperate were given the first news of important events—which, however, they soon learned to treat skeptically, for the government did not hesitate to convey false information if it could thereby promote its policies.[61]

Mandel had special means for dealing with recalcitrant journalists. Previously, directors of journals had been given automatic deferments from the draft. Mandel revoked this privilege, granting instead one-month deferments renewable only on written request.[62] When press representatives complained about this practice to Under-Secretary of War Louis Abrami, they were flatly told that Mandel considered deferments as a proper instrument of government for controlling the press.[63]

If Mandel's job by its very nature was bound to make him many enemies, his methods made him many more. What was worse, his personality did nothing to counteract this tendency.[64] People often disliked him instinctively. One of Clemenceau's American friends writes,

Never did I learn to feel friendly toward this extraordinary but singularly unpleasant individual. I once remarked to the Tiger that I would about as soon strike up an acquaintance with an adder as with his closest adviser, who was always hanging about, poised and alert. The old man grinned, and said that I did not appreciate Mandel. "I appreciate him, all right," I replied, "but I still don't like him."[65]

A censor who worked under him called Mandel a "bilious, suspicious, peremptory, vindictive secretary, made vice-dictator of France by the caprice of an old man."[66] Another writer pictured him as "thin, small, twisted, pale, with a long, thin nose planted askew, to either side of which a cold glaucous green eye glinted, hard and steady. On his forehead hung a damp wisp of hair. He was always cold for the same reason one expects a fish to be."[67] With reactions like these, it is no wonder that there were soon literally hundreds of journalists, bureaucrats, and members of Parliament waiting for the chance to discredit him and, through him, the government.

They got their first opportunity in February 1918 during the trial of Bolo Pasha. Bolo testified that in August 1917 he had given Mandel a letter of recommendation to General Quiquandon, commander of the 18th military region. This region included Bordeaux and the Médoc where Mandel hoped to be a candidate for the Chamber of Deputies after the war. It seems that Mandel wanted to increase his influence there by acting as intermediary between Quiquandon and some local officials who disliked the General's policies.[68] In a letter to the court, he explained that he knew the accused, but considered him to be an adventurer and had warned a number of deputies against him.[69] In Parliament shortly afterward, the deputy Camille Picard confirmed Mandel's account.[70]

The incident proved little besides the fact that Mandel was an enterprising politician. But in the atmosphere he himself had helped to create, mere acquaintance with a traitor proved to be embarrassing. Mandel required the help of Abel Ferry, chairman of the Chamber subcommittee on counter-espionage, to ward off attacks in Parliament, and he succeeded only with difficulty in keeping his name out of many newspaper accounts of Bolo's testimony.[71]

Nevertheless, until November 11, 1918, Mandel managed to muzzle press criticism of himself. Now and then a deputy would threaten to interpellate Clemenceau about his young assistant who was supposedly making trouble for the cabinet by abusing his authority, antagonizing deputies, and brusquely handling the prefects, but little ever came of these threats.[72] Discontent, however, was widespread, and mention of Mandel's name in political circles inevitably brought angry comments about the *éminence grise* and the *éminence grisée*.[73]

The press had hoped that the end of hostilities would mean the end of censorship and repression. Clemenceau decided otherwise. He maintained the censorship in order to control public opinion until after the signing of the peace treaty. The frustrated journalists, fearing to attack the Prime Minister because of his overwhelming popularity, attacked Mandel instead. According to one of the censors, Mandel tolerated these personal attacks because doing so gave the impression that the regime was a liberal one, and thus enabled him to control political ideas even more severely.[74]

For the leftist weekly *Les Hommes du Jour*, Mandel was the man of the year in 1919. The front cover of more than forty issues featured caricatures of him by Gassier over such captions as "Sa Majesté, Jéroboam II."[75] The entire opposition press—*L'Oeuvre, L'Humanité, Le Populaire, Le Journal du Peuple, Le Carnet de la Semaine*—joined in the campaign. They vied with one another in finding names for him and exercising their wit at his expense. *Le Roi de France, Raspoutinette*, and *le deuxième flic de France*[76] were among the favorites. They repeatedly asserted that "except for the peace conference, it is Georges Mandel who is governing."[77]

The outcry was taken up in Parliament by the former minister Charles Chaumet of the Alliance Démocratique, who declared that the government was controlled not by an "anonymous but by a pseudonymous power, who has turned the administration upside down and wants to put his fantastic schemes into effect throughout the government.... We want the important public services to be directed by a responsible individual, by a real prime minister; we do not want a dictatorship by proxy."[78]

The most remarkable outburst came at the Congress of the Radical Party on July 26, 1919, when Henry Franklin-Bouillon, president of the Foreign Affairs Committee of the Chamber, said that "there is neither a premier nor a minister of the Interior; there is a person I do not want to name who is directing by himself the policy of France. This man ... has everything at his disposal: 25 million francs of secret funds, Legion of Honor awards, offices, and markets. Everyone has to kowtow to him. France, even under the Directory, has never known such a corrupt regime."[79]

The account of Franklin-Bouillon's speech may have been censored, or the Paris press may have voluntarily ignored it. In any case, only one major journal reported it—in order to denigrate the speaker. *Le Radical* said:

It is understandable and not surprising that the deputy from Seine-et-Oise gets carried away by his bitter feelings, his disillusion, his disenchantment, and his disappointed ministerial ambitions. But we are astonished to see intelligent Republicans and Radicals applaud such nonsense and then vote approval of it.[80]

This flow of abuse and recrimination can be dismissed as nonsense, or as an ingenious means of discrediting Clemenceau without attacking him directly. Nevertheless, the President of France and the President of the Senate, Antonin Dubost, both believed that many of the charges were true. In May 1918 Poincaré noted in his diary:

Neither the Council of Ministers nor the War Committee ever meets. Neither the ministers nor I know anything. Clemenceau is governing like a dictator. But Dubost told me yesterday that he is a dictator subject to successive influences, who acts by fits and starts, sometimes under pressure from Foch, sometimes from Mandel.

In December of the same year Poincaré described Mandel as "a strange and disturbing creature who, together with Mordacq, controls Clemenceau."[81]

Furthermore, two of the men assigned to work under Mandel as censors report, with some exaggeration, that "he directs simultaneously the Ministries of War, the Interior, and Foreign Affairs, pulling the strings on the old Tiger and manipulating him as no one else could. Not a line, a word, a mutter escapes him. He reigns with a sharp manner, an absolute contempt for people, and treats all the ministers—even old Ribot, the ex-premier—with disdain."[82]

Although it would seem that Mandel had extensive authority, some of Clemenceau's assistants maintain that "no one exerted a decisive influence on the Tiger, except perhaps his brother Albert.... Mandel would have been the last one to have any illusions on that score. Nevertheless, understanding Clemenceau's psychology, he knew how to talk to him, and could achieve what he wanted, provided that his aims were in accord with the ideas of the Prime Minister."[83] In other words, Clemenceau, preoccupied with the conduct of the war, was willing to leave internal affairs in the hands of Mandel so long as he got the desired results, and did not exceed the bounds Clemenceau set for him.

On at least one occasion Mandel did overstep those bounds. In 1918 when the opposition was massing for an attack on the government over some scandals in the army health services, Mandel arranged an incident in the Chamber that caused the Under-Secretary of Health, Justin Godart, to resign. Mandel thus helped the cabinet to avoid a potential pitfall. But because he had acted on his own authority, Clemenceau considered dismissing him for fear of a cabinet revolt against his meddling. At the last minute, however, Poincaré requested that he retain Godart. Clemenceau, who took a perverse joy in antagonizing the President, decided instead to accept Godart's resignation and keep Mandel.[84]

Even if Clemenceau had dismissed him, there seems little doubt that Mandel would soon have been recalled, for, as François Albert pointed out, he was "the only link between M. Clemenceau and the external world. . . ." Without him the Prime Minister would no longer have known what was going on.[85] Clemenceau frequently insulted and ridiculed Mandel, but the deputy Abel Ferry noted: he "calls him an *asiatique*, asks if he is really French, but cannot get along without him."[86] The proof is that Clemenceau kept him on until the very end in spite of the great outcry against him and in spite of the many occasions on which Mandel undoubtedly acted on his own authority. He was far too useful both as an assistant and as a scapegoat, as Clemenceau once actually called him.[87]

Mandel not only deflected attacks directed at the Prime Minister, but, as mentioned earlier, he also relieved him of the burden of supervising internal affairs. Clemenceau rarely summoned his ministers, many of whom soon became accustomed to reporting to Mandel and receiving orders from him. Each morning he briefed Clemenceau on internal events and gave him a résumé of the press. General Mordacq, Clemenceau's military *chef de cabinet*, called him "the best informed on everything."[88] He was always to be found at his desk, receiving information and relaying orders by telephone, questioning visitors, or studying the mass of newspaper clippings and dossiers piled high in front of him. Even when sick and feverish, he refused to leave his post and insisted on being treated in his office.[89] The endless hours of work were at times almost too much for Mandel, who had always been physically frail. According to one report, he was virtually exhausted every day by 6 P.M. and could continue working beyond that time only after a daily injection administered by his personal physician, Dr. Maurice Isch-Wall.[90]

Although it is impossible today to trace all of Mandel's activities, there are incidents in which his influence is unmistakable. At the end of the war the Prime Minister decided to postpone elections and continue the censorship in order to be able to conduct negotiations at the peace conference without worrying about the demands of public opinion. He thus avoided the fates of Lloyd George and Woodrow Wilson: he was neither forced to demand more than he thought was reasonable nor repudiated in advance by the electorate. Throughout 1919 French "public opinion" was orchestrated by Mandel to harmonize with whatever policy Clemenceau happened to be following at the moment. Mandel censored any mention of Foch's ambitious plans and suppressed popular demand that France take over the Rhine-land.[91] When Wilson's assistant, Colonel House, complained to Clemenceau about press criticism of the American leader, "the effect was magical," he said. "All the Parisian papers appeared ... the [next] morning ... with the most enthusiastic praise of President Wilson."[92]

Mandel's second major task in 1919 and the one that earned him the title of *le deuxième flic de France* was the maintenance of order in the country in the face of a revolutionary threat far greater than that of 1906. In 1914 the workers had shared the patriotic emotions of the rest of the country, but by the end of the war they were thoroughly disillusioned by the reactionary and repressive measures of the government. Their meetings and press were held in close check, and their economic position had deteriorated seriously. While prices had leaped upward, wages had been relatively stable. In 1919, inspired by the revolutions in Russia, Germany and Hungary, and by the social agitation in Italy, they began to join unions, hold demonstrations and go out on strike, all in unprecedented numbers. During that year, more than 1,150,000 men stopped work in a series of strikes affecting every major city of France.[93]

Despite the mounting pressure, Clemenceau, who was still busy with the peace conference, left the burden of maintaining order on Mandel. Even two hostile critics who served under him had to admit that he showed great strength during this period. He handled everything, they said. Day and night he conferred with the police and the Ministry of the Interior, checking on the cities and districts not yet affected by disturbances, and telling the old Tiger almost nothing in order to spare his nerves.[94]

In April the General Confederation of Labor drew up a long list of demands for the government to meet and scheduled a general strike for May 1. An eight-hour day, a general amnesty for political prisoners, rapid and complete demobilization, a just peace, and disarmament were among the things they wanted. They were opposed to intervention in Soviet Russia, the current form of taxes, and the continued censorship.

The strike was an undoubted success as a demonstration against the government. Work stopped in many areas throughout France. But in Paris, where the strikers appeared in the streets despite the government prohibition, armed police were thrown against them, and in the fights that followed, one worker was killed and over 300 were injured. Moreover, little if anything was actually gained. The government had granted the eight-hour day shortly before the strike, but it ignored the rest of the workers' demands.

Shortly thereafter, French, Italian and British trade unionists and Socialists decided to hold an international general strike on July 21 to protest against Allied intervention in Soviet Russia.[95] To gain as much support as possible, the union leaders included domestic demands among the aims of the strike. The moderate leaders of the working class regarded the movement as a demonstration of strength, but for some of the extreme Left it was to be the beginning of the revolution. They hoped to continue the strike until the workers had assumed power.[96] Aware of the danger, the government took measures this time to suppress the demonstration altogether. It warned the railwaymen and the postal workers, two key groups, that if they struck they would be charged with crimes against the nation and sent before a court martial.[97] Clemenceau then summoned the leaders of the CGT on July 18 and promised to increase the rate of demobilization, grant a partial amnesty to political prisoners, and reduce the cost of living.[98] But he also told them that "if they wanted a fight, the government was ready and would reply with all the forces at its disposal."[99] Threatened with all-out repression, the CGT leaders were caught in a dilemma: either they led the workers into an open battle with the government, or they abandoned the strike without having obtained anything more than promises. To enable them to back down with more or less good grace, however, Mandel had arranged an incident that same day in Parliament. At his request, Pierre Laval joined in an attack on Minister of Supply Victor Boret, held responsible by the workers for the high cost of living.[100] Mandel saw to it that the Minister received no support from the government, and when the Chamber voted against him, Boret decided to resign. Thus that night the CGT was able to announce that "the vote of the Chamber of Deputies, which has finally listened to the voice of the working class, has created a new situation.... We believe that a reexamination of our plans has become necessary ... and have decided to postpone the demonstration scheduled for July 21."[101]

Although the strike movement was stopped before it had even begun, the Socialist editors of *L'Humanité* defended the decision taken by the CGT. They accused the "Mandel-Clemenceau regime" of seeking an opportunity for "*Père la Victoire* to play the role of providential messiah." But unfortunately for the government, *L'Humanité* said, Parliament had forced Boret to resign. "What the CGT expected from a general strike, it can now hope to obtain from the wisdom of the representatives of the people, who have finally shaken off their torpor and who understand that the new situation demands new solutions."[102]

Without the use of force, Mandel had helped the Prime Minister avoid a possibly bloody confrontation with the workers.[103]

Whatever one may think of Mandel or his methods, it must be admitted that if Clemenceau was able to achieve what he wanted in this instance, at least part of the credit belongs to his assistant. Georges Wormser, who shared his office for more than two years, has said that without Mandel's "foresightedness, without his network of contacts, Clemenceau would have encountered difficulties whose extent he did not even suspect. Mandel had smoothed his path for him."[104] But in aiding Clemenceau, he also created a reputation and a legend that both helped and hurt his future career. Previously unknown outside political circles, he now became one of the most familiar figures in France. Caricatures of the somberly dressed, slightly hunched, slender young man with a prominent nose became so impressed on the public imagination that the same features were still being used to portray him twenty years later when he was greatly transformed. Described as cold, hard, ruthless, and Machiavellian, he would always be so remembered.

4. The Reformer

*A la fois probe et au courant des affaires, grande intelligence
masquée par des apparences de haine et de vanité, il valait mieux que
bien d'autres qui ont été depuis chefs d'Etat. Son tort, vis-à-vis
des autres hommes politiques, était d'en rester aux questions d'homme
à homme; son tort vis-à-vis de l'opinion publique était de mépriser
les hommes avant que les hommes ne lui en eussent reconnu le droit.
Si l'on prétend regarder de haut avant de monter sur le piédestal,
on n'y monte pas.*

Jean Prévost

BY THE END OF THE WAR Mandel had become a strong political personality
in his own right. Two of his assistants said, "No one would treat him any
more like a pretentious young secretary ... as they did a year ago, and
especially not those of us who have experienced his penetrating stare and
felt the weight of his authority."[1] By this time also, he had developed his
own plans for a fundamental reform of the parliamentary system in France.
The year 1919 for Mandel was to be one long attempt to persuade Clemenceau, Parliament, and the country to accept his ideas.

Because he worked in Clemenceau's shadow and usually preferred to
exercise influence indirectly, it was not always easy for his contemporaries
to determine what he was up to. One of the few who saw the role that he
played was the Royalist historian Jacques Bainville, who wrote in 1920 that
Mandel's most important achievement as Clemenceau's assistant "was to
prepare with intelligent foresight the internal policy of the postwar period,
to impose his views, and to make them succeed." His ideas, Bainville said,

were the expression of his mature thought developed over the years. On the one
hand, he wanted the collaboration of all French patriots against Bolshevism, ...
and on the other, he wanted the end of prewar parties, of local domination, of
personal rivalries, and particularly of religious conflicts. The elections of 1919
were his work. The winners perhaps do not always remember it; the losers
never forget it. ...[2]

Mandel's plans were similar in some ways to the reforms enacted or proposed years later during the Fifth Republic. Basically, he called for the creation of a two-party system. "I work neither with the revolutionaries, nor
with the reactionaries," he once said. "But between those groups there is
room for two great parties, the Whigs and the Tories."[3] One of the merits
of Clemenceau's government, he told the Socialists, was that "there were
two parties, as in the British Parliament ..., as in the assemblies of the July
Monarchy, as under the Combes cabinet. ... Of all the premierships [of the

Third Republic], Clemenceau's was the longest, and his policy was free from equivocation. Clemenceau always had the good fortune ... of being assured of your hostility. You at least were always able to say to your friends, 'Vote against Clemenceau.' "[4]

It was this division of Parliament into two large groups—a coherent, dependable majority facing a united opposition—that Mandel wanted to create. He believed that France already possessed an incipient two-party system, but that tendencies in that direction had to be strengthened.

If we look at our political history since 1870, [he said,] we will see that people voted for or against Thiers, for or against Gambetta or Marshal MacMahon, for or against the policy symbolized by Jules Ferry, for or against General Boulanger, for or against Waldeck-Rousseau.... When the voters went to the polls, ... they very rarely voted for a party, but rather for men who represented other men who planned to carry out a certain policy. I want to see conflicts of ideas, but they cannot take place without men; an idea not represented by a person is a myth.[5]

In other words, while it was essential that parties have clearly defined programs, it was just as important that they have well recognized leaders, supported by all the party's candidates in an election. It was this leadership that would provide the cohesive force in any coalition.

For Mandel, Clemenceau was the obvious leader of the coalition he hoped to create. The first stage of Mandel's plan, therefore, was to see that the 1919 elections gave Clemenceau a majority in Parliament. This could happen only if the Prime Minister intervened decisively in the elections in favor of his supporters, no matter who they might be. Clemenceau, traditionally anticlerical, might find it difficult to support the Catholics, but they had given him his most dependable backing since 1917. Moreover, if a viable two-party system were ever to be achieved in France, the Catholics must be allowed effective participation in the government as they had been during the war. Mandel hoped to persuade the moderate Republicans of this, and to ensure Catholic allegiance to the regime by promising at least the reestablishment of diplomatic relations with the Vatican.

The second stage of Mandel's plans called for the election of Clemenceau to the presidency of the Republic where his personal leadership would enable him to transform French politics by creating a coherent majority and provoking the opposition to unite. In order to restore the authority of the president as a counterweight to Parliament, and assure that Clemenceau would be able to play the decisive role envisaged for him, Mandel hoped to revive the presidential power of dissolving the Chamber that no one had dared to use since 1877.

In addition, Mandel proposed to create fifteen or twenty administrative regions out of the existing eighty-six districts, with regional elective assemblies authorized to decide many questions then handled by Parliament:

The Chamber of Deputies will only have to deal with the most important problems of foreign and internal policy.... The government will govern, the assemblies will control, and ultimately the sovereign people will judge. In case of conflicts of opinion between the assemblies and the government, the Chamber will be dissolved. Within a month the people will decide between them.[6]

These measures were designed to transform the political system of France, which Mandel called "a mediocre caricature of a parliamentary regime."[7] If Clemenceau retired, as he often threatened to do, Mandel knew that change would be difficult. Deputies would quickly return to prewar allegiances and reestablish the former system of fragmented groups, multiple parties, and floating majorities. The success of Mandel's plans therefore depended on his ability to lead the perverse and cantankerous seventy-eight-year-old Prime Minister along the desired path.

II

The armistice had hardly been signed when some of Mandel's plans became known. Predictably, they caused great excitement. Paul Deschanel, the president of the Chamber, perceiving a threat to his own lifelong ambition to be president of the Republic, rushed to Poincaré to report a disturbing remark Mandel had made: "We are going to have an election like that of Pope Sixtus V, and we will make of the presidency what it has never been."[8] Hoping to enlist Poincaré's aid against Mandel, he returned to the charge several weeks later with Antonin Dubost, president of the Senate, who also feared a campaign was under way to elevate Clemenceau to the presidency.[9]

Though not unwarranted, their concern was premature. Before the presidential and parliamentary elections could take place, many questions had to be settled. The troops were still at the front, industry had not yet been reconverted, the peace conference had not even met, the press was still censored, and the state of siege was still in force. There was considerable support, moreover, for a change in the electoral law, the discussion of which occupied the Chamber for the better part of 1919.

The system of election in effect since 1889, known as the *scrutin d'arrondissement à deux tours*, provided for single-member constituencies with a runoff ballot in case no candidate won an absolute majority on the first vote. It favored local interests and independent candidates at the expense of national policy and organized parties. Reformers proposed to introduce a list system of voting with proportional representation by departments. Such a system, they said, would reflect national opinion more accurately by giving equitable representation to all groups, and would raise the level of political discussion since the electorate could choose among the programs of parties rather than among the personalities of individual candidates. It was thought that the system would favor organized parties committed to definite programs over independent deputies, elected for local reasons and with only vague allegiances.

The law, as it emerged after lengthy debate in the Chamber, gave all the seats in a department to the list receiving an absolute majority of the votes. Proportional representation would come into effect only if no list received a majority. Thus stated, the law seems simple enough, but in practice the procedures proved to be both highly complicated and unfair. Instead of providing equitable representation for all groups as its original proponents had intended, it gave a great advantage to parties able to form electoral alliances. Two or more parties combining to present a common list had a better chance of obtaining an absolute majority of the votes, depriving even large minorities of any representation whatsoever.

Mandel was one of the staunchest opponents of the new system. During his electoral campaign in November, he said that "he understands proportional representation, the *scrutin de liste*, and the *scrutin d'arrondissement*, but he admits frankly having been unable as yet to understand the law voted by the Chamber, which adopted the worst features of each of these systems. He will let those who passed the law try to explain it to the voters."[10]

Unable to speak against the bill in Parliament, Mandel had persuaded various deputies to introduce amendments in order to make the bill so confusing that the Senate would reject it.[11] When it passed anyway, Mandel had the Socialist deputy Pierre Laval present a motion to postpone the application of the law until the following election.[12] This maneuver failed as well. Laval then tried to get Clemenceau to admit in debate that he disliked the law. Mandel hoped that if the Prime Minister, who had decided to let the Chamber choose its own form of election, publicly denounced the law, the deputies could be brought to reject it.[13] Clemenceau, however, disappointed Mandel by informing the deputies that although he thought it was a bad law, they had freely chosen it and he would not ask them to change their minds.[14] Thus in spite of all Mandel's efforts, the elections took place under the new system.

Mandel's opposition to proportional representation was deep-seated and unchanging. He believed that it failed to evoke a clear decision from the electorate on any issue, merely transferring national divisions of opinion to the parliamentary level, where policy would have to be determined haphazardly on the basis of compromises and temporary coalitions. He always favored a majority system of voting because, he repeatedly asserted, it was the best means of discovering the will of the country on any given issue and of creating a majority in Parliament in order to carry out the decision of the electorate.[15]

In 1919 he opposed the new law also because it disrupted his plans to be a candidate for the Chamber from Lesparre in the Gironde. Under the old system of voting he would surely have been elected because he had un-officially represented the interests of the arrondissement in Paris ever since the cancellation of the by-election in 1914. By obtaining favors for the voters and accomplishing virtually everything that they might have expected from any duly elected deputy, he had established a nearly impregnable position for himself in the district.[16] The new law, however, would make it much harder for him to get elected. New district boundaries could be gerry-mandered against him. He would be forced to find allies in order to present a common list for the entire department of the Gironde. His many enemies took advantage of their opportunity. Four of the incumbent deputies from the Gironde, including the influential former minister Charles Chaumet, refused to join the list Mandel tried to form or to have anything whatsoever to do with him.[17] At the same time, Parliament took up a motion to divide the Gironde into two electoral districts in order to join Lesparre with all the areas where it was thought that Mandel might run poorly.[18]

While his enemies united to assault him in the Southwest, Mandel secretly conducted negotiations in other districts in order to provide an avenue of retreat should his plans in the Gironde collapse. To force his opponents to disperse their efforts, he also spread rumors linking his name with a large number of districts.[19] As a result, within a short time everyone was utterly confused about his intentions. The frequent mention of his name as a pos-sible candidate in Corsica led the Bordeaux Socialist paper to print in a ban-ner headline: "Mandel, juif errant! Corse ou Gironde?"[20] In the Chamber, the Socialist deputy Jean Bon said that "the average Frenchman opening his paper in the morning does not ask whether the government has been overthrown or whether Serbia agrees with Italy, but in what electoral dis-trict *He* has decided this morning to present himself."[21]

Unable to oppose Mandel in any specific district, his enemies mounted a frontal attack in Parliament. In early August twenty deputies signed a proposed amendment to the electoral law to prevent any *chef de cabinet* who had not resigned six months before the elections from being a can-didate.[22] As introduced in the Chamber in October by Jean Bon, it was made even more explicit:

1) Civil servants known as *chef, directeur*, or *attaché de cabinet* of a minister or under-secretary of State cannot be elected in any district.

2) All acts of candidacy are void if they are not made in the legal name of their authors.

It was so obviously aimed at Mandel that it might as well have read: "No person who has assumed the name Georges Mandel can be elected in any district." The amendment had little chance of passing, but the

Chamber devoted a lively morning session to discussing it.[23] In its support Bon said that "we must know the names of those who want to govern France; it must be known that the next Chamber will bear an indelible mark; ... it will be the Chamber of Rothschild."

At Mandel's request,[24] Anatole de Monzie spoke against the amendment and told the deputies not to exaggerate his influence. "I have been his friend for ten years, but our friendship has never made me change my vote." Léon Bérard, who was soon appointed minister of Education as a reward for his efforts, wittily opposed the amendment, saying that its passage would put Mandel in the same category as members of former reigning families, who were also forbidden to hold public office.

All of these attempts to block Mandel were futile. While conducting negotiations in several districts, he delayed declaring his candidacy in any one of them until almost the last minute. Finally, on October 25, just three weeks before the elections, it was formally announced that he had joined a list in Corsica.[25] Three days later it was suddenly revealed that he would be a candidate in the Gironde. Although Mandel later claimed that the Corsican negotiations had been only a feint to force his adversaries to spend time and money fighting him there while he quietly prepared his election in the Gironde, he had actually made considerable efforts to obtain the support of the Bonapartists who were still influential on the island.[26] It was true that he preferred to run in the Gironde, probably because it was a larger and more important department, and possibly because he felt that there was something vaguely disreputable about being the deputy from Corsica. But it was also true that he had encountered strong resistance in the Gironde—resistance that was overcome, finally, when Clemenceau was persuaded to back him.[27] With the Prime Minister's open support, there could be no further objections to him.

The list that Mandel joined was composed of Center Republicans and Catholics who had reconciled their former differences in order to benefit from the decisive advantage given to coalitions by the new electoral law.* They signed a secret agreement in which the Republicans promised to support laws regularizing the use of ecclesiastical property by the Church, allowing the Catholics to open schools freely, and reestablishing relations with the Vatican. In return, the Catholics promised not to raise the question of revising the laic laws during the coming legislature. Mutually em-

---

* Although Mandel was nominally a Radical and still, in 1919, president of a section of the party in the 16th arrondissement of Paris, his plans for reform caused him to break with the Left. That this was not mere opportunism is indicated by the fact that, after entering Parliament, he took up a position clearly on the Right, instead of joining one of the amorphous and colorless Center groups. For his affiliation with the Radical Party and his attempts to deny it, see debate in *PVCG*, April 27–May 1, 1923, pp. 252–55, 328.

barrassed by their reciprocal concessions, the two groups formulated an equivocal election statement that expressed Republican attachment to the separation of church and state at the same time that it vaguely promised Catholics the relaxation of the anticlerical laws: "We will remain faithful to republican principles while assuring to all, Catholics, Protestants, Jews, and freethinkers, the rights to which they are entitled."[28]

Although Mandel joined the list after this agreement had been signed, he undoubtedly subscribed to its main points. As Bainville had seen, and as Mandel's later policies would show, he was genuinely interested in re-integrating the Catholics into the political life of the Republic. In fact he was probably one of the strongest advocates of concessions to the Catholics in all of France. During the campaign, a writer for *La Croix* spoke skeptically of the promises his friends told him the Republicans were making to them: "the reestablishment of relations with the Holy See, a law establishing the position of the Church in France, the restitution of any unsold ecclesiastical property, proportional state aid to Catholic schools, the admission of chaplains to public schools, and still more." "Obviously," the writer told his friends, "all of that is excellent, and if we get it eventually, we will be well along the way toward achieving the religious peace that we all desire. But are these things going to be mentioned in your program or at least in public speeches during the electoral campaign? 'Ah! No,' they reply with a frightened air. 'That would wreck the alliance! But we have received assurances. Have you no confidence in M. Mandel?' "[29]

It is questionable whether Mandel had promised all of these things to the Catholics. The writer for *La Croix* said he had chosen Mandel as an example simply because he had been mentioned as a possible candidate in so many constituencies that in citing him no particular coalition was being compromised.[30] But there can be no doubt that Mandel made substantial promises to the Catholics and did everything in his power to encourage the formation in other districts of similar alliances between them and the moderate Republicans.

The passage of the new electoral law forced all the parties to seek alliances or risk almost certain defeat. Only the Socialists, whose belief in class warfare had been revived by the revolutions in Russia, Germany and Hungary, refused to join any coalitions, and showed their disdain for bourgeois parties by presenting independent lists. In contrast, the moderate Republicans of the Alliance Démocratique hoped to form a large anti-Socialist coalition, embracing both the Catholics and the anticlerical Radicals. In this way they expected to win a majority of the votes, and thus all of the seats, in a large number of departments, drastically reducing Socialist representation. Many Radicals, however, balked against running on the same list with Catholics. Although the moderate Republicans had traditionally sided with the Radicals against the Catholics, when forced to choose in 1919 between their erstwhile allies and their newfound friends, they decided for once that a right-wing coalition would best serve their interests.[31] As a result, in many departments the Radicals were forced to run isolated lists. In forty districts, however, they managed to form alliances with the moderate Republicans, and in twelve more they even agreed to forget their anticlericalism and run on the same lists with Catholics.[32] The most notable of these broad coalitions was created in Paris under the title of the Bloc National, the name subsequently given to the victorious majority in the legislature.

Leadership of the Bloc National was assumed by the former Socialist Alexandre Millerand, who had started his career in the 1880's on Clemenceau's paper, *La Justice*. An almost irreparable breach had been created between the two men by Clemenceau's ferocious attacks on Millerand as minister of War in 1914, but Mandel managed to reconcile them and succeeded in having Millerand appointed High Commissioner for the Liberated Territories of Alsace and Lorraine in March 1919.[33] Brought once again into the limelight after his momentary eclipse during the war, Millerand became the most prominent personality in the Bloc National and the most likely successor to Clemenceau.

Further in the background, but never completely out of sight, was Mandel, using the extensive administrative machinery of the Ministry of the Interior to encourage the formation of lists supporting the government. The Interior minister was traditionally expected to intervene in elections in favor of friends of the party in power. It was a policy that everyone publicly deprecated, but privately adopted. Mandel's distinction lay in making little attempt to hide the influence he was exerting on the elections and even publicly acknowledging it. Speaking in the local assembly of the Gironde in 1921, he accused the Briand government of hypocrisy for its denial that it was using the administrative system for political ends. As for himself, he said, he considered the prefects to be political agents of the government and admitted having given them political orders.

I did not tell them to maintain neutrality. No! I believe that all citizens are equal and that we must have justice for all. But since it is only possible to govern effectively by means of a political majority, it is to that majority that we must accord favors, for our anachronistic administrative system still permits us to do it. I have always said it, and I will say it again until we reform the administrative system.... I will not be so cynical as to say, "I had nothing to do with what happened." Having given orders and directives, I assume the responsibility for them.[34]

Although the victorious Right later claimed that "for the first time since 1871 ..., the government did not interfere in the legislative elections,"[35] many complaints were registered at the time about Mandel and his machinations.[36] Jean Bon said that he was influencing the formation of lists throughout France and ironically compared him to God because "he takes care of the smallest details."[37] The respected diplomat Paul Cambon wrote to his son that Mandel

is now manipulating all France for the elections, using threats, making all the decisions, sparing no one, and using all the means put at his disposal by the censorship and the state of siege. In this time of general weakness he compels attention and even liking. Your uncle and I enjoy watching him operate; he would have been very useful in the Committee of Public Safety. I doubt whether well-meaning visionaries like Bourgeois, skeptics like Briand, romantics like Viviani, or manipulators like Barthou, will be able to get the better of this little man. . . .[38]

The creation of an effective majority in Parliament, however, would require far more than administrative pressure. The candidates all over France who were appealing for Clemenceau's support would have no obligation to work together after the elections unless they were committed in advance to a common program. The lists being formed in each department by separate agreement could be unified only by Clemenceau's open intervention in the campaign. With Millerand at his side, he gave a speech at Strasbourg on November 4 that provided the disparate groups of the Bloc National with a common program.[39]

Mandel later said that he had inspired the speech, and it did in fact broadly express his own policy.[40] In it Clemenceau endorsed the alliances that were being formed, especially insofar as they seemed to foreshadow the disappearance of the old parties. Should the Catholics be reintegrated into the political life of the country, he said, "I would consider it one of the greatest victories of the Republic." Only the Bolsheviks were condemned. In Clemenceau's famous phrase, "Between them and us, it is a question of force. . . ."

The most memorable parts of Clemenceau's speech were this appeal for national unity and the denunciation of the Bolshevik danger. Equally important, however, was the picture of the new order that he sketched. The main question facing the country, he said, was "the creation of a governmental majority based on a clearly defined program of action." But to achieve this required strength of character, "much more rare in our public men ... than brilliance of mind." There was no need, however, to revise the constitution, for the best political machinery was useless without capable and energetic leaders. Although he had not mentioned the presidency explicitly, he was clearly appealing for the election of a strong president, willing to use all his constitutional powers, possibly including that of dissolving the Chamber should it oppose him.

Given a strong executive, Clemenceau considered only one reform necessary: the decentralization of administrative authority by the creation of regional, rather than departmental, assemblies with increased powers. Beyond that, the task facing the new legislature would be a practical one. Mandel soon spelled this out in a speech in the Gironde:

> To wipe out as much as possible the horrible effects of the war; to give the country the economic equipment necessary to its development; to construct roads, canals, and railways; ... to build up our merchant marine; to conquer the air, for that is as crucial today as building railroads in 1840; to profit from the tremendous advantages of the peace treaty that people criticize without knowing its terms; to restore respect for authority in our administrative and our public services; to develop all of our natural resources; in brief, to use all means to assure general prosperity.[41]

It is as difficult to say how much of Clemenceau's speech was inspired by Mandel as it is to determine how much Mandel ultimately owed his ideas to Clemenceau. It is enough to note that their policies were identical, except for the extensive concessions Mandel was willing to make to the Catholics.

Clemenceau's speech gave the Bloc National a common program and a decided advantage over its opponents, who had no single leader capable of embodying their ideas. Jaurès was dead, Caillaux was in prison, and Briand was either too shrewd or too fearful to attack Clemenceau openly. Thus the only real choice people had was to vote for or against Clemenceau, and there was little doubt of the outcome of such a plebiscite.

In the Gironde, the Liste d'Union Républicaine Clemenciste was headed by Mandel and Pierre Dupuy, the under-secretary of the Merchant Marine in Clemenceau's cabinet and codirector of the influential Paris daily *Le Petit Parisien*.[42] It also included seven moderate Republicans and three Catholics. They were opposed by a Socialist list, a dissident Republican list, and a Radical list with only four candidates, whose eclectic supporters advised the voters to fill out their ballots with names from the other three parties. Among their recommendations were Mandel and two others from his list, three of the dissident Republicans and two Socialists.[43] Mandel was thus in the enviable position of being endorsed by the Catholics, the Republicans, and the Radicals.

The dissident Republican list was headed by the four incumbent deputies who had refused to collaborate with Mandel. They adopted a "me-too" strategy, claimed that they shared Clemenceau's ideas, and directed their attacks against Mandel personally. They reproached him for his supposed friendship with Bolo Pasha, for his change of name, and for not being a native of the Gironde. Of political differences there was hardly a word, though they did criticize the Treaty of Versailles as being too lenient. The only important issue they raised was the appearance of clericals and anti-clericals on the same list.[44] It was obvious that except for Mandel these men would have been willing to join the coalition behind Clemenceau. It was equally obvious that his fellow candidates would rather have Mandel on their list than these four established political leaders.

Mandel's greatest asset was his association with Clemenceau, which was played up in brief campaign biographies appearing in the newspapers.[45] It was suggested that Mandel would be a particularly influential representative if the Prime Minister were elected to the presidency. But when Clemenceau refused the offer of the Alsatian Radical Party to be its candidate for Parliament with the comment that he was obliged by age and poor health to retire from political life,[46] Mandel's opponents were quick to conclude that if elected, he would enjoy no special influence, and might even be at a disadvantage because of his many enemies.[47] Mandel felt sufficiently threatened to issue a statement, probably on his own authority, denying that Clemenceau had any intention of retiring from politics. Even though he was not a candidate for Parliament, Mandel said, nothing required him to give up the premiership, where he could still serve for a long time.[48] The statement was interpreted to mean that "the Bordeaux voters can depend for a long time yet on the favors dispensed to assure the election of the all-powerful *chef de cabinet*, who is doing them the great honor of soliciting their votes."[49]

Mandel's greatest disadvantage was the fact that he was not a native of the Gironde. As a Parisian Jew, he had little in common either with the provincial bourgeois society of Bordeaux, the departmental capital, or with the predominantly wine-making hinterland of the district.[50] The support given his list by the influential *Petite Gironde*, one of the most important provincial dailies, and by the Catholic newspaper *La Liberté du Sud-Ouest*, helped to compensate for his origins. So did the composition of the rest of his list: four incumbent deputies, several provincial politicians, a distinguished war veteran, a university professor, an agricultural specialist, a few businessmen, and some landowners. Clearly, local appeal was not lacking. Only the working class of this semi-industrial area, already committed to the Socialists in any case, failed to find representation on Mandel's list.

He tried to overcome the prejudice against him by emphasizing in speeches and campaign biographies the long patriotic and republican lineage of his family: "He is the son of a republican and the grandson of a combatant of the *Trois Glorieuses* whose name is inscribed inside the Colonne de Juillet.... His grandparents were Alsatians. Ten of their grandchildren have fallen on the field of battle for the integrity of French territory." He said that his father, who had been "a volunteer in 1870, was seriously wounded at Buzenval, and made *Chevalier de la Légion d'Honneur* on the field of battle. At this moment he is on the verge of death following the loss of two of his sons, fallen at the Somme for the defense of the country."[51]

To the Paris papers, which sent out special correspondents, Mandel's was the most newsworthy of the provincial campaigns. According to *Le Matin*'s André Salmon, as Mandel walked onto the stage at Libourne on November 6, the crowd of a thousand shouted out the word "Rothschild." In reply Mandel nodded his head and said: "Voici le grand coupable!" It took some time for him to dominate the noise and the interruptions of the hostile audience, but he was finally able to deliver his speech. His conclusion was a memorable apostrophe: "I am appealing to your intelligence, not asking you to like me."[52] Even more memorable was Mandel's incredible reply to criticisms of the government: "You can blame me for any mistakes the government may have made." It was no slip of the tongue or inadvertent statement. He had made the same assertion in a speech at Pauillac at the beginning of the campaign.[53] The first time, the remark had gone virtually unnoticed, but its repetition was reported in *Le Matin*. Clemenceau was infuriated by the insufferable presumption of his assistant, and did not forgive him for months.[54]

The scene prepared for Mandel at Libourne had been only a rehearsal for his first appearance in Bordeaux on November 13. Henri Béraud, sent from Paris to report on the meeting for the leftist *L'Oeuvre*, said, "I have seen some famous public meetings; I have seen some that are almost legendary, but never have I attended anything like this one."[55] Police surrounded the Alhambra Hall, which was jammed with more than two thousand of his opponents. They had arrived early and taken all the seats in order to show just how unpopular Mandel really was. The crowd began to roar as soon as he appeared on the stage, and they never did allow him to speak. Every time he tried to begin, the noise increased in volume. After patiently and disdainfully standing his ground for some time, he left the stage by the side exit, where his car was waiting. Pushing through another shouting mob, he reached his car and was just beginning to pull away when the rear window was shattered.

The following day the Bordeaux and Paris papers announced that an attempt had been made to assassinate Mandel.[56] Someone in the crowd outside the hall, they said, had fired a bullet that broke the rear window of the car and just missed Mandel's head. The story spread quickly and was soon embellished. By the time the Paris correspondent of *The Times* sent his account to London, it was being reported that two bullets had grazed Mandel's head.[57]

The "assassination attempt" created a sensation in Bordeaux. It seemed as if the Socialists and his other opponents feared and hated him so much that, realizing they would be unable to defeat him at the polls, they had resorted to assassination to prevent him from entering Parliament. The leftist press immediately expressed doubts about the story, and bystanders claimed to have heard no shot, but no one discovered what had actually taken place until after the election.[58] It turned out that the window had been shattered not by a revolver bullet, but by a cane or stick swung too hard by someone in the shouting and shoving mob.[59] Knowingly or not, Mandel had complained to the police about an attempted assassination, and released the story to the press.[60] His explanation of the incident turned the Socialist attempt to demonstrate his unpopularity into a demonstration of their fear of him.

The results of the elections on November 16 were a surprise. No one had expected the conservatives to win by such a large margin. The fear of socialism, which had encouraged the union of the conservative parties, was dispelled by the massive triumph of the Bloc National throughout France. The representatives of the old political regime seemed to have been swept into the dustbin as 370 new deputies were chosen in a total of 616, more than in any other election of the Third Republic. Since some four hundred of the victors had campaigned in support of Clemenceau, his program seemed assured of a large majority in the new legislature.

In the Gironde Mandel's list received an absolute majority of the votes cast, which entitled it to all twelve of the seats for the department. The Clemencists averaged 81,000 votes, Mandel himself receiving the second highest number on his list, 83,141. The dissident Republicans averaged 29,000, the Socialists 25,000, and the Radicals 13,000. The addition of the 81,000 votes for Mandel's list to the 29,000 for the dissident Republicans, with their almost identical program, gives an example, though perhaps not the most typical one, of the strength of the conservative forces in France: 110,000 out of 160,000 votes.

Within the following weeks Mandel was elected mayor of the small coastal town of Soulac and representative of the arrondissement of Lesparre on the General Council of the Gironde. To his growing list of offices he decided to add the presidency of the General Council, a position one writer has called "the sole honor in French politics that is awarded to seniority, the supreme goal of local politics, the ultimate aim of provincial ambitions. . . ."[61] He was warned that he would offend local opinion if he demanded this office,[62] but Mandel was not to be denied and the councilors accordingly elected him president on January 5. Many of his recent running mates, however, growing restless under his rule and alarmed by his seemingly boundless ambition, decided to halt his drive for power before it was too late. At the senatorial elections a few days later, when he tried to push through his own list of candidates, his fellow deputy Pierre Dignac bluntly told him, "That's enough, Mandel. Leave us in peace. We can choose our senators without your help."[63] A revolt had begun.

III

With the election of a large conservative majority, the first stage of Mandel's plans had been realized. His second aim was to weld into a coherent political force the 400 deputies elected in support of Clemenceau's program, many of whom were entering Parliament for the first time. At the opening of the legislature in December, said François Albert,

All eyes converge on Mandel. . . . The new deputies have no difficulty recognizing him since even before the return of Parliament he has tried to indoctrinate them. The first to arrive and the last to leave, he has taken each of his colleagues aside for conversation. In the anterooms . . . he can be seen endlessly carrying on long and mysterious discussions. Dogmatic, didactic, subtle, aware of everything, speaking in bookish terms, he is creating an impression and making his presence felt. He is directing maneuvers and establishing his position. He has his plan: tomorrow at the tribune, and soon after in power, which he has the firm hope of keeping for half a century since he is still only thirty-four years old. . . .[64]

It was already rumored that Millerand would succeed Clemenceau as prime minister and that Mandel would be the minister of the Interior.[65] It seemed only natural that he would take over the office he had run for two years. Wild speculations even accorded him the ministry of Foreign Affairs,[66] and the leftist *Progrès Civique* mentioned him as one of the five men who would dominate the new Chamber. After dismissing Viviani, Briand, and Barthou as possible prime ministers, they said that Millerand's victory had designated him to succeed Clemenceau. Of Mandel, they commented that "it is really too soon for him, and moreover, he lacks personal support."[67] The remarkable fact, of course, was that even for a second they entertained the idea that Mandel might become prime minister.

During the entire month of December, with the authority born of the part he had played in the elections and the part it seemed he was going to play in the new legislature, Mandel tried to convince the deputies to break with the old system of forming themselves into numerous groups and to create simply a governmental majority and an opposition.[68] He advised the Radicals to establish an opposition party, and their new leader, Edouard Herriot, did in fact unsuccessfully attempt to unite the Left.[69]

For Mandel the main problem facing the country, as Clemenceau had stated at Strasbourg, was "the formation of a governmental majority based on a clearly defined program of action." The resurrection of the old groups would mean the perpetuation of prewar political divisions. The Catholics would remain isolated, the Center groups would continue to vote alternately with the Left and the Right, and cabinets would continue to be a prey to these shifting alliances. There would be no coherent majority, no consistent program, and no government with a life expectancy long enough to permit it to undertake long-range reforms.

Mandel believed, as he later told the local assembly of the Gironde, that representatives

must be on one side of the barricade or the other. I realize that it is embarrassing. There are those who would prefer to make promises to both sides, depending on which way the wind is blowing. These men are found in every assembly. Before voting, they wait to see what everyone else is doing. They are always on the side of the majority. They are the Plain. They are the ones, gentlemen, who guillotined your great ancestors, the Girondins, ... who were in the minority at that time. I profoundly despise the Plain. I respect all opinions when they are sincere, thoughtful, and reasoned, ... but the men I despise are those who do not know which way to vote, because their only objective is to serve their own interest in invoking when necessary the general interest.[70]

No groups were formed in December, but neither were the deputies organized into two large parties. It was obvious that strong and active leadership would still be necessary to weld them into an effective majority. Clemenceau, however, was extremely coquettish. Mandel tried to persuade him to campaign openly for the presidency and to stop acting as if he already had one foot in the grave. At long last he agreed to accept the office if elected, but he refused to solicit anyone's vote, believing that the country owed him the honor in recognition of his work during the war. "I have other things to do," he told General Mordacq, "besides concerning myself with backstage maneuvers and low politics."[71]

Not only did Clemenceau maintain this attitude until the very end, but he obstinately refused to take Mandel's advice or to give him a free hand in conducting the campaign. Unfortunately, Mandel's influence on the Prime Minister was at a low point. Their relations had been strained ever since the election in the Gironde when Mandel's public assumption of responsibility for the acts of the government had infuriated Clemenceau.

On Mandel's first visit after the campaign, Clemenceau tipped his hat to him and said, "My greetings to the Prime Minister." He then forced Mandel to resign as *chef de cabinet* and ordered him to leave his office.

By January they still were not completely reconciled. When ex-Premier Ribot asked him, "What do you think of Mandel? He is already president of the General Council of the Gironde. What will he be tomorrow?" Clemenceau had replied that "Mandel is a good subaltern. He is subtle, but he has no ideas, and he is not capable of being a minister."[72] Clemenceau's opinion was not solely influenced by his anger at Mandel's presumption. Mandel did not share Clemenceau's liking for philosophical speculation, and he lacked the physical presence and force which Clemenceau considered essential to dominate an assembly.

Mandel for his part was dismayed by the Prime Minister's petulant refusal to heed his advice. He knew that in spite of the lack of open opposition to Clemenceau's candidacy, it would be fatal to remain inactive. The only other candidate was the President of the Chamber, Paul Deschanel, who despaired of being elected but was persuaded by Aristide Briand to stay in the race.[73] Despite Deschanel's promise to the Catholics to reestablish diplomatic relations with the Vatican, he received the support of the left-wing anticlerical leaders, Edouard Herriot and Léon Blum. Deschanel told them that he was personally opposed to renewing relations with the Vatican.[74] They must have suspected that he was lying, but when faced with a choice between having Clemenceau in the Elysée or an ambassador in the Vatican, these staunch anticlericals decided it would be easier to deal with the Pope in Rome than with the Tiger in Paris.

For fear of antagonizing anyone, Deschanel had always refused to join any government.[75] His sole qualification for the presidency, therefore, was that since 1912 he had been president of the Chamber. Mandel believed that if he were defeated in his bid for reelection to that office on January 13, he would have to withdraw from the presidential election four days later. Thus Mandel set about finding someone to oppose Deschanel in the Chamber election. He chose the leader of the Bloc National, Alexandre Millerand, whose chances of winning were excellent. But Millerand had little to gain personally from defeating Deschanel, and might have endangered his own authority in the Chamber when he was already assured of succeeding Clemenceau. He agreed to Mandel's plan only on the condition that the Prime Minister ask him to be a candidate. Clemenceau refused.[76] Clemenceau also ignored Mandel's advice to support Jules Pams for the presidency of the Senate. As a result, Pams withdrew from the race, and the presidency of the Senate as well went by default to the opposition.[77] Clemenceau in fact obstinately refused to take any action to assure his own election. He was playing to the hilt the role of "candidat malgré lui," and try as he might, Mandel was unable to sway him.

On January 13 Deschanel was reelected president of the Chamber without opposition. The announcement of his election was the signal for the outbreak of a demonstration arranged by Briand and the deputy André Lefèvre.[78] Shouts of "A l'Elysée" immediately resounded in the Chamber. To reporters who asked him if he intended to be a candidate for the presidency against Clemenceau, Deschanel cautiously replied, "I won't say 'No.'" Briand, who was at his side, hurriedly interjected, "That means 'Yes.'"[79]

Until that moment Deschanel's campaign had remained under cover, and almost the entire press had spoken of Clemenceau's election as certain. Briand, however, had been quietly undermining him, telling the deputies that "the hour has finally come to breathe freely," and asking them if they intended to install "the Mandelian regime at the Elysée." "You can see what an abominable tyranny it is," he said, "from the secrecy with which we are obliged to conduct our campaign."[80] But with the knowledge that Deschanel would definitely be a candidate, reported *L'Oeuvre*, there was "a great sigh of relief."[81] The campaign was brought into the open.

For two days Briand and others used every imaginable argument against the Prime Minister. Deschanel told the Catholics, "You have only one mistake to make—not to vote for me. If Clemenceau is elected, Mandel will become master of France...."[82] Briand warned them that Clemenceau would refuse to reestablish relations with the Vatican, and that there would be the scandal of a civil funeral for the president of Christian France since his age made it probable that he would die in office. It was also said that he would probably get sick and be unable to represent France properly at official functions, balls and dinners. It was even reported that he wanted to get married again.[83]

Variations of these arguments were repeated in the leftist press and, surprisingly, in some of the most important moderate journals as well. Among these were *Le Matin* and *L'Intransigeant*, which had been threatened with prosecution during the war and still remained antagonistic to Clemenceau and Mandel. Even *Le Petit Parisien*, whose codirector was one of Clemenceau's ministers, gave him only nominal support.[84]

The Left planned to nominate its candidate for the presidency at a preliminary meeting held shortly before the regular election at Versailles. Not wanting to give the old groups a chance to re-form, and fearing that a purely leftist congress would repudiate Clemenceau and hurt his chances of being elected, Mandel succeeded in having everyone invited to participate, turning the meeting into little more than a rehearsal of the actual election.[85] By continual harassment Clemenceau was finally persuaded to announce that he would accept the nomination for the presidency if his friends wanted to vote for him,[86] and at the last minute he asked the Catholics to have confidence in his liberalism and in his determination to unite all Frenchmen.[87]

These measures, however, came too late. Clemenceau continued until the end to frustrate Mandel's maneuvers. On the eve of the preliminary meeting that was to take place in the Senate building, Clemenceau told him: "Mandel, you are a deputy. You belong in the Chamber, but you have no business in the Senate. I forbid you to go there." As Mandel left the office, he predicted to a friend that the Prime Minister would be beaten the following day.[88]

Despite the prohibition, Mandel went to the Senate, where he carefully noted how each representative was voting. Ex-Premier Louis Barthou angrily exclaimed: "You want to see who I'm voting for? Take a look. I'm voting for Deschanel!"[89] In all, 408 votes were cast for the President of the Chamber, while Clemenceau, on whose program some 400 deputies had been elected, received only 389. He then withdrew his candidacy despite the protests of his friends, who insisted that he could still win the following day at the formal election.

Clemenceau was defeated for many reasons, but the primary one was his refusal to take any action to assure his own election. A promise to restore diplomatic relations with the Vatican would have won the support of the Catholics, but he was too prominent an anticlerical and too proud to make any promises.[90] Mandel could have defeated Deschanel and neutralized the opposition, but Clemenceau would not let him. As a result, all the enemies he had accumulated during his long political career were finally able to take their revenge. Senator Jean Philip, who had worked for him on *L'Aurore* and at the Ministry of the Interior in 1906, said that almost all of his former associates voted against him. They had too often suffered from his malicious wit and his capricious actions.[91]

Some representatives apparently voted against Clemenceau in order to get rid of his entourage.[92] By this they meant primarily Mandel. They feared that if elected, Clemenceau would be "a figurehead, capable of stirring to life only occasionally and striking out with his paws. People shuddered at the thought that victorious France, which could play such a decisive role in Europe, might confide the direction of public affairs to a second-rate figure who more often employed police methods than governmental procedures."[93]

Mandel also cost Clemenceau the votes of some of the deputies from the Gironde. In December, the twelve representatives had agreed to act in union, but most of them, including Pierre Dupuy, the High Commissioner for the Merchant Marine, voted against the Prime Minister. They chose this method of destroying Mandel's influence for fear of being dominated by him during the rest of the legislature.[94]

Mandel tried to find a candidate of sufficient stature to run against Deschanel at the formal election, but no one was willing to step into Clemenceau's shoes. Deschanel was chosen president of France without formal opposition. Together with Poincaré, the outgoing president, he agreed to confide the mission of forming the new government to Millerand, the leader of the Bloc National. It might seem as if little had been changed, for Millerand had been Clemenceau's choice as well. Indeed, one journal explained to its readers: "Although M. Clemenceau has disappeared, his policy remains."[95]

In fact, however, everything had been changed. Before the end of the month the group system in the Chamber was firmly reestablished. The deputies who had been elected on Bloc National lists in 1919 formed four groups: the frankly conservative Entente Républicaine Démocratique, and the ostensibly moderate or centrist Action Républicaine et Sociale, Gauche Démocratique, and Républicains de Gauche. The distinctions between them, according to the deputy Edouard Soulier of the Action Républicaine, were superficial: "None of these four groups has a distinctive doctrine; and for most of the 370 members who compose them, there is no real reason why they should belong to one of the four groups rather than another." He added that even many of the Radicals could easily belong to one of them.[96]

The creation of groups meant that the moderate Republicans would retain the balance of power in the Chamber. Necessary to the creation of either a rightist or a leftist majority, the Center groups hindered the development of an effective two-party system. A division of the Chamber into a governmental majority and an opposition, on the other hand, would have forced them into a tight alliance with the Right, which they rejected for two reasons. First, as old republicans and supporters of the separation of church and state, they were uncomfortable with any Catholic alliance, and afraid that the taint of clericalism might hurt them at the next elections. The second and more important reason was that they feared a solid conservative alliance would encourage the union of the Radicals and Socialists, which, if it ever came to power, would apply a left-wing economic policy. This was the real nightmare that disturbed the sleep of the moderates and made them irreconcilable opponents of any purely conservative coalition.[97] They were astute but basically timorous, and would have repudiated even a Guizot whose program called for "moderate measures applied by energetic men."[98] They favored a government based on an unorganized majority extending from the Catholics to the Radicals. This situation permitted them to be masters of policy by voting with the Right on economic and social issues and with the Left on religious or educational issues.

In the course of time a determined and skillful president aided by an equally determined and skillful premier might have been able to force the moderates into a permanent alliance with the Right, as Mandel had wanted to do. With Clemenceau gone, however, leadership of the new Chamber devolved on Millerand, who had an entirely different conception of the necessities of the moment.

Although he had been Clemenceau's heir apparent, Millerand was no one's puppet. He had refused to be a candidate against Deschanel, and he had been reluctant to accept Clemenceau's recommendations for cabinet positions. On leaving office, the old Premier offered to brief him on the negotiations and programs in progress, but Millerand curtly replied, "Don't bother." Said Clemenceau bitterly, "I turned over Europe and the government of France to him as casually as if I had given him a pebble."[99]

Moreover, in an electoral speech in November, Millerand had outlined a program superficially similar to but fundamentally different from Clemenceau's and particularly from Mandel's. At Strasbourg Clemenceau had opposed revision of the constitution and said that the basic problem facing the country was the formation of a coherent majority. Millerand, however, had proposed enlarging the electoral college and increasing the powers of the president in order to make him less dependent on Parliament.[100] He envisaged a presidential regime in which the executive branch would formulate policy independently of the deputies and parties, whose only function would be to approve or reject that policy. In the system conceived by Millerand, who professed the desire to maintain the *Union Sacrée* established during the war, there would be no organized majority or opposition, but merely a large number of isolated deputies voting on each question as they saw fit.[101] In essence, his ideas coincided with those of the moderate Republicans, who would have retained control over policy under such a system.

Although Millerand was unable to effect these reforms immediately upon becoming prime minister, he indicated from the start the policy he intended to follow. When the representatives from the various parties of the Bloc National met to coordinate their plans for the coming legislature, Millerand sent his secretary to inform them that they didn't need to talk any more about the Bloc National; the elections were over, and individual deputies could act as they wished. Technical and economic questions were now more important than political considerations.[102]

In his cabinet he gave the ministry of the Interior to Radical Senator Theodore Steeg, and the ministry of War to André Lefèvre, who not only had voted against the Treaty of Versailles, but had helped to defeat Clemenceau for the presidency. When the Catholics protested, Millerand told them: "We are not party men. To serve France and the Republic, I want the aid of all men: I will not be the prisoner of anyone.... Neither today, nor ever, do I intend to make concessions to what is generally called 'politics.' "[103]

The nomination of a Radical to the ministry of the Interior, however, was a further affront to the Catholics of the Entente Républicaine Démocratique, the largest group in the Chamber, whom Millerand had already offended by restricting them to two minor ministerial posts. Even the Radicals, the party supposedly discredited by the recent elections, had received more. Millerand perhaps realized that unless he pleased the strong Radical group in the Senate, he would have to depend entirely on the Bloc National for support, and this would soon have brought him into conflict with the upper chamber. Although he was undoubtedly obliged to treat the Senate with some circumspection, the appointment of a Radical minister of the Interior was an open repudiation of his electoral allies. It immediately destroyed the cohesion of the conservative forces by pushing the Catholics into opposition. As a result, Millerand's investiture majority was composed of moderate Republicans and Radicals. The members of the Entente abstained, but they very shortly rejoined the majority, for they had nowhere else to go and were eager to collaborate in the task of reconstructing the country. Mandel called them "worthy men who conducted themselves magnificently during the war, but who have not yet begun to understand politics."[104]

Millerand's conceptions could not have been further from Mandel's own belief that "everything is politics, for it is the political point of departure that determines the solution."[105] In his first article for the *Journal du Var* in 1910, Mandel had observed that many of the assemblies of the last twenty years had, by their first vote, set for themselves a course that they would have rejected if they had foreseen its logical consequences.[106] The record of the Bloc National Chamber would not only confirm the continuing accuracy of this observation, but also support the conclusion that Mandel was one of the few men of his time to have understood the fundamental weakness of the French parliamentary system and to have made a realistic attempt to reform it.[107]

IV

The personal rivalries surrounding the presidential election had almost obscured its real meaning. On one level, it was a personal battle between Clemenceau and Deschanel, or rather between their supporters; on another level, it was a struggle between two conflicting ideas of the nature of the presidency. Behind Deschanel were those who wanted to retain the tradition of a weak president with nominal powers, an arbitrator rather than a ruler, a symbolic figure like the King of England. Opposed to them as *Le Temps* pointed out, were those who "believed that it was possible, with or without constitutional revision, to give the president a more prominent role, more active powers, and more visible influence."[108]

That Clemenceau would have tried to rule and not simply reign is beyond question. Of a journalist who advised him to stay at the head of the government instead of imprisoning himself in the Elysée, Clemenceau exclaimed: "The imbecile! Nothing would be changed."[109] After his defeat, he told his friends that he had wanted to establish the peace on a secure foundation. He had asked nothing, had not wanted to be a candidate, and had only agreed to run when they insisted that it was his duty.

In fact, [he said,] you were right; no one . . . has more influence on the Allies than I do. To complete the work of peace, more difficult now than ever, I needed the general consent of the country. It would have given me the necessary authority with the Allies to obtain for France all of her rights. . . . Now I am a controversial figure. Even if I were elected tomorrow, my authority would not be the same. And the work to be done required absolute authority. Since Parliament did not want to give it to me, my role is finished. I am leaving.[110]

He then maliciously added to his friends that, without attempting to dictate to Millerand, he had recommended three of them for cabinet positions. These three, he said, had been his best assistants, but he refused to divulge their names. Earlier, however, he had told General Mordacq that the three men were Tardieu, Ignace, and Loucheur.[111]

To Mandel, who understood Clemenceau too well to have any illusions about him, it would have come as no surprise that he had not been recommended to Millerand. Cutting comments had been Mandel's customary fare for two months. The prolonged hostility was an unmistakable indication that his influence with Clemenceau had lessened. It was also an indication that, even if Clemenceau had been elected president, he might not have adopted Mandel's plans for reforming French politics. Moreover, by this stage of his career, the Prime Minister was weary of political maneuvering and was largely concerned with preserving France's security. Nevertheless Mandel might well have brought Clemenceau to share his ideas. So long as he was able to produce the required support for a vigorous foreign policy, Clemenceau would have raised no objection to his methods or plans. Whether they would then have been able to create a stronger executive and a viable two-party system is another question.

Undoubtedly, Clemenceau would have made a more effective president than either Deschanel or Millerand, who eventually succeeded Deschanel. Although the Catholics had voted against him because of his anticlericalism, he still represented the conservative, nationalist values that they upheld. Under him, the Right and Center would have been forced to collaborate more closely. As Edouard Soulier remarked, the main reason the Bloc National did not become a united group was that "no one had the will or the ability to bring it about."[112]

On the other hand, if Clemenceau had become an active and partisan president, there is a good chance that he would have come into conflict with Millerand, who had his own plans, or with the Chamber. It is possible that he would have been forced out of office as Millerand was in 1924 by the Cartel des Gauches. The one thing that can be said with certainty is that France would have fared no worse under Clemenceau than it did under the vacillating and contradictory policies followed by the men who succeeded him.

That Clemenceau never had his chance was largely his own fault, for he had been foolishly naive and stubborn in ignoring Mandel's advice to campaign for the presidency. But it was also the fault of Mandel, whose overbearing attitude not only antagonized Clemenceau but also precipitated a revolt among the deputies from the Gironde, and drove a large number of influential politicians and journalists into opposition. As Jean Prévost remarked, "Anyone who looks down on people before having been put on a pedestal will never be placed on one."[113]

5. The Bloc National

L'intelligence ne sert de rien en politique quand on ne possède pas le don de se faire suivre.

Paul Cambon

"SINCE CLEMENCEAU is no longer anything, Mandel is no longer very much."[1] That is the way one Bordeaux paper, in banner headlines, interpreted the presidential election. But if his enemies expected that Mandel, deprived of Clemenceau's support, would simply disappear, they badly misjudged their man. To a speaker who once said that events are sometimes beyond human control, Mandel replied, "I do not share your Moslem fatalism. I am not ready to bow my head to the ground and cry 'Allah is great! Let his will be done!' No, I believe that men and nations create their own destinies."[2]

According to Jacques Bainville, Mandel's outstanding characteristic was his strength of will, "an energetic and tenacious will that must and finally does overcome all obstacles."[3] Decisively defeated in 1920, his immediate and sole thought was to establish his position as a political force independent of Clemenceau, and to carry out his plans as best he could under the changed circumstances. Alone, or almost alone, he had somehow to bring the Chamber back from its erring ways and regain its capricious support. He might have tried to make the deputies forget their unpleasant memories of him; he chose instead to remind them of the past and the promises they had made during the campaign of 1919. "It is easy to please everyone," he told the General Council of the Gironde; "you pay compliments to everyone, do favors, and thus obtain the most diverse and contradictory support. Well, gentlemen, you can get rid of me if you like, but I refuse to give up any of my opinions.... At least I will always have had the satisfaction of saying what I think."[4]

Emphasizing his isolation, Mandel refused, as he always would, to join any of the groups in Parliament except the *Réunion des membres qui n'appartiennent à aucun groupe*, created to allow independent deputies to participate in the work of the permanent parliamentary committees, whose members were elected by the various groups. In defense of the program of 1919, he was joined by four of Clemenceau's assistants: the immensely talented André Tardieu; former Under-Secretary of Military Justice Edouard Ignace; and two other former ministers, Lucien Klotz and Louis Loucheur. Klotz and Loucheur soon defected, discouraged by the long period of opposition, but Mandel, Tardieu, and Ignace worked so closely together that Léon Daudet dubbed them Mandace, Ignieu, and Tardel.[5] They created no official organization, but were among the most active deputies in the Chamber.

Tardieu was the outstanding figure in the group. He had all the natural qualities of a leader: the physical stature and constitution, the verve and eloquence, the brilliant mind and resourceful imagination, and the tremendous desire for action and achievement. As foreign affairs editor of *Le Temps*, he had been one of the most influential journalists in France before the war, when the German Chancellor von Bülow had called him the seventh great power of Europe.[6] As Clemenceau's chief assistant during the peace negotiations, he had provided the arguments and drawn up the reports to support France's position. Clemenceau himself was so well aware of Tardieu's contribution that he once called the agreement reached at Versailles "our treaty."[7] Tardieu, rather than Millerand, was the real heir of Clemenceau, and according to one newspaper editor, "the Bloc National should have acknowledged him as its leader. The logical result of the 1919 electoral victory should have been a government headed by André Tardieu with Georges Mandel as minister of the Interior."[8]

After the presidential election, Tardieu refused Millerand's offer of a cabinet position out of loyalty to Clemenceau. Conscious of his own superiority, he had no doubt that the Chamber would soon acclaim him as its leader. But the deputies in 1920, having repudiated Clemenceau, were far from ready to accept another self-assured, overbearing, disdainful premier. They resented Tardieu's haughty airs and his habit of challenging the Chamber, of preferring to fight and harangue rather than persuade. Senator Jean Philip said that "it was impossible to like so arrogant a man, who, instead of making you forget his unquestionable superiority, insolently and brazenly asserted it over you."[9]

What joined Tardieu to Mandel, whose ascetic frailty and intellectual intensity contrasted markedly with Tardieu's exuberance and love of life, was their common loyalty to Clemenceau and their determination to impose his program on the Chamber. They continued the division of labor begun under Clemenceau: Tardieu defended the Treaty of Versailles against a slowly mounting current of criticism, while Mandel devised their political strategy.[10]

According to Paul Reynaud, Mandel had one of the finest political minds of his time.[11] Superior to Tardieu in his knowledge of Parliament and of internal affairs, Mandel would have liked to direct him, but Tardieu was often far too independent and impatient to follow Mandel's tortuous thoughts and plans.[12]

When Millerand first presented his cabinet in the Chamber with the Radical Steeg as minister of the Interior, Tardieu abstained, while Mandel surprisingly supported the new government.[13] But the two men soon united again in opposition, particularly after the Prime Minister made some concessions to Germany in a conference at Spa in June. It was the beginning of France's long retreat from the advantageous position she had established at the Paris Peace Conference. From the rostrum, Tardieu made it clear that the Clemencists wanted the Treaty of Versailles applied without weakness or compromise.[14] Most of the Chamber undoubtedly agreed, but not strongly enough to overthrow Millerand and hand the government over to Tardieu. It was said that Millerand would be unbeatable so long as he could dismiss the Clemencists' criticism as "nothing but a political maneuver of the Tiger's former cohorts."[15]

While Tardieu attacked from the rostrum, Mandel made use of his new position on the Foreign Affairs Committee of the Chamber. He pressed the Committee to hasten its consideration of the bill for the reestablishment of diplomatic relations with the Vatican.[16] Although he hoped to reconcile the prewar discord over religious questions, he thought the issue ideally suited to split the Chamber into a coherent majority and a united opposition. In the past the clerical danger had often been used to recreate the alliance between the Center and the Radicals. Since the Center now favored, or at least had agreed to vote for, the reestablishment of relations with the Vatican, Mandel hoped to use it to force the anticlerical Radicals to oppose the government, which they had supported since the beginning of the legislature as faithfully as the members of the Bloc National.

The bill was not finally brought up for discussion until November. By that time President Deschanel, succumbing to a nervous breakdown bordering on insanity, had resigned. Almost without opposition Millerand was chosen to succeed him. His candidacy was supported by Briand, as well as by Mandel and Tardieu, for the obvious reason that Millerand's elevation would vacate the premier's office in a legislature where natural leaders were few and competition restricted. Moreover, ignoring his disappointing record, which led other Clemencists to oppose his election,[17] Mandel usually spoke well of Millerand and tried to support him whenever he could.[18] In fact, throughout the legislature, in spite of frequent differences of opinion, they maintained a tenuous alliance, the exact nature of which has never been revealed.[19]

In the electoral campaign of 1919 Millerand had proposed revising the constitution to strengthen the power of the president. That he himself intended to be more than a figurehead, even without revision, was evident by his choice of Georges Leygues to succeed him as prime minister.

Leygues was a respectable but not particularly distinguished moderate Republican who had served in a number of governments. As prime minister, he agreed to keep Millerand's cabinet and to fulfill Millerand's program, which made him seem little more than the President's delegate.

Although Leygues held office for only four months, he did get the Chamber to pass the bill reestablishing diplomatic relations with the Vatican. It was on this issue that Mandel chose to make his official debut in Parliament on November 18, 1920. He could hardly have found a more controversial topic for his first speech. The issue itself revived the anticlericalism of the Radicals, and Mandel's position on it assured him of their open opposition. In any case, it was the first public occasion his many enemies would have to demonstrate their dislike, and not even a less controversial subject would have protected him.

His speech was at least a *succès de curiosité*, for everyone turned out, not so much to hear him, as to watch the spectacle of what *L'Humanité* called "l'après-midi d'un singe."[20] As he walked to the tribune with a large dossier under his arm, noises and voices became audible throughout the Chamber. In the few seconds he took to mount the stairs, the disturbance became a clamor so loud that he could not be heard when he began his speech. Standing expressionless at the tribune, he tried once or twice to raise his voice above the commotion, but failed. The Socialist Paul-Boncour taunted him, "That's the Chamber you elected, M. Mandel."

A few deputies on the right contributed to the clacking of desk tops and the shouts from the left. The rest of the Right occasionally supported Mandel, but for the most part sat immobile, fascinated by the concerted assault. Faced with such deliberate obstruction, deputies in the past had been forced to retreat from the rostrum. Knowing what to expect, however, Mandel had minutely prepared his speech and was ready to stay there all night if necessary. When this became clear, the demonstration subsided, and he was able to begin.

Gentlemen, I have not climbed this Calvary . . . and exposed myself to the jeering I knew awaited me, in order to make amends for the crime of Golgotha. . . .

I belong to a race that in the course of centuries past has been the object of this kind of Inquisition, which, if it sometimes degrades its victims, always dishonors its agents. But I know also the duties of tolerance . . . and there is a point on which I am in complete agreement with M. Herriot: though the Church may appear in the mists of time like a force of oppression, the Republic is and must be a regime of freedom.

He proceeded to lecture the Chamber on the history of France. Documenting every point, he intended to prove that the reestablishment of relations with the Vatican was not at all incompatible with French law.

Occasionally, the noise would break out again, and the President of the Chamber would have to threaten to suspend the session before order was restored. At one point, Mandel commented about some papers he held in his hand, "I had these documents before coming to the prime minister's office," which meant that he was not making illegitimate use of information obtained as Clemenceau's *chef de cabinet*. To the Left, however, it seemed as if he were referring to himself as the former prime minister, and they took it as their cue for a new outburst. From any other speaker, the remark would have been merely a slip of the tongue or an abbreviated reference, but in a speech as well prepared as Mandel's, where he had foreseen everything, including the original disturbance, the remark could only have been a calculated provocation.

Even his manner of delivery provoked the Chamber. "He was too much at his ease," said Etienne Chichet, the former director of *L'Homme Libre*. "Sometimes he lounged about or leaned on his elbows; sometimes he bent double over the tribune, his head and chest protruding beyond the edge. In short, he ... seemed to be saying: 'At most, there are a dozen among you worthy of hearing me.' "[21]

Contemptuous of his fellow deputies, and knowing that he was going to be attacked in any case, he deliberately courted their antagonism, almost as if overcoming it would give added *éclat* to his final victory. "You like unpopularity," his friend Emile Buré once told him, "because you have read that it generally accompanies true statesmen in their rise to power. Besides, displeasing or disturbing your contemporaries always gives you a sadistic pleasure."[22]

Mandel argued that France should be represented at the Vatican because it was one of the most important listening posts in Europe. An embassy at the Vatican might also give France some influence over the nomination of bishops in the Rhineland and help her to create an autonomous Rhenish state. He did not say so, of course, but these possible diplomatic advantages were secondary to the internal benefits he hoped would result from establishing the embassy. The Catholics formed the bulk of the Entente Républicaine, the largest single group in the Chamber. They had to be appeased and brought into effective participation in the Republic, for they were necessary to the formation of a conservative majority, and without them France would return to a system of Center governments. To assure their collaboration, some of their demands would have to be met. The most important of these demands at the moment was the reestablishment of relations with the Vatican. Since the Center had already agreed to support that proposal, debate on it provided an opportunity to recreate the Bloc National majority and force the Radicals into open opposition.[23] Ultimately, Mandel and Tardieu hoped to push them into permanent opposition, making the government dependent on the right wing of its majority. This would oblige the Center to work more closely with the Right. It would also increase the likelihood that one of the Clemencists might become premier.

In the second half of his speech, therefore, Mandel attacked the Radicals and particularly their leader, Edouard Herriot. After attempting for some time to provoke Herriot, he said, "I would not think of starting a personal debate between us. We are discussing ideas. I do not even want to remember that in the year before the war you went to Berne to speak with the Germans. (Exclamations on the left and extreme left.) That is the kind of polemic you will never be able to get me to indulge in."

The remark, calculated to nettle the Radicals, got an immediate reaction: "You there at the tribune, what's your name?" Mandel ignored the interruption and continued his attack. "It is possible," he declared, "to be a republican without making a pact with the apostles of social revolution. There are 400 deputies in this assembly who take their cue neither from the Bolsheviks nor from the counterrevolutionaries." Because of their occasional collaboration with the Socialists, Mandel was including the Radicals among those dominated by the Bolsheviks. Although they took up his challenge, the Radicals and the entire assembly were tired, and after a few more exchanges of repartee, the session was closed. The speech had lasted over two and a half hours.[24]

Mandel's speech had no effect on the ultimate voting; the Chamber would have passed the bill in any case. Nor did it succeed in placing the Radicals in permanent opposition. After this one lapse, they returned to voting for the government. It had been a personal triumph of sorts, however. He had held his ground before the concerted attack and made the assembly hear him out. But if he had demonstrated his personal strength, he had certainly done nothing to abate the animosity of the Chamber. He was as insolent and assured as when he was Clemenceau's assistant, with the full force of the government behind him. Far from having taught him prudence, his multiple disappointments earlier in the year had only made him more aggressive. The situation itself, perhaps, required the qualities he had shown, for a less aggressive man would certainly have been swept from the tribune by the fury of the attack.

When the Leygues government was overthrown two months later, it seemed as if Mandel's last hope of directing the Chamber was lost. To form the new cabinet, Millerand summoned Aristide Briand, who even the Left admitted had been the big loser in the elections of 1919.[25] It was rumored that Briand was chosen because he had helped elect Millerand to the presidency in September,[26] but it is more likely that Millerand, as his secretary later explained, was merely responding to the political climate of the moment.[27]

In this case, the "political climate of the moment" was created by the Alliance Démocratique, the party to which almost all the members of the Center groups belonged. It had participated in the Bloc National for the elections and admittedly shared the economic policy of the Right,[28] but it preferred not to be too closely associated with the Catholics. Together with the Right it held a clear majority, but the last thing it wanted to see was the division of the Chamber into a coherent majority and an organized opposition. The union of the Radicals and the Socialists that Mandel favored was in fact the nightmare of the Center, for such an alliance might eventually lead to the adoption of a leftist economic policy. The Alliance Démocratique preferred therefore to court the Radicals, and to leave the Socialists and, if necessary, the Catholics to create a totally ineffective opposition. Albert Mamelet, the secretary-general of the Alliance Démocratique, wrote that "there are many reasonable and sensible Radicals and Radical-Socialists who are not separated from us by any essential idea, and who are no less resolved than we are to defend economic freedom, fight collectivism, respect all religious beliefs, and settle outdated quarrels; the Republican, Democratic and Social Party* is open to them, and without them, in our opinion, no true national union is possible."[29]

Thus, even if Millerand had wanted a right-wing leader to form the government, he would have had to contend with the opposition of the Alliance Démocratique, as the party informed him in advance. When the Leygues government was overthrown, Mamelet warned that if the Right or Right-Center tried to determine the orientation of the new cabinet, the Bloc des Gauches would be reconstituted immediately. Rather, all factions of the Republican Party should form a government with a clear and precise program, headed by a true statesman. He insisted, however, that the Left-Center remain in control.[30] The man he supported to lead the cabinet was Raoul Péret, a member of the Alliance Démocratique and Deschanel's successor as president of the Chamber. But when Péret failed to persuade Briand and Poincaré to work together in his cabinet, Millerand asked Briand to form the new government.

Briand gave the Right slightly more representation than it had received in the previous government, but still retained a Radical at the Ministry of the Interior, though one less markedly objectionable to the Right than Steeg

---

* The "Republican, Democratic, and Social Party" was the name adopted by the Alliance Démocratique during the years immediately after the war. I have continued to refer to it as the Alliance since the party soon reverted to this title.

had been. It was the Center, however, that received the greatest number of places in his cabinet.[31]

Although Mamelet was disappointed that Poincaré, the honorary president of the party, was not in the government, he was otherwise fairly well satisfied. "The Briand ministry contains too many of our friends for us not to approve of it. Briand is a master at extracting from any parliamentary assembly the broad lines of a governmental policy, and incarnating them in a skillfully balanced coalition, where all the elements of the government majority are exactly represented."[32] The Entente Républicaine group on the Right, with 180 members and only four ministries, would hardly have agreed that they were exactly represented, but they nonetheless gave their support to the new cabinet. Only the Socialists voted against it, Mandel and Tardieu preferring to abstain for the moment.

The summoning of Briand was a patent breach of French parliamentary practice, for he was neither a leader of the majority, nor a leader in overthrowing the Leygues cabinet. He was able to form a government only because the Center supported him and the Right, less willingly, went along. The members of the Entente were mostly Catholics who at one time may have opposed the republican regime, but had since rallied to it. Elected for the first time in 1919, most of them were suspicious of the old politicians and thoroughly befuddled by the political maneuvering of their opponents. In their inexperience, they had hoped to do away with purely political struggles and simply devote themselves to the economic reconstruction of the country. They wanted new and younger men to take charge of the government and were disappointed when they saw the reappearance of the old guard. But without experienced leaders themselves, they very frequently simply followed the Center, and allowed it to dominate the government.

Tardieu and Mandel in many ways represented the policies of the Right and sometimes succeeded in getting its support. It was even suggested to them by Robert Cornilleau of the Christian Democrats that they create a new political party of which the Entente would probably have formed the nucleus. "Clemencism," Cornilleau said, "to the extent that it represents the tradition of a democratic and national radicalism, but avoids its anticlericalism, could be the ferment of a new party that would rejuvenate the Republic. It is a great opportunity for vigorous and talented men like Tardieu and Mandel. If they accept it with determination, restraining their excessive individualism and their parliamentary maneuvers, they would rally a great number of men who dislike the insipid policies of the moderates and the Radicals, and yet do not want either Fascism or Communism."[33]

But both Mandel and Tardieu were too independent to work within a party and do not seem to have considered creating one. They modeled themselves after Clemenceau, who was never more than a nominal member of any party, and preferred to concentrate on gaining power and directing policy so as to create a coherent majority. Mandel had been correct in his belief that Clemenceau's general popularity and forceful will were necessary for this. It would have been difficult for the Center to oppose the old statesman openly. Once in office, Mandel and Tardieu themselves might perhaps have possessed the essential will power to weld the Bloc National into an effective political force, but they were unable to get into office. They had tried in vain throughout 1920, but the initial desire for change expressed in the 1919 elections had been thwarted by Millerand, and Parliament soon settled into its old, comfortable political habits. The choice of Briand in 1921 was a striking indication that they had failed to change the system. Briand at the head of Clemenceau's majority was more than even Mandel in his most cynical moments could have foreseen.

In his speech in November 1920 Mandel had criticized the majority for failing to carry out its own program. In 1921, with Briand heading the government, he was to lash out at the Right and Center. The bitterness had been slow in building up, but it finally erupted in August after he lost the presidency of the General Council of the Gironde.

On the strength of his association with Clemenceau and the role he had played in the 1919 campaign, Mandel had secured this office in January 1920. In August of that year, in the regular election for the normal term of a year, he was chosen again but with a greatly reduced majority. His prestige had declined in the Gironde more slowly but no less disastrously than it had in Parliament, and for the same reasons: he had been insolent, arrogant, and domineering. Again a candidate in August 1921, he spoke in advance to each of the fifty councilors, of whom thirty-five promised to vote for him.[34] On the day of the election, however, knowing that the promises would not be kept, he withdrew from the contest. After the vote for his successor, a well-liked local politician, one of the more vehement councilors cried out: "Long live the Gironde and the Girondins! Long live the General Council of the Gironde, which will now have as president a good republican and a native Girondin."[35]

Mandel was free for the first time to speak as an ordinary councilor and not as the president of the group. In a marathon bout of oratory stretched over four days, he told the councilors, seventeen of whom were also deputies and senators, what he thought of them, what he thought of their choice to replace him as president, and what he thought of their policies. Finally, not to end on a negative note, he gave them a plan for carrying out several of the department's projects.[36]

But first he wanted to say something about the meaning of the word *Girondin*. "I have been criticized for not being a Girondin," he complained. "If by not being a Girondin, you mean that I was not born in the department of the Gironde, you are right; and if by being a Girondin, you mean practicing an easy opportunism, making promises to everyone, spending one's time making toasts and attending banquets, you are right again: I am not a Girondin."

Having set the tone of his speech by this prelude, he continued:

Gentlemen, you are winegrowers and businessmen; I am a politician. I do not deny it. I have twenty, thirty or forty years ahead of me; and so long as I have a breath of life in me, I will be in politics. Until my last day I firmly hope to be able ... to say that I have not changed.... But there are some men of whom I cannot say as much; they are those Saxons* you spoke of; that band of domestics, opportunists of Right or Left, who go with one side or the other depending on which way the wind is blowing. They are those men who say in private conversation: "Yes, Mandel is right. But he is all alone. We can't go along with him. He is going to be beaten." Whether he is right or not is really unimportant to them; the general interest does not count for them; they have only one concern: to make a career, to advance, to obtain a promotion, to move one step higher....

The Council protested so loudly that it was difficult for him to develop his thought. He returned to the same points several times, however, as if to heap coals on a fire that was already blazing. "There is a barrier between us.... You are concerned with your own interests; you are preoccupied ..., miserably preoccupied with questions of vanity. You are worried whether X will shake your hand; you want to get along well with Z. Rarely ... during my campaign for the presidency of the General Council did I find any colleagues who asked me: 'What would be good for the people?' "

They already disliked him; now he was going to make them hate him. For once, he would tell them exactly what he thought despite the consequences:

At this moment I am making innumerable enemies. If I had gone to see you all individually and told you that you had given magnificent speeches, written remarkable reports, you would undoubtedly have said: "That Mandel, he's really an intelligent fellow." You would have said that I had great qualities. Men are like that. But I refused to demean myself by imputing virtues to you that you do not have. My fate was therefore sealed.

He said that it was unimportant that they did not want him to be their president, but they should have elected someone worthy of representing

---

* According to Mandel, "The characteristic of a Saxon is to keep his mouth shut in public, to make promises in private, and to break them at the polls."

the Gironde, one of the largest departments in France. He had told them in advance that "the president of the assembly in a department of a million people should be the most eminent and distinguished man among them." But they had refused to listen to him, they had refused to choose "a man with some gift for expressing himself, who is intelligent, who has some intellectual ability, who is talented and has achieved something." Instead, said Mandel, all but pointing at the new president, they had chosen "the most polite, the most pleasant man."

Rarely has any assembly ever been taken to task so harshly, or any group of men told so bluntly that "in an assembly under the democratic regime, fifty men have never been brought together without there being among them a certain number of imbeciles and a few thieves." His aim in the seemingly interminable speech, however, was not simply to demonstrate how much he despised the councilors, but to present them with a definite plan of action, though how he ever expected to gain their collaboration after having insulted every one of them is beyond comprehension. He recommended that the councilors attend public meetings, go among the people, discuss issues with them and draw up a list of demands. Then,

on the day when [your newly chosen president] will come to say to our members of Parliament, "This is our program; this is what our people want"; on the day that these demands seem justified, I will join all of my colleagues, without exception—on the condition, however, that we agree in advance to set a time limit for the government to give us satisfaction. If at the end of that time, we have received nothing but words, we will decide what to do. But if you are making a *démarche* only in order to receive letters from the ministers, then No! A *démarche*! Yes! With a time limit! Yes! And if at the end of that time limit, satisfaction has not been given to us, we will return before the General Council of the Gironde. There are seventeen senators and deputies among us, and if to defend a request of the district, these seventeen members of Parliament decide to fight, to raise questions, to interpellate every day, we will achieve our aims, and if we do not, the cabinet will not survive our failure.

Needless to say, his ideas were not accepted by the Council. Calixte Camelle, the former Socialist deputy defeated by Mandel in 1919, told him,

I am ready to accept your advice . . . , but you should preach a little more by example. Yesterday you drew a very bleak picture of the parliamentary system; you called some of the deputies from the Gironde and some of the men in this room domestics, valets. That's your policy, M. Mandel! It's the policy of M. Clemenceau! . . . When you have a policy like that behind you, when you have used and abused the system . . . , you should be more modest, M. Mandel. Just because you have descended from the tribune, you should not adopt such a haughty tone, wanting to give advice to everyone. Look at the faces of your colleagues; they are skeptical every time you speak. They say: "M. Mandel speaks well!" Yesterday evening you spoke superbly; you made a furious attack against those you called the "Saxons." I assure you that from the point of view of oratory, you were superb; and I congratulate you. But I repeat again, it is not you who should say these things.

Mandel's attack had indeed been furious, but it had not been unpremeditated. In spite of its emotional tone, the speech had not been caused by a spontaneous burst of anger, nor had it been inspired solely by his disappointed ambition; it was part of his fight to change France's political habits, to get the Council, to get Parliament, to get every political assembly to act rather than just discuss. As he told the councilors,

If the representative system is to work, it is essential that we once again enjoy the benefits of party conflict. And I ask those who have sometimes appeared to regret the liveliness of our discussions to reflect for a moment: The voters will go to the polls only if we fight for our respective ideas. If they believe that nothing will be changed no matter which candidate they vote for, they will not participate in future elections, and the Republic will be finished.

Having presented one plan of action to the councilors in the Gironde, Mandel left for Paris to present its national counterpart in the Chamber. Earlier in the year he had asked Briand to define his policy,[37] because as Mandel told Camelle, "If you were in the Chamber, you would not know whether to tell your friends to vote for or against M. Briand."[38] Now he would ask Parliament to turn Briand out of office.

The moment was propitious. Mandel's intervention against Briand in March had been fruitless. The skillful Prime Minister had gained the support of the Right by promising to get the Senate's approval for the resumption of relations with the Vatican, and to make Germany live up to her obligations under the Treaty of Versailles. Although the Chamber had been disturbed when Briand accepted the reduction of German reparations at the Paris Conference in February, his government had been bolstered by the Allied decision in March to occupy some cities on the right bank of the Rhine. The Germans had pressed their luck too far. The occupation had been decided upon when the German delegation at the London Conference suggested that reparations be reduced to one-fourth of what the French considered their due, and claimed to have paid half of that already. Even Prime Minister Lloyd George, generally favorable to mitigating the provisions of the Treaty of Versailles, was angry, and approved of occupying Düsseldorf, Duisburg and Ruhrort to encourage German compliance. Mandel's intervention in March, following the occupation by just a week, could do nothing to efface the impression of dynamism left by the movement of Allied troops into Germany.

By October the situation had changed. The Germans had failed to pay the twelve million gold marks due on May 1. Briand used aggressive language, but this time did nothing. In the meantime, Lloyd George had returned to a policy of conciliation. In his wake he drew Briand, who was afraid of leaving France isolated and was himself convinced that if Germany were ever to pay her debts, she could not be pushed too far. The Center and the Right, favorable to a stricter interpretation of the Treaty of Versailles, were seriously disturbed when Briand's forceful words were followed by weak actions.

It was at this point that Mandel intervened in Parliament, and for two days held the attention of the assembly. His tone was less bitter than it had been in the Gironde. The first day, in fact, he did little more than toy with the assembly, but in such a way that he had the Socialists all but climbing out of their seats to pull him from the rostrum. By suggesting that one of their members was an informer, he brought them to a fever pitch. "His name!" they cried. "Give us his name!" Only when the entire assembly was in an uproar did he reveal that the Socialist deputy Escoffier had given him some information that might embarrass the government.

The following afternoon, as Mandel walked to the tribune to continue his speech, Escoffier, who had been absent the day before, ran up and struck him. The two men were quickly separated, however, and Mandel was soon able to resume his speech. He then finally came to the point. In the elections of November 1919, he said, the country had not voted for a leftist or a rightist policy.

It voted for the Republic that had won the victory. It voted for a policy of order and of progress, and at the same time it expressed dissatisfaction with the men whom, rightly or wrongly, it considered responsible for the lack of preparation in far too many areas at the beginning of the war.

On the morning of November 17 ... everyone reading the papers remarked: "More than three hundred new deputies in the Chamber! Something is going to be changed! We will no longer see on the forefront of the stage that prehistoric personage who has been rationalizing his actions for a quarter of a century, or the one who for thirty years has always rushed to abstain from voting, or the other whose ability to forget has been taken for an indication of dexterity." The least we can say is that so far no such profound change has taken place.*

---

* The "prehistoric personage" was probably Millerand. The man who rushed to abstain from voting was Poincaré. Caillaux tells the story in his memoirs (III, 6–7). The man with the bad memory was Briand, who had begun his career as a union lawyer, advocating a general strike to overthrow the regime. Then as prime minister in 1910, he recalled the striking railwaymen to military service and used the army against them. Also, in 1904 he had been the reporter of the bill to break diplomatic relations with the Vatican, and was now supporting the renewal of those relations.

He turned to the Right and Center and told them that they should try to carry out the program they had outlined in 1919: the strict application of the Treaty of Versailles by means of a strong government backed by a coherent majority. They had either to force Briand to carry out their policy, or to replace him by one of their own men. "Members of the majority," he said, "don't let your opponents persuade you to commit suicide. Don't let them hold you responsible for acts they have committed, and for which they will one day blame you."[39]

In spite of all the peripheral issues with which Mandel almost obscured his point, the speech had been effective. François Albert observed that "with impressive vigor, Mandel broke decisively with seven years of *Union Sacrée* governments and raised the question of internal policy in a style as clear and blunt as in the time of Méline, Combes, or the first Briand ministries. Such language has not been heard since the day Ribot fell a few weeks before the war, under the attacks of the republican majority elected in 1914. But this time the positions were reversed. It was the electoral majority of the Bloc National which through Mandel asked Briand to delimit the majority on which he intended to base his government."[40]

The cabinet was shaken. The Right was upset, and even Albert Mamelet of the Alliance Démocratique called on Briand to define his policy.[41] But the Center had no intention of overthrowing Briand. The always moderate *Petite Gironde* did not approve of Mandel's criticisms. "It has always seemed to us that Briand was the statesman most qualified to conduct the negotiations with our allies and maintain the Entente. With a prudence adapted to the circumstances, excluding neither firmness nor results, he has realized his aims."[42]

A few days later Tardieu, against Mandel's advice,[43] renewed the attack. By an exaggerated denunciation of the Radicals, whom he held responsible for all the difficulties of the prewar regime, he brought them to support Briand's ministry openly.[44] The combined effect of the two speeches was to create a new majority for Briand, with the part of the Right that went into opposition being replaced by the Radicals. Paul Cambon noted that Briand "had been saved ... by Tardieu and Mandel. In spite of their great talent, the Chamber cannot tolerate either of them, and particularly not Tardieu."[45]

In explaining his party's vote for the cabinet, Herriot, the leader of the Radicals, was expressing the opinion of a large section of the Center as well. Little as his party might expect from the government, he said, he would vote for it in order to prevent Tardieu and Mandel from getting into power and to defeat their policy, which he considered disastrous for the country.[46]

The Clemencists had failed to oust Briand, but they were not discouraged, for they had just begun their campaign. In the past they had opposed the government; in the future, they would conduct open warfare against it. Negotiations were already under way for the foundation of a new journal, the *Echo National*, which would complement their action in Parliament, and enable them to take their case to the country. Their aim: "To reawaken in France the spirit that led us to victory and to support ... the men capable of translating it into action."[47]

II

On the masthead of the first issue of the *Echo National* on January 10, 1922, were the names of Clemenceau as founder and André Tardieu as political director.[48] Neither Clemenceau nor Mandel ever contributed a line to the paper, though Clemenceau eagerly lent his name to the task of national regeneration undertaken by his friends. For his part, Mandel assumed responsibility for everything published in the journal,[49] but preferred to devote his time to parliamentary activities. He could not hope in any case to rival the formidable journalistic talents of Tardieu.

When the *Echo National* appeared, Briand was in greater difficulty with Parliament than ever because of the weakness of his policy toward Germany, and his compliant attitude toward England. While he conferred with Lloyd George at Cannes in the beginning of January, Parliament considered ways to keep him from making further concessions to Germany. In the midst of the conference the *Echo National* appeared, repudiating French foreign policy since Clemenceau left office. "France," it proclaimed, "has been in the hands of governments of abdication for two years." The men in charge had been rejected by the electorate in 1919 and had treated each renunciation of France's rights as a success. They had hidden the truth from the public. "To establish the peace," the paper asked, "did we have to call on those who had almost lost the war?"[50]

Clemenceau was delighted with the new undertaking. "Tardieu," he wrote to a friend, "has thrown himself vigorously and courageously into the battle and clearly defined his position. If he continues along that line, he will be able to exercise great influence over the country, which seems to be waking up.... We are well launched; it remains to be seen whether the unfortunate French people will follow us."[51]

Coincidentally with the appearance of the paper, an apprehensive Parliament warned Briand at Cannes not to agree to any further reduction of France's rights under the Treaty of Versailles. Briand abruptly suspended the negotiations, and returned to Paris to defend his policies. Speaking before the Chamber, however, he sensed that he had lost its confidence, and in an unprecedented action, handed in his resignation from the tribune.

Millerand immediately summoned Poincaré to form the new government. Poincaré had been elected to the Senate in 1920 and had become the head of its Foreign Affairs Committee. Although he had rarely voted against the successive cabinets, his articles in *Le Temps, Le Matin,* and the *Revue des Deux Mondes* gave him a reputation as one of the most consistent critics of the concessions made by France during the past two years. Poincaré insisted on strict application of the Treaty of Versailles and refused to consider any revision of it. However, he criticized Clemenceau for having failed to obtain more benefits for France in the Treaty. "M. Tardieu," he pointed out, "wants to defend the Treaty of Versailles as a masterpiece. I defend it as energetically as he does, but as a last resort."[52]

In addition to representing, in French opinion, a more forceful policy toward Germany, he had the advantage over Tardieu of being able to disclaim responsibility for defects in the Treaty. Before the war, moreover, he had helped inspire French resistance to Germany and led the campaign for increasing France's armaments. The role he had played in the war only augmented the general esteem in which he was held. He was particularly popular with the nationalist Right, even obtaining the support of the Monarchists, including the antiparliamentary but staunchly patriotic Action Française.[53] By his accession to power in January 1922, he effectively stole the ammunition of the Clemencists before they even had a chance to load their guns.

For Poincaré, foreign affairs at that moment took precedence over internal affairs. Everything must be subordinated to the strict application of the Treaty of Versailles, for which he tried to get the support of the entire nation. What he wanted was not a parliamentary majority, but a National Union government. He offered ministries to both Tardieu and the Radical leader Herriot. Herriot refused, but three members of his party joined Poincaré anyway. The Right also received three posts. Most of the rest of the cabinet was composed of members of the Alliance Démocratique. Albert Mamelet was exultant: "For many years, no government has been so exact an expression of the national republican policy that we support."[54]

Many observers, however, were disappointed. Poincaré's cabinet "in no way reflected the views of those whose criticisms and repeated attacks had brought down Briand, nor even the views he himself had expressed for two years in his campaign against the failure to implement the Treaty of Versailles."[55] In fact, twelve of Poincaré's ministers had served with Briand, and the centrist Alliance Démocratique had been the mainstay of Briand's majority, first in alliance with the Right and then with the Radicals. The general had been replaced, but the staff remained the same.

Tardieu refused to join the cabinet. In a letter to the new prime minister, he expressed approval of his foreign policy, but wondered how it could be carried out since Poincaré himself had supported the policy of the previous governments and had even included in his cabinet many of the men responsible for it. There were also certain questions of internal policy that separated them. Poincaré's professed desire was to be above politics. In Tardieu's opinion, one had to play politics, to rely upon a certain majority, and to ally oneself with it. He himself could participate only in a government that promised to carry out the program approved by the voters in 1919. Because of their divergent views on these questions, he could not accept Poincaré's offer.[56]

Mandel, of course, had not been asked to join the cabinet, having neither the personal prestige nor the past authority of Tardieu. But like Tardieu he doubted Poincaré's ability to carry out a more vigorous foreign policy. He told a journalist that he had no confidence in the Prime Minister: "I know him; I collaborated with him indirectly for many years. He is a patriot, an honest man, a learned jurist, and an excellent lawyer. If I had a losing case to be pleaded, I would certainly give it to him. But I do not want to entrust him with the fate of France. Poincaré is a broken lath painted to look like iron, not a political force. . . ."[57]

Mandel and Tardieu, however, faced an almost impossible task in trying to convince the country that Poincaré was not the man of the hour. As a talented lawyer, he seemed likely to see that the Treaty of Versailles was carried out to the letter, saving the fruits of the victory Clemenceau had won. Although the intellectuals and the workers disliked him, he symbolized for a large part of the nation the qualities they thought had made the period before the war a time of unparalleled peace and prosperity, *La Belle Epoque*: he was intelligent, honest, conscientious, hard-working, and prudent. It scarcely mattered that he was also colorless and unimaginative.

Poincaré was less compliant toward the English and more aggressive toward the Germans, but he was no more successful than earlier prime ministers in forcing the Germans to abide by the Treaty of Versailles. His attitude, nonetheless, was irreproachable. In the field of foreign affairs, Mandel and Tardieu were reduced to criticizing details and promising that they would do better if given power. On internal affairs, they had a stronger case. Cantonal elections to the general councils were scheduled for May 1922, and all the parties were beginning to look ahead to the national elections in 1924. Supporting Poincaré unqualifiedly in Parliament, the Right felt entitled to his support in the country. But when they asked for his backing, he loftily replied, "I don't play politics."[58]

In return for his neutrality, many Radicals supported him in Parliament, although the party leaders usually abstained. In view of the national elections, however, some of the younger members created a new propaganda organization, *La Ligue de la République*. Their purpose was to elaborate a specifically Radical program to oppose the Bloc National and to create a union of the leftist parties to take advantage of the 1919 electoral law favoring coalitions. They toured the country, attacking the Bloc National and holding preliminary discussions with other leftist leaders.[59] The Radicals were slowly loosening their ties with the majority and heading towards a leftist alliance.

In the May cantonal elections the Left gained a few seats throughout France. The Right was disturbed by the action or rather the inaction of Interior Minister Maurice Maunoury. He and Poincaré had proclaimed their neutrality, but the prefects and agents of the government, most of them recruited by previous leftist governments, felt the climate of opinion changing and acted in favor of their former patrons. Of Maunoury, Mandel remarked, to the general hilarity of the Chamber, that "in the administration he has the illusion of directing, all of his agents play politics except him.... He thinks that the Place Beauvau, instead of being a center of action, should be a sort of observatory, and he, just a meteorologist. He limits himself to noting and registering the state of the political climate."[60]

Mandel himself had had a difficult election in Lesparre. In 1919 he had been chosen general councilor for the area without opposition. His position in the arrondissement was almost unbeatable, in spite of the fact that Briand had replaced most of the important government agents appointed by Mandel in 1919.[61] Of the new men, one had worked with the candidates opposing Mandel in 1919, another was an assistant of Malvy, a third was the nephew of the former Radical leader Emile Combes, and a fourth had run on the same list with the leftist Paul Painlevé in 1919.[62] Since these men had been kept in office by Poincaré, almost the entire administration of the Gironde opposed Mandel's candidacy in May 1922.

In spite of official support, however, his opponents still had some difficulty in choosing a candidate in Lesparre. Mandel had cultivated the constituency since 1914 and made it his political fief. Realizing that if they split their forces, he would easily defeat them, his opponents buried their political differences for the moment and chose a single candidate to represent them. Socialists, Radicals, and moderate Republicans all supported the venerable and respected conservative Catholic Th. Skawinski. He was a member of the Bordeaux Chamber of Commerce, and more likely than anyone else to draw votes from Mandel's Catholic supporters. During the campaign, of course, the Catholics were encouraged to vote for a practicing member of their faith in preference to a Jew, but alone of all the regional papers that had supported him in 1919, the Catholic daily *La Liberté du Sud-Ouest* continued to back Mandel.[63] With its help Mandel beat his opponent 1,921 votes to 1,526.

The action of the national administration against Mandel had been intensified for personal reasons. But enough similar incidents had occurred throughout France to disturb the Right. Their discontent would ordinarily have assured Mandel of a sympathetic hearing when he spoke on this issue after Parliament reassembled in October 1922. But instead of simply attacking Poincaré, Maunoury, and the Radicals, he also attacked François Arago and Laurent Bonnevay, the leaders of the Entente Républicaine, and finally the entire majority itself. In passing, he disposed of Briand and former Prime Minister Paul Painlevé as well.[64]

To Poincaré, Mandel said that he saw no difference between his internal policy and Briand's. He asked him if he had finally decided to choose between the Right and the Radicals and to return to "those wise rules of the parliamentary system that you yourself once defined: a unified cabinet based on a coherent majority, which will support the government in a crisis, ... even when it may be wrong. ..." Instead of providing a precise program and clearly drawn lines, the government had proposed, "under the pretense of national union, a series of half measures, half-baked solutions, and equivocal compromises designed to appease everyone."

Mandel then went on to attack the majority and particularly François Arago, a leader of the Entente Républicaine. The Entente had voted for all the governments since 1920 despite their consistent refusal to associate themselves openly with the Bloc National. He advised the majority to demand a clarification of the political situation, for the Radicals, who had also voted for every government, were openly attacking the Bloc National and holding it responsible for all the problems of the moment. Mandel warned that if the Left won the elections, it would play politics, vote an amnesty for Caillaux and Malvy, and evacuate the Rhineland. Nevertheless, he surprisingly advised the Right to continue supporting the government, at least while France was still engaged in negotiations with England over the Near Eastern question. One day, however, when they judged the moment opportune, they should express their will so decisively that the government would be bound to accept it.[65]

Mandel's speech, as usual, had lasted for more than three hours. "What he said," commented Robert Cornilleau, "he said without grace, but with an assurance that gave him authority. His words burned with political passion, and his calm and grave attitude in the face of violent interruptions—a mixture of *sang-froid* and disdain—impressed even his most hostile listeners. Despite his frailty, he gave an impression of force and of irresistible willpower that finally succeeded in dominating the Chamber."[66]

For the moment, Mandel had not asked the Chamber to overthrow the government; it would not have done so in any case. The members of the Bloc National defended themselves halfheartedly against his attacks: "We are a majority that does not want to play politics." One deputy, to the general applause of the Center, remarked that "so long as the question of peace is not settled, so long as reconstruction is not completed, we have better things to do than engage in political maneuvers."[67]

But in spite of their professed indifference to playing politics, the Right and Center were disturbed by Poincaré's exalted neutrality. Mandel's speech precipitated a serious discussion of internal politics in the press.[68] Even *Le Temps*, the semiofficial organ of the Center, said that "Mandel's speech has spotlighted with a cruel insistence the problem of the majority of the 1919 Chamber."[69] But the speech failed to move Poincaré, who still proclaimed in his reply to Mandel that he wanted "a republican majority of national reconstruction," excluding only the Socialists and the Communists.[70] Although his majority was slightly reduced for a time by the abstention of twenty-one members of the Entente, the 418 votes he received still gave him the necessary authority to continue as he had in the past, until a new crisis in foreign affairs brought back even those twenty-one votes.

After almost a year in office, Poincaré had been no more successful than previous premiers in forcing Germany to obey the Treaty of Versailles. Growing economic difficulties had obliged Germany to ask for a moratorium on payments in 1922. The English were inclined to grant it to help her establish a sound economy and a sound financial system. The French, on the other hand, provoked by the repeated necessity of making concessions, and disappointed by the German failure either to make payments or to deliver the promised quantities of coal, insisted that the Allies control the coal deliveries and collect tariffs on all products manufactured in the Ruhr, Germany's industrial center.

These measures were to guarantee payment and were to last only until Germany showed herself ready to meet her debts. England refused to be associated with this policy of force, which might lead to French annexation of the Ruhr, or at least to its prolonged occupation. In the past, to avoid diplomatic isolation, France had grudgingly followed England's lead, but her sense of frustration and injury were now so great that she resolved to act alone. On January 10, 1923, French engineers accompanied by three army divisions were sent into the Ruhr. Germany immediately organized passive resistance. The mine owners and the workers refused to cooperate with the French engineers. The Rhineland railroads stopped functioning. The French were forced to import workers and send more troops to keep the mines running. The result in Germany was disastrous. To provide for all the striking workers and those affected by the occupation, the government issued more and more money. The resulting inflation destroyed savings, bankrupted creditors, and weakened the entire financial structure of the country.

Despite critical world opinion, national sentiment in France solidified behind the government. No matter what the eventual result might be, Poincaré's measures had relieved France's sense of frustration at being unable to collect payments from Germany. Poincaré had acted, and for the moment that was enough. At least half the Radicals and the previously disaffected part of the Right would now vote for him.

The Clemencists, who had advocated forceful measures since 1920, were momentarily silenced. Mandel, however, soon recovered his tongue. He began to describe Poincaré's program as representing only the "minimum national requirements." As for Poincaré himself, he had destroyed his authority for enforcing the Treaty of Versailles by saying so often that it "contained more promises than benefits" and that it was unworkable. Mandel advised Parliament to try the experiment of having the Treaty enforced by men who had confidence in it.[71]

Tardieu also was soon attacking Poincaré daily in the *Echo National* and periodically in Parliament. In the Chamber, he reproached Poincaré for not conducting operations forcefully enough in the Ruhr. "After three years of weakness and retreat, I believe that the occupation of the Ruhr is a decisive moment.... It is the Verdun of the peace; it cannot be repeated."[72] Although the Right and the Center loudly applauded Tardieu, they voted for Poincaré. Obviously, attacks on foreign policy were futile. As Guizot had written almost a century before, "You may count on the fact that foreign policy does not concern the French at all and will not be the cause of any important event. Governments can do what they please. If they make foolish mistakes, they will ... be hissed at without anger, and without being overthrown as a result, as long as they are able to accomplish something in the domestic affairs of the country, the only ones taken seriously by the people."[73]

It was on internal issues that Mandel and Tardieu could hope to overthrow Poincaré, who continued to refuse either to repudiate the Radicals or to ally himself with the Bloc National. By hammering away at the government and repeatedly emphasizing the necessity of forming a coherent majority, they finally awakened the apprehensions of the Right. On June 1, in a vote implying confidence in Minister of the Interior Maunoury, the government received its smallest majority ever, 339 to 154 with 64 abstentions. And on June 15 the Right interpellated Poincaré on "the position that the government intends to take in the battle already being passionately fought between the Bloc des Gauches and the Bloc National." In the debate, they told Poincaré that the moment had come to choose between the Entente Républicaine and the Radicals.

For once, the Prime Minister seemed to have accepted the challenge. He said that the Communists and Socialists were excluded from the majority because they advocated class warfare, and he warned the Radicals that a republican majority could not include men who allied themselves with these parties. In reply, Herriot took his party into formal opposition, even though in the vote of confidence following the debate, twelve Radicals still supported the government and eight others abstained.[74]

In his speech, however, Poincaré had refused to assume the leadership of the Bloc National, and it was obvious that he had broken with the Radicals reluctantly. Nevertheless, half of the Right remained loyal to him, and Poincaré could afford to ignore the dissidents who either followed Tardieu or began to look toward the Royalist Action Française.[75]

Thus, despite serious disaffection on the Right, despite Poincaré's ambiguous attitude toward his majority and his dallying with the Radicals, despite the meager results of his foreign policy, and despite the fear generated on the Right and in the Center by the threatened alliance of the Radicals and Socialists for the coming elections, Mandel and Tardieu were never able to obtain the support of more than fifty to a hundred right-wing deputies—enough to cause considerable commotion, but not enough to endanger the government. Tardieu and Mandel were among the most dynamic and eloquent men in the Chamber. The Right consistently applauded them; the Center occasionally admitted they were correct in their analysis. But when it came to a showdown, the government inevitably won. What was wrong with the Clemencists?

6. The Most Hated Man in France

Ne craignez jamais de vous créer des ennemis. Si vous n'en avez pas, c'est que vous n'avez rien fait.

Clemenceau

IT HAS BEEN SAID that in the years immediately following World War I, Mandel was the most hated man in France.[1] When he entered the Chamber in 1919 the many enemies he had made during his collaboration with Clemenceau did not forget him. The press, which he had severely controlled for the two preceding years, took its revenge by writing unfavorable reports about him or ignoring him entirely.[2] Léon Bailby's *L'Intransigeant* refused even to mention his name. The Radicals had not forgotten that he was one of the men responsible for the conviction of Malvy and Caillaux, and they threatened to take him before the High Court of Justice if they came to power.[3] They called him "that disgraceful Jew, Jéroboam."[4]

Even after his election, Mandel made no effort to gain the esteem of his colleagues. He had a supreme disdain for them and took pleasure in showing it. On two occasions a councilor of the Gironde threatened to beat him up.[5] On another, Mandel's insolence provoked the General Council into censuring him. The incident was caused by the citation during a debate of a precedent established by the Minister of War and Pensions, André Maginot. At the mention of Maginot's name, Mandel interjected: "You cannot seriously use such a childish argument from authority in a debate like this. And I don't mean to discuss the person of the *mutilé complet* who has strayed into the Ministry of Pensions as its head."

The reference to Maginot, a popular national hero who had lost a leg in the war, caused a furor. After the debate Mandel realized that he had made a mistake and had his remark removed from the record of the meeting. But when the minutes were read the following day, thirty-seven of the fifty councilors voted to send a letter of sympathy to Maginot and have Mandel's exact words reinstated. Mandel was absent that day, but at the next session he explained:

I had no intention ... of attacking the *mutilé* Maginot. But when the Prefect spoke seriously of Maginot during the discussion, I was forced to say what I thought of the Minister of Pensions, namely, that he is a *mutilé intégral*. (Exclamations.) I will explain the term for those who do not understand, for there are some here who do not seem to have understood. ... If you take the trouble to read Littré, Vaugelas, Sylvestre de Sacy, ... you will see that there are men who have been mutilated without having been in the war. When I said that Maginot was a *mutilé intégral*, I was not referring to his wartime experience, but to his intelligence.... My opinion of the Minister of War has never changed: he was a brilliant soldier, a good sergeant-major, gifted with qualities that developed magnificently during the war.... But I deny that he is a man of great intelligence, and that during a political discussion anyone can seriously base his argument on a decision taken by Maginot.

At the end of this lesson in semantics, Mandel made a mistake that taught him to be more cautious in his assertions. "Having sat in the classrooms of the Faculty of Letters and of the Ecole Normale," he proudly told the councilors, "I remember the meaning of the word *mutilé*."

Never before having heard Mandel mention the prestigious Ecole Normale, his adversaries, searching for a way to embarrass him, checked the records of the school. Later they delightedly announced to the Council that these records carried no mention of Mandel under any name. He obtained a temporary respite by claiming that he had entered the school in a special class in December of 1903 and had withdrawn shortly thereafter. The spring session of the Council ended before this new story could be checked. Of course, when it was checked, it proved also to be false.

When the Council reassembled in September, Mandel was not allowed to change the recorded wording of his speech, as almost anyone else would have been permitted to do. The councilors would have laughed privately about the incident and then forgotten it. But Mandel was another matter. The opportunity to embarrass him, particularly with the elections only a year away, was simply too good to lose. For his part, Mandel implicitly recognized his mistake by trying to change the wording of his speech, but not once in public session did he admit he was at fault. One of his opponents gleefully declared, "We can show the country that this man, this self-styled public moralist...has violated the trust of the district that elected him."[6] What the series of incidents really showed, however, was that most of Mandel's colleagues hated him.

His interventions in the Chamber were equally tumultuous. Probably only half his time at the tribune was spent in delivering his speeches, the rest being consumed by interruptions and personal attacks. But Mandel could provoke attack even when he was not addressing the Chamber. One day when Mandel repeatedly interrupted him, Poincaré lost his usual composure and, livid with rage, shouted: "You are insufferable!"[7]

By contrast, according to Jacques Bainville, in private

no one is more courteous than Mandel, nor more tolerant in the exchange of ideas. But in public he is peremptory, curt and aggressive.... The atmosphere of hate, rancor and mistrust surrounding him has perhaps ... contributed to his cold and distant attitude. . . . By nature Mandel is not familiar; he detests familiarity. He has few friends because he wants few. He has nothing but disdain for insults and no concern whatsoever for popularity. He wants to owe his prestige only to his talents, and his authority only to his personal merits.[8]

Inevitably, the behavior of Mandel and Tardieu disturbed the bourgeois conservatives of the Bloc National. They were shocked by their almost systematic opposition to Poincaré, and regarded it as "less the opposition of two policies than of two temperaments."[9] They might applaud Mandel's courage and his skill in embarrassing his opponents, at least when the sallies were not too close to home. But they disliked him personally, and never knowing what he might do next, they also distrusted him.

Mandel's mind was tortuous and his maneuvers quite frequently unfathomable. One day when leaving Clemenceau, he said that he was going to continue the struggle. Clemenceau could not resist replying, "Yes, but which struggle?"[10] Eugène Lautier of *L'Homme Libre* said that it was not enough to hear Mandel's speeches; they had to be scrutinized under a microscope.[11] A councilor from the Gironde, urging rejection of a motion proposed by Mandel, remarked: "I know you quite well, my dear colleague, and I know that you do nothing without reason. . . . I am afraid of being led into a trap. With your shrewdness and your quick mind, one can sometimes be drawn much further than one would want to go. . . ." To his colleagues, the councilor added: "I am afraid of Mandel's maneuvers. He makes me suspicious. Even his most harmless-looking act has its purpose. We may be contradicting ourselves by passing his motion."[12]

There were, however, a few men who admired Mandel's qualities, among whom the Royalists, and particularly Léon Daudet, were the most prominent. Georges Bonnefous called Mandel and Daudet "the two most formidable debaters in the Chamber."[13] From the beginning of the legislature until his defeat in 1924, Daudet kept the Chamber in turmoil with his frequent and boisterous interventions. In his memoirs, he left practical advice to future disturbers of the parliamentary peace.[14] With Rabelaisian exaggeration and humor, he launched accusations of treason, corruption, and perversion against the administration, the government, and his colleagues, few of whom found favor in his eyes. Mandel was one of those few. His interventions exceeded even Daudet's in noise, disorder, and, sometimes, violence. Mandel, too, considered himself to be a master of "The Art of Interpellating," as he entitled a lecture he gave at the Sorbonne in 1925.[15] Unfortunately, no record of his advice can be found.

Daudet originally admired Mandel for his work with Clemenceau during the war. In November 1917, when Clemenceau became prime minister, the Royalist and superpatriotic *Action Française*, to which Daudet contributed a daily article, suddenly found itself in accord with the policies of the government. The coincidence was notable and, according to a former writer for the paper, not entirely accidental. Daudet's campaigns against defeatism after 1917 were supposedly carried on in conjunction with Clemenceau, and nourished by Mandel with information from government sources.[16]

In any case, Mandel, a Jew, and a firm republican in addition, achieved the remarkable feat of gaining the respect of some of the ultranationalist leaders of the Royalist Party. He found a ready welcome among them,[17] and favored them in return with critiques of their tactics, advising them what to do if they seriously wished to overthrow the republican regime.[18] It was the counsel of a connoisseur of politics, not of an adherent to their cause. Daudet knew very well that "for Mandel, the French parliamentary system was weak only because it had been perverted and misused. He believed that we do not have the true parliamentary system, the ideal system of Thiers and Guizot."[19]

Daudet was also attracted by Mandel's character. He explained that it was "the physical and moral courage of that frail and extraordinarily subtle man that made me sympathetic to him. Barrès described him as 'a soul of iron encased in glass.' ... He spoke of Mandel as Goethe spoke of Humboldt, with a mixture of surprise, fear and admiration."[20] For Daudet himself, Mandel was "a statesman (and not just a politician) of extraordinary ability, energy, and intelligence. He fears nothing and no one. Although some people are repelled by him, others find him sympathetic. I belong to the second group. Georges Mandel is one of the most interesting and singular persons I have ever encountered. Witty yet serious, harsh yet capable of compassion, ... his steel-like strength contrasts remarkably with his fragile appearance."[21]

The Royalists' respect for Mandel caused them to forget momentarily their traditional anti-Semitism. Their movement was partially a reaction against the weakness of France in the years following the Franco-Prussian War. Insofar as Mandel was a defender of national strength and independence, he was, in their eyes, a follower of Royalist policy. A nationalist Jew was infinitely preferable to an internationalist Frenchman, no matter how devout a Catholic he was or how deep his roots in the country went. The Royalists were Clemenceau's strongest supporters during the war because then he was the greatest defender of French national interests, as they conceived them. If they could easily swallow their hatred of the great republican anarchist because of his war-time leadership, they could even more easily ignore Mandel's republican convictions and Jewish antecedents because of his vigorous foreign policy.

The question rather is why Mandel devoted so much attention to them. The answer is that he sympathized with their nationalism, did not fear their antiparliamentarianism, and hoped to wean them away from Poincaré, who was also seeking their support.[22] But in spite of all his attention, and in spite of the esteem that Daudet, Maurice Barrès, and Jacques Bainville had for Mandel personally, he was never able to persuade them to support Tardieu. Tardieu was less inclined than Mandel to conciliate the Royalists, and often publicly attacked Charles Maurras, the director of the *Action Française*.[23] Maurras as a result, turned against the Clemencists, who, he said, "want only power and nothing else. What chance majority would be foolish enough to support them?"[24]

II

By antagonizing potential supporters, Mandel and Tardieu lessened their chances of leading the Bloc National. But even had they been more conciliatory, it is doubtful that they would have been able to create the coherent majority they so bitterly fought for. By 1923 the term "Bloc National" was a derogatory epithet used by the Left for the electoral victors of 1919. The coalition had begun to falter under Millerand, had been dislocated under Briand, and was being given the *coup de grâce* by Poincaré. Not one of the three premiers had seriously attempted to unite the conservatives against the Left. All of them preferred to straddle the fence and attract as much Radical support as possible.

What was worse, the members of the Alliance Démocratique had made every effort to disassociate themselves from their compromising Catholic allies. They denied that there had ever been any national alliance with the Catholics, or any intention to exclude the Radicals from the coalition.[25] As time went on, in order to demonstrate their anticlericalism, they called for the enforcement of the laws directed against the religious orders.[26] They also made repeated overtures to the Radicals for an alliance in order to prevent them from joining with the Socialists in a Bloc des Gauches that might implement a left-wing economic policy. The Radicals, well aware of the Center's strategy, encouraged these approaches in order to split the conservative forces. In December 1922 Joseph Caillaux, the former president of the Party, wrote to his successor, Edouard Herriot:

You are absolutely right in your belief that the essential thing is to give the Radical Party a program, and not to run after alliances, which will come of themselves. . . . It is important that our program appear to be an appeal to a part of the Bloc National. And it has been so interpreted by the moderate journals, such as *Le Temps*, which are overwhelming the party with compliments for its moderation, its restraint, etc. Moreover, I notice that the *Union des Intérêts Econo-*

miques is beginning to turn toward us. It is easy to see what their tactic is; in this business world that I know so well, they believe that the Bloc National is finished; they are looking for a new formation to replace it, to which they are ready to concede a measure of anticlericalism and some vague social laws, and from which they will demand only one thing in return: respect for the enormous contracts they have grabbed from the state—the maintenance, if not the extension, of their monopolies. Such is the danger that I foresee.[27]

As late as mid-1923 the Center still hoped to win the Radicals over. On July 29 Senator Charles Chaumet of the Gironde publicly appealed for a coalition of the Center and the Radicals in support of Poincaré.[28] Chaumet was president of the influential Comité Républicain du Commerce, de l'Industrie et de l'Agriculture, which had been associated with the Radicals before the war but had broken with them to join the Bloc National in 1919. The renewed alliance would have been ideal for the Center. Not only would it have averted the left-wing economic policies they feared, but it would have allowed them to campaign with the Radicals. Thus they would have benefited both from the recent shift in public opinion toward the Left and from the provisions favoring coalitions in the electoral law of 1919. Moreover, they could have isolated the Catholics and the Socialists, and perhaps even have saddled the Right with responsibility for the postwar financial and diplomatic difficulties of France.

Herriot, however, rejected the offer, and pressed instead for an alliance with the Socialists.[29] A new Paris daily, *Le Quotidien*, was founded to coordinate propaganda on the Left; and on the other side of the barricade, the majority finally found a leader in the most unlikely of places. After having done his best to break up the Bloc National in 1920, President Millerand now attempted to put it together again for the 1924 elections. Reversing roles with Poincaré, who maintained the political neutrality normally expected of the president, Millerand spoke out in a speech at Evreux on October 14, in defense of the Bloc National governments.[30] Reviewing their foreign policy, their financial measures, and their position on the religious question, he found them all good. His only criticism was directed at the system, and specifically at the weakness of the executive power. Repeating his proposal of 1919, he advocated constitutional revision to increase the authority of the government.

More than any action of Poincaré's, Millerand's speech divided the Chamber into a majority and an opposition. The Radicals ranged themselves against Millerand for stepping out of his constitutional role, and the Center accepted his speech as "the electoral platform of the national parties for the elections of 1924."[31] But to reenact the victory of 1919, the Bloc National needed more than the generous blessing of the President. It seemed likely that in 1924 the Radicals and Socialists would be united, and the conservatives would need the active intervention and support of the Prime Minister to overcome the drift of French opinion toward the Left.

With the Radicals now clearly in opposition, Mandel and Tardieu thought they might persuade enough conservative deputies to vote with the Left to overthrow the cabinet. In November Mandel prepared to interpellate the government on its internal policy, but Poincaré succeeded in having his intervention postponed until the end of February, just two months before the elections. In the meantime, realizing that this was their last opportunity to gain power during that legislature, the Clemencists conducted a final desperate battle against the government. While Tardieu led the attack from the tribune, Mandel cornered his conservative colleagues in the corridors of the Chamber. One by one, he tried to persuade them of the folly of Poincaré's policy and warned them of certain defeat if they fought the elections without government support.[32] His listeners were more attentive than usual, for Poincaré had been forced to introduce some extremely unpopular bills to remedy the country's deteriorating financial situation.

Since 1920 France had financed the reconstruction of her devastated regions while waiting in vain for the anticipated payments from Germany to cover the costs. By 1924 inflation had set in, and the value of the franc on the world market had dropped sharply. To deal with the situation, Poincaré asked Parliament for emergency powers to pass laws by decree, and for a 20 per cent increase in taxation. Mandel opposed granting decree power because to do so implied that the Chamber would not have enacted the necessary legislation and therefore tended to discredit the parliamentary system. He opposed the increase in taxation because it was madness to pass it on the eve of the elections.

In the many votes of confidence required to get the program through, Poincaré's supporters faltered. On one ballot, had it not been for the twenty-six Royalist votes, the government would have been overthrown.[33] Poincaré had put his majority to a trial by fire; it had come through singed and tattered but still basically intact.

Thus when Mandel's interpellation on internal policy finally came up at the end of February, it was an anticlimax. Mandel, however, was never one to admit defeat in advance. For five hours he indicted Poincaré for failing to carry out the internal policy of his majority, and for jeopardizing France's foreign policy by refusing to support his followers in the elections. "If speechmaking were governing," he said, "you would be a magnificent prime minister. I'm afraid that in the process of making speeches worthy of appearing in an anthology you are leading your majority to the slaughterhouse." Every change in the basis of internal policy had serious external consequences. "It is not enough ... to desire the greatness of France and praise the occupation of the Ruhr. You must also desire the reelection of those who made the operation possible." According to Mandel, there were two possible majorities and two possible policies, that of the Bloc National and that of the Bloc des Gauches. He wanted Poincaré to declare which of the two he favored.[34]

The point of Mandel's intervention was clear. But in the five hours he was at the tribune he passed judgment on the entire Chamber and incited the deputies to open battle. The correspondent for *Le Matin* gave a detailed description of the scene:

The Far Left and part of the Left rushed from their seats toward the Right, breaking through the line of ushers. Socialist Deputy Clausset leaped at the throat of Count Ginoux-Defermont, who grabbed him in turn by the collar. Fists beat down on Clausset's head, but he refused to let go. . . . Socialist Deputy Chaussy, running toward Maurice Binder, slipped and fell face forward on a desk. Blood gushed out. . . . More and more of the Far Left deputies struggled to get across the Chamber, one man even leaping across the secretaries' table, but the battle soon became a terrifying free-for-all. No one could be recognized in the mass of heaving backs, thrashing arms, and twisted faces. . . . The public in the gallery was embarrassed and dumbfounded. . . . Mandel, leaning over the edge of the tribune in an attitude of meditation, seemed far, far away from the turmoil.[35]

Mandel's contemporaries were unable to find any plausible explanation for his tactics. They agreed with Jacques Bainville's earlier judgment that as a deputy, Mandel had at least one great defect: "that of being an implacable fighter and a merciless adversary. Not only does he return blow for blow, but he likes to provoke the enemy. Never dropping his guard, always ready with an answer, he is unable to compromise on personal questions, and his systematic and often useless aggressiveness, repelling those who want to support him, hurts his own cause. . . ."[36]

Bainville was obviously right, but just as obviously Mandel wanted to awaken a Chamber that Poincaré preferred to lull to sleep. He wanted to clarify the political confusion resulting from Poincaré's ambiguous policy and from the ambivalent attitude of the Radicals, who held the Bloc National responsible for the difficulties of the moment but treated Poincaré with respect because of his continued popularity in the country. Herriot admitted that the Clemencists were far more critical of Poincaré than the Radicals, who were supposedly combating him in the name of a diametrically opposed policy.[37]

Poincaré's reply to Mandel was a masterpiece of its kind. "For three hours," said François Albert, "he spoke in balanced phrases whose false clarity of style was intended to hide their deliberate vagueness or even vacuity: national republican party; neither reaction nor revolution; the laws enforced with tolerance but without weakness; laicity reconciled with liberty; no unions for civil servants, but liberal conditions promised by way of compensation; no one to be excluded from the majority, which is invited to group itself under the government's direction."[38]

Poincaré's refusal either to disavow the Radicals or to declare his support for the Right eliminated the lingering possibility that the conservative forces could unite for the elections. His policy was a deliberate one, inspired, according to his latest biographer, by his fears of the antiparliamentary tendencies of the Catholics.[39] Although Poincaré may have been prescient, it should be noted that at this point the Right had not yet returned in large numbers to their earlier antiparliamentarianism and that they were eventually encouraged to do so precisely because the government continued to exclude them from effective participation in the regime.[40] It seems more likely that Poincaré shared the Alliance Démocratique's fear of being too closely associated with the clerical cause. He undoubtedly agreed with André Siegfried that "the Right never seems to realize that its influence is compromising and that it would do much better to give its help in silence."[41]

Moreover, Poincaré knew that if the conservatives won the 1924 elections, he would be allowed to remain in power. In the case of a Radical victory, he hoped that if he did not openly support the Catholics, the Radicals would keep him as prime minister rather than form a government with the Socialists. Shortly after the victory of the Left in May 1924, Poincaré told a journalist that he was still not certain the Radicals would force him out of office: "I have so many friends among them."[42]

Despite Poincaré's deviousness, however, the Right continued to support him. Mandel had failed to present the Chamber with an alternative policy. At best, his speech promised a change in tactics, a government that would support its majority with all the means at its disposal. Just two months before the elections, the conservatives were afraid to repudiate Poincaré. He still represented an electoral asset that they were unwilling to renounce in favor of the doubtful benefits of administrative support in the campaign.

Nevertheless, by their continual sniping, Mandel and Tardieu had awakened the apprehensions of the Right, and thus contributed to the surprise overthrow of the cabinet on a minor issue on March 26. In a fit of dissatisfaction, the Right voted with the Radicals and Socialists against Poincaré. The move showed what could have been done before, but it came too late to bring about a reorientation in policy. Millerand recalled Poincaré, who invited three of his leftist critics to join the government, reduced rightist repre-

sentation, and continued as if nothing had occurred. The Right, shocked
by its own audacity, apologetically returned to the fold.

III

By refusing to support his followers, Poincaré was protecting his own
political career. He hoped that the Radicals would help him to remain in
power after the elections, or at least recall him if their alliance with the
Socialists proved to be unviable. But in acting as he did, he helped to wreck
the last chance of welding the conservatives into a coherent group. Even
confronted by a left-wing coalition of Radicals and Socialists that seemed
likely to benefit from the majoritarian provisions of the electoral law, the
conservatives were unable to unite in 1924. They formulated no common
national program, concluded no national alliances, and received almost no
support from the government.

The Alliance Démocratique of the Center was as responsible as the government for this situation. Like the prime ministers since 1920, they had
been moving away from their embarrassing clerical allies on the Right and
courting the anticlerical Radicals. Although the Radicals had always put
them off, they too hoped that if the Left won the elections, the Socialists
might soon disagree with the Radicals, who would then be forced to turn
for support to the Center, and they wanted to be ready. During the electoral
campaign, the Radicals played their part in this game by blaming the
Right for the policies followed since 1920 and by treating the Alliance
Démocratique merely as a prodigal son. They also handled Poincaré cautiously, making Mandel and Millerand their particular *bêtes noires*, as if
they alone had governed France for four years.[43]

If the Right and the Center found it difficult to cooperate on the national
level they found it nearly impossible to work together in the Gironde, where
the situation was complicated by the personal antagonism that Mandel had
aroused. As early as 1922 it was clear that his enemies, including most of the
men he had been elected with in 1919, would do anything to defeat him.
Senator Chaumet, who proposed a national alliance between the Center
and the Radicals, tried to create a local alliance between them in the
Gironde. To thwart his maneuvers and isolate the Center, Mandel revealed
the promises made to the Catholics by the Center candidates in 1919.[44] The
Radicals would find it difficult to support men who had compromised
themselves with the Catholics, and the Catholics in turn would be alienated
from men who now wished to forget their promises. The national secretary
of the Alliance Démocratique, Albert Mamelet, severely criticized Mandel
in an article whose lengthy title summarized his tactics: "How Georges
Mandel, for the great benefit of the reactionaries, is arming the Radical-

Socialist extremists against the Left Republicans and attempting to divide the Republican party."[45]

Most of the negotiations preceding the formation of electoral lists in the Gironde seem to have revolved around the question of how to get rid of Mandel. At the national congress of the Radical Party in 1923, the delegates from the Gironde fought for a union of all the leftist groups as the only means of defeating him. Jean Odin, one of the unsuccessful Radical candidates in 1919, said that "in our department, to allow the quotient to come into effect ... is to desire the election of Mandel. We have had enough of Mandel. Even though the quotient system may help some Left Republicans, it is more important that we form the Bloc des Gauches, which is the only way that we can get rid of that scoundrel Mandel."* When some of the Radicals expressed reservations about an alliance with the Socialists, Herriot himself went to the Gironde to tell them that "you must fight in favor of the Cartel des Gauches. You will win the election only if you unite with the Socialists. In the interest of the country itself, which is the same as the interest of the Republican party, you must free yourselves from the disastrous policy that Mandel stands for."[46]

The only thing that saved Mandel from total isolation was the continued support of the Right. With the aid of the three Catholic deputies, André Ballande, Paul Glotin, and Elisée Frouin, he formed the *Liste de concorde nationale et d'action républicaine clemenciste*. This weak list was bolstered by the inclusion of Abbé Daniel Bergey, the immensely popular priest from St. Emilion, who was highly regarded by the veterans because of his war record. Although Bergey at first had rejected their offer, Cardinal Andrieu, the Archbishop of Bordeaux, ordered him to join the list.[47] He advised the reluctant Abbé to consult with Mandel and told him: "I will approve everything that you two decide in common."[48]

Nevertheless, many Catholics found it difficult to accept a Jew as the leader of their party. Shortly before the elections, a young professor in a Catholic lycée, Philippe Henriot, attempted to answer the objections made against the French Disraeli. "Mandel is Jewish," he said. "Everyone knows it. Neither he nor his friends have ever attempted to hide it. But beyond

---

* *Congrès du parti républicain-radical et radical socialiste tenu à Paris les 18, 19, 20 octobre 1923* (Paris, 1923), pp. 139, 185. According to the electoral law of 1919, a list receiving an absolute majority of the votes would get all of the seats for the department. If no list received an absolute majority, the seats would be allocated according to a system of proportional representation, i.e. according to the quotient, which was determined by dividing the total number of voters by the number of seats to be filled. A list receiving five times the quotient would receive five seats, and so on. By presenting a common list, the Radicals and Socialists had a chance to get a majority of the votes in the Gironde. If they presented separate lists, it was certain that the seats would have to be distributed proportionally, thus almost ensuring Mandel's election.

that? No one knows exactly. No particular complaint is made against him. No one criticizes him for breaking his word or changing his program. He has one fault, only one: he is Mandel." Henriot claimed that a campaign of insults and insinuations was being carried on against him. People are asked, "How can you have any sympathy for a man as surly, unsociable, irascible, and intransigent as he is?" Henriot's article was his answer. He gave high and almost lyrical praise to Mandel's courage, will power, and ability to dominate an assembly.[49]

Despite the official support of the Church, however, Mandel was unable to obtain the aid of the Royalists, who had received 8,000 votes in 1919 but were not presenting candidates in 1924. The Catholic journalist Louis-Georges Planes, who acted as intermediary in the negotiations, told Mandel that the Royalists recognized the contribution he had made to winning the war and admired his courage in defending his ideas even in the most hostile places, but they disliked supporting a Jew and were disturbed by his systematic opposition to Poincaré. They would support Mandel only if he agreed to repudiate the laic laws and allowed someone else to head the list, two conditions that he was unable to accept. The Royalists therefore refused to vote for him.[50]

Besides the Catholics supporting Mandel, and the Communists, four groups presented lists for the elections. One was composed of Radicals and Socialists. A second included four deputies from Mandel's 1919 lists, two candidates from the dissident Republican list of that year, and Jean Odin from the Radical list. This heterogeneous assemblage was led by Joseph Capus, whom Poincaré appointed minister of Agriculture in April in order to give more prestige and authority to the list opposing Mandel.[51] Also in the field was a dissident Radical list formed by Henri Labroue, who had campaigned with Jean Odin in 1919. Finally, some dissident Republicans presented a list, headed by two deputies from Mandel's 1919 coalition. In brief, the Radicals were now allied with the Socialists, who had formerly opposed them; Mandel's allies of 1919 were campaigning on three different lists; and even the four Radical candidates of 1919 were now running on three separate lists. This both confused the voters and helped Mandel. No party was likely to obtain an absolute majority, and under the quotient system Mandel and the Catholics seemed certain to elect at least one deputy.

As usual, Mandel conducted a vigorous campaign. By the time of the election, his weight, never great in any case, had dropped to less than one hundred pounds. He was forced to have an operation on his throat to restore his weakened voice.[52] The journalist Louis-Georges Planes described his campaign as "Homeric."

His meetings were extremely disorderly. Everywhere he encountered an opposition inspired by hatred. The night at the Alcazar in La Bastide, one of the Communist quarters of Bordeaux, was remembered for a long time. Mandel had to get out of his car at the end of the stone bridge and pass through a threatening mob. Hostile people shoved him and shook their fists under his nose. He passed by haughtily and indifferently. When he got to the stage, he could not speak for the uproar. The crowd seemed ready to yell forever. From time to time he was hit by a rotten egg or a tomato. He merely wiped his coat with a disdainful hand and resumed his immobile stance. At two o'clock in the morning, when everyone else was finally worn out, he gave his speech.

Before hostile crowds of workers and peasants, said Planes, "Mandel discussed the most difficult subjects of finance and foreign affairs, and the audience, in spite of its prejudices, was flattered to be taken seriously." One night when Mandel had difficulty making himself heard, he concluded by saying: "Tomorrow, you will vote for me, if you realize your duty. I would like to have confidence in your intelligence and determination, but I cannot forget that I am in the country of the Girondins and that your ancestors let Pétion be devoured by dogs!"* Said Planes, who was there, "Insolence, when it reaches that degree, touches the sublime."[53]

Mandel's prime targets in the campaign were the Center Republicans, whom he called "the Saxons without faith, without ideas, without conscience, who are concerned only with their own interests."[54] Throughout the district he posted reprints of the articles that the *Petite Gironde* had published in 1919 in praise of him. The paper, whose editor had sworn never to print his name again, was forced to break its silence about "Judas," and to try to explain why it had not spoken out about "the distressing changes of opinion of this renegade and degenerate Jew: his repeated betrayals, his blatant cynicism, and his complete lack of political morality.... It seemed only proper to pay no attention either to the acts and words of a man like Mandel or to the physical and moral weaknesses that nature has combined in that abnormal personality."

The same series of articles criticized Mandel's policy on the Treaty of Versailles. "From the very beginning of the legislature, we saw a strange and odious comedy: Mandel, on the pretext of saving the work of Clemenceau, refused to take into consideration its shortcomings, and obstinately sabotaged the efforts of men who were trying to enforce the Treaty." And

---

* Jérôme Pétion (1756–94) was a French revolutionary leader who was condemned by the Convention in 1793. Fleeing Paris, he sought refuge in the Gironde but was unable to find a secure hiding place. His body, the face half devoured by dogs or wolves, was eventually discovered in a forest, where he was presumed to have committed suicide.

when Poincaré took power, instead of supporting him, Mandel, "that grotesque pygmy, set himself up against the great statesman in whom France and a part of the world had placed their confidence...." The judgment of the *Petite Gironde* on the election was summed up on the front page:

Action Clemenciste equals Reaction, Fascism
Bloc des Gauches equals Revolution, Civil War
Concentration Républicaine equals Peace, Order, Security[55]

At the end of the campaign a bitter controversy arose between Mandel and Jean Odin, a candidate on the Republican list. Odin, a former Radical, had earlier defended Joseph Caillaux, whom Mandel and Clemenceau had prosecuted for treason during the war. But as a Center candidate in 1924, he was forced by electoral considerations to denounce Caillaux and even to deny having known him. Caillaux, who had kept Odin's sympathetic letters and even one asking for a loan, decided to take revenge on the unfaithful friend. He sent one of the letters to Mandel to use as he wished.

It was a perfect opportunity to discredit Odin and his entire list, and Mandel took a showman's advantage of it. To announce the impending revelation, he had leaflets dropped from airplanes, and posters placed on practically every wall in the Gironde. Odin protested his innocence, denied writing the letter, and called both Mandel and Caillaux liars. But his chances of winning the election were crushed. Only one candidate on his list received fewer votes than he did.[56]

Undoubtedly, everyone was glad to see the end of this particular campaign. On election day, Mandel's list averaged a respectable 31,340 votes.[57] The averages for the other lists are as follows:

Bloc des Gauches 73,904
Concentration Républicaine 55,473
Dissident Radicals 10,108
Communists 5,792
Dissident Republicans 5,591

Because no list received an absolute majority of the votes, the seats had to be apportioned among the parties. The Bloc des Gauches, with four times as many votes as the electoral quotient—16,822—was entitled to four seats. The Republican list obtained three seats and Mandel's list one. This seat went to the Abbé Bergey, who had received several thousand votes more than Mandel. Had their list averaged 2,304 more votes, it would have had twice the electoral quotient and have been entitled to a second seat. Mandel would thus have been reelected although he had received fewer votes than any member of the Bloc des Gauches or the Concentration Républicaine. Some of the extra votes for Bergey had come from the Royalists, whose leaders in the Gironde had instructed their followers to vote for Bergey, but to cross Mandel's name off their ballots.[58] Mandel's brilliant idea of putting the popular Abbé on his list had backfired. Once again, as in 1920, he was defeated not so much by his enemies as by his own stratagems, for his list would probably have won a seat even without Bergey.

Since only eight of the Gironde's seats had been apportioned according to the quotient system, the other three seats were given to the Bloc des Gauches as the list with the highest average. The Left thus received seven seats to three for the Center and one for the Right, despite the fact that the Left had actually obtained fewer votes than the Right and Center.

Bloc des Gauches	73,904	Center	55,473
Dissident Radicals	10,108	Right	31,340
Communists	5,792	Dissident Republicans	5,591
TOTAL	89,804	TOTAL	92,404

The conservatives fell short of an absolute majority by only 118 votes.[59] If they could have united, presumably they would once again have swept the Gironde, depriving the Left of seven important seats in the ensuing legislature. The cost of dissidence was high. Had this situation occurred only in the Gironde, it might be blamed on Mandel's divisive activities, but it occurred in other districts as well.[60] In the country as a whole, the Right and the candidates of groups that had usually supported Poincaré, together received more votes than the combined Left.[61] But these votes, when translated into the new mathematics of the electoral law, produced 313 left-wing deputies and 274 moderate and right-wing deputies.[62] The inability of the conservatives to present common lists in the elections cost them several seats. Also, forty-two of the newly elected moderate deputies extricated themselves from the defeat of the Bloc National, formed a new group, the Gauche Radicale, and threw their support to the Cartel des Gauches.

Had Poincaré seriously attempted to unite the Right and Center for the elections, some seats would have been saved, and most of the forty-two members of the Gauche Radicale would have toed the line.[63] The conservatives and Poincaré might have stayed in power, and—who knows?—France might also have begun to develop a viable party system. Instead, as Mandel said, Poincaré had "methodically organized the defeat of those who were insane enough to have confidence in him."[64]

7. Local Politics

*Soupçonnez-vous quel peut être le sort d'un politicien qui, pour
être resté fidèle à ses idées, a perdu l'oreille des pouvoirs
publics? Le malheureux, il n'a qu'à disparaître! C'est ce qu'on
ne s'est pas fait faute de me signifier de toutes parts au
lendemain du 11 Mai.*

Mandel

THROUGHOUT the Bloc National legislature, Mandel had repeatedly criticized the internal policy of the various governments, but his primary concern had always been with foreign affairs. If he chose to attack on internal policy, it was first of all because he knew that French governments were rarely overthrown on military or diplomatic issues.[1] The second and more important reason, however, was his belief that "domestic politics invariably determine foreign policy."[2]

The essential problem for Mandel, therefore, had been the creation of a coherent majority willing to support a vigorous foreign policy. Everything he did during the legislature was directed to this end. He advocated concessions to the Catholics to eliminate the traces of their recent antirepublicanism and make it easier for them to cooperate with the Center. He personally associated himself with the Right and even attempted to get the support of the Monarchists because it was among these men that nationalist sentiment was strongest. He aroused the antagonism of the Radicals against the majority in order to prevent them from working with the Center, and he tried to drive them into permanent opposition in order to make the government absolutely dependent on the right wing of its majority. Finally, he tried to force the government to support its followers in the elections, for should they be defeated, he believed that the Left would inevitably adopt a more pliable foreign policy.

Against Mandel's contentions, Poincaré had argued that questions of foreign affairs should take precedence over internal politics.[3] In order to obtain a massive vote of confidence as a demonstration to world opinion of French unity and determination, he refused to play the game of partisan politics. The result, as Mandel had predicted, was that the Bloc National majority was led to the slaughterhouse, and the Cartel des Gauches was able to put into effect its own foreign policy.

Despite the precariousness of its electoral victory, the Left acted as if it had received a large popular mandate. At home it was combative, forcing President Millerand to resign because of the open support he had given to the Bloc National. Abroad, it was conciliatory, determined to rely on negotiation and compromise rather than force and threats. The new left-wing government accepted the Dawes Plan, reducing Germany's annual payments to France. The French army evacuated the Ruhr. Germany was admitted to the League of Nations and freed of the Armaments Control Commission. All of these measures indicated Germany's return to the family of nations and the beginning of her restoration to a position of equality with other countries. They also foreshadowed the early evacuation of the Rhineland and the elimination of the other restrictions placed on Germany by the Treaty of Versailles.

To Mandel, the foreign policy of the Cartel government was pure folly. At his first opportunity in the General Council of the Gironde, he protested publicly against the Dawes Plan. Had there been no government and no prime minister since 1920, he said, France's position could not have been worse. And yet the councilors had repeatedly voted congratulations to the successive governments. "To Millerand we have said, 'You are a genius!'; to Georges Leygues, 'You are outstanding'; to Briand, 'You are covering yourself with glory'; for Poincaré we never had praise enough. And what is the result of all these pseudosuccesses? That at the present time we are asking for only sixteen billion gold marks from Germany." France, he estimated, had already spent 100 billion francs on the liberated areas and would have to spend eighteen billion more. Pensions to war victims would cost another fifty billion. Even without her debts to England and America, France would still have to meet a bill of 168 billion with the sixteen billion gold marks from Germany. That was the situation supporters of the Dawes Plan were asking them to accept. As for himself, he declared, "I cannot agree to this new surrender that sanctions the biggest robbery in history."[4]

He opposed any concessions to Germany because they only encouraged her to make further demands. "Whether the majority in the Reichstag is leftist or rightist, socialist or nationalist," he said, "Germany will keep only those agreements she is forced to keep."[5] He was particularly opposed to reductions in reparations because so long as Germany did not meet her payments, France had the right to maintain troops in the Rhineland. But if payments were scaled down or guaranteed in some way by the various powers, then France might be forced by world opinion to evacuate the Rhineland on schedule or even prematurely, thus lowering the last physical barrier to German aggression.[6]

It was not, of course, that he feared an immediate attack, but he considered it axiomatic that Germany would strive to become a great military power again. In that event, she would try to change the territorial provisions of the Treaty of Versailles. He predicted that "she would begin, in agreement with the Soviets, by occupying Austria or by having bands recruited on her territory attack the new states established in 1919. In that case we would not be able to remain neutral any more than we could have permitted the annihilation of Russia in 1914. It is not so much our agreements with Warsaw, Belgrade or Prague that require us to intervene, as concern for our own preservation." His greatest regret was that England was not willing to guarantee the provisions of the treaty in eastern Europe.[7]

In 1919 Great Britain and the United States had promised France immediate military aid in case of German aggression, in return for which France gave up her claim to a permanent occupation of the Rhineland. When the American Senate rejected the treaty, however, France was left unprotected, for England's aid had been conditional on that of the United States. In subsequent years, the question of a new agreement was broached, but England would never commit herself to intervening in Eastern Europe, where France in the meantime had concluded alliances with Poland and Czechoslovakia to compensate for the loss of Russia as her eastern ally.

Renewed negotiations eventually led to the signing of the Locarno Pact in October 1925. Under the terms of this agreement, England, Belgium, and Italy agreed to guarantee the Franco-German frontier. For her part, Germany gave up Alsace and Lorraine in return for admission to the League of Nations. For England, the pact was the fulfillment of the promise she had made to France in 1919 of immediate military aid in case of German aggression. The failure to mention the eastern frontiers, however, raised doubts about Germany's peaceful intentions toward Poland and Czechoslovakia, and also seemed to imply that England regarded German aspirations in this area as legitimate. For France, the pact was a calculated risk. On the one hand, she effectively renounced the right to intervene in the Rhineland save in the case of German remilitarization of the area or of a direct German attack on French territory. But on the other, the elimination of Franco-German differences might lead to the reconciliation of the two nations and a peaceful future for an exhausted Europe. In any case, France now had a definite English commitment in the event of German aggression. On balance, most Frenchmen regarded it as a good bargain.

Mandel disagreed. "To the desire for peace, they have sacrificed the most certain guarantees of peace," he wrote in a remarkably prophetic article. He considered it obvious that "if there is another war, it will be provoked as in 1914 by difficulties in the east. In that event, of what use would the British promise about the Rhine be to us? Could we let Poland and Czechoslovakia be annihilated?" Furthermore, the pact failed to give France the right to intervene in the Rhineland if Germany annexed Austria. "What would our legal position be if we then began an occupation? Would the English have to fight us?"

Both Mandel and the adherents of the accords thought that Locarno opened up a new era. For them, however, it meant the peaceful settlement of disputes, whereas for Mandel it meant the end of Franco-British unity. He believed that in spite of her differences with France, England had always felt herself morally bound by the promise of aid she had made in 1919.

It was certain that in the event of war she would be on our side. The situation has now been changed. Locarno has both committed her and freed her. In imposing precise duties on her, the pact . . . has clearly limited the very rare cases in which she must intervene. With our full consent, she ceases to be our ally in order to become a sort of arbitrator between Germany and us. The English enthusiasm for the pact is therefore quite understandable. The advantages of "splendid isolation" could not have been more shrewdly combined with the guarantees of the Entente Cordiale. England has succeeded in paying her moral debt to France without losing her freedom of action; and if in the future she takes any interest whatsoever in continental affairs, she will be able to choose whichever side she pleases.[8]

Striking confirmation of Mandel's analysis is found in the diary of Lord D'Abernon, the British Ambassador in Berlin, who noted that the signing of the Locarno Pact "marks the turning point in the postwar history of Europe. . . . It restored the necessary balance of power."[9]

For France, however, Mandel saw no advantages at all. In addition to renouncing her moral claim on England, she gave up the right to intervene in the Rhineland or to prolong the occupation as a sanction except under certain very strict conditions. As for Germany, "it is clear. Their plan is being carried out with irresistible logic. After the Ruhr, the Rhineland, then the eastern front. Germany is methodically revising the Treaty of Versailles."[10]

Although the German plan may have been obvious to Mandel, to his contemporaries it was not so obvious. Nor is it perfectly clear even to a later generation that in 1925 Germany had irrevocably determined on a policy of expansion. In any case, under the growing influence of Aristide Briand, who was to direct French foreign policy under both leftist and rightist governments from 1925 to 1932, the country was committed to compromise and conciliation. Symbolic of the change was the reversed public estimation of the two old antagonists, Briand and Clemenceau. Briand, now minister of Foreign Affairs, was popularly called the "Pilgrim of Peace," while as Robert Cornilleau of the Christian Democrats noted, it was "no longer in good taste to be the friend of *'Père la Victoire,'* . . . who in certain circles is referred to only with scorn and disdain as 'the author of the Treaty of Versailles.'"[11]

In the face of this reversal of opinion, Mandel attempted to remind the nation through speeches and interviews of "the German responsibility for the war, the atrocities of fifty months of occupation, and the treason that was widespread in the press and in Parliament," but he recognized that "anyone who dares to remember these things is called a dreamer, a mystic, a madman or an enemy of the peace."[12] He was almost the last, even of the Clemencists, to regard the Treaty of Versailles as the cornerstone of French security. Even André Tardieu, who had retired from politics after his defeat in 1924, but was back in Parliament as a result of a by-election in February 1926, agreed to join with Briand in the National Union government formed by Poincaré in July when the Cartel des Gauches finally collapsed.

As Tardieu later explained, from 1920 to 1924 he had attempted to reform the regime while in opposition. His failure had convinced him that reform could be accomplished only from a position of control. Therefore, he did "what was necessary" in order to acquire control and accepted the ministry that Poincaré offered him.[13] Tardieu's talents were such that within three years he came to be regarded as Poincaré's natural successor.[14]

In taking the road to power with Poincaré, however, he lost the friendship of one of the few men he ever really respected. Some time after Tardieu became minister, Clemenceau sent him a copy of his latest book, *Au soir de la pensée*, with the inscription: "A André Tardieu. Souvenirs et regrets." In reply Tardieu wrote: "I was very happy to receive your two volumes—a little saddened by the dedication. Memories? I would prefer contact between us. Regrets? I have done nothing to justify them. And if there are differences of opinion, friends can always discuss them. If you are willing, I will come to visit you."[15] This appeal for renewed relations apparently went unheeded, for Tardieu was not to see Clemenceau again until November 1929 when the old man lay on his deathbed and Tardieu himself had become prime minister.

After Clemenceau's retirement his former associates at first awaited his return to active politics and then began to make their own way. Despite the rebuffs and insults always directed at him,[16] Mandel was one of the few who still came to see him. In a man otherwise as hardened and unsentimental as Mandel, this devotion is surprising, but it has been noted by all who met him. Emmanuel Berl remarked that Mandel virtually rose from his chair every time he said "Clemenceau," as if it were improper to say the name without standing up.[17] Clemenceau, who was possibly even more cynical than Mandel, appeared to be grateful for the attention. Mandel was the last of his political friends, he said, adding, "He has his faults, but he is faithful."[18] Embittered about the direction of French politics, he often said that he no longer wished even to discuss it with anyone. General Mordacq, his former *chef de cabinet*, reminded him, "You will certainly make an exception for Mandel, the best informed man in Paris." Clemenceau smilingly replied, "Ce n'est pas sûr."[19]

Unlike Tardieu, Mandel had announced his intention to remain in political life after the 1924 election, squelching rumors that he planned to follow his friend into retirement. "It is only those who never fight who are never beaten," he declared. "Whoever loves his country and wishes to serve it knows in turn the joy of success and what is called the bitterness of defeat.... But one is really defeated only when one gives up. And when the present situation is most disturbing, it is more than ever necessary to continue the struggle...by word and by pen and to prepare for future elections as our opponents did four years ago."[20]

In complete isolation for the first time, he set out to reestablish his political position. He devoted himself to building a solid base of power in Lesparre, dependent neither on the gratitude of fellow deputies he might have helped to elect, nor on their expectations of favors if he achieved power, an event that now seemed remote. He temporarily exiled himself from Paris and acquired control of a small weekly, *Le Réveil Médocain*. The entire regional press had opposed him in the elections except for the *Liberté du Sud-Ouest*. After his defeat, even its directors were uncertain whether to support him any longer. Paul Duché, the editor and one of the founders, retired in December because of the dispute.[21] Thereafter Mandel could count only on the sympathetic neutrality of the *Liberté*.

One of the principal arguments against Mandel during the elections—and one of his tactical errors—had been his neglect of local affairs. He had not attended the banquets and celebrations of his constituents and had concerned himself little with the area. More effort devoted to local politics might have brought him the few thousand votes he needed to be elected.

He had always held enough meetings to explain to the farmers and workers of the area his views on national and international events, but he had neglected the personal side of politics—the shaking of hands, the inquiries about the business and health of his constituents, all of the little touches that might have brought him the necessary support. He had wanted the people to back him because of his policies and the favors he was able to obtain for them. Although he had attended most of the sessions of the General Council, he had spent as little time as possible in the region and had failed to create any popular sympathy. His entire life was centered in Paris and in national politics, and he made a strange picture on the beaches of Soulac and in the vineyards of the Médoc with his black suit, his high stiff collar, and his derby hat. Worst of all, perhaps, was the fact that he was "the only mayor in the Gironde who drank nothing but Vichy water."[22]

Although his recent defeat made him realize the necessity for courting his constituents, he was temperamentally incapable of being a local politician in the ordinary sense. He disliked the empty, banal statements of so many political meetings. His conception of a speech was that it "should not be a simple exercise of rhetoric; it must be an act."[23] It was a declaration of his principles, and he usually agreed to speak only to define his policies. Every speech was minutely prepared and memorized. Through weeks of study and many drafts, it was made as tightly reasoned and as accurate as possible. Unfortunately, however, every speech was also crammed with so many details and nuances that his audience could easily lose the thread of his argument.

Even though he would never really have the common touch, Mandel began to attend local celebrations, presiding over an agricultural banquet for the first time, speaking at a dinner in honor of the local firemen, and even distributing the prizes and delivering the commencement address at the school in Soulac. He also tried to turn the seaside town of Soulac into a fashionable summer resort. This attention to local affairs was rewarded in the municipal elections of 1925. Although opposed by the entire slate of candidates he had been elected with in 1919, he managed to have his own men chosen for twelve of the sixteen places, thus assuring his own reelection as mayor.[24] He also soon built up a local machine that included mayors and councilors in the various municipalities and arrondissements. His followers did not form a party or become affiliated with any national organization, but their personal support allowed him to withstand and defeat, just barely at first, and then overwhelmingly, the united opposition of all the organized parties in Lesparre. By 1936 not even the union of the Republicans, Socialists, and Radicals could overcome Mandel's personal party in the Gironde.

Nationally, he began to write occasional long articles for the conservative *Revue Hebdomadaire*, which, together with the interviews he arranged in various papers, served to keep his name in circulation during his exile from politics in Paris. Journalism may have been only a substitute for the direct influence he would have preferred to exercise in Parliament, but he thoroughly understood the power of the press. Early in his career, he had chosen journalism as an avenue to power; under Clemenceau, he had controlled the censorship; and each time that he lost power, he turned to journalism as a forum for his ideas even though writing was not easy for him. But as soon as the door of authority opened for him again, he deserted the exposition of ideas for the more immediate satisfactions of political power. "Action," he held, "is the source of all pleasure."[25]

For the moment, he had to be content with criticizing both the Cartel des

Gauches and the former members of the Bloc National. In contrast to other conservatives, and even though opposed to the Cartel, Mandel approved its attempt to take full power. He praised

the masterly political lesson [it] has given its adversaries. It has not made the same mistake as the victors of 1919 who never dared to take power; it has known how to use victory. In succession, it has expelled the head of the state, elected one of its own men to the presidency of the Chamber, taken over the entire government and replaced most of the important officials.... Except in its action against the Elysée, it has abided by the rules of parliamentary politics. It is the absolute duty of a majority to carry out its program, for which it needs the full cooperation of the agents of the executive power as well as of Parliament. The Cartel has the majority. It has alone assumed the burdens of power. If it succeeds, let it have all the rewards; if it fails, let it suffer as well all the consequences.[26]

II

The Cartel des Gauches was primarily an electoral alliance. The Radicals and Socialists never formulated a common program. Herriot formed the first government with the support but without the participation of the Socialists, who refused to join any cabinet they did not control. For a while the electoral victors managed to maintain their precarious alliance on the basis of secondary issues. They voted an amnesty for Joseph Caillaux and Jean Malvy, withdrew all financial support from the embassy at the Vatican, attempted to suppress the special religious and administrative independence enjoyed by Alsace because of its separation from France between 1870 and 1918, and in general resurrected the clerical issue that had always united the Left in the past.

But because of fundamental disagreement between them and the Socialists on economic and financial questions, it was obvious that the Radicals would be able to keep power only with the aid of moderate votes on these issues. Unfortunately for Herriot and his successors, the financial difficulties left unsolved by the Bloc National were the most important questions of the day. For two years, one Cartel government after another wrestled unsuccessfully with the financial question, while the franc steadily deteriorated, falling to one-tenth of its prewar value by July 1926. At this point the Radicals finally admitted defeat, abandoned the Socialists, and turned over the government to Poincaré.

For the first year of the coalition, most of the Center, like the Right, had actively opposed it. Former President Millerand's National Republican League, founded to organize nation-wide propaganda against the Cartel, received their wholehearted support. While sympathetic to its aims, Mandel nevertheless preferred to remain aloof from the new league because "they seem to be looking for the first pretext to return to the bosom of the majority instead of . . . remaining systematically in opposition throughout the legislature."[27] He was afraid that some moderates would vote for the government on financial questions when the Socialists withdrew their support, thus saving the left-wing alliance from total discredit and permitting it to stumble along for a while longer.

This is precisely what happened in April 1925 when Prime Minister Paul Painlevé, who succeeded Herriot, appointed Joseph Caillaux Finance minister. The reappearance of Caillaux outraged the conservatives at the same time that his reputation for financial orthodoxy reassured them. Desire for financial salvation, however, outweighed considerations of exacerbated patriotism, and the opposition several times saved Painlevé from defeat when the Socialists refused to support him.

Painlevé was not finally defeated until he attempted to adopt the Socialist proposal to postpone payments on the national debt. The Gauche Radicale, the Center group that had maintained a tenuous alliance with the Cartel since the elections, immediately rejoined its former allies on the Right in opposition. Parliament was stalemated. Leftist governments could not obtain a majority for financial measures proposed by the Socialists, and could pass measures acceptable to the Right only at the risk of being opposed by a majority of their own supporters. To solve the crisis, President Gaston Doumergue called on Briand, whose ability to fashion a working majority out of the most disparate elements was almost legendary. He put together a cabinet composed of thirteen members of Radical or allied groups, four members of the Gauche Radicale, and two representatives of the Center who had been in opposition since the beginning of the legislature, Georges Leygues and Paul Jourdain.

Some of the conservatives saw in Briand's cabinet the indications of a new orientation in policy and gave their support to it. Since all but two of the ministers had collaborated either with Herriot or with Painlevé, Mandel did not believe that the inclusion of Jourdain and Leygues—"who had adopted such contradictory policies that they could not be said to represent any"—indicated a real change. The composition of Briand's cabinet showed merely that he intended to base his government "on alternating majorities, depending on circumstances." Mandel advised the conservatives to remain in opposition, because "no financial reform or diplomatic action . . . can lead to satisfactory results if it is not part of a general policy."[28] Most of the Center, nevertheless, voted for Briand, who proved to be as incapable of solving the financial crisis as his predecessors.

The continued failure of the Cartel to restore financial stability caused a revival of the antiparliamentarianism that had subsided during the war and had been perpetuated afterwards only in the propaganda of the Royalist *Action Française*. New groups, admirers of Mussolini's Fascist state, now added their voices to the demand for more authority in government. For the first time, in Camille Aymard's noted *Bolshevisme ou Fascisme? Français, il faut choisir*, the country was called on to decide between the rival forms of government.

Mandel had no sympathy with any of these groups, nor with those who recommended constitutional reform or emergency powers for the government. With arguments that he was to repeat throughout the following decade, he declared his belief that "the country will be saved by the parliamentary system."[29] Clemenceau's successful conduct of the war under the existing constitution had convinced him that no change was necessary. "Authority cannot be conferred by decree. The office does not make the man.... Out of more than a thousand ministers we have had in half a century, how many of them were ministers in more than name? It is vastly more difficult to resolve the problem of recruiting leaders...than it is to compose constitutional texts that will be worth only as much as the men who have to put them into effect."[30]

Mandel's own solution to the problem of obtaining an effective and coherent majority was simple: new elections. To the conservatives who hoped to gain power by weaning the Radicals away from the Socialists, he pointed out that their error was "to let themselves be hypnotized by the group system in the Chamber. General policy is determined primarily by electoral alliances, and since the Cartel persists in the country, it must necessarily continue in Parliament." Many of them believed that the Cartel was merely an electoral alliance and that there was therefore no reason why a Radical ministry should depend on Socialist rather than conservative support. "This would be true," said Mandel, "if the Radicals elected on common lists with the Socialists were no longer forced to campaign with them."[31]

He recommended that the President and the Senate dissolve the Chamber and call new elections, a solution also supported by the Socialist leader Léon Blum, who said that between the Cartel and the Bloc National there was room only for "confusion and disorder." But since the Senate would agree to dissolution only if the Chamber returned to the former method of electing deputies from single-member constituencies, Mandel argued that the conservatives should attempt to reestablish the *scrutin d'arrondissement*. Instead, they actually opposed returning to the former method of voting for fear that any changes would enable the leftist majority to tamper with electoral boundaries.

The fears of the conservatives were well founded. The number of deputies had been reduced for the 1924 elections. A simple return to the *scrutin d'arrondissement* would therefore require the redrawing of a large part of the electoral map of France—inevitably to the benefit of the majority. To avoid this difficulty, Mandel proposed the reenactment of the 1889 electoral law, which would also resurrect the old electoral districts. This would increase the number of deputies, but it would also prevent extensive gerrymandering. Obvious inequities could then be rectified by means of special laws.[32]

Although Briand had been one of the foremost supporters of the 1919 electoral law, on becoming prime minister in November 1925, he had recommended that the country return to the *scrutin d'arrondissement*—not in order to prepare the way for dissolution of the Chamber, but in order to separate the Radicals from the Socialists. Elections were not scheduled to take place until 1928, but the passage of the law would permit the Radicals to desert the Socialists immediately and support a Center government without suffering any electoral consequences.

Preoccupation with financial and diplomatic problems prevented Briand from getting the reform passed before the Cartel finally collapsed in July 1926. The fall in the value of the franc was so disastrous that the Radicals were forced to join Poincaré's National Union government even without any revision in the electoral law. At the time, Poincaré's refusal to back the Bloc National in the 1924 elections gained him the indulgence of the Radicals. Now it permitted them to support him as a nonpartisan premier.[33]

When the franc began a rapid rise in value under Poincaré, the Radicals found themselves trapped in the new coalition. It was impossible for them either to withdraw support from the successful government or to campaign in 1928 in formal alliance with the Socialists who were opposing that government. Only the return to the *scrutin d'arrondissement* could resolve their dilemma by permitting them to remain in the cabinet without courting electoral disaster.

By this time everyone realized that party confusion in the Chamber would prevent the 1919 law from functioning satisfactorily. The return to the *scrutin d'arrondissement* was therefore passed by an overwhelming majority, the problem of drawing the boundaries of the electoral districts being solved more or less as Mandel had proposed. The number of deputies was increased, and the Universal Suffrage Committee, on which all parties were represented, was instructed to correct inequities in districting. It was tacitly agreed that all decisions would be made by the Committee and merely ratified by Parliament. The deputies would thus keep the bitter debates and the embarrassing compromises always entailed by redistricting behind closed doors.

Although not a member of Parliament, Mandel proved to be one of the major stumbling blocks in this arrangement. Under a simple return to the old constituencies, his election in Lesparre seemed assured. He had worked the district for fourteen years and had spent the last four carefully cultivating his electors. The only hope his opponents had of defeating him lay in gerrymandering the district to include people who would be sure to vote against him. Mandel, however, not only thwarted their attempt in the Universal Suffrage Committee, but managed to have Lesparre made an exception to the provision of the law requiring that each district have a population of at least 40,000.[34] Their only recourse then, in spite of the prior agreement to bypass discussion, was to take their case to the Chamber itself, where the leftist majority and Mandel's unpopularity would assure them of success.

Jean Montigny, the Radical deputy from La Sarthe and a close friend of Joseph Caillaux, who represented the same district in the Senate, was chosen to introduce an amendment attaching the canton of Castelnau to Lesparre. Superficially, there was some justice in this change. The Bordeaux district that included Castelnau had a population of 93,000 whereas Lesparre had only 39,000. Therefore, the addition of Castelnau's 16,000 to Lesparre might seem to be only a question of equalizing the population in the two districts.

Nevertheless, everyone knew this was actually an attempt to defeat Mandel.[35] Castelnau was a moderate Republican stronghold where he had made his poorest showing in 1924.

	Republican List	*Cartel*	*Mandel*
Lesparre	2,527	3,404	3,224
Castelnau	2,187	714	664
TOTAL	4,714	4,118	3,888

Although Mandel was absent the day Montigny introduced the amendment, his spirit was present. It was a confusing and at times comical session. Montigny was constantly interrupted by the Right and particularly by Abbé Daniel Bergey, Mandel's running mate in 1924. When someone referred to Mandel as "mort," Bergey replied that "if he were dead, you would be making less noise." He forced two of the deputies from the Gironde to withdraw their assertions that Castelnau had always been part of the district of Lesparre. But in spite of his lengthy and amusing intervention, in which, as a native of the area, he pretended that each reference to the "haute personnalité politique" from Lesparre was actually to him, the Chamber overruled the Universal Suffrage Committee and attached the canton of Castelnau to Lesparre by a vote of 310 to 210.[36] Thus, more successfully than in 1919, Mandel's enemies had used the cumbrous machinery of Parliament against him.

To benefit from the new arrangement, the Center chose as its candidate Alain du Périer de Larsan, Castelnau's representative on the General Council and the son of a former deputy from Lesparre. He was supported by the *Journal du Médoc*, the local organ of the Alliance Démocratique, which began its campaign toward the end of 1927. Week after week the entire front page was devoted to chauvinistic and anti-Semitic attacks on Mandel, using such slogans as "A Médocain is better than a Jew." They claimed that Mandel was the candidate of "the Royalists, the Bonapartists, the Fascists, and of all the enemies of the Republic."[37]

Representing the Radicals was incumbent Deputy Lucien Teyssier, whose campaign, though less virulent than that of the Center candidate, was also conducted primarily against Mandel.[38] He, too, never let the electors forget that Mandel was a Jew, but more often he accused Mandel of being "an agent of international capitalism" and of receiving the financial support of the Comité des Forges.[39] Mandel replied by producing a letter that Teyssier had written to him in March 1916 asking his aid in obtaining a munitions order for a factory of which Teyssier was co-owner. It was only on Teyssier's behalf, Mandel said, that he had met with the Comité des Forges. He also published a letter that du Périer had written to him in 1919 asking to join his list.[40] It was a long time before his opponents learned what Mandel had always known: never put anything in writing.

The Paris daily *Le Matin* reported that there were hardly four districts in France where the campaign was being conducted as fiercely as in Lesparre. The paper quoted Albert Bacquey, the President of the Radical Party in the area, as saying that his party had a single idea: "Anything rather than Mandel and his 'petits papiers.'" The influential *Petite Gironde*, which had not mentioned his name in its columns for four years, addressed a front-page editorial to Mandel announcing its intention to combat him "to the extent that your public duties permit you to apply your disastrous policies." To complete his isolation, even Abbé Bergey informed the Catholic readers of *La Liberté du Sud-Ouest* that the paper had no official candidate in Lesparre.[41]

Despite his failure to get support from the local political leaders, Mandel refused to give up hope of regaining a place in Parliament. The Prefect of the Gironde wrote to the Minister of the Interior: "Need I tell you what kind of adversary Mandel is and what strength of will he has, combined with finesse, audacity and talent ...? In short, he is so determined to succeed that he will let nothing stand in his way."[42] Mandel's main aim was to discredit du Périer in order to win over the necessary votes from the Center. He first proposed to du Périer that since they both backed Poincaré and opposed the Radicals, whichever one had fewer votes on the first ballot should withdraw in favor of the other. When du Périer refused, Mandel began to campaign against him, at one point almost forcing him to withdraw.[43] One of the tricks Mandel played on him has entered local legendry. Du Périer was such a poor public speaker and so unaccustomed to electoral battles that he memorized one talk and gave it at every meeting. As soon as Mandel realized this, he hired a stenographer to copy the speech, which he then had printed and distributed to the audience as they entered the hall at du Périer's next meeting.[44]

The result of Mandel's four-year campaign for reelection was that he received more votes than any other candidate—6,370—but not enough to win on the first ballot. Moreover, his opponents' combined total of 8,788—Teyssier, 3,929; du Périer, 3,625; Martet (Socialist), 1,234—made it seem certain that he would be defeated on the second ballot because both the Socialists and the Center advised their supporters to vote for Teyssier. Even the senators from the Gironde, members of the Alliance Démocratique, used their influence on behalf of the Radical candidate.[45]

Because Mandel was a supporter of Poincaré's National Union government,[46] the Alliance Démocratique was forced to justify its decision to back a potential opponent of the cabinet. They were not opposed to Mandel's principles, they said, but "to his manner, his methods, and his temperament, which do not seem to be suited to a policy of union."[47]

On the second ballot, however, more than one thousand of du Périer's supporters defected to Mandel, who received 7,765 votes to Teyssier's 7,725. It was a remarkable victory, achieved in the face of the combined opposition of the Center and the Left and despite the gerrymandering of his district by the Chamber of Deputies.[48] His opponents claimed fraud and tried to get the Chamber to invalidate his election. But Clemenceau, who may have financed Mandel's campaign, told a friend that "contrary to certain rumors, his election will certainly be validated, and he well deserves it, for he fought a courageous battle."[49]

8. Back to Parliament

Il faut consentir à être seul de son avis.

Mandel

THE PRECISE ROLE that Mandel would play in the new legislature was uncertain. He was far from the days of 1919 when everyone expected him to become minister of the Interior. The hostility of Parliament was now mixed with indifference and curiosity, for there were many deputies who had never known him, and the disintegration of the Clemencists seemed to have rendered him harmless. He refused to join any of the regularly constituted groups, and instead took his place among the "sauvages," those deputies, mostly antiparliamentarians, who kept aloof from the group and party struggles in the Chamber. Only the Monarchists seemed to share his intransigent nationalism. He became Parliamentary commentator for *Candide*, the reactionary literary and political weekly edited by Pierre Gaxotte and published by Arthème Fayard.[1] As immoderately as ever, Léon Daudet praised him as "very probably the only statesman among the Republicans," and deplored the fact that he had not become prime minister after 1919 instead of "Millerand, Briand, Poincaré, Herriot, Painlevé, and all those second-rate men." Under Mandel's direction, Daudet believed, "the affairs of France would certainly have taken a different turn and we would not once again be on the eve of a catastrophe."[2]

Aside from these compromising friends, however, Mandel was isolated. His only asset was his notoriety. He was still one of the favorite targets of the caricaturists and chansonniers.[3] But this reputation was an inadequate weapon with which to defend the Treaty of Versailles. As a maverick, he could have only marginal influence. His power would depend entirely on his famed instinct for corridor politics and on his ability to intervene in a debate at the proper moment.

His task was made doubly difficult by Poincaré's continued popularity after two years in office. Prosperity had been restored, the Germans were meeting their payments, and the peace began to look permanent. In gratitude, the voters had returned 440 deputies who claimed to be Poincaré's supporters. Yet many of them were restless in his coalition. Because of the financial crisis in 1926, the Radicals had deserted the Socialists to join the National Union government, but they had given Poincaré no mandate to tamper with the foreign policy of conciliation and compromise inaugurated by Herriot and Briand. To maintain their support, he had prudently allowed

Briand to continue, thus committing the country to the anomalous combination of a left-wing foreign policy and a conservative financial policy. It was obvious that the situation could not last.

Since the elections had given the conservatives a slight majority, the Right began to press for greater influence in the government. On the other hand, the Radicals, who blamed the recent losses in the election on their enforced collaboration with the Catholics, suggested to Poincaré that he get rid of these embarrassing allies and rely solely on what they called a "Republican" majority. Caught between the parties when he wanted to be above them, Poincaré rejected these entreaties. He intended to be a national leader and not the prisoner of either the Radicals or the Right.

As he usually did after each election, Mandel outlined the conditions for successful government in the ensuing legislature. Since no occasion in Parliament seemed to warrant his intervention, he gave the speech at a banquet in Lesparre as a virtuoso performance in political analysis. As usual, for the next four years the Chamber did its best, by not following his advice, to prove that he had been right.

Although recommending the continuation of National Union, Mandel predicted that the Radicals would soon desert Poincaré because they believed that they themselves would be able to form the next government with the aid of either the Center or the Socialists. This belief Mandel considered to be chimerical. On the basis of parliamentary arithmetic, he declared that the Radicals would never be able to form a viable government during that legislature. Therefore, if they did break up the National Union, the only alternative was not some ingenious combination of groups in the Chamber, which would be transient and incohesive, but the creation of a new conservative majority led by men willing to act. "The problem of government is above all one of leadership. . . . Will power is the essential condition for the restoration of French grandeur."[4]

A few days after the speech at Lesparre, the Radicals withdrew from the government and were surprised to find themselves in opposition. Poincaré simply replaced their ministers and continued in office with the support of a Right–Center majority. Mandel advised the new government to act clearly and decisively: "Let it lead its majority and proclaim solidarity with it before the country, and it will be in power for a long time—but only on that condition." He also expressed his confidence in André Tardieu, who had become minister of the Interior: "He is not a man to sit on the fence."[5]

But despite the disastrous defeat of his apolitical policy in 1924, Poincaré still preferred to be a national leader, above party and above politics. Although the balance of power had shifted, he retained Briand as foreign minister in order to appease the Radicals. The paradoxical result was that the conservatives supported a left-wing foreign policy because of their general approval of the government, whereas the Left voted against their own policy because they disliked the Right–Center majority. Poincaré also refused to increase the influence of the Right in the government, giving them only one additional post even though he was now absolutely dependent on their backing. In addition, he persuaded the conservatives not to claim the fruits of victory by replacing the left-wing presidents of the important Chamber committees with their own men.[6] Worst of all in Mandel's eyes was Tardieu's conversion to Poincaré's philosophy of government. Mandel had hoped that Tardieu's presence at the Ministry of the Interior would mean the division of the country into two large blocs, as they both had advocated during the 1919 legislature. But instead of helping the conservatives by the traditional method of appointing friendly prefects, Tardieu nominated men favorable to the Radicals.[7] Hoping to succeed the ailing Poincaré, he did nothing to alienate potential Radical supporters. In speeches posing his candidacy, he did not even mention party politics. His sole refrain was that France should follow the example of the United States and concentrate on building roads, canals and ports, "the only policy worthy of victorious France." Mandel commented that it was also "a policy that would further aggravate our political confusion by permitting an appeal for the collaboration of all parties."[8]

Mandel had previously advised the Right and Center that "power and opposition are only means, and the worst mistake a political group that has a majority can make is not to know how to use power to realize its program." He had also warned the government that in attempting to gain the questionable support of a few Radicals, it ran the risk of alienating some of the men who would otherwise be among its strongest backers.[9] Neither advice nor warning had been heeded. He therefore openly sought an occasion of upsetting the cabinet to recall it to a conservative foreign policy and to remind it of its dependence on a Right–Center majority.[10] Several issues were at hand. The first was the ratification of the agreements with the United States concerning French war debts. Negotiated but not ratified by the Cartel des Gauches, they were opposed by the Right because they failed to link these debts legally with Germany's obligations to France. Thus France might be forced to honor her debts to the Allies without any guarantee of being repaid in turn by Germany.

Knowing that the Socialists and Radicals would reject the accords in order to undermine Poincaré, Mandel hoped to persuade enough conservatives to vote with them to overthrow the government. "The operation would not be a glorious one. But who can be surprised? The working of our institutions is distorted when the Center and Right are forced to carry out the foreign policy of the Left. There is no doubt that a majority can be found in the present Chamber to ratify the accords, reduce once again the debts owed to France, and abandon the Rhineland guarantees without compensation, but to ask Nationalist deputies to do it is just too much."[11]

Despite serious illness, however, Poincaré was still able to play the Pied Piper. The Right blustered and threatened, but the Prime Minister's daily pleadings rallied enough of them to ratify the accords in July 1929 by a vote of 300 to 292. Although Mandel's opposition, limited to the corridors, had proved ineffective, his chances of overthrowing the government improved when Poincaré resigned shortly afterward for reasons of health. Tardieu was bypassed for the moment in favor of Briand, who simply took over his predecessor's cabinet.

The new prime minister immediately asked for a political truce until the details of a plan for the settlement of reparations could be worked out at an international conference at The Hague in August. Negotiations on the Young Plan, as it was called, had begun under Poincaré, who had been willing to reduce Germany's annual payments if the debt were commercialized, i.e. if Germany issued bonds for the entire sum, which her creditors could then sell on the world market. It had also been proposed that the Allies evacuate the Rhineland in 1930, five years ahead of schedule.

Mandel opposed the plan because he believed that the evacuation of the Rhineland was only the first aim in Germany's foreign policy. Next it would be the *Anschluss*, and then the question of colonies or of the eastern frontier. France, therefore, had to stay in the Rhineland.[12] His right-wing colleagues agreed, but they were reluctant to bring down the cabinet for fear of turning power over to the Radicals. Mandel himself was confident that any leftist government would be short-lived and that in any case the Right should resume its traditional role of defending French security. "If the Cartel is really a national peril," he declared, "this is primarily because of its foreign policy, which will not be any less harmful for being implemented by its former opponents."[13]

When Parliament reassembled in October, the conservatives were disturbed by the concessions that Briand had made at The Hague. He had agreed both to the reduction in payments and to the early evacuation of the Rhineland. Several speakers demanded an immediate debate on foreign policy. Among them was Mandel, whose intervention, Tardieu said, was "far more precise and pertinent" than the others.[14] One journalist was particularly struck by his style: "Slowly, carefully, his long body rises from his bench. His voice, thin and monotonous, has a surprising resonance. He leans toward the assembly as if to attract and hold its attention. And for a moment, his coldness and reserve disappear; carried away by his precise calculations and complicated schemes, he no longer seems to be in possession of himself. After quoting from a paper drawn from his pocket, he affects surprise, protests his good faith, assures Briand of his esteem, and insists there must be some mistake."[15] Surely, Briand could not be deviating from Poincaré's policy. As his predecessor had always demanded, he must certainly have subordinated the evacuation of the Rhineland to the commercialization of the debt. Undoubtedly, the Prime Minister would like to enlighten the Chamber on this point.[16]

Briand never enjoyed the respect and confidence that the Right had given Poincaré. They had been willing to see him at the foreign ministry over the preceding years, because they believed that Poincaré would keep him in line and prevent him from making any irreparable mistakes. Mandel wanted to show them that Briand, freed from any tutelage, was deviating from Poincaré's policy.

Briand maintained a guilty silence because he *was* making more concessions than Poincaré. As a liberal gesture to the Germans, he had agreed to a reduction in reparations and to an early evacuation of the Rhineland without demanding the prior commercialization of the debt. Therefore, instead of answering Mandel, he posed the question of confidence against holding an immediate debate on foreign policy. When the result of the vote was announced, "the assembly was at first stunned, and then exploded in murmurs."[17] Fifty-two nationalists had united with the Left to defeat the government 288–277. Mandel had warned that nationalist deputies could be pushed only so far in making concessions to Germany.[18]

As the largest group in opposition, the Radicals were asked to form the new government, but they were unable to get the aid of either the Socialists or the Center and had to retire. A Right–Center majority seemed the only viable one, and André Tardieu the logical candidate to head it.

In 1924 Tardieu had urged Poincaré to take the leadership of his majority. Presented now with a similar opportunity, he failed to follow his own advice, and instead adopted Poincaré's pretension to being above party politics. He immediately opened negotiations with the Radicals to bring them back into the government. "Constitutionally," he told the press, "parties do not exist." Friends were dinning in his ear that he had "the makings of a statesman," who could heal the old Right–Left division and build a modern, healthy, and vigorous France. "Using the combined resources of mother country and empire, he could create a harmonious economic and social structure, a France capable of giving the world the principles of international organization and of being the beacon of Europe."[19]

The vision was enticing, but if he were to gain Radical support he could not afford to be compromised by close collaboration with the Right. Thus, although the Radicals rebuffed him, he still restricted the Right to two ministries, kept Briand as minister of Foreign Affairs, and gave fourteen places in his cabinet to Left-Center groups that had previously supported the Cartel des Gauches. He then announced a whole series of reforms, so many of which had originated with the Left that one deputy exclaimed, "It's the Radical program!"[20]

Sure of the nobility of his own plans as compared to the petty political considerations of the Chamber, he dared the deputies to overthrow him, but warned them that in doing so, they would be acting against their own best interests. He told the Left that they would once again in effect be destroying Briand's policy. And to those most afraid of a leftist government, he said that in overturning him they would probably be preparing the way for one.[21]

Tardieu was playing on the Chamber's fears, and for the moment he struck the right chords, receiving a seventy-vote majority. Even though Mandel had frequently denounced Tardieu's tactics, he voted for the government. He apparently hoped that under the direction of Tardieu it would adopt a more intransigent policy toward Germany. After all, who was more capable of defending the Treaty of Versailles than Tardieu himself, its coauthor?

In any case, in December when Mandel was finally able to complete the interpellation begun against Briand two months earlier, he tried to recall the conservatives to their duty. He pointed out that the occupation of the Rhineland was to have been a guarantee that Germany would abide by all the clauses of the peace treaty. Yet Germany had balked not only at paying reparations, but also at disarmament. She was having weapons manufactured in Russia and elsewhere, was forming paramilitary organizations such as the Stahlhelm, and was spending five times as much on military equipment as was necessary for the forces allowed her by the Versailles Treaty. Why then was France evacuating the Rhineland?

Mandel believed that so long as France held the bridgeheads on the Rhine, she would be safe from a new and deadly attack, because the Germans would never deliberately unleash the horrors of war on their own territory. To those who objected that France would have to evacuate her troops in five years anyway, he quoted what Tardieu had earlier said: "Who cannot see that in fifteen years we will still be on the Rhine, for one reason among others, because at that time Germany will not have faithfully fulfilled the conditions of the peace treaty?"

Mandel then concluded his long speech with an apostrophe to the deputies on the Right, who have inscribed in their program the strict execution of the Treaty and who call themselves nationalists, undoubtedly to indicate that, disregarding all the contingencies of internal politics, they place concern for the grandeur and the security of the country above everything else. After having protested against the evacuation of the Ruhr, they will be contradicting themselves in accepting that of the Rhineland in return for a new and grave reduction of the debt Germany owes us. In any case, I know there are some who, without playing their opponents' game, will show at the proper time that they are not capable of it.[22]

It was a pertinent intervention that demonstrated all of his debating qualities: a minute knowledge of the facts, an inexorable logic, and an impeccable control of the discussion. But the speech had no effect. In reply, Tardieu affirmed his solidarity with Briand and said that there were three defects in the arguments of Mandel and the other critics: "No proof of what they have asserted; no program in place of what they have criticized; no vote as a sanction of what they have said."[23] Tardieu could hardly admit it at the time, but he himself opposed the Young Plan. Nevertheless, he considered the country committed by the negotiations begun under Poincaré.[24] France could not draw back at the last moment without causing a serious international crisis. In these circumstances, Mandel's criticisms were merely irritants. He had only warned the government and not even called for a vote of no confidence. Tardieu himself had to provoke a ballot to clear up the malaise the attacks had caused. Mandel abstained along with the Radicals and Socialists, and the Prime Minister returned to the conference at The Hague with a majority of 342 to 17.

The right-wing deputies basically agreed with Mandel, but they were in an embarrassing situation. They opposed the evacuation of the Rhineland, but for fear of giving the Left an opportunity to regain power, they refused to keep overthrowing their own governments on questions of foreign policy.[25] Therefore, instead of voting against the government, they attacked Mandel. The conservative journals gave him a poor review. He had been far too critical, his tone was too harsh, and he had failed to offer a constructive program. About his arguments there was not a word.[26]

Mandel was growing accustomed to isolation. In 1928 he had been among the eighteen die-hard deputies who voted against the stabilization of the franc at one-fifth of its prewar value. In March 1930, at a combined meeting of the Finance and Foreign Affairs Committees, he was the only one to oppose ratification of the Young Plan and the only one to vote against it.[27] When the Chamber accepted the plan, Mandel once again found himself in a very small minority. In July 1931 he voted against accepting the Hoover moratorium on international payments and opposed lending money to Germany to help her through the spreading world depression.

How would a deputy have been greeted in 1928, [he said,] if he promised to obtain: 1) the evacuation of the Rhineland; 2) the reduction of Germany's payments; 3) the payment to the English and the Americans for fifty-nine years of five to seven billion francs; 4) the acceptance of Hoover's proposal to suspend reparations for one year, and undoubtedly forever; 5) the agreement to lend money to Germany that will never be repaid? Such a deputy would not have received a single vote! And yet that is what the Chamber has accepted; that is what the policy of Briand has accomplished![28]

But without friends or authority, Mandel was unable to bring about a change in policy. Since his return to the Chamber, he had proved that he was a trenchant critic and a dangerous adversary, but the conservatives were afraid to follow him. One writer remarked that "if his interventions were not mistrusted, if the least of his words were not greeted with suspicion because of his reputation, his role would be more important."[29] And so after two years of futile opposition, Mandel decided that if he could not change his principles, he would at least change his style.

II

In November 1930 Mandel gave one of the few speeches of his career in support of government policies. The deputies had come expecting to hear another acid critique of the ministry. Instead they heard a qualified defense of Tardieu's bill for supplementary armaments credits. By evacuating the Rhineland, France had lost the last tangible guarantee against German aggression. But in spite of all the concessions she had already received, Germany still spoke of further revisions of the Treaty of Versailles, particularly at the expense of France's allies in the east. Mandel believed that "no informed Frenchman would ever permit such a betrayal of the nations that we have liberated," and denied that defending them would necessarily mean war. "In order to avoid such a possibility, we have only to build up the threat of an imposing force against those who might be tempted to disturb European order."[30] Yet for twelve years successive governments had failed to draw up a comprehensive plan of defense requirements. Tardieu's bill, although inadequate because it covered only the next few months, was the first to provide for the modernization of equipment and the reconstitution of war stocks. Because France had given up all of the guarantees against Germany, she was going to have to build up her defenses.

The speech has more importance in retrospect than it had at the time, for it laid down the fundamental policy that Mandel was to advocate throughout the bewildering events of the succeeding decade, events which would find him first on the Right and then on the Left while remaining faithful to his own principles. At the time, it was the relative moderation of the speech that attracted attention. The Royalist Charles Maurras, in fact, blamed him for not driving his criticisms home: "I call it Tardieuism."[31]

There was no doubt that a change had occurred. The Left had previously complained of "the cracked and nasal voice escaping from that livid mask while M. Mandel's hands trace ridiculous gestures in the air."[32] *Le Populaire* now remarked that "it is no longer the old Mandel. He has put on weight and become more assured. But he has lost some of his insolence.... The voice is still nasal, but the arms no longer move, or so little that one no longer recognizes M. Mandel."[33] Henri de Kérillis was soon to recommend that Léon Blum learn to imitate Mandel's immobility at the tribune.[34] Eventually he was to gain a reputation as one of the most self-possessed men in the Palais-Bourbon.[35]

With advancing age—he was now forty-five—Mandel had learned to discipline his tongue and restrain his actions. His features were becoming less angular and his manners less abrasive—in public at least, for in private, he had always been the soul of politeness. He was seen more frequently in society now, moving freely in the salons of the old aristocratic families. Without giving up his apartment on the avenue Mozart, he established a residence at the Ritz, where he liked to receive visitors.[36] He was becoming almost human. No longer would Tardieu be able to refer to him as "the monk of politics."[37]

But even adopting his more benign and statesmanlike image did not at once overcome deep-seated animosities toward him. When Pierre Laval formed his first cabinet in February 1931, he considered offering a post to Mandel. The mere mention of his name, however, brought forth such a roar of protest from old enemies, including President Gaston Doumergue, that Laval was forced to withdraw the offer.[38] Nevertheless, Mandel was able to exercise more influence on Laval's government than he had on its predecessors. According to Laval's secretary, he was the only deputy who had immediate access at all times to the new prime minister—though it was by the back door, "for he was still a compromising person."[39]

That Mandel himself had not forgotten the past was shown in May 1931, when he paid off an old score by helping to defeat Aristide Briand's bid for the presidency of the Republic. In secret alliance with Tardieu, and with Laval, who could not openly work against his own minister of Foreign Affairs, Mandel drummed up support for Paul Doumer, Briand's opponent.[40] This defeat marked the beginning of the end for Briand, who was watching the revival of German nationalism slowly destroy his hopes for peaceful reconciliation. In January 1932 he was dropped from the cabinet. Two months later, he died.

One thing that kept public attention focused on Mandel until the end of the legislature and advanced his new public image without entirely eliminating the old one was his prominent role in the Oustric investigation. In November 1930, a provincial bank controlled by the financier Albert Oustric collapsed. A parliamentary investigation was demanded when it was discovered that Tardieu's minister of Justice, Raoul Péret, had been Oustric's lawyer and had authorized the sale on the stock exchange of some unsound bonds sponsored by the bank. Péret was forced to resign along with two under-secretaries of State, Falcoz and Lautier, who had also been on Oustric's payroll. The government itself fell a few days later.

Mandel became one of the leading members of the commission set up to investigate the scandal, pressing for a total exposé of the affair and threatening to denounce the government publicly if it refused to turn over all of the relevant documents in its files.[41] Inevitably, the investigators themselves were subject to criticism. *Le Temps* complained that names were being used loosely, and *L'Ere Nouvelle* accused the Oustric Commission of muckraking.[42] One witness who had been roughly handled turned a venomous pen on Mandel, accusing him of being involved in the scandal.[43]

But despite attacks and opposition, the Commission continued its investigation. In March 1931 a preliminary report was issued. By May three ex-ministers and one former ambassador had been sent before the Senate sitting as a high court. By then, however, public interest was beginning to lag, and the four men were cleared of charges for lack of sufficient evidence. The final report of the Commission in March 1932 was not even published. It had been adopted unanimously by the Commission, but the right-wing majority voted not to publish it for fear of shaking public confidence on the eve of the election.[44] The hearings had dragged on for so long that no one even noticed. After more than thirty years it still has not been made public.

Although the Commission failed to have any of the accused punished, it at least threw the light of publicity on the relationship between the government, the press, and financial interests. It also helped Mandel to reestablish his position in Parliament. For months on end, his name appeared on the front page of the Paris journals. His clashes with witnesses provided a constant source of anecdotes. Of one former deputy who finally admitted having received a check, Mandel asked, "What did you say when it was given to you?" The harassed witness replied: "I said 'Thank you.' "[45] When Mandel asked a former civil servant if he were still employed at the Ministry of Commerce, he replied, "No. I am in business now." "In other words," quipped Mandel, "you have regularized your situation."[46]

By the time the Commission finished its hearings, Mandel was once again a feared and respected deputy and not just a relic from Clemenceau's regime.

If he had made new enemies, he had also won for himself a public image as an incorruptible and fearless representative. He had only to show what he could do as a political leader to become one of the outstanding figures on the Right.

III

In November 1929, shortly after Briand's government fell, Mandel was chosen president of the Universal Suffrage Committee. It was the first position of authority he had held since 1919 and the first opportunity he had to influence policy in an area he considered vital.

From the very beginning of the Third Republic there had been controversy over the electoral law of the nation. The first regular Chamber of Deputies had been elected in 1875 under the system known as the *scrutin d'arrondissement à deux tours*, which provided for single-member constituencies with a run-off ballot in case no candidate won an absolute majority of the votes on the first ballot. The Monarchist majority of the time had chosen this system because it favored local notables, who tended to be conservative, over their Republican opponents. In 1885 a Republican majority adopted the *scrutin de liste*, which provided for multi-member constituencies with a single ballot. This system was dropped after one election because of the threat that a man like General Boulanger, running at the head of a number of lists, might create a popular current that would sweep him and his supporters into power. The *scrutin d'arrondissement* was restored because it now favored the Left by permitting Republicans, Radicals, and Socialists to present separate candidates on the first ballot and then to unite on the second ballot against the reactionary candidate. In practice it worked to the advantage of all middle-of-the-road parties, especially the moderate Left, whose candidates were chosen on the second ballot against extremists of both Right and Left. It thus became the official "Republican" mode of election. Because of their underrepresentation, the Right and eventually the Socialists denounced the system and campaigned for proportional representation. As the reader will recall, in 1919 the Chamber adopted a hybrid system of proportional representation with majoritarian provisions, satisfying no one. Several years later when the Radicals were participating in Poincaré's government and thus could not campaign with the Socialists, they resolved their dilemma by returning to the *scrutin d'arrondissement*. This enabled Radicals and Socialists to present their own candidates on the first ballot and then, without too much embarrassment, jointly support the most favored left-wing candidate on the second. The system had its advantages for the Left, but it prevented clear identification of a given policy with any one party; indeed, it tended to prevent the formulation of any clear policy at all. For example, just what policy could a financially conservative Radical be said to represent when he had been elected with the aid of Socialist votes?

Despite the benefits derived by their party, even some Radical deputies deplored the ambiguous results of the system. In 1930 Charles Lambert, Herriot's running mate six years before, introduced a proposal in the Universal Suffrage Committee to abolish the second ballot. He argued that it had formerly been useful to prevent a return to a reactionary regime.

But at the present time we no longer have to fear this danger. The necessity of saving a regime that is not threatened therefore cannot justify the continuation of Parliamentary anarchy and of the disastrous confusion of parties. The time has come for the leaders to organize their followers, formulate their principles, state clearly their aims, and assure the country a stable, coherent and forceful policy. This can be accomplished only by suppressing the second ballot.[47]

As president of the Universal Suffrage Committee, Mandel adopted Lambert's proposal, removed others from consideration, and began to draft a bill providing for the election of deputies on a single ballot by a simple plurality. He believed that such a system would force each side to agree on a common program and a single candidate in each district. There would be no more purely electoral alliances between such disparate parties as the Radicals and the Socialists, whose programs were contradictory and whose members would go their own ways as soon as they reached the Chamber. Ultimately, he hoped, the reform would bring about the polarization of Parliament and the constitution of "the two great traditional governmental parties, the party of movement and the party of resistance."[48]

According to François Goguel, Mandel knew that the Left would find it more difficult than the conservatives to agree on a common program and common candidates, and therefore supported the reform merely in order to bring about a right-wing victory in the 1932 elections. He would thereby gain the gratitude of the Right and reestablish himself in Parliament.[49]

Undoubtedly, these considerations played a role in Mandel's plans. Even if he had been unaware of them, the anguished cries of the Socialists that they would lose sixty to seventy seats would soon have enlightened him. But it should be noted that his bill was consistent with the ideas of political organization he had formulated under Clemenceau and repeatedly advocated during the intervening twelve years. It was also consistent with his position on the electoral law over the years, and was not merely an expedient conceived in haste in order to defeat the Left.

With the help of the conservatives, who were persuaded to renounce their cherished plan for proportional representation, Mandel pushed the reform through the Universal Suffrage Committee. There was, however, one change: to be elected on a single ballot, a candidate would have to get at least 40 per cent of the vote, failing which a second ballot would still be held.

Mandel then had to get the reform put on Parliament's agenda. Because budgetary discussions had a high priority at that moment, the Chamber would agree to consider the proposed electoral law only in special sessions at night, on weekends or on odd days. There would be no continuous debate. Each extraordinary session had to be individually approved, which meant that Mandel had to be prepared for a long struggle against leftist delaying tactics even to get the measure debated, let alone passed.

On December 10, 1931, the bill came before Parliament for the first time. Despite determined resistance from the Radicals and Socialists, who tried to postpone discussion until the end of January, the Chamber voted 306 to 252 to hold a special session the following week.[50] Henri de Kérillis attributed the success solely to Mandel, who had worked for months to obtain support for the reform. "He has killed the legend of the Mandel who opposes everything and favors nothing, of Mandel the eternal and systematic adversary, of Mandel the great destroyer. Adding to the curious combination of traits in his complicated, enigmatic and bizarre personality, he has revealed to us a positive and constructive Mandel, capable of formulating plans and pushing them through against determined opposition." Kérillis predicted a seventy-vote majority for the law, but he feared that the Senate, not subject to Mandel's influence, might reject it. He concluded, however, that the senators could hardly repudiate a measure that they themselves had recommended ten years earlier.[51]

Although the Left accused Mandel of trying to put something over on the Chamber, in a moment of candor the Socialist Ludovic-Oscar Frossard declared:

I know what M. Mandel wants: he wants a majority and a minority. He wants to shackle the country to the two-bloc regime. . . . In this debate, he cannot be accused of being too subtle. He wants us to be either on the Right or on the Left, to fight the elections in massive formations; he wants the country, without any regard for nuances, to declare for the Right or for the Left so that a coherent, disciplined majority will be constituted, which will not be able to avoid its responsibilities, as it too often does, and which will form a government in its likeness. That's what M. Mandel wants.

But we have the right to ask the Chamber and the country not to condemn us to this system. That is the question; there is no other.[52]

The Left began a campaign against the bill, planning to propose amendments, demand public ballots, insist on the prior discussion of the budget, and sign all their deputies up to speak. They intended to wear down the resistance of the conservative deputies by repeated night and weekend sessions.[53] Léon Blum said that the reform would be extremely dangerous to his party and openly advocated the use of any method of obstruction.[54] Attempting to sow panic among his followers, he declared that the bill would cost the Socialists seventy seats.[55] Edouard Herriot announced his intention to campaign throughout France "in defense of the Republic." More important, he let it be known that if the bill passed, the Radicals would definitely unite with the Socialists to choose a single candidate in each constituency.[56] This threat frightened some of the Center deputies who had hoped that the Radicals and Socialists would be unable to reach an agreement. They now feared that the law might work to the advantage of their opponents.[57]

The result of the concerted opposition was shown on December 16 when, after an inconclusive debate, Mandel persuaded the Chamber to continue discussion by a majority of only 240 to 231. There had been no increase in the opposition; some of the Center deputies simply failed to show up. On December 17 Mandel's request for another debate was turned down by a vote of 234 to 228. A few more Center deputies absented themselves that day, but also certain ministers abstained from voting. These men, including Briand, were working to defeat the bill despite the official backing given it by their government.[58]

Technically, the vote meant only that the Chamber would not discuss the electoral reform law again until after the Christmas holidays. But everyone considered it to be dead, if not yet buried. The Left rejoiced that "the attempt of the Fascist thieves" had failed.[59] Even Henri de Kérillis, one of his most outspoken supporters, thought Mandel was beaten.[60] Faced by a united opposition, the timorous Center deputies had deserted Mandel, and there was no reason to suppose they would reverse themselves in the future. In addition, Prime Minister Laval informed him that the government would no longer support his bill or a demand for the renewal of debate.[61]

Mandel, however, had no intention of admitting defeat. Friends like Jacques Bainville soon revealed that he was working to have the electoral reform put back on the agenda.[62] Late in December, he persuaded the heads of the conservative groups to consider ways of imposing discipline on their members. The list of deputies abstaining was to be published, and both the Alliance Démocratique and the Fédération Républicaine promised to use every means to bring recalcitrant members into line.[63] When Laval learned in January that Mandel controlled enough votes to overthrow his government, he decided to support the bill once again.[64] The electoral reform was put back on the agenda.[65] The Left repeatedly tried to have debate postponed, but Mandel managed to maintain a thirty-vote majority through-out the balloting, and on January 28 his majority went up to eighty as the Chamber agreed to discuss the bill once more the following day.[66]

In the meantime, Charles Lambert, who had originally proposed the re-form in the Universal Suffrage Committee, resigned from the Radical Party. In a letter to Herriot, he stated that in December the party had agreed to oppose the bill simply as inopportune. But since then it had vio-lently denounced the reform, which was basically the system England had used for centuries. He wanted to know why they now considered it to be "an attack on universal suffrage," when at one time it had received the approval not only of President Daladier and the executive committee of the party but of Herriot himself.[67]

The two Radical leaders immediately denied having supported Lam-bert's proposal,[68] but it was relatively easy for their opponents to cite articles in which they had done so.[69] At one point, when it had seemed that bad relations between the Radicals and Socialists might prevent them from co-operating at all, their leaders had favored the single ballot. By December 1931, however, relations had improved, and the necessity for changing the electoral law had vanished.[70] The rationale was simple: as someone once said, the best system of election is the one that assures your election.

On February 3, 4, 5, 9, 11 and 12, Mandel's thirty-to-fifty-vote majority held together in sessions lasting until one or two o'clock in the morning. On the fourth the Chamber finally voted to end the general discussion and begin debate on specific articles of the bill. On the fifth, the Left pre-sented a proposal for proportional representation in an attempt to wean the Catholics, who favored it, away from Mandel. But the Right, realizing that the Senate would reject proportional representation in any case, re-fused to fall into the trap and continued to back Mandel.[71] Some proposed amendments were finally adopted. The required plurality on the first ballot was reduced to 25 per cent of the vote. Women's suffrage was included, as was the obligatory vote.

In a last desperate attempt to prevent passage of the bill, the left-wing members of the Universal Suffrage Committee resigned. The president of the Chamber Finance Committee, Jean Malvy, and the Reporter of the Budget, Lucien Lamoureux, also sent in their resignations, hoping to pre-vent a vote on the budget, for which they intended to blame the government at the elections.[72]

This time, however, the opposition failed to shake Mandel's hold on the majority even though, as François Albert remarked, the Center was still suspicious of him, as it had been of Tardieu at first. Although he con-trolled it by his political intelligence, "Mandel . . . remains an outsider;

his ambitions seem too personal, too mysteriously Machiavellian, not to be disturbing.... As a result there is almost as much distrust in the Center as blind faith on the Right." Albert claimed that Mandel had no respect for either group. "He considers the Right to be imbeciles, capable of discipline and action, but absolutely unable to lead themselves.... As for his colleagues in the Center, he knows that intellectually they are vastly superior, but he has no illusions about their weak will. He believes that he must drive them with a stick and force them to join the compact bloc on the Right." The Center, Albert added, was not really interested in the reform, because it usually received votes from both the Right and the Radicals. It also did not like the idea of defying the Senate, which had already expressed its opposition to the reform. Albert concluded that the Center deputies would eventually desert Mandel again as they had in December.[73]

But when the crucial moment came, Mandel won, thwarting every stratagem devised by the Left. To those who feared Senatorial opposition, he declared that it could be overcome, "if from one trial to another the Chamber remains resolute on questions which are of more concern to it than to the Senate."[74] To those who feared left-wing coalitions, he replied that the Radicals and the Socialists would unite in seventy-five districts anyway. "It is better...that it happen immediately, for the parties will negotiate directly on the basis of a precise program that will not vary from district to district."[75] Then, in a titanic final session lasting twenty-two hours, during which there were twenty-four ballots and thirty speeches, the Chamber approved the reform 322 to 4. Before the final vote, Herriot had declared, "You are imposing...majority rule on us. That is Fascism." The entire Left then walked out of the Chamber in protest.[76]

The victory was clearly Mandel's.[77] After twelve years he had finally driven a wedge between the Center and the Radicals. No longer would deputies be able to float back and forth between the Right and the Left. The Center had stood firmly with the Right, despite Radical taunts and threats, and Mandel could turn to Prime Minister Laval and say, "The majority is crystallized, well in hand. The government has only to make use of it."[78]

Mandel had also proved himself as a leader. Emile Buré commented, "It will now be difficult for the determined enemies he still has...to prevent him from becoming a minister. Like his mentor Georges Clemenceau, he has won his position in combat.... No one will now be able to deny that he has the qualities of a true statesman."[79]

Buré, however, was too optimistic. The Senate, which housed such bitter enemies of Mandel as Charles Chaumet and Joseph Caillaux, hated both the man and his bill. One Senator immediately demanded a discussion of the general policy of the government. Laval asked for an adjournment until February 26, when Minister of War André Tardieu would be finished presenting France's case at the disarmament conference in Geneva. The Senate refused. Laval then posed the question of confidence on an adjournment until February 19. Again he was refused and the government was overthrown. Rarely had the upper chamber expressed its disapproval with such determination.

The Senate was an essentially conservative body, whose members disliked any government in which either the Catholic Right or the Socialist Left played an influential role. They always favored a concentration of moderates that would exclude these two groups from power. The Socialists, however, were regarded as good republicans, whereas the Catholics, including the republicans among them, were treated as political lepers. This ideological predisposition was shared by the Radicals and Socialists and gave the Right a feeling of exclusion from the political community that would eventually make it receptive to antiparliamentary propaganda. The Monarchist Pierre Gaxotte expressed the opinion of many Catholics when he exclaimed that the vote of the Senate meant that "the single ballot is legitimate if it assures the victory of the Left but is an attack on the sovereignty of the people if it works for the Right. The Republic is a divine-right regime (without God). The holders of a certain body of doctrines have been invested in perpetuity with the government of France. The others do not count, were they a thousand against one, and everything else is just a farce."[80]

After Laval's defeat, the Radicals, with the aid of the Center, tried to form the kind of government favored by the Senate, but once again merely proved, as Mandel had asserted in 1928, that a Center government was impossible in that legislature. André Tardieu then formed a new government. Anxious to avoid Laval's fate, he agreed with the Senate to drop the electoral reform in return for a speedy passage of the budget.[81] He also publicly denounced Mandel and the Socialist deputy Frossard, who had led the opposition, for causing the ministerial crisis: "When I saw from afar, day after day and night after night, those two infernal duelists, Mandel and Frossard, struggling implacably, ... and when I saw the Chamber divide behind them, ... I thought to myself in Geneva, 'What a misfortune for France!' I could feel a cabinet crisis coming."[82]

Mandel tried vainly to persuade him to support the reform bill, or at least not to hold the elections before the end of May, by which time he expected that a victory of the Nazi party in the Prussian elections would swing the vote to the Right in France.[83] Wanting to get rid of the existing Parliament as soon as possible and supremely confident of victory in the coming elections,[84] Tardieu not only turned Mandel down on both counts, but even encouraged the Chamber to reject the electoral reform when, in spite of everything, Mandel reintroduced it.[85]

In the meantime, the Senate had defeated the bill by a vote of 193 to 0. With hardly a chance of getting it passed, Mandel still insisted on the Chamber's debating it once more. He wanted one last opportunity to explain his position to the country, and he also wanted to pin responsibility on the weak-kneed Center deputies and on the vacillating members of the government. As François Albert put it, "Instead of Machiavelli he would play Guizot."[86]

In his speech, after reviewing French electoral history, he came to the defense of his own bill. It would, he told the Chamber, help to create stable majorities, enabling the government to carry out a coherent policy. "Our political struggles will gain in clarity and nobility, and we will no longer have to witness the distressing spectacle, seen in this legislature, of opposed groups tearing each other apart in order to get power and carry out the same program." It was true that the bill seemed to favor the Right, but that was only because the Left did not unite until the second ballot. If they were unable to agree on a common candidate in an election, he asked, how would they ever be able to govern together?

The second ballot only encouraged deputies to neglect their programs in favor of the special interests of their constituents. To obtain the largest number of votes, they were forced to make numerous promises to every economic group and professional organization. "Thus, when elected, they represent no precise segment of public opinion, but become the official representatives of every local interest ... and are committed in advance to every demagogical demand without exception."

The current legislature, where the conservative majority had appeared stable and coherent but actually was not, was a good example of the effects of the second ballot. Governments had been regularly overthrown because they were dependent for their existence on the votes of some Center deputies periodically tempted to vote with the Left in order to appease a portion of their electorate. "It is impossible to govern," he said, "if one has to ask ... what Monsieur X or Monsieur Z thinks when quite often he has no opinions whatsoever. What is important, ... whether a right-wing or a left-wing government is in power, is that it be followed by a majority ready to support it, even if in certain details it is wrong." But the only way to create such a majority was for the Right and the Left each to agree on common candidates and a common program. In a prophetic conclusion, Mandel warned the Center deputies whose greatest fear was the creation of a coherent left-wing coalition that "it is better to have a leftist majority than no majority at all." And he told the Chamber that by not changing the electoral law, they might drive their successors to resort to decree laws or to get around the constitution in some other way.[87]

Mandel had adopted the tone of a statesman for the speech and had not really tried to change the result of the ballot that followed. The reform was beaten by a vote of 299 to 227, and the Senate bill retaining the second ballot was accepted by a weary Chamber, 152 to 111. Tardieu and most of his ministers voted for Mandel's bill so that he could not charge them with having deserted him, but it was clear that they had actually fought it.[88]

The Right of course lamented its lost opportunity to exercise influence proportionate to its strength and denounced the Center for its weakness.[89] But the Center welcomed the end of the bitter fighting over a reform that had threatened their ability to float between Right and Left. The moderate *Le Temps* expressed its relief that the vote had ended "an agitation particularly inopportune on the eve of the general elections...."[90] And *Le Matin*, another stalwart supporter of the status quo, was grateful that "the Parliamentary scene is finally rid of one of the debates oppressing the atmosphere at the Palais Bourbon."[91]

Henri de Kérillis, on the other hand, called Mandel's bill "the only serious attempt at reform" during that session of the legislature.[92] If the elimination of the second ballot would have helped to create a coherent majority and encouraged the formation of a two-party system, then Kérillis was correct. Mandel and the Left, of course, believed that this would be the result. Since then Maurice Duverger has asserted that "reason as well as observation permits . . . the formulation of a triple sociological law: the double ballot leads to multiple and incoherent parties; proportional representation, to multiple and coherent parties; the single ballot, to the two-party system."[93] More recently, however, Peter Campbell has argued from the continued existence of multiple groups even after MacMahon's dissolution of Parliament polarized the country in 1877, and from the rapid disintegration of the electoral coalitions of 1919, 1924, 1928, 1936 and 1951, that Mandel's reform would not actually have led to the formation of a united majority in Parliament. It would not have eliminated the divisions among the parties, particularly on the Left, created by historic and social factors.[94] Yet Campbell's analysis ignores the possible effect of the single ballot on coalitions. Had the parties known that in subsequent elections they would be forced to reach agreement with the same allies on single candidates and a single program, these coalitions would not have broken up so easily. It was the two-ballot system that permitted some Center deputies to fluctuate between Right and Left and enabled the Radicals to rely on Socialist votes in the elections and then frequently to collaborate with the conservatives in the legislature. In 1927, in fact, the Radicals had pushed the return to the double ballot through the Chamber precisely so that they could play this game.

In 1932, because of basic disagreements between the Radicals and the Socialists, the single ballot would probably not have produced a two-party system. But it might have clarified the situation by forcing the left-wing parties to form a definite alliance and agree in advance on a common program. Instead, these parties went into and came out of battle in dispersed order, so that the verdict of the electorate was ambiguous, indecisive, and ultimately disastrous. It resulted in eighteen months of weak and ineffective government that encouraged the growth of antiparliamentarianism and led to the riots of February 6. It is also possible that the new electoral law might have returned the conservatives to power, and even from a left-wing point of view it could be said, to paraphrase Mandel, that "it is better to have a right-wing majority than no majority at all."

By a quirk of history, not only is Tardieu frequently credited with responsibility for Mandel's bill,[95] but he is considered to be the outstanding advocate between the wars of the two-party system in France.[96] No doubt he had fought for this system during the 1919 legislature, but only in alliance with Mandel and possibly under his guidance. In their division of labor at that time, internal policy had been Mandel's province. But as soon as Tardieu returned to Parliament, he adopted Poincaré's philosophy and placed himself above party politics, minimizing the influence of the Right and trying to court the Radicals. According to Beau de Loménie, he never recognized the pivotal role played by the Center in shifting the majority between Right and Left.[97] Nor did he realize, as Mandel did, that without the Catholics no conservative majority and no viable two-party system was possible. Tardieu always disliked the Right and said to a friend, "I will never fall into their hands."[98] It is true that he refused to repudiate them in favor of the Radicals, but that was because he did not want to be the prisoner of either group.

Tardieu envisaged a majority composed of the Right, the Center, and the Radicals that would follow him wherever he decided at any moment to go. The opposition was to be composed of a small number of Socialists railing impotently at him from the other side of the barricade. In short, while ostensibly favoring a two-party system, Tardieu in fact, after 1924, did nothing to help and everything to hinder it.

Even in the elections he continued his Janus-like policy, assuming the leadership of his conservative majority at the same time that he appealed for a coalition with the Radicals. He also refused to give the ministry of the Interior to Mandel,[99] which admittedly would have raised a storm of protest, and instead named an innocuous senator to the post. With these tactics, he was fully confident of winning thirty new supporters.[100] Instead, like Poincaré in 1924, he led his majority to defeat. The Radicals, rejecting Tardieu's appeals, encouraged their candidates to maintain "republican" discipline, i.e. to vote for Socialists on the second ballot against conservatives. As a result, the Left won a large but incohesive majority of 356 to 268. The Radicals and Socialists had reached no agreement before the elections and were utterly at odds on most of the important issues of the day. The new legislature would see a succession of cabinets grapple impotently with the problem of creating an effective majority, until finally, as Mandel had predicted, the Chamber would resort to decree laws.

IV

In his own constituency, Mandel faced a more serious threat than in 1928. The moderate Republicans were so adamantly opposed to him that even though they were followers of Tardieu, they decided not to run their own candidate, but instead to support the Radical-Socialist candidate, who opposed Tardieu. They adopted the battle cry of the Radicals—"defeat Mandel!"[101] If the same tactics had been employed in 1928, he would probably have lost the election on the first ballot.

The campaign began in April 1931 when René Thorp, former secretary of the Socialist leader Paul-Boncour, arrived in Lesparre. Because a local candidate might have found it difficult to get the support of groups that had fought each other for years, he had been dispatched from Paris to unite opposition against Mandel. Thorp became the official candidate of the Radicals, receiving the support of the Center. The Socialists preferred to run their own candidate on the first ballot.[102]

Despite the unity of his opponents, in one way Mandel was in a stronger position than he had been in past elections. Although he still spoke to the peasants and workers primarily about national issues, he also took care of their local demands. In 1931 he reported to the electors that in the preceding three years the Médoc had received

68 million francs in grants, more than any other district in France. From 1924 to 1928, you only received 180,000 francs. Every time a city asked me to obtain a grant, it received immediate satisfaction. And where did the money come from? Did it come from your pockets? No! Each year since 1920 the Chamber has voted 300 million francs for public disasters. It is from these funds that I obtained the 68 million for you.[103]

If Mandel's figures are correct, the government must have ranked him among the most important or at least the most dangerous deputies in France, and there is little wonder that despite the opposition of almost the entire local press, he received 7,695 votes on the first ballot to Thorp's 5,206 and the Socialist Mesnard's 3,120. Nevertheless, Mesnard's withdrawal in favor of Thorp made Mandel's defeat on the second ballot seem likely, since he could hardly expect Socialist support, and it would be difficult to find the 650 extra votes he would need to win. But on the second ballot the unexpected happened, and Mandel received 8,325 votes to Thorp's 8,176. Without his attention to local affairs and particularly to those of Soulac, he would have been defeated. That small coastal town of which he had been mayor since 1919 gave him a majority of 275, his margin of victory.

On his return to the Chamber Mandel was faced by a three-pronged attack mounted by his opponents. First, Thorp persuaded fifty Radicals to contest the election, whereupon Mandel countered by signing up to speak on all the other contested elections in France. This of course would have delayed indefinitely the organization of the Chamber and the formation of a government. As a result, Mandel's election was the first one validated, and he then withdrew his requests to speak.[104]

Second, the Socialist deputy Pierre Renaudel tried to unseat Mandel from the Universal Suffrage Committee by introducing a motion to restrict official recognition to those groups whose members signed a common political declaration. The point was to keep the Groupe des Indépendants, headed by Mandel and composed of Monarchists and other mavericks, from electing representatives to the various committees. Mandel thwarted this maneuver fairly easily by proposing that the members of his group sign a declaration of independence. "No one," he said, "can claim that a declaration of independence is not a political declaration."[105]

The third move, to eject Mandel from the presidency of the Suffrage Committee, seemed certain to succeed, for the Left now had a majority, and there was no possibility that they would return him to the position from which he had just led the fight for electoral reform. For some reason, the choice of a new president was postponed until the end of November, but it was understood that the post would go to the Radical Guernut. In the interim, however, the Socialists decided to present their own candidate, Bracke. On the first ballot, Bracke's fourteen votes to Guernut's thirteen fell short of an absolute majority, but the Radicals refused to maintain republican discipline by withdrawing their candidate because they were annoyed at the Socialists' attempt to usurp a presidency that had been allocated to them. When Bracke received sixteen votes and Guernut twelve on the second ballot, however, Guernut was persuaded to withdraw. Mandel then posed his own candidacy and on the third ballot defeated Bracke 18 to 16. Mandel's friends had voted for Bracke on the earlier ballots, knowing that not all of the Radicals would vote for him when their candidate desisted, whereas if Guernut had led, Mandel would have had no chance to win.[106] The following day a nationalist journal joyously announced that "the Cartel, which once accused Mandel . . . of committing a crime against universal suffrage, yesterday elected him president of the Universal Suffrage Committee."[107]

After his recent defeat on the electoral reform, these successes did something to restore Mandel's tarnished reputation as a tactician. But whereas the new session started off for him on a light-hearted and triumphal note, the same was not true for the Chamber itself. The deputies were immediately faced and very quickly overwhelmed by economic, political, and diplomatic problems requiring the strong government and effective majority Mandel had fought so long to create.

9. Back to Power

*L'homme habile qui veut acquérir de l'influence sur la Chambre est
tenu de passer beaucoup de temps dans les couloirs. Le plus beau discours
du monde ne vaut pas cent conversations particulières; il ne faut pas
s'en étonner. Le discours est fait pour l'extérieur et les conversations sont
destinées aux seuls parlementaires. Ils doivent donc y être plus sensibles
qu'à une manifestation publique.*

Louis Latzarus

THE VICTORY of the Left in 1932 was an illusion. The Radicals and Socialists were incapable of formulating a common program or of governing
together. They particularly disagreed on economic questions. Whereas the
Socialists advocated larger government expenditures to counter the effects
of the depression, the Radicals, adherents of traditional financial procedures, proposed deflation, higher taxes and smaller government expenditures. The Cartel des Gauches was stillborn, and the division of the Chamber into two blocs an electoral rather than a parliamentary reality.

As the largest party in Parliament, the Radicals naturally assumed power,
which they hoped to keep with the alternate support of the Socialists and
the Center. It took eighteen months of governmental instability climaxed
by rioting in the streets to convince them of the impossibility of their undertaking. The parliamentary arithmetic, however, had been clear from the
beginning to Mandel. After one glance, he announced that the Radical
plan was bound to fail. "From one difficulty to another," he predicted, "we
will go on to a National Union government."[1]

Mandel urged the conservatives of Right and Center to form a systematic
opposition, forcing the Radicals to choose between a National Union government with them and a firm alliance with the Socialists. In any case, a
government compelled to depend alternately on the Center and on the
Socialists for its majority would be unable to carry out an effective program. Thus the Center would be ill paid for any support it might give the
Radicals, receiving part of the responsibility for their failure but no real
voice in determining policy. Even the consistent collaboration of the Center
and the Radicals in a government of "Republican concentration"—excluding both the Socialist and the Right—would be ineffective. A purely rightist or leftist cabinet might exist with a small majority, he said, but a Center
government required a large one, for it would be torn apart on its two wings
by the attraction of the groups in opposition. Since there was no large
Center majority in the present Chamber, only a National Union govern-

ment formed on the basis of a specific program would be capable of solving France's economic, political, and diplomatic problems.[2] Nevertheless, he expected a "cascade" of ministries before the Radicals could be driven to break completely with the Socialists.[3]

For the first time in several years Mandel found himself in agreement with Tardieu. They both did everything possible to persuade the conservatives to remain in opposition.[4] But under the guidance of Pierre-Etienne Flandin, many of them preferred to support the Radical government in order to break up the leftist coalition by infiltration rather than by open attack. Even after thirteen years of enforced collaboration with the Right and of unsuccessful approaches to the Radicals, the Center still hoped to return to the prewar pattern of "concentration" governments—a pattern that had excluded both the Socialists and the Right from power.[5]

For Tardieu the defection of some of his former ministers and followers was the last straw. He concluded that the existing parliamentary system was warped, corrupt, and incapable of giving France the leadership it needed. His confidence in the system had been waning for years, but he had still thought after his long campaign during the 1919 legislature that he could reform it by gaining control of the levers of power. Where others had failed before him, Tardieu had expected to be able to carry out long-range programs. His failure as prime minister to achieve his aims, and his failure now to weld the Right and Center into an effective opposition, convinced him of the necessity for constitutional changes.

In January 1933, after several months on vacation in Spain and Italy, he began a campaign for the reform of the constitution. First in articles in the weekly *L'Illustration* and then in a series of books he argued his case. According to Tardieu, French governments were unable to carry out their policies because of the instability of their parliamentary majorities. Cabinets and budgets were at the mercy of deputies, and deputies in turn were at the mercy of their electors, who were concerned only with local questions. Thus the general good of the country was subordinated to the requirements of small interest groups.

To liberate both deputies and governments from the demands of local interests, he suggested that representatives be deprived of the right to propose expenditures. In order to facilitate the passage of necessary legislation in the face of an unwieldy or recalcitrant assembly, the president of the Republic was to be given the right to dissolve the Chamber at the request of the prime minister and without the consent of the Senate, as was then required. In addition, the government could appeal directly to the people by means of referendums. These were Tardieu's major proposals. Two others, the extension of suffrage to women and the prohibition of strikes by civil servants, could have been handled by ordinary legislation, but he considered them important enough to be included in constitutional amendments.[6]

On the issue of reform Mandel and Tardieu once again parted company. Mandel attributed the weakness of government to lack of leadership rather than to defects in the constitutional machinery. In an open attack on his former friend, he said in an interview in March 1933 that "we only thought of changing the constitution when those who governed us had shown themselves inferior to their tasks. They then naturally attempted to blame the institutions for their own weaknesses."[7] He recommended a return to traditional parliamentary rules: a unified government bound to its majority by a definite program. The recent national governments, ashamed of their own supporters, had adopted the program of the Left. They had given up the last of France's gains in the war. Their time had been spent in passing tax reductions and other popular measures demanded by the opposition. And finally, when shown that they could prevent a Left coalition government by getting rid of the second ballot, they had been incapable of fighting to the end.

Mandel claimed that the war had demonstrated the resiliency of French institutions. They needed only men of will and initiative to make them function. Government was less a question of ideology than of character. For him the proof of this principle was that, except for the Socialists, there was general agreement on the necessity for a policy of deflation to ease the financial situation and for a vigorous reaction to counter the threat from Germany, and yet nothing was being done.

He concluded that the constitution should not be changed to give more power to weak hands. Recent governments had not even used all their existing powers. Although they had the authority to do so, ministers had failed to dismiss civil servants who had gone on strike. Such dismissals, he believed, would have had a much more salutary effect than all the special laws that had been proposed. Even if new laws were passed, they would still have to be applied, and those who had not yet used existing powers would hardly dare to use any new ones given them. It would be time enough to speak of reform when some one who had exerted all his constitutional authority had been thwarted.[8]

Tardieu quickly replied to Mandel in the April issue of *L'Illustration*. He spoke of *beaux esprits* who argued that reforms were unnecessary because Clemenceau and Poincaré had succeeded in governing without them. Tardieu said these men had ruled a France ridden by fear—fear of defeat and fear of financial failure—and their authority had not outlived that fear. Furthermore, Clemenceau had had the wartime controls at his disposal and

Poincaré the power of governing by decree. Their successors had had neither of these. Those who rejected his reforms, he predicted, would lead France straight to disorder and dictatorship.

Tardieu's argument that Clemenceau and Poincaré had been able to govern so effectively because of fear was only partially true. The same fear had not permitted their predecessors to govern successfully. It was because these two prime ministers were born leaders that they had been able to rule without being obstructed by Parliament. But Mandel's own argument was equally weak. He failed to specify who was to provide the leadership and how the parties might be persuaded to accept it. Influenced by Clemenceau's achievement during the World War, confirmed in his beliefs by Poincaré's success in 1926, he was convinced that will power and intelligence alone would suffice to solve France's problems. He undoubtedly thought that he had enough of both.[9] But he was still in no position to form a government. Moreover, he had more faith than Tardieu in the parliamentary system that he knew more intimately, and greater confidence in using parliamentary tactics to achieve his ends. Thus he continued to work for a National Union government, not only because no viable cabinet could be formed without the aid of all the parties from the Radicals to the Right—though that was reason enough—but also because no decisive action could be taken to counter the growing threat from Germany without the support of these same groups.

Strangely enough, Hitler's accession to power in January 1933 had not provoked a strong reaction in French public opinion.[10] Some thought of him as just a particularly blatant exponent of an invariable German policy. Others believed he would quickly fail and disappear. But most people were simply more absorbed by domestic problems. Since June 1932 the Radicals had formed one government after another, obtaining the support now of the Center and now of the Socialists. They stayed in power, but could not carry out any consistent policy. Internally, they had cut spending in order to obtain a majority. Externally, even though Herriot and many other Radicals wanted to reject the ever greater German demands, they felt compelled to make concession after concession.[11] They had agreed to the temporary suspension of reparations and recognized, at least in principle, Germany's right to equality in armaments. They had also accepted Mussolini's proposal for a European conference composed of France, England, Germany, and Italy to discuss the revision of other clauses of the Treaty of Versailles.

Mandel, of course, had opposed all of these concessions. He believed that the only way to preserve peace was "to resist obstinately and to hold on to what remains of the peace treaties."[12] But he did not intervene in Parliament until November 1933. His failure to speak out earlier, despite his intransigent opposition, had been noticed.[13] Thus the announcement that he intended to question the government on foreign policy aroused considerable interest.

The intent of Mandel's interpellation, it immediately became apparent, was not merely to embarrass the cabinet, or to attack the Left for its policy of conciliation. As he pointed out at the start, this policy was only the continuation of that followed by all the governments since 1920. But he did want to know what the Prime Minister intended to do in face of the almost open rearmament being undertaken by the Third Reich. Rather than enter into a conference with Germany to discuss equality in armaments, the government should have denounced her failure to disarm. It was no longer up to France to demonstrate her peaceful intentions. She had reduced her army, curtailed military service, and cut her military budget for 1933 by two billion francs. How had Germany reacted to these concessions? By building up her army. "Unless we take a stand now," he declared, "they will wipe out the margin of military superiority we still have, and will attempt to profit from the period of our *classes creuses* ... to present us with the tragic dilemma: general revision of frontiers or war."

Mandel then gave an itemized account of German rearmament that, according to the press, sent a shiver of fear down the deputies' backs. The precise figures on the number of men being trained, the amount of arms being produced, and the kind of raw materials being imported impressed the Chamber as fiery denunciations could not have done. Those who thought to prevent German rearmament, he said, reminded him of the generals who were preparing today for the war of 1914. They could no longer speak, as Léon Blum constantly did, of rearmament as a future occurrence, but must see it as a present reality. According to his information, which he believed corresponded to that received by the government, Germany was capable of mobilizing forty-five divisions in five days, and would be able by June 1934 to produce 2,500 planes a month. In these circumstances, there could no longer be any hesitation. If France were not to be drawn into an arms race, and ultimately into war, she must denounce the impending danger before world opinion at the League of Nations, demand an international investigation, and if Germany refused, ask for collective sanctions. Great Britain might hesitate, but he believed that once public opinion there had been alerted by resolute action, "sooner or later, following conservative leaders like Austen Chamberlain or Winston Churchill, and under pressure from the most pacifist elements of the Labor Party, the hand of the British Government will be forced."[14]

Mandel had seldom had such a strong immediate impact on the Chamber. A number of deputies were "stunned" by his revelations.[15] According to the

Journal des Débats, it was the first time that the danger from German rearmament had been brought out into the open and stated in such precise terms.[16] It was believed that Mandel's information came from reports of the French War Office and could not be dismissed lightly.[17]

The British military attaché in Paris immediately checked Mandel's figures with the French general staff, who asserted that "if anything, they were understated." Recent information had forced the French to revise their estimate of Germany's preparedness for war. They had assumed for some time that Germany would not be ready for five or six years, but they now thought that she would be capable of waging war by January 1935 or at the beginning of 1936 at the latest.[18] The attaché learned, however, that Mandel's information had not come from the War Office. Colonel Koeltz, head of Intelligence, pointed out that Mandel had his own private Deuxième Bureau made up of Mandel himself, Senator Eccard of Alsace, and General Bourgeois, president of the Senate Army Committee.[19]

One journalist observed that "watching the Palais Bourbon yesterday, where applause rose from three-fourths of the benches, just stopped at the edge of the Socialist seats by the glacial features of Léon Blum, one realized the magnificent responses that a leader worthy of the name, worthy of France, could obtain from a French assembly . . . when external danger threatens."[20] Mandel had consciously sought to achieve this large agreement on the question of foreign affairs. Jacques Bainville revealed that he had not wanted merely "to warn the country, and like Thiers after Sadowa, go down in history as the man who had been right." His speech was also a strategic maneuver. He had wanted to break up "the disastrous Cartel" in order to make way for a National Union government. Mandel had advised going to the League of Nations not because it would do any good, but because he knew that if he had advocated unilateral action by France, he would only have driven the Radicals into the arms of the Socialists and delayed the formation of a National Union government.[21] Colonel de Lattre de Tassigny told Mandel that his speech "had created a certain emotional feeling in the Chamber and elevated the debate onto a national and nonparty plane, and the effect on the government had been good."[22] War Minister Daladier even congratulated Mandel and expressed his satisfaction that he had placed the debate on a nonpartisan level.[23]

The speech had no permanent effect, however, for Foreign Minister Paul-Boncour refused to register a complaint at Geneva. He declared that France needed the support of other nations in order to apply sanctions, and probably would not be able to obtain it.[24] With Mandel and Tardieu in opposition, the Chamber then voted confidence in the government's foreign policy, 394 to 144. A few days later *Le Matin* published an interview with

Hitler by Fernand de Brinon, who was reported to be an emissary of Daladier. The interview revealed a peace-loving Hitler with friendly intentions toward France.[25] Soon afterward the government undertook direct negotiations with Germany for a settlement of the armaments question.

Despite his failure to change either external or internal policy, Mandel continued to press for a National Union government. He might vote against Radical cabinets, but he did nothing to create an irreparable breach with the party. Reflecting on his speech in his new post as parliamentary commentator for the nationalist illustrated weekly, *1933*, he wrote:

It is important to note . . . that for a moment almost the entire Chamber, for the first time in many years, seemed to experience the same concerns, and share in the same sentiment of patriotic anxiety; and although that atmosphere of union has been dissipated, . . . the impression remains that at the first danger it would be quickly recreated. But . . . it cannot represent the revenge of a party or group, which would be less than just because the present crisis is the result of the policy of giving up the gains won at Versailles that almost everyone has followed for twelve years. . . .[26]

His task of achieving a consensus on foreign affairs, however, was rendered more difficult that winter by the Chamber's increasing preoccupation with internal problems. Daladier's purely Radical government was followed by another of a similar stripe led by Albert Sarraut, who was in turn succeeded by yet a third Radical, Camille Chautemps. The inability of these governments to solve the economic crisis, and the alarming rate at which they were falling, led to a recrudescence of antiparliamentarianism. The Action Française, almost alone in the campaign for several years, was now joined by such organizations as the Jeunesses Patriotes of Pierre Taittinger and the Croix de Feu, a veterans' association led by Colonel de la Rocque. Various rightist leagues began to send their supporters into the streets at the slightest provocation to demonstrate against Parliament. The Radicals, Mandel said, could not complain about the campaign since they were not themselves practicing the system faithfully when they merely redistributed ministerial posts among themselves after each crisis instead of permitting a different group to form a government. In reality the Chamber was not ungovernable; it was always the same government that it overthrew.[27]

The vague discontent in the country became focused in December when reports began to appear about a new financial scandal involving a naturalized Russian Jew by the name of Stavisky. His activities, which ranged from writing bad checks to issuing almost worthless bonds, seemed to have been abetted by various cabinet members and administrators. The antiparliamentary groups seized on the affair, took up the cry of corruption in the government, and throughout the month of January agitated in the streets against Parliament. Although Stavisky's activities dated back to 1926 and had benefited from the complaisance or negligence of both rightist and leftist governments, the Right acted as if the affair had begun on June 1, 1932, when the Radicals took over. Prime Minister Chautemps supported this interpretation by posing the question of confidence against a motion for an investigating committee instead of promising action against those involved. The Chamber voted on a partisan basis, and the motion was defeated, 332 to 209. To the public it seemed that Chautemps was trying to cover up the scandal. The government was even accused of murder when Stavisky was found dead in his mountain retreat.

Although Mandel joined with other members of the Right in demanding an investigating commission, he criticized his conservative colleagues for exploiting the scandal for partisan purposes. The affair had not started under the Radicals. It was the result of the general amorality and weakness in government that all the cabinets had allowed to continue. He insisted that any investigation had to go back to the origins of the affair, which clearly meant that some members of the Right might be implicated as well.[28] His plea for a nonpartisan investigation was obviously an attempt to avoid a rupture between the Radicals and the Right that might prevent the formation of a National Union government.

When Chautemps was succeeded on January 27 by another member of his party, Edouard Daladier, who failed to obtain Center support and was forced to form yet one more Radical government, Mandel predicted that it would "die without ever having lived." The only remedy for the situation would be "finally to establish a government worthy of the name, including men of action from all parties, who would agree in advance on a common program consisting of these few essential points: the elimination of the scandals by purging Parliament and the administration; the rapid approval of the budget; and the preservation of peace by demanding respect for the peace treaties, particularly with reference to German armaments." This was a limited program that could be realized in a short time. If a new cabinet promised to resign at the end of that time, it would get a momentary truce. Party struggles might then resume, but France in the meantime would have regained her equilibrium.[29]

By the time Mandel's article appeared in print, Daladier's government had already resigned. The antiparliamentary leagues, veterans groups, and even some Communists had gathered on the Place de la Concorde on February 6 and tried to invade the Chamber of Deputies. The police fired on the rioters, killing fourteen and wounding many others. Daladier resigned and former President Gaston Doumergue, after frantic appeals, agreed to leave his country home at Tournefeuille in the south and come to Paris to form a government.[30]

On his arrival in the capital on the eighth, Doumergue immediately began consulting the leaders of Parliament—all but Georges Mandel. Although Mandel was president of the Groupe des Indépendants, and Doumergue had known him since the time of Clemenceau's first cabinet, the new Premier refused to see him. "Knowing Mandel's formidable destructive faculties as well as his gifts of observation, he felt that a two-hour conversation with him would be so discouraging that he would immediately take the train back to Tournefeuille."[31] Tardieu, Herriot, and men who had formerly opposed a National Union government were included in Doumergue's cabinet, while Mandel, who had fought so long to bring it about, was left standing on the doorstep.

Mandel could be pardoned if he believed that there was a plot to keep him out of the government. No one denied that he had extraordinary abilities, or that he was one of the most intelligent men in Parliament, as his remarkable analyses had repeatedly demonstrated. Yet it was virtually impossible for him to become a minister. In the 1920's Tardieu and Laval, coming from opposite sides of the Chamber, had soon reconciled themselves with the men in power. Each of them first obtained a minor cabinet position, then within a few years became head of the government, and thereafter would be called on repeatedly in cabinet crises.

During recent years Mandel had tried to disarm opposition by toning down his aggressiveness, by establishing friendly relations with Radicals like Herriot and Yvon Delbos,[32] and by showing himself a capable leader as well as a caustic critic, but all to no avail. In 1931 the mere mention of his name for a ministerial post caused a storm of protest, and in 1934 Doumergue would not even talk to him, let alone have him in the cabinet.

Mandel was kept out of the government partly because of his close association with the Right, which unlike most of the Center, he emphasized rather than played down. The right-wing Paris journal *La Liberté* called him "the strategist of the nationalist parties,"[33] and in the fall of 1933, as already noted, he became parliamentary commentator for the illustrated weekly *1933*, which blended the traditional conservatism of the Academicians Abel Bonnard, Henri Bordeaux, Abel Hermant, and André Chaumeix with the new nationalism of Thierry Maulnier and Robert Brasillach. Jacques Bainville continued to write favorable articles about him in *Candide*, and even Pierre Gaxotte's anti-Semitic *Je Suis Partout*, which one of its writers would later call "the flagship of French Fascism," still referred to Mandel as "cet Israélite de haute classe."[34]

Yet this identification alone should not have kept Mandel out of the government, for Catholic leaders like Louis Marin were often asked to join conservative or National Union cabinets. Mandel was ostracized primarily because of his own character. Over the years he may have succeeded in eliminating the most abrasive qualities, but the essence remained unchanged. The Radical writer Pierre Dominique noted that although he and Tardieu were the only two outstanding conservative deputies, Mandel was not fully accepted by his colleagues "because of his secretiveness, his mysteriousness, and the mixture of Fouché and Jesuit that is his mark. The moderates . . . are frightened by the extent of Mandel's plots and maneuvers, whose aim we will one day understand, but whose secrets we will never discover."[35]

In addition, to many deputies increasingly preoccupied with economic problems and the Fascist threat to democracy, Mandel seemed to be a relic of the past. The left-wing pacifist Pierre Bénard of the *Canard Enchaîné* said that for a long time Mandel had created an illusion:

He was considered an apprentice dictator at a time when we knew neither Mussolini nor Hitler. Today he is laughable, and it is surprising that we could have taken him seriously and even tragically. He is a romantic café conspirator, a melodrama Fouché, a comic-opera Machiavelli. He is out of date and already a museum piece. He is the last parliamentarian. He knows all the maneuvers when no one is any longer interested. . . . He will teach you the art of overthrowing a government in less than ten lessons. . . . The connoisseurs of the corridors—another fossil race—say admiringly: "He is cunning." So what! Georges Mandel invariably reminds me of a strange object in a museum that one looks at curiously for a time and says, "But what did they ever use it for?"[36]

In many ways Mandel *was* an anachronism. He concentrated too exclusively on political and parliamentary issues and almost totally disregarded social and economic questions. He was essentially a nineteenth-century liberal, devoted to the parliamentary form of government, but skeptical about the possibility of large-scale social reform. A self-made man, he believed that individuals and nations alike were responsible for their own fate. To him, the demand of the working classes for greater justice was merely special pleading on the part of one interest group, whose claims would have to compete with those of other groups. He seems to have devoted little attention to the increasing impact of the world depression on France, sharing the conventional wisdom of most of his colleagues in opposing devaluation and supporting deflationary measures.

Nevertheless, by the end of 1934 Mandel would show that his extensive knowledge of politics and his mastery of parliamentary techniques, which gained him the wary respect of many of his colleagues, if not of the general public, were still of considerable importance. Doumergue would learn that he had made a serious mistake in ignoring Mandel. And Mandel would finally break the barriers that had encircled him since 1919, becoming, except for the Popular Front interlude, a member of every government thereafter.

II

Although excluded from the cabinet in February, Mandel was elected to the parliamentary commission charged with investigating the Stavisky Affair. The inquiry was dominated by partisan considerations. The Right wanted to discredit as many left-wing leaders as possible, while the Left hoped to implicate the conservatives and defend their own men. Mandel refused to consider the Left solely responsible for the scandal just as he refused to blame France's economic and political difficulties solely on them, but he did not want the investigation to end with a whimper, as the Oustric Commission had. "In this country," he said, "we spend ... our time starting investigations that are never heard from again."[37] To stimulate public pressure, he began to leak information to the press and predicted that if the left-wing majority succeeded in covering up for the guilty, they would destroy parliamentary institutions in France.[38]

The Left was thus delighted when Stavisky's secretary, Romagnino, revealed that Mandel had once dined with the swindler. Even some members of the Right reproached him for not having mentioned this before presenting himself as a candidate for the commission and demanded that he resign.[39] Mandel refused. In explanation, he produced a letter from a M. Castanet, who had arranged the dinner with Stavisky in the fall of 1932. Castanet, owner of some land in Soulac, said that he had been approached by General Bardi de Fourtou, head of a construction firm, with a plan for developing the town as a summer resort. At the dinner, to which they invited Mandel as Mayor of Soulac to discuss the project, Bardi introduced a M. Alexandre as his financial partner. M. Alexandre turned out to be Stavisky. Afterward, according to Castanet, Mandel warned him of his suspicions of the group, and nothing further came of the plan.[40]

Mandel's explanation was later confirmed by Bardi de Fourtou and Romagnino,[41] but the Commission was reluctant to accept it at the time because of another incident that seemed to connect Mandel with Stavisky. Fernand Décis, a former editorial secretary at the Stavisky-controlled Paris daily, *La Volonté*, volunteered to testify about Mandel's relations with the swindler. According to Décis, Stavisky had asked him to transfer from *La Volonté* to *Le Rempart*, another one of the newspapers he backed. He had made the move, only to be fired ten days later. Stavisky told him that Mandel could not accept his presence at *Le Rempart* and that "the deputy from Lesparre was too influential a person for Stavisky to dare oppose him. Stavisky added that my terminal leave pay came in large part from Mandel."[42]

Décis' testimony, of course, was hearsay. He could not prove his claim that Mandel was the real political director of *Le Rempart* or that he had had "important and prolonged" relations with Stavisky. Also, as a long-standing opponent of Mandel in the Gironde, he was obviously biased. His testimony had to be discounted by the Commission, although there were other grounds for believing that Mandel was associated with the daily, *Le Rempart*. Its founder, Paul Lévy, supported Mandel's nationalistic anti-German policy, and his weekly, *Aux Ecoutes*, frequently quoted Mandel and printed favorable stories about him. It was generally assumed that Mandel provided the information for many of the articles appearing there,[43] and, in fact, those about him were written by his friend Maurice Nau.[44] Lévy, however, denied that the deputy from Lesparre had any control over his newspapers: "We shared certain ideas and met sometimes for dinner. But the Commission was convinced that Mandel was all-powerful at *Aux Ecoutes*. In attacking its director, they were trying to discredit the most prominent member of the Commission."[45]

Under the Third Republic, French politicians were notably unfortunate in their associations, particularly with journalists and financiers. The press was inevitably venal since few of the newspapers could have survived on their own, and were subsidized either by businessmen or by the government itself from the "secret funds" voted by Parliament every year. Deputies, whose careers depended on a favorable press, were forced to support men whose pens could be bought by the highest bidder.[46] It was perhaps impossible to be sufficiently cautious, and almost every leader became involved with shady characters at one time or another. Mandel had been embarrassed during the war because of his acquaintance with Bolo Pasha. Clemenceau's career was temporarily wrecked by his friendship with Cornelius Herz, a prominent figure in the Panama Canal scandal of the 1890's. And no one had ever been more compromised by his associates than Joseph Caillaux; they almost brought him before a firing squad. In ordinary times these relations caused no comment, but once a swindler had been unmasked, it was dangerous even to have passed the time of day with him. No one ever proved anything against Mandel, but the testimony enabled opponents to claim that he was somehow or other mixed up in the Stavisky Affair,[47] and left him vulnerable to embarrassing comments. When Mandel asked one underworld figure known as Jo-la-Terreur whether he knew Stavisky, the witness replied, "I already told you and I repeat: I only saw Alexandre once in my life and I assure you that *I* never dined with him."[48]

Once this early contretemps was over, however, Mandel assumed a dominant role on the Commission. He was one of the most faithful in attendance and diligent in questioning. *Je Suis Partout* vividly described a session with André Hesse, a Radical deputy and one of Stavisky's lawyers.

In his role of inquisitor, [said the paper] Mandel surpassed himself. For an hour and a half, he interrogated the parliamentary lawyer with the method and precision of a professor of surgery dissecting a corpse. And when Mandel was through, Hesse was like a corpse. He came out of the duel exhausted, weeping, almost a human wreck. His physical strength and his cynicism could not resist a sovereign intelligence and a frightening tenacity.... One experienced and could almost touch human decadence. We thought we had seen the peak of the drama in watching René Renoult; alone, searching for a hand in the crowd, he seemed to act out a famous scene from [Maurice Barrès'] *Leurs figures*. Hesse surpassed all that when, after hearing the verdict, he fell trembling and gasping into the arms of Albert Dalimier, who was awaiting his turn.[49]

For the conservatives, Mandel was the real president of the Commission.[50] The *Alliance Démocratique*, the official organ of the Center party said that the investigation would have died of discredit had it not been for the "courageous tenacity of some of its members, notably of M. Mandel.... Thanks to him, Bonny is inculpated, the Dalimier file has been sent to the minister of Justice, and René Renoult has been charged with influence-peddling."[51]

His work on the Commission enhanced Mandel's already formidable reputation as "the Grand Inquisitor of politics."[52] *Le Canard Enchaîné* printed a caricature of him wearing a bandit's eye mask. The caption read: "Investigations. Speed and discretion. Jéroboam's Agency. Palais-Bourbon. Branch: Lesparre (Gironde)."[53] In the Radical weekly, *Le Cri du Jour*, there appeared an article entitled "Georges Mandel: Ministre de la Sûreté Publique," which was written anonymously by a member of the Commission. The author proposed reestablishing the Ministry of Public Safety and confiding it to Mandel, "a merciless connoisseur of the methods for controlling weak and pitiable mankind." He asserted that although Mandel was supposed to be a man of the Right, he actually belonged to neither side. "At one time Mandel was a rightist, but the desertion of his conservative friends has shown him what to expect from them in political life: ingratitude and cowardice. Mandel is motivated more by a sense of duty to the office he holds than by political prejudice."[54]

Le Cri du Jour was one of the many political gossip sheets already mentioned that flourished in Paris with the aid of the government, political parties, or businessmen. Copies were usually distributed free to members of Parliament, who devoted inordinate attention to them. Until January 1934 *Le Cri du Jour* was owned by the Radical Albert Livet, who described it as "un journal politique de combat, franchement à gauche."[55] Under Louis Thomas, the new owner, it kept the Radical stamp, but soon began to take an extraordinary interest in Mandel. At first he was praised for some things and mocked for others.[56] But critical comments were soon dropped and Thomas was no longer able to find anything but good to report about him. He became "a born statesman," and as Thomas said, "true statesmen cannot be reactionary. Mandel is too intelligent to be the ally of the most stupid people in France."[57] Pages were devoted to his activities, and he was so copiously quoted that Thomas was finally forced to justify the preoccupation: "It may seem strange that a leftist journal would report the comments of the man that some of our newspapers have anathematized, excommunicated and cursed. But as journalists eager to inform our readers about the Stavisky Commission, we could not neglect the deputy from Lesparre. He refuses to give interviews, ... but speaks with complete freedom about all current topics when he meets a journalist sufficiently objective to repeat his words without distorting them."[58]

Le Cri du Jour is a valuable source of information about Mandel's ideas and activities during this period. Although a minor Radical journal seems an unlikely vehicle for his opinions, it should be noted that it was not Mandel who chose *Le Cri du Jour*. Nonetheless, for years Thomas visited his office and diligently and accurately quoted him for the benefit of his Radical readers. Mandel only once found it necessary to correct him,[59] and so well did he do his work that when Mandel acquired the Paris daily, *L'Ami du Peuple*, in 1936, Thomas was hired as editor.*

There are several reasons why Mandel utilized Louis Thomas's weekly. He was only slightly less concerned about his reputation than Poincaré, who used to answer criticisms appearing in the most insignificant newspapers. But there was no way of answering a journal like *Le Cri du Jour*, which could only be supported or ignored. Moreover, in recent years Mandel had become accustomed to having his ideas and opinions communicated to the political world by *Aux Ecoutes*. He took a virtuoso's pleasure in explaining his maneuvers in advance.[60] In using a gossip sheet like this, he could say what he wanted and then, because it was reported at second hand, deny the accuracy of the account if his statements for one reason or another proved to be unfortunate. However, after the revelation that Stavisky was one of the financial backers of Paul Lévy's other publication, *Le Rempart*, Mandel could no longer use *Aux Ecoutes*. It was at this point that the *Le Cri du Jour* offered its services, of which the most important perhaps was to

---

* Thomas was another man whom Mandel would one day regret having known. By 1938 he had turned *Le Cri du Jour* into one of the most violently anti-Semitic journals in France, which, strangely enough, still refrained from attacking Mandel.

gain a hearing for Mandel in Radical circles normally hostile to him. The message was that Mandel was no longer a rightist and that he "was motivated more by a sense of duty to the office he holds than by political prejudice."[61]

Through *Le Cri du Jour* and by other means Mandel conveyed the word that he was a changed man. In May his future speech writer Pierre Lafue declared that for a long time Mandel had falsely been considered "a man of 'petits papiers,' petty maneuvers, and minor intrigues. Just because he wanted to know something about men before relying on them, it was thought that he enjoyed rummaging in private dossiers." Lafue predicted that Mandel would not become "minister of Commerce or of Posts in just any cabinet without prestige and without future. But if power comes to him from the right source, he will not reject the instrument that is given to him, and those who thought the regime weak and debilitated will be surprised at the vigor that it will recover in his hands."[62]

By May, in other words, Mandel was preparing for the formation of a new cabinet. The results of the 1932 elections had convinced him that only a National Union government would be viable in that legislature. But it had taken eighteen months of cabinet instability to make the Radicals admit defeat and agree to join with the Right. The Doumergue government, however, did not live up to Mandel's expectations. It excluded him from power and it also failed to provide the leadership that, in his opinion, the situation demanded. A combination of personal ambition and political principle therefore drove him to work against the government, at first quietly, then openly. His efforts were not without success.

Alone, of course, he was powerless. He needed the help of the Radicals both to overthrow Doumergue and to form the National Union cabinet he wanted to replace Doumergue's. Tactics and strategy alike demanded an entente with the Radicals.

In February Mandel had voted for Doumergue, but he quickly began to criticize the government's policies. He particularly opposed the use of decree powers to effect budgetary savings. In bypassing Parliament in this way, Mandel said, Doumergue was only further discrediting the regime that he had been called to save. Furthermore, the government had refused to give judicial powers to the Stavisky Commission, thus preventing it from seizing documents and forcing witnesses to testify. Without these powers, the investigation was likely to be no more effective than the Oustric Commission. The only way to regain the respect of the public, Mandel believed, was to prosecute the men involved in the scandal. But it was evident to him that "such action would upset the Prime Minister. It is not that he misunderstands the necessities of the moment. He is far too intelligent and far too shrewd for that. But he is by nature more inclined to temporize than to act speedily."[63]

Mandel was also opposed to the attempt by some members of the Right, including Tardieu, to use the Stavisky hearings to discredit the Radical Party. He defended some of the Radicals, particularly his old friend, the late François Albert,[64] and thus inevitably was himself attacked by the Right. Léon Bailby accused him of covering up for the Radicals. He said he had known Mandel for a long time but "had never seen him act clearly, loyally, without reservations, and for the sole good of the nation. This man whom the moderates consider an ally does them more harm than if he were their declared enemy."[65] François Le Grix in the conservative *Revue Hebdomadaire* said that one of the members of the Commission, "the most prominent perhaps, to whom many of our friends attribute the implacable will of an incorruptible judge and the audacity of a Clemenceau or a Fouché, was placed there only in order to cover Chautemps on the essential while attacking him on the incidental."[66]

Other issues were also beginning to separate Mandel more and more from the government and from its staunchest right-wing supporters. He succeeded in defeating their proposal for proportional representation, warning the deputies that Doumergue would dissolve the Chamber if they ever passed it.[67] His fellow right-wing deputy from the Gironde, Philippe Henriot, publicly accused him of scuttling the bill for purely personal reasons, because he needed the *scrutin d'arrondissement* in order to assure his own reelection.[68] In turn, Mandel criticized the antiparliamentary campaign being carried on throughout the country by Henriot, who was vice-president of Louis Marin's Republican Federation. His speeches denouncing the Radicals and freemasons were causing riots in almost every city where he appeared. Mandel noted that his campaign "proves there is really no government," for Doumergue had not ordered Louis Marin either to resign from the cabinet or to stop the provocative speeches of Henriot. He added knowingly that Clemenceau would not have hesitated for a moment.[69]

Despite all of these issues, however, Mandel did not openly act against the cabinet until August, when he attacked Henry Chéron, the minister of Justice, for failing to prosecute the cases against Stavisky's friends. On Mandel's initiative the investigating commission voted a motion demanding that Chéron tell what he had done with the twenty-six dossiers sent to him for further investigation and possible prosecution.[70] *Le Cri du Jour* then revealed that if Chéron did not resign and nothing were done about the cases, Mandel planned to overthrow Doumergue to prepare the way for a new and more vigorous National Union government.[71] Doumergue took the hint, dismissed Chéron, and thus briefly prolonged the life of his cabinet.

Nonetheless, opposition was building up. It finally broke out on the issue of constitutional reform. Although Doumergue had created a parliamentary commission in March to study the question, thereafter he seemed to have forgotten about it. Then suddenly in September in two radio speeches, he recommended that the prime minister be given the right to dissolve the Chamber without having to obtain the consent of the Senate, that deputies be prevented from proposing expenditures, that the budget be enacted by decree if Parliament had not passed it before the end of the fiscal year, and that civil servants be forbidden to join unions or to strike.

The Socialists immediately sprang to the defense of the Republic, denouncing Doumergue's reforms and his use of the radio as demagogical and fascistic procedures. Mandel joined them in opposition. The cover of the November 3 issue of *Le Cri du Jour* announced in large type: "MANDEL OPPOSES DISSOLUTION." He believed that the Prime Minister, "the shrewdest tactician of the old guard,... had arranged the whole affair of constitutional reform... solely in order to prepare a remarkable exit."[72] According to Mandel, Doumergue thought to himself, "Either I pass the reforms and then resign, leaving someone else with powers that will force him to act, or if I fall on the question of dissolution, I can resign on that honorable pretext after having done some useful work." He obviously did not want the reforms for himself, because he had used neither the powers vested in his office nor the freedom of action granted him by the country and by Parliament, which between February and September would have done anything he asked. Mandel thought that Doumergue was

covering up not only his own weakness and lack of determination, but all the faults of his predecessors. It is as if he were saying to the country: "You have had a succession of governments composed of admirable, patriotic, intelligent, active, disinterested men devoted to the public good. They accomplished nothing, or almost nothing, because Parliament paralyzed them, hampered them, and prevented them from acting."

It was Mandel's own belief that "Parliament has never prevented an energetic man from acting...." And he wondered rhetorically whether the Radicals were going "to renounce their traditional doctrine of the sovereignty of the people... in favor of a personal power that would put the Chamber at the mercy of one man's caprice. If so, within several months we will have a dictatorship...; the Radicals will have offered themselves up for the sacrifice like the Social Democrats in Berlin."[73]

It is uncertain whether Mandel really was afraid of the consequences of a stronger executive as his friend and assistant Georges Wormser claims,[74] or whether he was sounding the alarm simply in order to frighten the Radicals.

In any case their real dilemma was how to replace Doumergue with a more congenial prime minister without driving his right-wing supporters into opposition and the antiparliamentary leaguers into the streets. To help them resolve the dilemma, Mandel reportedly warned the Right that the dissolution of the Chamber would immediately recreate the Cartel des Gauches.[75] He also tried to reassure the Left. "Why are you afraid of the demonstrators?" he asked. "I know these men. It will be enough to terrorize them, and there is no need to spill blood for that."[76] He also worked directly on Herriot and other Radical leaders to persuade them to overthrow the government.[77] Finally, on November 8, after days of debate and maneuvers, the Radical ministers withdrew from the government, forcing Doumergue to resign.

Although most historical accounts fail to note the role played by Mandel, it was clear to contemporaries that he had been instrumental in defeating the government. Doumergue publicly denounced his opponents without naming them. It was understood that his remarks were directed at Mandel.[78] And the Prime Minister's personal advisor called the defeat of the government "the tactical triumph of a deputy who in spite of his recognized personal value had never yet been a minister." Mandel's campaign had been a masterpiece of its kind in which he had played on the fears of those deputies who needed their salaries to pay off their debts and could not afford a new election. He had also warned others who would become eligible for a pension in 1936 that they would risk losing it if Doumergue dissolved the Chamber and they were defeated in their bid for reelection.[79]

One reporter noted that "since Mandel is particularly responsible for Doumergue's fall, there is much talk of him as minister of the Interior."[80] The rumor had spread several days earlier that Pierre Laval would succeed Doumergue and give Mandel this ministry "in order to break the nationalist leagues."[81] Laval, however, declined the opportunity, and the task of forming a new government fell to Pierre-Etienne Flandin, President of the Alliance Démocratique, who had begun negotiations for Radical support several weeks earlier. Although Flandin was not on speaking terms with Mandel, who had openly attacked him in 1931, he immediately offered Mandel a post in the government.[82] It was said that his activities in recent months and particularly his maneuvers against Doumergue had made him an indispensable element in *any* government that followed.[83]

It is probable in fact that the cabinet would never have been formed without Mandel's support. He represented one of the last links in Parliament between the Radicals and the Right. His conciliatory attitude, his part in the Stavisky investigation, and his opposition to constitutional reform reassured the Radicals about him, and everyone agreed that his participation was a sign the new government would drop Doumergue's projects and place more reliance on Parliament.[84] There would be no more threats of dissolution or "Fascist" speeches on the radio.

Strangely enough, Louis Marin's right-wing Republican Federation, which favored constitutional reform, also found Mandel's presence "reassuring."[85] While the cabinet was being formed, a heated dispute arose when Mandel's perennial adversary from the Gironde, the Neo-Socialist Adrien Marquet, balked at collaborating with him. Forced to choose between them, Flandin decided to keep Mandel, for Louis Marin refused to join the government without him. Without the support of Marin's group the government would have been unable to secure a majority in Parliament.[86]

10. Machiavelli as Postman

Il en est des politiciens comme des arrivistes: ils cessent d'être méprisables dès l'instant où ils sont arrivés.

Mandel, 1928

TO THE GENERAL PUBLIC the most surprising thing about Flandin's cabinet was Mandel's acceptance of the Ministry of Posts, Telephones, and Telegraphs, usually held by a younger and more inexperienced deputy. Mandel explained to one journalist that his title was unimportant. What he cared about was getting to participate in the council of ministers. To another he said that it had taken years, but at last he had been "cleared through customs" (*dédouané*). He wanted nothing more.[1]

Despite his explanations, however, the public was still amazed. Mandel in charge of the telephones and post office? He once again became the butt of the chansonniers[2] and the target of the Left, which had always liked to picture him listening at doors and rummaging through wastepaper baskets.[3] The Right was especially indignant at his taking such a minor post in that particular government, and vented its anger in the antiparliamentary press. Henri de Kérillis said that "when the attraction of power blinds even the best men to the most elementary notions of political honesty and casts them unseeing into the rush for portfolios, one can only despair of our institutions."[4] But the most bitter reaction came from another of Mandel's old friends, Pierre Gaxotte of the Monarchist *Candide*, who wrote:

On the basis of outmoded caricatures, the public still pictures Mandel as a tall, thin young man with an acute knife-like profile. What a mistake! Mandel is fifty years old, short, plump, and as rosy as a canned ham. He wears stiff collars in the style of Royer Collard and has given himself the appearance of Guizot. He is the Parliamentarian with a capital P. . . . The great mass of people still remember him as the man who governed France under the pseudonym of Clemenceau, arranged the treason trials, dismissed prefects and presided over the elections of 1919. He is the inquisitor of the committees and the Torquemada of the corridors. Torquemada has installed himself at the radio, the listening post and the *cabinet noir*. It is enough to make one laugh. Fifteen years of effort, intrigues, "petits papiers," cabals, maneuvers, snares, traps, daring calculations and profound reflections; fifteen years of plots and mystery. And for what? To get the beginners' ministry, the insignificant office that the Sarrauts give to the young men of Tarn after six months in the Chamber. People used to say: "Mandel will be minister of the Interior. When Mandel is minister of the Interior. . . . If Mandel were minister of the Interior. . . ." Mandel was not as demanding as that. He stupidly wanted to be just another minister. Nothing more, nothing less. Minister of something or of anything. People called him "the Machiavelli of the Republic." Machiavelli had an ambition. Machiavelli wanted to be postman.[5]

Mandel had been parliamentary commentator for *Candide* in 1929 and still met Gaxotte occasionally for an epicurean repast at Lapérouse.[6] Even after the riots of February 6, when Gaxotte became one of the leading armchair Fascists in France, he still seemed to have some vague hope that the incorrigible parliamentarian might be able to restore more effective government. The bitterness of his reproach to Mandel was the measure of this hope, apparently shared by Kérillis and other extremists on the Right.

Mandel, who had always opposed Doumergue's plans, saw no betrayal or even a contradiction in accepting office in the government that succeeded him. As for becoming minister of the Interior, Radical prejudices precluded that. It was enough for the moment that the Radicals, who had made him their *bête noire* for years, agreed to accept him at all. Moreover, he had learned that before he could aspire to a more important role, he would have to create a new image and a new legend. The PTT gave him an opportunity, without affronting political susceptibilities, to put into effect the ideas he had so often expressed about the necessity for restoring authority in government through energetic action. At last he would be able to show not only what could be done, but more important, what *he* could do.

Although usually given to a junior member of the cabinet, the PTT was one of the most important branches of the administration because of its budget and the number of its employees. Only the Ministries of War and Education had more employees, and the Ministries of War and Finance larger budgets.[7] Mandel had first been offered the Ministry of Commerce but had refused it in favor of the PTT which would give greater scope to his administrative abilities.[8]

The day he took office, he placed a wreath at the statute of Clemenceau on the Champs-Elysées, symbolically putting the ministry under the protection of his patron saint.[9] Within two weeks, in a speech before the Conseil Supérieur des PTT, he laid down the general lines of the policy he intended to follow. He promised to improve the administration "by modernizing the regulations and breaking the chains of an archaic and rigid organization, which paralyzes initiative and too often leaves the minister no other power than that of registering almost automatic promotions." He intended to give more authority to the heads of departments to reward good work and initiative. To assure satisfactory service, he would establish a central complaint bureau. In general, he wanted to contribute to the revitalization of the country by better organization and discipline.[10]

As an example of the speed and efficiency with which things could be accomplished, he had his budget passed in December with virtually no debate, an unprecedented event. With 158,000 employees and offices in every district in France, the Ministry was usually besieged by requests from deputies with constituents who wanted jobs or new post offices. These deputies used the budget debate to show what difficulties they could create, were their demands refused. Discussion often dragged on for days. To avoid this tiresome procedure, Mandel had spoken to the individual deputies and tried to satisfy their requests in advance. On the day of the debate, no one asked to speak, not even the Socialists and Communists, who usually presented union complaints at this time.[11]

The press was soon inundated with stories and communiqués about the new Minister of Posts. He was a tireless worker who arrived at his office at 8:30 in the morning and remained until midnight. To assure efficient service, he frequently paid surprise visits to the PTT offices in Paris. He took but half an hour for meals, and read his mail while he ate. He was reported to be sleeping at the Ministry itself, though he actually retired to a little room on the second floor of the Ritz. He spent Sundays and holidays at the office personally hearing the complaints of the public and the employees.[12]

Hardly a week went by without the announcement of some reform or innovation. New subscribers would get their telephones within a few days instead of having to wait several weeks. Rural areas, previously deprived of service from noon until two and after six when the local office shut down, would be provided with automatic telephones. An information and messenger service was inaugurated. By dialing "SVP" a subscriber could get any easily available information for a charge of one franc or any information requiring research for charges up to ten francs. A messenger service would make reservations for theaters, planes, trains, or steamships, and would buy and deliver anything for a nominal fee. By the time Mandel completed his work at the PTT, said one American journalist, telephone service in France, once a source of constant complaints, was as good as it was in New York.[13]

Postal services as well were to be improved. One office in Paris, the Bureau de la Bourse, would remain open all night. Air mail delivery was provided between major cities without adding an extra franc to the budget. Mandel arranged for a private firm to perform this service. On each letter there would be a surcharge of three francs of which one would go to the government. Should the firm fail to carry out its agreement, one half of the facilities it had built would be turned over to the state.[14] Everything, it seemed, was to be transformed, including the workers, who were ordered to improve the appearance of their uniforms. Even his enemies applauded this last reform. As one of them explained, after first judiciously expressing his dislike of Mandel, "A good appearance is not a political question."[15]

Every postman thereafter, as he made his rounds in the villages and towns of France, was a living reminder of Mandel. And anyone who was unreached by a postman probably heard of Mandel over the radio, which was also under his jurisdiction. This was the most powerful means at his disposal for conveying the impression he wanted to create of himself as an efficient administrator. One of his first acts was to stop all advertising on the state network. To make up for the loss in revenue, he started a campaign to compel listeners to declare their radios and pay the tax required since 1933. Henceforth, the fee could be collected by the postman, who would receive two francs for each new registrant. Within a year the number of registrations leaped from 1,700,000 to 2,700,000, and receipts from 80 to 150 million francs.[16]

Mandel also increased the hours of broadcasting from eight to sixteen and extended the range of the various stations. The *Radio-Journal*, little changed since the spontaneous and informal early days of radio, was given a definite format, one more in line with the increased sophistication and importance of the broadcasting medium. Besides the news and commentary, it began to include a review of the press, which quoted the Monarchists as well as the Communists. The various political parties without distinction were given air time to present their views. Exchanges of programs were arranged with other countries, and a center was established for recording and rebroadcasting French and foreign programs. Productions from the state theaters were scheduled more frequently, and the performances of the *Comédie Française* were broadcast every night.[17]

The last major project to which Mandel turned his attention was television. French television had been so neglected that it was virtually nonexistent before that time. Mandel established the first public television studio, scheduled daily programs, and ordered the installation of a powerful transmitter on the Eiffel Tower. When it began functioning in November 1935, people could receive programs forty kilometers away. Previously the range had been limited to the immediate environs of Paris. The quality of the picture received by the viewers was improved by increasing the number of lines in the transmitted image from sixty to 180. Since few Frenchmen yet owned sets, Mandel had sets installed in public places throughout the capital. During his administration, according to one historian, French television not only caught up with but advanced beyond television in the rest of the world.[18]

Mandel had realized from the beginning that in order to accomplish these reforms, he would need public support. Thus he contrived to appear responsive at all times to the interests and complaints of the public, multiplied minor improvements when he had no major ones to suggest, and unhesitatingly made both major and minor improvements known through the press.[19] For Mandel himself, however, the material improvements he made were only a means to an end. "I believe that men are more important than matériel," he said. "Rules, laws and decrees remain ineffective so long as they are not put into effect by individual men. The Ministry of Posts is important not only because of the size of its budget, but also because it controls the activities of a great number of men, and because through it and all the people it employs, one can and must influence the moral spirit of the entire country." Although he directed a "technical" ministry, Mandel asserted that the work he was doing was not that of a technician: "I am working above all to restore the authority of the state."[20] Inevitably, then, he devoted as much concern to the personnel as to the administrative machinery of the PTT.

On taking office he interviewed the six directors of the various services and replaced four of them with his own appointees. He then turned his attention to the 158,000 employees, who had some of the most powerful unions of civil servants in France and a long tradition of unruliness. These unions had succeeded in getting promotion boards established that removed from the minister in charge almost all authority over his subordinates.[21] Mandel showed from the first that he intended to reassert control over them. Besides seniority, other factors, including recommendations from members of Parliament, would be taken into consideration in making promotions. Contests would be held to stimulate the zeal of the workers, and agents who distinguished themselves would be rewarded and promoted rapidly.

The day after Mandel became minister, *L'Humanité* called for "the defense of workers' liberties and trade union rights against the machinations of the Flandin-Mandel crew."[22] A union journal, *Le Ralliement des PTT*, more cautiously advised Mandel not to let political considerations influence his decisions. Although they were disturbed by the idea of appointment by recommendation, what really provoked them was the publicity given to the central complaint bureau and to the punishment of inefficient employees.[23]

For the first month or so, however, their protests were muted. They did not quite know what to make of this new minister who consulted the unions before making any decisions and who told them he was not concerned with their political opinions or activities. They could sing the *Internationale* as much as they liked—so long as they did it after working hours. The future Socialist minister Robert Lacoste wrote that "contrary to what one might believe, Mandel is not prejudiced against his employees; he showed as much by deciding in their favor several pending questions and by making reparations to some thirty union men who had previously been punished." However, Lacoste did complain about Mandel's use of the jobs at his disposal to create friends in Parliament. The minister had explained his ideas to the union leaders: "Parliament is a fact; I have to take it into consideration. The deputy is a representative of the nation; if he expresses a wish, I must give him satisfaction if I can." But since Mandel wanted deputies' requests answered within twenty-four hours, Lacoste said, "the entire central administration is completely occupied with answering their letters."[24]

Union criticism continued to be cautious until February when Mandel made his second speech before the Conseil Supérieur des PTT. After announcing a few of the reforms he intended to make, he said that the publicity given to the complaint bureau would continue, "for it is important for people to know that in the future employees giving poor service to the public will be punished." He defended parliamentary recommendations as coming "from responsible representatives of the people, who sometimes are forced to justify them under embarrassing circumstances." Moreover, union or department heads frequently influenced the classification and promotion boards by their own recommendations, which for being unwritten were none the less decisive. Many department heads, he said, were afraid of their subordinates. In 1933 every single worker had been rated at least "très bien" by his superior. There was no law requiring promotions to be made by seniority, and henceforth half of them would be made at the discretion of the minister.[25]

From the beginning, Mandel's reputation had made the workers uneasy. The failure of the Communist and Socialist deputies to speak out during the budget debate in December worried them. They were alarmed by the action he took against a few men who struck for an hour and a half in Dijon in January. But it was not until February that the battle lines were drawn. After Mandel's speech they knew precisely where they stood, and the weekly column in *Le Ralliement des PTT*, which had been sarcastically entitled "Le Ministre Miracle," (The Superminister) became "Le Ministre Néfaste" (The Sinister Minister).

The paper claimed that Mandel, who had a "sens de la publicité," was simply trying to gain popular favor. His use of the radio "would make M. de Tournefeuille green with envy." In Parliament, "more discreetly, more insidiously, the same work is going on, to consolidate an already well-established reputation for courteous aggressiveness. There is not a single deputy who is not well received in the minister's office, and every request or letter of recommendation from a deputy is acted on immediately. Mandel is thus creating friends in all the parties, for, alas, all the parties contain these unscrupulous servants of electors no less unscrupulous."[26]

Protest meetings were held; Léon Jouhaux, the head of the CGT, led a delegation to see the prime minister; but all to no avail.[27] Every two weeks the press inexorably printed communiqués about the complaint bureau. The one of August 1, 1935, announced that 1,696 complaints had been received and 202 employees had been punished, the punishments ranging from a simple reprimand to temporary suspension from duty. During the off week there would be articles praising the wisdom, authority, and ingenuity of the new minister. In reply to this deluge of propaganda, there was not a word of protest from Parliament, not even from the Socialists and Communists, the official representatives of the working class. Backed by public opinion, Mandel now had a free hand with his employees. They could vent their frustrated anger only in the columns of the trade union press.

There had been bad ministers before, they said, but Mandel surpassed them all. Their writers were especially enraged by the complaint bureau, announced, they said, "with the same hullabaloo as a patent medicine.[28] Everyone with sore feet, indigestion, a sour stomach, a lazy intestine or a perennial migraine headache; the nervous, the constipated, the bored, the neurotic, all henceforth had an outlet for their bad humor, a remedy for what ailed them, a salve for their irritations: the ability to complain about anything or anyone." They had but one threat in their mouths: "We will write to M. Mandel." The workers could only exclaim with their paper: "C'est assez!"[29]

Le Ralliement des PTT admitted that

it would be vain to deny the almost universal favor that our present minister enjoys. His toadying to the public, the clever and voluminous publicity that accompanies the least of his acts, the support that he has found in the press thanks to certain favors he has granted ... have incontestably made of him the best known figure of the Flandin cabinet. This sudden reversal of public opinion, which was not always so favorable to him, is one of the most surprising events of the strange period we live in. In order to aspire to the highest offices, however, Mandel had always needed that final recognition given by the masses only to exceptional men. He has just acquired it almost effortlessly, thanks to one of those chance events that influence the destinies of men more than their own wills.[30]

The chance event referred to was the postal strike of April 18. Some two hundred postmen in Nice stopped work to protest the announced layoff of temporary workers hired to handle the heavy winter workload. On receiving the news, Mandel suspended all the strikers, sent an inspector by plane to investigate, and ordered 150 Paris postmen to take the night train for Nice. Arriving on Friday morning, they immediately began deliveries. By Monday they had reestablished normal service. There had been some talk that the Paris replacements might quit work or that the strike might spread throughout southern France. Mandel announced that he had taken precautions against both eventualities. Neither occurred. When the Nice postmen tried to return to work *en bloc*, Mandel forced them to apply individually for reinstatement. The leaders of the strike were to be identified and punished.[31]

For several days the Nice affair occupied the front pages of the Paris papers. *Le Ralliement des PTT* thought that the strike could have been settled peacefully without all the publicity. On the strength of the unnecessarily forceful measures he had taken, they asserted that Mandel had become, for the public, "one of the three or four possible dictators. He still comes after Tardieu, but he is already ahead of M. de la Rocque."[32]

II

Within six months, by hard work and constant publicity, Mandel had made himself one of the most prominent and popular members of the cabinet. His relationship to the other ministers, however, and in particular to Flandin, was ambiguous. All the theatrics and publicity could easily be thought to mean that he wanted to become prime minister. His Machiavellian reputation, once perhaps an asset, was now a liability. Everyone began to suspect that having lifted the anathema and become a minister, he would be eager to move on to a more important position. Every threat to the cabinet caused rumors that he was working against Flandin in order to succeed him or take over the ministry of the Interior in the next government.[33]

Mandel repeatedly found it necessary to protest his good faith. With an injured air he would exclaim, "My position is very strange. There is a legend about me. I can do nothing to get rid of it ... and must resign myself to being slandered."[34] But while continuing to affirm his allegiance to the cabinet, Mandel did little more to dispel his supposedly unwanted reputation for Machiavellianism. To reporters he might say that people pictured him as being more complicated than he really was: "I always defended my opinions openly, speaking to everyone frankly, telling journalists what I thought. ... I was not maneuvering." He had merely explained his analysis of the situation in advance, and people were surprised when he was quite often proved right.[35] Yet any effect that Mandel hoped to achieve by these denials was immediately destroyed by such stories as the one told by Doumergue's minister of Posts, André Mallarmé. Apparently when Mandel came to take over the administration, he refused Mallarmé's offer to explain some of the technical problems involved with a "Don't bother." But Mandel did ask him: "Do you know the code that is used for the official telegrams sent to the Ministries of the Interior, War, and Foreign Affairs?"[36] Mere denials could not efface the impressions created by his apparent desire to know all the secrets of the government.

Moreover, at the same time that Mandel was saying there was no reason for the cabinet to fall, his friends in the press were noisily proclaiming that he would make an ideal minister of the Interior, minister of Air, or possibly even prime minister.[37] He was "one of Parliament's last hopes." Louis Thomas in the *Cri du Jour* had a special column entitled "Mandeliana." In the nationalist *1935*, Pierre Lafue, who had become Mandel's speech writer in November 1934, continued to praise Mandel's qualities in both signed and anonymous articles.[38] The talented journalist Georges Suarez almost made a living from his writings about Mandel.[39] The refrain was taken up more modestly by journals that had usually been reserved or hostile toward Mandel. The influential *Europe Nouvelle* wrote:

> As the situation becomes worse, there will be no preventing public attention from turning toward men who appear capable of taking extreme decisions. During the last eighteen months of crisis, which has not yet reached its peak, the position of Mandel is comparable to that of his patron Clemenceau during the war. The politicians are being used up little by little; the desire for authority is growing. One day perhaps there will come a moment when the members of Parliament and of the leagues together will call on a man capable of controlling them. That day they will not go to Mandel with enthusiasm, but they will look around them and they will see no one else.[40]

Among the newspapers that joined the chorus was *La Petite Gironde* of Bordeaux, which ten years earlier had sworn never to print his name again. The strait-laced *Le Temps*, which had formerly been shocked by his antics or found his ideas too intransigent or pessimistic, now thought that he made an excellent minister. The opposition suggested that the newspaper was merely repaying Mandel for scheduling afternoon mail deliveries so that *Le Temps* and *Le Journal des Débats* could be carried to subscribers by the postmen. He had also arranged for the mailmen to make special Sunday afternoon deliveries of *Le Temps*.[41] Even Léon Bailby's *Le Jour*, which usually preferred to ignore his existence when not attacking him, began to publish pictures and stories about the new Minister of Posts.[42]

Through the haze of the conflicting reports, denials, and propaganda, it could be seen that while Mandel wanted to allay suspicions of his loyalty to the cabinet, he also wanted to reserve a more important place for himself in the next government. His friends were already reporting in the press his growing acceptance by the Radicals.[43] It was noted that the leftist journals, which once had treated him sarcastically, were beginning to adopt a more "objective" tone.[44] *L'Europe Nouvelle* said that he was not a man of the Right but a true Radical: "A man like Caillaux, who has 'le sens de l'Etat'—partially because he thinks: 'L'Etat c'est moi.' "[45]

Soon after becoming a minister, Mandel had set about repairing some long-broken political fences. He renewed old ties with two friends from his early days with Clemenceau, Albert Bayet and Georges Gombault, now editors of the important left-wing weekly *La Lumière*.[46] He also asked Emile Roche, editor of the Radical *République* and close friend of Joseph Caillaux, to arrange an interview for him with the man he and Clemenceau had tried for treason during the war. No longer head of the Radical Party, Caillaux still wielded great influence as the president of the Senate Finance Commission. Caillaux at first refused: "Never! You can't seriously think that I would receive Mandel? Have you forgotten the trial?" But when it was pointed out that as president of the Finance Commission he would sooner or later have to deal with the Minister of Posts, he agreed to an interview on the following day. When Mandel arrived, he told Caillaux, "You always thought that it was Clemenceau who wanted to have you shot. It's not true. I have the proof here." He then gave Caillaux a letter that Poincaré had written to Clemenceau in 1918. After reading the letter Caillaux exclaimed, "La canaille!" Mandel's revelation was followed by a friendly conversation during which he explained what he planned to do as minister of Posts. Caillaux approved.[47]

Mandel also seems to have been assured of the discreet support of Emile Roche's *La République*. Besides publishing his communiqués as regularly as the conservative press, Roche wrote after Mandel's speech in February 1935 that the ideas of the new Minister of Posts about revitalizing the state were the very ones *La République* had always supported. The following week, former Radical minister Georges Bonnet added his approval of Mandel's "remarkable speech."[48]

At that time, besides calling for greater authority and discipline in the PTT and in the State, Mandel had announced the creation of a Conseil Supérieur de la Radiodiffusion, which was to supervise the intellectual, moral, and artistic qualities of all broadcast programs and assure their non-partisan nature. To this commission were named all former prime ministers and ministers of Posts, which meant a Radical preponderance. It would include Caillaux, Chautemps, Daladier, Herriot, Steeg, and Albert Sarraut, to name only the former Radical premiers. To represent the public interest, a number of other men were chosen, including Henry Simon, director of the Catholic *Echo de Paris*, Richard Chapon of the moderate *Petite Gironde*,

Maurice Sarraut of the Radical *Dépeche de Toulouse*, the Socialist leader
Léon Blum of *Le Populaire*, and Jean-Richard Bloch of *L'Humanité*. A
second commission was to coordinate the activities of the various national
and regional stations. As president of the Conseil, Mandel named the
Radical Jean Mistler, who had been minister of Posts at the time of the
February 6 riots.

The composition of the commissions once more inspired Mandel's ex-
friend Pierre Gaxotte, who wrote:

> People are trying to make us believe, simpletons that we are, that Mandel and
> Blum are opposed to one another, that to go from Blum to Mandel is to go from
> darkness to light and that the victory of Mandel over Blum would be a great
> nationalist success.... The crowd becomes enthusiastic, fights, struggles. "A
> bas Mistler! Vive Mandel!" Mandel wins and takes Mistler as his advisor. We
> had no need of Clemenceau's secretary to have Caillaux and Malvy named to
> a radio commission! I do not know whether the country is tired of this bad farce,
> but as for me, it has lasted long enough. Fight against [the rule of] parliament,
> Yes. Fight for another system, Yes. Fight to get new men, Yes. Fight for one
> parliamentarian against another parliamentarian, No.[49]

Gaxotte's, however, was a lone voice on the Right. It may be significant
that he published his article in the more violent *Je Suis Partout*, which he
also edited, rather than in *Candide*, where Jacques Bainville and others
still seemed to be friendly. In any case, Mandel won wide acceptance among
conservative Radicals without seriously alienating his right-wing supporters. While Gaxotte fulminated in *Je Suis Partout*, sometimes called *Je
Suis Nulle Part* because of its lack of readers,[50] the equally violent and antiparliamentarian but far more successful *Gringoire* referred to Mandel as
"one of the rare ministers France can count on." The editors of *Gringoire*,
which was owned by Horace de Carbuccia, son-in-law of Jean Chiappe,
former prefect of police and friend of right-wing extremists, thought that
Mandel would make an excellent minister of the Interior.[51]

In seeking a rapprochement with the Radicals, however, Mandel could
have been accused of the very kind of political opportunism practiced by
the Center that he had denounced for so many years. He seemed to have
changed drastically since the time of his electoral reform bill in 1931 when
he preached the necessity of forming homogeneous governments based on
united majorities. Nevertheless, there was a presumption in his favor, for
any mere opportunist would have made his peace with the powers that be
long before Mandel did. Admittedly it had been easier for Tardieu, whose
leadership qualities were more apparent and who generated dislike rather
than hatred, but he had required only three months after his reelection in
1926 to become a minister. In fact, Mandel was moved by the same consid-

erations that had led him to call for a National Union government ever since the 1932 elections. Although the leftist electoral majority in the Chamber numbered 350 out of 600 deputies, a voting majority could be found only for conservative financial and defense measures. This meant that if the Chamber were not to fall back into the impotency that preceded the February 6 riots, Radical support for what were actually rightist governments had to be maintained. Only if all the parties from the Radicals to the Right shared responsibility equally could the necessary but unpopular financial and military measures be passed.

Mandel's determination that responsibility be shared was demonstrated on the question of the two-year military service law. One of the major problems facing Flandin was the drop in the number of draftees predicted for 1935 as a result of the drastic decline in the French birth rate during the war. It was expected that the annual contingent would be cut in half, leaving the French forces woefully undermanned in comparison with the resurgent German army. Mandel favored enacting a bill increasing the term of compulsory military service to two years. The Socialists vehemently opposed any such bill as a plot on the part of the General Staff to build up a professional army of long-service troops. The Radicals, loath to alienate the Socialists, would have preferred to postpone the bill until after the nationwide municipal elections in May, when they would be safe from Socialist denunciations.

Mandel was suspected of leaking information to the press in order to force the Radicals to take an immediate stand and share responsibility for the law before the electorate. The dispute ended in a personal argument between Herriot and Mandel during which both threatened to resign. Out of that argument, however, came a compromise. Action would be taken immediately, but instead of asking the Chamber to enact a two-year law, the government would utilize Article 40 of the 1928 draft law, which allowed the service of draftees to be extended "in case of necessity." Those drafted in April would serve an extra six months, and those drafted thereafter, beginning in October, would serve for two years.[52] By means of this compromise, the conservatives were able to enact a measure they favored without bearing all the blame for it as they had for the three-year military service law passed the year before the 1914 elections.

To demonstrate his concern for national unity, Mandel arranged that only one list would be presented in Soulac in the May municipal elections. The list included representatives of all the parties participating in the government, including some of his oldest local enemies. To the electors, Mandel declared, "It is more than time to proclaim a political Edict of Nantes."[53] He told a reporter that "in the terrible period in which we are living, electoral struggles are dangerous. They crystallize latent oppositions and re-inforce open hostilities. They thus undo on the electoral level the work that the government is trying to do." There was no longer time for fruitless and endless quarrels. The German threat, the budgetary difficulties complicated by reduced tax returns, and the unprecedented economic and agricultural crisis made unity absolutely necessary. No single political group could hope to solve the problems by itself. Recovery would be the work of all the parties.[54]

Besides the political necessity of cooperating with the Radicals, there was also the greater necessity of maintaining moral unity. For him there were not two Frances; the country was not divided into

believers and nonbelievers, veterans and those they saved, employers and em-ployees, peasants and city-dwellers, taxpayers and tax collectors, Right and Left, admirers of Rome and servants of Moscow. All these distinctions are useless.... There is only one France, and all Frenchmen must cooperate wholeheartedly in its salvation under the direction of men for whom the grandeur of the country is the supreme duty and the only law.[55]

For the moment, Flandin represented that indispensable unity, and Mandel praised him as one of the most informed and intelligent men in Parliament.[56] But there were serious differences of opinion between them that could not be concealed. Mandel was repeatedly quoted as advocating a vigorous foreign and domestic program, but the cabinet seemed to prefer more dilatory procedures.[57] Their differences were brought into the open by Flandin's decision, following his failure to balance the budget by ordi-nary legislation, to ask Parliament for the authority to undertake deflation-ary measures by decree. Opposed on principle to rule by decree, Mandel also thought it would be fatal to the cabinet and said so as soon as he learned of Flandin's plans.

The cabinet had not been invested to adopt Doumergue's methods, he stated, but rather "to show that Parliament could save the country and meet any difficulties, even very serious ones.... A minister should be able to do anything." For example, he said, "a real government should be in a position every morning to have two thousand Parisians shot and to get Parliament's approval that night." Anyone who could not do this simply did not know how to govern. Unlike Flandin, he believed that Parliament should be confronted with its responsibilities: either it would vote the de-flationary measures or it would have to devalue the franc. To encourage the deputies to vote the measures, he proposed lengthening their terms of office by two years. "Have the Senate vote the six-year term, and you can get whatever you want from the Chamber." Public opinion of course would have to be prepared, but as he said at the beginning of May, "from now until

June 1, when Parliament meets again, we have the time to move worlds. We need only will and foresight. Public opinion can be created. It is a battle to be fought, and one loses only the battles that one wants to lose."[58]

Despite Mandel's warnings and advice, however, Flandin went ahead with his plans to ask Parliament for decree powers. Sensing the overthrow of the cabinet, Mandel began to sound out opinion about his own chances of forming the next government. Three weeks before Flandin was defeated, Louis Thomas printed an interview with "the editor of a large journal" who sounded suspiciously like Mandel. The "editor" called Mandel "the hope of tomorrow. The only question in case Flandin cuts his own throat is whether President Lebrun will dare call on Mandel...." If he did, the "editor" predicted:

A ministry would be formed in twenty-four hours. He would be a calm, firm, and daring leader. Some men would be dismissed and new ones tried.... Reforms would follow one another in rapid succession. Parliament would be held over for two years and would share credit for the reforms.... With Laval at the Foreign Ministry, peace would be defended. The weak-willed and incapable would be dismissed from the Ministries of War and Air. An intensive armaments program would be inaugurated to frighten Germany. The battle against unemployment would be conducted with new measures and new ideas each day....

When the "editor" was interrupted with the objection that Flandin could accomplish all that, he replied, "Certainly. Let him do it and the public will immediately follow him. Parliament will be forced to go along. Success depends in the long run on public opinion, and public opinion can be created. It is only a question of will power."[59]

On May 31 when Flandin asked Parliament for the power to issue decree laws, he was defeated by a vote of 353 to 202, the Radicals having withdrawn their support. In spite of a few rumors that he would form the new government or become minister of the Interior,[60] Mandel seems to have realized, as *Gringoire* reported, that "his hour had not yet come."[61] His own paper announced that the rumors were unfounded.[62] In the National Union government formed by Fernand Bouisson, Mandel remained at the PTT. His friends reported that he had refused to accept a change, and Mandel himself explained, "I am not a jack of all trades."[63]

The novelty of the new cabinet was the presence in it together of Mandel and Caillaux, who became minister of Finance. Caillaux, in his own way as resourceful and determined as Mandel, was even less diplomatic and more overbearing. Although he realized that many members of the cabinet disapproved, he advised Bouisson to ask Parliament for decree powers. It was just such a request that had been Flandin's downfall. After a stormy session, the Chamber once again defeated the government, but this time by only two votes, 264 to 262. The task of forming a cabinet next fell to Pierre Laval, who had been foreign minister since October 1934. Laval's cabinet was farther to the right than either Bouisson's or Flandin's. Nevertheless, when he, too, asked for decree powers, the Radicals decided to give him the authority he wanted, not because he was more trustworthy than his predecessors, but simply because there had to be a government.

Although Mandel might have expected promotion from Laval, who had been the first to offer him a post in 1931, he remained at the PTT, either to squelch rumors of his ambitions or because opposition was still too great to his taking a more important office. In either case, in spite of his sudden rise in popularity and the wide acclaim of his abilities, Machiavelli was still postman.

11. Homme de Droite? Homme de Gauche?

*Il y avait des fois où j'avais envie de l'empoigner aux épaules et de
lui demander en le secouant un peu: "Mais enfin, qu'est-ce que vous pensez?
Qui êtes-vous, hein? Qui êtes-vous exactement?"*

Odette Pannetier

EVER SINCE THE WAR when Mandel had used Laval as a spy in the Socialist Party, the two men had helped each other out on various occasions. They do not seem to have been bound by anything more than political interest, however, for even after Laval became premier, Mandel's friends continued to write articles praising Mandel as "one of the great reserve forces" of the country.[1] During the cabinet crisis, Pierre Lafue had said that the more serious things got, the more people thought Mandel might be the answer.[2] Later he predicted that if Laval failed, "there will no longer be any recourse except to let Tardieu establish a new political system, more responsive to the will of the rulers, or to let Mandel, in one last experiment, show that nothing can resist human will power...."[3] *Le Cri du Jour* quoted Senator Emile Sari of Corsica: "One, two, or three premiers will be used up. Then one day public opinion will demand Mandel as it demanded Clemenceau in 1917.... There will be a Mandel government and perhaps in the not too distant future."[4]

This was the same type of propaganda that had helped to bring Clemenceau to power. It shows that Mandel now wanted to be premier, not just minister of the Interior, and that he did not consider his fate to be linked to that of the Laval government. He might not try to overthrow it, but if it fell, he wanted to be ready to succeed it.

The most important immediate problem facing the new government in June was the continued deterioration of France's economic and financial position. The devaluation of foreign currencies had made French goods uncompetitive in the world market, and the general decline in business activity, which reduced tax revenues, had seriously unbalanced the budget. French governments had followed a deflationary policy since 1932 without, however, reviving the economy. Doumergue had issued decree laws. The Chamber had turned Flandin and Bouisson out of office when they asked for the same powers, but finally gave them to Laval simply because there was no majority for any alternative policy, and Parliament could not endlessly overthrow governments.

Over the summer Laval issued a large series of laws aimed, by cutting governmental expenditures ten per cent, at balancing the budget and reducing the prices of French goods in the world market. Mandel asked the PTT unions to cooperate with him in a reorganization of the services so that wages would not have to be cut. But when the workers refused, their salaries were cut, and other economies announced.[5]

The decree laws caused considerable agitation throughout France that summer. Civil servants demonstrated at Tours, Mulhouse, Strasbourg, Montauban, and Lille, and struck at Bordeaux, Brest, Toulon, Lorient, Cherbourg and Oran.[6] The PTT workers also organized protest meetings against the decree laws and "the Fascist methods" of Mandel, but refrained from striking. Mandel had warned them that for some time he had been accepting and classifying job applications. He now had over 60,000 applicants, many of whom had been assigned to, and instructed in, the specific jobs they would fill in case of a strike. The applicants were ordered to be ready to report to work at a moment's notice.[7]

There was also some talk of a general strike of all state employees like the one successfully organized on February 12, 1934, in reaction to the riots on the Place de la Concorde. These rumors were denied by Adrien Marquet, a leader of the Fascist-influenced Neo-Socialists. A general strike, he said, was impossible without the postal workers, and they refused to go out because they were convinced that Mandel was trying to provoke them into striking in order to break their power.[8] Whatever the reason, there was no strike that year, and Mandel was able to take credit in a speech in October for having prevented "a movement which could have had serious consequences."[9]

Mandel's actions, however, disturbed his newfound friends on the Left. Georges Gombault of *La Lumière* protested that the PTT workers would have struck only if the Fascists had attempted to take power. They could have thwarted the coup by cutting off communications with the provinces. He concluded that Mandel's use of strikebreakers favored the Fascists, and asked how he could reconcile this with his declarations of loyalty to the Republic and his promises to leftist friends to break the antiparliamentary leagues if he were made minister of the Interior.

The following week Gombault reported Mandel's reply: The measures adopted were designed to prevent a professional strike and not to crush a movement of republican resistance. Mandel also assured Gombault that in case of a Fascist coup, he would not be found on the wrong side of the barricades.[10]

This fencing match between Mandel and *La Lumière* seems to have been put on for the benefit of the workers, who complained throughout the year about the failure of the left-wing press to criticize Mandel. In a pamphlet, the Syndicat National des Agents des PTT commented:

The members of Parliament, whether from the Right, Left, or Center, say nothing. They seem to be afraid. Moreover, for many of them, Mandel is the great man, the coming man, the Savior. . . . What does all this mean? Has a mysterious cloud surrounded and favored the inexplicable rise of the man who used to be called "Raspoutinette"? What strange spell has hypnotized the wisest of our deputies? Are we on Mount Sinai?[11]

L'Action, representing the political extremists among the PTT workers, protested that "some leftist politicians, whose names would surprise our friends, have been won over by Mandel. Some leftist journals are maintaining a sympathetic silence about him. He has told them that he would dissolve the leagues, and our friends believed him." The journal said that Mandel was not a good republican and would not dissolve the leagues. He had violated the rights of the workers and appointed conservatives as department heads. "It is not by placing reactionaries in a formerly republican administration that Mandel has acquired the right to be considered the hope of the republicans." George Boris, Léon Blum's future *chef de cabinet*, replied for *La Lumière* that the editors were not toadying to Mandel and had in fact often criticized him, but that they differed with the workers "on the wisdom at that moment of systematically opposing a certain politician."[12]

Actually the editors of *La Lumière* were critical of Mandel, but not when they thought it would embarrass him.[13] To them, Mandel was not a reactionary but a late-nineteenth-century Radical, who may have had little concern with social questions, but whose loyalty to the Republic was unquestionable. And in the second half of 1935, the republican Left was far more worried about the threat of the leagues than about social questions, and found more cause to rejoice than to despair in Mandel's authoritarianism. Increasingly, their own journals called him "une des grandes réserves de la France," and mentioned him as possibly the only man capable of controlling the leagues.[14] Mandel himself refused to be quoted, but his assistants told a journalist that he had made preparations against any attempt to take over the communications system, which would be one of the principal objectives of a revolutionary movement. They apparently also told him, however, that the Croix de Feu would take action only in the event of an attempted Communist coup.[15]

It might appear that Mandel was guilty of duplicity. But if he told the Left he was faithful to the Republic, it was only the truth. And if he told them that he would know how to handle the leagues, that was very likely also true. However, the Left probably thought he meant to suppress them by force, whereas he himself intended merely to see that they did not get out of hand. Even though he had no sympathy with rightist attacks on the republican system, he was still tied to the Right by years of collaboration in a common cause. Ever since 1919, in fact, the Right had been an essential element in his political plans. Only if they accepted the Republic and in turn were accepted by the republicans, could a viable two-party system be established. They also provided the necessary patriotic leaven to heighten national feeling and provide for national security. Without their support in 1913, the three-year military service law would never have been passed, and France would have found herself even less prepared for the conflict than she had been. During the war itself, the Right had been totally committed to victory over Germany while much of the Left had leaned toward a compromise peace.

To an associate who asked him why he maintained his friendship with them, Mandel replied that "the parties of the Extreme Right and the nationalist groups in France have always been the most ardent defenders of the national idea.... They contributed ... by their writings, their speeches, and their warnings to reawakening national feeling and to maintaining French opinion at a high level of vigilance and of devotion to national duty."[16] To a journalist he once said that even if Léon Daudet attacked and insulted him every day, he would not defend himself. "There are certain things in the past that I will never forget."[17]

National security was Mandel's first consideration at that time. To get any military measures passed, he would need Radical votes, but he believed that national security would not be advanced by driving the Right into opposition or by suppressing leagues such as the Croix de Feu, which was composed of war veterans. During the 1920's Mandel had amused himself by advising the Monarchists how to overthrow the Republic if they were really serious about it, but he never thought they were really serious. Nor did he now consider the new leagues a real danger. He had many admirers in the Croix de Feu,[18] and he undoubtedly knew that Colonel de la Rocque had accepted subsidies from the government when Tardieu was prime minister, and was possibly also receiving them from Laval.[19] He considered the riots of February 6 an expression of discontent and not a plot against the Republic, and thought that a strong and energetic government would be able to restore order.[20] According to one of his assistants, Mandel severely reprimanded Jean Chiappe, the right-wing Prefect of Police in Paris whose dismissal helped precipitate the riots, and obtained from him a guarantee of good conduct for the future. "You can be sure that he will not make the same mistake again," said Mandel. "He will not do anything any more without my approval."[21] Chiappe was probably not so subservient to Mandel as this statement suggests. But the consideration shown him year after year by the weekly *Gringoire*, which was owned by Chiappe's son-in-law Horace de Carbuccia, indicates that the former Prefect of Police must have thought it wise not to antagonize Mandel. Throughout the 1930's, despite *Gringoire*'s strong antiparliamentarianism, its anti-Semitism, its total disagreement with Mandel on foreign policy, and its violent denunciation of all of its other opponents, Mandel miraculously escaped criticism. In *Gringoire*, he was always "one of the rare ministers France can count on."[22]

Mandel was out of sympathy with the aims and methods of extreme right-wing leaders and propagandists like Chiappe, Daudet, Gaxotte, La Rocque, Maurras, and Taittinger,[23] but somehow or other was able to keep either their friendship or their wary respect, and he certainly never feared them. Undoubtedly influenced by his wartime experience as Clemenceau's assistant, controlling the police powers of the country, he might consider the threats and demonstrations of the nationalist leagues bothersome, but as he said at the time of Doumergue's fall, "I know those people. It is enough to terrorize them."[24]

Combining in his person the devotion to authority and national security characteristic of the Right with the devotion to the Republic characteristic of the Left, Mandel seems to have hoped, by winning the confidence of both sides, to be able to maintain and to incarnate national unity. One great obstacle was the fact that the opposing groups did not want to be reconciled. When an otherwise responsible journalist like Georges Gombault could seriously state that the entire Right in France was Fascist, the time for reconciliation was almost past.[25] The epithets Fascist, reactionary, Bolshevik, and Communist had been used far too freely for the rivals to distinguish Frenchmen under their own caricatures of each other.

Mandel's plans were complicated and eventually rendered vain by developments in foreign affairs that made pacifists of the Right and turned their opponents into the leading advocates of forceful measures. As a result, while still maintaining, as he had since 1919, that France must act vigorously against the threat from Germany, Mandel found himself pushed into alliance with the Left, to the great scandal of his former friends.

II

Doumergue's foreign minister, Louis Barthou, a conservative nationalist of Poincaré's era, had rejected the policy of conciliation and compromise France had followed for so many years under the inspiration of Briand. He set out instead to reinvigorate and expand France's system of alliances, which had been weakened by her repeated failure to react to German violations of the Treaty of Versailles. By January 1934 Poland had signed a treaty of nonaggression with Germany. Yugoslavia had also become doubtful of France's willingness to defend her friends in the east. By the time Barthou was assassinated in October 1934, he had travelled to Poland, Czechoslovakia, Rumania, and Yugoslavia in an attempt to revitalize existing alliances and had brought Russia into the League of Nations as a prelude to signing a defensive treaty with her. He had also laid plans to include Italy within the projected system of alliances.

On becoming foreign minister, Laval continued these negotiations, but he had less faith than Barthou in a grand alliance and a greater horror of the consequences of war. His policy was to prevent war rather than to be sure of winning it in case it broke out. He relied heavily on compromise, and fancied that he could settle any dispute in private conversation. An uninspiring speaker in Parliament, he was a past master, like Mandel, of working the corridors to obtain the votes he needed. As foreign minister, he tried to apply the same methods of conversation and compromise that had proved so successful for him in domestic politics.

Until the Abyssinian crisis late in 1935, Laval's foreign policy seemed an almost unmitigated success. In January he settled the colonial differences that had long disturbed relations between France and Italy. The agreement released French troops on the southeastern frontier and in the African colonies for duty on the Rhine in case of difficulties with Germany. In April at Stresa he got England and Italy to declare with France that unilateral revisions of the Treaty of Versailles would not be tolerated. In May he closed the defensive ring around Germany by signing a mutual assistance treaty with the Russians. Although its provisions for immediate assistance in case of unprovoked attack were hedged with so many qualifications as to render them useless, the treaty at least served as a warning to Germany. Until the summer of 1935, Laval's only setback had been England's agreement with Germany allowing her a fleet thirty-five per cent the size of the English naval forces. Negotiated without the knowledge of the French, it sanctioned German rearmament and virtually repudiated the Stresa accords signed just two months before.[26]

The issue that finally wrecked Laval's imposing diplomatic edifice and destroyed whatever internal unity remained in France was Mussolini's plan to conquer Abyssinia. The move was carefully timed, for France obviously needed Italy's aid against Germany and could be expected to wink at such a classical, if anachronistic, colonial expedition. In January Laval had expressed disinterest in the economic exploitation of Abyssinia, which Mussolini had interpreted as French acquiescence in his plans to conquer it.

Opposition to Italian plans came mostly from England and from the French Socialists, who seemed to find Fascist Italy more horrible than Nazi Germany. For England, Italian aims in Abyssinia were both a threat to her interests in the Near East and an affront to the League of Nations and the idea of collective security. The French Left supported the English position partly out of deference for the League, but also because of an ideological hatred of Fascist Italy. As one historian commented, "The anti-Fascist crusade...sometimes seemed to be led by men who were determined to get rid of Mussolini's regime at all costs."[27]

The French government, however, was in the hands of Pierre Laval, who had no intention of losing potential Italian support against Germany for the sake of the League of Nations or of a backward African state that still practiced slavery. He was backed by the French Right, partly because of its ideological sympathy for Fascism, but mostly because it was appalled at the thought of applying military sanctions against Italy for a colonial expedition while Germany was able to violate the Treaty of Versailles with impunity. For the Right, the enemy was across the Rhine, not over the Alps.[28]

On October 2 Mussolini finally invaded Abyssinia. A few days later when the League of Nations voted to apply economic sanctions, Laval went along in order to please England but succeeded in limiting the embargo to things Italy did not really need. Oil, iron, and steel were excluded. In effect, sin was condemned but not punished.

The Socialists demanded that the sanctions be extended, and Léon Blum even announced his willingness to go to war. "Eventually," he said, "peace may require the use of armed force. A defensive war is just as atrocious as a war of aggression; but it is still better than if the world made a cowardly surrender to wars of aggression."[29]

To the Right, this seemed absurd and outrageous. The Socialists, who refused to act against Germany and always voted against military expenditures, were now talking about war with Italy. A furious Charles Maurras called for the assassination of the 140 French members of Parliament who had signed a manifesto protesting Mussolini's expedition. The rest of the Right was equally outraged. In *Gringoire*, Henri Béraud wrote an article blaming England, not Italy, for the trouble. *Candide* launched a slogan destined for considerable success in various forms: "How would you like to die for the Negus?" it asked.[30]

On the Abyssinian affair, Mandel's position was ambiguous. In September he had expressed complete confidence in the way Laval was conducting negotiations at Geneva, and said that "if, after bargaining, Mussolini accepted what he could get from the League of Nations, he would obtain a foothold in Abyssinia, just the way we did in Morocco in 1907 when we landed at Casablanca.... With time, money and good negotiators, the Italians would win over the native chiefs, and the Negus himself would undoubtedly end by understanding that his personal interests would be safeguarded by an Italian protectorate."[31] Yet at the time sanctions were voted,

Mandel was considered to be "in total disagreement with Laval's pro-Italian policy."[32] Léon Bailby reported that "there is no secret at London that in case of Laval's overthrow they are counting on a Herriot-Flandin-Mandel government, clearly favorable to the Foreign Office's policy towards Italy."[33]

In the midst of the tension generated by the invasion of Abyssinia, the appeals for assassination, and the threat of a right-wing coup, Mandel decided to speak out. In the company of two prominent Radicals, Lucien Lamoureux and Finance Minister Marcel Regnier, he delivered a speech at the inauguration of a new post office at Vichy. The entire press agreed that it deserved close attention because of the rarity of his public addresses. As *L'Oeuvre* remarked, "He never speaks for the sole pleasure of speaking."[34] And in fact the papers the next day gave it precedence over the Abyssinian affair. It was probably one of the few times in history that the inauguration of a post office got bigger headlines than the current international crisis.

After paying due attention to the beauty and importance of the city of Vichy, Mandel defended his work at the PTT, justifying the complaint bureau and the sanctions he had taken by the necessity "of putting an end to the state of general irresponsibility that people are too often inclined to confuse with democracy." If the Right the following day praised this reassertion of the principle of authority, the Left took note of the comment that followed, that "the restoration of authority is in no way incompatible with the normal functioning of our liberal institutions." Both sides ignored his claim not to have been inspired by any ideology: "My only ambition has been to serve the public."

Mandel then went on to the substance of his speech, the justification of the financial measures taken by the Laval cabinet. Without them, he asserted, France would have been driven either to inflation or to devaluation. The only fault of the government had been to neglect the preparation of public opinion. Thus people did not know that besides cutting salaries by ten per cent, the decree laws had also given municipal governments the means of undertaking public works, and raised the taxes on incomes and stocks higher than they had ever been before. The measures had also ended the flight from the franc and reduced the interest rate.

Only one conclusion could be drawn: the work undertaken must be continued. In the present European situation, a truce among the French political parties was more than ever necessary—if only to assure the country a minimum of political stability. No single party was responsible for the financial crisis because every party had voted for measures that would be popular rather than measures that might have been effective. Thus the people themselves were equally responsible, and he urged them to demand that all questions affecting national defense, including finances, be treated as nonpartisan. "Only if the people learn to discipline themselves will they be able to continue to fulfill, for the good of the world, their mission of justice and human emancipation."[35]

After the speech, the press, which had waited impatiently for a clarification of Mandel's position, knew no more than before. Everyone agreed that the speech was significant, but no one was able to decide precisely what it meant. He had not even mentioned foreign affairs or the threat of the leagues, the burning questions of the moment. *Le Temps* solved the problem by calling it "the speech of a statesman." The Right generally applauded its appeal for authority and discipline, and Jacques Bainville praised Mandel for defending Laval at such a time. On the Left, *L'Humanité*, *Le Populaire*, and *Le Ralliement des PTT* saw in the speech the program of a man who sensed the imminent overthrow of Laval and was making a bid to succeed him.[36]

For *L'Oeuvre*, *L'Ami du Peuple*, and *La Nation* the important question was to determine whether it was a *discours de gauche* or a *discours de droite*. The leftist *L'Oeuvre*, like *L'Humanité*, interpreted it as a warning to the leagues that the state's authority must be respected. Louis Marin's *La Nation* was more puzzled. No doubt Mandel was "one of the pillars of order and national ideas." He belonged to the Groupe des Indépendants, "the authentic representatives of the French conservative party." Yet he was doctrinally opposed to the Right on the question of proportional representation and constitutional reform, and was often led by his penchant for maneuvers to play the game of the Left against his true friends on the Right. After weighing all the evidence, this organ of the conservative party was still unable to decide whether Mandel was *un homme de gauche* or *un homme de droite*.[37] The significant fact, of course, was that until then there had been no doubt.

What made Mandel's position even more difficult to determine was his ambiguous relationship with Laval. The day before the speech, he and Laval had travelled together to Vichy, where they spent part of the night drawing up a communiqué announcing that there had never been any question of applying military sanctions against Italy and that France and Britain would always work together.[38] At the same time as he seemed to be working so closely with him, however, Mandel was encouraging rumors that Laval, unable to carry the dual burden of the premiership and the Foreign Ministry, was thinking of turning direction of the government over to him.[39] As the *Cri du Jour* later revealed, these rumors were a hint to Laval that this was the only way he could remain at the Quai d'Orsay.[40] Foreseeing the fall of the cabinet, Mandel repeatedly warned Laval that "any separation of France from England, no matter how small . . . , would create opposition not only in the Chamber, but within the cabinet itself." France had to choose between England and Italy. While England had made many mistakes and France had good reason to be annoyed, she still could not afford to choose the weaker nation rather than the stronger.[41]

In other circumstances Mandel might have had no objection to Mussolini's campaign against Abyssinia. But once it aroused English antagonism, he believed that France was obliged to side with her former ally. Because England did not demand military sanctions, Mandel and Laval had no difficulty in agreeing on that point. But they clashed over the question of extending economic sanctions to include strategic materials[42] and over the general attitude of the government towards England. Laval was continually temporizing, hoping somehow or other to keep the friendship of both England and Italy. According to Emmanuel Berl, a frequent visitor to Mandel's office at this time, "the Minister of Posts believed that Laval was causing us to lose the friendship of England and thereby exposing us to the danger of German domination."[43]

Under constant prodding to change his policy or turn the government over to his postal minister, Laval struck back with one of the most potent weapons at hand. When the rumors that Mandel might become prime minister were repeated to him, Laval apparently retorted, "You don't really want a Jew, do you?"* Until then it had been rare in parliamentary circles for people to refer to Mandel's Jewish origins, as they often did to Blum's.[44] It would become more common thereafter.

Several years earlier when Mandel had been mentioned as a possible prime minister, Aristide Briand told a friend, "France is a Christian country. . . . She would never tolerate an Israelite at the head of the government. Moreover, Mandel is too intelligent ever to entertain such an ambition."[45] Briand of course was wrong on both counts. Blum and Mendès-France have since headed the government, and Mandel at that time still hoped to be the first Jewish prime minister of France. In what might have been an answer to Laval, the Catholic *Liberté du Sud-Ouest* of Bordeaux stated that the man who succeeded him would have to be "rightist in spirit, but have his friends on the Left." The writer suggested that in spite of objections that might be made to his Jewish origins, Mandel was the man. "Many Jews have harmed

---

* *Le Canard Enchaîné*, Nov. 20, 1935. The same story is told by Georges Gombault (as Pierre du Clain, *La Lumière*, Nov. 16, 1935), who probably heard it from Mandel himself.

A friend of Laval's recounts a milder incident of the same sort, but places it in 1939. To someone who said that Mandel would make a good prime minister, Laval replied: "No, I don't believe he has a chance, solely because he is a Jew." Mandel was infuriated by Laval's comment. See Jean Durtal, *Les coulisses de la politique* (Paris, 1966), p. 299.

our country," he wrote. "If there is one who can redress the harm and put the country back on its feet again, we would be the last to criticize him for not having belonged to the French race from the time of Clovis and the Crusades."[46]

While his friends continued the campaign of rumors against the cabinet,[47] more and more people expressed their belief that Mandel was "the coming man."[48] It was still being said, moreover, that the Radicals were willing to invest him with power in order to crush the leagues and reorient French foreign policy.[49]

The Radicals in fact held the key to the situation. Without some Radical votes, the cabinet could not last a day, but ever since Laval's investiture in June the Party had been split over the issue of supporting him. While Herriot and several other members participated in the government, the left wing of the party under Daladier worked for an entente with the Socialists and Communists. In October the party joined the Popular Front, placing Herriot in an awkward position. By all rights he should have resigned, not only because his party had now joined the opposition—at least in an electoral sense—but also because he himself opposed Laval's Italian policy. On the other hand, he supported the deflationary measures taken by the cabinet, and was afraid of the consequences of the economic policy that a left-wing government might institute. Moreover, having twice before suffered abuse for resigning from National Union governments—Poincaré's and Doumergue's—he was in no hurry to do it again. He hoped instead to have the cabinet defeated in Parliament, thus relieving him of personal responsibility for its downfall.[50]

While Herriot agonized over his dilemma for three months, Laval used all of his skills as a parliamentarian to remain in power. In December he persuaded Jean Ybarnégaray, La Rocque's assistant, to offer to disarm the Croix de Feu if the leftist groups would also renounce recourse to arms. There was a momentary reconciliation of Right and Left, which temporarily settled the issue of the leagues, and incidentally eliminated any need to summon Mandel to suppress the Fascists.

Simultaneously, Laval negotiated an agreement with Sir Samuel Hoare, the British foreign minister, to settle the Abyssinian crisis. He proposed ceding a large portion of Abyssinia to Italy and guaranteeing her economic control over the rest. The premature revelation of these terms by the press, however, caused a furor in England that forced Hoare to resign and Prime Minister Baldwin to repudiate the plan. It is sometimes said that except for the leak, Laval might have settled the crisis and been able to continue in power. But the Abyssinian emperor was certain to oppose the plan, and Herriot, outraged by it, became convinced of the necessity to resign.[51] At the same time Mandel became convinced of the necessity to get rid of Laval. Through his friend Georges Wormser, he encouraged the Radical deputy Yvon Delbos to attack Laval's ambiguous foreign policy and sketched the line of argumentation that he should adopt.[52] Delbos' speech on December 27 was well received by the Chamber, as were similar interventions by Léon Blum and Paul Reynaud, but Laval still managed to secure a slight majority in the vote which followed. He was able to hold out until Herriot and three other Radicals finally withdrew from the government on January 22, leaving Laval no other choice but to resign.

The Right and Center were furious at the defeat of the man who best represented their policies, and they were also afraid, just three months before the elections, of being held responsible for all the unpopular measures they had passed jointly with the Radicals during the preceding two years. They hoped, therefore, to force the Popular Front to take power, rendering it responsible on the eve of the elections for all the difficulties of the moment. Failing this, they intended to prevent the formation of an amorphous Center government in order to force the Radicals to join a new government with Laval.[53]

For the Radicals, the resolution of Herriot's personal dilemma confronted the Party with a greater one. They wanted to retain control of the government for the elections, but could not do so without the participation of either the Socialists or some conservatives. A purely Radical cabinet, merely supported by the Socialists, would have placed the party in the ridiculous position of demanding reforms from a government that they themselves controlled. Although Blum announced that he was willing to form a Popular Front government, no one took him seriously.[54] The only alternative to another Laval cabinet, therefore, was a caretaker government in which conservative ministers provided the necessary aura of nonpartisanship.

It was Mandel who frustrated the plans of the Right and Center and helped the Radicals resolve their dilemma. After Herriot and Yvon Delbos had refused to form a cabinet, President Lebrun summoned a third Radical, Albert Sarraut, who had conferred with Mandel in advance and left all the negotiating up to him. Working through the night, Mandel, with the help of Flandin, had a coalition formed by morning. It was basically a Radical government, enlarged on one wing by the inclusion of three independent Socialists, and on the other by the participation of Flandin, Mandel, and several other conservative deputies who joined it against the advice of their parties. The entire press from *Je Suis Partout* to *Le Populaire* agreed that the Minister of Posts was the linchpin of the combination. It was called "Mandel's government" and Sarraut was referred to as "his delegate at the premier's office."[55]

The question arises, of course, why Mandel was so anxious to form a government and thereby save the Radicals from the consequences of their own disunity. One reason, Mandel said, was his friendship for Sarraut, whom he had served as *chef de cabinet* thirty years earlier: "I had typhoid when I was twenty-two years old, and Albert Sarraut came to see me twice a day. I was no one at that time."[56] A more satisfactory explanation, to the Right at least, was that Mandel wanted to influence the elections. Although the conservatives did not get the ministry of the Interior, Mandel pointed out that a conservative (Flandin) was to be foreign minister. Thus the conservatives would control the secret funds always granted to him and to the High Commissioner for Alsace-Lorraine, an office Mandel himself took over in addition to the PTT. With the ministries of Agriculture and Health in their possession as well, the conservatives would be able to subsidize their friends. "If we had had a homogeneous Radical government dominated by the Socialists," Mandel asked, "what would have happened? Considering the way the administrative machinery functions, ... the conservatives would have been massacred. The elections will not be good, that's certain, but they will not be as bad as they would have been otherwise."[57]

There is no account of what Mandel told the Radicals, but he was undoubtedly thinking of what would happen after the leftist coalition broke up. Mandel was as certain as everyone else that there would be a Popular Front government after the elections, but he was also certain that it would not last indefinitely. By helping to form Sarraut's government, and thus gaining the confidence of the Radicals and Socialists, he was reserving a prominent place for himself in the broad coalition he was convinced would follow the collapse of the Popular Front. In November already, *Le Cri du Jour* had quoted a Center deputy: "After May we are going to have a very left-wing government, which, following the normal rhythm of French political life, will be succeeded by a government of concentration. That will be the real Mandel government, for only he will be able to repair the damage done by the Extreme Left in power."[58]

Mandel may also have hoped that the results of the elections would be ambiguous. In that case, conservative Radicals, who had only halfheartedly accepted the alliance with the Communists, might be induced to desert the Popular Front in sufficient numbers to support a Center coalition.[59] In fact, according to François Piétri, who became naval minister, the whole purpose of the Sarraut government was to destroy the Popular Front in advance by attracting the support of these Radicals.[60]

The formation of the Sarraut government was the most complex of all Mandel's maneuvers. While still attempting to act as a bridge between the Right and the Left, he hoped to salvage some seats for the conservatives, possibly break up the Popular Front, and at the same time ingratiate himself with the Radicals, thus improving his own position as well. It is hard to say which factor predominated in his plans: tactics, strategy, or ambition. His diverse aims may not have been contradictory, but they left him open to the charge of duplicity from both sides of the political fence. In the circumstances, the Radicals refrained from expressing any suspicions they might have had, but some rightists, whose plans Mandel had frustrated, furiously denounced him as a traitor.[61] *L'Action Française* suddenly recalled his Jewish origins and asserted that "to trust Alsace-Lorraine to a Jew could be dangerous for our prestige in the recovered provinces."[62] *Le Canard Enchaîné* and *Marianne* noted that on the Right, "when Georges Mandel was a Lavalist, he was called an Israelite. . . . But now that he has become a Sarrautist, he is a dirty kike. . . . They are beginning to say that he gets too much publicity. Soon they will admit that the telephones worked even before he came to power."[63]

That some of his former friends attacked Mandel was not surprising, for feelings were running high among the conservatives, who foresaw defeat for themselves and victory for the Marxists in the coming elections. The remarkable fact, as one journalist noted, was that whereas Flandin was vehemently denounced, "Mandel, who was really responsible for the success of the cabinet, was treated with a good deal of caution."[64] Men like Pierre Taittinger, Philippe Henriot, and Henri de Kérillis furiously attacked the cabinet and advised their friends to vote against it, but refrained from attacking Mandel personally.[65] Jacques Bainville, who died in February, retained confidence in Mandel to the end, approving of his actions on this occasion.[66] By keeping substantial personal support on the Right while effecting a rapprochement with the Left, Mandel had accomplished an undeniable *tour de force*. He might still hope someday to bridge the ever-widening gap between the conservatives and the Popular Front.

III

The first major act of the Sarraut government was to submit the Franco-Soviet mutual assistance treaty to Parliament for ratification. Although Laval had signed the treaty in May 1935, he had put off submitting it for fear of antagonizing the Germans. In contrast, the Sarraut government, despite indications that Hitler would use ratification as a pretext to remilitarize the Rhineland, and without having decided on what countermeasures France should take, immediately brought the bill up before the Chamber. The cabinet seems to have believed that further delay would only make the Russians suspicious of French intentions, and encourage German belief in French weakness.

The ratification of the treaty, however, exacerbated internal divisions in

France. A portion of the Right, including the Action Française, had always denounced the pact. Their opposition stemmed from the belief that any war would be disastrous for France, leading either to German hegemony or to Communist expansion in Europe.[67] After the formation of the Popular Front, the entire Right and Center lined up behind the Action Française because they feared that a government dominated by the Socialists and the Communists might drag France into a war for the preservation of Soviet Russia.[68] Their suspicions were only confirmed when Parliament ratified the pact on February 27, 1936, by a massive left-wing majority, including the Communists, who had given the government their qualified support since its investiture.

Conservative opposition to the pact and to the Sarraut cabinet itself meant that the government was in no position to rally the country behind it when the German army marched into the Rhineland on March 7. Nor was it in any position to react immediately to the reoccupation, even though warnings had been coming in for months from French diplomats in Germany. Because the Quai d'Orsay treated his dispatches apathetically, the Consul in Cologne, Jean Dobler, came to Paris in January to see Mandel. "He had the reputation of being a determined man," said Dobler, "and I wanted to meet a determined man." Thereafter the Consul reported to Mandel on the situation in Germany, sometimes sending him duplicate copies of his telegrams to the Foreign Office. On February 23 he wrote a personal letter advising Mandel of Germany's definite decision to reoccupy the Rhineland.[69] Surprisingly enough, there is no evidence that Mandel did anything with this information, any more than did the French General Staff, which was also receiving warnings. Solely preoccupied since 1919 with questions of defense, the General Staff was reluctant to prepare even a limited offensive against Germany. Thus, when Hitler's army entered the Rhineland, France was both politically and militarily unprepared to act.

On the morning of March 7 Sarraut summoned General Maurin, the minister of War, and General Gamelin, the commander in chief, to a special meeting, also attended by Flandin, Paul-Boncour, and Mandel, who was regarded by other members of the cabinet as Sarraut's *éminence grise*.[70] He and Flandin were the Prime Minister's preferred advisers throughout the crisis.[71] According to Gamelin, Paul-Boncour and Mandel were determined to respond to Germany decisively and with force if necessary. But at that initial meeting the discussion was limited to generalities.[72] An appeal for support was made to the Locarno powers, and a few precautionary measures such as alerting the railroads and recalling soldiers on leave were ordered, but no decision was made to resort to force. It was understood that this question would have to be discussed by a plenary session of the cabinet.

At the cabinet meeting on March 8,[73] according to one account, Mandel declared:

If we permit this provocation to go unanswered, Hitler will feel confident that he can try anything with impunity. And he will try everything. A year ago he reestablished compulsory military service. Today he is erasing the last of the Military Clauses of the Treaty of Versailles. Be careful! The decision we are called upon to make will be a historic one, for if we tolerate the Chancellor's present move, we shall be denying ourselves the right to intervene in the future. We shall then no longer be in a position to give aid to the States we have promised to help. And we shall be obliged to reorient our entire foreign policy.... A military setback would almost certainly have serious repercussions within Germany—and that might very well mean the beginning of the end of Hitler.[74]

General Maurin, however, explained that France had no troops ready to undertake an expedition into the Rhineland, and that before anything could be done three classes of reserves would have to be called up. If Germany offered any resistance, he said, general mobilization would then have to be decreed. He made it clear that he was opposed to mobilization because he thought it would bring about a war, for which the French army was not prepared.

There is some dispute about the reaction of the ministers that day, but the only firm decision taken was to bring a complaint before the League of Nations. According to Foreign Minister Flandin, most of the cabinet "feared that energetic measures by the government might create a threat of war at a time when the mood of the country was, above all, pacific." In short, everyone was thinking what effect any action might have on the elections.[75] Flandin thus blamed the other ministers for the failure to act, but Mandel blamed Flandin himself because he did not attempt to impose a decision on the cabinet. After Maurin's exposition, Mandel said, the Foreign Minister turned to Sarraut and commented: "I see that there is nothing that can be done."[76] In Mandel's view, as he later said, the French army should have been mobilized, but "it was asking too much of Sarraut and Flandin.... It would have meant a break with the Socialists, who were opposed to mobilization, and who demanded that the opening of the electoral campaign not be deferred."[77]

Yet, despite this criticism of Flandin and Sarraut, over whom Mandel apparently did not exercise as much influence as many people assumed, for some reason he still believed on March 8 that France was going to take steps to repulse the Germans. On leaving the cabinet meeting, he told his entourage: "We are going to act. There was bitter discussion in the cabinet. We had to combat the military imbeciles who do not want to fight....

Sarraut is going to speak over the radio tonight in terms we have agreed on together, and after which there will be no going back."[78] Sarraut's speech that night contained the famous phrase: "France is not disposed to leave Strasbourg under the threat of German cannon." It was calculated to arouse French public opinion and it did at least succeed in frightening the Germans.[79] Mandel now began to urge Sarraut to follow his words with action. The German chargé d'affaires in France reported that Mandel and his supporters wanted

to go to the limit in resisting the Third Reich, including, if necessary, the use of armed force. They believe that, faced with such a threat, Germany could not stand firm. Germany's financial and economic position is held to be extremely weak, and her military preparations incomplete. In their opinion, the internal political situation in Germany is also very tense; they are convinced that Germany's action was taken against the will of the responsible economic, foreign affairs and military authorities, and that this supposed opposition is bound to react to Germany's disadvantage as the situation develops. The supporters of this point of view are thinking in the first place of a diplomatic struggle *à l'outrance*, including, if necessary, a threat to Britain that France will withdraw from the League of Nations. As a last expedient there is also talk of military action by France without the active participation of Britain; this might be initiated by an ultimatum demanding the withdrawal of troops from the Rhineland zone.[80]

For several days Sarraut met with the military leaders to see what action short of mobilization could be taken. But they hemmed and hawed and insisted that nothing could be done unless the government was prepared for full mobilization if necessary.[81] Pleas for British support were equally fruitless. Finally, after having had a chance to assess public reaction, the government concluded that neither from the press, nor the Parliament, nor the public, nor France's allies would the necessary support for forceful measures be forthcoming. Sarraut and Flandin therefore bowed to the inevitable and accepted the German remilitarization of the Rhineland. This failure to act doomed France's system of alliances. It led ultimately to the *Anschluss*, the annexation of Czechoslovakia, and the invasion of Poland. It eliminated the great advantage France had enjoyed since 1919 of being able to put troops immediately on German soil to counter any attack against her eastern allies. Henceforth, she would be able only to watch helplessly from behind the Maginot Line while Germany devoured her allies one by one.

Despite his belief that France had reached a turning point, Mandel too accepted the inevitable and did nothing to arouse resistance once it became evident that the government would limit itself to verbal protests. He even praised Flandin, who returned from a meeting of the Locarno powers in London with a British promise to aid France in case of aggression, and to coordinate military plans in the future by arranging joint staff conversations.[82] "What he brought back from London is positive," said Mandel, "and we must know how to profit from it, contrary to what we have done so many times. The battle is not over: we will only lose it if we relax our vigilance a single day."[83]

It was all very well to talk of not relaxing vigilance, but France had just suffered her gravest defeat since the war, and Mandel proposed to do nothing about it. He does not even seem to have considered resigning. One could well ask if this was the legendary Mandel, Clemenceau's dictatorial *chef de cabinet*, who overrode objections and brooked no opposition, who believed that governing was just a question of will power? Was this the man who insisted that "the best means of governing is to tell the truth to people, no matter how unpalatable it may be"?[84]

According to Georges Wormser, one reason for his caution was his unwillingness to embarrass Albert Sarraut, in whom he had more confidence than in many other leaders. Another reason, Wormser suspects, may have been a desire to retain his cabinet position for the forthcoming elections. But Wormser concludes that Mandel's political isolation and his Jewishness were probably the most important factors in preventing him from trying to lead a campaign against Nazi Germany in the face of a reluctant General Staff and a public opinion almost totally opposed to adopting forceful measures.[85]

Public reaction to any suggestion that France march against Germany had been extremely adverse. All the conservatives were hostile to any measure that might lead to war "for the profit of Moscow."[86] The Left wanted economic sanctions at most,[87] and even *L'Humanité* affirmed that "only the coordinated peaceful action of the powers can defeat Nazi Germany's use of force."[88] The Christian Democratic review *Politique* sang a refrain that would be repeated more frequently and more insistently in the years to come: "If we were going to start a preventive war, we should have done it earlier when the situation was infinitely more favorable."[89]

Mandel was personally attacked for wanting to drag France into war.[90] Colonel de la Rocque declared that while he hated anti-Semitism, he was nonetheless keeping an eye on some Jews in high places.[91] Mandel's friends in the press who had earlier reported him as favorable to decisive action against Germany, now began to backtrack. Emmanuel Berl's *Marianne* denied the rumors being spread about the Minister of Posts by "Hitlerophiles and anti-Semites."

If Mandel had wanted France to seize guarantees and take securities in reaction to Germany's diplomatic aggression, he would have shown himself to be the heir of Clemenceau rather than the descendant of Solomon. But the fact is that Georges Mandel did not demand the mobilization of four classes in the council of ministers and the rumors spread to that effect are absolutely false.[92]

It was true that Mandel had not asked for the mobilization of four classes "in the council of ministers." Maurin's demand for the mobilization of three classes, if anything was to be done, had shocked the cabinet and had not even been seriously discussed. But there is no doubt that Mandel favored military intervention of some sort and privately encouraged Flandin and Sarraut to take action. The disclaimer was mere quibbling.

Mandel has often been described as intransigent, but the term more properly applies to his ends, not to his means, which were subject to infinite variations. The question he had to ask himself was whether he could achieve more by remaining in the cabinet and working quietly toward bolstering France's security, or by departing noisily in an attempt to arouse public opinion. He seems to have concluded that the French people were so thoroughly opposed to taking action against Germany that his resignation not only would have had no effect, but might even have encouraged an anti-Semitic movement.

Although Mandel may have been intransigent, he was never quixotic. In January the Right had openly warned him that if he acted against Laval or collaborated with the Left, his future career would suffer.[93] He ignored these threats because he believed that France would fare better under Sarraut and because he knew that he could form the government. In March, however, he refused to risk the anger of the country by a dramatic but useless and possibly harmful resignation. He may have been wrong, but even after thirty years it is difficult to see what his withdrawal from the cabinet might have accomplished.

12. The Popular Front

*Votre arrivée au pouvoir, M. le Président du Conseil, est incontestablement
une date historique. Pour la première fois, ce vieux pays gallo-romain
sera gouverné par un juif. . . . J'ajoute que, contrairement aux espérances
de M. Jéroboam Rothschild, il ne se sera pas appelé Georges Mandel.*

Xavier Vallat

LESS THAN A MONTH after the remilitarization of the Rhineland, the
French Parliament recessed on schedule to allow its members to campaign
for the elections. In Lesparre, despite Mandel's participation in a largely
Radical government, the local section of the Party united with the Socialists
to present a single candidate against him. They were joined by the Alliance
Démocratique, which told its supporters to "take anyone but him."[1] In 1928,
when the three parties had presented separate candidates, Mandel won on
the second ballot with a thirty-five-vote majority. In 1932, realizing that
disunity would assure his reelection, the Center had decided to support the
Radical candidate. Mandel won on the second ballot with a 132-vote majority. In 1936, in desperation, the Radical, Socialist, and Center parties held
a joint meeting on February 23, presided over by Paul Vigneau, Mandel's
secretary from 1916 to 1923. They decided to present only one candidate, the
Socialist mayor of Pauillac, Dominique Garby. The Communists promised
to vote for him on the second ballot.[2]

Despite the heated atmosphere elsewhere in France, where Popular Front
candidates squared off against their National Front adversaries, Mandel had
one of the most uneventful campaigns of his career. He was of course called
a Fascist, but his opponents campaigned largely on local issues.[3] Paul Vigneau's paper asked,

What difference does it make to winegrowers like us that Mandel devotes himself to politics and nothing but politics, that he spends his time discrediting a
minister in order to take his place, that he mounts the tribune to speak of armaments in order to increase the business of his friends the armaments manufacturers, who put him in as minister? All that doesn't mean anything to us, and
it was not for this reason that the people of the Médoc sent him to the Chamber.[4]

Mandel spoke almost exclusively on foreign affairs. One reporter noted
that "to an audience composed mostly of vineyard workers and artisans,
he explained the great problems of the day as if he were at the tribune of
the Chamber. It was not a campaign speech but a lecture on high policy."[5]
He called for union among Frenchmen and warned his audience that the

only way to maintain peace was to be able to ensure it if necessary by themselves.[6] At the end of his speeches, only a few people approached him to offer their congratulations. They applauded and respected him but there was little of the warmth and friendliness usually shown to candidates.[7]

In his more than fifty speeches about high policy, however, Mandel did not forget that his listeners were people who also had more immediate concerns. He always took care to answer the charge that he had done nothing for the region. "I have had more credits accorded to this area," he told them, "than the other twelve districts of the Gironde have received." As a reporter said after one of his speeches, "he proved once again that he was a statesman *de grande classe*. . . . But he did not disdain to recall that he was also a useful and influential deputy."[8]

In this election Mandel did not have to contend with the opposition of the regional press. Renouncing neutrality, the Catholic *Liberté de Sud-Ouest* supported him, and *La Petite Gironde* also came back to the camp of the man whose name it had sworn ten years earlier never to mention again. Backed by the important local dailies, and sustained by his prestige as minister, Mandel easily defeated his Socialist opponent on the first ballot by 8,514 to 6,217, winning every canton except Garby's own Pauillac. His victory was all the more remarkable in that the Popular Front won nine of the thirteen seats in the Gironde.

Elsewhere in France, the moderate parties—the Radicals and the Center—lost heavily, the Right maintained its strength, but the Socialists jumped from 97 to 146 deputies and the Communists from 10 to 72. As the head of the largest party in the Chamber, Léon Blum formed the new government with Radical participation and Communist support.

The decisive left-wing victory meant of course that Mandel would have to leave office. The leftist leaders may have regarded him as a good republican, but the rank and file still considered him to be the worst of reactionaries. In February some Monarchists attending the funeral of Jacques Bainville had pulled Léon Blum from an automobile and given him a severe beating. The government then dissolved the Action Française organizations, and the Left held a massive demonstration on February 16 to protest against the attack on Blum. Uniformed postal workers turned out in large numbers and noisily shouted "Hang Mandel!" ("Mandel au poteau!").[9]

During the electoral campaign, the national union of the PTT workers had denounced Mandel in a seventy-two page tract that was widely distributed and widely quoted in the leftist press.[10] After the victory of the Popular Front, the National Council of Postal Employees loudly celebrated his anticipated departure. When Mandel's successor, the Socialist Robert Jardillier, arrived at the Rue de Grenelle, the workers sang the *Internation-*

ale and then accompanied the new minister to his office. The demonstration had been arranged by Robert Quénot, the technical director of the PTT, who had remained in office under Mandel but had seen his authority curtailed by a minister who really ruled instead of letting himself be controlled by the permanent officials of the administration.

When Mandel left his office, the workers still surrounded the door and lined the staircase down to the street. Mandel departed alone and passed smilingly through the jeering mob. As he entered his car and drove away, the workers once again held up their clenched fists and sang the refrains of the *Internationale*.[11]

The celebration of the National Council and the demonstration at the PTT caused even some of the left-wing journals to protest. *Notre Temps* remarked that although Mandel could not be considered one of their political friends, "for a long time now he has not been counted among those whom one facilely calls 'enemies of democracy.' " The Left should have had the objectivity to recognize that he had been an excellent minister who would be difficult to replace. It would no longer be possible to put just anyone at the head of the PTT, for he had turned it into an important ministry.[12]

Mandel took advantage of his freedom from ministerial responsibilities to visit Holland, Belgium, and England in the summer of 1936, and Italy and Switzerland the following year.[13] His companion on these trips was Madame Béatrice Bretty of the *Comédie Française*, whom he had met in 1935 while he was head of the French radio and television system. Thereafter Madame Bretty always went with him to dinners and public functions. She also took charge of raising his six-year-old daughter Claude, of whose existence almost no one had been aware until that time.[14]

Once called "the monk of politics" by Tardieu, Mandel was now one of the prize dinner guests in Paris. He had always been welcome in the homes of the Rothschilds and other wealthy conservatives,[15] but after becoming a minister, he moved in a much wider circle of friends and acquaintances. Together with his former archenemy Joseph Caillaux, he often dined with Emile Roche, editor of the Radical *République*,[16] and he became a regular guest at the home of Geneviève Tabouis, whose articles were published in another left-wing journal, *L'Oeuvre*. Madame Tabouis thought to score one of the minor social successes of 1936 by inviting Mandel, Maurice Thorez, and Gabriel Péri, the foreign affairs editor of *L'Humanité*, to a luncheon party. But when Mandel arrived, the two Communists hurriedly left, explaining that "M. Mandel is a great enemy of our party. Really, we cannot possibly sit down at the same table with him."[17]

Simultaneously, he achieved international prominence, becoming one of the French politicians most often sought out by visiting dignitaries. For his part, he tried to meet as many foreign diplomats, statesmen and journalists as possible in order to impress on them the growing danger from Nazi Germany.[18] At his office, he received the international financier Basil Zaharoff, the Archduke Otto of Austria, Lloyd George of England, and Foreign Minister Antonesco, Ambassador Titulesco, and King Carol of Rumania, who awarded Mandel the Grand Croix de l'Etoile.[19] He could be found at the American Embassy with Herriot, Reynaud, Czech Ambassador Stefan Osusky, and Spanish Defense Minister Alvarez del Vayo; or at small British Embassy dinners in honor of Winston Churchill with Daladier, Flandin, Reynaud, Chautemps, and Alexis Léger, the permanent secretary at the Quai d'Orsay;[20] or at the home of Senator Maurice Rothschild with the Russian Ambassador or the Duke of Windsor.[21]

By 1936, it might be said, Mandel had finally arrived. He even left his rooms at 72 avenue Mozart, where he had moved in 1908 so as to be close to Clemenceau, for a more fashionable apartment at 67 avenue Victor Hugo. After being an outsider for so long, within two years he had obtained everything but the official position of a national leader. It seemed likely that the breakup of the Popular Front, whenever it occurred, would give him even that.

II

The Popular Front had won primarily because of internal problems. The electoral collaboration of Radicals, Socialists, and Communists, the threat to the Republic from the "Fascist" Right, the economic crisis, the widespread discontent with Laval's decree laws, and the denunciation of the "gun merchants" and the "Two Hundred Families" reputed to control the French economy, all helped bring about a left-wing majority. But the electoral campaign had two unfortunate results: attention was riveted on internal issues when the greatest danger was external; and the nation was divided into two irreconcilable blocs on the basis of those internal issues, making national unity on foreign affairs almost impossible.

When the Communists and other leftist elements became the leading proponents of resistance to Germany, the Right began to reevaluate its traditional nationalistic anti-German policy. Many conservatives concluded that it would be impossible for France to be really victorious in a war against Germany, for the defeat of her ancient enemy would only lead to the spread of Communism across Europe. They were driven by their own logic to the conclusion that France must avoid war with Germany at all costs.

Mandel was caught between the extremes. "Politically," he said, "I am with the Left on foreign affairs, but I support the Right on internal policy.

How can I reconcile these divergences when I do not want to change any of my convictions?"[22] Actually, Mandel never had any difficulty in subordinating internal affairs to national interests. He had begun his career as a Radical and could easily have remained in that amorphous party after 1919. Instead, with Clemenceau, he had shifted to the Right because of its overriding concern with national security. The shift was clear, decisive, and irrevocable, for he took his seat with the Groupe des Indépendants, called by Louis Marin's *Nation* "the authentic representatives of the conservative party in France." It was his firmest conviction, as he repeatedly told Poincaré in those years, that "the orientation of foreign policy is always determined by the orientation of internal policy."[23]

Logically, then, his concern with national security should now have brought him into closer alliance with the Left, which for ideological reasons was becoming the center of resistance to Germany. Practically, because the workers had classified him as an utter reactionary, this was impossible. More important was the fact that a government of Socialists and Communists, inspired by ideological rather than national considerations, tended to throw the Right into opposition to a policy of resistance to Germany. What Mandel wanted to do was unite the new anti-Nazism of the Left with the traditional anti-Germanism of the Right, which could only be achieved by someone who had the confidence of both sides. He hoped that the Left, which respected his republicanism and now tended to agree with his policy of opposing Germany, and the Right, which recognized him as a conservative and still admired his authoritarian temperament, would eventually agree to accept him as the leader of a National Union government formed to confront the danger from Germany. Before such a realignment could take place, however, the Popular Front would have to run its course. He would have to wait until events should focus attention once again on the threat from Germany.

When Mandel returned from his vacation in Holland in the summer of 1936, France was in the process of a rapid and almost revolutionary transformation. The victory of the Popular Front had caused a flight from the franc, and brought about a massive sit-down strike by the workers even before Blum could take over the government. The strike movement was the largest and longest France had ever known, involving at its peak more than a million workers, and lasting several months. The workers made many immediate gains: collective bargaining, a forty-hour week, paid vacations, and wage increases. But they achieved these gains at the price of thoroughly frightening the conservatives. The reforms also increased production costs, reducing exports to a new low and slowing down the manufacture of weapons just when French rearmament was getting under way.

Mandel did not systematically oppose the Popular Front government. He abstained on a number of important issues—the investiture of the cabinet, paid vacations, collective bargaining, and the forty-hour week—voted for the bill authorizing the government to nationalize any industry engaged in the production of armaments, and voted against the devaluation of the currency that Blum was forced to carry out in September in spite of campaign promises to the contrary. Aside from his votes in Parliament, however, Mandel's public role was negligible. After the elections in 1936, he shunned publicity as diligently as he had previously sought it. He later explained that "if I had spoken in the Chamber, I would no doubt have had some influence. I might have persuaded a few deputies to change their votes, but it would have made no difference. A speech has significance only as a means of action."[24] In the circumstances, he did not believe that speeches would have any effect on the deputies or on the country. "Born of a movement of discontent," he said, "the Popular Front will not be overthrown by ballots, but by events."[25]

The one thing he did do while waiting for events to discredit the new government was to attempt to reorient public opinion on the Right. In September 1936, with Pierre-Etienne Flandin as a silent partner, he acquired control of *L'Ami du Peuple*.[26] This Paris daily had been founded in 1928 by the perfume manufacturer François Coty, who had used it as an organ for the group he regarded as his personal antiparliamentary league, Jean Renaud's Solidarité Française. Since 1935 it had been owned by another leading antiparliamentarian, Pierre Taittinger, head of the Jeunesses Patriotes. Taittinger's column on the front page was replaced by a daily editorial signed *AP*, inspired and closely reviewed by Mandel, but written by Pierre Lafue, who had first collaborated with Mandel on the illustrated weekly *1933*, and then followed him to the Ministry of Posts as speech writer.[27]

If it was strange that Mandel should acquire one of the leading antiparliamentary journals, it was stranger still that Pierre Taittinger and Jean Renaud, though no longer entitled to the front page, continued to contribute articles to it. One might conclude from Mandel's association with these leading antiparliamentarians either that he was not so great a defender of parliamentary institutions as he pretended to be or that these right-wing extremists were not so great a danger to the Republic as the Left feared. Mandel had never shared that fear and obviously still thought of the league supporters as a part of the national community whose collaboration was essential to meet the increasing danger from Germany.

Mandel bought *L'Ami du Peuple* in order to counter the "defeatist" influence of conservative journals such as *Le Matin* and *Le Jour*. He wanted

to revive patriotism on the Right, to recall the conservatives to their traditional preoccupation with national security, and to strengthen in them the
desire to resist German aggression. Yet, probably because he was afraid of
being discredited in moderate and left-wing circles,[28] he never publicly
acknowledged ownership of the journal. The most important fact, however,
is that he obviously still enjoyed the respect of men like Taittinger even after
such issues as sanctions against Italy and the formation of the Sarraut cabinet
which had temporarily separated him from the Right and driven him
toward the Left.

L'Ami du Peuple had once been a formidable rival to the five great Paris
dailies. But after Coty's death in 1934, the paper's circulation sank from a
peak of 700,000 to 300,000 under Taittinger in 1935 and to 120,000 by the
time Mandel obtained control in September 1936. Nevertheless, with 120,000
readers of whom 40,000 were subscribers, *L'Ami du Peuple* was still an important journal. Mandel retained most of the former staff, which included
the Monarchists Simon Arbellot and Louis Truc, and François Hulot, a
member of the Jeunesses Patriotes and the founder of the anti-Semitic
Porc-Epic.[29] But he also changed *L'Ami du Peuple* from a party organ into
a newspaper—biased perhaps, but no more so than the other large papers
in Paris. No longer were Taittinger's, Hulot's and Renaud's voices the only
ones heard in its columns. Georges Suarez, Léon Treich, Gaetan Sanvoisin,
Augur, the diplomatic correspondent of the London *Times*, and other professional journalists were hired. Literary and political figures such as
Georges Goyau, André Bellesort, Germain-Martin, and Fernand Laurent
were commissioned to write articles. Special week-end supplements on the
movies, radio, the theater, fashion and sports were added. While trying
to keep the old readers, Mandel was broadening the paper's appeal.

From the beginning, however, he was plagued by administrative and
financial difficulties. As editor-in-chief he hired Louis Thomas of *Le Cri
du Jour*,[30] who lasted less than a month, being replaced at the end of October
by a Pierre or Robert Dubard, who in turn was succeeded in December by
a Belgian journalist named Koister. Mandel never found the editor who
could turn *L'Ami du Peuple* into a popular journal. His financial manage-
ment of the paper was equally unsuccessful. Charles Michelson, formerly
of Emile Roche's *La République*, was the first director. According to Louis
Truc, it was Michelson who assured the paper the financial support of a
group of industrialists from the north.[31] When he was replaced after several
months by Martial Louit, a friend of Mandel from the Gironde and a former assistant at the Ministry of Posts, the industrialists withdrew their
support, and the paper encountered serious problems. There was talk for a
time of merging it with Léon Bailby's *Le Jour*.[32] Eventually the special sup-

plements were eliminated, and the number of editions and the size of the paper reduced. Finally in October 1937, just a year after Mandel had assumed control, the paper closed its doors. Mandel's self-appointed task of revitalizing and reorienting opinion on the Right had been hopeless from the start. People were too upset by internal problems to be swayed by his rational exposition of the danger from Germany.

Even at his best, he never approached Clemenceau as a journalist, but the daily editorials in *L'Ami du Peuple* show his intelligent and informed concern for French national security. These articles are also the only guide to his thought during this period. The stream of information about him which had flooded Paris papers for years had been shut off at the source after Mandel left the Ministry of Posts. For a year, *L'Ami du Peuple* was his almost exclusive means of propaganda and received the same minute attention he gave to all of his activities. He closely watched its content, having all political commentary read to him over the telephone each day before the paper went to press. Louis Truc, who spent twenty to thirty minutes each day in this fashion, said that "when I hung up, I was sweating. I felt as if I'd been talking to a cobra."[33]

Mandel had continued the paper's policy of attacking the domestic program of the Popular Front. His principal criticism was that it divided the nation into two warring camps. "Based on the class struggle, generating hate and mistrust, [it] is leading the country to a catastrophe that can destroy the regime."[34] The spirit of discord was exemplified by the vicious attack of the Extreme Right on Minister of the Interior Roger Salengro, who had forbidden the Right to hold public meetings. In retaliation he was accused of having deserted during the war. A special army commission found Salengro innocent of the charge, but the calumny had been too much for the lonely and childless Minister of the Interior, whose wife had died the previous year. He committed suicide on November 17, 1936.

Mandel blamed both sides for the tragedy. The advocates of class struggle who had never refrained from slanderous attacks on their opponents were now reaping what they had sown. In a milder tone, he advised Salengro's enemies, if they really had the best interests of the country in mind, to remember the need for internal harmony in the face of the external danger threatening France.[35]

Mandel considered Blum incapable of imposing order on the nation and bitterly inquired of him: "What good is it to be head of the government, if you don't intend to govern?"[36] Worst of all, the government's lack of authority had an unfortunate effect on French foreign policy. Mandel believed that "internal order is an absolute necessity for the security and honor of France. . . . Pan-Germanism frightens people, but Communism horrifies them. Posing as the champion of order, Germany ... can gain the sympathy of states which, not being on her borders, do not feel immediately threatened. Others will submit to Germany, despairing of obtaining aid from a France they believe on the verge of disintegration."[37] In order to resist, France had to be strong, which was not possible "as long as a disastrous economic and financial policy prolongs internal instability and prevents the union of all Frenchmen."[38]

He also objected to the foreign policy of the Popular Front, which he believed was guided by party politics rather than by concern for national security.[39] At the beginning of the Spanish Civil War in July 1936, Blum's first inclination was to help the Spanish Republican forces, but he was restrained by British disapproval and by fear of precipitating war throughout Europe, and finally decided on a policy of nonintervention. His government, however, could not refrain from expressing its sympathy with the Republican forces, and doing what it could in an unofficial and unobtrusive way to aid them.

Like Winston Churchill, whose reactions were remarkably similar to his own during these years, Mandel at first approved the policy of nonintervention. By 1938, again like Churchill, when it seemed that Germany and Italy would turn Spain into an Axis base, Mandel came to favor aid to the Republicans. At the beginning, however, he warned that if France became involved, "we would be heading straight for a war, and a war without the aid of the English, for they do not want to see the Spanish War spread across the Pyrenees.... In this battle of two extremist mystiques, the democracies should not interfere." France must keep a cool head and defend her national interests.[40]

When Italian and German aid to the nationalists tipped the balance in their favor, he still opposed direct intervention to save the Republic: "If we must fight, it will be for ourselves and not for the *Frente Popular*." But he wanted France and England to warn Germany that they would not tolerate "a virtual invasion of Spain by the Reich. That is the only language Hitler can understand. On this issue our own interests are involved. We do not want a second frontier with Germany."[41] The two democracies had to determine whether or not Germany and Italy intended to make a military ally of Spain. If so, French lines of communication with North Africa as well as British sea routes to parts of her empire would be under the control of the dictators. London and Paris could not permit that for one second.[42]

Mandel could see only one way to force the Axis powers out of Spain and and that was for France to become the strongest power in Europe and show herself resolved to resist their territorial ambitions. "We must at last organize resistance to pan-Germanism. We must fill the gaps in our system of alliances, reinforce it and give it its full value by concluding military accords. We will thereby gain the aid of Italy and we will pay less dearly at Berlin for the right to live in peace."[43] This was not to be a "croisade des démocraties," as his opponents claimed. He rejected "any idea of a crusade, whether anti-Bolshevik or anti-Fascist. The internal regime of foreign countries is of little concern to us. Our own gives us enough to worry about. We are ready to conclude an alliance with anyone who wants to defend us and we are ready to fight anyone who wants to attack us."[44]

These words applied particularly to Italy. Although he had favored sanctions against Italy during the Abyssinian war, he still hoped not so much to win as to force Italy over to France's side. He did not share the Left's instinctive repugnance for the Fascist dictatorship, and criticized Blum for having denounced Fascism at a public meeting. "Whatever may be our sentiments toward the dictatorial governments or our judgment of Mussolini's policies, we must not forget that Fascism is the regular form of government in Italy.... The tone of public speeches has risen to such a pitch that if we do not take care, we risk ... aggravating the international situation."[45]

While recognizing that "Italy is working out a vast plan for dominance in the Mediterranean and that she wants to turn the expression *mare nostrum* into a reality,"[46] he believed, as he had written in 1911, that "Italy ...traditionally allies herself with the strongest power."[47] He thought it possible therefore to maneuver her back into the Allied camp in opposition to Germany. For that purpose, he advocated that France

close off Eastern Europe to Germany by concluding military accords giving us guarantees where at present we have only risks. ... Until now we have not dared to conclude a pact with Yugoslavia for fear of provoking Italy. Today it is Mussolini who is provoking us. Barred in the east and in the west, the Reich will turn toward the south, where she has already established strong positions at Vienna and Budapest. Under pressure, Rome will break away from Germany and will seek aid in Paris and London. For such a policy, repairing the damages of years of errors and weakness, a little resolution would suffice. But can we expect that little from the weak-willed men who govern us?[48]

Mandel condemned the Popular Front for adopting its opponents' policies and not carrying out its own aim of resisting Germany.[49] The government never attempted to reinforce the mutual assistance treaties with Czechoslovakia, Poland, Yugoslavia, and Russia by concluding military agreements to spell out precisely the conditions and extent of aid in case of attack. Thus, rather than being strengthened under the Popular Front, France's system of alliances began to break up. In October 1936 Belgium renounced her pact with France and declared herself neutral. Mandel blamed the rupture on the French failure to resist German remilitarization of the Rhineland and also on the mistrust aroused by the reliance of Blum's government on Communist support. "If we want to maintain our alliances, . . . if we want to break the *cordon sanitaire* with which the Reich, under the pretext of anti-Bolshevism, is surrounding us, we must assume our responsibilities in foreign affairs, and decide in internal affairs to drive the Communists from the majority."[50]

The aim of Mandel's policy was the formation of a National Union government that would exclude or at least not be dependent on the Communists, whose mere presence in the government caused Great Britain and other nations to mistrust France. Externally, he wanted France to negotiate military agreements with the powers in Eastern Europe, particularly Soviet Russia.[51] Signed in 1936, such an alliance would immediately have raised the question that later proved so thorny—how Russian military might could be brought to bear against Germany. Russia had no common frontier with the Reich, and both Rumania and Poland refused to permit the passage of troops. Although the French government recognized the problem, it did nothing to get a definite Russian commitment of aid or to change the mind of the Polish government.[52] As a result, the Allies were so uncertain of Russian aid and so suspicious of Russian motives that they allowed Austria to be annexed, abandoned Czechoslovakia, and entered World War II without ever making a serious effort to discover whether Russia sincerely wished to cooperate with them in stopping German expansion.

Mandel felt so strongly about the necessity for completing the Franco-Soviet mutual assistance treaty by a military alliance that it was the one issue on which he spoke out during this period. In his Armistice Day speech at Soulac in 1936, he declared that France had to decide whether she preferred restful indolence to an independent foreign policy. She could withdraw from Central and Eastern Europe and gain a few years of relative peace in which to broaden and intensify the sociological experiments she had already begun, but sooner or later she would have to confront a Germany enlarged and strengthened by conquest. The policy of withdrawal and postponement had the one great merit that it required no immediate effort, whereas the other policy, which Mandel recommended, required vigilance.

We must hold on to what remains of the treaties to preserve the European equilibrium and the independence of nations. . . . We must be ready to collaborate with any country, without worrying any more about its internal regime than did Francis I or Richelieu when they concluded alliances with the Sultan or with the Protestant Princes of Germany; if necessary, we must ally ourselves with the worst enemies of democracy—be they Bolsheviks or Fascists—in order

1. Clemenceau and Mandel arriving for a debate
in the Chamber, *c.* 1906.

2. Mandel in 1910 at the time of his first
campaign for Parliament.

3. Clemenceau's first speech in the Chamber as wartime prime minister, November 1917.
Mandel stands at the extreme right, arms crossed.

5 and 6. "Georges" and "A Contribution to the National Homage," cartoons by H. P. Gassier,
appearing in *Les Hommes du Jour* for August 16 and January 4, 1919.

4. *Opposite*. Clemenceau and Wilson (top hats) leaving Versailles after signing the peace treaty in 1919. Mandel (hatless) is near the left of the picture.

7. Georges Mandel as Clemenceau's *chef de cabinet*, 1918.

8. Mandel speaking to his constituents in Lesparre during the electoral campaign of 1924.

9. Georges Mandel as president of the Universal Suffrage Commission of the Chamber of Deputies, 1930.

10. PTT Minister Mandel and Foreign Minister Pierre Laval in 1935.

11. "This way, boys," a cartoon by Jehan Sennep on the proposed electoral reforms, appearing in *L'Echo de Paris* for December 19, 1931.

12. Meeting of the Sarraut cabinet on March 11, 1936, to decide how France would respond to the remilitarization of the Rhineland. Mandel is at the right. Albert Sarraut is left of center, flanked by Joseph Paul-Boncour and Pierre-Etienne Flandin.

3. Mandel campaigning in Lesparre, c. 1936.

14. Georges Mandel at the time of the overthrow of Laval's cabinet, January 1936.

15. "Machiavel," a Sennep cartoon from a book entitled *Le Diable au Palais-Bourbon*, 1938.

16. Mme. Béatrice Bretty of the *Comédie Française*, appearing on the first public television program transmitted from the new studio established by Mandel, November 10, 1935.

17. Georges Mandel as minister of Colonies.

18 and 19. Interior Minister Georges
Mandel in May 1940, as he was
caricatured by Bib (Georges Breitel) in
Gringoire (May 23), and as he really
looked, plump and fifty-five, seated at
his desk in the Place Beauvau. French
cartoonists had clung for so long
to their original image of him as a thin
young man with an outrageous nose,
that it had become more of a symbol
than anything else. Bib's caption calls
Mandel the man France is counting
on to wipe out the Fifth Column.

LE CORBEAU

REPUBLIQUE FRANÇAISE
POSTES

1885-1944
GEORGES MANDEL

0.30

21. Commemorative stamp
issued in the early 1960's.

20. *Left.* A cartoon by Ralph
Soupault in *Je Suis Partout*, July 21,
1944, after Mandel's assassination.
The caption reads: "So you have
finally come to see your old friend?"

22. Claude Mandel receives the Cross of the Legion of Honor in the name of her father from
President Auriol in 1945. Mme. Auriol is at the right.

to resist any attempt at domination. Furthermore, if the danger becomes more pressing, we must side immediately with the first states threatened, without waiting to be attacked directly.

Because the government in France continued in power only with the aid of the Communists, however, German propaganda could easily make Frenchmen believe that they were being asked to fight for Russia, which they did not want to do, any more than they wanted to fight for Yugoslavia, Czechoslavakia, or Rumania. But there could be no one-sided alliance. "A country can find aid when it is attacked only if it shows itself ready to aid other states in case of aggression. To fight for one's allies is to fight for oneself."

He advocated that all the nations threatened by Germany be united into an alliance. France should immediately "plan the establishment and coordination of military agreements, taking steps to organize a unified command and a common pool of all resources, including men, armaments, and raw materials." A military alliance with Russia, however, did not mean that France had to let herself be overrun with revolutionaries. Turkey, for example, he said, had an alliance with Russia, but it had also outlawed Communism. "Whenever a Communist is found, he is hung." It was not necessary to go so far in France, but the government had to show by its ability to maintain order that the Communists were not in control. In conclusion, Mandel appealed for the end of internal divisions, the creation of a National Union government and, above all, strong leadership.[53]

During these years Mandel lacked only eloquence to become the French Churchill. Determination and farsightedness he possessed in abundance, and he shared the isolation and mistrust which were the lot of his English counterpart. It can be said of his speech that it outlined the only plan of action that might conceivably have prevented World War II or at least have assured France of effective allies against Germany when war finally did break out. At the time, however, his appeal for a vigorous foreign policy failed to arouse anyone. To the converted, its wisdom was evident. Emile Buré said that if people wanted to know what Clemenceau would have said about the situation, they had only to read Mandel's speech. "He is the only one who has always followed the line traced by our old leader."[54] Gabriel Péri in *L'Humanité* approved the idea of a Franco-Soviet pact, but condemned Mandel's opposition to the Popular Front. Péri asked how a government could oppose Hitlerism externally if it did not also try to eliminate it internally. "How can it defend French security and international law if it cannot act against the forces of financial capitalism that are paralyzing the economy of the country and against the employers who are violating the social laws? Contrary to what M. Mandel believes, the rigorous observance of the Popular Front program is the most solid guarantee of national security and European peace."[55]

The answer, of course, was that Mandel was not opposing Hitlerism, but German imperialism. The Communists, like the Right, utterly failed to distinguish between internal and external policy. *Candide* made the same mistake when it remarked that "to suppress Communism internally while supporting it externally is a chimerical undertaking."[56] Events were to prove that Mandel had evaluated the French as well as the Russian national interest more accurately than Péri. In 1936, when the German industries were working day and night to create a powerful war machine, France did not have the time for sociological experiments. The English journalist Alexander Werth, himself sympathetic to the social aims of the Popular Front, said later that "Stalin's desire for a *strong* France ... was very poorly served by the encouragement the French Communists gave to the stay-in strikes and the 40-hour week."[57] In other words, the surest means of containing Hitler was not the rigorous observance of the Popular Front program.

The nationalist press either failed to mention Mandel's speech, or gave it only a few lines on the inside pages.[58] The Royalists at *L'Action Française* ignored the speech but explained why they no longer had any confidence in Mandel. They had criticized Flandin for supporting Sarraut, but "M. Mandel is infinitely more culpable for having done so. He has been a greater disappointment because this type of treachery and compromise seemed more alien to his temperament. That day a number of patriots lost confidence in him." The writer agreed that the country needed a strong government, and said that Mandel was obviously thinking of himself to lead it, but "the parliamentary and ministerial career of M. Mandel does not show a great deal ... of consistency or of continuity of purpose. The appearance of energy is vain if its sole aim is to create a reputation as a strong man. Behind the appearance, there should be real energy applied to a determined policy. M. Mandel, who has wandered from the Center to the Radicals, who has gone from Clemenceau to Tardieu, to Flandin, and then to the Freemason Sarraut, has not shown by his changeableness that he has the ability to command."[59]

What the Royalists did not see, or, blinded by their own prejudices, refused to see, was that Mandel's concern for French security and his opposition to Germany had remained unchanged. More than that, his concern had dictated collaboration with anyone who held similar views, regardless of the reasons. It was the Right itself, preoccupied with internal events, that had changed, giving up its traditional policy of maintaining France's position in Europe.

Considering the negative reaction to his speech, the question arises why

Mandel decided to speak out, fixing his position clearly. An Armistice Day speech at Soulac called for nothing more than patriotic rhetoric. There was no need even for that, it seems, for Mandel did not deliver the address himself, but had his assistant André Coudy read it from the steps of the city hall.[60] In other words, he had deliberately chosen that moment to state his policy. The reason must be sought in the situation in Parliament, for Mandel's speeches were not philosophical dissertations, or affirmations of faith, but political acts which can be understood only in the context of events.

By November 1936 the Communists were in open disagreement with Blum's policies on a number of points. Strangely enough, they criticized him for ruling in the interest of a class, and for not broadening the governmental coalition to include conservative leaders like Paul Reynaud. To counter the danger from Nazi Germany, they advocated the union of all the people in a "French Front." They were also critical of the government for failing to aid Republican Spain and for refusing to conclude a military alliance with Soviet Russia. Realizing, however, that a National Union government would not help the Spanish Republicans, they played down this issue when they demanded the formation of a "French Front."[61]

Seen in this context, Mandel's speech seems to have been a warning to the Communists that a more vigorous foreign policy, including a military alliance with Russia, could be carried out only by a government that was not dependent on Communist support, and would be possible only if the Communists refrained from pressing for further social reforms. The speech was an invitation to the Communists to desert Blum, who rejected any idea of uniting with the conservatives in order to resist Nazi Germany.[62]

In December 1936 Georges Gombault of *La Lumière* reported that Mandel and Paul Reynaud were conducting a campaign against Blum, who had repeatedly said that he would resign if the Communists failed to support him. They hoped to persuade the Communists to abstain, forcing Blum to resign, or at least to broaden the base of his government.[63] For a moment their plan seemed to have succeeded when the Communists abstained in a vote on foreign affairs on December 4. But Blum, instead of resigning, treated their action as a temporary lapse, and decided to remain in power.

Throughout this period, Mandel was obviously and understandably attempting to overthrow the government. According to Blum's authorized biographer, he was "the cabinet's most redoubtable enemy," who "played a lone hand, lurking in the shade, waiting for an opportunity after the manner of his old chief, 'Tiger' Clemenceau, to leap at the government's throat."[64] For many reasons, it was difficult for Mandel to intervene personally. He probably did not want to antagonize the Left publicly, and in any case he could not have influenced enough votes in the Chamber where the government enjoyed a solid majority. Only in the Senate, that conservative body designed to serve as a moderating force, could Mandel hope to overthrow Blum. In 1932, over the question of the electoral reform bill, he himself had felt the anger it expressed whenever policy threatened to swing too far to the left or to the right. The Senate had been opposed to the Popular Front since its inception, and Mandel did not have to search very long to find a man who would attack the government in his stead.[65] Joseph Caillaux, the powerful President of the Senate Finance Committee, was easily persuaded to lead the opposition in June 1937 to Blum's request for special decree powers. When the Senate refused to grant him the powers he had requested, Blum resigned.[66]

Most of Mandel's other activities at this time were equally covert, so that it is difficult to say what he was trying to do. On the one hand he collaborated with Paul Reynaud, who agreed with his views on French foreign policy. But on the other hand he also supported Pierre-Etienne Flandin, Reynaud's enemy within the Alliance Démocratique, who now urged that France withdraw from Eastern Europe. In *L'Ami du Peuple*, Mandel invariably praised Flandin's speeches.[67] In return, Flandin's party organ announced after Mandel's Armistice Day speech that "he is one of those who must necessarily be summoned to collaborate in the work of recovery in the days of peril."[68]

Throughout this period, Mandel's policies were obviously as tortuous as ever. He was still attempting the impossible task of uniting all the divergent elements on the Right while maintaining relations with forces on the Left that were willing to resist Nazi Germany.

III

The one open attack Mandel made on the government concerned his successor as minister of Posts, the Socialist deputy Robert Jardillier. A professor of history and an excellent musician, Jardillier seems to have lacked both common sense and administrative ability. He set out at once to satisfy the workers' complaints and remedy the injustices Mandel had supposedly committed. During the first days of the Popular Front government, André Morice, one of the editors of *Le Petit Parisien* and head of an association of journalists, asked Jardillier to continue the practice of allowing the association to broadcast several concerts each year for the benefit of its retirement fund. The Minister inquired who had authorized the programs. When Morice informed him that permission had originally been granted by Mandel, Jardillier exclaimed: "Then I am canceling them. I have come here to do the exact opposite of my predecessor." As Morice ruefully commented, Jardillier was "a peculiar minister."[69]

One of his first acts was to set up a "Reparations Commission" to review all the nominations and promotions Mandel had made. Actually, the commission, whose membership was never revealed, limited itself to examining the cases of the employees whose names were submitted by the PTT unions. It was a sort of kangaroo court. Over three hundred employees were dismissed or transferred on the authority of the commission without having had an opportunity to be heard. Just before boarding a ship for the United States, Jardillier, without investigating the cases himself, signed the decree authorizing the changes. He also fired 160 auxiliary postmen who had received their appointments from Mandel, and discharged some thirty journalists from the national broadcasting system in order to replace them with men favorable to his own party. In addition, a number of higher officials who had not been appointed by Mandel, but had worked closely with him, were removed from office.[70]

In December 1936 Mandel began a counterattack against the Socialist minister who had been foolish enough to denigrate his work by deliberately adopting a contrary policy. When the Chamber Finance Committee examined the PTT budget, Mandel kept Jardillier until dawn, questioning him in detail about the new rural telephone system, the allocation of funds, the air mail service, and the expansion of the radio network. Jardillier, who had just returned from the United States, was unable to answer many of the questions. Instead, he criticized Mandel's work, particularly his nominations. Mandel replied that he had been responsible for more than 36,000 appointments, but

not one of your friends either questioned or interpellated me, not even you. And yet you came to see me fairly often. Moreover, if the nominations had been irregular, the people concerned could have protested to the Conseil d'Etat. But there were no more complaints to the Conseil d'Etat than there were interpellations in Parliament. You waited until I left the ministry to decide to denounce the pseudo-injustices.[71]

Mandel's campaign against Jardillier continued the following month when three Radical Senators, Jean Philip, Babaud-Lacroze, and Paul Laffont, asked the Senate to establish a special commission to investigate Jardillier's work as minister. They accused him of having "put the French broadcasting system at the service of a party," and said that the workers he had fired or transferred were all guilty of two crimes: being recommended by members of Parliament and being appointed by Mandel. Philip stated that Radicals, Communists, and even Socialists, including Blum and Jardillier, had made recommendations to Mandel. According to Paul Laffont, Mandel, while in office, had been "the least questioned, the least criticized, the least attacked of all ministers of Posts."[72]

Clearly mounted by Mandel, it was a deadly attack. Blum came scurrying to the Palais du Luxembourg to defend, not his minister, but his government. He asked the Senate to refer the question to the regularly constituted Commission du Commerce, de l'Industrie, du Travail et des Postes rather than to create a special investigating commission. The Senate complied by naming a subcommittee to examine the accusations made against Jardillier.[73] Fifteen months passed before the committee turned in its report and another year before it was discussed in the Senate. In the meantime Blum resigned, and his successor as leader of the Popular Front, Camille Chautemps, thought it prudent to replace Jardillier as minister of Posts.

The report, drawn up by Paul Laffont, confirmed all the charges originally made. Condemning the Reparations Commission, Laffont noted that Mandel's nominations had not caused any formal complaints, but many of Jardillier's "have been annulled as arbitrary and illegal by the Conseil d'Etat." After investigating all cases of political appointments, including but not limited to those denounced by the unions, the committee concluded that "everyone has used and perhaps abused the system of political recommendations. M. Mandel accepted them...and M. Jardillier was just as guilty." The only difference the committee found between the two was that "M. Jardillier accorded favors much more exclusively to his political friends."

The report also criticized Jardillier for dismissing many of the journalists on the state radio system in response to a campaign started by the leftist press, which was "indignant that there were still some men on the radio who did not praise the Popular Front every day. An immediate purge was demanded." The left-wing Socialist Marceau Pivert and Jardillier's *chef de cabinet* took charge of the radio system and eliminated most of the former employees. Thereafter, said Laffont, the radio became a weapon in the political struggle and lost all objectivity.[74]

La Lumière immediately protested against the report, which, "with incredible violence, charged Jardillier with arbitrariness and muddle-headedness and accused him of having put his ministry into a state of total anarchy."[75] In a long series of articles entitled "Mes Crimes," beginning in June 1938 in *Le Populaire* and in his local Dijon paper, Jardillier attempted to defend himself against the accusations. Calling the report "a tissue of inaccuracies and a monument of partiality," he claimed that his appointments were simply attempts to rectify the injustices of the Mandel administration. He admitted that he had purged the radio system and was proud of it. He would not allow the French radio to remain anyone's "fief," nor did he want the essential posts in the hands of reactionaries. Before June 1936 the programming was supposedly eclectic, but neither he nor any impartial listener thought so. He wanted the radio to become "the image of living France."[76]

Le Populaire, after printing a number of Jardillier's articles, suddenly discontinued them in July 1938. The readers perhaps were getting tired of his long-winded defense. Or perhaps the decision had been taken because Mandel had once again entered a government supported by the Socialists. After almost two years, the Popular Front, as Mandel had anticipated, was finally forced to create a semblance of national union, and Mandel was one of the first conservative leaders called on to join Daladier's government in April 1938. As it became apparent after the annexation of Austria that Hitler's designs on Czechoslovakia might lead to war, some of the Socialist leaders may have realized that they were now on the same side of the barricade as Mandel. They may have decided that it was more important to support this valuable ally in the government than to satisfy the grievances of Jardillier, or of the ordinary party members who still regarded Mandel as the enemy of their class.

At the Socialist congress in June 1938, Blum asked the delegates to support Daladier's government. They had no reason to fear that it would betray the Republic, he said. "Even the men in the cabinet from the Center, Mandel and Reynaud, are not Fascists." The remark brought immediate protests from the delegates, who were unaccustomed to hearing Blum defend Mandel. The chairman of the meeting was forced to call for silence, and Blum exclaimed: "I assure you! (Effervescence in the hall.) I am aware that I am asking for trouble in telling you that. But don't get the habit of stretching the meaning of the word 'Fascist.' I am not saying that the men I have just named are not reactionaries; I am only saying that they are not Fascists. I am saying that they are men who will not be the agents or accomplices of a plot against the Republic. (Some disturbances.)" The audience was unable to comprehend such a subtle distinction, for after what were described as "manifestations diverses," the chairman was once again forced to ask the delegates to stop holding discussions among themselves. "After all," he shouted, "France does not revolve around M. Mandel's navel!" Dismayed and fatigued, Blum could only add his own injunction: "Please calm yourselves. (Noise.) Calm yourselves, and do not attribute that last remark to anything but a need for a bit of fantasy, explicable and pardonable at the end of a very long speech."[77]

Some of the leaders of the Socialist Party may have come to recognize Mandel as an ally against Nazi Germany, but even in the summer of 1938, a few months before Munich, it was still impossible for the rank and file to regard him as anything but an enemy. Blum had learned that the greatest danger to France was external, but many of his followers were obviously still preoccupied with internal differences.

13. Munich

*Il ne servirait à rien d'armer, de surarmer, si l'on n'était pas résolu à faire,
le cas échéant, usage de ses armes. La leçon du 7 mars ne doit pas
être oubliée. C'est pour avoir alors laissée réoccupé la Rhénanie que la
France a vu quelques-uns de ses plus fidèles amis l'abandonner. . . .*

Mandel, March 1938

IN SEPTEMBER 1936 Léon Blum had rejected the Communist demand for the formation of a "French Front" to meet the danger from Nazi Germany. But by January 1938, when his successor Camille Chautemps resigned, Blum had changed his mind. He proposed the creation of a broad coalition, headed by Edouard Herriot, to extend from Paul Reynaud and Mandel on the right to the Communists on the left.[1] There was no mistaking the import of Blum's suggestion. Herriot, Mandel, and Reynaud were the main proponents of a military alliance with Russia. Such a government would have proclaimed to the world that France was determined to resist German ambitions.

Blum's proposal was rejected because the Right and the Left would not collaborate.[2] It was only in April, after two short-lived ministries, that Edouard Daladier was able to form a government with widespread support. His cabinet was composed primarily of Radicals but was enlarged on the left by the addition of some independent Socialists and on the right by the inclusion of Mandel, Reynaud, and the leader of the Christian Democrats, Champetier de Ribes. Mandel had been correct in his assumption that the Left would turn to him when the Popular Front began to dissolve. He wanted the Air Ministry, but certain generals, who still resented his bitter remarks about them in March 1936, objected to that appointment, and Mandel accepted the relatively minor Colonial ministry instead.[3]

Curiously, the presence of Mandel and Reynaud did not gain the government any conservative support. On the contrary, the conservatives repudiated them,[4] seeing their serving in the cabinet as a guarantee to the Left and to France's allies that Daladier would not change the country's traditional foreign policy.[5] According to Georges Bonnet, the new foreign minister, Litvinov told the French ambassador in Moscow that Mandel and Reynaud were the only two men he trusted in the government.[6] And the German chargé d'affaires in Paris concluded from their presence in the cabinet that "France still considers the Soviet Union as an important factor in her political system, and though the relationship may not be founded on mutual sympathies, she does not at present intend to discard this card in her hand."[7]

It was to balance their influence that Daladier had made Bonnet foreign minister. Bonnet was suspected of wanting to give up France's alliances in the East in order to reach an agreement with Germany. One journalist commented accurately that there was method in Daladier's madness: "The presence of Georges Bonnet reassured the Axis powers, while Georges Mandel reassured Czechoslovakia and the USSR."⁸ Thus Daladier was able to retain his freedom of action. He committed himself neither to appeasement nor to resistance on the major problem facing the cabinet: the German threat to Czechoslovakia. From a symbolic point of view, he was the perfect man to head the government; he represented the inability of the country to make a definite decision.

The Czechoslovak crisis had been building up for two years. In 1936 the three million Sudeten Germans, supported by Hitler, began to make serious demands for local autonomy. Their agitation immediately preoccupied Mandel, who devoted a number of articles to the question in *L'Ami du Peuple* and visited the country in the summer of 1937.⁹ He believed that the primary issue was European and ultimately French security, not minority rights. Hitler was trying to destroy Czechoslovakia's internal unity and break the alliances that protected her.

The campaign of threats that he has inspired is designed to frighten us into separating ourselves from Prague. If we abandon the Czechs, they will submit rather than perish, and thus will open the way to German expansion toward the south and to the creation of a formidable empire, which will press irresistibly on our eastern frontier.¹⁰

By 1938 Mandel and Reynaud had become convinced that war with Germany was inevitable. Their opinion was no secret in the inner circles of government. Flandin himself, having heard Mandel explain their position innumerable times, later gave a fair summary of it. They believe, he wrote, that

war is inevitable because Hitler will always demand more than he has. One day France will have to stop the Third Reich in its attempt to establish hegemony over Europe. Therefore we must choose the most opportune moment to go to war, and, according to these two ministers, the most favorable moment is now.¹¹

Although he believed war to be inevitable, Mandel found it difficult to speak publicly about his conviction, for this would have jeopardized a possible settlement with Germany and have left him open to the charge of favoring a preventive war, or of simply wanting war for some reprehensible reason. He expressed himself freely to his colleagues, but no matter how rational or logical his explanation, he could still be accused of acting not as a disciple of Clemenceau but as a Jew. When Mandel and Herriot advocated a military alliance with Soviet Russia in November 1936, the independent Socialist Fernand Bouisson, a former president of the Chamber and a former prime minister, angrily exclaimed: "Those men are leading us straight to war—Herriot because of his inordinate pride and his desire to regain power, and Mandel because he is ambitious and because he is a Jew. Like all the Jews, he is pursuing Hitler with his hatred."[12] In March 1938 Yvon Delbos, who had been Blum's foreign minister, tried to dissuade some of the conservative deputies from supporting a motion made by Mandel in favor of Blum's proposal for a National Union government. He explained that "the Communists, frightened by their defeat in Spain, and the Jews, hunted down almost everywhere, are searching for salvation in a world war."[13] Even Flandin, with whom Mandel had collaborated so closely since 1934 and who seemed to have a theoretical understanding of his position, nevertheless attributed his policy to his racial origins. In an interview in 1942 in which he condemned Reynaud unequivocally, he showed more sympathy for Mandel, whom he considered to be "very intelligent and endowed with many qualities," but added: "Unfortunately, he is a Jew and he has allowed his own interests to take precedence over those of the country."[14] If Mandel received so little understanding from usually liberal men, some of whom claimed to be his friends, what could he expect from his enemies?

In January 1937 already, *Je Suis Partout* declared: "It is grave and dangerous that in circumstances that threaten European peace, men like Léon Blum and Georges Mandel, who are not just simple citizens, can have reflexes that are not purely French, and that men who must decide the question of war or peace can be influenced by something resembling clan vengeance or racial hatred. . . . French blood should be spilled only for a French cause."[15] Starting in January 1938, as international tension heightened, the rightist press increased its denunciations of Mandel for his *bellicisme* and his "pro-Russian" activities. Charles Maurras regretted that Mandel, whose "Clemencism had formerly recommended him to many good people," was now working for the interests of Israel and Russia. The *Action Française* commented that it was quite natural to have a Jew as minister of Colonies: "Isn't France itself a Jewish colony?" On May 10 *Je Suis Partout* demanded that Blum, Mandel and Reynaud be shot for warmongering. For the next four months, the same journal carried a weekly column devoted to every unfavorable comment that had ever been made about Mandel and every incident that could reflect discredit on him. The venomous articles finally stopped in September, in the midst of the Czech crisis, even though the last one published was marked "to be continued."[16] The editors would later boast that Mandel had unsuccessfully tried to silence them. In fact he did succeed, though it took him a few months.[17]

As the year progressed he became the object of attacks from a wider variety of sources. In June Colonel de la Rocque demanded that Mandel deny the persistent rumor that he advocated a preventive war.[18] Henri de Kérillis, the nationalist deputy and writer, defended Mandel,[19] but the rumor continued to spread. In August Emmanuel Berl devoted a large part of two issues of his small weekly, *Les Pavés de Paris*, to the topic: "M. Mandel, ses amis et la guerre." Berl said that he had known Mandel for a long time and both liked and respected him. "I believe that he sincerely loves his country, that he is capable of making the greatest sacrifices for it, and that no public figure is capable of more civic courage and devoted work. He rendered great services to France under Clemenceau. At the Ministry of Posts he was an outstanding administrator; in the Chamber of Deputies he is a great parliamentarian who carefully studies every question." Mandel, however, was not being honest with the country. "This minister believes that France is more ready for war today than she will be in four years." Holding this conviction, Berl said, Mandel had the duty not only to state his position but "to desire war and to work for it."

As for himself, Berl believed that since it was impossible to foretell the future, it was impossible to say that war was inevitable. He believed that France should give up her attempt to maintain the peace treaties of 1919. Once Germany had achieved her long-delayed unification, the German problem would disappear, whereas a new war would mean the end of European civilization. For Berl, war itself was the greatest danger.[20] His position was a carry-over from the previous decade, when it was hoped that if enough concessions were made to Germany, a lasting peace might be established. It was reinforced by an absolute horror of war that was shared by many Frenchmen. In a letter to a friend in September 1936, the novelist Roger Martin du Gard exclaimed that he preferred "*Anything, rather than war! Anything, anything!* Even Fascism in Spain! And do not press me, for I would also say: 'Yes...and even Fascism in France!'... Nothing, *no experience, no servitude* can be compared to war and all that it entails.... *Anything*, Hitler rather than war! And, moreover, war would also mean civil war, the triumph perhaps of Communism after years of blood, ruins and unspeakable horrors."[21]

Mandel might have replied to Berl that he had not concealed his policy but had announced it openly in his speech in Lesparre in November 1936, and that in any case he was far less secretive than Bonnet, who publicly declared that France would fulfill her commitments but did everything possible to see that she did not. Mandel might also have repeated what he said in an interview in 1936, that "we will always have war so long as there are men on earth. Therefore it is not a question of peace or of war at this moment. It is a question of invasion, and of knowing whether we are going to take the means to avoid it. War cannot be avoided if someone else wants it. What must be avoided is defeat."[22]

In the circumstances, he could not answer Berl, but let Emile Buré's *L'Ordre* defend him instead.[23] It did little good. When the British Ambassador, Sir Eric Phipps, heard alarmist rumors from Flandin that Mandel, Herriot and Reynaud were working for war, he sought out Bonnet, who informed him that "M. Mandel, though not M. Reynaud, was bellicose, but he alone in the cabinet could not do much. His feelings were doubtless prompted by his Jewish origins."[24] Even Daladier heatedly told Mandel one day as German pressure on Czechoslovakia built up that "he did not intend to sacrifice the entire youth of France merely to whitewash the criminal errors that had been committed by Mandel and his friend Clemenceau and the other members of the Big Four during the conference that produced the Treaty of Versailles."[25]

Though every one was able to repeat Mandel's arguments almost word for word, no one except the German Ambassador seemed to understand them. Writing to his government in February 1938, Count Welczeck reported that although strong opposition to a pact with Russia had arisen, the idea was supported not only by the Socialists and Communists, but also by "bourgeois defenders acting for military reasons and out of considerations of national security...in the sense of its originator Barthou."[26] To Bonnet, Flandin, and a host of others, however, Mandel's desire to resist Germany seemed to be inspired by sympathy for his fellow Jews. To Daladier, he seemed motivated by an egotistical desire to defend his own and Clemenceau's work in the Treaty of Versailles. To the British Ambassador, his presumed motives were possibly even more reprehensible. Adopting the views of the Extreme Right, Phipps wrote to his government advising it not to encourage "the small, but noisy and corrupt, war group here. All that is best in France is against war, *almost* at any price...." The permanent officials at the British Foreign Office were outraged that "the Ambassador should hold that those who thought like Georges Bonnet were the best of France and that those who thought like Georges Mandel were to be stigmatized as belonging to a corrupt war group." Questioned on the point, the Ambassador explained that by "small but noisy and corrupt war group" he meant "the Communists, who were paid by Moscow and have been working for war for months." He then insidiously added, however, that "a well-known French minister has also been advocating a preventive war for many months."[27]

Faced by almost total incomprehension in the cabinet and in the country, Mandel fought a losing battle against concessions to Germany. He was restrained by his cabinet position and even more by his Jewish origins from conducting an open campaign. Bonnet was equally hindered by his position from engaging in open controversy, but he had the advantage as foreign minister of being able to exercise considerable influence on the press. In April the German Ambassador had noted incipient hopes among the French that they might be absolved from discharging their treaty obligations to Czechoslovakia. He added, however, that "if the government knew how to inculcate in the people the conviction that sooner or later hostilities between France and Germany were inevitable, the 'bulwark of Czechoslovakia' would assume an entirely different significance in the minds of the people."[28]

This, of course, was precisely what Bonnet wanted to prevent. In August the German Ambassador reported that Bonnet was satisfied with the attitude of both the French and the German press, which had shown "a sensible relaxation of tension. . . ." Welczeck also reported Bonnet as saying that "if I had any complaints regarding the newspapers here which he was in a position to influence, he was always at my disposal; but he did not wish to conceal that he could undertake no action against left-wing newspapers of the caliber of the *Humanité* and the *Populaire*."[29]

Even when the government was attempting to impress Germany with its determination to defend Czechoslovakia, Bonnet seems to have been undermining its position through the press. At one point Mandel was forced to ask in a cabinet meeting if measures were finally going to be taken to see that the newspapers supported the government's policy.[30] There is no doubt that the press had a disastrous effect on public opinion. The American journalist Edmond Taylor remarked that "the alarmism of the French and British press was not curbed, though means to curb it existed in both France and England. Not only was the imminence of war played up by the defeatist papers, but the horrors of this war were graphically depicted."[31] After war broke out in 1939, Taylor wrote that "though it is journalistic treason to say so, the truth is that the political censorship was indispensable in France at the beginning of the war and would have done a lot of good if it had existed earlier, especially at the time of Munich."[32] In November 1938 even the liberal periodical *Politique* favored censorship. "A government cannot carry out its policy effectively," it said, "if it is thwarted by the press, the radio and the movies."[33]

Mandel's policy was not unrepresented in the press, but its advocates could not match the means deployed against them by Bonnet. The real battle to determine French policy, however, was fought out subtly and surreptitiously within the cabinet. At the end of April, before Bonnet and Daladier left for a conference in London, Mandel got the cabinet to insist that no agreement be made contrary to France's treaty obligations with

Czechoslovakia or Russia.[34] But in London, after attempting to get a British commitment to aid Czechoslovakia, the French agreed with Chamberlain to persuade the Czechs to meet as many of the Sudeten German demands as possible.[35] Thus began the policy that was to culminate in Munich. By April France and Britain had already accepted Germany's contention that this was primarily a minority problem and not, as Mandel asserted, primarily a problem affecting European security. All year the emphasis was placed on the rights of the German minority and not on the Nazi threat to Czechoslovakia and ultimately to France.

By September, Britain and France had forced President Beneš to accept almost all of the Sudeten German program. On September 12, however, at a mass rally in Nuremberg, Hitler increased his demands. He furiously denounced Czech brutality and promised to aid the German minority if they were not granted autonomy. He did not demand annexation yet, but it was clear that this was his aim.

Hitler's speech had a disastrous effect on Daladier and Bonnet. The British Ambassador reported that Bonnet seemed "to have lost his nerve and to be ready for any solution to avoid war."[36] Mandel and Reynaud, on the other hand, pressed Daladier to order an immediate partial mobilization to show Hitler that France would not permit the integrity of the Czech state to be violated or her defenses to be destroyed by the separation of the Sudetenland from the rest of the country.[37] This was the incident that provoked Daladier's bitter comment about the criminal errors made by Mandel and Clemenceau at Versailles. Instead of reacting forcefully to the German threat, Daladier and Bonnet decided rather to settle the Czech problem and then, as they told American Ambassador William Bullitt, "enter at once into negotiations designed to bring together Germany and France in genuine friendship."[38] The Prime Minister's edgy rejoinder to Mandel and his comments to Bullitt indicate that no matter what ineffectual hopes he may once have entertained about saving Czechoslovakia, he had now decided to desert her.

Daladier and Bonnet proposed to Chamberlain to call a three-power conference, but Chamberlain preferred to fly to Germany for a private conversation with Hitler. At Berchtesgaden on September 15, he accepted the principle of self-determination for the German-speaking areas of Czechoslovakia, and promised to press the Czechs to accept this solution if the British and French cabinets approved it. He then returned to London for a conference with the French on September 18, and presented them with his plan for the cession to the Reich of all areas where the population was more than fifty per cent German. Daladier agreed to transmit the plan to the Czechs, but said that he would first have to obtain the assent of his cabinet. When rumors of the London plan began to circulate in Paris that night, it was expected that Mandel would provoke a governmental crisis by resigning at the cabinet meeting the following day.[39] People believed that Hitler, having his plans frustrated, would then invade Czechoslovakia, and France would either have to go along with the invasion or go to war under a new resistance cabinet. Camille Chautemps told Ambassador Bullitt that if Germany attacked, "the French people would become so aroused that there would be strikes and revolutionary demonstrations and in the end public opinion might decide for war."[40]

On the nineteenth, when Daladier and Bonnet put the London plan to the French cabinet, they warned the ministers that British aid was uncertain except in case of a direct attack on France and that French military forces were inadequate to defend Czechoslovakia. Surprisingly, no one protested against the concessions to the Sudeten Germans, which would destroy Czechoslovakia's ability to defend herself and render her ineffective as an ally. It meant conceding what Mandel had fought against for so many months. Only by their demeanor did Mandel and Reynaud reveal their disapproval, but they did insist that no pressure be brought to bear on the Czech government to force acceptance of the plan. They also sought and received assurances from Daladier that should the plan be rejected, France would still consider herself obliged to aid Czechoslovakia.[41] The only plausible explanation of their seeming acquiescence in the London plan is that they believed Beneš would reject it and that France would then be forced to help her ally against a German attack.

Despite Daladier's promise in the cabinet meeting, however, Bonnet told Bullitt afterwards that if Beneš rejected the plan, "France positively would not march in support of Czechoslovakia."[42] When Beneš did at first reject it, Lacroix, the French Ambassador at Prague, volunteered his opinion that France in that case probably would not come to his aid.[43] Premier Hodža then asked for official confirmation that this was French policy, and Daladier and Bonnet, on the night of September 20, authorized Lacroix to state that France would feel relieved of all responsibility if the plan were rejected. Deserted by their ally, the Czechs could no longer resist, and on the afternoon of the twenty-first the Prague radio announced that the plan had been accepted under pressure from Paris and London.[44] Angry because Daladier had broken his promise not to pressure the Czech government, Mandel, Reynaud, and Champetier de Ribes drew up letters of resignation. This news spread quickly and generated the fear that the cabinet might be overthrown at the very moment Chamberlain was flying back to Germany to make final arrangements with Hitler. There was a danger that France would have to face war without a government and without the united support of the nation.

Before seeing Daladier, Mandel and Reynaud spoke to Winston Churchill, who had flown to Paris the preceding day to coordinate policy with them. He was against their resigning, "as their sacrifice could not alter the course of events, and would only leave the French government weakened by the loss of its two most capable and resolute men."[45] Herriot, still possessed by his phobia about resigning, also tried to persuade Mandel and Reynaud to postpone their decision because of the gravity of the situation. The three ministers finally agreed, but nevertheless kept their resignations in their pockets when they went to see Daladier on September 22 for an explanation. Daladier told them the Czech government had requested the French declaration in order to justify acceptance of the plan to the Czech people. He promised to deny the report that France had deserted her ally and also promised that in case of attack by Germany, France would back Czechoslovakia.[46]

After the meeting Daladier issued a communiqué to an anxious public, denying that the three ministers had resigned. Distinct sighs of relief were immediately heard among the Radicals and the Left Republicans.[47] The overthrow of the cabinet had been postponed; war might still be avoided. Only the Communists voiced their discontent. Gabriel Péri warned the three men that "if their indignation is known only to a few associates, public opinion will make no distinction between those guilty of high treason and their accomplices."[48]

While the French cabinet was barely holding itself together, Chamberlain flew to meet Hitler at Godesberg and discovered that the German Chancellor had again increased his demands. Refusing Chamberlain's proposal to have an international committee draw the frontiers, he demanded that all German-speaking areas, including those containing a large proportion of Czechs, be ceded at once. He also insisted that the claims of the Hungarians and Poles be settled as well. Chamberlain was dismayed but agreed to transmit the new demands to the Czechs if Germany in the meantime would refrain from attack.

Hitler's excessive demands stiffened the backs of the French and English. On the twenty-fourth, Daladier ordered a partial mobilization, and on the following day declared at a cabinet meeting that the Godesberg plan was unacceptable. It included areas that were clearly Czech and that even the Sudeten leader Henlein had never demanded. Questioned by Mandel, the Prime Minister said that he would refuse to go beyond the London agreement. He declared that he was willing to make all possible concessions, "but if there is an unprovoked attack, our obligations remain in force. I will remain faithful to them."[49] Even the British seemed to have changed tack. On the twenty-sixth they issued a press release stating that "if, in spite of the efforts made by the British Prime Minister, a German attack is made upon Czechoslovakia, the immediate result must be that France will be bound to come to her assistance, and Great Britain and Russia will certainly stand by France."[50]

For the moment, it seemed as if the *bellicistes* had won out. Bonnet was being openly accused not only of weakness, but of treason, and Mandel was pointing him out as the man who was working for Germany.[51] Pale, shaken, and tearful, the Foreign Minister told his friends in Parliament that he was being overwhelmed in the cabinet by Mandel, Reynaud, and the other advocates of resistance. "They are crazy. You in the Chamber must do the impossible and stop this war; we are heading for a disaster. This war would be a crime."[52]

Frightened but not idle, Bonnet and his friends treated the British declaration of solidarity with France and Czechoslovakia as a fabrication or as the work of a subaltern.[53] On the twenty-eighth, Flandin covered Paris with posters announcing: "You are being deceived. . . . For weeks and months, a plot has been organized by secret forces to make war inevitable. Tendentious and false reports are the weapons of those who are working for war. You are being told that an unbridgeable gap separates the demands of Hitler from the plan already accepted. That is false. The only disagreement is over a procedural question."[54]

Above all, Bonnet and Chamberlain refused to accept the inevitability of war. Both proposed an international conference to settle the Czech problem peaceably. Accepted by Germany, the conference met at Munich on September 29–30. There Daladier and Chamberlain gave Hitler virtually everything that he had demanded at Godesberg. No longer did the Czechs first have to accept the plan and no longer did France promise to back them if they rejected it. Gone was all pretense of protecting the integrity of a useful ally, or even of honoring commitments. Peace was to be preserved at any price.

In protest against the Munich agreements, Duff Cooper resigned as British Lord of the Admiralty, and advised Mandel of his decision. Mandel and Reynaud once again considered resigning, but decided to stay in the cabinet on the advice of friends who said that their withdrawal would have been badly received in Parliament, and would have aroused a lasting anger against them.[55] They limited their public protest to loudly applauding in the Chamber the speech of Henri de Kérillis, the only rightist deputy to vote against the Munich pact.[56]

Paul-Boncour has claimed that their resignations might have shaken the euphoria of Parliament.[57] This is unlikely. The entire nation was so relieved to escape war that by resigning they might only have increased the abuse that was already being heaped on them. For *L'Action Française*, Mandel was "le grand chef de la parti de la guerre." *Je Suis Partout* commented: "One must always return to this devil of a man when trying to explain the plot directed ... against France and against peace." Pierre Gaxotte in effect read them out of the nation. He declared that henceforth there were only two parties: "Those who are for France, and those who are for war. Nothing else counts or ever will count."[58] On September 29 *L'Action Française* paraphrased a verse from the *Internationale*:

> S'ils s'obstinent, ces cannibales
> A faire de nous des héros,
> Il faut que nos premières balles
> Soient pour Mandel, Blum et Reynaud.[59]

Of far greater significance, perhaps, because representative of normally more moderate opinion, were the articles appearing in *La République*, the Radical daily. On October 2 the former Secretary-General of the Radical Party, Edouard Pfeiffer, wrote:

The time for settling scores has come. More than the leaders of the Communist Party, who openly fought for war, the guilty ones are those few men, who, in agreement with them, wanted war and did everything to involve the country. These men used every underhanded weapon: truncated telegrams, biased radio and press campaigns, false reports about the attitude of America, Poland, Yugoslavia, and Rumania, maneuvers, intrigues, etc. Hour by hour, we fought against these men of whose criminal actions the country is as yet unaware. We were risking our skins, for we knew that in wartime M. Mandel, who already saw himself as dictator, would have attacked us just as he attacked M. Caillaux in 1918. Now that peace has been saved, these men must be put where they will no longer be able to do any harm.

In the same journal, Pierre Dominique warned foreigners and Jews not to mix in French politics: "The affairs of France are none of your business." A more subtle warning lay in the rueful remark of Emile Roche, the editor of *La République* and later president of the Conseil Economique de la France: "It will be very difficult for us ... to forget, if we can, the crimes against peace committed these last few days by M. Georges Mandel. Fortunately, there is also M. Léon Blum, who, in contrast, was working for peace."[60]

It was obvious that these men would have been delighted to see Mandel leave the government. Those who only a few days earlier had been so fearful of the consequences of his resignation were now demanding his immediate departure.[61] In view of the state of public opinion, Mandel may have been right when he told Reynaud, "Resignation is justified only when it serves some purpose. Ours would have served no purpose."[62] He was afraid that their departure would only give Bonnet a free hand to commit the country completely to a policy of retreat, and he also could not see at that moment a viable alternative to a government led by Daladier. He believed that his only choice was to remain in the cabinet in order to help prepare the country for war and to minimize the influence of his "bête noire," Georges Bonnet.[63]

Under similar circumstances Clemenceau would have resigned without hesitation. But Mandel was no Clemenceau. Even as Clemenceau's assistant, he had always preferred indirect means of action. He excelled at manipulating people through conversations, rumors, threats, and promises, and usually tried to avoid direct confrontations. From 1920 to 1924, he and Tardieu had both tried unsuccessfully to follow their mentor as great orators, but both eventually turned to other means of gaining power. For Mandel, the road had been long and arduous, and after he "arrived" in 1934 there seemed to be a lessening of tension in him, a decline in aggressiveness, a sort of "settling in," and a greater enjoyment of what Wormser called "les futilités mondaines."[64] It is possible that this change may have had something to do with his decision not to resign.

Another factor that seems to have influenced Mandel was the powerful current of anti-Semitism then running in France. Revived as a result of the influx of Jewish refugees from the East after 1933, it had been relatively unimportant as a national problem until Blum became prime minister.[65] Then it "reached a degree of violence that made the writings of Edouard Drumont seem moderate."[66] In October 1936 the writer Marcel Jouhandeau declared: "I always instinctively felt myself a thousand times closer ... to our former German enemies than to all those Jewish riffraff who call themselves French, and although I have no personal sympathy for M. Hitler, I am disgusted by M. Blum."[67] Blum's enemies could easily accuse him of resisting Hitler because of his sympathy for fellow Jews in Germany. During the September crisis, demonstrations occurred in Alsace and elsewhere. Jews were attacked in the streets and their shops looted by mobs shouting "Down with the Jewish war."[68] Blum himself was reduced to writing an article entitled "Je suis Français," in which he protested against assertions that he had not been born in France.[69]

Because of his origins, Mandel had for some time restricted his public activities. He had given up hope of becoming prime minister except in extreme circumstances. In 1935 there had been a barrage of rumors that he would be chosen. But there was not a single rumor again mentioning this possibility from 1936 until the spring of 1940. During that time he did everything possible to play down the issue of anti-Semitism. It is significant that he never once denounced Hitler for it or even mentioned the question publicly.[70] According to his assistant Pierre Lafue, he used all his influence to reduce anti-Semitism in the press, cutting off or arranging subsidies, as the case required, and attempting to persuade the most important journals to publish articles denouncing racism.[71]

Mandel was sensitive to the issue not because he suspected his colleagues and countrymen of being fanatics or of being particularly susceptible to the virulent German type of anti-Semitism, but because he knew from experience, dating back to the Dreyfus Affair and to his first days in politics, that many Frenchmen did not regard Jews as full citizens.[72] In normal times, when being Jewish could have little or no effect on the determination of policy, anti-Semitism was a minor irritant rather than a source of worry. But these were not normal times. Men who were not really anti-Semitic, at least not in the Nazi sense, began to suspect the motives of their Jewish colleagues. Were they moved *exclusively* by concern for the national interest in calling for resistance to Nazi Germany, which might lead ultimately to war, or were they moved as well, and possibly primarily, by the plight of their fellow Jews? Even liberals such as Bouisson, Delbos, Flandin, and Roche had such suspicions, though they seldom expressed them openly.

Under the circumstances, Mandel preferred to remain in the background. To a friend who even before Munich suggested that he should take over direction of the country, Mandel replied, "It's impossible and you know very well why." When his friend persisted, Mandel added that there were other factors as well that hindered him: the deputies would accept him only in case of civil disorder, and the generals only after they were beaten in battle.[73] Mandel may have been right in thinking he could not get enough support in Parliament to become prime minister, but this should not have prevented him from trying to arouse the country to the dangers from Nazi Germany. What really stopped him was his fear that if he played a more prominent role, he would hurt his own cause, for his opponents would then have found it even easier to persuade people that France was being driven into war for the sake of Jewish interests.[74]

After Munich, some of the *bellicistes* may have considered trying to overthrow Daladier in order to place Mandel at the head of the government; at least Blum felt obliged to oppose the idea publicly. In a speech given at Lille in November, without explicitly mentioning Mandel, Blum said in effect that he should not become prime minister. "Is it still possible in this country to send a 'Jew' to power? It is not a question of me, or of anyone in particular at this moment. But if you asked this Jew, I assure you that he himself would feel that in the present circumstances it is his duty not to increase the international difficulties of his country."[75] Obviously, in Blum's opinion, a Jew could not lead French resistance to Nazi Germany.

II

For a brief moment in September Mandel and Reynaud had hoped that a national reaction would sweep Daladier and Bonnet from power. But until March 1939, when Hitler occupied Slovakia, the tide of opinion ran against the advocates of resistance. Bonnet continued a policy of appeasement, following up his "success" at Munich by inviting Foreign Minister Ribbentrop to Paris to sign a nonaggression pact. It was rumored at the time, and believed by Mandel, that Bonnet had promised Germany a free hand in the East.[76] No doubt Bonnet was not so imprudent, but the Germans took his obvious desire to conciliate them as a sign that France would no longer interfere in Central Europe.[77]

Bonnet's policy angered and disheartened Mandel. When France should have been rearming and strengthening her agreements with Russia, she did nothing. Mandel wondered despairingly whether she would ever decide to resist Germany or would just withdraw into her colonial empire as many people wished.[78]

The rightist press, moreover, continued to attack Mandel. There were articles demanding that he resign from the government, accusing him of being the head of a war party and of spreading false rumors, claiming that he wanted to take over the ministry of Foreign Affairs or the ministry of Aviation, or even that he was trying to overthrow the Daladier government altogether. If he wanted the ministry of Aviation, it could only be in order to protect the Jewish aircraft manufacturers. If he laid a wreath at Clemenceau's statue, it was because he wanted to become the second "Père la Victoire." If he succeeded in getting publicity for the colonies, it was only in order to build up his own reputation. *Candide* referred to him as the "Chef de publicité de la firme Mandel." It was suggested that he be thrown out of the government and tried for his treasonous activities.[79]

Although unable to change the policy of appeasement being followed by the government, Mandel did everything possible to counteract its influence. At times during this period France seemed indeed to have two foreign policies—one directed by Georges Bonnet and carried out by the diplomatic corps, the other directed by Georges Mandel and carried out by an unofficial staff of agents throughout the world. He had always maintained contact with a large number of informants abroad, and as minister of Colonies he expanded the intelligence services in the overseas possessions.[80] It is impossible to trace his activities, but there are indications that they were extensive. Mandel was particularly interested in Spain. Although he had earlier opposed intervention, by April 1938 it was common knowledge that he favored helping the Republican forces.[81] He was convinced, said *Le*

Jour, that "the Spanish War must be prolonged. The longer it lasts, the more it will weaken the Fascist powers."[82] As minister of Colonies, he could do little directly, but Alvarez del Vayo, the Republican foreign minister, considered him one of their most dependable friends in Paris.

I had more respect for the ultra-conservative Georges Mandel than for many who considered themselves the cream of the French progressive movement. During the Spanish War he had been more disposed, more determined even, to aid us than had many Socialists. He was the one member of the French cabinet whom our ambassador in Paris felt free to call on, at any hour of the night, if some difficulty arose about the passage through France of arms for the Loyalists. When I went to see him in Paris to express our government's appreciation of his help, he indicated very clearly that, apart from the high value he placed on the Spanish effort to withstand the Nazi-Fascist attack, he was actuated by a desire to serve his own country.[83]

Mandel also tried to keep the government from making any concessions to Italy. In November 1938, encouraged by French weakness at Munich, Mussolini began a campaign to acquire Nice, Savoy, Tunisia and Djibouti, the capital of French Somaliland. When Daladier suggested that Djibouti be turned into a free port in order to meet Mussolini's demands halfway, Mandel replied: "We'll give the Italians a pier and that's all."[84] Whenever Bonnet and Daladier attempted any conciliatory move, he released information to friends in the press in order to cause a public outcry.[85] In turn, the Right held him responsible for the failure of negotiations and attacked him for spreading alarmist rumors about Italian ambitions in Africa.[86]

Mandel believed that Italy always followed an opportunistic policy and would ally herself with the strongest power.[87] Concessions, therefore, would only encourage Mussolini to make more demands without assuring his assistance against Germany. To divert Italian attention, he financed the Ethiopian nationalists who revolted in December 1938, and laid plans with Haile Selassie for a full-scale insurrection of his people.[88] These were dangerous moves, but he was convinced that Italy would ultimately declare war on France in any case.[89]

A third area of French policy on which Mandel and Bonnet differed was the Far East. France had been helping China in the Sino-Japanese War by sending war materials over the Red River railway into Yunnan province, and allowing other nations to do the same. But in October 1937, after Japanese protests, the French government agreed to stop sending war materials itself and to close the railroad to all such shipments. Unlike Bonnet, who preferred not to antagonize the Japanese, partly for fear that they might attack France's Far Eastern colonies, Mandel believed that the best way to prevent such an attack was to keep the Japanese engaged in China. He therefore decided to continue to aid Chiang Kai-shek as much as possible. He sent a military mission to advise the Chinese government, arranged for a loan, and ordered his assistants to draw up plans with the Chinese for military cooperation in case Japan attacked the French possessions.[90] He may even have authorized the continued shipment of war materials on the Red River railway. According to his chief of staff for the colonies, General Bührer, the supplies sent to China after October 1937 were limited to non-strategic goods. But in June 1939 it appears that arms and ammunition were also being sent.[91] Whatever the case, until June 1940 the Red River railway was China's single most important supply route. The Japanese would have liked to close it down altogether. By keeping it open, even if only for civilian goods, France provided substantial assistance to China.

Despite Mandel's efforts to change French policy, his influence as minister of Colonies could only be peripheral. Nevertheless, the position had certain compensations. The colonies afforded great scope for his administrative abilities, and gave him the opportunity of contributing to France's defense effort by preparing the empire for war. The minister of Colonies controlled all of the French overseas territories except Algeria, Morocco, and Tunisia in North Africa, and Syria and Lebanon in the Near East. The territory for which he was responsible was larger than the homeland, though most Frenchmen hardly gave the empire a thought. It had been acquired in the nineteenth century by a few enterprising statesmen and generals as a source of raw materials, an outlet for manufactured products, and an addition to French power and prestige in the world.

Mandel, like Clemenceau, had once been vigorously anticolonial. In 1938, however, the colonies were no longer just the prey of rapacious capitalists, but a source of potential strength to a threatened nation. Mandel was now prepared to make the most of the advantage given to France by her empire. France's self-confidence had been sapped by her great casualties in World War I and by her tremendous inferiority to Germany in population. Mandel conceived of the empire as a means of restoring her confidence. In his eyes, France was not just a European nation of 40,000,000 people but a vast empire of 110,000,000, whose potential resources far exceeded those of Germany. He wanted to make the country conscious of its empire and aware of its own strength.

For that purpose, he reorganized the information services of the ministry and obtained considerable publicity for the colonies. The press soon began to talk of France's "national mission." *L'Ordre* declared:

We must tell the people that our colonial empire is a primary element of our grandeur, that we are the second colonial power of the world, that our colonies are an economic asset, that they are an element of strength, a reservoir of products, of men and soldiers, and that France can no longer do without them; that our work is admired and our territories coveted, and that one day perhaps we will have to defend them.[92]

One of Mandel's assistants at the ministry published a book whose sole purpose was "to teach the French that they have an immense empire overseas.... It can only be a great comfort to us to know that we are no longer alone, that in peace, as in war, we have behind us the resources of an entire world, of an increasingly prosperous and civilized world."[93] Mandel himself gave two major radio addresses to inform the public about the colonies' contribution to the homeland.[94] He also organized a colorful colonial exhibition, for which many of the stores in Paris decked out their show windows with goods produced in the overseas territories.

Mandel's task, of course, went beyond mere propaganda. As he had done at the PTT, he set out also to make his ministry both efficient and effective. He ordered all colonial officials, many of whom were in the habit of taking extended vacations in Paris, back to their posts immediately. To ensure that high officials would be thoroughly conversant with the problems of the country to which they were assigned, he raised the minimum tour of duty to five years. Civil servants were henceforth to be recruited on the basis of competitive examinations and not by recommendations. A special salary scale was set up for those who learned the language of the country in which they worked. For the first time, native officials were assigned for one-year terms to the central administration in Paris.[95]

This last measure resulted from Mandel's concern to guarantee the allegiance of the native populations in the colonies in case of war. He also proposed to grant them a greater degree of independence and self-government. That this was no sudden and Machiavellian conversion to liberal principles is indicated by his support, even before he became minister, for Senator Maurice Violette's bill to grant more than 20,000 Algerians the right to vote without renouncing Arabic law as had hitherto been required. In February 1938 the Right, even then opposed to any concessions, denounced Mandel as a "zealous partisan of the extension of political rights to the native populations."[96]

Ellen Hammer has said that he was known among people from the empire for his attempt to make the colonial administration more liberal.[97] As minister, he passed one measure providing for the election, rather than the appointment by the governor general, of the municipal councilors of Madagascar. In Indochina, Mandel increased the authority of the local councils in the colony and mitigated the sentences of five hundred political prisoners.[98] These are relatively insignificant measures, but apparently he had plans to grant considerable autonomy to the colonies,[99] plans that had to be postponed at the outbreak of war. Although in this area of liberalizing the administration of the colonies he had accomplished little more than his Popular Front predecessor Marius Moutet,[100] one student of the question maintains that "Mandel's achievement remains remarkable, if only for the many lines of action he was able to initiate."[101]

Among the first to conceive of the French colonies in terms of a commonwealth of nations rather than as possessions, he tried to create a co-ordinated imperial economy and may be considered the godfather of the short-lived French Union created after World War II. In 1939 *The New York Times* wrote that history would remember Georges Mandel for creating the idea of a French colonial empire comparable to that of Britain.[102]

At the time, Mandel's plans for reform were subordinated to the admittedly more important task of increasing the colonies' contribution to the defense of Metropolitan France. His efforts were inspired by the visions of old colonial officers and administrators, who for a half century or more had thought of the colonies as a means of restoring French supremacy in Europe. At the Versailles Peace Conference, Clemenceau declared that the only thing he wanted in the colonies was an unlimited right to levy black troops to help defend France against any future attack by Germany.[103] Mandel's ideas were more liberal than Clemenceau's, and his task was complicated by the fact that the colonies were no longer merely pawns on the European chessboard but for the first time might themselves have to be defended against possible attack.

In attempting to build up the military strength of the empire, however, Mandel faced great administrative obstacles. Although charged with the defense of the colonies and the logistical support of the troops stationed there, he had no control over the size of the army or the deployment of the troops, both of which were determined by the minister of War. Moreover, he had no authority whatsoever over the air and naval forces assigned to the colonies. In effect, he was deprived of the very means of carrying out his mission. To remedy this, Mandel first got his ministry represented on the Permanent Committee of National Defense, which gave him a voice, along with the ministers of War, Aviation and Navy, in military decisions affecting the colonies. He then had the colonial army organized as a separate entity with its own chief of staff, who was given the right to levy troops and to organize the defense of the colonies. Mandel thus acquired the authority to carry out his plans without more than passing reference to the War Department, whose attention was fixed on Europe.[104]

In World War I the colonies had called up 356,000 troops, of which some 275,000 were sent to France along with 56,000 workers. In 1938 the colonial army comprised 100,000 men, of whom only 60,000 were natives. Mandel estimated that in case of war it would be possible to increase this number to two million without disrupting the colonial economies.[105] As a start, in May 1938 he ordered the recruitment of 50,000 extra troops: 25,000 from French Africa, 20,000 from Indochina, and 5,000 from Madagascar. To create armies entirely staffed by natives, he passed a decree granting Indochinese the right to attend French military schools without losing their nationality.

By calling the new units into being, Mandel forced the War Department to supply him with the necessary cadres for training them. But with the budget of Metropolitan France already being strained to meet the burden of rearmament, he had difficulty in obtaining funds for some of his projects. He decided to have the colonies pay for their own defense. Either by increasing taxes or issuing bonds, they were to finance the training and equipping of troops, and the construction of new roads, industries, and fortifications. Making it a point of honor not to rely on the financial resources of the mainland, he was able to disregard the economy-minded objections of his ministerial colleagues. But colonial officials, understandably, had their own objections to Mandel's policies and methods. Governors were suddenly ordered to recruit, house, train, and equip 20,000 extra troops, improve ports, build roads through desert and jungle, and to finance most of these projects themselves. Mandel overrode all objections by threatening to replace recalcitrant administrators, as he was finally forced to do in a number of cases.

Even with the necessary money, Mandel found it impossible in 1938 to purchase all the modern equipment he needed for the troops he was raising. French and foreign manufacturers had more orders than they could fill. From official channels he received only what could be spared from the European theater, which at that time was very little and usually outmoded. He was forced to improvise. In 1939 he was able to acquire the equipment of the Spanish Republican forces that had been disarmed on French soil. A permanent solution, however, demanded that armaments industries be established in the colonies themselves. Factories were set up in Indochina to produce infantry mortars, bombs, cartridges, uniforms and gas masks, and work was begun on a plant capable of turning out 150 aircraft and 400 motors annually. These measures raised serious problems for the colonies, where social unrest was caused by the introduction of industries, and for the Ministry of Aviation, which refused to supply training personnel for aircraft that were presumed to be unsafe. Mandel ignored all objections and ordered the factories completed. He purchased training planes in England, and sent instructors under the command of Colonel Louis Castex to establish a school of aviation in Indochina.[106]

By June 1940 over 500,000 native troops had been called up, more than the colonies had raised throughout World War I.[107] Roads had been constructed across the Sahara linking Morocco, Algeria, and the French possessions in Central Africa. The defenses at the Port of Dakar were strengthened. French Somaliland had been turned into a fortress that prevented Mussolini from seizing it even after the collapse of France.[108] Plans had been made with the British for the pooling of the resources of the two empires, for their military and economic coordination during the war and their eventual cooperation after the war. Rivalries were to be reduced and the two empires made as complementary as possible.[109]

Mandel's one notable failure, due more to lack of time than to lack of will or planning, was in the creation of a colonial air force. In April 1938, to defend the entire empire, he had 109 aircraft, of which only twenty-two were modern. By December 1939, he had increased this number to 209, of which seventy-seven were late models, but the colonial air force was still entirely inadequate. Most of the planes were assigned to Djibouti, and the rest of the colonies left unprotected.[110] In time the aircraft factory in Indochina would have provided that colony with an adequate air force, but by June 1940 it had not even started production.

The colonies could not have saved France in 1940, but Mandel's efforts, only beginning to bear fruit when the country surrendered, had been undertaken with a long and exhausting war in view. Cyril Falls has said that one factor in France's endurance in World War I, "half forgotten today, but which at the time the Germans realized to their cost, was the part played by colonial troops, especially from North and Central Africa. I doubt whether she would have survived without them."[111] Had the French Army been able to hold out in World War II, the colonial contribution would have been of overwhelming importance. As it was, the colonial army formed the largest part of the Free French Forces that fought in Italy and in France in 1944.[112] Some of the credit for this army, which helped to restore France's prestige and self-esteem, must be given to Mandel. General Bührer, chief of staff of the colonial army, dedicated his account of their work to Mandel. "The empire," he said, "... was brought to its apogee during the war by the persistent, forceful, unremitting efforts of a minister of Colonies endowed with all the qualities of a great statesman."[113]

14. The Phony War

*Historical examples . . . show that nations which lay down their arms
without compelling reasons prefer in the ensuing period to accept the
greatest humiliations and extortions rather than attempt to change their
fate by a renewed appeal to force. This is humanly understandable.
A shrewd victor will, if possible, always present his demands to
the vanquished in installments. And then, with a nation that has lost its
character—and this is the case of every one which voluntarily submits—
he can be sure that it will not regard one more of these individual
oppressions as an adequate reason for taking up arms again.*

MEIN KAMPF

WHEN HITLER OCCUPIED PRAGUE in March 1939, even the most ardent
appeasers had to admit that Germany could not be trusted. At a cabinet
meeting Daladier declared that nothing could be done now but prepare
for war.[1] Emmanuel Berl wrote: "The die is cast, and it is clear that force
alone will resolve the problem. There will be no peace for France or Europe
until Germany, either exhausted or conquered, gives up her plans."[2]

Some of the pacifists, with amazing resilience, quickly recovered from
their shock, and returned with other arguments to their fight against war.
Now they said that although war might be inevitable, everything must be
done to postpone it as long as possible.[3] The great difference between October and March was that public sentiment was now on the side of the
bellicistes.[4] It was no longer so easy to attack Mandel for wanting war or to
denounce him for his Jewish origins. In April a law was passed forbidding
anti-Semitic attacks. The minister of Justice declared that the aim of the
law was "to call a halt to the abominable press campaigns, for anything that
stimulates hatred or sets Frenchmen against Frenchmen can only be considered treasonous."[5] Henceforth, Mandel's opponents would tread warily.
They might risk an occasional attack, but the tone would be less violent.
With war approaching, he was bound to exercise more influence in the government, and there was not one of his enemies who did not remember
Mandel's role during World War I in the arrest of Caillaux, Malvy and
many journalists. At the time of Munich, Edouard Pfeiffer had openly
expressed their fears in *La République.* Laval's friends were convinced that
Mandel would not hesitate to have Laval shot,[6] and according to some reports, Mandel said that in spite of his friendship for Flandin, he would
have no qualms about ordering him executed if events required it.[7]

Mandel's enemies may have feared his coming to power, but his friends
regarded it with hope and expectation. Emile Buré called Mandel "the su-

preme hope of all French patriots."[8] Henri de Kérillis openly regretted that the country was governed by Daladier and Bonnet instead of by a Tardieu, a Reynaud, or a Mandel. "France must find a Clemenceau," he wrote. "His origins, his past and his errors are unimportant. France must be galvanized, driven forward by daring energy, and exalted by an ardent patriotic faith."[9] Others agreed with Kérillis that Mandel might be the man.[10] Mandel himself, said one of his assistants, "had known the intoxication of total power during the last years of the 1914–1918 war. Although he was a born parliamentarian, the dictatorship necessarily accompanying a state of war did not frighten him. In 1917–1918 under Clemenceau he had acquired the necessary experience for governing a country at war, and he was convinced that this experience would put him in the forefront of the political scene."[11]

At the moment, however, Mandel's power in the government was less than his enemies feared. They considered him the evil genius in the cabinet leading the country into war. Outwardly, at least, his importance was secondary. He rarely spoke out in cabinet discussions. Everyone knew what he thought, in any case. He limited himself to demanding that France take a stand against Germany, or to calling for clarification when the irresolution within the cabinet threatened to make French policy even more ambiguous than it already was. The determination of policy ultimately depended on Prime Minister Daladier, who was inclined to resist but feared war. Mandel exercised little direct influence over Daladier, one of the few men in Parliament with whom he had never had long discussions.[12] He repeatedly told friends that Daladier was better than Bonnet. "He is an honest man, but unfortunately he is a maneuverer. He is indecisive and acts only when he is driven to the wall and cannot do anything else." For his part, said a mutual friend, Daladier was usually reticent about Mandel. "He admired his intelligence and his strength, but remained suspicious of him."[13]

France finally went to war in 1939 not because of her determination to stop Hitler, but because she felt obliged to follow Great Britain. After the occupation of Prague in March, Chamberlain resolved to make no further concessions, and promised to aid Poland if she were attacked by Germany. Bonnet and the pacifists were dragged, protesting, into the war. Even after the outbreak of hostilities they tried to extricate France from her commitments. Reynaud and Mandel, on the other hand, fought to keep France faithful to her allies. Daladier as usual was caught between the two factions, but this time was more inclined to resist than to capitulate.

When word of the proposed Russo-German nonaggression pact reached France on August 22, Mandel and Reynaud insisted that Daladier order general mobilization as the only means of restraining Hitler.[14] Daladier, still hoping to postpone war, preferred to continue with the partial mobilization that was already under way. On the twenty-fifth, Bonnet tried to send Anatole de Monzie, the minister of Public Works and a well-known Italophile, to Rome. He was to persuade Mussolini to intercede with Hitler, but Mandel's opposition reportedly killed the plan.[15] The message nonetheless got through to Mussolini, who proposed on the thirty-first that an international conference be summoned to settle the Polish question. Bonnet favored the idea, but Reynaud and Mandel opposed a new Munich and the cabinet postponed any decision.[16] On September 1 German troops entered Poland, and France finally decided on general mobilization. On the second, the French Parliament voted war credits. On the third, after one final delay in the cabinet, the government sent Germany an ultimatum stating that unless she evacuated Poland, France would be forced to aid her ally. Hitler ignored the ultimatum, and France found herself once again at war with Germany.

For some time Mandel had believed war to be inevitable. He had been unwilling, therefore, to make any concessions that would strengthen Germany or to postpone confrontations in the hope of obtaining peace. He believed that France's position became relatively weaker each year, for while Germany prepared her economy for war, France remained foolishly preoccupied with internal problems. He repeatedly declared that "democracies prepare for war only after having declared it,"[17] and maintained that the only way France could overcome Germany's growing superiority in armament was by resisting German demands and accepting the war that would follow. Each month that Bonnet thought to have gained by making concessions was for Mandel a month lost. His announced preference for "war tomorrow rather than in a week, in a week rather than in a month, in a month rather than in a year" may have shocked his contemporaries but it concisely expressed his opinion.[18]

At the time of Munich, Mandel seemed to be optimistic about French chances in a war with Germany. Yvon Delbos quoted him as saying: "We will hold out on the Maginot Line; the Russian divisions will seize or destroy the Rumanian oil fields and Germany will collapse, once again strangled by the blockade."[19] In September 1939, after Russia's desertion and the loss of Czechoslovakia, he was no longer so hopeful. "The war will be long—very, very long," he told Paul-Boncour. "It is impossible to foresee the end! France will be invaded as far as the Bidassoa [small river running along part of France's frontier with Spain], and all sorts of catastrophes will strike our poor country.... But you will see, from catastrophe to catastrophe, we will go on to final victory."[20]

The outbreak of war brought little change in the balance of political forces in France. The press might celebrate French unity and determination to put an end to Hitler's adventures, but at the highest levels sentiment was as divided as ever. On August 27 Flandin had told Daladier that "war would be a crime."[21] Flandin's efforts to keep France out of war were supported by a committee of deputies who had thirty of their colleagues sign an appeal to the government for an international conference. After the declaration of war they continued their activities, trying to persuade the government to ask for peace before real hostilities against Germany began.[22]

The only real change in the situation since Munich was that Daladier was now determined to fight. At heart he had never been an advocate of appeasement, but believing in 1938 that France was too weak to act without British support, he had reluctantly and remorsefully followed Chamberlain in his policy of conciliating Hitler. In 1939 he once again followed Britain, this time into war; but in doing so, he also followed his own inclinations to resist German aggression.

In deserting his pacifist friends, however, Daladier by no means joined the camp of the *bellicistes*, who advocated an immediate attack on Germany. His own policy was to hoard France's precious and limited resources until the air force had been built up and the British could join her in strength. He refused to authorize a major offensive or even to allow air attacks on Germany, fearing to engage the country in battle before French and British rearmament had been completed. Thus in September, while Germany annihilated Poland, France limited herself to a token campaign in the West.

To maintain control of policy, Daladier guarded himself as carefully against the *bellicistes* as he did against the pacifists. He kept Mandel and Reynaud in their relatively subordinate positions, and refused to eliminate the pacifists from the cabinet. Their dismissal would have driven them into open opposition, risking the life of the government and leaving Daladier completely dependent on the support of the *belliciste* faction.[23]

Mandel was among the most vehement of those favoring an immediate attack. "If we do not launch a full-scale offensive against the Germans while they are occupied in Poland," he said, "we may never again have such a chance."[24] He did not specify how or where the offensive was to be undertaken, but he later backed General Bührer's plans to use a colonial army as the spearhead of an attack on the Siegfried Line.[25] He also favored an attack on Italy "to put an end to Mussolini's blackmail."[26] He later told a friend that he had fought in vain day after day for an active policy:

We declared war in order to save Poland. Then we sat and twiddled our thumbs until Poland was crushed. We should have fought at the start. We should have created a warlike spirit in the army. Without regard for anyone, we should have rid the general staff of the incompetent and those with outmoded ideas, and replaced them with new men, men with modern ideas, with will power and character. We needed a commander in chief and not an infantry captain.... The men of 1914, magnificently commanded, were magnificent soldiers. It has been proven that those of 1939 were their equals. But there was a spirit of demoralization to overcome; a few executions would have sufficed. Absolutely! A country in war cannot be governed by imbeciles. Like Clemenceau, I wage war, and in order to assure victory, all obstacles must be swept away without pity. The nation comes before everything.[27]

At the Nuremberg Trials the German generals agreed that a real offensive in the opening days of the war when most of the German army was in the east would have had considerable chance of success, and the most recent study of the question concludes that in September 1939 France and Britain lost a magnificent opportunity to defeat Germany at small cost.[28] At the least, it seems clear that if France had been able to undertake an offensive of some importance before May 1940, the army and the nation would not have collapsed so quickly. The troops would already have experienced battle, incompetent generals would have revealed their deficiencies and been replaced, and the entire nation would not have sunk into the mentality of the phony war, hoping that victory could be achieved without bloodshed.

The early outbreak of hostilities would also have silenced the pacifists. As Mandel put it, "In order to stop the peace maneuvers, a river of blood must once again separate France and Germany."[29] Any suggestions of retreat would then be shouted down as treason and their authors imprisoned as they had been during World War I. Mandel opposed a negotiated peace because France had declared war "to stop German conquests and remove the German threat to French security. Even if a compromise peace had been concluded in November, the threat would still have existed, and a year later there would have been another mobilization."[30]

To encourage a more vigorous prosecution of the war, Mandel advocated harsh treatment for defeatism on the home front. Several times he demanded the arrest of the principal members of the Comité France-Allemagne.[31] British journalists heard rumors that he had also wanted Flandin, Laval, and Bonnet arrested, but that the Prime Minister hesitated to take such drastic action.[32] Daladier denies any knowledge of this and says that in any case it would have been impossible to arrest anyone as important as Flandin or Laval.[33] Mandel was undoubtedly aware of Daladier's reluctance to act and possibly inspired the rumors in order at least to inhibit defeatist activities.

Because he talked of repressive measures, because he opposed the government's do-nothing policy and openly criticized Daladier and Gamelin—"those men don't want to fight"[34]—Mandel was rumored throughout the winter to be trying to overthrow the cabinet.[35] But even without the rumors, Daladier would have been suspicious of Mandel. Louis Aragon puts it well in his historical novel *Les communistes*:

[Daladier] is haunted by the thought of a successor.... The one he suspects is Mandel. Whoever says Mandel, says Clemenceau, and what do you expect, when people are always comparing this war with the other one? In 1914 a Radical of sorts, Viviani, was there to declare war. Daladier does not want to be replaced like Viviani. Yet there are many people who are saying that Mandel is waiting for his chance, and that the war will take a different turn the day Mandel is summoned. Daladier is determined to play all the roles: he was Viviani, he will be Clemenceau. There is no need for Mandel.[36]

To allay the Prime Minister's suspicions, Mandel spoke to him several times. "You are the only possible man [to lead the government] under the present circumstances," he told Daladier. "[Even] if you were not, it could not be me, because I'm an Israelite and on account of Hitler. He does not like Jews, and there are so many people hereabouts who are anxious to humor him."[37] Nevertheless, it is clear that Mandel would have liked to replace Daladier with a more vigorous leader. In April 1939 he tried to prevent the reelection of President Lebrun in order to eliminate Daladier. His own choice for the presidency would have been President Jules Jeanneney of the Senate or another advocate of resistance, who would have nominated a like-minded man as prime minister.[38] Then, when Daladier's government began to weaken in February 1940, Mandel actively helped to arrange for its successor. At dinners at Maurice Rothschild's home, he and Reynaud argued with Senator Lémery for a more dynamic war policy and tried to get Senate support for a government led by Reynaud.[39] Finally, in March Mandel encouraged right-wing leader Louis Marin to attack Daladier in Parliament for not pursuing the war more actively.[40]

Daladier's position deteriorated over the winter because of criticism from both sides. After Russia invaded Finland in November 1939, the French conservatives, in one of the strangest reactions of the war, demanded that the government aid the Finns and declare war on Russia. Here, at last, was a crusade in which they could participate wholeheartedly.[41]

Under pressure from the *bellicistes* as well to do something—anything—

to break the grip of apathy and inertia on the country, Daladier decided to send an expedition to Scandinavia. The decision came too late, for the Finns surrendered on March 13 before the troops had even embarked. Both factions in France then seized the occasion to attack the government in secret sessions of Parliament for its conduct of the war. Daladier made a weak effort to salvage his government. He proposed a reorganization of the cabinet, but an adverse vote in the Chamber caused him to resign before any changes could be made. He refused President Lebrun's request to form a new government because he was worn out by his constant struggles, but also perhaps because he hoped that Reynaud, his expected successor, would fail to find a majority in the Chamber and thereby be discredited, leaving the way clear for Daladier's own eventual return to power.[42]

Reynaud's majority was, in fact, uncertain. As a result, he was forced to form a government that was as disunited as Daladier's. He dismissed Bonnet but kept de Monzie in order to demonstrate the new government's friendly disposition toward Italy. Six Socialists were included in the cabinet, but not Léon Blum, for fear of alienating rightist support. Without Blum, it was impossible to add Louis Marin, his right-wing counterpart, and thus rightist support was lost in any case. The Radicals held the key to the situation, and Reynaud had to court them. He gave them eleven portfolios in compensation for losing direction of the government, and allowed Daladier to remain minister of War, although Reynaud would have preferred that post himself.

There were two important appointments that Reynaud tried to make but had to delay until a more propitious time. Daladier's objections forced him to retract his offer to make his unofficial military advisor, Colonel de Gaulle, secretary to the war cabinet. De Gaulle's ideas clashed with those Daladier had carried out as minister of War since 1936. Once again Reynaud had to defer to Daladier and the Radicals.

Reynaud had also wanted to appoint Mandel minister of the Interior, but Mandel refused the post for two reasons. First, although legend pictured him as avidly coveting the office, he believed that "the moment was not yet at hand when he could really do a thorough job of it and uncompromisingly strike at the very roots of defeatism."[43] A sort of Jewish reflex may have warned him that it would be impossible for him to adopt any serious measures before the country felt itself menaced. As he told Emile Buré, "I will be minister of the Interior when things are at their worst and no one cares any more about the shape of a minister's nose."[44]

The second reason was that the new government, in order to survive, needed the support of Daladier and his followers in the Radical Party, already antagonistic to Reynaud for having supplanted them in power. Loss of the ministry of the Interior, traditionally given to a Radical, would only have increased their antagonism and possibly have led to the defeat of the government. Thus Mandel refused to accept the ministry without Daladier's approval. This proviso was made in order to remove any lingering suspicion from Daladier's mind that Mandel had been involved in a plot with Reynaud in order to advance himself personally.[45]

Mandel's concern was not unwarranted, for Daladier momentarily considered refusing to join Reynaud's government, knowing that it could not stand without him. To encourage Daladier's participation, Mandel, after consulting with Maurice Sarraut, the *éminence grise* of the Radical Party and a close friend in recent years, announced that his own participation was dependent on Daladier's.[46] He thus clearly fixed responsibility for the fate of the cabinet on the ex-premier, and incidentally reserved a place for himself in any cabinet that Daladier might form in the future.

The weakness of Reynaud's government was that it lacked the sense of inevitability and necessity that had swept Clemenceau into office. Lloyd George believed that Reynaud had come to power too soon and that, like Clemenceau, he should have waited until France was in grave danger.[47] The crisis that gave him his opportunity was parliamentary, not national, and he had been forced to form a large, unwieldy, and disunited cabinet. Every ministerial post, he said, had to bring him some support.[48] In parliamentary terms, all the maneuvers surrounding the formation of the government were justified, for on his first vote of confidence he received just 268 votes while 156 deputies opposed him and 111 abstained. Emmanuel Berl has said that without Mandel, even this majority would have been impossible. According to Berl, no one except Mandel would even have tried to force Reynaud on a Chamber so thoroughly opposed to him.[49]

The utter confusion of the times is indicated by the fact that a right-wing leader like Reynaud could receive most of his support from the Left. Only the Socialists voted for him as a group. The Right and Center, led by Laval and Flandin, formed the bulk of the opposition. The advocates of appeasement naturally rejected him. Marcel Déat asserted that "behind Reynaud there is Mandel, and behind Mandel there is General Bührer" with his scheme to throw a million men against the Siegfried Line.[50] Despite all the maneuvers, the Radicals split, as usual, the majority abstaining even though Daladier, Chautemps, and Albert Sarraut were in the cabinet.

To demonstrate the country's determination to fight the war to the end, and to counteract any lingering desire for peace, Reynaud immediately flew to London to sign an agreement with the British in which both nations promised not to conclude a separate peace. The two governments also decided to mine Norwegian waters to cut off the German supply of iron ore from Scandinavia. The Allied operation was stopped by the German invasion of Denmark and Norway on April 9 and ended in a quick retreat.

Reynaud then tried to get rid of General Gamelin whom he considered to be incompetent and held responsible for the failure of the Norwegian operation, but he was twice thwarted by Daladier. After the second attempt had failed on May 9, Reynaud was on the point of resigning, but the beginning of the German offensive the following day forced him to remain in office. Thus France faced the gravest crisis in her history as a disunited nation, with a disunited Parliament, led by a disunited government on the verge of disintegration.

Despite eight months of preparation, the German invasion took France by surprise. On the very day of the attack, all soldiers who had been born in 1912 and 1913 were being sent to the rear for demobilization.[51] The Germans very quickly broke through the Allied front and threatened for a moment to descend on Paris. Reynaud decided to evacuate the government and authorize the population to leave the city. Emotion rapidly subsided, however, and the government remained in Paris when it was learned that the Germans had turned toward the Channel. Reynaud then decided to profit from the disaster to construct a strong war government. He replaced Gamelin with General Weygand, Foch's chief assistant; he called Marshal Pétain into the cabinet; and he placed Mandel in charge of the Ministry of the Interior in order to produce "a psychological shock."[52] Public opinion was overwhelmingly favorable to the changes. The three men symbolized France's victory in World War I and inspired absolute confidence.

Mandel's promotion was celebrated by foreign and national journals alike. *The New York Times* asserted that he "will make good the premier's warning that henceforth in France weakness will be punished by death." According to Léon Blum, what most impressed public opinion was "the installation at the Ministry of the Interior of M. Georges Mandel, whose foresight, authority, and firmness are legendary and almost mysterious." Even his former enemies on the right suddenly rallied behind him. Léon Bailby, whom Mandel had threatened to prosecute during World War I, now found it wise to praise Mandel's abilities publicly. *Je Suis Partout* declared: "We never spared our criticism of that intelligent and complex man when he influenced foreign policy . . . (censored). But it is impossible to deny his administrative ability and his sense of authority. M. Mandel does not attempt to evade responsibility. . . . The forces of disorder and treason will find their match in him."[53]

The crisis also brought about a reconciliation with Maurras, who devoted a long, almost affectionate, article to describing his relations with Mandel over the years, regretting Mandel's departure from nationalist circles where he had been respected, and concluding that at the Ministry of the Interior, "like all of his predecessors, he will be confronted with an impossible situation. He is perhaps the only man who can handle it without harming the regime."[54]

Although Mandel had acquired implacable enemies in the course of his career, he had also acquired—and retained—the personal respect of men who bitterly opposed his policies. Flandin was one, and Anatole de Monzie, who had opposed Mandel at the time of Munich, was another. Monzie wrote in his memoirs that of the three advocates of resistance, Reynaud, Mandel and Champétier de Ribes, he preferred Mandel, "diable sans équivoque."[55] The oddest relationship, perhaps, was with Pierre Gaxotte. For years Gaxotte had venomously attacked Mandel in *Je Suis Partout* for his evil influence on the government. Yet once war broke out, Gaxotte visited him every week in order to discuss developments. After the war he wrote that he regarded Mandel as having been "une force mal utilisée."[56]

It is clear that many conservatives, though they disagreed with his policies, still respected him. The poisonous propaganda that had been poured out day after day had not utterly destroyed all the confidence he had so laboriously built up. When he became minister of the Interior, the anti-Semite Count Armand de Puységur was provoked by the "stupid *bienpensants* and *salonards*" who were pleased by the appointment because they knew that he would control the Communists.[57]

For obvious reasons, discordant notes like this did not appear in the press, except in the clandestine *L'Humanité*.[58] Any disapproval of Mandel's appointment was expressed in private. Alain Laubreaux of *Je Suis Partout* considered it symbolic: "For a Jewish war, we needed a Jewish Clemenceau."[59] Lucien Rebatet of the same journal reported the reaction of some of the army officers stationed with him: "He's a bastard, but at least he is an energetic bastard." For his own part, Rebatet was disgusted with the praise being lavished on Mandel by Maurras and others, but said nothing about the hypocritical comments of his own paper.[60]

The irony in the situation was that Mandel had achieved his reputed lifelong ambition, but at a time when he believed it would be difficult to accomplish anything. Many of the functions of the Interior had been taken over by the Ministry of War, and he would have little authority. But he could hardly refuse to accept the office when his very presence there might aid in reestablishing the morale of the country.[61]

Everyone counted on him to assure that the war would be fought with greater determination. Many people had already seen him in action in World War I and the rest knew him by reputation or had heard him make ominous demands for the arrest and possible execution of defeatists. "Individual cases can be saddening," he once said. "But a statesman cannot be sentimental when the life of the country and of millions of honest families is at stake. Weakness in government results in disorders that create terrible misery."[62]

One American journalist noted that the first reaction to the German breakthrough had been disastrous, but the people were "vaguely confident, because they at last have the feeling of being governed by capable hands. The extraordinary effect on morale of Reynaud's speech and Mandel's toughness can't be overlooked."[63]

Mandel's first concern was to assure the internal security of the country. He began by taking charge of the censorship[64] and dismissing the director of the Sûreté Nationale. In his place Mandel appointed Maurice Winter, who had held the position under Clemenceau. Dance halls and gambling dens were then closed down. Patrols were sent through the Paris sewers. The police, newly equipped with rifles, bayonets, and helmets, began a roundup of all suspicious persons. In the first week, two thousand cafés and hotels were checked, over 62,000 people interrogated and five hundred arrested.[65] Military courts were given authority to try civilians for acts against the security of the state. Judgments were to be executed without appeal and without delay. The effect of all these measures was immediate. A Canadian businessman remarked at the end of the month that

Paris is changing its appearance more and more. The metamorphosis begun on May 18 with the nomination of Georges Mandel to the Ministry of the Interior continues. . . . Numerous arrests have been made in the street. Traffic is strictly controlled. . . . Policemen, bayonets fixed, stop passers-by and ask for identification. Cafés are constantly visited by the police. . . . Service on public telephones has been cut off. A telegram cannot be sent without special permission from the police. Surveillance is so strict that everyone feels himself guilty of some mysterious crime.[66]

Mandel also tried to stop the flow of refugees from the northeastern departments. Anticipating a long war, the government had planned the evacuation of the population in advance in order to spare the people the long occupation they had suffered from 1914 to 1918. But so many people had decided to leave that roads were blocked, troop movements hindered, and refugees left without food and shelter. In a radio address, Mandel urged the people to stay at home, and ordered all administrative officials to stay at their posts in order to halt the emigration and maintain essential services. Those who panicked or failed to obey directives were dismissed.[67] He and Weygand agreed not to order any further evacuations,[68] and during a lull in the fighting Mandel even attempted to get some of the people to return home.[69] The mass movement of population, however, was too great to be stopped, and continued until the armistice.

Mandel was more successful in Paris, where after the first bombing of the city on June 3, he prevented a flight by ordering all public officials and workers to remain at their posts under threat of severe penalties.[70] Nevertheless, there was a spontaneous emigration a week later after the government left Paris. Mandel had wanted to defend the capital,[71] but at the last minute, Weygand, in charge of military operations, had it declared an open city. Unfortunately, the population was not informed of this decision until the night of June 12, by which time large numbers had already fled under the impression that Paris was going to be defended to the last stone. Because their *jusqu'auboutiste* sentiments had helped create this impression, and because they did not prepare for the evacuation, Mandel and Reynaud have sometimes been held responsible for the confusion and suffering that followed.[72] The real responsibility, however, lies with Weygand, who later took credit for having spared the capital.[73] He himself made the decision at the last moment and only belatedly informed the military governor of Paris, who was then unable to notify the people in time to stop them from leaving.[74]

Mandel's third great concern during this period was the problem of right-wing defeatism about which little had been done until that time. *Belliciste* papers like *La Lumière* and *L'Epoque* had called for repressive measures, but the government had acted largely against Communists and aliens. The Communist Party was suppressed, its newspapers banned, its deputies tried, and its supporters purged from the administration. In September 1939 thousands of foreigners were arrested, and after May 10 all persons of German origin were ordered to report for internment.[75]

In comparison with the immense effort deployed against Communists and foreigners, relatively little seems to have been done about German sympathizers and right-wing defeatists.[76] In September 1939 a few small anti-Semitic papers had been closed down and Fernand de Brinon, future Vichy representative to the Germans in Paris, was confined to his residence.[77] But in October, Minister of the Interior Albert Sarraut had refused the request of the counter-espionage services to arrest Marcel Déat, Jean Luchaire, Jacques Benoist-Méchin, Fernand de Brinon, and others who were later to become leading collaborators.[78]

Mandel seems to have been reluctant to act against the Communists.[79] According to Louis Aragon, he opposed the measures already taken against them by Daladier because he hoped for a rapprochement with the Soviet Union.[80] He also protected the Russian writer Ilya Ehrenburg from harassment by the French police.[81] The Communists, for their part, seem to have had mixed feelings about him. He was officially denounced in *L'Humanité*.[82] But if one is to believe Aragon's historical novel *Les communistes* and Ehrenburg's memoirs, the Soviet leaders, at least, regarded him with a different eye. In Aragon's novel, Mandel appears both under his own name and as an anonymous figure called simply "Le Ministre." In both roles, he is portrayed more or less sympathetically until, as "Le Ministre," he disillusions one of the principal protagonists by advocating an attack on the Russian oil fields. Aragon's hero is depressed by the fact that "such an intelligent man" could fail to realize the seriousness of what he was proposing. Then, as Mandel, the minister of the Interior, he also proves to be a disappointment. "Many people," the narrator says, "had trembled at the thought of Clemenceau's disciple at the Interior, because they believed that Mandel in power meant action taken against *L'Action Française, Je Suis Partout,* the Doriotistes, and the Cagoule. Yet it seemed that his appointment was interpreted by the police ... as an order to renew the offensive against the Communists."[83] His lapses seem to be noted with regret, and one has the feeling that ultimately he is the man with whom the Communists hoped to come to an understanding.

But whatever their attitude toward him may have been, and despite his own hopes about future Russian involvement in the war, in the circumstances Mandel could not allow the French Communists to go on denouncing the war as a capitalist and imperialist venture and urging the workers to sabotage war production.[84] He interned a number of them, including the wives of Gabriel Péri and André Marty.[85] Other party members were arrested and shot for acts of sabotage in airplane factories.[86] Mandel's principal efforts, however, were directed to dramatizing the fight against right-wing defeatism, which he considered to be a greater danger at the moment, for it might lead the nation to hope for a negotiated peace. On taking office he declared, "We must put an end to weakness. A purge is necessary."[87] He began an immediate investigation of *Je Suis Partout*, and on June 5 had its two directors, Alain Laubreaux and Charles Lesca, arrested along with three salon Fascists, Armand Thierry de Ludre, Robert Fabre-Luce, and Clement Serpeille de Gobineau, grandson of the nineteenth-century writer. Also arrested was Pierre Mouton, head of the Prima-Presse Agency, whose Berlin agent had been Paul Ferdonnet, the French Lord Haw-Haw.[88] Other German sympathizers or anti-Semites like Henry Coston of *La Libre Parole* were questioned or had their apartments searched.[89] Those arrested were charged with "acts likely to impair the external and internal security of the state." The police report specifically charged *Je Suis Partout* with being "one of the principal centers of the Hitlero-Fascist campaign carried on in France for years."[90]

When people began to leave Paris a few days later, the prisoners were first sent to the Camp des Graves near Orleans and there chained together and marched south. Along the way de Ludre disappeared. His body was never found, but he was later reported to have been shot and killed by the guards.[91] The rest of the prisoners were transported to a camp at Gurs near the Pyrenees from which Lesca and Laubreaux were rescued by Marshal Pétain on June 28.[92] The Vichy government dismissed the charges against them, enabling them to resume publication of *Je Suis Partout* under the Nazis in Paris. It became one of the major journals in France sincerely committed to collaboration with the Germans.

Fascist sympathizers have frequently held Mandel responsible for de Ludre's death, the usual charge being that he had given the order to shoot any prisoner who lagged behind.[93] The truth, however, was known even before the end of the war. On his release from prison, Charles Lesca made an investigation and discovered that General Héring, the military governor of Paris, and not Mandel, was responsible for the evacuation of the prisoners.[94]

After the arrest of the salon Fascists, it was an open question just how far Mandel might go in his campaign against defeatism. In World War I, the imprisonment of the editors of *Le Bonnet Rouge* had served as a prelude to the arrest of Caillaux and Malvy, two of the most important political leaders in the country. Was the action against *Je Suis Partout* to be followed by the arrest of Flandin, Bonnet, and Laval? Earlier Mandel had told a foreign caller that it would be possible to act decisively only when war had really started. His visitor would know that the moment had come when some of the leading defeatist statesmen were arrested.[95] It was said that he brought with him to the Ministry of the Interior a list of two hundred important Frenchmen who had compromised themselves by negotiations with enemy agents.[96] Rumors specifically mentioned Flandin, Laval, and Jacques Doriot as marked for arrest.[97]

Those in favor of fighting the war to the end were impatient with Mandel's failure to act,[98] but his campaign against defeatism was limited to putting out of circulation a few third-rate journalists and some minor social figures. *Candide* later asserted that he had garrulously tipped his hand in advance and thereby prevented his plans from being carried out.[99] This is unlikely. Mandel was a master of the art of manipulation by rumor. His friend André Stibio said that the calculated leak was one of his most powerful political tools.[100] Any revelations were deliberately made, possibly to restrain the defeatists while waiting for a more opportune moment to arrest them.

But not arresting some of them, particularly Laval, whom Mandel considered the most dangerous of the defeatists,[101] had serious consequences. In the last days of Reynaud's government at Bordeaux, these men helped persuade the wavering ministers of the necessity for an armistice. Laval was also instrumental in preventing the departure of President Lebrun and most of Pétain's cabinet for North Africa.

General Spears has written that both Mandel and Reynaud felt that Laval should be arrested, but "they threw back at each other the responsibility for so drastic a step, which neither had the courage to take."[102] The statement is simply naive, for the minister of the Interior could not have arrested any important figure without Reynaud's prior approval. It was widely known that Mandel favored taking such action. Camille Chautemps has said that he was "ready to go the limit against the *paniquards*, the *fuyards* and the defeatists, no matter how important they might be."[103] Even General Franco knew that Mandel had many times called for "the application of draconian laws against the Communists and defeatists."[104] It would seem that the real reason no action was taken was that Reynaud would not give his approval. He was afraid of the objections that President Lebrun and others would have raised, splitting the cabinet just when he was trying to unite it to carry on the war. Even the arrest of the journalists from *Je Suis Partout* had brought strong protests.[105]

If this is true, it indicates that Mandel and Reynaud were not working together so closely as people assumed. One opponent wrote, "They are a team. They form a tandem, a sort of duumvirate with joint ideas, dividing external and internal affairs between them."[106] Georges Wormser says that after the German invasion Mandel was always consulted before any important decision was made.[107] Reynaud himself states:

In the course of my political life, I have always had a perfect communion of thought with Georges Mandel. . . . It was for this reason that I asked him to be my most immediate collaborator. Every night he came to see me at the War Office. I gave him the military news, and he informed me of the internal situation, which was equally serious.[108]

In fact, however, the accord was not as close as Reynaud claims or as others assumed. The two leaders were cold, ambitious, self-sufficient men, accustomed to working alone and not afraid of being alone in their opinions. They were among the few members of Parliament who never used the "tu" form of address. They might share the same aims, but they did not share one another's thoughts, nor did they formulate policy in common.

Some of their differences were minor. Mandel, for example, disliked Reynaud's insensitivity to political amenities. Reynaud was imperious, disdainful, brusque, enormously vain, and thoroughly disliked by most of his colleagues. Although Mandel had no high opinion of the members of Parliament, he treated them individually with the utmost courtesy. Unlike Reynaud, he carried on no personal vendettas in the Chamber. Yesterday's enemy might be, and often was, today's friend. He was a consummate parliamentarian who neglected none of the marks of respect due to the powers of the regime. On becoming minister of Posts, he had immediately reconciled himself with Joseph Caillaux, the influential president of the Senate Finance Committee, whereas Reynaud as minister of Finance had totally ignored this potentially dangerous adversary.[109] For some time Mandel had also kept in close touch with Maurice Sarraut, and was disturbed by Reynaud's failure to consult this elder statesman of the Radical Party either before or after the formation of the cabinet.[110]

There were other more important differences. Reynaud has been severely criticized for appointing Pétain and others who later maneuvered him into resigning and then went on to conclude an armistice with Germany. In his defense, he states that no one, not even Mandel, objected to the nomination of Pétain.[111] But according to Louis Marin, several ministers had reservations that they were not given the opportunity to express.[112] Moreover, Mandel had earlier opposed Daladier's plan to bring Pétain into the government: "It would be a mistake, for he was a defeatist during the war."[113] And after his appointment to the cabinet, Mandel told a friend, "I believe that we are heading for an armistice; the presence of Pétain is the proof. In 1917 he wanted to sue for peace, for he thought the war was lost. Without Foch and Clemenceau we would have lost the war."[114]

Reynaud has tried to shift some of the responsibility for the unfortunate appointment to Mandel by recalling his advice of June 5 to name Pétain minister of Foreign Affairs. This, however, was two full weeks after Pétain had been called into the government, and would have involved giving him nominal responsibility for tasks actually carried out by someone else. The great mistake was not in giving him this or that post, but in having him in the government at all.[115]

A second incident of the sort involved the appointment of Paul Baudoin, a known defeatist and future Vichy minister of Foreign Affairs. Reynaud says he named Baudoin secretary to the war cabinet,[116] but made him under-secretary of State to the prime minister, and thus a member of the cabinet itself, only at Mandel's suggestion. He claims that he had hesitations about the appointment because Baudoin had published an article in the *Revue de Paris* supporting views on foreign policy at variance with his own. Only after Mandel told him that Baudoin had undergone a change of heart, Reynaud claims, did he agree to his appointment as under-secretary. Then when the cabinet was reshuffled on June 5, Reynaud promoted Baudoin to the post of under-secretary for Foreign Affairs. In commenting on this in his memoirs, Reynaud says with a certain lack of candor, "It will be remembered that it was on Mandel's recommendation that I had taken him as an assistant."[117]

On another occasion, Mandel got word in advance that Reynaud intended to dismiss Alexis Saint-Léger as secretary general of the foreign office. Léger was known to favor a vigorous prosecution of the war, and Mandel warned Reynaud: "You and he are the very embodiment of the spirit of determined resistance. If you dismiss him now, your move will be interpreted as the first step toward the policies you have hitherto fought."[118] Nevertheless, for reasons that are still unclear, Léger was replaced.

In all of these decisions, despite Reynaud's devious explanations, it is clear that he did not consult Mandel in advance. If they had been working together as closely as Reynaud says, if they had held informal conferences every evening to exchange ideas and information, they would have reached agreement on these issues, and Reynaud today would be able to state: "Mandel and I thought...", or "Mandel and I decided...", instead of "Mandel made no objections."

No one could expect two such independent men to agree on everything, but the appointment of Pétain and of Baudoin and the dismissal of Léger were not minor issues. They show, no matter what members of the cabinet may have thought, that it was Reynaud's government and it was he who made the decisions. Reynaud may have respected Mandel and relied on his support, but he did not always seek his advice or that of the cabinet.[119] The lack of confidence, moreover, was not one-sided. For his part, Mandel apparently did not fully trust Reynaud's ability to lead the government and rally the nation behind him.[120] In February Mandel had predicted to Admiral Jean Fernet that Reynaud would soon succeed Daladier, but said that "when the situation becomes extremely grave, we will have to have recourse to a prime minister who is even more energetic."[121] On May 9 when Reynaud at a full cabinet meeting attempted to have Gamelin replaced as commander in chief, Mandel remained silent while Daladier frustrated the Prime Minister's plan. It was not that he had any respect for Gamelin or opposed replacing him; he had often enough said that Gamelin was nothing but "a very intelligent prefect and a generalissimo for large-scale maneuvers."[122] But he considered the move to be untimely, and after the meeting criticized Reynaud: "On June 9 he could have closed the session of Parliament and sent the chambers on vacation for six months. It would have been possible then to make certain political changes that are manifestly inopportune now."[123] It is obvious that Mandel had not been informed of Reynaud's plans. The absence of accord was so clear that Lucien Lamoureux, the minister of Finance, thought Mandel failed to support the Prime Minister dur-

ing the meeting because he wanted to reserve a place for himself if Reynaud
had been forced to resign and Daladier been called on to form a new government.[124]

The most important difference between the two men was in their attitude
toward the war. In this respect Reynaud was far more equivocal than Mandel. In March he criticized Churchill, and in effect Mandel, who was like
Churchill in many ways, for being "utterly intransigent." As Sumner
Welles, the American under-secretary of State, reported after a visit to Paris,
"M. Reynaud felt that while Mr. Churchill was a brilliant and most enter-
taining man, with great capacity for organization, his mind had lost its
elasticity. He felt that Mr. Churchill could conceive of no possibility other
than war to the finish—whether that resulted in utter chaos or not. That,
he felt sure, was not true statesmanship." Reynaud twice repeated his conviction that "the possibility of negotiations on the basis of security and disarmament should not be discarded."[125]

After the German breakthrough in May, Reynaud told Ambassador Bullitt that "if the French army should be defeated, Great Britain would be
strangled in short order. . . ."[126] In contrast to the Prime Minister, Mandel
never for a moment doubted the ultimate victory of the Allies. Shortly before the armistice, he said to a friend: "Hitler will soon be in Paris, but he
is nonetheless beaten. We are going to the colonies; we are going to fight
everywhere. The Anglo-Saxons are the strongest powers. This war is above
all a war of tanks and planes. In a given time the English and the Americans
will manufacture 50,000 tanks, 100,000 planes—more if necessary—and in
the end Hitler will be beaten." He was absolutely convinced that the United
States and probably Russia would eventually enter the war on the Allied
side.[127]

Despite Reynaud's pessimistic moments, however, there is no doubt that
he hoped to keep France in the war. He himself had insisted on the signing
of the agreement with the British not to conclude a separate peace. And on
May 27 he told Chautemps that he would fight the final battle of the war
in Paris. He planned to have the government remain in the capital until the
last moment and then leave for London. Chautemps was to prepare secretly
for the departure, but the plan was dropped when Mandel opposed it.[128]
Mandel also opposed Reynaud's idea of fighting the last battle of the war
in Brittany, where evacuation to England would be a simple matter. He
favored instead a withdrawal first to Bordeaux and then to North Africa.
Thus the government could remain in control of France until the very end.
If they left before then, the people might feel abandoned. A widespread
feeling of this sort might enable the pacifists to form a rival government and
make a separate peace with Germany.[129]

These plans for continuing the war indicate the positive and energetic side

of Reynaud's character, but there was also the vacillating side. This may
have been in Mandel's mind when he told General Spears on May 25, "I
shall go on fighting in North Africa," but a moment later curiously added,
"I speak for myself alone. You may be sure that so long as I have the power
to do so, I shall advocate fighting on to the bitter end everywhere."[130] There
is also the strange note written by Mandel in prison: "Asked Lebrun end of
May—after surrender of Belgium—to appeal to the country and to proclaim
that we will never surrender. Refusal. June 17, government fell in dis-
grace."[131] Apparently Mandel had so little confidence in Reynaud that he
went directly to the President in the vain hope that Lebrun, on his own
authority, would proclaim France's refusal to surrender.

In any case, Reynaud says that by May 25 he had become convinced that
Pétain and Weygand were working for an armistice, but that he was unable
to dismiss them for fear of the repercussions. He resolved to avoid a rupture
with them, put off any discussion of ending the war, and strengthen his
cabinet by eliminating some of the men he thought might favor an armistice.

I hoped that if we were beaten in the battle for France, Pétain and Weygand
would be won over by the unanimous decision that my strengthened cabinet
would take. Thus I would avoid a break with them that I considered disastrous.
Until the end I tried to avoid that break, which would have divided France into
two camps.[132]

According to Philip Bankwitz, who has written the most authoritative
study of the question, Reynaud was in an impossible situation. He was unable to persuade Weygand to adopt a policy of continuing the war from
North Africa, and lacking the prestige of Clemenceau, he was unable to
dismiss Weygand so shortly after having summoned him, without sowing
panic and destroying national unity. He had only once choice: "to resign,
after a decent interval of suppressed conflict with the military power."[133]
In fact, Reynaud's inability to act guaranteed that power would gravitate
into the hands of the generals as the military situation deteriorated. By the
time a confrontation did take place, Weygand, in sole command of the military forces, had become the arbiter of the political situation and was able
to force Reynaud to resign.

III

From May 25 until June 16, Reynaud managed to postpone any decision
about continuing the war. During that time, on June 5, he reshuffled his
cabinet once again. The new appointments, like the earlier ones of Pétain,
Weygand and Baudoin, were to have disastrous effects. Of the new men,
only Yvon Delbos and the recently promoted General de Gaulle, now under-

secretary for War, would favor continuation of the struggle, whereas Jean Prouvost, Yves Bouthillier, and Georges Pernot would support demands for an armistice. Instead of strengthening the cabinet to carry on the war, Reynaud was unknowingly weakening it.

By June 10 the Allied defenses before Paris were broken, and the battle for France was virtually over. The question of an armistice would soon be raised seriously. When it was decided to evacuate the government from the capital, Mandel invited all the members of Parliament and the municipal councilors to leave with the cabinet in order to assure that no prospective Talleyrands remained behind to negotiate with the Germans.

The cabinet first headed for Tours, undecided as yet whether to go next to Brittany or Bordeaux. At a meeting with Churchill and Reynaud on the eleventh, Weygand described the depressing military situation and raised the issue of stopping the war. Reynaud cut him short with the remark that this was the concern of the government, not of the commander in chief. But despite Weygand's evident desire to end hostilities, Reynaud allowed him to attend a meeting of the cabinet on the twelfth at Tours. At this meeting, Weygand, supported by Pétain, demanded that the government ask Germany for an armistice. Until that moment few of the ministers had realized the extreme gravity of the situation. They were taken aback by Weygand's demand, but did not support him.

Instead of trying to get the cabinet to commit itself to continuing the war, Reynaud accepted Chautemps' suggestion that a new conference be held with Churchill to consider what to do about the collapse of the French army. Still afraid of the consequences of dismissing Weygand, Reynaud was being trapped by his own indecision. While Weygand and Pétain were determined on an armistice and doing everything possible to obtain it, the Prime Minister was playing for time and hoping for a miracle.

On June 13 Reynaud conferred once again with Churchill. For some time he had been suggesting to the British that unless they threw all their forces into the desperate battles then being fought, France might be forced to sue for an armistice. He always said that he personally would never surrender, but that a government headed by someone else might. On this occasion he explicitly asked Churchill what the British reaction would be if France were forced to ask for peace. In reply, Churchill refused to release France from her agreement not to sign a separate peace, but he also said that he understood the French predicament and promised that no matter what happened, England would restore France after the war "in all her power and dignity." He expressed himself so sympathetically that Baudoin was able to interpret his statement as approval of France's withdrawal from the war.

Although Reynaud states in his memoirs that he spoke to Mandel, Jeanneney and Herriot before the meeting and found them once again in complete accord with him,[134] it is obvious from their reaction when they learned what he had done, that he had not told them in advance what he planned to say to Churchill. The three leaders, who had been waiting in an adjoining room during the conference, criticized him immediately afterward for even bringing up the possibility of an armistice.[135] What Mandel called "the tragic word that never should have been spoken" was being used by Reynaud as well as by the advocates of peace.[136]

To forestall the possibly disastrous effects of Reynaud's action, Mandel spoke to Churchill for a few minutes before he flew back to England. There is no record of the conversation, but Mandel's sentiments were clear, and he undoubtedly told the British leader that instead of expressing his understanding of the French position and thus encouraging those who wanted to withdraw from the war, he should reject absolutely any idea of an armistice.[137] At least, that was the essence of his advice to the British Ambassador that night. Word of Reynaud's conversation with Churchill had spread quickly. Within hours it was being rumored that Great Britain would release France from her promise not to conclude a separate peace. Mandel consequently told the British to make it clear in a formal note that they did not intend to do so.[138]

Following the conference with Churchill, the French cabinet held another meeting. The ministers had expected Churchill to address them personally and objected when Reynaud said he had informed the British of their decision to continue the struggle. Weygand once again repeated his demand for an armistice. As if to reinforce his argument that hostilities must stop if order were to be maintained, he announced that Maurice Thorez had established a Communist government at Paris. Mandel immediately telephoned the Paris Prefect of Police, who denied Weygand's report.[139] But this did not stop Weygand, who then accused the government of ignoring the sufferings of the army and the country. When Mandel smiled at something he had said, the General, insisting he had been insulted, "gathered up his skirts like a furious prima donna and, without even a bow before the curtain, flounced out." As Weygand left the room, Mandel's secretary heard him say the ministers were mad and ought to be arrested.[140]

Once again, Reynaud postponed any decision about an armistice. This time he said he was waiting for a reply to a message he had just sent to Roosevelt, appealing for American intervention in the war. In Mandel's opinion, "although a vote for continuing the war would probably have been obtained yesterday, today, had one been taken, it would in all probability have been in favor of surrender." Weygand's demonstration and a speech by Pétain supporting him had swung a number of ministers over to the side of an armistice.[141]

The conference with Churchill brought the differences between Reynaud and Mandel into the open. Reynaud was weakening under the burden of responsibility. He was unable to make a clear-cut decision and would soon lose himself in a morass of maneuvers which he has since spent a quarter of a century attempting to justify.[142] Mandel, on the other hand, as Churchill noted that day, "was in the best of spirits. He was energy and defiance personified. . . . He was a ray of sunshine. . . . His ideas were simple, fight on to the end in France, in order to cover the largest possible movement to Africa."[143]

Alvarez del Vayo, former foreign minister of the Spanish Republic, and former Ambassador Albert Kammerer have both written that if Mandel had been prime minister instead of Reynaud, the destiny of France would have been different.[144] Their belief is shared by many journalists, statesmen, diplomats and scholars. Denis Brogan, the British historian, summed up the fairly widespread opinion when he wrote that "only Georges Mandel was of the stuff of which Gambettas are made."[145]

What impressed everyone was his calm and composure throughout the war in the midst of the most disturbing and disheartening news and events. On May 16, when it seemed for a moment as if the Germans were going to occupy Paris, the government was thrown into a panic. Bundles of documents were dumped from the upper-story windows of the Quai d'Orsay into a fire on the lawn. Mandel was among the few to keep his wits about him.[146] The journalist André Géraud, better known as Pertinax, wrote that together with the Presidents of the Senate and Chamber, Mandel was "the only public man on hand responsive to the Jacobin tradition of 1793. And he kept immune from the despair which made helpless men of Jeanneney and Herriot."[147] General Spears states that

he was the only Frenchman I met who proved quite impervious to circumstances, who remained detached, objective and even-tempered whatever befell. I have met many men who did not shrink from calamity, others who bore misfortune stoically, and yet more in whom danger kindles courage, but very few of the kind you could not "rattle," whose pulse and mind remained unaffected by events however unforeseen, sudden or shattering. It is a reptilian quality, not endearing but wholly enviable.[148]

The great question in the minds of his friends was whether Mandel would be able to take over the government and continue the war from North Africa. Mandel himself seems never to have had any hope of doing so. He reminded one friend that President Lebrun had always been hostile to him.[149] To another who inquired on June 10 about rumors that he might become prime minister, Mandel replied, "They are false. And even if they were true, I would refuse because I am Jewish."* Everyone seems to agree that this was a determining factor in preventing him from becoming prime minister and from taking action against the defeatists.[150] General Spears "expected him to pounce on the defeatists at any moment. But the opportunity did not come in time, or perhaps the fear that his religion might weaken his authority held him back."[151]

On the eve of the war, anti-Semitism had risen to heights unequalled in France since the Dreyfus case. After Sumner Welles spoke to Léon Blum in March 1940, he received more than three thousand letters from Frenchmen complaining of the honor he had bestowed on a Jew by his visit.[152] As a result of the bitter racial feeling, Mandel had been forced more than ever to leave the center of the stage to others, and to act through intermediaries. Although he quite obviously thought himself qualified to lead the country, he made no attempt to become premier in 1938–39. In 1940, if he worked for anyone's advancement, it was Reynaud's. As mentioned above, he believed no Jew should be at the head of the French government when blood was first shed. It would make the task of the defeatists far too easy. Already, one pamphlet published early in 1940, whose author was not a member of the lunatic fringe but was a Conseiller d'Etat and the president of the Comité France-Amérique, had called Mandel "a veritable calamity for our dear country," and charged him with responsibility for the fact that France must once again sacrifice the blood of her youth for foreign interests.[153] Laval reportedly was ready to incite an outburst of anti-Semitism in order to immobilize Mandel.[154] In these circumstances, it was impossible for him to become prime minister and equally impossible for him to act independently of Reynaud, who was continually temporizing. Moreover, the Prime Minister was clearly playing his own game, not consulting Mandel and hardly

---

* Bleustein-Blanchet, p. 196. Zaleski, the Polish foreign minister, even reportedly suggested that he take over the state. Mandel replied that he would not hesitate to do so, "but you must not forget that I am a Jew. . . . I could not get a sufficient following to oppose the defeatists. I am already being closely watched by them, lest I do what you suggest and what I would have no hesitation in doing if among our politicians and military leaders I could rally enough sound and determined men to support me. Unfortunately, it cannot be done." Jan Ciechanowski, *Defeat in Victory* (London, 1949), pp. 22–23. Reynaud contests the authenticity of this conversation. He told the investigating commission after the war, "Mandel was too patriotic to agree to stop the war when there was still a chance to continue resistance, and too proud to say that he was obliged to give up because he was Jewish." *Les Evénements*, VIII, 2420–21. Nevertheless, the reported conversation with Mandel is in keeping with his sentiments as recorded by other observers.

even informing him of his plans. Mandel had no recourse but to back Reynaud fully while trying to strengthen his resolution to resist.

IV

The day after the conference with Churchill, the advance of the German army forced the government to leave Tours. Despite Reynaud's earlier plans for a Breton redoubt, in the end it was decided to go to Bordeaux. Mandel, who had been the last one to leave Paris, was also the last one to leave Tours. He was evidently making certain that no one remained behind to negotiate with the Germans.

That morning in Tours, Drexel Biddle, the United States representative to the French government (Ambassador Bullitt had decided to stay in Paris), saw Reynaud and reported to the State Department that he was "in a state of profound depression and anxiety." Reynaud wanted an immediate reply to his appeal for American intervention. "He emphasized the fact that the possible collapse of the French armies was a question not of days but of hours. The single hope of France and in his opinion England rested in immediate declaration of war by the United States. Only in such event would it be possible for the French armies to continue the struggle from Northern Africa."[155] The trip to Bordeaux did nothing to revive Reynaud's spirits. On the morning of the fifteenth, he gave General Spears the impression of "lassitude." Reynaud told Spears that everything depended on Roosevelt's answer to his telegram. Spears believed that "at heart he knew these hopes were an illusion which served no other purpose than to postpone decision."[156]

That day Reynaud thought of another strategem. He proposed to General Weygand that the soldiers in the field lay down their arms without signing an agreement as the Dutch had done earlier, while the government went to North Africa to continue the war. General Weygand adamantly refused, asserting that it was the task of the government to end the war by obtaining an armistice. Reynaud raised the question again at a meeting of the council, but was opposed by some of the ministers. Chautemps proposed what he called a conciliatory solution. He suggested that the Germans be asked for the terms of an armistice, which he felt could not fail to be dishonorable. Such terms would demonstrate to the nation that an honorable peace was impossible and would unite the government in its determination to continue the war.

Visibly annoyed with the constant delays, Mandel spoke out for the first time since the government had left Paris. He opposed any request for an armistice and criticized Baudoin, Bouthillier, and Prouvost, who had only recently joined the cabinet to carry on the war, and now wanted to conclude peace. Mandel said it was time to end the interminable debate. Each minister should state his opinion clearly.[157]

Chautemps' proposal was obviously insincere. He had already said privately that an armistice was necessary.[158] Nevertheless, ignoring Mandel's demand, Reynaud agreed to ask Great Britain for permission to sound out the Germans on the conditions of an armistice. He thought that a majority of the cabinet favored this solution. Only by adopting it while hoping that it would fail, he believed, might he still be able to get the government to go to North Africa. If he resigned, Pétain would become premier and resistance would end.

That morning Mandel still seemed to hope that Lebrun would ask Reynaud to eliminate the defeatists from his government.[159] He wanted Weygand replaced either by General de Gaulle or by General Bührer, the commander in chief of the colonial army.[160] After the cabinet meeting, however, he told a friend that he was afraid Reynaud was weakening, and that if he resigned, Lebrun would turn the government over to Pétain.[161]

To strengthen the position of the Prime Minister, Mandel again strongly advised the British government through Ambassador Ronald Campbell not to approve the French demand. "To condone the request for an armistice," he said, "is to make an abject surrender inevitable."[162] Although Chautemps' proposal had been supported by a majority of the ministers, Mandel obviously hoped that if the British held France to her agreement not to sign a separate peace, most of them could be persuaded to continue the war.

In any case there was no doubt where Mandel stood. According to General Spears, he was "the bravest man in Bordeaux."[163] On arriving in that city, Mandel took over the prefect's office and set up a network of telephones in order to stay in touch with the situation in the rest of France and keep the government from being caught unaware by false reports from Weygand or others.[164] He asked Léon Blum to exert influence on several Socialist ministers who were still wavering, and put Herriot to work on the Radicals. He sent a friend to see Public Works Minister Frossard, but Frossard had firmly decided that an armistice was necessary. Furthermore, he explained, because of the strong feeling against Jews and the fear of complicating the international situation, he did not believe it was time for "une opération Mandel."[165] Frossard later wrote: "If I had thought that war could have been carried on, in spite of everything I would have backed my friend Georges Mandel, the only man whose intelligence, character, lucid energy and statesmanlike qualities inspired in me an absolute confidence."[166]

For the next three days, Blum, Herriot, Jeanneney and others virtually lived in Mandel's office at the prefecture.[167] He became the focal point of resistance. "During those hours," said Blum, "we all recognized him as the leader that he truly was."[168] They hoped he would finally be able to get the government to go to North Africa, and half expected him to take some dramatic action against the defeatists.[169] But it was impossible for Mandel to do anything. On the fifteenth, the commanding general of the region, Lafont, in accordance with wartime regulations, had taken over the state and local police. Though he was minister of the Interior, Mandel had no forces at his disposition even for the maintenance of order.[170] General Lafont was virtual military dictator of the region and his first loyalty was not to the government but to his close friends Pétain and Weygand. On June 16, when his intelligence services recorded an important telephone conversation between de Gaulle in London and Reynaud in Bordeaux, he immediately reported the conversation to Pétain.[171] After Pétain formed his government, Lafont explained to President Lebrun, "I am entirely devoted to the Marshal, not only because he is the head of the government, but because he is my military superior."[172] By 1940 the French army had already developed a strange conception of its duty and its loyalty to the civilian authorities.

It is quite probable that if General Lafont had been ordered to arrest Pétain and Weygand, he would have refused to do so. Lafont's forces were in fact being used to protect them against any measures Mandel and Reynaud might take. On the fifteenth, Raphaël Alibert, Pétain's *chef de cabinet*, and two of Baudoin's assistants told Lafont they feared a plot to arrest Pétain and some other ministers. It was as a result of their warning that Lafont applied the full provisions of the state of siege, giving him absolute control over the police forces in the area, and withdrawing them from Mandel's jurisdiction.[173]

In order not to alarm the people, Lafont at first stationed twenty armed reserve officers dressed in civilian clothes, in a house opposite Pétain's. Civilian members of nationalist organizations were assigned to protect some of the ministers. Eventually this informal militia, armed by Lafont without the knowledge of the government, was replaced by officer candidates from the airfield at Merignac, close to Bordeaux.[174] They were told that some members of the government, determined to surrender, intended to arrest Pétain and Weygand, who wanted to continue resistance. Armed with rifles and machine guns, they were assigned to guard strategic points in Bordeaux, including the prefecture where Mandel's office was located. The Minister of the Interior was indeed being watched closely by the defeatists.[175]

The situation at Bordeaux was dangerous. But the danger to the state came not from the Communists, on whom Weygand lavished so much concern, nor from the people, who were stunned by events, but from the commanding officers of the army. These men were determined to take power, obtain an armistice, and then perhaps abandon the republican form of government, which Weygand blamed for the defeat. Early in June Pétain had informed the Spanish representative in Paris that he was waiting for the proper moment to force President Lebrun to resign in his favor. From "a completely reliable source" the Spaniard also learned that after gaining power, Pétain and Weygand would blame the military catastrophe on the Popular Front and tell the French people that a separate peace with Germany was essential.[176]

The military leaders were aided in their plans by the defeatist politicians whom Mandel and Reynaud had failed to arrest earlier. Pierre Laval hurried from his home in Chateldon in order to have a hand in forming the new government and negotiating with the Germans.[177] Establishing his headquarters in the mayor's office at Bordeaux, he tried to persuade all the arriving ministers and deputies of the need for an armistice. Georges Bonnet stationed himself in the courtyard of the prefecture, where he told everyone who came in that Reynaud and Mandel were crazy to want to continue fighting and move the government to London or Morocco when actually the French army was beaten.[178]

Pressed by both sides, Reynaud was finally cornered on the sixteenth and forced to make a decision. That morning he had received a telegram from the British agreeing to let the French request the terms of an armistice, provided their fleet was first sent to safety in British ports. Before he had a chance to meet with his cabinet, however, the telegram was cancelled and Reynaud received a call from London proposing a political union of France and Britain. For a moment, he thought that this was the miracle he had been waiting for. But when he presented this startling offer to the other ministers, the majority rejected it outright. They had been forewarned by General Lafont, and objected that the plan would make France a British dominion. The cabinet then began to quarrel bitterly.

Mandel believed that most of the ministers favored Chautemps' proposal.[179] It had the enormous advantage of allowing them to evade responsibility. They could claim that they were asking for the terms of an armistice only in order to demonstrate the impossibility of an honorable peace with Germany and thus unify the government to carry on the war. To prevent them from using this subterfuge, Mandel intervened in the debate to force them to vote on the issue of the armistice itself. Confronted with direct responsibility, the ministers might still reject the armistice. Reynaud might then be able to dismiss the defeatists and move the government to North Africa. In any case, it was the last hope for Mandel and his friends, for the rejection of the proposed union with Britain had completely deflated Reynaud and left him with neither the will nor the energy to continue the struggle.[180]

Mandel bluntly told the ministers that there were two groups in the cabinet, the brave men and the cowards. He demanded that the useless delays come to an end and that each minister stand up and be counted for or against the armistice.[181] President Lebrun was opposed, for he wanted the cabinet to make a unanimous decision and thought Chautemps' proposal a useful means of establishing unity. Instead of following Mandel's lead, Reynaud adjourned the meeting until ten o'clock that night, and presented his resignation to Lebrun.

Reynaud has explained in his memoirs that he expected the President to reinvest him, thereby enabling him to eliminate the defeatists and take the government to North Africa. He ignored Mandel's suggestion that a vote be taken for fear an adverse decision would discredit him in advance and prevent him from reorganizing the cabinet.[182] Once again, however, Reynaud failed to inform Mandel and the other resisters of his plans. They were convinced that a vote would finally be taken at the cabinet meeting that night and continued to try to influence hesitant colleagues.[183]

The period following the cabinet meeting was one of hectic consultations. General Spears asked Jeanneney, the president of the Senate, to advise Lebrun to reappoint Reynaud, or possibly Mandel, in order to eliminate the defeatists. Jeanneney, however, did not think Mandel would be able to form a government and believed Lebrun agreed.[184] Lebrun asked Jeanneney and President Herriot of the Chamber to advise him on the appointment of a new prime minister. Both of them suggested Reynaud, but because Reynaud still opposed an armistice, Lebrun asked Marshal Pétain to form a new government.

Reynaud had lost the battle he had been fighting for three weeks. He was a beaten man. Despite his repeated assertions that he was anxious to carry on the war, everyone who saw him after he had decided to resign remarked how relieved he was to be rid of the burden of responsibility. He was no longer depressed and anxious but seemed almost gay.[185]

His defense is weak. Since May 25, by his own admission, he had been aware that Pétain and Weygand were working for an armistice. He had not dismissed them for fear of splitting the country and destroying his cabinet just when he was trying to strengthen it to carry on the war. Then at the last minute, when the two military leaders had done everything possible to thwart his policy and brought a majority of the ministers and the President of the Republic around to their point of view, Reynaud explains, he was resolved to do what he had been afraid to do earlier in more propitious circumstances. Who stopped him? Lebrun, the typically colorless French president, who believed that a majority of the ministers favored Chautemps' proposal and therefore refused to reinvest Reynaud to form a resistance government.

His desire to explain away his failure is understandable, but it is probably true, as Philip Bankwitz has said, that the outcome was inevitable from the start.[186] Without the prestige or temperament of a Clemenceau, Reynaud was unable to take the extreme measures necessary and resorted instead to maneuvering.[187]

Would Mandel have been able to do any better? Did he even have a chance to become premier? Baudoin insists that if Reynaud had really wanted to continue resistance, he would have advised Lebrun to appoint Mandel.[188] Baudoin, however, is almost alone in believing that the President would have agreed to do so. Jeanneney was dubious, and if the possibility even crossed Reynaud's mind, he quickly dismissed it, for Lebrun's antagonism toward Mandel was well known.

It seems clear that Mandel was effectively barred from office, and it is doubtful in any case that he would have been able to resist the military leaders and persuade the government to go to North Africa. His interventions in cabinet meetings had been unsuccessful and he had no more control over Weygand and Pétain than Reynaud did. The most that can be said is that Mandel probably would have confronted the issues more squarely, as he repeatedly tried to do.

The main difference between the two leaders was not that Mandel would necessarily have been more successful, but that Reynaud only half believed his own rhetoric and half feared that the occupation of Metropolitan France would mean the end of the war. Both Mandel and de Gaulle criticized him for being too much influenced by his entourage.[189] His mistress, Hélène de Portes, his military *chef de cabinet*, and the personal friends he appointed to the cabinet—Baudoin, Bouthillier, Prouvost—all came down decisively on the side of an armistice. Mandel, on the other hand, never doubted for a moment that Britain would continue to fight until, with the aid of the United States and possibly Russia, Germany was defeated. On June 13 he had persuaded de Gaulle not to resign from the cabinet: "Who knows whether we shall not finally get the government ... to go to Algiers? ... In any case, we are only at the beginning of a world war. You will have great duties to fulfill, General!"[190]

The difference between them is evident in their reactions to the advent of the Pétain government on June 17. Whereas Reynaud momentarily considered becoming ambassador to the United States and wrote a letter to Churchill asking him not to be vindictive toward France, Mandel was determined to oppose Pétain and keep on fighting. In a last attempt to keep France in the war, he went to North Africa to rally the colonies. He failed, but his attempt showed a Churchillian sense of the drama of history. Reflecting later on his unsuccessful venture, he remarked: "What a magnificent epic [it would have been]: alone against everyone!"[191]

15. The First Resister

Ce qui compte dans la guerre, ce n'est pas un échec, c'est
l'implacable volonté de ne jamais plier.

Mandel

AFTER THE FIRST German breakthrough in May, France was compelled to consider seriously the possible consequences of losing the war. If Paris were evacuated and the government transferred to North Africa, for instance, the way might be left open for a revolutionary movement or a coup d'état. This particular possibility was so disturbing to many government leaders, that they allowed it to influence their behavior even before defeat was certain. Reynaud hesitated to dismiss Weygand and Pétain because they might establish a rival government and split the country. For similar reasons, Mandel instructed all members of Parliament to leave the capital with the cabinet and stayed in Paris and Tours until the last moment to ensure that his instructions were carried out. Later, he also advised the deputies and senators in the provinces to join the government in Bordeaux so that they would be available to support a decision to leave for North Africa,[1] and also possibly so that he could watch them.

That Mandel had indeed once feared a revolutionary outbreak seems clear from Ambassador Bullitt's report of May 28, that "both Reynaud and Mandel now expect a Communist uprising and butcheries in Paris and other industrial centers as the German army draws near." He added that Mandel had asked personally that morning whether the shipment of American submachine guns could not be speeded up.[2] Mandel seems to have changed his mind, however, for General Spears reports that he finally discounted the danger of a revolutionary movement because the people had been shocked into passivity and their leaders had been drafted.[3]

By contrast, a fear of disorder remained uppermost in the mind of General Weygand.[4] One reason he insisted on an armistice was that, like Bazaine in 1870, he believed part of the army had to be kept intact to preserve order in the country. To enforce his point of view, he was willing to go to any lengths. His unverified announcement to the cabinet that Maurice Thorez had established a Communist government in Paris may only have been a mistake, but to his opponents it seemed more like a trick. More serious was his personal revolt against the government. To overthrow Reynaud and have Pétain or someone else invested, he pitted his personal prestige and authority against the Premier's, refusing to surrender to the Germans and refusing to leave the country. His supporters were aware of the revolutionary nature of his acts, and expected the government to retaliate. They feared that Reynaud and Mandel might try to arrest or assassinate Pétain and Weygand, and appealed for protection to the commanding general of the Bordeaux region, who complied by placing guards at strategic points around the city.

On the night of June 16, when Pétain left his residence to form the new government, further precautions were taken. His car was escorted by General Lafont, the colonel in charge of the local gendarmerie and half a platoon of motorcycle guards. General Lafont had been warned that the *jusqu'auboutistes* would make a last-minute desperate attempt to prevent Pétain from taking power.[5] No such attempt had been planned, and Pétain, carefully guarded by the army, had no difficulty in composing his cabinet. His government's first act was to ask the Germans for the terms of an armistice. Almost simultaneously, a detachment from the local gendarmerie replaced the informal militia surrounding Mandel's office at the prefecture, where the resisters continued to consult with him. The police at first tried to turn visitors away, but after protests, finally allowed them through.[6] Although in complete command of the army and the police, the new authorities still seemed to fear Mandel and only Mandel, for similar precautions do not seem to have been taken against anyone else.

Their fears were groundless, for there was little that Mandel could do, short of personally assassinating Weygand and Pétain. But the government was alarmed by the stream of visitors who sought him out that night at the prefecture and the following morning at his room in the Royal Gascogne Hotel.[7] They were frightened by Mandel's reputation for decisive action rather than by anything he actually did, and were ready to interpret any incident in the worst sense. Jean Prouvost, who stayed on in the government as Pétain's minister of Information, later charged that Mandel on the night of the sixteenth had "flooded the Havas Agency with false news about the composition of the new government."[8] Yves Bouthillier, another legacy from Reynaud, and Raphaël Alibert, Pétain's *chef de cabinet*, had more serious charges. As Bouthillier explained, he and Alibert had learned "from a very good source, that after Mandel returned to the Royal Gascogne Hotel that night, he distributed arms and money to gunmen and instructed them to assassinate some of the ministers...."[9] Without verifying the rumor, Pétain issued a warrant on June 17 for the arrest of Mandel and his former assistant, General Bührer. General Lafont suspected that the accusation was false, but in clear violation of Mandel's parliamentary immunity, he sent a colonel to arrest him at the Chapon Fin, a famous restaurant where he was having lunch with Madame Béatrice Bretty. The incident took place in full view of the diplomats and politicians assembled there discussing the events of the preceding day. Count Sforza, who watched the arrest, admired Mandel's stoic calm. He first finished his cognac, then kissed the hand of his companion, and only then left with the officer.[10]

The public arrest of Mandel quickly spread fear and confusion throughout the city. No one was quite sure who was attempting to take over the state. Many officers armed themselves in order to protect Pétain against a plot. Louis Rollin, Reynaud's minister of Colonies, suspected the Marshal's followers of a coup d'état.[11] Others believed that Mandel's arrest had been the first of the German requirements for granting an armistice.[12] One English journalist more accurately concluded, "They must all be scared (word deleted by publishers) of Mandel."[13]

All afternoon, while rumors of plots and conspiracies disturbed the city, President Lebrun, Herriot, Jeanneney, Pomaret, and others besieged Pétain to release the prisoners. At 5 P.M., Mandel and General Bührer were finally brought to Pétain's office, where he explained that they had been accused of having distributed arms in preparation for a coup d'état.[14] An investigation had proved the information to be erroneous, and they were therefore free to go. In reply, Mandel irately denounced the new Prime Minister and told him that "it was regrettable in such a serious situation for France to be governed by a man who was the puppet of his entourage." He demanded a written letter of apology, which Pétain quickly supplied. Mandel, however, pronounced it unsatisfactory and proceeded to dictate a more acceptable version, which the Marshal obediently copied out.[15]

Monsieur le Ministre,
    On the basis of information given to the Central Intelligence Bureau, according to which M. Mandel and General Bührer had set up an arms depot for a coup d'état against the government, I ordered these men arrested.
    I am convinced that the information was unfounded and was designed to provoke disorder. I apologize for the arrest and insist that this unfortunate incident have no further consequences.

The letter and particularly the last sentence indicate Mandel's increasing mistrust of the intentions of Pétain and his followers. At first, along with many members of the cabinet,[16] he had thought that the German armistice terms would be so harsh that the government would be unable to accept them. "There is not a single Frenchman who would put his signature on such a document," he declared.[17] Expecting that Pétain would resign and that Reynaud would then be reinvested in order to carry on the war from North Africa, he had rejected suggestions that he leave the country. On the night of June 16, General Spears, Churchill's personal representative, asked Mandel to come with him to London the following morning by plane, or later via the British destroyer that was in the harbor. Spears argued that the voice of French resistance must be heard immediately. The authorities in the French colonies must be persuaded to continue the war. "Someone whose name was known and carried weight must make them see the shame of accepting defeat while they were undefeated and it was still possible to fight for France." Mandel, conscious of his Jewish origins and still hoping to regain power, preferred to wait for a few days. Otherwise, he maintained, "it would look as if I were afraid, as if I were running away."[18]

He knew that as a Jew he would be particularly vulnerable to the reproach of having fled France. Living on foreign soil, he might be discredited and whatever authority and influence he possessed be greatly diminished. But his arrest showed him that the new government would stop at nothing to carry out its policy. He decided to leave France.

He first contacted Lord Lloyd, the British minister of Colonies, who arrived on June 18 on a special mission to discover what Pétain intended to do about the French fleet. Mandel asked if he could return on the British plane with Lord Lloyd to England, explaining that he also had "des bagages." Interpreting this to mean Mandel's mistress, Lloyd told Lord Halifax when reporting on his mission that "he had drawn the line."[19] After this refusal, incredible at any time but catastrophic at a moment when Great Britain was desperately seeking for any means to keep the French Empire in the war, Mandel momentarily considered leaving by way of Spain, but finally decided against it because of the risk of being imprisoned by Franco.[20] He then thought of departing on the British destroyer in the harbor, but changed his mind when he learned that day that the government itself might be transferred overseas.[21]

As the German army continued its advance toward Bordeaux, the fear had grown that the cabinet might fall into the hands of the enemy and be unable to negotiate freely. Pétain had promised that he personally would never leave the country, but he was willing to let President Lebrun and the presidents of the Senate and Chamber, Jeanneney and Herriot, along with Vice-Premier Chautemps and some of the ministers, go to North Africa. Mandel believed that with part of the government overseas, it would be possible to repudiate the remnant and have France continue the war officially. As he told Ambassador Biddle, "the public powers, reduced to their elements, were the president of the Republic, the presidents of the Senate and the Chamber, and a minister."[22]

Like Daladier, who also rejected a suggestion from the British Ambassador to leave for England, Mandel had learned that the colonies were demanding the continuation of the war. They knew that General Noguès, resident-general in Morocco, was pleading with the government to carry on resistance from North Africa. As Daladier testified, he, Mandel and others who were soon to leave the country, believed that no matter what happened in France it would still be possible to organize resistance overseas.[23]

On the evening of the nineteenth, their bags packed, Mandel, Blum and other *jusqu'auboutistes* gathered with Herriot to await instructions for departure. They thought that the cabinet intended to fly to Algiers and that the members of Parliament would embark on the *Massilia*, a steamship that had recently arrived. After waiting most of the night, they were finally informed that the government had postponed departure until after a cabinet meeting to be held that morning.[24]

At the meeting on the twentieth it was decided that instead of leaving directly for Algiers, the government would depart in the afternoon for Perpignan, close to Port Vendres on the Mediterranean, where they would be out of German hands but still in a position to go to Algiers if the enemy advanced too far or the armistice terms proved too severe. On the basis of this information, Jules Jeanneney and Léon Blum left immediately for Perpignan, believing that Parliament was to join the government there. But shortly afterward Admiral Darlan told Herriot that facilities at Port Vendres would be inadequate to embark all the deputies. He suggested that they leave as originally planned on the *Massilia*, which unfortunately had been unable to reach Bordeaux because the Germans had mined the Gironde River during the night. But cars would be provided to take them to Le Verdon, a port one hundred kilometers along the coast, where the *Massilia* was anchored.[25]

Following Darlan's instructions, some thirty of the representatives at Bordeaux made their way on the afternoon of the twentieth to Le Verdon. Among them were Mandel, Daladier, César Campinchi, Jean Zay, and Pierre Mendès-France. Mandel was accompanied by Madame Bretty and his daughter. The fact that so few deputies showed up has frequently been taken by Pétain's followers as an indication that most of the representatives wanted to stay in France, and that only a frightened few—mostly Jewish—anxious to save their lives, fled on the *Massilia*.[26] It is true that many of the passengers were Jewish, but it is also true that some of the deputies in the confusion at Bordeaux had not received word of the embarkation.[27] Others, whose baggage was loaded on the ship, either were prevented from getting to Le Verdon or changed their minds at the last minute. All of the senators, except Tony Révillon, decided not to embark for fear of being separated from the government while important decisions were being taken. They resolved instead to follow the ministers to Perpignan.[28]

The representatives at Le Verdon, however, unaware of what had happened to their colleagues, were concerned that so few were ready to depart. The complete absence of any of Pétain's supporters should have warned them that the government might not leave Bordeaux after all. Louis Marin, in any case, expressed his fears of this to Mandel, who replied, "I have no more confidence in the government than you do, but I must get to North Africa."[29] Clearly he had given up all hope of accomplishing anything in France, and was determined to leave, whatever the other cabinet members or anyone else did. The absence of Blum, Jeanneney, and Herriot disturbed him not in the least. Reynaud's failure to join the other advocates of resistance seems to have been taken for granted. The one man whom Mandel tried to persuade to accompany him was General Bührer, the commander in chief of the colonial army.[30] But even his refusal did not change Mandel's plans. "The *Massilia*," he later told a friend, "was not a flight. It was above all a mission."[31] To a deputy who wondered why so few of their colleagues were with them, Mandel said, "There are enough, and even perhaps too many, to constitute a resistance government."[32] The time of delay and doubt was over. Mandel had decided to act.

II

While the deputies were traveling to Le Verdon and embarking on the *Massilia*, the leaders in Bordeaux who favored an armistice were doing everything possible to delay the departure of the government. When General Weygand received word on the morning of June 20 that the French armistice negotiators would be received by the Germans sometime after 5 P.M., he persuaded Pétain that this information warranted a postponement of the move to Perpignan.[33] The delay gave the opponents of departure time to organize. On the twenty-first Pierre Laval led a delegation of deputies and senators to browbeat President Lebrun into either remaining in France or resigning from office. Unlike Pétain, Laval was as well aware as Mandel of the crucial nature of the president's office. He told Lebrun:

If the head of the state, the ministers, and the presidents of the assemblies leave France, the ministers who remain behind will no longer have the authority to speak in the name of the country. What is worse, the president of the Republic, in taking the seals of the state with him, will also take with him the government of France; he will be the sole master of policy.[34]

Lebrun and the ministers in favor of departing were unable to overcome the obstacles placed in their way by Weygand, Laval, Pétain and others, and finally were forced to remain in Bordeaux. Blum and Jeanneney, already en route to Perpignan, were told to return, as was the staff of the Ministry of Colonies.[35] But no one bothered to tell the deputies at Le Verdon about the change in plans. Expecting to leave immediately, they waited on their ship from the evening of the twentieth until the orders to depart arrived shortly after noon on the twenty-first.

Charles Pomaret, Pétain's minister of the Interior, has charged that the *Massilia* incident was a trap set by Admiral Darlan to get certain deputies out of the way while the armistice was signed.[36] It was Darlan who had insisted that they leave on the *Massilia* while the government went to Perpignan. And it was Darlan who allowed the orders to be sent to the commander of the ship on the twenty-first to leave for Casablanca. The least that can be said is that he, Pétain, and the other ministers were not opposed to the departure of the most active advocates of continued resistance and did nothing to keep them in France.

It was only after two days at sea, on the evening of the twenty-third, that the passengers on the *Massilia* learned the government had stayed at Bordeaux and concluded an armistice. Campinchi's suggestion that the ship be turned about and head for England was not acted on, for they realized that Commander Ferbos, openly antagonistic toward the passengers, would refuse.[37] It was also impossible to return to Bordeaux because of wartime regulations forbidding a request for new orders. They had no choice but to proceed to Casablanca where some of the deputies still hoped to organize resistance.[38]

The ship arrived on the morning of the twenty-fourth and was met by M. Morize, deputy governor of Morocco, who would not let the passengers debark.[39] That afternoon, however, Mandel and Daladier received permission to visit Resident-General Noguès at Rabat. They were given an official car and accompanied by M. Fourneret, the head of the Sûreté Générale in Morocco. In Rabat, when they learned that Noguès was in Algiers, they placed a call to his office there, only to be disappointed once again. The general was out but would call back when he returned. While waiting to hear from him, Daladier went to see Madame Noguès and Mandel made a fateful visit to British Consul General Hurst. Later, when they were finally able to talk to Noguès, Mandel tried to persuade him to act immediately, but he replied that nothing could be done before they had more precise information about the armistice and knew what the Bordeaux authorities were doing. Mandel angrily told him that "Bordeaux represents nothing," and ended the conversation. He and Daladier then returned to the *Massilia* in Casablanca as they had promised.[40]

Until that moment Mandel had hoped that Noguès would carry on the war. For days the General had been sending telegrams to the Bordeaux government advising it to come to North Africa and to transport all available men and equipment across the Mediterranean. On the seventeenth he had wired Weygand:

The army, air force, and navy all demand the continuation of the struggle in order to preserve our honor and keep North Africa for France.... If the government has no objection, I am ready to take responsibility, without formal authorization, for the continuation of the war with all the risks that that action involves.[41]

Although he was convinced they would be able to hold out in North Africa, he was desperately short of men and equipment. He asked the British to send reinforcements and received the discouraging reply that it was impossible for the moment to dispatch an expeditionary force.[42] On the night of the twenty-third he was further disheartened by the news that the Pétain government had stopped the shipment of men and matériel across the Mediterranean. What finally convinced him that resistance would be impossible was the refusal of the naval authorities to support him once they learned that the armistice agreement left the colonies and the fleet in French hands.

In view of the circumstances, Noguès' acceptance of the armistice is completely understandable. What is remarkable, however, is his animosity toward Mandel, who shared his belief that resistance should have been continued. Because of him, Mandel was prevented from leaving for England. He was arrested, never to know freedom again, and set on the road to his assassination in 1944. The ostensible cause of Noguès' action was the visit Mandel had made to the British Consul in Rabat.

On the night of the twenty-fourth London had learned, probably from Hurst, that Mandel and a number of other deputies had landed in Morocco. Churchill immediately decided to send Lord Gort and British Minister of Information Alfred Duff Cooper, an old friend of Mandel, to persuade them "to form a new French government in North Africa to carry on resistance."[43] There was no secrecy about the mission. On the morning of the twenty-fifth, when Hurst and General Dillon, British liaison officer in North Africa, were notified that Duff Cooper and Gort would arrive at Rabat that evening, they informed General Noguès, who refused to receive the British representatives and ordered the *Massilia* sent into the harbor so that they could not contact the passengers.[44] He also instructed Admiral Harcourt, the naval commander at Casablanca, to use all means, "including force," to prevent Mandel from leaving the ship or telephoning.[45]

Thus when Duff Cooper and Gort landed at Rabat on the evening of June 25, they were advised by Deputy Governor Morize not to try to see Mandel, for otherwise "he would be compelled to take steps that he would much regret." Duff Cooper agreed, but he asked Hurst to tell Mandel that everything possible would be done to get him out, and a ship would be sent from Gibraltar the next day if necessary.[46]

A close guard was kept on the two Englishmen until, finally convinced that nothing could be accomplished in Morocco, they left on the twenty-sixth for Gibraltar. Noguès, returning that morning to Rabat, then sent orders to Admiral Harcourt to allow the passengers to leave the *Massilia,* except for Mandel, who was to be placed under house arrest.[47]

To the authorities at Bordeaux, Noguès reported that Hurst had asked him for permission to embark the passengers from the *Massilia* on a British destroyer. "I expressed my surprise and my indignation at such a request and formally rejected it."

> In answer to my questions, M. Hurst told me that Mandel had made the request to him the day before yesterday. . . . I informed M. Hurst that on behalf of my government I forbade M. Mandel to leave for England. I ordered the Admiral [Harcourt] to watch for the arrival of the English destroyer and to prevent any clandestine landing. I have informed M. Mandel through General Michel that at the least incident, at the first attempt to contact the British consul, I would not hesitate to have him arrested.
>
> The remarks of M. Hurst and the results of the investigation into the visit to Morocco of M. Duff Cooper establish that M. Mandel after his arrival contacted the British consulate and that it was at Mandel's instigation that the Minister of Information made the trip.
>
> Separating the case of the former Minister of the Interior from that of his colleagues, I am considering sending Mandel away and placing him in a residence under the control of the police.[48]

In accordance with Noguès' orders, when the *Massilia* was allowed to return to shore on the twenty-seventh, the other passengers were set free, but Mandel, in a new violation of his parliamentary immunity, was placed in police custody. Along with Madame Bretty, he was sent to Ifrane, a fashionable summer resort in Morocco, where he was lodged in a hotel under guard.

At his trial after the war, Noguès tried to defend his actions as measures to protect Mandel against demonstrations being organized by the supporters of Jacques Doriot's Parti Populaire Français. He was sent to Ifrane because it was "the most agreeable place for him to wait." The man assigned to guard him, said Noguès, was "the friendliest, the nicest policeman in Casablanca." The General concluded: "I don't think he suffered. On the contrary, he was protected there, and I think he was better off at Ifrane."[49]

In spite of Noguès' professed concern for Mandel's well-being, it is evident from his report to Bordeaux on the twenty-sixth that he placed Mandel under house arrest and sent him to Ifrane to prevent him from escaping to England. One would have expected a more sympathetic attitude from the military commander in chief in North Africa, who himself believed that the war should have been continued. But through fear of the wrath of the Bordeaux government should Mandel be allowed to escape, or because of a personal resentment of politicians, widely shared by military men in 1940, or because he could not conceive of opposing the constituted authorities,[50] Noguès did everything in his power, legal and illegal, to restrain Mandel.

A few days later, believing that Mandel was still on the *Massilia*, Churchill ordered the admiralty to attempt to capture the ship. The British navy, however, was unable to work out a plan, and Mandel, in any case, was already at Ifrane. "Thus," writes Churchill, "perished the hope of setting up a strong representative French government either in Africa or in London."[51]

On June 18 de Gaulle had made his famous speech calling for the continuation of the war, but the British government was reluctant to recognize the relatively unknown General as the head of French resistance. The growing French refugee colony in London also had serious reservations about de Gaulle. Some of them were opposed to supporting a military man, others disliked his assumption of personal leadership, and still more were waiting to see whether some organization would not be formed in the colonies that would enjoy greater authority and legitimacy.[52] Even de Gaulle was hoping that a more prominent leader would appear. "If *any one* of influence would come forward!" he exclaimed. "Any one—any one!"[53]

Mandel's arrival in Casablanca had revived waning expectations that he would be the man. When Lord Perth learned that the *Massilia* had reached North Africa, he declared to French friends, "I have great hopes for Georges Mandel.... That man can be a Clemenceau." For two days the French émigrés shared his hopes and were optimistic that Mandel would be able to form a government in North Africa, with which General de Gaulle would then have collaborated. They believed that Marshal Pétain and Mandel had a secret agreement to divide the responsibility for governing France while disavowing one another in public.[54]

Mandel's arrest dashed these hopes and led the English on June 28 to accept General de Gaulle as head of all free Frenchmen. It was at best a *mariage de convenance*, and Churchill always regretted the failure to liberate "the first resister."[55] In 1944, in the midst of his perennial difficulties with de Gaulle, he was heard to murmur: "Ah, if only I had been able to rescue Mandel."[56]

16. Prisoner of Vichy

La Haute-Cour est un tribunal fait pour condamner les
adversaires du gouvernement, non pour les juger.

"A realistic statesman"

WHILE MANDEL and his colleagues were trying to persuade officials in
North Africa to continue the war, the Bordeaux government was preoccupied with the problem of maintaining its authority throughout the empire
and preventing the division of Frenchmen into opposing factions. On June
18 General de Gaulle had appealed to his countrymen and particularly to
the colonial governors to continue resistance. Word had begun to come in
from Syria, Tunisia, and Algeria that Britain was offering money and equipment to any colonies willing to stay in the war. The government then received General Noguès' report of June 26 accusing Mandel of conspiring
with the British. The cabinet concluded that his action in North Africa was
the second half of a two-pronged attack by Reynaud's former ministers,
the complement of de Gaulle's appeals from London. Pierre Laval, who had
entered the government on June 23, demanded an immediate investigation
into this "plot against the safety of the state." He talked Marshal Pétain into
appointing Mandel's long-time enemy Adrien Marquet as minister of the
Interior so that the investigation would be conducted with determination.[1]

Any government receiving a report such as Noguès', clearly accusing
Mandel of plotting with the British government, would have acted in a
similar fashion. But because his arrest was the first in a long series of events
leading to his assassination in 1944, everyone was later anxious to deny responsibility for the measures taken against him. Laval would repeatedly
invoke their long friendship as proof that he had no malicious intentions
against Mandel.[2] Marquet's lawyer was also to deny his client's responsibility. He laid the blame on the military authorities, who wanted "to take
revenge on a man whom they considered to be the most dangerous of all,
and who they knew would denounce them publicly before the nation as
incompetents for having gotten France into the mess she was in. It was
impossible for Mandel to escape."[3] General Noguès would likewise argue
in his trial: "I am in no way responsible for the actions against M. Mandel."
It was the French government, he said, "that pursued him with its hatred."[4]

The truth is that they were all ready to pursue Mandel—General Noguès,
Marquet, Laval, the military authorities, and the Bordeaux government—
not only because he may have summoned Duff Cooper to North Africa,
but for various personal and political reasons. For some it was because he

was a Jew, a deputy, and a minister, and thus triply responsible for the defeat. For others it was because he was the leading opponent of their own policy of appeasement and negotiation. All of them were filled with bitterness and intended to revenge themselves on their antagonists, of whom Mandel was one of the most notable. Knowing this, Herriot had earlier warned Mandel and Blum to leave the country: "Do not remain within the grasp of our current masters; I know too well how much they hate you."[5]

Already on June 24, before any news of the events in North Africa could have reached Bordeaux, Jean Prouvost, the minister of Information, denounced the *Massilia* passengers over the radio. "Public opinion will have no indulgence for them. In fleeing the responsibilities they assumed toward the nation, they have withdrawn from the French community."[6] Several days later when Léon Blum tried to defend them, Laval refused to listen to his explanations: "They are the men who wanted this war, this crazy, criminal war."[7] According to one of Pétain's assistants, the greatest enemies of the "deserters" were Laval, Marquet, and Raphaël Alibert, soon to become minister of Justice, who had been involved in Mandel's first arrest in Bordeaux. "The Marshal readily adopted their opinion, as these deserters were represented to him as systematic detractors of his work and enemies of the armistice."[8]

Laval feared Mandel more than he hated him. Despite policy differences, their relations over the years had generally been good. He had a keen respect for the abilities of Mandel, who was perhaps his only equal as a backstage politician. In September 1939, when Laval was working to establish a Pétain government, Mandel was the one man he specifically wanted to exclude from the projected cabinet.[9] His actions in June 1940 were obviously designed to eliminate the only French leader he considered a threat to the new government.

The first obstacle encountered in acting against Mandel was his parliamentary immunity. While the Chamber of Deputies was still officially in session, no deputy could be arrested or tried for any offense without the authorization of the Chamber, unless he had been caught in the act. Although Parliament was scheduled to reassemble on July 10, the government had no intention of requesting permission to try Mandel. They feared that even the cowed and disheartened representatives who met at Vichy would refuse to prosecute Mandel simply for not wanting to surrender. Moreover, such a request might arouse their suspicions about the nature of the regime to come and make them unwilling to grant Pétain the power to govern by decree and to change the constitution.

In order to detain Mandel without alerting Parliament, the government prevented all the *Massilia* passengers from returning to France and told the National Assembly that the Germans would not let a ship cross the Mediterranean.[10] It was an obvious lie, for the Algerian representatives had been allowed to return to France.[11] Parliament, however, failed to protest against the enforced absence of so many deputies because it was preoccupied with more urgent business, and had no reason as yet to suspect the government of hidden motives. Herriot and others limited themselves to defending the departure of the *Massilia* passengers and did not raise any embarrassing questions about why they had not been allowed to come back.[12]

The full extent of the government's duplicity is shown in its order to General Noguès on July 8, two days before the meeting of Parliament, "to begin judicial proceedings immediately against X at the Permanent Court at Casablanca. As soon as the session of Parliament is closed, the case can be changed into one naming Mandel expressly."[13] In accordance with these instructions, on July 15 Mandel was formally accused of having attempted to establish a government in North Africa with English help, and three days later the other *Massilia* passengers were allowed to return to France.

Mandel's trial was conducted by Colonel Loireau of the Military Court at Meknes. He was astounded to learn from the dossier that the case rested on nothing but a telegram mentioning the visit Mandel had made to the British Consul General at Rabat and the subsequent arrival of Duff Cooper and Lord Gort. He rapidly established that Deputy Governor Morize of Morocco had advised Mandel to see the Consul General, and that he made the visit in an official automobile put at his disposal for that very purpose. Loireau concluded that "as Mandel had never contacted the British ministers, there was obviously nothing for which he could be indicted."[14]

Loireau wanted to dismiss the case immediately, but he was ordered to postpone any decision. Further evidence might be forthcoming. The government was having the archives of the Ministry of Colonies searched for incriminating documents.[15] Also, on June 24 the French authorities had intercepted Hurst's telegrams to London after his conversation with Mandel. They were attempting to crack the British code and hoped that the telegrams, when deciphered, would give positive evidence that Mandel had asked Duff Cooper to come to North Africa. Loireau, increasingly suspicious of the government's motives, concluded that this was only a trick to delay the dismissal of the charges.[16] His skepticism was warranted, for after more than a quarter of a century the telegrams still have not been deciphered.[17]

Disturbed by the government's methods, but unwilling as yet to defy instructions by dismissing the charges, Loireau tried to release Mandel provisionally, but was prevented by General Noguès, who ordered that Mandel be kept under house arrest and closely watched. When Loireau nevertheless gave Mandel permission to visit his sick daughter in Algiers, Noguès revoked the permission and wrote a report to Vichy criticizing Loireau. He accused the Colonel of being too much impressed by Mandel's reputed power and influence to prosecute the case firmly, and suggested that he needed a reminder of the government's policy on it.[18]

Besides pressuring the court in Morocco, the French government was preparing to send Mandel before a more important tribunal. At Vichy on July 10 the National Assembly had granted Pétain full powers to rule the country and revise the constitution. Among the laws he soon promulgated was one establishing a Supreme Court at Riom to judge

1) ministers, former ministers, and their immediate civil and military subordinates accused of having committed crimes or offenses in the exercise of their functions or of having betrayed the duties of their office in the acts which contributed to the passing from a state of peace to a state of war ... or in the acts that later aggravated the consequences of the situation thus created;

2) all persons accused of attempts against the security of the state. . . .[19]

Although decrees transferred jurisdiction from lower tribunals to the Supreme Court for any cases involving these offenses, the government allowed Colonel Loireau to continue proceedings against Mandel. A trial before the multimember Supreme Court might be lengthy and less conclusive, and in any case, Mandel could be tried again no matter what Colonel Loireau did.

At Vichy there had been conflicting opinions about the precise purpose of the forthcoming trial of the former ministers who had "betrayed the duties of their office." One group, considering Germany responsible for the war itself, wanted the trial to be limited to determining responsibility for France's inadequate preparation. They were opposed by the military authorities, who were afraid that they themselves would be compromised by an investigation into the causes of the defeat, and by men like Laval and the historian Jacques Benoist-Méchin, who had favored a rapprochement with Germany before the war and wanted a trial that would condemn those responsible for the actual declaration of war.[20] This second group succeeded in having their ideas embodied in the law establishing the Supreme Court.

On July 29 Laval explained to the American Chargé d'Affaires, Robert Murphy, his reasons for prosecuting Mandel and the other leaders—Daladier, Reynaud, and Blum—who were soon to be arrested:

I do not want their lives but the country demands that the responsibilities for the errors committed in persuading France to enter the war for which she was not prepared and the aims of which she did not clearly understand be fixed and those responsible be punished. If this is not done voluntarily by the Government in an orderly fashion the country will rise up and accomplish it by revolutionary force and violence.[21]

There is some justification for Laval's statement. Reynaud's lawyer has admitted that feeling was running high against the former ministers in the summer of 1940.[22] And the Dominican priest Raymond Bruckberger later wrote that animosity against these leaders was so great that Pétain possibly saved them from lynching by having them arrested.[23] But there are several qualifications that should be made.

First, there are indications that Mandel did not share in the general opprobrium. André Weil-Curiel, one of the first to rally to de Gaulle in London, states that Mandel's popularity was never greater than in the summer of 1940. He "was on the verge of becoming a legendary figure. Of all the French leaders, he alone emerged from the events with his prestige enhanced, for he had never shown a moment of weakness."[24] A note in a French officer's diary for June 28 seems to confirm Weil-Curiel's judgment. After an attack on the former ministers by the Stuttgart Radio, the French officer wrote:

I have never admired Paul Reynaud, whom, wrongly perhaps, I have always considered a political opportunist. But if he has the guts that he seemed to express in his message to Roosevelt he is better than his reputation; in any case, he and Mandel (whom I have always taken to be an energetic, able and honest man) have had the courage not to yield to the savage enemy.[25]

Even more indicative that Mandel was not so thoroughly discredited as Laval would have liked to believe, is the comment made by Father Bruckberger immediately after the passage cited above: "France is unfortunate. We would gladly have welcomed Mandel back, and he is the only one from that worn-out crew who did not return."[26]

A second qualification should be added to Laval's statement: even Pétain's friends saw that the Riom trials had not been set up merely to satisfy public opinion. General Serrigny, one of Pétain's associates, remarked:

It is strange to see a trial of the political leaders of the former government who are only guilty to a lesser degree, while the conduct of our generals is left in the shadows. I have the impression that some people are satisfying their thirst for revenge and others are protecting their friends in order to defend their own administration from 1932 to 1940 (Weygand).[27]

Finally, it should be remembered that in the summer of 1940 public opinion was strictly controlled and directed by the government. A cursory examination of the press for the period shows that before the end of July not a single newspaper, aside from the clandestine *L'Humanité*, demanded that the former ministers be punished.[28] Suddenly at the end of the month, when the government judged the moment opportune, a violent campaign against the republican leaders began.

It started with an announcement of a full judicial inquiry into the responsibility of Daladier, Mandel and other ministers for the defeat.[29] *Le*
Petit Parisien immediately began a series of articles supporting the government's decision. Headlines announced that "Those responsible for our inadequate preparation, for the war, and for the disaster must be judged."
The editor, Charles Morice, declared that the country's ministers, members
of Parliament, and journalists had been madmen under "international" influence who had thrown the country into a war for which it was not prepared.[30] As if synchronized, the rest of the press took up the cry.[31]

On July 26, in the midst of this organized clamor, the news was released
that Mandel had been charged before the court at Meknes with plotting
against the security of the state.[32] At once he became the prime target of the
press. He was denounced as a "deserter," and the government let it be known
that he and other deputies from the *Massilia* would probably be stripped of
their French citizenship and have their property seized under a new law
providing these penalties for anyone who left Metropolitan France between
May 10 and June 30 without orders or good reasons.[33]

Le Temps then published a story from its correspondent in Tangiers indicating that Mandel had indeed been involved in a plot against the security
of the state. The correspondent, René Richard, reported that while in Casablanca Mandel had attempted to send a message to France through the
Havas Agency announcing that he had taken over the government and
that he was going to contact agents of the English government. Moroccan
officials had intercepted the message and prevented Mandel from meeting
with the English representatives he had summoned. Richard then gave an
account of Duff Cooper's arrival in North Africa and his demand to see
Mandel, whom he called "the head of the French government."[34]

The story could only have been concocted with the aid of the Vichy authorities, who wanted public justification for trying Mandel. Having received daily reports from the officials in North Africa, they knew that he
had made no attempt to form a government in Morocco. Nevertheless, as
the *Journal du Médoc* reported, "wide publicity" was given to the account
published in *Le Temps*.[35] The story was picked up by many journals, elaborated on, and finally accepted by most historians of the incident.[36] The government had resorted to false propaganda in order to prepare public opinion
for the coming trials, and also possibly in order to exert pressure on Colonel
Loireau. This determined magistrate, however, finally losing patience, informed Vichy that for want of evidence he was dismissing the case. In his
verdict, he listed the three charges against Mandel: 1) that he contacted the
British consuls at Rabat and Casablanca on June 24 and 25;* 2) that he in-

* On June 25 Mandel had visited the British Consul at Casablanca.

spired the mission of Duff Cooper and Lord Gort; 3) that he asked the consul at Rabat to have a British destroyer take him to England. First of all, according to Loireau, Mandel's visits to the British consuls had been made with the knowledge of the authorities in Morocco. Second, Duff Cooper had come to Morocco "in order to get Mandel's opinion and to examine with him and the other members of Parliament the possibility of continuing the struggle in North Africa. This desire on the part of the British government to study the situation at first hand . . . is understandable, but the accused cannot be held responsible." Third, Loireau said, even if Mandel had wanted to leave for England on the twenty-fourth, which the accused denied, "this cannot be considered reprehensible, since the armistice had not yet been signed and the essential clauses were not made public in Morocco until the twenty-eighth." Finally, he noted, Mandel had embarked on the *Massilia* on the twenty-first in order to come to Algiers, and if he had wanted to go to England rather than to a French territory, he had been granted permission to do so by President Herriot four days before, on June 17.

In view of these facts, Loireau concluded,

it is not necessary to await the possible decoding of the telegrams exchanged by the British authorities. . . . If, after decoding, these telegrams prove that M. Duff Cooper was summoned to Rabat by M. Mandel, then this can be considered as new evidence permitting the reopening of the case. . . . But in the meantime there is no evidence to show that the accused communicated with the agents of a foreign power in order to harm France militarily or diplomatically. . . . Therefore the case is dismissed.[37]

The decision must have shocked the Vichy authorities, who suppressed the news until they could decide what to do with Mandel. In the meantime, before he could be freed, five policemen were dispatched by plane to bring him back to France. There he was imprisoned, or "administratively interned," as the government phrased it, in the Château de Chazeron with the other prisoners awaiting trial before the Riom Supreme Court.

When Loireau's decision was finally made public early in October, the *New York Times* correspondent in Vichy called it "a major blow to the hopes of making the former Interior minister the chief criminal in France's forthcoming war-guilt trials. . . ."

The Riom prosecution had prepared against M. Mandel charges which included treason as well as general war-guilt allegations, upon conviction of which he might have been sentenced to death. But hopes for obtaining the extreme penalty, it was said, appeared to have been dashed by what occurred before the court-martial at Meknes.[38]

There is no proof that this was what the Vichy authorities had planned, but Mandel, charged with treason, was the only one of those eventually accused who was threatened with the death penalty.[39] In any case, along with Reynaud, he always remained "public enemy number one" for Laval and Alibert.[40] Unable to convict him of plotting with the British, they still hoped to try him and Reynaud for betraying the duties of their office "in the acts that contributed to the passing from a state of peace to a state of war ... or in the acts that later aggravated the consequences of the situation thus created." This wording in the decree establishing the Riom Court was aimed directly at the two former ministers. However, in the course of the preliminary investigation, the judges changed the purpose of the trials. From inquiries into responsibility for the war, they were turned into inquiries into responsibility for the defeat, i.e. of responsibility for France's inadequate preparation. As a result of this change, the judges excluded the cases of Mandel and Reynaud, because as Procurator-General Cassagnau later explained, "they cannot be blamed for the lack of preparation. On the contrary, if there are two men who should be congratulated, they are M. Mandel and M. Paul Reynaud, for they wanted to prepare for the war and defend France at all costs."[41]

Thwarted in their attempt to convict Mandel of treason, blocked by the Riom Court from trying either him or Reynaud for war guilt, the government had to find some other grounds on which to condemn them. Accordingly, on September 24, the jurisdiction of the Supreme Court was enlarged to cover the cases of "ministers, former ministers, or their immediate subordinates ... accused of embezzlement, corruption or misuse of funds, or of having betrayed the duties of their office by speculating on the value of the national currency or by misappropriating funds with which they were entrusted." Shortly afterward Reynaud was charged with the misuse of public funds, and Mandel with "irregularities in the administration of funds entrusted to him as minister of Colonies, and reprehensible speculations on the value of the national currency."[42] "Thus," writes one historian of the Riom trials, "not being able to accuse them of high treason, the government vilely attempted to dishonor them."[43]

II

The Supreme Court had refused to act against Mandel and Reynaud, but it had indicted Léon Blum, Edouard Daladier, General Gamelin, and the former Minister of Aviation Guy La Chambre for "having betrayed the duties of their office, either in failing to prepare the national defense, or in compromising it directly by a policy or by decisions contrary to the essential interests of the country."[44] These men were imprisoned with Reynaud and

Mandel in the Château de Chazeron, a medieval fortress refurbished in the seventeenth century for an expected visit of Louis XIV. Accommodations seem to have been adequate, but the prisoners were kept in solitary confinement and allowed to receive only one visit a week from their families. Mandel, always extremely sensitive to the cold, and having just spent three months in the heat of North Africa, suffered from the sudden change of climate. He was also physically run-down. He had lost weight in Morocco, and was seriously bothered by his teeth.[45]

In November, when Blum, Daladier, and Gamelin were transferred to Bourrassol near Riom to await appearance before the court, the Château de Chazeron was closed down, and Reynaud and Mandel were sent first to a former hotel for pilgrims at Pellevoisin, then to Aubenas, and finally to Vals in the Ardèche. One of Mandel's assistants, who visited him during this period, reports that "he had lost none of his assurance, his caustic spirit, or his insolence towards his jailers."[46] One evening, when Mandel was talking with Reynaud, the prison director, Courrier, told him that because of some insulting remark, he would not be allowed to receive visitors the following day. Mandel turned on him and replied: "Mark my words, Courrier. You are going to die like your namesake of Lyons: on your knees and begging for mercy."[47]

Perhaps the strangest fact about Mandel's case is that he was never officially informed of the charges against him, nor was he ever questioned by the court. He knew, nevertheless, that the government was still attempting to decipher the telegrams sent by the British Consul from Rabat, and hoped eventually to try him again on a charge of treason. To help him in his defense, Duff Cooper sent a written statement affirming that "his visit to Casablanca in June was in no way inspired by M. Mandel, who had no prior knowledge of it. . . ."[48] At his trial, Mandel intended to have General Gort, Duff Cooper, and the two British consuls offer to testify in person. He had no hope that Pétain would allow them to come, but he expected that the announcement of their offer would shake the government's case.[49]

Mandel also managed to learn the reasons for the other charges against him. The corruption charge referred to the construction of a large tourist hotel in Guadeloupe, from which Mandel had supposedly profited. According to Mandel's lawyer, responsibility for graft in the letting of the contracts rested with local officials in Guadeloupe and not with Mandel, who had simply ordered that the hotel be built and was not involved in the details. The speculation charge was based on the decision Mandel had made to devalue the Indochinese piastre at the same time as the French franc. However, Paul Baudoin, Vichy foreign minister and former governor general of the Banque d'Indochine, had given Mandel a written statement clearing him of responsibility in this affair.[50]

In January 1941 Mandel's lawyer visited the American Embassy in order to give President Roosevelt first-hand information about his case. Unable to publicize his own defense in France, Mandel sent the Embassy a statement which he hoped the Americans would have broadcast in French. There is no indication that the broadcast was made, but a week after the visit, President Roosevelt asked Pétain to free Mandel and Reynaud.[51] At the same time, Cardinal Gerlier of Lyons and Father Peter Gillet, the Superior General of the Dominican order, also requested their release.[52]

These interventions were of no avail. The Vichy authorities were determined to punish their opponents. Reportedly, for Pétain, the very memory of the struggles against Paul Reynaud on the eve of the armistice was enough to arouse his anger toward the *belliciste* clan—the *jusqu'auboutistes sans canons*, as he called them—who seemed to him to have been led by Reynaud and Mandel.[53] Xavier Vallat, head of the Vichy Commission for Jewish Affairs, wrote to the German officials that he had no sympathy for Mandel, "whom I consider to be one of the most despicable specimens of the Jewish race."[54] Jean-Louis Tixier-Vignancourt, Laval's director of the national radio system, declared: "The first thing we must do is to rip out the guts of those responsible. I want to see a Jew hung from every branch in the park. As for Blum and Mandel..."[55]

To persuade public opinion of the justice of its policy, the government permitted the press to vilify the prisoners. Professional anti-Semites like Count Armand de Puységur were turned loose,[56] and all of Mandel's enemies, the old as well as the new, were able to vent their hatred without fear of a libel suit. The most venomous of the journals in the unoccupied zone was Horace de Carbuccia's *Gringoire*, which had not printed a word of criticism of Mandel since 1932 in spite of its violent opposition to his policies. Now the journal blamed the war on the machinations of the Jewish politicians Blum, Mandel, Mendès-France, and Zay, and demanded, in the words of Philippe Henriot, Mandel's former colleague from the Gironde, that Pétain "free us from the Jews."[57]

Although the *Gringoire* writers were the most vehement in the south until a change in the tides of war in 1943 caused them to veer about, they were never able to match the ferocity of the collaborators in the occupied zone. *L'Atelier*, the Paris journal of Mandel's Socialist adversaries in the Gironde, Gabriel Lafaye and René Mesnard, denounced Mandel as "a pederast," "a speculator," and "an agent of the London banks and the international Jewish committee of New York." "A tyrant to the postal and colonial employees, a liar and a corruptor, a traitor to his chosen country, an agent of foreign interests, Georges Mandel must be judged and punished with exemplary severity."[58]

Not to be outdone, the avowed Fascists of *Je Suis Partout* also took Mandel and Reynaud as their chief targets. The poet Robert Brasillach wrote that if he were forced to choose just two enemies of the country to be hung, he would have no hesitation in selecting Mandel and Reynaud. "Their crime is more deliberate, of longer duration, and more sadistic than anyone else's. They began their abominable task before the others, they wanted to continue it after the others.... In these circumstances, what are we waiting for?"[59]

Mandel symbolized all that the collaborators hated in the old regime. Jacques Doriot, a confirmed Nazi, declared: "The condemnation of Mandel will serve as the line of demarcation between the Third Republic and the National Revolution. When we see this sign, we will believe that the great turning has been made. It is thus we will know that France has committed herself to the new policy."[60]

As the trials of the former ministers were continually postponed, and as it became evident that Mandel would not even be judged by the Riom court, the collaborationist press became enraged. It suggested, in the words of *Je Suis Partout,* that Mandel be taken out and "shot like a dog."[61] Throughout 1942 Doriot organized demonstrations in various parts of France demanding the punishment of "those responsible for the war and the defeat." Before a large audience at Bordeaux on April 26, 1942, he demanded that the Jews Mandel and Blum be stood up against a wall and shot. Leading the claque at this demonstration was the former Socialist Adrien Marquet, the mayor of Bordeaux, who personally gave the signal for applause at the end of Doriot's diatribe.[62]

Although the government announced that Mandel's trial was being held up because of the failure to decipher the telegrams sent by the British consul at Rabat, the press refused to accept this excuse.[63] They generally concluded that the postponement of Mandel's trial was due to the fear that his famed, but probably nonexistent, collection of incriminating dossiers generated in ruling circles. Everyone presumed that they had been hidden away or shipped abroad.[64]

The Nazis hated Mandel as much as their French collaborators did. Before the war, German writers had called him the most important man in France and accused him of organizing a Jewish plot to drive France into war.[65] Later, Otto Abetz, the German Ambassador in Paris, told Reynaud's lawyer: "We are not very much interested in the Riom trial, but we are interested in the men who were responsible for the war, Reynaud and Mandel. If I had them in my power, I would strangle them with my own hands."[66] When the Germans entered Paris in June, they immediately began to search for evidence connecting Mandel with the "warmongering" American government or with Jewish international organizations.[67] His apartment was raided for the first time on June 19, and then more method-ically searched on August 27 by agents for Alfred Rosenberg's Einsatzstab, who collected thirty-two boxes of books and papers. In October the remain-ing thousand books in the apartment were packed and sent off to Ger-many.[68]

The documents were turned over to the Institut zur Erforschung der Judenfrage in Frankfurt. They were systematically classified by the faculty and students of Frankfurt University, but seem to have produced little of any use, for there is no record of their being employed in a propaganda campaign. Unfortunately, German interest in Mandel was not limited to his papers. The German government was as anxious as the French to see him imprisoned and possibly eliminated. For three years he was the subject of negotiations between the two governments, which passed him back and forth as a hostage, until someone was finally willing to assume responsi-bility for assassinating him.

The first of the negotiations began in March 1941 when Otto Abetz, the German Ambassador in Paris, suggested to Ribbentrop that Reynaud and Mandel be extradited and executed in place of the special groups of French territorial guards formed in May 1940 to combat German parachutists. The German government, considering these men to be guerrillas and not part of regular military formations, had sentenced them to death for firing on German soldiers. Abetz argued that Mandel and Reynaud, who were re-sponsible for the formation of these units, should be punished rather than the guards themselves, who were merely carrying out orders.[69] Thus, the Ambassador wrote, "the execution of Reynaud and Mandel would hit two men who are chiefly responsible for the war and be a just expiation for the crimes committed against German fliers and parachutists."[70]

Ribbentrop, who was not yet ready to defy world opinion, replied to Abetz that "pursuance of this proposal would not be expedient."[71] There the matter rested until June 1941 when Marshal Pétain formally protested the proposed execution of the territorial guards. In delivering the letter of protest, Admiral Darlan, who was attempting to curry German favor at this time, adopted Abetz's earlier suggestion and made it his own. He in-formed the German Embassy in Paris that he was "in agreement with the surrender of former Ministers Reynaud and Mandel....He would sur-render them at any time if such a demand were made by the German gov-ernment for criminal prosecution by German authorities in exchange for the holding of separate trials of members of the Gardes Territoriaux."[72]

Despite Darlan's agreement, however, Ribbentrop was still unwilling to order the execution of Reynaud and Mandel. He replied to the German Em-bassy on July 5:

With reference to your telegram No. 1909 of June 26.

Please tell M. Darlan orally that we are prepared to consider a pardon for the territorial guards in our custody as requested by Marshal Pétain in his letter to the Führer, although from the legal point of view we would certainly be justified in treating them as snipers. We are also prepared to renounce the extradition, *offered us by Darlan*, of Reynaud and Mandel, who were the intellectual instigators of the activities of the territorial guards.[73]

Ribbentrop, however, made the pardon dependent on two conditions:

1) that the French Government on its part impose imprisonment for life on Reynaud and Mandel and that it assume the strict responsibility that the two former Ministers never escape from detention and flee abroad.

2) that the French Government place at our disposition all the documents in its hands that would furnish information about the political collaboration of Reynaud and Mandel with the American Government. We already have evidence that the two former Ministers together with Roosevelt and his followers, especially the former American Ambassador Bullitt, had worked towards war. We are moreover interested in strengthening our material by the exhibits in the French files, which are, no doubt, voluminous and convincing.[74]

On August 8 Admiral Darlan accepted these conditions. As he explained to the Germans, "Marshal Pétain proposes to assume jurisdiction over the cases now being examined by the Supreme Court of Justice, ... and to proceed by means of ... political sentences. He is resorting to this method in order to be able to condemn Reynaud and Mandel to perpetual imprisonment."[75]

The French government, however, found it embarrassing to reveal that it was condemning Reynaud and Mandel at the request of the Germans. To avoid this, the Vichy authorities decided to use the power granted Pétain by Constitutional Act Number 7, allowing him to punish with penalties ranging up to imprisonment in a fortified place any high official who, in his estimation, had "betrayed the duties of his office" within the preceding ten years. On August 12, therefore, four days after Darlan's agreement with the Germans, Pétain announced that by virtue of the powers given him by this act, he personally was going to judge those responsible for "our disaster." To advise him on his decision, a Council of Political Justice would be established that would report to him by October 15.

Another device adopted by Pétain to hide what was really going on was to put all of those accused before the Riom Court in the same category as Mandel and Reynaud. Pétain could scarcely sentence Mandel and Reynaud to life imprisonment on the basis of the charges of corruption and embezzlement, nor could he find them guilty of responsibility for the defeat unless those already officially indicted before the Riom Court on these charges were also found guilty. The only way he could hide the German intervention was to judge all of the former ministers together.

Ironically enough, Pétain's Council of Political Justice tried to live up to its name. At least one of the judges was given to understand that, no matter what their decision, Pétain intended to find all of the prisoners guilty.[76] The majority of the seven-member Council concluded that if Pétain were certain of Reynaud's and Mandel's responsibility for the disaster, Constitutional Act Number 7 gave him the power to judge them. But the two men should then be indicted immediately on the same charges before the Supreme Court. The three minority members of the Council advised Pétain not to condemn Mandel and Reynaud at all. "The only grounds for blame ... sprang from their actions in the critical hours of May to June 1940." They stated that if Pétain went ahead and sentenced them anyway, he should at least have the Supreme Court at Riom open a new inquiry and issue a warrant for their arrest.[77]

Knowing that the Supreme Court would refuse to reopen the cases against Mandel and Reynaud for war guilt, Pétain ignored the Council's advice, and decided to sentence them without specifying the reasons. His judgment was announced on October 16, 1941. For their responsibility in the defeat, Blum, Daladier and Gamelin were sentenced to imprisonment in the Fort du Portalet. "As for M. Paul Reynaud and M. Georges Mandel," Pétain went on, "who have been subjected to a preliminary examination before the Court of Riom, I have decided on the advice of a majority of the members of the Council of Political Justice, that the grave presumptions against them justify their imprisonment in a fortress. I have ordered this measure to be taken."

Pétain then concluded his radio address with the following words:

A first step has been taken toward rendering the justice due to the nation. Undoubtedly, the normal course of the judicial procedure would have dispensed me from using Constitutional Act Number 7, since those ... who were punished today may receive a more severe sentence at the close of the trial. But in the times we are living in, each one must assume his responsibilities. I am setting the example. I assume mine.[78]

Thus, in spite of the judgment he had just rendered, the Riom Court was to continue its investigation into the cases of the former ministers. Jacques Benoist-Méchin, who was conducting the negotiations with the Germans for the Vichy authorities, informed Otto Abetz that Pétain had allowed the Riom trial to continue because recent investigations had uncovered grounds for new charges against Mandel and Reynaud, "the gravity of which might be sufficient to condemn these two men to perpetual imprisonment and even, perhaps, to death." In reply Abetz told Benoist-Méchin that the German government was concerned about the conditions under which Mandel and Reynaud were imprisoned. They wanted the French government to take all appropriate measures to prevent their escape from the Fort du Portalet, which was situated close to the Spanish frontier. Abetz added that they also expected the Riom Court to formally sentence the two leaders to life imprisonment by March 1, 1942.[79]

Whatever new information had been discovered, it must have been as insubstantial as the old. Although Vichy informed the Germans in December of its intention "in January 1942 to start regular criminal proceedings against the two ex-ministers, for which the minimum penalty is life imprisonment,"[80] no new indictment was drawn up, and Reynaud and Mandel never appeared before the Riom Court, which finally convened in February 1942.

The French government had tried to convict Mandel of treason, of war guilt, and finally of financial corruption; they had investigated his political activities, his personal relations, and his financial situation. The German government had made its own investigation, using Rosenberg's Einsatzstab as well as the faculty and students of Frankfurt University to classify and analyze Mandel's papers. All of this effort revealed exactly nothing. Few men have had their lives investigated by their enemies as thoroughly and as methodically as Mandel. But neither the French nor the German government was ever able to find any evidence that could be used for propaganda purposes or for a case in court, even according to the new rules of justice established by Pétain.

After the war Pétain explained that he had decided to judge Reynaud and Mandel himself because public opinion did not understand the delays in the procedures of the Riom Court.

I believed and continue to believe that those whom I punished are gravely responsible for the misfortunes of France. My decision, of a political nature, was in response to the political necessities of the time; it had the merit of doing nothing irreparable, since it left the Riom Court free to render a definitive decision on the judicial level. It also allowed for a retrial later on if time and the discovery of new documents showed that one was warranted. Thus my decision was not opposed, when the time came, to the necessary reconciliation of Frenchmen, which has always been the supreme aim of my policy.[81]

But in spite of all his brave talk of accepting responsibility, when the time came at his trial to explain the reasons for the decision, Pétain and his lawyer lacked the courage to admit that, as on so many other occasions, Vichy had bargained with the Germans in order to save French lives. It was known that they had sentenced Communists in order to save other

Frenchmen; that they had turned over foreign Jews to the Germans in order to save native-born Jews; but neither Pétain nor his lawyers were willing to admit that the Marshal had made a sacrificial offering to the German gods of some of France's former ministers. Nor was he willing to admit that he had condemned Mandel and Reynaud at the request of the enemy when the Germans proved afraid of the consequences of executing them. All of Pétain's actions, from the establishment of the Council of Political Justice to the misleading defense at his trial, were designed to cover up this fact. One may approve Pétain's desire to save the lives of the territorial guards, but it should be recognized that he was ready to turn Mandel over to the Nazis for trial and possibly execution, and that he made a hostage of him in bargaining with the Germans, who would one day claim their victim.

17. German Hostage

Si vos maîtres ne nous rendent pas Mandel vivant, vous aurez à payer
ce sang juif d'une manière qui étonnera l'histoire—entendez-vous bien,
chiens que vous êtes—chaque goutte de ce sang juif, versé en haine de notre
ancienne victoire, nous est plus précieuse que toute la pourpre d'un
manteau de cardinal-fasciste—est-ce que vous comprenez bien ce que je
veux dire, amiraux, maréchaux, Excellences, Eminences et Révérences?

Georges Bernanos

NEWS OF THEIR SENTENCE reached Mandel and Reynaud in Vals via the Vichy radio. Their fellow prisoners were shocked at the unprecedented sentencing without indictment or trial, but they observed no change in the features or demeanor of the two ministers, who merely thanked their friends for their expressions of sympathy.[1] Mandel had never expected to receive a fair trial, but he had hoped for the opportunity to defend himself publicly. Now even that possibility seemed to be gone. In the circumstances, he could only protest to Pétain by letter:

I learn that on the basis of charges of which I have never been informed, you have decided.... [left blank]

That is the equivalent of condemning me without having heard my defense. In other times, everyone would have considered such a denial of justice as a crime, but it would be foolish to misunderstand your position. By the armistice you made yourself completely dependent on our enemies, and everyone knows the particular interest they have shown in me for a long time.

I am honored to have deserved this attention because, as a faithful disciple of Clemenceau, I have always been absolutely committed to the task of maintaining for France the place which she won in the world by the victory of 1918....

For thirteen months now I have been imprisoned. In that time your legal experts were ingenious in creating new offenses and crimes by arbitrary laws which they then made retroactive, and under which they indicted me before the Court at Riom. The Court got the strangest people to help it; undertook numerous inquiries; minutely investigated not only my life but that of my family and of my assistants, who were discharged from their positions; and examined all the malicious rumors coming from the press, the administration, and political circles—but all in vain. It never succeeded in discovering the least bit of evidence that would have justified interrogating me. In case you did not know it, in the course of the investigation which has lasted for more than a year already, I have never been questioned; in fact, no one has even bothered to inform me of the charges against me! ...

I have just one thing further to say: I will be waiting for you at the downfall of the Axis forces. It is the best revenge and also the only reparation that a Frenchman can desire who up until his last breath had only one religion—that of his country.[2]

On November 15, 1941, Mandel, Reynaud, and the other prisoners were transferred to the Fort du Portalet, located in the Pyrenees some fifteen kilometers from the Spanish frontier. This nineteenth-century fort, built to defend the Col de Sempart, the famous pass used by the Arabs to invade France in the eighth century, had been abandoned for some years and had to be hurriedly prepared for its new guests. Marshal Pétain, who was condemned in 1945 to the same cell that Mandel had occupied, was appalled by the primitive conditions and wrote to his wife: "If I had known what it was like . . . , I would not have sent my worst enemies here."[3]

For the first seven months at Portalet, although Mandel and Reynaud were prevented from seeing or speaking to each other, they were not kept in total isolation. Mandel's twelve-year-old daughter Claude and Madame Béatrice Bretty, who took up residence in the village of Urdos, a few kilometers from the prison, were allowed to visit him almost daily. His Negro servant Baba Diallo, a former soldier in the French army, brought his breakfast from Urdos in the morning, and Madame Bretty carried his lunch with her when she came to visit him for the afternoon. She and his secretary, Raymond Amar, were Mandel's main sources of information and contact with the world. Madame Bretty would hide messages from General de Gaulle and others in her coiffure, and then use all her gifts as an actress to get past the guards without being searched. Amar frequently brought him long résumés of foreign broadcasts. On days on which he had no other visitors except Madame Bretty, Mandel was allowed two brief walks with her in one of the yards of the fortress, which he had to climb 150 steps to reach. On these occasions, he would always say, "Put on your hat, we are going out."[4]

Besides his lawyers Armand Goëau-Brissonière and Maurice Garçon, another of his secretaries, Maître Besselère, was an approved visitor as well. Some of his friends and former colleagues were also occasionally allowed to visit him, though only after long delays. Others remembered him in his exile with packages and letters. Among the most faithful were two friends from the Gironde—André Coudy, his assistant as mayor of Soulac, and Martial Michel, the director of his weekly newspaper in Lesparre. To Coudy he wrote in June 1942 thanking him for a recent letter: "I was all the more touched by it in that it was almost an act of faith. You know that my crime is to have opposed the armistice. It is all too certain that Clemenceau would not have acted otherwise. The only difference is that in his time, it was the defeatists who were punished. But if I had need of consolation or encouragement, I would receive it from the attachment of friends like you."[5]

It was months before Mandel could finally get permission for Martial Michel to visit him. At one point he told him: "I am going to make another request for authorization for you to visit me, but don't nourish any hope. For some people I am a living reproach; they only regret that I have not yet disappeared. They do not want me to have the least contact."[6]

In the fall of 1942 Mandel received permission for Michel Clemenceau, the son of the former Premier, to visit him. Despite difficulties in crossing zones, Clemenceau managed to get to Portalet, where he was able to stay with the prisoners for two days. Mandel asked him to inform Pétain of the conditions under which they were imprisoned, and to insist that they either be given a public trial or be set free. When Clemenceau fulfilled his mission a few days later at Vichy, he also suggested that they be allowed to escape. Pétain replied that nothing could be done for them because it was the Germans who demanded their imprisonment.[7]

The location of Portalet, perched on the Spanish frontier, tantalized both friends and enemies. With the slightest initiative, it seemed, the prisoners could be freed. When the American radio announced Mandel's arrival in England in February 1942, *Je Suis Partout* denied the report but said that "his escape remains possible because Portalet is so near the Spanish frontier and Mandel still has so many accomplices in the antechambers of power.... Only corpses do not escape."[8]

To prevent his escape, the Vichy authorities soon tightened security precautions. When Clemenceau visited the fort in the fall of 1942, it made "an extraordinary impression" on him: "The entire mountain was illuminated by searchlights shining on a two-hundred-meter section of rocky wall in which the fort was situated. Below it was a torrent running through a ravine, and a little above it were barbed-wire entanglements, machine guns and eighty policemen."[9] Except for artillery, Portalet had been fitted out like a permanent fortification in order to guard two men.

After Laval returned to power in April 1942, many people proposed that he allow Mandel and Reynaud to escape. One friend asked: "Why don't you let Mandel go to London; or better still, why don't you send him there yourself? An escape can be arranged easily.... He at least would be qualified to talk about the government. You would thus avoid the travesties of de Gaulle and the stranglehold of the Communists. Mr. President, in that way you would save France, the Republic, and yourself into the bargain."[10]

Laval's biographer Alfred Mallet reports that he rejected all these suggestions as "chimerical."[11] Similar suggestions were made to the Minister of Justice, Joseph Barthélemy, who had been a frequent dinner guest of Mandel before the war. All of these proposals were turned down, not because they were chimerical, but because they would have infuriated the Germans.[12] Laval, however, did say that if men like Doriot took over the government, he would help Mandel to escape. Laval reportedly added: "He deserves it, and he will be needed."[13]

In sentencing Mandel at the request of the Germans, the Vichy government had in effect tied its own hands and turned Mandel into a hostage. Until October 1941, his imprisonment had been what might be called a family affair, and his escape, although it would have provoked the Germans, would not necessarily have brought down any reprisals on the unoccupied zone. But having formally agreed to condemn him, Vichy felt compelled to keep its side of the bargain for fear that his escape would bring German retaliation. All of Laval's good will cannot change the fact that he, Pétain, Darlan, Benoist-Méchin and the rest gambled with the Germans for Mandel's life—and lost.

Equally unfortunate was the failure of the Free French in London to try to liberate Mandel. The journalist Henri de Kérillis, who had left France in June 1940, received a report in December that Mandel, Reynaud, Daladier, Blum and Gamelin could easily be freed. He sent the report to General de Gaulle, along with the offer of $20,000 or more to help arrange the escape. His letter went unanswered. Much later he learned from a friend in London that his plan had been rejected by some of de Gaulle's advisers. His friend wrote:

The prospect of having three ex-premiers, a former minister, and the former Generalissimo show up in London struck them as catastrophic for the General's future. These important figures would have promptly become the outstanding representatives of France and would have been qualified to speak in her name here. . . . This, you understand, was not a pleasant thought. It was better to quash your plan. I have heard it said that you are quite insufferable with your eccentric ideas.[14]

Mandel's assistant Philippe Roques, who acted as his liaison agent with the London authorities, seems also to have found de Gaulle unwilling to help Mandel escape.[15] That such plans were not totally unfeasible was shown by the escape of many Resistance leaders from French prisons and of General Giraud from Koenigstein, some five hundred miles inside Germany. But according to Maître Besselère, Mandel himself did not want to escape at first and turned down several opportunities. "I am not guilty of anything," he explained.[16]

Nevertheless, the failure of the Free French to attempt to rescue Mandel is surprising, for his collaboration would have been of considerable help. He was highly regarded by diplomats and statesmen of many nations. Sumner Welles, the American under-secretary of State, said that Paul Reynaud and Georges Mandel were the only two French leaders in the critical years of World War II who showed themselves to be true statesmen.[17] It would seem that Mandel could easily have gained the international recognition that was so reluctantly and so belatedly accorded to de Gaulle.

Moreover, in contrast to de Gaulle's Maurrasian background, which aroused fears that he was a Fascist, Mandel's republicanism was unimpeachable. Many Frenchmen who were suspicious of the General would readily have supported Mandel. In fact, to gain a wider following, de Gaulle was eventually forced to seek Mandel's endorsement. Messages were exchanged with the prisoner at the Fort du Portalet through Philippe Roques.[18] In May 1942 Roques succeeded in escaping to England, where he met with de Gaulle and André Diethelm, another of Mandel's former assistants.[19] He returned to France with a proposal from de Gaulle that the two leaders collaborate in the postwar restoration of the Republic. The exact nature of the proposal is unknown, for the General has not seen fit to reveal the contents of his own letter, but Mandel replied:

Although the first political act which will launch the provisional Government of the liberation will necessarily be important, I accept your judgment in advance. Above all, it is of the greatest importance that you should be the *leader, the uncontested leader* of this Government with *complete freedom of action.* When, in order to save France's honour, you resolved to continue the struggle beside the Allies, there was no competition; it would be intolerable that you should be subjected to competition when the deliverance begins to be in sight.

As for me, I suffer, and suffer cruelly, from my many persecutions only because they prevent me from seconding your effort. I have only one ambition, to make up for lost time. I hasten, therefore, to accept your proposal to establish a link [une conjonction] between us, without interference from anyone (always taking into account, of course, the risks of my present situation).

I only make one condition: it is that I always have the right to express my *frank* opinions to you, and the reasons for which I hold them. But, on the other hand, rest assured, that *once you have made a decision,* no one will support it more firmly than myself.

It seems to me that this strict collaboration will give rise to a unity of action which alone can hasten the liberation and national rebirth.[20]

Collaboration was never effectively established, of course, because Mandel remained in prison. By the fall of 1942, however, according to Georges Wormser, Mandel was anxiously looking for a way to escape.[21] Several plans were formulated. Colonel Groussard, his former fellow prisoner at Vals, released in January, 1942, hoped to free the prisoners with the help of some of the military personnel stationed at Portalet. Because of his friendship and former army service with the commander of the fort, Major

Vidala, Groussard at first anticipated no difficulties. To his surprise, however, Vidala refused to help him either directly or indirectly.[22]

By November 1942, two other groups were laying plans for freeing the prisoners. One was organized by Philippe Roques after Laval told another of Mandel's former assistants, Francis Varenne, that the guards at the fort were not heroes and would not get themselves killed merely to prevent Mandel's escape. Roques gathered a number of men together, but his plans were thwarted by the German occupation of the south in November 1942.[23]

The occupation also forestalled a plan being worked out by some of Reynaud's friends in conjunction with Churchill's government.[24] They smuggled in two metal saws, along with a two-hundred-foot rope, with which Reynaud was to descend the side of the fort to the road running through the ravine alongside the swift stream. On the night of the escape, it was planned to blow up the electrical transformer, throwing the entire fort into darkness. The plan was feasible for Reynaud, who kept himself in good physical shape by daily exercise. But for Mandel, who despised sports and had never taken any exercise in his life, it was impossible. As Reynaud was unwilling to leave without his friend, on whom the Vichy authorities might have taken revenge, he had to postpone the plan until alternative arrangements could be worked out for his fellow prisoner. On the night of the escape, it was hoped to smuggle Mandel out disguised in the cloak of Madame Bretty, who was to remain behind in the cell.[25]

These plans were upset by the Allied landings in North Africa on November 8. Mandel, who always seemed to know precisely what was going to happen, wired to Pétain:

I want to remind you that when you took power in order to surrender, you had me arrested, and for twenty-nine months, without having tried me or even heard my defense, you have kept me imprisoned in defiance of all law. Leaving me in Portalet when all of France is going to be occupied is equivalent to turning me over to the enemy. I want to warn you of this so that it will be clearly established before the court of history that you are responsible for this crime.[26]

When the Germans occupied the south of France three days after the landings, an SS battalion supplied with tanks and armored cars was sent to seize Mandel and Reynaud. Its Commander, Colonel Knochen, was ordered to take the prisoners peacefully if possible, but by force if necessary.[27] The Germans were temporarily repulsed by Major Vidala, however, who refused to allow them to enter the fort until he had received instructions from Vichy.[28] During the respite, friends of the prisoners spoke to Laval and demanded that he prevent the Germans from taking them. After telephoning to Paris, Laval told Joseph Laniel, "So long as I am in power, the prisoners will not be handed over to the Germans."[29]

Despite Laval's promise, on November 20 Colonel Knochen took the two ministers from Major Vidala, who had received orders from Vichy to resist the Germans passively, and without bloodshed. Although Reynaud concluded that the French government must have agreed to the transfer,[30] Pétain registered a complaint with the Germans, and Laval sent a personal representative to protest to General Oberg, the head of the security police in France. The emissary, Jean Leguay, reports that Oberg furiously rejected the protest, stating that "he had proof that M. Reynaud and M. Mandel with the complicity of the Vichy government were maintaining close relations with England and America."[31] The next day Laval came to Paris to make a personal protest, which was equally unavailing. He told Maître Maurice Ribet, however, that he had obtained a promise from the Germans that the prisoners would eventually be returned unharmed: "There is nothing to fear. I have a receipt in my pocket."[32]

Until April 1943 no one knew what had happened to the prisoners. From Portalet they had been taken to Oranienburg, a camp some twenty-five miles north of Berlin, where Mandel and Reynaud were put in separate cells and kept in total isolation. But after three months Reynaud succeeded in establishing contact with his friend. He noticed that only one other cell besides his own was specially screened. While taking his daily walk in the courtyard shortly thereafter, he called up to the window of the cell, "Who is there?" When a shadowy figure appeared at the window, Reynaud reports, "I was so moved that for the first and last time in my life I addressed him in a familiar style: 'C'est toi, Mandel?'" Until they were transferred in April 1943, they were able to talk for two or three minutes each day in this fashion.[33]

Aside from the brief talks with Reynaud, however, Mandel was completely cut off from the world. For months he was allowed neither to receive nor to send any correspondence. With no idea of what the Germans had in store for him, he expected the worst, and as was his habit, sought to fix clearly the responsibility for whatever might happen. Two weeks after he arrived, he jotted down on a piece of paper which he hid in his clothes, "I want it known that if I die in my cell, it will not have been a voluntary death."[34]

In April 1943 Mandel was finally allowed to communicate with Madame Bretty and Claude, who were staying in a hotel in Pau. One of his primary worries while in Germany had been the fate of Madame Bretty and his daughter. He was relieved at having reestablished contact with them, but was still concerned about their health, their morale, and the conditions under which they had to live. His letters to Claude reveal a degree of paternal solicitude surprising to those who knew only the public side of his life.

From time to time he had to tell her not to worry about him. He was anxious to see her again and was doing everything he could to take care of himself. But he, too, was concerned because of long interruptions in the correspondence. He often wondered where she was and what she was doing. He was particularly interested in her school work, and asked for a list of the books she was reading, so that he might be able to reread them along with her. In September 1943 he congratulated her on the progress she was making, but added that the word *progrès* is not spelled with a *t*.

As much as he could in brief letters, he tried to impart to her his own philosophy of life. Four recurrent words—intelligence, knowledge, character, and tenacity—might well have been his motto. On February 1, 1944, he wrote that although the work she was doing might seem hard, it was easier to bear than the humiliations she would have to suffer later if she failed to acquire the necessary knowledge and develop the character that would enable her to control her own life.[35]

The conditions of Mandel's imprisonment improved in April 1943 after the Germans seized Blum, Daladier, and Gamelin. The newcomers were treated as political prisoners, and it was decided to give the same treatment to Reynaud and Mandel. Reynaud was accordingly transferred to a camp in Austria where he was confined with Daladier and Gamelin. For racial reasons, Blum was separated from the rest and sent to Buchenwald where he was soon joined by Madame Jeanne Reichenbach, who had received permission to marry him and share his fate. Several weeks later Mandel was also transferred to Buchenwald and interned with the Blums in a small hut set apart from the rest of the camp.

On learning of the permission granted to Madame Reichenbach, Madame Bretty asked Mandel's old friend Anatole de Monzie to help her send an open letter through official German channels requesting similar permission for herself. De Monzie forwarded the letter through Fernand de Brinon, the Vichy representative in Paris.[36]

Although word of her request got through to Mandel, he did not send for her at once. In September Mandel put off asking for permission until the spring, because he did not want Madame Bretty to have to face the severe winter in Germany.[37] And in January, after new restrictions were imposed, leading him to fear that he might be sent to a concentration camp, he definitely decided against having Madame Bretty join him.[38]

His life at Buchenwald was nevertheless a considerable improvement. "One is always better treated by the masters than by the servants," he wrote.[39] He had a radio, and although his visits to the Blums at first were limited, he was later allowed to see them freely. Much of his time was spent in reading modern historians, but he also liked the classical writers, especially Plutarch.[40] Among the authors and works mentioned in his notes are Montesquieu, Voltaire, de Maistre, Ernest Renan, Jacques Maritain, Charles Benoist's *Machiavelli* and Casanova's *Memoirs*. He wrote to André Coudy in December 1943, "I suffer only from the total lack of activity. I read about one volume per day. But nothing compensates for the joys of action or the company of good friends."[41]

According to Blum, who shared his life for fourteen months, Mandel's habits and outlook remained unaltered:

> Nothing had changed in his face, in his bearing, in his attitude, or in his dress. He even continued to wear those high stiff collars which for lack of starch my wife was eventually unable to maintain.
> He always wore his gloves whenever he went for a walk on the little path between the barred walls of the prison and the barbed wire entanglements. . . .
> Toward the officers of the camp he was more imperious than he ever had to be with his assistants at the ministry. In everything, at every moment, he maintained an arrogant and contemptuous dignity, which in that place and at that time was truly a form of heroism.[42]

His guards, of course, made him pay for his intransigence. He failed to receive packages that had been sent to him, and his mail was held up for months at a time. On January 6, 1944, he was informed that if his letters continued to be written in provoking terms, they would no longer be forwarded. The following day he wrote in his notebook: "Spent a very bad night because of worries.... Am concerned about correspondence. Expect total interruption and perhaps transfer to a camp. Poor B. and Claude." Shortly afterward he was limited to two letters a month and told that he would have to write to the Gestapo and promise to change the tone of his letters.[43]

By 1944 he was beginning to suffer seriously from the effects of his long imprisonment. He was able to sleep at night only with the aid of soporifics. On April 16 he noted: "Slept six hours, but woke up every hour. Continual dreams. Pains in the stomach getting worse. The result of four years of captivity, and especially of the food in German camps." By July his condition was deteriorating, as the last note in his diary indicates: "With the camp sleeping pills, I slept only five hours.... Woke up sick, with pains and nausea. Had a great deal of difficulty in getting up and dressing. Took only a cup of weak tea in the morning. In these circumstances, I feel very much alone. Cannot count on anyone. Every move I make is watched...."[44]

What sustained him throughout his imprisonment was his unwavering belief in the ultimate victory of the Allies and the liberation of France. He wrote his daughter in December 1943 that he constantly tried to distract himself from his sufferings and his immediate concerns by focusing attention on the final goal.[45] That goal always remained the same. He noted in his diary, "During the months of isolation in my cell, I have had but a single thought, a single hope: the defeat of Germany. To have lived to see it will console me for everything."[46]

He lived long enough to learn of the Allied landings in Normandy, but he was never to experience the joy of final victory. Safely confined to a camp in Germany, he should have been far from the thoughts of the Vichy French and German leaders. But he was apparently not forgotten by Otto Abetz, the German ambassador in Paris, who in the spring of 1944 came up with a macabre scheme involving Reynaud and Blum as well as Mandel.

To oppose the Allies in North Africa after November 1942, the Germans had organized the African Phalange, composed of French and native troops. When captured by the Free French forces, some of these men were tried and executed. In reprisal, and in order to stop the trials, Vichy judged and shot some members of the Resistance movement. The Algiers government nevertheless on May 10 began the trial of Admiral Derrien, the commander of the Bizerte naval base. Abetz then suggested that reprisals would work only if those to be executed were important leaders either of the Resistance movement or of the prewar French government. The first three names on his list were Léon Blum, Paul Reynaud, and Georges Mandel.[47] On May 30 Hitler announced his intention to turn Blum, Reynaud, and Mandel over to the French government to be shot if any further executions took place in North Africa.[48] Informed of the impending transfer by Laval, Algiers commuted Admiral Derrien's sentence.[49] The three hostages in turn received a reprieve, though a short one, for they had been singled out as choice victims in the holocaust of executions and reprisals that were the result of four years of civil war in France. Mandel in particular became the unknowing center of plots and negotiations so complex that they have yet to be unraveled.

On June 30 an Algiers court condemned Colonel Magnien, leader of the African Phalange, to death. Two days later Abetz notified Laval that the three prisoners would be turned over to the Vichy government to be shot in reprisal. Laval again informed the Algiers authorities, who canceled the execution of Colonel Magnien.[50] But Mandel did not get a second reprieve.

In Buchenwald on the morning of July 4, he was ordered to pack his bags in preparation for his return to France. Neither he nor Blum seems to have had any doubts about the fate that was in store for him. They were unaware, of course, of all the negotiations, but they knew that on June 28 Philippe Henriot, minister of Information in the French government and the most effective speaker on the Vichy radio, had been assassinated by members of the Resistance. On learning the news, they suspected that they themselves might be killed in retaliation, and this thought was uppermost in their minds when the order came for Mandel to return to France.[51]

Mandel needed little time to get ready. He had always put everything carefully back in his suitcase after use, as if he expected just such a sudden departure. He breakfasted with the Blums, who were the last friends to see him alive. "He had not the slightest illusion about the fate that awaited him," said Blum. Yet "the most attentive observer would not have been able to see the least change in the gestures of his hands, in his bearing, in his speech, or in the intonation of his voice. We never saw him more calm, more poised, more lucid." His last words to Blum were, "Tell Béatrice Bretty and my daughter that I regret nothing of what I have done, that I know I have acted well, and that no matter what happens, they will not have to be ashamed of me."[52]

Mandel was flown to Rheims and then taken by car to Paris, where he was kept for three days in the Gestapo offices located in the rear at 5 Square du Bois de Boulogne. What happened during that time is still uncertain. However, it seems most likely that after Abetz informed Laval on July 2 that the prisoners were being returned to France, the German government simply went ahead with its plan without waiting to see whether Laval would be able to stop the execution of Colonel Magnien in North Africa.[53] Then when Mandel arrived in Paris, Colonel Knochen of the Gestapo called Joseph Darnand, under-secretary of State for the maintenance of order, and tried to persuade him to take charge of the prisoner. Darnand rejected the proposal.[54] Knochen, in a hurry to return to Germany on personal business, was in a quandary. At that point, either he or his assistant, a mysterious Dr. Schmidt who was acting on his instructions, ordered the Milice, Darnand's paramilitary organization charged with the repression of the Resistance movement, to accept the prisoner.[55] For three days Schmidt and Max Knipping, Milice chief in the northern zone, discussed Mandel's fate, until the Frenchman finally agreed to accept responsibility for him. According to the head of the Gestapo in France, General Oberg, Mandel was handed over to Knipping because as Darnand's assistant he could be considered a formal representative of the French government. He says that before taking charge of Mandel, Knipping conferred by telephone with his superiors in Vichy.[56]

In any case, on the evening of July 6 Knipping called André Baillet, director of the penal system, to inform him that the Germans were turning Mandel over as a hostage and that he was to be locked up temporarily at La Santé Prison. The next day, Schmidt brought Mandel to the prison, where Knipping wrote out an order to commit him, stipulating that the prisoner could be released only to him personally. Baillet objected because there was no official court order, but Knipping insisted that Mandel be kept in custody for a few hours until he could be transferred to the Château des Brosses near Vichy where he was to be formally tried by the French government. It was 2:00 P.M. when Schmidt and Knipping left Mandel at the prison. They returned at 5:30 P.M. accompanied by three carloads of Miliciens.[57]

Mandel, of course, had no precise knowledge of their plans, but he seemed to realize that either openly or secretly he would soon be killed. When he arrived, he told the director of the prison, "So long as I am within your walls, I will probably not be killed. But I don't think I will be left under your protection for very long."[58] Before leaving with Knipping that afternoon, Mandel turned to the director and said: "To die is nothing. What is sad is to die without seeing the liberation of the country and the restoration of the Republic."[59]

Mandel was placed in the first car with four Miliciens—Jean Mansuy, the driver, Pierre Boéro, a shoe salesman from Nice, Georges Néroni, a bartender, and Pierre Lambert, a mechanic. In the second car were Paul Fréchoux, head of security for the Milice in the northern zone, and two other Miliciens, Vernon and Temple. The third car, which remained in Paris, contained the German officer Schmidt in civilian clothes, Knipping, and the chauffeur.

After a short time, in the midst of the forest on the Fontainebleau road, Mansuy brought the first car to a halt. Something seemed to be wrong with the motor. All of the passengers got out. While Boéro tried to find out what was wrong, Mandel began to walk away from the car with Néroni at his side. From a distance of thirty feet, Mansuy fired an automatic pistol at Mandel, barely missing Néroni. Boéro shouted: "You're crazy. What's wrong with you?" Mansuy replied: "You're not in command. Both sides are agreed." To make sure that Mandel was dead, Mansuy then approached the body and fired two shots into his neck and head.

The whole thing had obviously been planned in detail, for Mansuy immediately turned on the car and sprayed it with bullets to make it appear that they had been attacked. Fréchoux, from the second car, then said: "I have orders. Put Mandel in the car and take him to the morgue at Versailles."[60] They had hoped to be able to bury Mandel in an unmarked grave, but the doctor called to examine the body notified Maître Besselère, Mandel's private secretary for fifteen years. Besselère arranged for a private burial in the Versailles cemetery, which was attended by a few friends.[61] Among Mandel's possessions were found a suitcase and various notes and bits of paper, one of which asked that his body be buried wherever he died and only be brought to Paris after the end of the war.[62]

On July 8 Laval learned of Mandel's death from Fernand de Brinon, who had been told of it by Knipping. Laval summoned Joseph Darnand, the head of the Milice, who seemed to know little more than he did, and who advised him to call Knipping in Paris for further details. Knipping tried to tell Laval that Mandel had been killed when the car taking him to the Château des Brosses was attacked on the road to Fontainebleau. Laval realized immediately that Knipping was lying.[63] Everyone who saw him that day reports his anger and indignation at the assassination, which was all the greater in that he thought he had prevented it by warning the Algiers authorities not to execute any more prisoners.[64]

Laval told Knipping and Darnand not to accept the transfer of Blum, Reynaud, or anyone else under any conditions, and he instructed Brinon to present a formal protest to Abetz. The German Ambassador, however, insisted that Laval had been informed in advance: "I told him myself in the course of a conversation at the Hôtel Matignon that the German government had decided to turn Mandel over to him.... As for the manner in which Mandel was executed, I find it deplorable. My government would have preferred that the death of a man who had been one of those principally responsible for the war between France and Germany be given a solemn character, particularly after the assassination of Philippe Henriot."[65]

The reaction of the French Fascists in Paris coincided perfectly with that of their German brethren. *Je Suis Partout* wrote: "We regret that the Jew Mandel, who had deserved death a thousand times for having pushed France into war, was not publicly judged and shot. But the most important thing is that the Jew Mandel no longer exists."[66]

Despite the reactions of the Germans, and of some members of his own government, who thought that he was acting too hastily,[67] Laval ordered the minister of Justice to begin an investigation of the case and to arrest those responsible. Pierre Taittinger, president of the Municipal Council of Paris, asked him: "Even if the guilty one is a member of the government?" and Laval replied: "Even if the guilty one is a member of the government."[68]

An investigation was begun but had not proceeded very far before the Allied advance caused the evacuation of the Vichy authorities to Germany. The investigation was reopened by the government of General de Gaulle after the liberation of Paris, when Boéro, Néroni, and Lambert were captured. They were tried in October 1944 and found guilty of giving aid to the enemy. Boéro and Néroni were executed shortly afterward, and Lambert was sentenced to twenty years at hard labor. Of the premeditated murder of Mandel they were found not guilty, for they were apparently brought into the plot at the last moment and had no foreknowledge of what was to occur.[69]

Jean Mansuy, the actual killer, was never tried. Two accounts place his death in late August of 1944. According to one account, he was involved in a plan to assassinate General de Gaulle at the Hôtel de Ville in Paris. Captured on August 26, 1944, he was executed the following morning.[70] According to another account, he had somehow managed to join the Resistance movement and was killed on August 26, 1944, fighting against the Germans.[71]

One of the key figures in the affair, Max Knipping, was tried in 1947 and executed, not so much for his part in Mandel's assassination as for all of his activities as head of the Milice in the northern zone.[72] Unfortunately, only very sketchy reports of his trial appeared in the newspapers at the time, and no official stenographic record has been preserved in the archives of the Cour de Justice.[73] Knipping, however, declared that he was innocent of Mandel's murder.[74] Knipping thought that it was Mansuy, in agreement with Dr. Schmidt, who decided to do it, possibly for money. He claimed that he never gave the order to execute Mandel.[75]

Knipping's precise role in the murder still remains obscure, as does that of his superior, Joseph Darnand, who was also executed after the war for his activities in the Milice. Many people doubt that Knipping would have ordered Mandel's assassination without first consulting Darnand, who expected to be charged with the crime at his trial: "I am held responsible for the assassination of Georges Mandel. I have not yet been questioned, but I expect to be. I have witnesses. I was at Vichy when it happened. My colleagues at Paris, who were unable to communicate with me, have testified in writing to that effect. They have declared that they signed the order for transfer because they were unable to consult me."[76] Despite Darnand's expectations, however, the prosecutor did not question him, and in fact clearly stated that he did not hold him responsible for Mandel's death.[77]

There are several indications, however, that Darnand may have known more about the negotiations concerning Mandel's return to France and his assassination than was realized. According to Prosecutor Flicoteaux, Darnand testified that Knochen first tried to persuade him to accept responsibility for the prisoner.[78] He refused, but according to his assistants, he expressed no surprise when he heard about the assassination.[79] Oberg's defense attorney claims that the whole affair could have been arranged by Abetz who on May 13 had discussed with Darnand the proposal to use Mandel, Blum, and Reynaud as hostages.[80]

In defense of Abetz, his lawyer René Floriot affirmed that Mandel had been murdered in retaliation for the assassination of Philippe Henriot. At the request of the Milice, Himmler had agreed to send him back to France, and had ordered Oberg to turn him over to the French paramilitary organization. Thus, Mandel's death was the result not of Abetz's scheme, but of a plan formulated entirely apart from him by the Milice and higher German authorities.[81] In his own defense, the former German Ambassador said that both in 1941 and in 1944 he had proposed that Mandel and Reynaud be shot only because he knew that the German government would be afraid to execute anyone as important as the two ex-ministers. By this means, he claims, he was able to save the lives of the territorial guards and of the Resistance members who were to be shot in reprisal for the executions in North Africa.[82]

Abetz was condemned to twenty years at hard labor for his part in the looting of Jewish possessions in France, the deportation of Jews to Germany, and the assassination of Mandel.[83] The sentence was surprising. As Pierre Scize remarked in *Le Figaro*: "If, in the mind of his judges, Abetz is guilty of everything he is accused of in the indictment, the sentence is too light; if one accepts the thesis of the defense in any degree whatsoever, it appears to be too severe."[84]

Abetz's trial had been hastily prepared. According to his lawyer, only one in a hundred of the telegrams concerning him was examined.[85] Such was not the case in the trial of Karl Oberg and Helmut Knochen. The prosecution spent ten years collecting evidence against the man known as "the Butcher of Paris" and his assistant. They were interrogated 386 times; the indictment ran to 240 pages; and the written evidence weighed almost two hundred pounds.[86]

Prosecutor Flicoteaux accused Oberg and Knochen of having ordered the Milice to assassinate Mandel after Laval had refused to accept the hostages or execute them officially. Despite indications of their involvement, however, he was able to present no conclusive proof of their guilt.[87] Nevertheless, for all of their other acts in France during the war,[88] they were condemned to death. By a curious irony, because the prosecution had delayed their trial in order to have an airtight case, the two Gestapo leaders benefited from the more relaxed atmosphere prevalent in France nine years after the war. Execution of the sentence was repeatedly postponed until President Coty finally commuted it to hard labor for life in April 1958.[89] Four years later, in the fall of 1962, they were pardoned by President de Gaulle and released from prison.

The failure to try anyone specifically and exclusively for the murder of Mandel has left an aura of mystery surrounding his death. He is mentioned in every trial, evidence is referred to, witnesses are quoted posthumously, others report at length what they were told by some third party unfortunately now dead, and then the matter is dropped.[90] The presiding judge must hurry on to more important charges. There is no real cross-examination—most of the potential witnesses, in any case, were executed years before—and no rigorous attempt to establish or refute a point. Thus, twenty-five years later, no one can yet be absolutely certain who arranged the assassination and was ultimately responsible for it: Knipping, Darnand, Abetz, Knochen or Oberg. Abetz's lawyer suggests that it was Himmler and the Milice; Oberg's lawyer thinks that it may have been Abetz and Darnand; Darnand seems to have believed that it was Knipping;[91] and Knipping says that it was Mansuy and Schmidt. There the chain ends, for Mansuy and Schmidt, of course, have disappeared.

As Jacques Delperrie de Bayac states in the most recent account of the assassination, however, Knipping seems to be one of those clearly responsible.[92] He was the key man in arranging Mandel's transfer from German to French hands, and it was his assistants who organized the escort for Mandel. The details of the assassination were obviously planned in advance, and it seems highly unlikely that the gunman Jean Mansuy would have been able to do this on his own account or even in collaboration with the Germans.

What is not so clear is the motive. According to Delperrie de Bayac, the assassination was the result of a plot formulated by certain French Fascists and Germans in Paris shortly after the Allied landings in Normandy early in June.[93] The plan was to compromise the Pétain government by assassinating Mandel, Reynaud, and Blum and thus to commit the Vichy authorities irrevocably to the German side. There is little evidence for this, aside from the message from Knipping to Darnand's *chef de cabinet* at Vichy the day after the assassination:

This morning I had a visit from Dr. Schmidt, who came to tell me that the whole SS would back us up in case of trouble with the President [Laval]. Tell that to the Chief [Darnand]....My opinion is that while we should remain loyal to the government, we must be the revolutionary element which pushes it to do what it is temperamentally reluctant to do. The policy followed by the government for three years has led us into the impasse we find ourselves in today. Not to have acted in yesterday's affair would have lost us the trust of the SS entirely.[94]

On the other hand, if the plan had been formulated in June, there would have been no reason for the three-day delay in handing Mandel over to the Milice. This delay would seem to indicate that the decision to assassinate Mandel was taken at the last minute by Knipping, possibly at the instigation of Oberg and Knochen. They may have hoped to compromise the Vichy government, or to avenge Henriot, or simply to eliminate a man they detested. The Milice had for similar reasons already assassinated Jean Zay, Maurice Sarraut, and other French leaders.

In any case, the only one who seems clearly absolved of direct complicity is Pétain, who by this stage of the war was barely informed of events and can hardly be said to have been responsible for anything. Laval, too, seems to be innocent. He may even have tried to get Mandel and Blum returned to French custody for fear that as defeat loomed closer the Germans might take revenge on them as Jews.[95] His grief at Mandel's death was real, and as Alfred Mallet suggests, all the greater in that he realized that "he lost the only friend capable of interceding effectively for him on the day of reckoning."[96]

In prison, Laval wrote:

I had been Georges Mandel's friend for thirty years. I had backed him when, for the first time, he became a cabinet member. He also had backed me to enter the Clemenceau Government, which I was unable to do, as the Socialist Party, of which I was then a member, had refused to collaborate with M. Clemenceau. Our friendship had strengthened as years went by, and our ties remained firm even when we did not agree on certain political points. If he were alive today I know that he would defend me. His death was a great shock—all the more tragic because for a time I thought I had saved his life.[97]

But if Pétain and Laval bear no direct responsibility for Mandel's death, owing to their readiness to compromise and bargain with the Germans they bear an indirect responsibility for it. Perhaps the best judgment on them was passed by Mandel's daughter, or by those who advised her, in a letter she sent to Pétain after the assassination: "For the sake of your conscience," she wrote, "I want to tell you, Monsieur le Maréchal, that I bear you no grudge. You have immortalized the name that I have the immense honor of bearing. Thanks to you it will shine like a beacon in history. For the name will not evoke the memory of surrender, or of treason toward one's allies, or of compromise with the enemy, or of all the lies of your equivocal policy that has done us so much harm."[98]

18. Conclusion

Il était un politique et non un politicien. . . . Si Mandel vivait, il serait ici, aujourd'hui, à côté de moi. Gardons son souvenir. Nous en avons besoin.

Charles de Gaulle, 1949

MANDEL IS DIFFICULT to place on the French political spectrum. He began his career at the turn of the century as a moderate Radical when clericalism was the main issue, gradually moved to the right as the question of national security gained importance before World War I, and afterward became a spokesman for the Right in alliance with the Catholics and even with the extreme nationalists. In the 1930's he moved back toward the left. At the very end he coordinated policy with Herriot and Blum, two of the titular leaders of the Left, and even gained the hesitant support of the Communists. It is easy to see why many people considered him a traitor or an opportunist and felt such animosity toward him. Yet to judge Mandel by the company he kept is to use a very poor criterion, for the twists and turns of his career were dictated by considerations having little to do with the normal meanings of the terms Right and Left. Even though his association with Léon Daudet and other extreme right-wingers was long and close, their support no more made Mandel a Royalist than the later support of Léon Blum and the Communists made him a Socialist or a revolutionary.

Basically, his social, economic, and political views placed him in the Right-Center with the members of the Alliance Démocratique. Like them, he favored a laissez-faire economic policy, disapproved of state intervention in the economy to aid the working class, believed in the efficacy of liberal parliamentary democracy, opposed the proportional representation advocated by the conservative Right, rejected constitutional revision to increase the power of the executive at the expense of Parliament, and never denounced the institutions of the country, as the Right and Left sometimes did, when measures he supported were defeated.[1]

He differed from the moderate Republicans, however, in two important respects. He wanted above all else to create a majority in Parliament that would carry out an energetic foreign policy, and he was willing to make concessions to the Catholics on domestic questions in order to get that majority. His nationalism was in the nineteenth-century Jacobin tradition of Gambetta and Clemenceau. But in 1920 a republican nationalist who believed that the security of the country outweighed everything else could find strong allies only on the Right, among the former enemies of the Republic. It was this same concern with foreign policy that brought him to collaborate with the Left during the late 1930's.

The second thing that distinguished Mandel from the moderate Republicans was the attention he gave to questions of political tactics and strategy and his determination to use the levers of power to achieve his goals.[2] In this he revealed his left-wing origins. For both Mandel and the Radicals, one of the key posts in the government was the ministry of the Interior, for the man who held it could influence the political direction of the country. The moderate Republicans, however, once assured that their economic position was not endangered, usually asked for nothing better than to be accepted by their Radical opponents and to share the honors of office with them.[3] They had no taste for combat, and feared arousing left-wing hostility if they took too clear a stand on any issue. In contrast, Mandel tried to weld all the conservative forces into a coherent bloc in order to put definite policies into effect and establish a clear division between Right and Left.

Because of his strong nationalism, his desire for firm leadership within the parliamentary system, and his willingness to use the power at the disposal of the government to effect his ends, Mandel is perhaps best described as an authoritarian Radical, a category to which Albert Thibaudet also assigns his mentor Clemenceau.[4] Although the Young Turks of the party would hardly have claimed him, an old Radical like Albert Bayet had no hesitation in classifying Mandel as a nineteenth-century Radical, who was devoted to the parliamentary system of government but was more interested in political than in economic or social questions.[5]

Roger Stéphane has said that "the fundamental vice of the parliamentary system is that the qualities necessary to obtain power are incompatible with the qualities necessary to exercise it."[6] Whatever the truth in Stéphane's statement, it is clear that Mandel's personality and methods ultimately made it very difficult for him to become prime minister or to play the role that he had cut out for himself.

The tragedy of France during the 1930's was that in a crisis demanding decisive leadership, she found herself ruled by a governmental system that almost excluded decisive men from power. Multiple parties and the two-ballot electoral system encouraged compromises, and favored the supple, shrewd, but also indecisive leaders who agreed to them. Occasionally, *in extremis*, men like Clemenceau, Poincaré, or, later, de Gaulle came to power in spite of the system, because of the faith they inspired in the people. It was to this class of men that Mandel aspired, but unfortunately he never possessed the éclat, the charisma, or the indefinable element in leadership that de Gaulle speaks of in *Le fil de l'épée*.[7] In fact, the very qualities Mandel had developed to gain power frequently served in the end to alienate people and keep him from power. The arrogance, disdain, and air of superiority he had cultivated as a young man as well as the measures that he took as Clemenceau's assistant made him so unpopular that for fifteen years it was impossible to give him even the most minor ministerial post, and he virtually had to use force to break down the doors that were barred to him.

His mastery of tactics, his ability to manipulate public opinion, and his penchant for backstage politics, although they were definite assets at various stages of his career, all tended to reinforce his isolation—and also to confirm his cynical evaluation of men. He enjoyed studying the members of Parliament and using them for his own purposes. After the beginning of the German invasion, General Spears had many interviews with Mandel and found

his detachment and objectivity in all this confusion . . . astonishing. A very curious man. One side of his mind was watching the antics of his colleagues with ironical amusement. The spectacle of all this weakness fascinated him, while the problem of unraveling the motives of each one absorbed him, for it was a game he had become expert in long ago when serving Clemenceau, and had practiced ever since. The other side of his mind was watching events through those eyes that were like thimbles full of sea water, behind which lay the cold alertness of a barracuda always ready to pounce with startling rapidity on anything that passed within its vision. If it was possible to be fond of a fish I should have been fond of Mandel. For he was like a fish if you could imagine one with the straight damp locks of black hair hanging like seaweed over its gills.[8]

Like Spears, many men respected Mandel's abilities, but did not warm to him. Both his Machiavellian tactics and his secretive, enigmatic self-possession prevented him from inspiring the devotion and trust that Clemenceau and de Gaulle were at times able to evoke. During the last days of Reynaud's government, Spears says, Mandel was "too aloof, too cutting, almost too inhuman to provide that faith which was the quality in shortest supply, after courage, at Bordeaux."[9]

Yet despite his cynicism Mandel never became a pure opportunist; he retained a strong faith in the destiny of France that motivated him throughout his life. From the beginning he supported de Gaulle's efforts as leader of the Free French. At Portalet in 1942 he told a friend that he was still convinced France should have continued the war in 1940:

I do not deny the drawbacks of such an alternative; but a country condemned to death by the occupation, bound by a solemn agreement not to conclude a separate peace, at war to preserve its liberty, must accept everything—all the suffering, all the sacrifices—in order to gain victory. Otherwise it is a country on the road to decadence. . . .

What will our place be at the peace conference if we have not participated in the battle? . . .

What will we have to show for ourselves at the end? Some magnificent individual acts, a few epic incidents, and the tenacious struggle of General de Gaulle. It will not be enough. You are going to regret our surrender and refusal to fight because of the effects on the commercial, industrial, and imperial future of this nation that monarchs, emperors, and the Third Republic made so great. As for myself, I regret nothing. One must either conquer or die. . . .

How long will it take France to raise herself from this humiliating position?

How much more preferable is the virile language of General de Gaulle. At least it is the affirmation of the French presence in the war. I do not know what the future has in store for M. de Gaulle, but in these hours of national weakness, the nobility of his words, the grandeur of his position, his faith, and his patriotic ideas merit the gratitude of the nation and of history.[10]

Mandel's total and unqualified support of de Gaulle reveals one of his most remarkable traits: his readiness to accept a secondary role if he believed, for any reason, that other men might be able to provide more effective leadership to the country. Because he was ambitious and supremely confident of his own ability, his multiple disappointments could easily have made him bitter and jealous. But he never allowed his personal misfortunes to blur his vision of the national interest. He even seems to have accepted the failure of the Free French to make any attempt to liberate him, for nowhere in his letters, notes, or reported conversations is there a word of reproach against the leaders of French resistance.

A second remarkable trait was Mandel's willingness to learn and his ability to change. At the beginning of his career he had been an extremely awkward public speaker, but in time he mastered the art of addressing Parliament, becoming one of those most remembered today for his "presence" at the tribune.[11] He also learned to temper the harshness of his character, gaining an almost avuncular image with the general public and those who did not remember him during the days with Clemenceau.[12] Similarly, the events of 1940 and the war seem to have changed his thought, transforming him from a Social Darwinian into a social democrat. He was a nineteenth-century individualist, a latter-day Guizot who believed in the virtues of struggle and in the right to rule of those who had raised themselves to the top of the heap. But the failure of the bourgeoisie to react vigorously to the German danger discredited them in his eyes and turned his thought in a new direction. The notes he made in prison give us only an outline of his ideas, but there is enough to indicate that a radical change was taking place. In the spring of 1944 he wrote: "We would more surely have avoided war ... if we had always been ready to accept it in order to save political liberty and the idea of respect for the human person, without which life is not worth living, and by which man is distinguished from the beasts."[13]

In what his friends have called his "political testament," Mandel said that his program was "to liberate man from the double servitude of war and misery." France, which had "often had the mission of showing the way for the rest of the civilized world," must send forth new ideas "to improve the world and make it more just and humane."[14]

More details of what his program would be were left on a sheet of paper found on his body after his death. It is entitled simply "Notes."

The country has to be rejuvenated, the institutions recast and organized; above all we have to reestablish the moral credit of the country. . . .

By their heroic resistance, the workers have acquired new and important rights.

The workers—the people—were at the center of resistance. They supported Jeanne d'Arc; it was on them that Henry IV relied in order to restore national unity, broken by the wars of religion. They made the Revolution, saved France with the Committee of Public Safety, founded, defended the Republic against factious attempts for half a century. They held out in the trenches from 1914 to 1918, and, after a moment of blindness in June 1940, they quickly discerned the treason of the military leaders and by their resistance rendered national liberation possible. . . .

We must create a regime of liberty without tyranny, neither the tyranny of capital, nor of the workers, nor of any class whatsoever. We must have a social renovation: assure (not only proclaim) the rights of women. We have been engaged in a total war. Women have been employed in the factories and fields, and have not been spared by the bombs. In a new world, we must treat them as equals.

There must be a rapprochement between owners and workers, a solidarity between patriotic owners and workers. We must bind up our wounds through the union, the concord, and the love of Frenchmen for one another.

There were two wars: one which began on September 1, 1939 and which is going to be won; and the other, secret, hidden, but no less formidable which, without France being aware of it, began well before '39 and is going to continue.

This one will not be ended by the victory, and we must win it as well. Otherwise, the victorious end of the first will be in vain. Its goal: political freedom, equality for all citizens, the improvement of the lot of the masses by the peaceful means that democracy must assure.[15]

Like many other leaders of modern France, Mandel failed to achieve his ambitions. He failed to become prime minister, to reshape French political institutions, to unite the country in preparation for conflict with Nazi Germany, and to keep France in the war. Many things contributed to his repeated defeats: his high-handed use of power under Clemenceau, which created many bitter, life-long enemies; his complicated maneuvers, which made everyone suspect his motives; his cynical view of men, which repelled even those most ready to follow him; his preoccupation with parliamentary matters to the exclusion of social and economic problems; and, finally, his Jewish origins, which helped prevent him from acting more decisively during the last years of the Third Republic.

His failure was perhaps inevitable, for he aimed high, and some of the problems almost defied solution. The Third Republic was a graveyard of praiseworthy ambitions. Clemenceau, Tardieu, and Blum are among its notable failures. Whether, given the opportunity, Mandel would have been able to fulfill his potential after the war is an unanswerable question. However, the transformation in his thought during the war, de Gaulle's attempt to secure his support and collaboration, and the general esteem he had earned in the Free French and Resistance movements by his stand in 1940 all indicate that he would have played a substantial role in the Fourth Republic. On this point at least, if on little else in his career, both Mandel's friends and his enemies seem to agree. As Léon Blum put it, Mandel's death was "one of the most serious losses that France suffered during the war."[16]

Notes

Notes

Following is a list of the abbreviations used in the notes. Authors' full names, complete titles, and publication data for all works appearing in short form in the notes will be found in the Bibliography, pp. 365–75.

BDIC   Bibliothèque de Documentation Internationale Contemporaine.

CDJC   Centre de Documentation Juive Contemporaine. 17, rue Geoffroy-L'Asnier, Paris, 4ᵉ.

DBFP   *Documents on British Foreign Policy, 1919–1939.* Edited by E. L. Woodward and Rohan Butler. Second Series (1929–38), Vols. I–VII; Third Series (1938–39), 9 vols. London, 1947–.

DDF   *Documents diplomatiques français, 1932–1939.* Second Series. Vol. I (1 janvier–31 mars 1936); Vol. II (1 avril–18 juillet 1936). Paris, 1963–.

DDI   *I documenti diplomatici italiani.* Eighth Series (1935–39). Vols. XII–XIII. Ninth Series (1939–43). Vols. I–IV. Rome, 1952–.

DGFP   *Documents on German Foreign Policy, 1918–1945.* Series C (1933–37). Vols. I–V. Series D (1937–45). Vols. I–XIII. Washington, 1949–.

FDGO   *France During the German Occupation, 1940–1944: A Collection of 292 Statements on the Government of Maréchal Pétain and Pierre Laval.* 3 vols. Stanford, 1957.

FRUS   *Foreign Relations of the United States, 1932–1941.* Washington, D.C., 1948–62.

JOC   *Journal Officiel. Chambre des Députés. Débats parlementaires.*

JOS   *Journal Officiel. Sénat. Débats parlementaires.*

PVCG   *Procès-Verbaux des délibérations du Conseil Général du Département de la Gironde, 1920–1940.*

Chapter 1

Epigraph: Bernard Lazare, "Le nouveau ghetto," *La Justice,* Nov. 17, 1894.

1. Wormser, *Mandel,* p. 15. Georges Wormser became Clemenceau's assistant in 1917, and succeeded Mandel as his *chef de cabinet* in 1919. From that year until Wormser became Mandel's own *chef de cabinet* in 1934, the two men seem to have had only infrequent contacts. Wormser resigned from Mandel's staff in 1935, but maintained close relations with him until 1940. Wormser's biography of Mandel unfortunately mixes memoirs and history without clearly distinguishing between them. For the period before 1917 and from 1919 until 1934, his work is a useful but uncertain guide.

2. In Paris, births and deaths are registered at the mairie of the arrondissement. The

death certificate gives the names of the parents and the deceased's date and place of birth. For Adolphe Rothschild, see the death certificate at the Mairie of the Third Arrondissement. For Nanette Nether and Edmond and Hermine Rothschild, see the death certificates at the Mairie of the Ninth Arrondissement. For Mandel, see the birth register at the Mairie of Chatou. The house where he was born, 10 avenue du Général Sarrail (formerly avenue du Chemin de Fer), is now marked with a commemorative plaque.

3. Louis-Jaray, p. 11; Pol, p. 157; Pascal Maurel, *Les grands hommes de l'Union nationale* (Paris, n.d.), pp. 19-20; *Les Hommes du Jour,* Oct. 25, 1919, p. 12.

4. Alexandre Varenne in *Annales,* Nov. 18, 1920, p. 69.

5. Nov. 1, 1919, p. 19.   6. Louis-Jaray, p. 11.

7. See Vallat, *Le procès,* p. 166.   8. Reynaud, *Mémoires,* I, 140.

9. Benda, pp. 36–43.   10. See Byrnes, *passim.*

11. Quoted in Malcolm Hay, *Europe and the Jews* (Boston, 1961), p. 214.

12. Interview with Adrien Rothschild. Paul Coblentz, who received the same information, erroneously records his name as Louis-Georges Rothschild; see Coblentz, pp. 16–21.

13. Varenne, *Mon patron,* pp. 31 and 95.

14. See the account of Mandel's speech at Pauillac in *La Petite Gironde,* Oct. 29, 1919, and his campaign biography in *La Liberté du Sud-Ouest,* Nov. 14, 1919.

15. See Mandel's campaign biography in *La Liberté du Sud-Ouest,* Nov. 14, 1919 and *La Petite Gironde,* Nov. 9, 1919. To my knowledge, no names are inscribed inside the Colonne de Juillet. The names of those killed during the July Revolution were engraved on the outside of it. In an interview, Mandel's brother Adrien Rothschild informed me that the story is part of family tradition. It is possible then that some member of the family may have been killed during the July Revolution, but there is no Mandel, Rothschild, Nether (the maiden name of Mandel's paternal grandmother), or Kahn (the maiden name of his maternal grandmother) listed among those killed. See the list printed in the *Bulletin des lois du Royaume de France,* 9ème Sér., XXI, No. 746 (July 22, 1840), pp. 79–86.

16. See Mandel's speech in *Annales,* Nov. 8, 1920, p. 19, and report in *La Petite Gironde,* Oct. 29, 1919.

17. See account of his speech at Blanquefort in *La Liberté du Sud-Ouest,* Nov. 8, 1919, and report in *Le Petit Médocain,* April 18, 1920. He referred to the death of one brother in speeches in the Conseil Général de la Gironde, *PVCG,* May 3, 1920, pp. 48–49 and April 30, 1923, p. 264.

18. Henri Massis, *Evocations: souvenirs, 1905–1911* (Paris, 1931), pp. 103–6.

19. Varenne, *Mon patron,* p. 32.

20. Wormser, *Mandel,* p. 18.

21. Archives of the Lycée Condorcet for 1901–3.

22. Albert Thibaudet, *La république des professeurs* (Paris, 1927).

23. See above, p. 80.

24. Letter to Pétain (*ca.* Aug. 1941), in *France-Amérique* (New York), July 1, 1945.

Chapter 2

1. Mandel said that his father had been one of the organizers of Jules Favre's electoral committee. See Mandel's speech in *Annales,* Nov. 18, 1920, p. 69. Also the campaign biography in *La Liberté du Sud-Ouest,* Nov. 14, 1919, and the account of his speech at Pauillac in *La Petite Gironde,* Oct. 29, 1919.

2. Interview with Adrien Rothschild.

3. Blum, *Souvenirs*, pp. 26–27.

4. *Le Siècle*, Aug. 29, Sept. 6, Oct. 22, and Dec. 11, 1902; Jan. 1, Jan. 16, and June 11, 1903.

5. Buré, *Clemenceau et Mandel*, p. 43.   6. Wormser, *Mandel*, p. 19.

7. Interview with Albert Bayet.   8. Buré, *Clemenceau et Mandel*, p. 44.

9. Philip, "Souvenirs," *La France Active*, July/Aug. 1935, p. 26. The author wrote for *L'Aurore* and later became one of Clemenceau's assistants at the Ministry of the Interior.

10. Buré, *Clemenceau et Mandel*, p. 44.

11. Buré, "Georges Mandel."

12. Interview with Albert Bayet; also Varenne, *Mon patron*, p. 36.

13. Wormser, *Mandel*, p. 17.   14. Abensour, p. 36.

15. Buré, *Clemenceau et Mandel*, p. 45.   16. *L'Aurore*, March 10, 1905.

17. Coblentz, p. 34.

18. Buré, *Clemenceau et Mandel*, pp. 44–45: "to what heights could I not climb!"

19. *Ibid.*, p. 47.

20. Lazareff, *De Munich à Vichy*, p. 281.

21. Interview with Albert Bayet; Coblentz, pp. 39–44.

22. Albert Sarraut, speech before the Société Historique d'Auteuil et de Passy, March 4, 1957 (mimeographed copy).

23. Pierre Lafue in *La Tribune des Nations*, July 25, 1935.

24. Langeron, pp. 7–8. Langeron was a member of Clemenceau's staff at the time.

25. Gatineau-Clemenceau, p. 83.

26. Emile Buré in *Je Suis Partout*, Nov. 11, 1933.

27. Buré, *Clemenceau et Mandel*, pp. 47–48; *L'Aurore, La Petite République, La Libre Parole, Le Radical, Gil Blas*, March 5–10, 1908; Chichet, pp. 134–35. Chichet was Mandel's second in the duel.

28. Philip, "Souvenirs," *La France Active*, Sept./Oct. 1935, p. 21; see also Buré, *Clemenceau et Mandel*, pp. 47–48; Sarraut, speech before the Société Historique d'Auteuil et de Passy, March 4, 1957 (mimeographed copy).

29. Philip, "Souvenirs," *La France Active*, Sept./Oct. 1935, p. 21.

30. *Ibid.*, p. 29.

31. *Ibid.*, pp. 29–30.

32. This account of Mandel's campaign is based on articles in *Le Courrier du Parlement*, which devoted more space to Levallois in its review of the election than to any other district in France, and in the following local newspapers: *Le Journal de Clichy et de Levallois, Le Républicain de Levallois, Le Clichy Républicain*, and *La Liberté de Levallois*, Jan.–April, 1910.

33. Philip, "Souvenirs," *La France Active*, Sept./Oct. 1935, p. 24.

34. Varenne, *Mon patron*, pp. 36–39.

35. *Le Journal du Var*, March 28–April 2, 1911; *JOC*, April 1, 1911, pp. 1638–43; Varenne, *Mon patron*, pp. 56–60.

36. Varenne, "Une célèbre collaboration," p. 73.

37. Varenne, *Mon patron*, p. 49.

38. Abensour, p. 35.

39. Varenne, *Mon patron*, pp. 84–86. When Clemenceau returned to power in 1917, Mandel had Hudelo dismissed from his position as head of the Sûreté Nationale and transferred to a minor post in Nantes. See *ibid.*, p. 87 and Poincaré, X, 391. Charles Arnaud, the sub-prefect in the Var who had encouraged Mandel's candidacy, was ap-

pointed Prefect of the Gironde when Mandel became a candidate there in 1919. See Pierre du Clain (unless otherwise specified, a pen name of François Albert), *Le Progrès Civique*, Feb. 14, 1920, p. 18.

40. James K. Pollock, *Money and Politics Abroad* (New York, 1932), p. 298. Paul Reynaud, a native of the region, said that "Castellane had a liking for opulent candidates." See his *Mémoires*, I, 131. The department of the Basses-Alpes is still known as a "rotten borough." See Pierre Viansson-Ponté, "Prélude à la campagne," *Le Monde*, Sélection Hebdomadaire, July 7–13, 1966.

41. *Le Petit Niçois*, April 24, 1914.

42. *Le Progrès de Castellane*, March 1, 1914.

43. In 1919 Vacquier was appointed to the Gironde when Mandel became a candidate in that department. On the influence exerted by the government in favor of official candidates, see Georges Lachapelle, "Le ministère et les elections," *Le Journal des Débats*, Feb. 20, 1914.

44. *Le Républicain de Castellane*, April 9, 1914.

45. *Le Progrès de Castellane*, April 5, 1914.

46. Varenne, *Mon patron*, pp. 91–92. Varenne accompanied Mandel on his speaking tour of the district.

47. *L'Homme Libre*, May 5, 1914. It was estimated that the election cost Stern 600,000 francs. See *Je Dis Tout*, June 1914, p. 8.

48. See statements of Mandel and Teyssier in *PVCG*, April 27 and May 1, 1923, pp. 241–49, 323–25.

Chapter 3

1. *L'Aurore*, March 20, 1905.

2. *Ibid.*, July 20, 1904; Oct. 10, 1905.

3. *Ibid.*, Feb. 23, 1904. Although opposed to colonization, he believed that France, having acquired colonies, had to establish order and assure their defense. *Ibid.*, May 22, 1904.

4. De Gaulle, *War Memoirs*, I, 3.

5. *L'Aurore*, Jan. 4, 1906.

6. *Bulletin du Parti Républicain Radical et Radical-Socialiste*, Feb. 26, 1910.

7. Alexandre Zévaès, *Clemenceau* (Paris, 1949), p. 219; Georges Louis, *Les carnets* (Paris, 1926), I, 21.

8. *L'Homme Libre*, May 21, 1913.   9. *Ibid.*, May 24, 1913.

10. *Le Journal du Var*, July 17, 1910.   11. *Ibid.*, Oct. 22, 1910.

12. *Ibid.*, Aug. 6, 1910.

13. *Ibid.*, Nov. 5, 1910; March 13, 1911; Sept. 26, 1912.

14. *Ibid.*, Aug. 13, 1910.

15. *Ibid.*, Oct. 22, 1910.

16. Mandel reserved for himself the foreign affairs column of the *Journal du Var*. For the Radical position on foreign affairs, see John C. Cairns, "Politics and Foreign Policy: The French Parliament, 1911–14," *Canadian Historical Review*, XXXIV (Sept. 1953), pp. 253–54.

17. *Le Journal du Var*, Sept. 24, 1910.

18. Pierre Lafue in *La Tribune des Nations*, July 25, 1935. In the 1930's Lafue was Mandel's personal assistant and speech-writer.

19. *Le Réveil Médocain*, Aug. 7, 1927. Mandel was uninterested in metaphysical questions (Wormser, *Mandel*, p. 22), but his basic philosophy, like Clemenceau's,

seems to have derived from the mid-century positivists. See Mandel's obituary notice for André Lefèvre, professor at the Ecole d'Anthropologie, in *L'Aurore*, Nov. 18, 1904: "He replaced the gratuitous claims of spiritualism and the *a priori* assertions of theologians with a clear explanation of the world as a series of mechanical events. In his *Renaissance du matérialisme* and in *Religions et mythologies comparées*, he continued and developed La Mettrie's and d'Holbach's tradition of scientific materialism."

20. Poincaré, V, 187–91.

21. Guy Pedroncini, *Les mutineries de 1917* (Paris, 1967).

22. Poincaré, IX, 382.

23. *Annales du Sénat*, July 22, 1917, p. 866.

24. Emile Herbillon, *Souvenirs d'un officier de liaison pendant la guerre mondiale* (Paris, 1930), II, 152; Ribot, p. 236.

25. Mordacq, *Le ministère Clemenceau*, I, 2–3; Charles Andler, *Vie de Lucien Herr* (Paris, 1932), p. 245; Chichet, p. 238.

26. *Le Figaro*, Nov. 2, 1917.

27. Poincaré, IX, 370.

28. Lacave La Plagne, *Souvenirs de la troisième République* (Avignon, 1950), p. 175.

29. *L'Oeuvre* declared in headlines: "The war must be over, for no one is talking about it any more." Quoted in Romain Rolland, *Journal des années de guerre, 1914–1919* (Paris, 1952), p. 1397.

30. Corday, II, 199.

31. Henry de Jouvenel in *Vu*, Dec. 4, 1929, p. 1000.

32. Pierrefeux, p. 29. Under the ominous title "Rubicon" (recalling not only Caesar's venture but the coup d'état of Louis Napoléon, who had similarly entitled his plans), Caillaux had drawn up during the war an outline of the measures he would take if called to power. Besides obtaining virtually dictatorial powers for the government, he intended to issue a call for peace and prosecute "the direct and indirect authors of the war." See Binion, pp. 73–76.

33. In a Senate speech on November 18, 1924, Poincaré gave him a rather belated clearance, saying, "No act of Malvy's that revealed a lack of patriotism was ever brought to my attention." Quoted in Jacques Kayser, *L'Action républicaine de M. Poincaré* (Paris, 1929), p. 29.

34. Georges Clemenceau, *Grandeur and Misery of Victory* (New York, 1930), p. 367.

35. Caillaux, III, 191; Berger and Allard, *Dessous du Traité*, p. 67 and *Secrets*, p. 283; Mordacq, *Le ministère Clemenceau*, IV, 182; Coblentz, pp. 65–71. According to Mandel's private secretary, one of the reasons why the government was able to act against Caillaux but not against Briand was that the former was very unpopular in Parliament, whereas Briand had many friends. Interview with Paul Vigneau.

36. Erich Ludendorff, *My War Memories* (London, 1919), II, 513.

37. Ferry, pp. 225 and 230.

38. Abensour, p. 36; Varenne, *Mon patron*, 36.

39. Gatineau-Clemenceau, p. 148; about the question of Mandel's influence on Clemenceau, see Corday, I, 37. According to Wormser (*Mandel*, p. 42), Mandel stayed in Paris when Clemenceau went to Bordeaux. It should be noted, however, that Wormser's first-hand information about Mandel dates from 1917 when he joined Clemenceau's staff.

40. Chichet, pp. 211–12.

41. Gatineau-Clemenceau, p. 136; also Frederic Eccard, *Le livre de ma vie* (Paris, 1951), p. 117; and Spears, I, 57–58.

42. *L'Homme Libre*, July 3, 1913.

43. Gatineau-Clemenceau, pp. 156–57; also Paul Carrère, *Profils* (Paris, 1935), pp. 115–16; see also Mandel's article, "Le devoir de l'Europe," *Le Journal du Var*, Oct. 17, 1912: In discussing the expected war between the Balkan states and Turkey, Mandel noted that it might provide the occasion for the expansion of Austrian power, which Russia would not permit. Germany, although annoyed with her ally, would nonetheless support her. France would then be forced to intervene, setting off "the most frightful of all wars. The duty of the diplomats is therefore clear: to avoid at all costs any cause for conflict between Russia and Austria. To that end, we must strive to maintain the status quo in the Balkans, regardless of the outcome of the war that is about to break out, and find the means to force the victor to respect that status quo. The peace of the world depends on it."

44. Wormser, *Mandel*, pp. 46–55.   45. *Le Pays*, Nov. 17, 1917.

46. Poincaré, X, 259.   47. Berger and Allard, *Secrets*, p. 275.

48. Chichet, p. 238; Charles Andler, *Vie de Lucien Herr* (Paris, 1932), p. 245; Martet, pp. 32–33; Buré, *Clemenceau et Mandel*, pp. 48–49; Wormser, *Mandel*, pp. 63–65.

49. *Le Pays*, Nov. 16, 1917; Wormser, *Mandel*, pp. 63–65. The Socialist deputy Aristide Jobert, in *Souvenirs d'un ex-parlementaire, 1914–1919* (Paris, 1933), pp. 154–55, reports that after the meeting Laval exclaimed: "The party stopped me this time, but the next time I won't be in the party and will be able to accept a post." See also *Les Documents Politiques, Diplomatiques et Financiers*, Feb. 1921, pp. 11–12; the comments of the Socialist deputy Calixte Camelle in *Le Cri Populaire* (Bordeaux), Jan. 18, 1920; "Rayon X" (until further notice, a pen name of François Albert) in *L'Oeil de Paris*, Feb. 20, 1932, p. 5. Mandel is reported to have denied offering Laval a post in the government. See Torrès, *Campaign of Treachery*, pp. 181–82; also Warner, pp. 13–14. The contemporary evidence, however, indicates that Mandel had promised Laval some position in the cabinet.

50. Henry Torrès, *Pierre Laval*, pp. 50–53; Emile Buré, *L'Ordre*, June 7, 1945. Laval's friend Alfred Mallet, *Pierre Laval* (Paris, 1954), I, 20, denies the accusation, but according to Paul Vigneau, Mandel's private secretary, who reports having dined with Mandel and the Socialist deputy twenty or twenty-five times during the war, Laval was Mandel's principal informant in the Socialist Party. Laval was supposedly induced to aid Mandel by threats of arrest. It is impossible to prove a charge of this sort, but it seems clear that Laval tried to get Socialist support for the government, that he made several speeches in Parliament at Mandel's request, and that he acted as the government's intermediary with Alphonse Merrheim, Secretary of the Metal Workers' Union. See Wormser, *Mandel*, p. 64; Wormser, *Clemenceau*, pp. 364–65; Privat, *Pierre Laval*, p. 137; Pierre du Clain, *Le Progrès Civique*, Oct. 1, 1919, pp. 18–19; and Maurice Labi, *La grande division des travailleurs* (Paris, 1964), p. 87.

51. Privat, *Pierre Laval, cet inconnu*, pp. 45–46.

52. B. W. Schaper, *Albert Thomas: trente ans de réformisme social* (Paris, 1959), p. 176.

53. Maurice Martin du Gard, *Les mémorables* (Paris, 1957), I, 27–28.

54. Interview with Mandel's private secretary for the years 1916 to 1923, Paul Vigneau.

55. Pierrefeux, p. 113.

56. Poincaré, X, 56.

57. Georges Valois, *L'Homme contre l'argent* (Paris, 1928), pp. 106, 154, 211. Georges Wormser, Clemenceau's secretary, denies that the Prime Minister ever had

any dealings with the *Action Française*. See Weber, pp. 108–9. According to Paul Vigneau, however, Mandel, though possibly not Clemenceau, maintained close relations with the paper.

58. Testimony of Herriot in *Le procès du Maréchal Pétain* (Paris, 1945), I, 330. See also Herriot's speeches in *JOS*, Feb. 12, March 27, April 2, 1919, pp. 92–97, 350, 467–83; Bailby, pp. 89–91; Eugène Lautier in *L'Homme Libre*, Oct. 23, 1922; Soulié, pp. 71–72.

59. *Le Journal du Var*, Nov. 26, 1910.

60. Jean Hennessy in *L'Oeuvre*, Sept. 26, 1918.

61. *Le Petit Parisien*: see *L'Oeuvre*, Sept. 4, 1919; *Le Progrès Civique*, Oct. 1, 1919, p. 30. *L'Intransigeant*: see Bailby, p. 91. *Le Matin*: see *La Petite Gironde*, May 5, 1924; *L'Oeuvre*, Sept. 4, 1919; Wormser, *Mandel*, pp. 80–81. Cooperating journals: see the account of Mandel's treatment of the *Journal des Débats* in Pierre Miquel, "Le Journal des Débats et la paix de Versailles," *Revue Historique*, CCXXXII (Oct.–Dec. 1964), 379–414.

62. René de Livois, *Histoire de la presse française* (Lausanne, 1965), II, 413.

63. *L'Oeuvre*, June 12, 1919; also Pierre du Clain in *Le Progrès Civique*, July 1, 1919, p. 13. Pierre Renaudel confirmed *L'Oeuvre*'s account of the conversation with Abrami in *JOC*, Oct. 2, 1919, p. 4711. For Mandel's treatment of Henri Fabre of *Le Journal du Peuple*, see Livois, II, 413.

64. Even before his accession to power, Mandel had made a number of bitter enemies. In 1914 someone in the Ministry of War maliciously issued an order to arrest him as an enemy alien. Wiser heads prevailed, however, and the order was never carried out. See Gheusi, IV, 55.

65. Wythe Williams, *The Tiger of France* (New York, 1949), p. 146.

66. Berger and Allard, *Secrets*, p. 276.

67. Spears, I, 57. The author was a liaison officer in France during the war.

68. See Bolo's testimony in *La Revue des Causes Célèbres*, March 9, 1918, p. 60. No official stenographic reports of most of the treason trials were made. Unofficial abbreviated accounts are given in *La Revue des Causes Célèbres*, 1918–1921.

69. See Mandel's letter in *L'Oeuvre*, Feb. 10, 1918. In his letter to the court, Mandel neither admitted nor denied having been given the recommendation by Bolo. Eighteen months later, during the electoral campaign, he did deny it, but only in a local newspaper. See *Les Girondins* (Bordeaux), Nov. 1, 1919.

70. *Annales*, March 8, 1918, p. 782.

71. Ferry, p. 222; Berger and Allard, *Secrets*, p. 279; *L'Oeuvre*, Feb. 11, 1918.

72. Marcellin, II, 273.

73. Graux, V, 352. The pun, of course, refers both to Mandel's reputed role as Clemenceau's secret advisor—*éminence grise*—and to his abuse of his authority—*éminence grisée*, drunken eminence, i.e. drunk with power.

74. Armand Charpentier, "Mémorial d'Anastasie," *Le Pays*, Nov. 5, 1919.

75. The name "Jéroboam" was first used on August 10, 1919 by *L'Oeuvre*, which asserted that it was Mandel's real name. It caught on so quickly that even the correspondent for *The Times* of London used it (Nov. 11, 1919). Some writers still believe that his name was Jéroboam Rothschild. See Montigny, p. 18.

76. When Clemenceau was minister of the Interior from 1906 to 1909, he was known as "*le premier flic* (cop) *de France*."

77. Pierre du Clain, *Le Progrès Civique*, July 1, 1919, p. 13; *L'Humanité*, Nov. 10, 1919. Gustave Téry called Mandel "the malicious little tyrant who is governing France under the pseudonym of Clemenceau." *L'Oeuvre*, May 14, 1919.

78. *Annales,* July 22, 1919, p. 3277.
79. *Bulletin du Parti Républicain Radical et Radical-Socialiste,* Aug. 16, 1919, p. 5.
80. *Le Radical,* July 28, 1919.
81. Poincaré, X, 196, 441. General Mordacq was Clemenceau's military *chef de cabinet.*
82. Berger and Allard, *Dessous du Traité,* p. 21. Clemenceau's friend Alphonse Aulard wrote that Mandel exercised "a preponderant influence" on the Prime Minister. "He was a born policeman whose memory, stocked with a rich collection of anecdotes about everyone, was always at the service of Clemenceau's grudges. His thorough knowledge of parliamentary intrigues made him indispensable. He was more powerful than a minister." *Histoire politique de la grande guerre* (Paris, 1924), pp. 288–89.
83. Chichet, pp. 241–42. When Clemenceau became prime minister, he chose Chichet to replace him as editor of *L'Homme Libre.* See also Varenne, *Mon patron,* p. 100, and *Miroir de l'Histoire,* Feb. 1953, pp. 78–79; Pierre du Clain in *Le Progrès Civique,* July 16, 1919, p. 10. Albert had worked on both *L'Aurore* and *L'Homme Libre* with Mandel and Clemenceau; Jean Martet, "Avec Georges Clemenceau," *Les Annales Politiques et Littéraires,* Dec. 15, 1929, pp. 545–47; Wormser, *Mandel,* pp. 73–75.
84. Poincaré, X, 32; Coblentz, pp. 58–64; *Annales,* Feb. 1, 1918, pp. 245–46.
85. *Le Progrès Civique,* July 1, 1919, p. 12.
86. Ferry, p. 203. There was no end to Clemenceau's sarcastic and disparaging remarks about Mandel, which were delightedly retailed throughout Paris. See Chichet, pp. 244–45; Berger and Allard, *Secrets,* p. 276; Gheusi, IV, 54; Martet, *Les Annales Politiques et Littéraires,* Dec. 15, 1929, pp. 548–49, and *Clemenceau, passim.* According to Chichet, pp. 244–45, and Emile Buré in *L'Eclair,* March 2, 1924, these witticisms should not be taken seriously. In particular, the accounts of Jean Martet, who rarely records a favorable remark, should be considered not skeptically, for Clemenceau had an acid tongue, but in perspective. Martet hated Mandel. See Gatineau-Clemenceau, pp. 155–56. On the other hand, General Mordacq, Clemenceau's military *chef de cabinet,* rarely reports an unfavorable remark. See *Le ministère Clemenceau, passim,* and *Clemenceau au soir, passim.*
87. Léon Treich, *L'Esprit de Clemenceau* (Paris, 1925), p. 74.
88. Mordacq, *Le ministère Clemenceau,* I, 28–30, 55.
89. Wormser, *Mandel,* p. 69.
90. *Aux Ecoutes,* Nov. 2, 1919, p. 5. The fact that Mandel was at times forced to resort to drugs in order to maintain his killing pace was confirmed to me by several persons who knew him well. See also Favreau, pp. 8 and 97. Another one of Mandel's personal physicians, Doctor Beausoleil, informed Favreau that Mandel always had to have injections before giving speeches or during periods of intense political activity.
91. George B. Noble, *Policies and Opinions at Paris, 1919* (New York, 1935), p. 249; Berger and Allard, *Dessous du Traité,* pp. 17–18, 28–29, 56–57; Frederick J. Cox, "The French Peace Plans, 1918–1919: The Germ of the Conflict between Ferdinand Foch and Georges Clemenceau," in *Studies in Modern European History in Honor of Franklin Charles Palm* (New York, 1956), pp. 88–89.
92. Charles Seymour, ed., *The Intimate Papers of Colonel House* (New York, 1928), IV, 407–8.
93. Marjorie R. Clark, *A History of the French Labor Movement, 1910–1928* (Berkeley, 1930), pp. 68–77; Roger Picard, *Le mouvement syndical durant la guerre* (Paris, 1927), pp. 204–14; Edouard Dolléans, *Histoire du mouvement ouvrier* (Paris, 1953), II, 298–304.

94. Berger and Allard, *Dessous du Traité*, pp. 213–14.

95. For an excellent account of the general strikes in 1919, see Mayer, pp. 667–72, 853–69.

96. Edouard Dolléans, *Histoire du mouvement ouvrier* (Paris, 1953), II, 313; also Annie Kriegel, *Aux origines du communisme français, 1914–1920* (Paris, 1964), I, pp. 298–303; Maurice Labi, *La grande division des travailleurs* (Paris, 1964), pp. 108–9, 120–23; Wohl, p. 138.

97. Marjorie R. Clark, *A History of the French Labor Movement, 1910–1928* (Berkeley, 1930), p. 76. According to the law of August 9, 1849, while the state of siege is in effect (as it was until October 1919), "the military courts may take jurisdiction over crimes and offenses against the safety of the Republic, against the Constitution, against peace and order, whatever be the status of the principal perpetrators and their accomplices." See Clinton Rossiter, *Constitutional Dictatorship* (2d ed., New York, 1963), p. 83.

98. Wohl, p. 138.

99. *L'Echo de Paris*, July 19, 1919.

100. Privat, *Pierre Laval, cet inconnu*, pp. 137–38; Torrès, *Laval*, p. 53; *JOC*, July 18, 1919, pp. 3597–3614.

101. *L'Humanité*, July 19, 1919.

102. *Ibid.*

103. He had also, of course, effectively frustrated most of the workers' aims. Mandel was not systematically hostile to the workers, however. He maintained contacts among the Left, and performed services as readily for the unions (see Virgile Barel, *Cinquante années de luttes* [Paris, 1967], pp. 33–34) as he did for their right-wing opponents (see Louis Dimier, *Vingt ans d'Action française* [Paris, 1926], p. 300). He simply considered them another factor in the game of politics. According to Wormser (*Mandel*, p. 293), who unfortunately gives no details, it was Mandel's very ability to manipulate the unions that caused him to underrate their strength and to ignore their demands for reforms.

104. Wormser, *Mandel*, p. 84.

Chapter 4

1. Berger and Allard, *Dessous du Traité*, p. 21.

2. "Georges Mandel," *Revue Universelle*, Dec. 1, 1920, p. 664. The article is unsigned, but Henri Massis informs me that Bainville wrote it. A series of political vignettes written by Bainville for the *Revue Universelle*, including the one about Mandel, was published anonymously under the title *Ceux qui nous mènent* (Paris, 1922).

3. *PVCG*, Oct. 6, 1921, p. 654.

4. *Ibid.*, p. 670.

5. *Ibid.*, April 27, 1923, pp. 230–34.

6. Speech at Pauillac (Gironde) in *La Petite Gironde*, Oct. 29, 1919.

7. *Annales*, Feb. 29, 1924, p. 979.

8. Poincaré, X, 425 (Nov. 21, 1918).

9. *Ibid.*, p. 441.

10. *La Liberté du Sud-Ouest*, Nov. 8, 1919.

11. Wormser, *Clemenceau*, p. 366.

12. *Ibid.*, pp. 364–65; *Annales*, Sept. 4, 1919, p. 3725. In one debate, Briand openly accused Laval of being Mandel's spokesman. See *JOC*, Sept. 19, 1919, p. 4454. Without

specifically naming Laval, Robert de Jouvenel wrote: "Everyone knows that a certain Socialist, at the end of the debate, will run to Mandel to arrange the next maneuver with that implacable enemy of his party." *Bonsoir*, Sept. 6, 1919.

13. *L'Europe Nouvelle*, Sept. 27, 1919, p. 1854.

14. *JOC*, Sept. 19, 1919, p. 4456.

15. See Mandel's articles against proportional representation in the *Journal du Var*, May 28, 1910; Sept. 13, 21, 28, Oct. 26, Nov. 2, 16, 30, 1912.

16. Pierrefeux, p. 148; MS memoirs of Charles Morice, "Quarante ans de journalisme: presse et parlement; souvenirs et anecdotes," vol. II, tome I, p. 109. These memoirs of the former editor of *Le Petit Parisien* are deposited in the Bibliothèque Nationale.

17. See statements by the deputy Gabriel Combrouze, *PVCG*, April 27, 1923, pp. 247–52; also Charles Chaumet, "Comment l'étranger a divisé les républicains girondins," *Les Girondins*, Nov. 14, 1919.

18. *L'Oeuvre*, Aug. 28, 1919; "Un piédestal," *Le Cri de Paris*, reprinted in *Bastia-Journal* (Corsica), Aug. 22, 1919.

19. Graux, VII, 333; *Le Progrès Civique*, May 16, 1919, p. 52; *L'Oeuvre*, July 9, Oct. 2, 21, 1919; *Courrier de la Corse*, Aug. 14, 21, 1919.

20. *Le Cri Populaire*, Oct. 26, 1919.

21. *JOC*, Oct. 2, 1919, p. 4708. Bon insisted on the capital letter.

22. *La Petite Gironde*, Aug. 4, 1919. The amendment was supposedly inspired by Chaumet. See *La France de Bordeaux et du Sud-Ouest*, Oct. 3, 1919.

23. *JOC*, Oct. 2, 1919, pp. 4707–12.

24. Interview with Mandel's secretary, Paul Vigneau.

25. *Bastia-Journal* (Corsica), Oct. 25, 1919.

26. See statements of Mandel and Paul de Cassagnac in *Annales*, Feb. 29, 1924, pp. 976–78; also Beau de Loménie, III, 235–36.

27. Mordacq, *Le ministère Clemenceau*, IV, 169; *La Petite Gironde*, May 5, 1924, April 19, 1928; interview with Paul Vigneau.

28. The secret negotiations and agreement with the Catholics were revealed by Mandel a few years later in an attempt to discredit the Republicans who had since broken with him. See debate in *PVCG*, April 30, 1923, pp. 310–85; A. Mamelet, "Le nouveau pacte de Bordeaux," *La République Démocratique*, July 8, 1923.

29. *La Croix*, Oct. 24, 1919, reprinted in *La Documentation Catholique*, Nov. 8, 1919, p. 571.

30. *Ibid.*

31. A. Mamelet, "La vérité historique opposée à la légende du 'Bloc National,' " *La République Démocratique*, June 18, 1922.

32. Schlesinger, pp. 56–57.

33. Wormser, *Mandel*, pp. 81–82; Pierre du Clain, *Le Progrès Civique*, Dec. 22, 1923, p. 21; interview with Francis Varenne.

34. *PVCG*, Oct. 4, 1921, pp. 408–10.

35. Lachapelle, *Elections . . . du 16 novembre 1919*, p. 35; also Cornilleau, p. 38.

36. *L'Oeuvre*, June 13, 14, 16, Sept. 13, 1919; *Les Hommes du Jour*, July 6, Oct. 25, 1919; Eugène Lautier, *L'Homme Libre*, Oct. 23, 1922.

37. *JOC*, Oct. 2, 1919, pp. 4707–12.

38. *Correspondance*, III, 355.

39. The speech was printed in *Le Journal des Débats*, Nov. 6, 1919.

40. See Mandel's comments in *Le Cri du Jour*, Nov. 10, 1934, p. 9. For his use of this parliamentary gossip sheet, see above, pp. 143–45.

41. See Mandel's speech in *PVCG*, Jan. 5, 1920, p. 15.

42. Beau de Loménie, who is attempting to establish the close connections between members of Parliament and business interests, erroneously says that by agreeing to join Dupuy's list, Mandel was "pris en main." *Les responsabilités des dynasties bourgeoises* (Paris, 1954), III, 235–36. On the contrary, by 1924 Mandel had embroiled Dupuy in conflicts with his fellow Republicans, brought about his defeat in the senatorial elections and finally forced him to give up his political career in the Gironde, his home district. See Pierre du Clain, *Le Progrès Civique*, Jan. 19, 1924, p. 21.

43. *La France de Bordeaux et du Sud-Ouest*, Nov. 3, 1919.

44. *Les Girondins*, Oct. 31–Nov. 14, 1919.

45. *La Petite Gironde*, Nov. 9, 1919; *La Liberté du Sud-Ouest*, Nov. 14, 1919.

46. *La France de Bordeaux et du Sud-Ouest*, Oct. 28, 1919.

47. "M. Clemenceau renonce à la politique," *Les Girondins*, Oct. 31, 1919.

48. *Le Journal*, Nov. 9, 1919; *L'Oeuvre*, Nov. 10, 1919.

49. *L'Eclair* in *La Presse de Paris*, Nov. 14, 1919.

50. A journalist reported that "à ceux qui reprochaient à Mandel d'être juif, ses colistiers répondaient que c'étaient un israélite, avouant avec candeur, à des électeurs naïfs, toute la différence qu'il y a entre un israélite lorsqu'il est notre ami, un juif lorsque nous nous brouillons avec lui, et un sale 'youpin' lorsque nous lui en voulons à mort." Pierrefeux, pp. 149–50.

51. See articles and reports of speeches in *La Liberté du Sud-Ouest*, Nov. 8, 14, 1919, and *La Petite Gironde*, Oct. 29, Nov. 9, 1919. His father died on February 8, 1920 and was buried in Montmartre cemetery.

52. "Je fais appel à votre intelligence, je ne demande rien à votre coeur." "La curiosité du jour: M. Mandel," *Le Matin*, Nov. 9, 1919. The article is unsigned but it was written by the art critic André Salmon. See his memoirs, *Souvenirs sans fin* (Paris, 1955–56), II, 290. Henri de Jouvenel, the editor of *Le Matin*, who, according to Salmon, "in the name of *Le Matin* if not for himself…detested Mandel," had sent the politically inexperienced Salmon to Libourne with the expectation that he would write an unfavorable article.

53. See *La Petite Gironde*, Oct. 29, 1919.

54. Ribot, pp. 282–83.

55. "Mandel devant le peuple," *L'Oeuvre* in *La Feuille Commune*, Nov. 15, 1919.

56. *La Petite Gironde*, *La Liberté du Sud-Ouest*, *La Presse de Paris*, Nov. 14, 1919.

57. Nov. 14, 1919.

58. *La Feuille Commune*, *Les Girondins*, Nov. 15, 1919; *Le Cri Populaire* (Bordeaux), Nov. 16, 1919.

59. *Aux Ecoutes*, Dec. 7, 1919, p. 8.

60. Interview with Mandel's secretary, Paul Vigneau. According to Mandel's running mate Pierre Dignac, however, it was Mandel himself who had arranged the attempted "assassination." See Favreau, p. 96.

61. Fournol, *Le moderne Plutarque*, p. 95.

62. Interview with Pierre Dignac.

63. *Le Cri Populaire* (Bordeaux), Jan. 18, 1920.

64. "Les nouveaux as du Palais-Bourbon," *L'Oeuvre*, Dec. 26, 1919.

65. Morice, vol. III, tome I, pp. 12, 18; *Le Cri Populaire* (Bordeaux), Jan. 18, 1920; *L'Europe Nouvelle*, Dec. 6, 1919, p. 2239; *Le Courrier du Parlement*, Dec. 6, 1919.

66. See speech by former Socialist deputy Calixte Camelle, *PVCG*, Oct. 6, 1921, p. 666.

67. *Le Progrès Civique*, Dec. 1, 1919, p. 5.

68. Wormser, *Clemenceau*, p. 402.
69. *Le Progrès Civique*, Dec. 27, 1919, p. 26; Buell, p. 138.
70. *PVCG*, April 24, 1923, p. 55.
71. Mordacq, *Le ministère Clemenceau*, IV, 217.
72. Ribot, pp. 282–83; see also Wormser, *Mandel*, pp. 88–89.
73. Bailby, pp. 187–93.
74. Soulié, p. 80; Wormser, *Clemenceau*, pp. 421–23.
75. To Mandel, he was the incarnation of mediocrity: "I've never taken M. Deschanel seriously because in thirty-five years of public life he has never taken a stand on any issue." See interview with Mandel in *La Liberté du Sud-Ouest*, April 23, 1924.
76. Wormser, *Clemenceau*, pp. 399–400; Coblentz, pp. 83–85.
77. Wormser, *Clemenceau*, p. 409.
78. René Malliavin, *La politique nationale de Paul Deschanel* (Paris, 1925), p. 154; Louis Sonolet, *La vie et l'oeuvre de Paul Deschanel* (Paris, 1926), pp. 263–65.
79. *L'Oeuvre*, *La Petite Gironde*, Jan. 14, 1920.
80. Pierre du Clain, *Le Progrès Civique*, Jan. 24, 1920, p. 16; also Suarez, *Briand*, V, 66–70.
81. *L'Oeuvre*, Jan. 14, 1920.
82. Joseph Brugerette, *Le prêtre français et la société contemporaine* (Paris, 1933–38), III, 642.
83. *L'Oeuvre*, Jan. 15, 1920; Graux, VII, 354–55; Morice, vol. III, tome I, pp. 18–26; Emile Buré in *L'Eclair*, Jan. 15, 1920.
84. Wormser, *Clemenceau*, p. 419.
85. *Ibid.*, p. 403.
86. Martet, *Georges Clemenceau*, p. 313; Wormser, *Mandel*, p. 89.
87. Wormser, *Clemenceau*, p. 406.
88. *Ibid.*, p. 404.
89. *L'Oeuvre*, Jan. 17, 1920; Cornilleau, p. 60.
90. According to Cornilleau, pp. 59–60, Clemenceau admitted to one Catholic emissary that he recognized the necessity of reestablishing diplomatic relations with the Vatican.
91. Jean Philip, *La France Active*, Sept.–Oct. 1935, p. 28.
92. *L'Europe Nouvelle*, Jan. 24, 1920, p. 118; Cambon, *Correspondance*, III, 372.
93. Bailby, pp. 184–93. The left-wing historian Georges Michon wrote that "this defeat signified especially a personal distrust of Clemenceau and a great deal of hostility toward the methods of those about him, particularly Mandel, who, since November 16, 1917, had been the true master of the internal policy of France. Controlling and governing in place of Clemenceau, he had caused all the petty officials and politicians to tremble with fear." *Clemenceau* (Paris, 1931), p. 252, also Morice, vol. III, tome I, p. 12.
94. Pierre du Clain, *Le Progrès Civique*, Feb. 14, 1920, pp. 17–18; Mandel's speech in *PVCG*, Oct. 6, 1921, p. 654.
95. *La Liberté du Sud-Ouest*, Jan. 20, 1920.
96. Soulier, p. 17.
97. See above, pp. 63, 83–84.
98. Quoted in Emile Faguet, *Politiques et moralistes du dix-neuvième siècle* (Paris, 1891), Première Série, p. 310.
99. Jean Martet, *Clemenceau peint par lui-même* (Paris, 1929), p. 218.
100. The presidential electoral college proposed by Millerand was similar to the one first adopted by the Fifth Republic.

101. See Millerand's speech in *Le Journal des Débats*, Nov. 9, 1919. For a discussion of his ideas, see Wurzburg, pp. 51–54.

102. Cornilleau, p. 55.

103. *Annales*, Jan. 22, 1920, pp. 12–13.

104. See Mandel's speech in *PVCG*, Oct. 6, 1921, p. 654.

105. *Le Réveil Médocain*, May 26, 1929.

106. *Le Journal du Var*, May 21, 1910.

107. For a historical analysis of the reasons for the persistence of rule by the Center from the French Revolution to the present, see Maurice Duverger, *La démocratie sans le peuple* (Paris, 1967). According to Duverger, the French Revolution created both left-wing and right-wing extremists determined to eliminate their opponents. As a result, except for short periods of time, a purely left-wing or purely right-wing government became unacceptable to the majority of the people because of the intense fear and passion it would arouse. In these circumstances the only possible government was one in which the Left-Center and the Right-Center collaborated. Unfortunately, however, this was also the kind of government that was least likely to introduce needed reforms.

Mandel's analysis of the French parliamentary system would tend to support Duverger's thesis. It is noteworthy that, like Mandel, Duverger recommends the establishment of a two-party system to overcome the weaknesses of government by the Center. The difference between them is that Duverger is concerned with ending the isolation of the Communists and creating a united left-wing party, whereas Mandel was concerned with gaining acceptance for the Catholics in order to create a viable conservative party. In this respect, Mandel's attempts from 1919 to 1932 to rehabilitate the Catholics parallel the efforts of François Mitterand from 1965 to 1968 to form an alliance with the Communists.

108. *Le Temps*, Jan. 18, 1920.

109. Wormser, *Clemenceau*, p. 396.

110. *Ibid.*, pp. 407–8.

111. Mordacq, *Le ministère Clemenceau*, IV, 221, 238.

112. Soulier, p. 54.

113. See the epigraph at the head of this chapter from Jean Prévost, *Histoire de France depuis la guerre* (Paris, 1932), pp. 41–42.

Chapter 5

1. *Le Cri Populaire*, Jan. 25, 1920. "M. Clemenceau n'étant plus rien, M. Georges Mandel n'est plus grand'chose!"

2. *PVCG*, Oct. 6, 1921, pp. 655–56.   3. *Revue Universelle*, p. 662.

4. *PVCG*, May 1, 1923, p. 329.   5. Daudet, *Paris vécu*, p. 155.

6. Binion, p. 242.   7. Tardieu, *La paix* (Paris, 1921), p. ix.

8. Cornilleau, p. 106.

9. *La France Active*, Nov.–Dec. 1936, p. 32.

10. Pierre du Clain, *Le Progrès Civique*, Feb. 12, 1921, p. 22; Daudet, *La Chambre*, pp. 14 and 55.

11. Reynaud, *Mémoires*, I, 140.

12. Wormser, *Mandel*, p. 109; *Aux Ecoutes*, Dec. 24, 1922, p. 4; Pierre du Clain, *Le Progrès Civique*, Nov. 5, 1921, p. 16. After becoming prime minister in 1929, Tardieu told a friend, "As a parliamentarian I'm not worth two cents.... I'd like to believe that I am a good minister, but I am a bad deputy. I've been lucky enough to be

trusted by the finest men of my day. I have been able to be of some service and, with the help of circumstances, to accomplish something. But if, in order to succeed, I had had to flatter deputies, or to maneuver in their world, I never would have succeeded." Sisley Huddleston, "Mon ami, André Tardieu," *Ecrits de Paris*, March 1955, pp. 35–36.

13. *Annales*, Jan. 22, 1920, pp. 22–23.

14. Bonnefous, III, 152–53.

15. Pierre du Clain, *Le Progrès Civique*, July 31, 1920, p. 16.

16. *Ibid.*

17. *Aux Ecoutes*, Oct. 3, 1920, p. 13.

18. See Mandel's speeches in *PVCG*, Aug. 30, 1920, pp. 14–18; Jan. 3, 1921, p. 6; April 30, 1923, p. 304; also the account of one of his speeches in *Le Réveil Médocain*, Nov. 4, 1923.

19. Pierre du Clain, *Le Progrès Civique*, Dec. 22, 1923, p. 21; March 22, 1924, p. 14; June 12, 1924, p. 19; *Aux Ecoutes*, Oct. 3, 1920, pp. 5 and 13; Sept. 26, 1920, p. 7; "L'Aventurier" in *L'Impartial Français*, reprinted in *Le Républicain* (Bordeaux), March 16, 1924.

20. "The afternoon of a monkey." *L'Humanité*, Nov. 19, 1920.

21. Chichet, p. 244.

22. "Lettre ouverte à M. Georges Mandel," *L'Eclair*, Oct. 22, 1922.

23. Fournol, pp. 102–3.

24. *Annales*, Nov. 18, 1920, pp. 62–69.

25. *Le Progrès Civique*, Dec. 1, 1919, p. 5.

26. Beau de Loménie, III, 293–94, 305; Bonnefous, III, 207.

27. Raoul Persil, *Alexandre Millerand* (Paris, 1951), p. 139.

28. See article by Albert Mamelet in *La République Démocratique*, May 7, 1922.

29. "La véritable union nationale," *La République Démocratique*, Jan. 30, 1921.

30. *La République Démocratique*, Jan. 16, 1921. The Alliance always referred to itself as the "Left-Center," although in fact it was usually situated on the Right-Center.

31. The Radicals received six portfolios and the rightist Entente, four: Bonnevay, Dior, Lefebvre du Prey, and Leredu. But Dior and Leredu belonged to the Left wing of the Entente and were also members of the Alliance Démocratique, which received eight other ministries. Four other ministers were from the center groups as well. Thus the Right actually received only two places (or four if Dior and Leredu are counted), the Center fourteen (or twelve), and the Radicals six. In Millerand's cabinet, the Right had received two, the Center fourteen, and the Radicals four.

32. *La République Démocratique*, Jan. 23, 1921.

33. *Le Petit Démocrate*, March 9, 1924; Cornilleau, pp. 143–44.

34. See Mandel's speech in *PVCG*, Oct. 6, 1921, p. 634.

35. *PVCG*, Sept. 5, 1921, p. 10.

36. The quotations on the following pages are taken from the debates on October 3, 4, 5, and 6, 1921, *PVCG*, pp. 272ff.

37. *Annales*, March 16, 1921, pp. 1052–59.

38. *PVCG*, Oct. 6, 1921, p. 670.

39. *Annales*, Oct. 19–20, 1921, pp. 38–55.

40. *Revue Politique et Parlementaire*, Nov. 10, 1921, pp. 254–55.

41. In *Le Radical*. Quoted in the Press review of *La Petite Gironde*, Oct. 21, 1921.

42. *La Petite Gironde*, Oct. 22, 1921. Most of the center journals, including *Le Petit Parisien*, *Le Matin* and *L'Intransigeant*, supported the government. The rightist *L'Echo de Paris* and *Le Figaro* were more favorable to Mandel.

43. François Albert, *Revue Politique et Parlementaire*, Nov. 10, 1921, pp. 254–55. Tardieu lost "the advantage that Mandel had gained by his greater finesse." Also Pierre du Clain, *Le Progrès Civique*, Nov. 5, 1921, p. 16.

44. *JOC*, Oct. 25, 1921, pp. 3672–79.

45. Cambon, III, 398–99. Also Pierre du Clain, *Le Progrès Civique*, Nov. 5, 1921, p. 17.

46. *JOC*, Oct. 26, 1921, p. 3708.

47. *L'Echo National*, Jan. 10, 1922.

48. See Wormser, *Clemenceau*, pp. 442–47 for details of the negotiations preceding its appearance. According to Mandel's secretary, Paul Vigneau, it was Mandel who obtained the financial support for the paper (interview with Vigneau). According to Wormser, however (*Mandel*, p. 110), Mandel refused to have anything to do with financing the paper.

49. See Mandel's statement in *PVCG*, April 27, 1923, p. 243.

50. "Notre but," *L'Echo National*, Jan. 10, 1922.

51. Mordacq, *Clemenceau au soir*, I, 186.

52. Quoted in Gaston Riou, *L'Après-guerre* (Paris, 1926), p. 302.

53. Miquel, p. 443; Weber, pp. 136–38.

54. Albert Mamelet, "Le ministère Poincaré," *La République Démocratique*, Jan. 22, 1922.

55. Beau de Loménie, III, 359.

56. Tardieu published his letter in *L'Echo National*, May 15, 1924.

57. Planes, "Mes rencontres" (MS memoirs). The author was a reporter for *La Liberté du Sud-Ouest* (Bordeaux) for many years.

58. Cornilleau, p. 173.

59. Bonnefous, III, 302.

60. *JOC*, Oct. 20, 1922, pp. 2765–66.

61. In 1919 Mandel appointed Charles Arnaud as Prefect of the Gironde, Paul Vacquier as Secretary-General, and Paul de Caunes as subprefect of Lesparre. De Caunes was a school friend of Mandel's. For an account of his activities during the 1919 elections, see the speech by Calixte Camelle in *PVCG*, Oct. 4, 1921, pp.405–7. Vacquier was the subprefect Mandel had had transferred to Castellane in 1914, just before the elections. See above, p. 14. Arnaud was the subprefect who had supported Mandel's candidacy in the Var in 1914. See Pierre du Clain, *Le Progrès Civique*, Feb. 14, 1920, p. 18.

62. See Mandel's speeches in the *Annales*, Oct. 20, 1922, p. 154 and in *PVCG*, Oct. 6, 1921, p. 639; also *L'Echo National*, May 19, 1922.

63. Paul Duché, "La journée du 14 mai," and "Le siège de Lesparre," *La Liberté du Sud-Ouest*, May 16, 17, 1922.

64. When Mandel mentioned the work of several previous prime ministers, Poincaré interrupted: "And M. Painlevé?" Mandel replied: "He was never prime minister. He was the only one who ever thought he was."

65. *JOC*, Oct. 20, 1922, pp. 2765–2777.

66. Cornilleau, pp. 209–10. Tardieu called it "le maître discours politique de la Chambre." *L'Echo National*, Oct. 21, 1922. As one of the most significant speeches of the year, it was reprinted in the *Encyclopédie parlementaire: La politique française en 1922*. (Paris, 1923).

67. *JOC*, Oct. 20, 1922, p. 2774.

68. André Chaumeix, "La crise des partis politiques," *Revue de Paris*, Nov. 15, 1922,

pp. 435–44. François Albert, *Revue Politique et Parlementaire*, Nov. 10, 1922, p. 330. Henry de Jouvenel in *Le Matin*, Oct. 23, 27, 31, 1922. The issue was discussed as well in *L'Homme Libre, L'Eclair, Le Journal des Débats, La Croix*, and *L'Ere Nouvelle*. See excerpts in *Le Réveil Médocain*, Nov. 26, 1922.

69. *Le Temps*, Oct. 22, 1922.   70. *JOC*, Nov. 10, 1922, pp. 3052–56.

71. *PVCG*, May 1, 1923, pp. 356–58.   72. Bonnefous, III, 354.

73. *Lettres de M. Guizot à sa famille et à ses amis*, ed. Mme. de Witt, (Paris, 1884), pp. 270–71.

74. Bonnefous, III, 373–76.

75. Louis Loucheur, *Carnets secrets, 1908–1932* (Brussels, 1962), p. 128. François Arago resigned as president of the right-wing propaganda organization, the Action Nationale Républicaine, because some of its members supported Tardieu while he himself backed Poincaré. See his letter of resignation in *Le Républicain* (Bordeaux), July 15, 1923.

Chapter 6

1. Suarez, *Nos seigneurs et maîtres*, p. 109; Ignotus (Georges Suarez?), "Georges Mandel," *Revue de Paris*, Feb. 1, 1936, p. 508; J. F. Louis Merlet, "M. Georges Mandel," *La France de Bordeaux*, April 29, 1932.

2. *L'Action Française*, Oct. 22, 1922; Villette, pp. 6–7; *La Petite Gironde*, April 27, 1924.

3. *Annales*, Feb. 29, 1924, p. 982.

4. *L'Ere Nouvelle*, March 20, 1923.

5. *PVCG*, April 26, 1922, pp. 228–33; Sept. 8, 1921, p. 159.

6. *Ibid.*, April 26–27, 1923, pp. 204–10; April 30, 1923, pp. 265–71; May 2, 1923, pp. 384, 448; Sept. 3, 1923, pp. 12–25.

7. *Annales*, Nov. 23, 1923, pp. 151–52.

8. Bainville, p. 661.

9. Reynaud, *Mémoires*, I, 158; Bonnefous, III, 305.

10. Mordacq, *Clemenceau au soir*, II, 24.

11. *L'Homme Libre*, Oct. 23, 1922.   12. *PVCG*, April 30, 1923, p. 302.

13. Bonnefous, III, 334.   14. Daudet, *Député, passim*.

15. See article by Maurice de Waleffe, *Paris-Midi*, March 24, 1925. Reprinted in *Le Réveil Médocain*, April 5, 1925.

16. Georges Valois, *L'Homme contre l'argent*, pp. 106, 154, 211.

17. Charles Maurras in *L'Action Française*, May 21, 1940.

18. Charles Maurras, *Pour un jeune Français* (Paris, 1949), p. 143.

19. Daudet, *Moloch et Minerve*, p. 190.

20. Daudet, "Un tribun."

21. Daudet, *L'Agonie du régime*, pp. 140–41.

22. Weber, pp. 136–38; Miquel, p. 443.

23. Daudet, *Moloch et Minerve*, pp. 200–201; *L'Agonie du régime*, p. 21. On September 22, 1922, Tardieu wrote in *L'Echo National*: "M. Charles Maurras . . . has shown us how foresighted he is by trying to make a crazy man president of the Republic." Quoted in Cornilleau, pp. 216–17. Maurras had supported Deschanel's candidacy for the presidency in 1920.

24. "La manoeuvre clemenciste," *L'Action Française*, March 20, 1923.

25. See article by Albert Mamelet, "La vérité historique opposée à la légende du 'Bloc National,' " *La République Démocratique*, June 18, 1922.

26. Jean Carrère and Georges Bourgin, *Manuel des partis politiques en France* (Paris, 1924), pp. 71–73. Also Wurzburg, pp. 145–46, 151–56.

27. Herriot, *Jadis*, II, 112. In his multi-volume study of the "dynasties bourgeoises," Beau de Loménie quite rightly focuses attention on the pivotal position of the Center and the unfortunate effect it has had on French politics. *Les responsabilités des dynasties bourgeoises* (Paris, 4 vols., 1943–63). On the other hand, Frederick Wurzburg considers the Radicals "the main artisans... of the collapse of the Bloc National" (p. 304). In his view, not only the Right but the Center as well "muddled along in ingenuous bewilderment that things were not going their way.... Only the Radicals played the game of maneuver." (p. 309). The evidence, however, indicates that the Center Republicans were maneuvering as much as the Radicals, though perhaps less successfully.

28. Speech reprinted in *Le Républicain* (Bordeaux), Aug. 15, 1923. For the reaction of the Right to Chaumet's speech, see the article "Un discours de plus" by Albert Orry in *L'Action Nationale Républicaine*, Aug. 9, 1923.

29. Herriot's reply was published in *Le Républicain* (Bordeaux), Oct. 15, 1923.

30. Millerand's speech was published in *Le Temps*, Oct. 15, 1923.

31. *La République Démocratique*, Oct. 21, 1923.

32. Pierre du Clain, *Le Progrès Civique*, Dec. 1, 1923, p. 18; Feb. 16, 1924, p. 12.

33. *L'Echo National*, Feb. 7, 1924; cited in Weber, p. 150.

34. *Annales*, Feb. 29, 1924, pp. 979–87.   35. *Le Matin*, March 1, 1924.

36. Bainville, p. 662.   37. Herriot, *Jadis*, II, 130.

38. *Revue Politique et Parlementaire*, April 10, 1924, p. 100.

39. Miquel, pp. 478–85.

40. On the reconciliation of Catholics with the Republic, see Harry W. Paul, *The Second Ralliement: The Rapprochement Between Church and State in France in the Twentieth Century* (Washington, D.C., 1967).

41. André Siegfried, *France: A Study in Nationality* (New Haven, 1930), pp. 91–92.

42. Pertinax (André Géraud), "The Coming French Elections," *Foreign Affairs*, Jan. 1928, p. 225.

43. Schlesinger, p. 145; Jacques Dupont, "La campagne de presse du Cartel des Gauches" (Thèse de la Fondation Nationale de Science Politique, 1950), p. 60.

44. *PVCG*, April 30–May 1, 1923, pp. 310–15, 357.

45. *La République Démocratique*, July 8, 1923.

46. *Congrès du parti républicain-radical et radical socialiste tenu à Boulogne-sur-Mer les 16, 17, 18, 19 octobre 1924* (Paris, 1924), pp. 103–4.

47. Marcel Espiau, "Avec l'Abbé Bergey," *L'Eclair*, May 27, 1924.

48. Henri-Michel Hillaire-Darrigrand, *L'Abbé Bergey* (Paris, 1956), pp. 26–27.

49. Henriot, "Mandel."

50. Planes, "Mes rencontres." The Royalists said that Mandel was a "Français légal" and not a "Français légitime." See Georges Suarez and Joseph Kessel, *Le onze mai: au camp des vaincus* (Paris, 1924), p. 222.

51. *Aux Ecoutes*, April 6, 1924, p. 13.

52. Interview with Mandel's secretary, Jacques Miqueau. Miqueau replaced Paul Vigneau as Mandel's secretary in 1923.

53. Planes, "Mes rencontres."

54. *L'Echo National*, April 26, 1924. For Mandel's definition of a Saxon, see above, p. 66.

55. *La Petite Gironde*, April 26, 27, 29, May 4, 1924.

56. On the Odin incident, see especially Pierrefeux, pp. 148–73. Odin's attacks on

Mandel and Caillaux are printed in *La Petite Gironde,* May 6 and 10, 1924, and in *Le Républicain,* May 7, 1924. Mandel's replies are in *La Liberté du Sud-Ouest,* May 9 and 11, 1924.

57. Lachapelle, *Elections legislatives du 11 mai 1924,* pp. 111–12.

58. Planes, "Mes rencontres." Mandel received 33,720 votes and Bergey 37,686.

59. Lachapelle, *Elections legislatives du 11 mai 1924,* pp. 111–12. Exactly 185,043 valid ballots were cast. An absolute majority was therefore 92,522. The total number of valid ballots differed from the total average because many people failed to vote for a full list of candidates. Voters crossed off 31,185 names.

60. Beau de Loménie, III, 461–62.

61. The figures were 4,539,063 to 4,270,228. See Lachapelle, *Elections legislatives du 11 mai 1924,* p. 28.

62. *Le Temps,* June 20, 1924.

Socialists	104	Independents	28
Radicals	139	Right	103
Republican Socialists	44	Républicains de Gauche	44
Communists	26	Gauche Républicaine	43
TOTAL	313	Christian Democrats	14
		Gauche Radicale	42
		TOTAL	274

63. Of the forty-two men who composed the Gauche Radicale, thirty-four had been incumbents. Of these, twenty-five had belonged to either the Républicains de Gauche or the Gauche Démocratique, which had consistently supported Poincaré. Five were Radical Socialists who had been ousted from the party for supporting Poincaré, and four were Republican Socialists. Of the eight new deputies, *Le Temps* (May 14, 1924) classified six as Républicains de Gauche and two as Radical Socialists. These men were clearly trimmers, most of whom could not even invoke electoral considerations to explain their fluctuation between Right and Left. Thirteen of them had been elected with the help of the Right against the Cartel, and ten against both the Cartel and the Right; nine had been elected with the help of the Left against the Right, and eight against both the Right and the Socialists with the aid of the Radicals. (I have left two overseas deputies out of consideration because party alignments in the overseas territories did not always coincide with those in Metropolitan France.)

64. Interview with Mandel in *La Liberté du Sud-Ouest,* June 12, 1924.

Chapter 7

1. *JOC,* Feb. 29, 1924, p. 1094.

2. See his interview with Marcel Hutin published in *L'Echo de Paris,* Sept. 20, 1924.

3. In his investiture speech, Poincaré had declared: "We believe that at the present time, questions of domestic politics must be resolutely subordinated to the grave problems that face us in foreign affairs. In order to keep the peace abroad, let's try first to keep it at home." *JOC,* Jan. 19, 1922, p. 48. He repeated this idea on many occasions, and read the statement again to the Chamber in November 1922. *JOC,* Nov. 10, 1922, p. 3052.

4. *PVCG,* Sept. 12, 1924, pp. 580–83.

5. Interview with Marcel Hutin, *L'Echo de Paris,* Sept. 20, 1924.

6. *PVCG,* Sept. 12, 1924, pp. 583–84.

7. Georges Mandel, "Au carrefour de deux politiques," *Revue Hebdomadaire*, Dec. 20, 1924, p. 352.

8. "La philosophie de Locarno," *Revue Hebdomadaire*, Nov. 14, 1925, pp. 202–14. Mandel's conclusion was almost uncanny: "M. Chamberlain can be proud. Lord Beaconsfield never concluded 'peace with honor' in better conditions." The Chamberlain referred to was not, of course, Neville, but his half-brother, Austen, who was Foreign Secretary in 1925.

9. *An Ambassador of Peace: Lord D'Abernon's Diary* (London, 1930), III, 199.

10. "La Philosophie de Locarno," *Revue Hebdomadaire*, Nov. 14, 1925, pp. 202–14.

11. Robert Cornilleau, *De Waldeck-Rousseau à Poincaré: chronique d'une génération, 1898–1924* (Paris, 1926), p. 6.

12. Interview in *La Liberté*, Nov. 18, 1924.

13. Interview with Pierre Lafue, "André Tardieu nous a dit...," *1935*, June 12, 1935.

14. François Piétri, "Tardieu, homme d'état," in Aubert, pp. 79–80.

15. Tardieu's letter is in the Musée Clemenceau in Paris. Mandel's copy of the book was inscribed "A Georges Mandel en souvenir de nos désaccords cordiaux." Wormser, *Mandel*, p. 293.

16. *Ibid.*, pp. 101–2, 119.

17. Berl, p. 63.

18. Benoist, III, 468.

19. Mordacq, *Clemenceau au soir*, II, 129.

20. Georges Suarez, "Une interview de M. Mandel," *Le Journal*, June 4, 1924.

21. See article entitled "Paul Duché" in Jean and Bernard Guérin, eds., p. 248.

22. Henri de Kérillis in *L'Echo de Paris*, July 21, 1925.

23. *PVCG*, May 11, 1920, p. 448.

24. His opponents claimed that their list was better than Mandel's, "for its composition assures that some of its members will always be friends of the government in power, no matter what government. It will thus be able easily to obtain—within the limits of the possible—the favors and subsidies it needs." *Le Journal du Médoc*, April 5, 1925.

25. Jean Bernard, "M. Georges Mandel, homme d'action," *Le Réveil Médocain*, Jan. 6, 1925.

26. "Quel doit être le role de l'opposition?" Interview with Mandel in *Le Courrier du Centre*, Nov. 11, 1924. Reprinted in *Le Réveil Médocain*, Nov. 23, 1924.

27. Georges Mandel, "Rappel aux principes," *Revue Hebdomadaire*, Feb. 21, 1925, p. 359.

28. Georges Mandel, "Cartel = Ignorance," *Revue Hebdomadaire*, Jan. 9, 1926, pp. 207–18.

29. *PVCG*, May 8, 1926, p. 386.

30. Georges Mandel, "La révision de la constitution," *La Renaissance Politique et Littéraire*, Oct. 4, 1924, pp. 3–4.

31. Georges Mandel, "Pour sortir du gachis," *Revue Hebdomadaire*, Oct. 24, 1925, pp. 452–53; also interview with Mandel in *Le Réveil Médocain*, Nov. 29, 1925.

32. See Mandel's speech in *PVCG*, May 7, 1927, pp. 332–39; also his articles in *Revue Hebdomadaire*, Oct. 24, 1925, pp. 446–56, and Jan. 9, 1926, pp. 207–21.

33. Jacques Chastenet, *Raymond Poincaré* (Paris, 1948), p. 268. "He now reaped the benefits of the caution he had shown during the election campaign of 1924. No one seriously considered calling him a reactionary; his reputation as a firm republican had

stayed intact; his contempt for Fascism was well known, as was his distrust of the Wilsonian ideology. To console themselves for his return to power, the old guard of the Left repeated to themselves the remark he had flung at the conservative Charles Benoist in 1912: 'We are separated by the full extent of the religious question!' "

34. Only Lesparre with 39,000 and two other districts were exempted. When these exemptions were challenged in the Chamber, Joseph Barthélemy, the president of the Committee, begged the question: "Surely you don't think that the Committee, whose majority also represents the majority of this Chamber—that is to say a Left majority— would have wanted to favor that strong and remarkable, although somewhat contentious person?" *Annales*, July 11, 1927, pp. 2522–23. Despite Barthélemy's disclaimer, however, this is precisely what the Committee did do. How Mandel persuaded the Committee to make the exemption is unknown.

35. *L'Echo de Paris*, July 10, 1927; *Le Journal des Débats*, July 13, 1927; *Paris-Radical*, July 22, 1927.

36. *Annales*, July 11, 1927, pp. 2537–40.

37. *Le Journal du Médoc*, April 1, Feb. 5, 1928.

38. *Le Démocrate et Petit Médocain*, March 18, 1928.

39. The National Association of Steel Producers. *Ibid.*, Feb. 26, March 11, April 29, 1928. Also *Le Journal du Médoc*, Feb. 26, March 4, 11, 1928.

40. *Le Réveil Médocain*, March 11, Feb. 26, 1928.

41. *Le Matin*, March 27, 1928; *La Petite Gironde*, April 19, 1928; *La Liberté du Sud-Ouest*, April 18, 1928.

42. Favreau, pp. 22–23. See also pp. 139–49 for an account of the 1928 campaign.

43. *Le Journal des Débats*, April 10, 1928; *Le Réveil Médocain*, April 22, 1928.

44. Several people from the region recounted this story to me.

45. *Le Républicain* (Bordeaux), April 29, 1928.

46. See Mandel's program in *Le Réveil Médocain*, April 15, 1928.

47. *Le Républicain*, May 20, 1928.

48. The addition of Castelnau to Lesparre almost defeated Mandel. The results in Castelnau:

	First Ballot	Second Ballot
Mandel	1,522	2,017
Du Périer	1,803	
Teyssier	708	2,230
Martet	312	

In the final analysis, Mandel's margin of victory came from Soulac, where he received 353 votes on the second ballot to 174 for Teyssier. Mandel's case makes it clear why deputies in France accumulate seemingly minor positions in local politics and devote so much time to them.

49. Mordacq, *Clemenceau au soir*, II, 186.

Chapter 8

1. Mandel wrote for the paper only from January to July 1929. In January 1930 Jacques Bainville, under the pseudonym of "L'Observateur," succeeded him as parliamentary commentator. See Pierre Gaxotte in *Candide*, Feb. 13, 1936.

2. Daudet, *Paris vécu*, p. 158. See also his book *Vingt-neuf mois d'exil*, p. 275, and his introduction to Fernand Neuray, *Entretiens avec Clemenceau* (Paris, 1930), p. 12.

3. Clement Vautel in *Le Journal*, May 1, 1928.

4. The speech is printed in *Le Réveil Médocain*, Nov. 4, 1928.

5. Interview in *La Liberté*, Nov. 22, 1928.

6. Georges Mandel, "La malaise politique," *Candide*, Jan. 24, 1929.

7. Georges Mandel, "Un paradoxe," *Candide*, Feb. 28, 1929.

8. Georges Mandel, "Le remède," *Candide*, March 7, 1929.

9. Georges Mandel, "La chimère de la participation Socialiste," *Candide*, Feb. 21, 1929. Also, "Où allons-nous?" *Le Réveil Médocain*, Dec. 23, 1928.

10. *Aux Ecoutes*, March 23, 1929; *Gringoire*, March 22, 1929.

11. Georges Mandel, "Un comble," *Candide*, June 27, 1929.

12. Georges Mandel, "Pas d'interversion de rôles," *Candide*, July 18, 1929.

13. *Ibid.*

14. André Tardieu, *La revolution à refaire*, vol. I, *Le souverain captif* (Paris, 1936), p. 44.

15. Georges Suarez, "La tragédie d'une chute," *Gringoire*, Oct. 25, 1929.

16. *JOC*, Oct. 22, 1929, pp. 2971–76.

17. *Gringoire*, Oct. 25, 1929.

18. See above, pp. 110–11.

19. Ivan Martin, "Tardieu au ministère" in Aubert, p. 171.

20. *Annales*, Nov. 7, 1929, pp. 47–48.   21. *Ibid.*, Nov. 8, 1929, p. 99.

22. *Ibid.*, Dec. 24, 1929, pp. 1602–8.   23. *Ibid.*, Dec. 27, 1929, pp. 1683–88.

24. Debû-Bridel, p. 67.   25. *L'Ami du Peuple*, Dec. 25, 1929.

26. *Le Temps, L'Homme Libre*, Dec. 26, 1929; *Le Figaro, Le Matin*, Dec. 25, 1929; *Gringoire*, Jan. 3, 1930.

27. *Le Matin*, March 23, 1930.

28. *Aux Ecoutes*, Aug. 1, 1931, p. 5.

29. Privat, *Les heures d'André Tardieu*, p. 21.

30. *JOC*, Nov. 25, 1930, pp. 3548–53.

31. *L'Action Française*, Nov. 26, 1930.   32. *Le Peuple*, March 17, 1921.

33. *Le Populaire*, Nov. 26, 1930.   34. Kérillis and Cartier, pp. 25–26.

35. Roger Priouret, *La république des députés* (Paris, 1959), p. 47.

36. *Carrefour*, Feb. 14, 1931, p. 11; Stephen Watts, *The Ritz* (London, 1963), p. 79.

37. *Le Réveil Médocain*, May 4, 1930.

38. Wormser, *Mandel*, p. 131; Mallet, I, 31; Kérillis, *L'Echo de Paris*, Jan. 27, 1931; Pierre du Clain in *La Lumière*, Jan. 31, 1931; Varenne, *Mon patron*, p. 140.

39. Pierre Tissier, *I Worked with Laval* (London, 1942), p. 58; Wormser, *Mandel*, pp. 130–31. See also *L'Oeil de Paris*, Feb. 20, 1932, p. 5.

40. Wormser, *Mandel*, pp. 132–33.

41. Bonnefous, V, 54; Coblentz, 165–73; anonymous article, "La Commission d'enquête vue par un parlementaire," *L'Europe Nouvelle*, March 21, 1931, pp. 378–80. See also Emile Buré, *L'Ordre*, Feb. 20, 1931.

42. *Le Temps*, Jan. 21, March 8, 19, 1931; *L'Ere Nouvelle* in the Press review, *Le Temps*, Jan. 23, 1931.

43. Privat, *Oustric et Cie.*, p. 165; Privat, *La Commission d'enquête*, p. 60.

44. See letter of Marc Rucart, who drew up the report, in *La Lumière*, July 6, 1935. *Le Temps* published abridged accounts of the daily testimony. The official version of the testimony, corrected by the witnesses, was published in the *Bulletin des Commissions*, Chambre des Députés.

45. Prévost, p. 329; Debû-Bridel, pp. 119–20.

46. *L'Oeil de Paris*, Feb. 28, 1931, p. 6.
47. *La Renaissance*, April 19, 1930, p. 2.
48. See Mandel's speech in *JOC*, March 17, 1932, pp. 1588–92, and the interview with Mandel in *L'Echo de Paris*, Feb. 13, 1932.
49. *La politique des partis sous la troisième république*, pp. 256–57.
50. *Annales*, Dec. 10, 1931, pp. 537–39.
51. *L'Echo de Paris*, Dec. 12, 1931.
52. *JOC*, Feb. 3, 1932, p. 335.
53. Henri de Kérillis, "L'Obstruction socialiste contre le projet Mandel," *L'Echo de Paris*, Dec. 14, 1931; *Je Suis Partout,* Dec. 19, 1931; *L'Oeuvre*, Dec. 13, 16, 18, 19, 1931.
54. *Le Populaire*, Dec. 17, 1931.
55. Sanvoisin, p. 160.
56. L'Observateur (Jacques Bainville) in *Candide*, Dec. 24, 1931. Until his death in 1936, Bainville used this pseudonym for his articles in *Candide*.
57. *Le Temps*, Dec. 13, 1931; Pierre du Clain in *La Lumière*, Dec. 19, 26, 1931; L'Observateur in *Candide*, Dec. 24, 1931.
58. *Annales*, Dec. 16, 1931, pp. 709–16; Dec. 17, 1931, pp. 742–49; see also *Aux Ecoutes*, Dec. 26, 1931, p. 17.
59. Pierre du Clain in *La Lumière*, Dec. 19, 1931.
60. *L'Echo de Paris*, Dec. 18, 1931.
61. L'Observateur in *Candide*, Dec. 24, 1931.
62. *Ibid.*, Dec. 17, 24, 1931; also, *Aux Ecoutes*, Dec. 26, 1931, p. 17 and *L'Action Médocaine*, Jan. 3, 1932.
63. *Aux Ecoutes*, Dec. 26, 1931, p. 17.
64. Rayon X (François Albert) in *L'Oeil de Paris*, Feb. 20, 1932, p. 5; Pierre du Clain in *La Lumière*, Feb. 6, 1932; Lucien Lamoureux "Souvenirs politiques," *Le Bourbonnais Républican*, Oct. 2, 1955.
65. *L'Ordre*, Jan. 23, 1932; *Je Suis Partout*, Jan. 30, 1932.
66. *JOC*, Jan. 28, 1932, p. 213.
67. *La Nation*, Feb. 6, 1932, p. 126; *L'Echo de Paris*, Feb. 3, 1932.
68. *L'Echo de Paris*, Feb. 4, 1932.
69. *La Nation*, Feb. 20, 1932, pp. 177–78; *L'Echo de Paris*, Dec. 17, 1931.
70. Pierre de Pressac in *La Revue Politique et Parlementaire*, Jan. 10, 1932, p. 124.
71. *La Nation*, Feb. 6, 1932.
72. Bonnefous, V, 110.
73. Rayon X, *L'Oeil de Paris*, Feb. 13, 1932, p. 6.
74. *Le Matin*, Feb. 13, 1932.
75. *L'Echo de Paris*, Feb. 13, 1932.
76. *JOC*, Feb. 12, 1932, pp. 645–48.
77. Louis Marin in *La Nation*, Feb. 20, 1932, p. 169.
78. *L'Echo de Paris*, Feb. 13, 1932.
79. *L'Ordre*, Feb. 16, 1932.
80. *Je Suis Partout*, Feb. 20, 1932.
81. Bonnefous, V, 115.
82. *JOC*, Feb. 23, 1932, p. 762.
83. Pierre du Clain, *La Lumière*, March 5, 1932.
84. Debû-Bridel, p. 153.
85. Bonnefous, V, 115; L'Observateur, *Candide*, March 10, 1932.
86. Rayon X, *L'Oeil de Paris*, March 26, 1932, p. 3.
87. *JOC*, March 17, 1932, pp. 1586–1605.

88. Pierre du Clain, *La Lumière*, March 26, 1932.

89. Louis Marin in *La Nation*, March 26, 1932, pp. 289–91.

90. *Le Temps*, March 19, 1932.

91. *Le Matin*, March 18, 1932.

92. *L'Echo de Paris*, March 19, 1932.

93. Quoted by François Goguel, "L'Influence des systèmes électoraux sur la vie politique d'après l'expérience française," in *L'Influence des systèmes électoraux sur la vie politique* (Paris, 1950), p. 81. Duverger has since modified this "law." See his book, *La VIème République et le régime présidentiel* (Paris, 1961), pp. 102–6. In 1955 Philip Williams said that "the most important of constitutional reforms is a change in the electoral law to encourage stronger, more coherent, and more lasting coalitions." *Politics in Post-War France* (London, 1955), p. 405.

94. Campbell, pp. 34–37.

95. Gordon Wright, *France in Modern Times, 1760 to the Present* (Chicago, 1960), p. 469; Binion, p. 313.

96. Jean-Jacques Chevallier, *Histoire des institutions politiques de la France moderne, 1789–1945* (Paris, 1958), pp. 565–66.

97. See Beau de Loménie's comments after a lecture by Jacques Debû-Bridel, "La vraie figure d'André Tardieu," *Société d'histoire de la troisième république*, Bulletin No. 13, Jan. 1955, p. 262.

98. Debû-Bridel, p. 95.

99. *Le Cri du Jour*, March 28, 1936, pp. 14–15.

100. Debû-Bridel, p. 153; Michel Missoffe, "Notre ami Tardieu, 1876–1945," in Aubert, p. 38.

101. *Le Démocrate et Petit Médocain*, Feb. 21, 1932. See also Favreau, pp. 161–68.

102. *Le Journal du Médoc*, April 26, May 24, Dec. 6, 1931; *Le Réveil Médocain*, March 13, 1932; *La Concentration Républicaine*, Sept. 29, 1931.

103. *Le Réveil Médocain*, April 12, 1931. For a gossipy account of Mandel's largesse in the Médoc, see "M. Mandel ou le pactole Médocain," *Les Annales Politiques et Littéraires*, Sept. 8, 1933, pp. 268–69.

104. *Carrefour*, June 15, 1932; *Aux Ecoutes*, June 11, 1932.

105. *Aux Ecoutes*, June 18, 1932, p. 20.

106. *L'Homme Libre, L'Ordre, L'Oeuvre*, Dec. 1, 1932.

107. *L'Ordre*, Dec. 1, 1932.

Chapter 9

1. *Aux Ecoutes*, May 14, 1932, p. 7.

2. See Mandel's speech in Lesparre, *L'Action Médocaine*, Oct. 16, 1932. Large extracts are printed in *La Liberté*, Oct. 10, 1932.

3. *Aux Ecoutes*, Nov. 19, 1932, p. 8.

4. Rayon X, *L'Oeil de Paris*, Oct. 15, 1932, p. 3; *L'Homme Libre*, Dec. 16, 1932; *Aux Ecoutes*, Jan. 21, 1933, p. 20, and May 14, 1932, p. 7.

5. See "Les méthodes du Centre," *L'Alliance Démocratique*, Jan. 3, 1934.

6. See particularly *France in Danger* (New York, 1935) and *La révolution à refaire* (Paris, 2 vols., 1936–37). Tardieu's ideas are discussed by Alfred Pose, "Les idées politiques d'André Tardieu," in Aubert, pp. 116–63. His contribution to the constitutional reform movement that culminated in the establishment of de Gaulle's regime in 1958 is discussed by Nicholas Wahl, "Aux origines de la nouvelle constitution,"

Revue Française de Science Politique, March 1959, pp. 58–66. For his activities in general at this time see Binion, pp. 310–20.

7. Fabre-Luce, "Conversation avec M. Georges Mandel," pp. 15–16.

8. Interviews with Mandel in *Le Pamphlet*, March 17, 1933, pp. 15–16 and April 28, 1933, pp. 12–14; *Le Petit Journal*, March 24, 1933. Also, Emile Buré, "Faut-il réviser la constitution?", *L'Ordre*, April 1, 1933.

9. See article entitled "L'Heure de Mandel" in his local paper, *L'Action Médocaine*, Dec. 17, 1933.

10. Micaud, pp. 24–26.

11. By 1932 Herriot no longer believed that agreement could be reached with Germany. See *FRUS*, 1932, I, 476–86.

12. See Mandel's speech at Lesparre in *L'Action Médocaine*, Oct. 16, 1932.

13. *Le Pamphlet*, March 17, 1933, p. 15; *Aux Ecoutes*, March 11, 1933, p. 14.

14. *Annales*, Nov. 9, 1933, pp. 4039–43. The Plon publishing house later printed the speech in pamphlet form.

15. *La Nation*, Nov. 18, 1933, p. 728.

16. *Le Journal des Débats*, Nov. 11, 1933.

17. Werth, *France in Ferment*, p. 72.

18. *DBFP*, 2nd Series, VI, 49, statement of General Corap, Weygand's Chief of Staff, reported by the British attaché Colonel Heywood to Lord Tyrrell, Nov. 11, 1933.

19. *Ibid.*, VI, 158, report of Colonel Heywood to Lord Tyrrell, Dec. 4, 1933.

20. Camille Aymard in *La Liberté*, Nov. 10, 1933.

21. L'Observateur, *Candide*, Nov. 16, 1933.

22. *DBFP*, 2nd Series, VI, 50; Colonel Heywood to Lord Tyrrell, Nov. 11, 1933.

23. *Ibid.*, and p. 54, Lord Tyrrell to Sir. J. Simon, Nov. 17, 1933.

24. *JOC*, Nov. 14, 1933, p. 4101.

25. *Le Matin*, Nov. 17, 1933. See John W. Wheeler-Bennett, *Munich, Prologue to Tragedy* (London, 1948), p. 239.

26. "La leçon d'un débat," *1933*, Nov. 22, 1933.

27. Georges Mandel, "Le dernier de la série," *1933*, Dec. 6, 1933.

28. Georges Mandel, "Une hypothèque sur l'avenir," *1934*, Jan. 31, 1934.

29. Georges Mandel, "La meilleure des solutions," *1934*, Feb. 7, 1934. See also Mandel's statement in *Le Matin*, Jan. 29, 1934.

30. As early as April 1933, the writer Pierre Lafue had published a biography of Doumergue calling for him as the leader of a National Union government.

31. Fischer, pp. 44, 201. Fischer was a close friend and personal advisor of Doumergue.

32. Wormser, *Mandel*, pp. 120–21.

33. *La Liberté*, Sept. 22, 1932; see also *L'Action Médocaine*, Dec. 3, 1933.

34. *Je Suis Partout*, Sept. 30, 1933. See Pierre-Antoine Cousteau, *En ce temps-là* (Paris, 1959), p. 71.

35. *Le Pamphlet*, April 28, 1933, p. 3.

36. *Noir et Blanc*, May 13, 1934.

37. *Commission Stavisky*, I, 929.

38. *Aux Ecoutes*, March 3, 17, 1934; Paul Lévy, *L'Affaire Stavisky: justice pourrie* (Paris, 1935), pp. 8, 21–22.

39. Vallat, *Le nez de Cléopâtre*, pp. 123–24. The Monarchist Vallat, who had been more or less friendly with Mandel, broke off relations as a result of this incident. When

Vallat was tried after the war for collaboration, his lawyer praised him: "It took courage, inside Parliament, to break with M. Mandel." *Le procès de Xavier Vallat,* pp. 428–9.

40. *Le Matin,* March 14, 1934; *Le Canard Enchaîné,* March 14, 1934; *Le Populaire,* March 15, 1934. Accounts of incidents between members of the commission are not included in the published testimony and have to be dug out of the newspapers.

41. *Commission Stavisky,* II, 2301–2; IV; 4487, 4513. Romagnino testified that Mandel had met Stavisky twice, once for dinner and another time for just ten minutes. Mandel denied the second meeting. See *Le Matin,* March 16, 1934.

42. For Décis' letter to the commission volunteering to testify, see *Le Journal du Médoc,* April 22, 1934. For his testimony, see *Commission Stavisky,* II, 1374–78. See also the account of his testimony in *Le Temps,* April 27, 1934. There are numerous differences between the accounts published immediately after the hearings by *Le Temps* and the final versions. For example, in *Le Temps* Décis seems to claim that Mandel controlled the policy of both *La Volonté* and *Le Rempart,* whereas the final report mentions only *Le Rempart.*

43. *Le Canard Enchaîné,* Feb. 13, 1935.

44. Wormser, *Mandel,* p. 7. When Mandel became a minister, he made Nau his parliamentary secretary. Although the articles during the 1930's may have been written by Nau, from 1918 to about 1924 the articles in *Aux Ecoutes* were decidedly hostile and could hardly have been composed by a friend. Nevertheless, they were obviously written by someone who knew Mandel well and followed his career closely. In any event, after 1924 this parliamentary gossip sheet came over to Mandel's side, quoting him at length and reporting extensively on his activities.

45. *Commission Stavisky,* II, 1381–83; Lévy, *L'Affaire Stavisky,* p. 21. Lévy's dossier was later sent to the minister of Justice for further investigation. He was annoyed with Mandel for not defending him, but said: "I do not hold it against him. Mandel is a politician. He had to look out for his political career. He wanted to become a minister; he has become a minister. He wants to become prime minister; he will become prime minister. I wish him good luck."

46. See testimony of Edouard Daladier, Camille Aymard, Camille Chautemps and others, *Commission Stavisky,* I, 1135; II, 2085; III, 3134–44. Daladier said that four-fifths of the press was subsidized.

47. See particularly the local opposition paper, *Le Journal du Médoc,* which from March through August 1934 reprinted all the unfavorable articles it could find in other papers about Mandel.

48. *Commission Stavisky,* III, 2706.

49. *Je Suis Partout,* May 12, 1934; *Commission Stavisky,* II, 1927–49.

50. "Chez les juges de Stavisky," *Candide,* March 15, 1934; also, Fayard, *Candide,* March 8, 1934.

51. *L'Alliance Démocratique,* July 18, 1934; also *Le Matin,* March 24, 1934.

52. *Le Mois,* December 1934, pp. 109–111.

53. *Le Canard Enchaîné,* July 25, 1934.

54. *Le Cri du Jour,* June 30, 1934.

55. See Livet's testimony in *Commission Stavisky,* II, 2202–5.

56. *Le Cri du Jour,* March 10, 1934, p. 4; March 17, 1934, p. 6.

57. *Ibid.,* April 7, 1934, p. 6.

58. *Ibid.,* March 31, 1934, p. 4; also Feb. 2, 1935, p. 6.

59. See *ibid.*, Dec. 15, 1934, p. 10, and for correction, *Le Ralliement des PTT*, Dec. 30, 1934.

60. Fabre-Luce, *Journal de la France*, I, 227.

61. See above, p. 143.

62. *Noir et Blanc*, May 13, 1934.

63. Georges Mandel, "Oeuvre utile," *1934*, Feb. 28, 1934, and "Trêve durable," *1934*, Feb. 21, 1934. Also *Le Cri du Jour*, March 31, 1934, p. 5.

64. *Commission Stavisky*, I, 1069.

65. *Le Jour*, May 5, 1934.

66. *Revue Hebdomadaire*, July 14, 1934, p. 242.

67. *Je Suis Partout*, June 2, 1934; *La Lumière*, June 2, 1934; *L'Echo de Paris*, June 1, 1934; also Bonnefous, V, 252–54; Gicquel and Sfez, pp. 66–67. For Mandel's justification of his opposition, see Pierre Lafue, "La réforme électorale, serait-elle un instrument de rénovation? Entretien avec M. Georges Mandel," *1934*, June 20, 1934; and *Le Cri du Jour*, June 9, 1934, p. 5. Although Mandel stopped writing for *1934* when he was elected to the Stavisky Commission, he continued to provide the information for most of the political *"échos"* through Pierre Lafue, who remained on the staff. Interview with Lafue.

68. See Henriot's speech to a local party congress on May 26, quoted in *Le Journal du Médoc*, June 17, 1934.

69. *Le Cri du Jour*, July 7, 1934, p. 5.

70. Debû-Bridel, 270–71.

71. *Le Cri du Jour*, Sept. 15, 1934, p. 3; Sept. 29, 1934, p. 5.

72. Mandel was only partially correct in his analysis of Doumergue's motives. His personal friend and advisor, Jacques Fischer, later revealed that after working on his proposals all summer, Doumergue presented them to the cabinet on September 20. Then, realizing from the reaction of his ministers that the reforms would not be passed, he decided to take his case to the people before he could be overthrown. Fischer, pp. 20–21, 177.

73. *Le Cri du Jour*, Nov. 3, 1934, pp. 14–15; Nov. 10, 1934, p. 9.

74. Wormser, *Mandel*, p. 155.

75. *Je Suis Partout*, Nov. 3, 10, 1934.

76. Maryse Choisy in *Noir et Blanc*, Nov. 11, 1934.

77. Wormser, *Mandel*, p. 154.

78. *Je Suis Partout*, Nov. 10, 1934. Doumergue said: "My proposal [to revise the constitution] encountered strong opposition from those who consider themselves the most fervent supporters of popular sovereignty. It is because of their pressure that some members of the government did not vote approval of my project." Quoted in Wormser, *Mandel*, p. 155n.

79. Fischer, pp. 200–204.

80. Maryse Choisy in *Noir et Blanc*, Nov. 11, 1934.

81. Henri de Kérillis in *L'Echo de Paris*, Nov. 8, 1934; *L'Oeuvre*, Nov. 4, 1934; *Je Suis Partout*, Nov. 10, 1934; *Le Canard Enchaîné*, Nov. 7, 1934.

82. Varenne, *Mon patron*, p. 140.

83. Pierre de Pressac in *Revue Politique et Parlementaire*, Dec. 10, 1934, p. 522.

84. *Ibid.*; Alfred Fabre-Luce in *L'Europe Nouvelle*, Nov. 17, 1934, p. 1132; *Je Suis Partout*, Nov. 17, 1934.

85. *La Nation*, Nov. 17, 1934, p. 759.

86. *Candide*, Nov. 15, 1934; *Le Temps*, Nov. 10, 1934.

Chapter 10

1. *Paris-Soir*, Nov. 10, 1934; *Le Cri du Jour*, Nov. 17, 1934, p. 4; see also Wormser, *Mandel*, pp. 160–64.

2. *Le Mois*, Dec. 1934, pp. 110–11.

3. *L'Oeuvre*, Nov. 11, 1934; *L'Humanité*, Nov. 10, 13, 1934; *Le Populaire*, Nov. 11, 1934.

4. "Un ministère sorti de la trahison," *L'Echo de Paris*, Nov. 10, 1934. Also "La revanche des vaincus du 6 février," *La Liberté*, Nov. 9, 1934.

5. *Candide*, Nov. 15, 1934. Louis XIV established a secret office, *le cabinet noir*, in the Hôtel des Postes, where private letters were read by government agents. This practice of opening private correspondence was not finally abolished until 1828.

6. Odette Pannetier, *Quand j'étais Candide* (Paris, 1948), pp. 265–66.

7. The figures were as follows:

Employees		Budget	
PTT	158,000	PTT	4,658,000,000 francs
Education	158,474	War	5,125,000,000 francs
War	185,464	Finances	20,017,000,000 francs

See Document Parlementaire 5612, Chambre des Députés, Session de 1935. Annexe du procès-verbal de la séance du 28 juin 1935. *Rapport. Budget Général de l'Exercise 1936 (Budget annexe des Postes, Télégraphes et Téléphones)* par M. André J. L. Breton, Député (Paris, Imprimerie de la Chambre des Députés, 1935), pp. 3–4.

8. Coblentz, pp. 177–78.

9. *Le Temps*, Nov. 11, 1934.

10. The speech is printed in *L'Action Médocaine*, Dec. 2, 1934.

11. *Le Cri du Jour*, Dec. 8, 1934, p. 10; *1934*, Dec. 26, 1934; *Je Suis Partout*, Dec. 15, 1934. *Je Suis Partout* (Dec. 29, 1934) also reported that it was the postal union itself, to which Mandel had granted so many favors, that asked the Socialist deputies not to question him. See also Reynaud, *Mémoires*, I, 140.

12. Odette Pannetier in *Candide*, Dec. 6, 1934; Paul Reboux *in Gringoire*, Feb. 22, 1935; *Le Cri du Jour*, Dec. 15, 1934, p. 10; *Le Petit Journal*, Nov. 30, 1934.

13. Wythe Williams, p. 23.

14. *Current History*, April 1936, p. 109; "Un ministère qui marche," *1935*, Jan. 23, 1935; *Le Cri du Jour*, Jan. 5, 1935, p. 9; *L'Ami du Peuple*, May 15, 1936.

15. Charles Braibant, *Lumière bleue: journal de la guerre* (Paris, 1940), p. 148.

16. Huc and Robin, p. 103; speech by Marcel Pellenc, National Broadcasting Director, at Limoges, Dec. 22, 1935, printed in *L'Action Médocaine*, Jan. 5, 1936; *Documentation Catholique*, May 30, 1936, columns 1373–76.

17. Edouard Champion, *La Comédie Française 1935* (Paris, 1936), p. xix; Tabouis, *Vingt ans*, pp. 380–81; Henri Jeanson in *Le Canard Enchaîné*, Jan. 8, 1936. The *Comédie* was paid for broadcast rights to these performances, and was thus saved from serious financial difficulties.

18. Huc and Robin, pp. 95–114, 137–51; see also speech by Marcel Pellenc at Lille, printed in *La Petite Gironde*, April 8, 15, 1936; *L'Ami du Peuple*, Sept. 19, 1936; *Marianne*, June 3, 1936; *L'Express*, Jan. 26, 1961; *Rapport . . .* par M. Breton, p. 282 (see Note 7 above).

19. Louis Thomas in *Le Cri du Jour*, March 16, 1935, p. 9.

20. *1935*, Jan. 23 and May 1, 1935.

21. Pertinax (André Géraud) said of the postmen that "it is sufficient, in order to convey an idea of their influence, to state that the secretary-general of their union over-rules the Postmaster-General every day." "The Coming French Elections," *Foreign Affairs*, Jan. 1928, p. 227.

22. *L'Humanité*, Nov. 10, 1934.

23. *Le Ralliement des PTT*, Dec. 30, 1934.

24. *La Tribune des Fonctionnaires*, Jan. 5, 1935.

25. The speech is printed in *L'Action Médocaine*, Feb. 17, 1935.

26. *Le Ralliement des PTT*, Feb. 20, 1935.

27. *La Tribune des Fonctionnaires,* cited in *Le Journal du Médoc*, July 21, 1935.

28. Henri Jeanson of *Le Canard Enchaîné* wrote that "since Mandel has become a minister, not a day goes by without publicity stories appearing about him. Mandel here. Mandel there. Mandel everywhere. Mandel is advertising himself like a patent medicine." Quoted in *Le Démocrate et Petit Médocain*, Dec. 8, 1935.

29. *Le Ralliement des PTT*, April 20, May 20, 1935.

30. *Ibid.*, May 5, 1935.

31. *La République*, April 22, 1935; *Le Cri du Jour,* April 27, 1935, p. 7; Wormser, *Mandel*, pp. 176–77.

32. *Le Ralliement des PTT*, May 5, 1935.

33. *Gringoire*, May 24, 1935; *Marianne*, May 22, 1935; *Je Suis Partout*, Feb. 2, 23, 1935; L'Observateur in *Candide*, Feb. 7, April 4, 1935; Pierre du Clain (Georges Gombault) in *La Lumière*, March 16, 1935. Georges Gombault took over the pseud-onym of Pierre du Clain after François Albert's death. Henceforth, the name will refer to Gombault.

34. *Le Cri du Jour*, Feb. 9, 1935, p. 8; Jan. 26, p. 10; March 23, p. 5; March 30, p. 7; April 13, p. 5; May 11, p. 9. See also *1935*, May 29, 1935, and *L'Europe Nouvelle*, Feb. 23, 1935, p. 175.

35. *Le Cri du Jour*, Dec. 8, 1934, p. 10.

36. *Commission Stavisky*, Jan. 17, 1935, V, 4988–89. After the 1932 elections, Stavisky had telegraphed congratulations to some of the successful candidates. But when the investigating committee asked to see copies of them, Mallarmé replied that they had been lost. On taking office, Mandel's second question to Mallarmé had been, "Where are the Stavisky telegrams?" He accused Mallarmé of having taken the tele-grams with him when he left office.

37. *Le Cri du Jour*, Jan. 5, 1935, p. 9; Feb. 23, p. 9; March 2, p. 6; April 13, p. 6. See also *1935*, Jan. 31, May 1, 1935.

38. On Lafue and Mandel, see Note 67, to Chapter 9.

39. See Suarez's articles in *Le Temps*, March 30, 1935, *La Petite Gironde*, Dec. 7, 1935, and *L'Action Médocaine*, Dec. 8, 1935, which reprinted an article from *Le Courrier du Centre*. Suarez had earlier worked for Tardieu's *Echo National,* but sub-sequently became embroiled with Mandel. In 1928 he helped to found *Gringoire,* which was hostile to Mandel so long as Suarez worked for it. See particularly his article en-titled "L'Insexué," Feb. 8, 1929. By 1931, however, he had become reconciled with Mandel, and thereafter published numerous articles praising him.

40. *L'Europe Nouvelle*, Feb. 23, 1935, p. 175. Mandel seems to have had some friends on this journal, which had recently come under the direction of Alfred Fabre-Luce. Shortly before Doumergue's overthrow, it had announced the forthcoming pub-lication of an article by Mandel, which never appeared once he became minister. For Mandel's relations with Fabre-Luce, see his *Vingt-cinq années de liberté*, I, 233–36.

41. *Le Populaire*, Nov. 15, 1934; Jean Galtier-Boissière, "Les mystères de la police secrète," *Crapouillot*, July 1936, p. 166; Syndicat National, pp. 54–57.

42. *Le Jour*, Nov. 9, 14, 1934. See also *Le Canard Enchaîné*, Nov. 7, 14, 1934, for comment on the change.

43. *Le Cri du Jour*, Jan. 5, 1935, p. 9; *1935*, Jan. 31, 1935.

44. *Je Suis Partout*, Feb. 23, 1935.

45. *L'Europe Nouvelle*, Feb. 23, 1935, p. 176. Fabre-Luce had recently published a biography of Caillaux.

46. Interviews with Bayet and Gombault.

47. Emile Roche, *Caillaux que j'ai connu* (Paris, 1949), pp. 99–100. Mandel later gave him other letters from Poincaré, two of which Caillaux published in his memoirs. *Mes mémoires*, (Paris, 1947), III, 361–82.

48. *La République*, Feb. 10, 19, 1935.   49. *Je Suis Partout*, April 13, 1935.

50. Lazareff, *Deadline*, p. 182.   51. *Gringoire*, Feb. 22, April 26, 1935.

52. *Candide*, March 14, 1935; *Le Journal du Médoc*, March 17, 1935.

53. *Le Cri du Jour*, May 4, 1935, p. 8. Also *Paris-Soir*, May 4, 1935; *La République*, May 2, 1935.

54. *Le Petit Journal*, May 6, 1935.

55. *Le Cri du Jour*, June 29, 1934, p. 11.

56. *Ibid.*, June 1, 1935, p. 5.

57. *1935*, March 27, 1935; *Paris-Midi*, May 5, 1935; *Le Cri du Jour*, March 30, 1935, p. 7; April 13, 1935.

58. *Le Cri du Jour*, May 4, 1935, p. 8; June 8, 1935, p.11. Also *1935*, May 29, 1935.

59. *Le Cri du Jour*, May 11, 1935, p. 6.

60. *Marianne*, May 22, 1935; *L'Action Française*, May 31, 1935.

61. *Gringoire*, May 24, 1935.

62. *L'Action Médocaine*, June 2, 1935.

63. *Gringoire*, June 7, 1935; *Candide*, June 6, 1935.

Chapter 11

1. Francis Varenne, *Vendémiaire*, Aug. 14, 1935. Varenne and Mandel collaborated from 1909 to 1912 on Clemenceau's *Journal du Var*. Varenne then joined Mandel at the PTT in 1934 and continued as his assistant until 1940.

2. *1935*, June 5, 1935.

3. "Le dialogue Tardieu-Mandel," *1935*, June 26, 1935; also Lafue, "Georges Mandel."

4. *Le Cri du Jour*, June 29, 1935, p. 11.

5. *1935*, June 26, 1935; *The Times* (London), Aug. 1, 1935.

6. Bonnefous, V, 346–47.

7. *Gringoire*, July 12, 1935; *1935*, July 17, 1935; interview with Mandel in *L'Avenir de Médoc*, July 14, 1935; *Le Jour*, July 7, 1935.

8. *Le Courrier de la IVème République*, cited in *L'Action Médocaine*, Aug. 25, 1935; also Paul Allard in *Vu*, Nov. 30, 1935, pp. 24–25.

9. His speech was printed in *Le Temps*, Oct. 14, 1935.

10. *La Lumière*, July 13, 20, 1935.

11. Syndicat National, pp. 6–7, 52–53.

12. *L'Action*'s protest and Boris' reply were both printed in *La Lumière*, Dec. 21, 1935.

13. Interviews with Albert Bayet and Georges Gombault.

14. *Marianne*, Sept. 18, 1935; Pierre du Clain in *La Lumière*, Oct. 19, 1935; see also Pierre de Pressac in *Revue Politique et Parlementaire*, Nov. 10, 1935, p. 318; *La Petite Gironde*, Oct. 15, 1935; *Le Cri du Jour*, Oct. 19, 1935, p. 4 and Nov. 2, 1935, p. 15.

15. *Vu*, Nov. 30, 1935, pp. 24–25.

16. Unpublished notes of one of Mandel's associates, who prefers to remain anonymous.

17. Planes, "Mes rencontres." I have been unable to find any criticism of Mandel by Daudet, even after the extreme divergence of their opinions on such issues as the Munich Conference. Moreover, even though lesser writers on the *Action Française* were allowed to denounce Mandel violently, Maurras' own criticism was usually restrained, at least until France's defeat in 1940. Obviously, there were things in the past that Daudet and Maurras also found it difficult to forget. Mandel, for instance, had been among the supporters of a pardon for Daudet, finally signed by Doumergue in 1929 (Weber, pp. 272–73).

18. Gurvitch, p. 546.

19. For Tardieu's testimony about La Rocque, see Pozzo di Borgo, *La Rocque, fantôme à vendre* (Paris, 1938), pp. 147–63.

20. Wormser, *Mandel*, p. 144. On the problem of Fascism in France, see the discussion and the bibliography in Robert J. Soucy, "The Nature of Fascism in France," *Journal of Contemporary History*, Vol. I, No. 1 (1966), pp. 27–55.

21. Wormser, p. 152. On Chiappe, see Weber, pp. 324–31.

22. See *Gringoire*, Feb. 22, April 26, 1935; April 15, 1938.

23. For his relations with Taittinger, see above, pp. 189–90.

24. See above, p. 148.

25. Pierre du Clain in *La Lumière*, April 11, 1936.

26. For Laval's foreign policy, see Warner, pp. 56–131.

27. Yves Simon, *La campagne d'Ethiopie et la pensée politique française* (Paris, n.d.), pp. 97–98.

28. *Gringoire*, Sept. 6, 20, 1935; Pierre Gaxotte in *Candide*, Sept. 26, 1935; Micaud, pp. 52–66.

29. *Le Populaire*, October 8, 1935, quoted in Werth, *Which Way France?*, p. 191.

30. *L'Action Française*, Sept. 22, 1935; *Gringoire*, Oct. 11, 1935; *Candide*, Oct. 17, 1935.

31. *Le Cri du Jour*, Sept. 28, 1935, p. 5.

32. Werth, *Which Way France?*, p. 187.

33. *Le Jour*, Oct. 12, 1935; also *Je Suis Partout*, Nov. 9, 1935; *Candide*, Oct. 31, 1935.

34. *L'Oeuvre*, Oct. 14, 1935.

35. The speech was printed in *Le Temps*, Oct. 14, 1935.

36. *Le Temps*, Oct. 15, 1935; L'Observateur in *Candide*, Oct. 17, 1935; *L'Humanité*, Oct. 14, 1935; *Le Populaire*, Oct. 14, 1935; *Le Ralliement des PTT*, Oct. 20, 1935.

37. *L'Oeuvre*, Oct. 14, 1935; *La Nation*, Oct. 19, 1935, p. 735–36. See also François Le Grix, "Un discours-programme? Ou un discours-rébus?" *L'Ami du Peuple*, Oct. 15, 1935. Le Grix commented that "the France that intends to defend itself and fight has been accustomed to consider Mandel as one of its ultimate resources. We would like to give him a friendly warning: Do not confuse publicity with popularity, or believe that one is founded on the other. Convince yourself that the time has come to drop your reservations and be completely frank."

38. *Le Cri du Jour*, Oct. 19, 1935, p. 6; Charles Maurras in *L'Action Française*, Oct. 14, 1935. The communiqué was published in *Le Temps*, Oct. 14, 1935.

39. *Le Cri du Jour*, Oct. 19, 1935, p. 4; Pierre de Pressac in *Revue Politique et Parlementaire*, Nov. 10, 1935, p. 318; *La Petite Gironde,* Oct. 15, 1935.

40. *Le Cri du Jour*, Feb. 1, 1936, p. 5.

41. *Ibid.*, Jan. 25, 1936, p. 5; *La République*, Oct. 18, 1935.

42. Debû-Bridel, p. 339; *Je Suis Partout*, Oct. 19, 1935; *La Lumière*, Oct. 19, Nov. 9, 1935.

43. *Les Pavés de Paris*, Oct. 7, 1938, p. 9. Berl, the editor of the left-wing weekly *Marianne*, was undoubtedly responsible for the publication in this journal of favorable articles about Mandel. He would later publicly break with Mandel at the time of Munich over the question of resistance to Germany. For his relations with Mandel, see Berl, pp. 61–66.

44. Léon Guerdan, *Je les ai tous connus* (New York, 1942), p. 55.

45. Charles Daniélou, *Dans l'intimité de Marianne* (Paris, 1945?), p. 159.

46. *La Liberté du Sud-Ouest*, Dec. 12, 1935.

47. *Le Cri du Jour*, Dec. 21, 1935, p. 6.

48. Jean Philip in *La France Active*, Nov.–Dec. 1935, pp. 22–28; also Henri de Kérillis, *L'Echo de Paris*, Oct. 15, 1935; Emile Buré, *L'Ordre,* Oct. 15, 1935; Marcel Lucain in *Dictionnaire national des contemporains*, ed. N. Imbert (Paris, 1936), p. 413; Williams, p. 10. Ignotus, *Revue de Paris*, Feb. 1, 1936, pp. 500–514.

49. François Le Grix in *Revue Hebdomadaire,* Dec. 7, 1935, p. 123.

50. Larmour, 188–89.

51. Soulié, pp. 474–76.

52. Wormser, *Mandel*, pp. 192–95.

53. *Le Cri du Jour*, Feb. 1, 1936, p. 6; *Marianne,* Jan. 29, 1936.

54. Lamoureux, Feb. 5, 1956.

55. *Je Suis Partout*, Feb. 1; *Le Populaire*, Jan. 24–25; *Candide*, Jan. 30; L'Observateur, *Candide*, Feb. 6; *Le Canard Enchaîné*, Jan. 29; *Gringoire*, Jan. 31; *L'Action Française*, Jan. 25, 26, 27; Pierre du Clain, *La Lumière*, Feb. 1; Pierre de Pressac, *Revue Politique et Parlementaire*, Feb. 10, p. 336; *Vendémiaire*, Jan. 31. Also Jean Fabry, *De la Place de la Concorde au Cours de l'Intendance* (Paris, 1942), pp. 74–97; Debû-Bridel, p. 339.

Mandel may have hoped to head the government himself, but seems to have encountered the unalterable opposition of President Lebrun, who, according to *Aux Ecoutes* (Jan. 25, 1936, p. 6), declared that "his name has often been recommended to me, and by people from whom I did not expect such an initiative. But I will never consent. His coming to power would create two precedents for which I refuse to take responsibility. Since the beginning of the Third Republic, a man has never gone from a technical ministry to the presidency of the council, and France has never been governed by a Jew."

Such a story is difficult to accept without further evidence, but it seems likely that it was Mandel himself who reported it to his friends, and it is hard to see what he could gain from such a fabrication. There is no doubt, in any case, that Lebrun seriously considered summoning Mandel. In December when Herriot discussed his personal dilemma with the President, Lebrun asked him what he thought of Mandel as a possible successor to Laval (Soulié, p. 468). Although Herriot at that time suggested the name of Marcel Regnier, the following month he actively supported Mandel's candidacy (interview with one of Mandel's assistants, who preferred to remain anonymous). Also, several of Mandel's friends in the press said that Sarraut repeatedly intervened in his favor (*Le Cri du Jour*, Feb. 1, 1936, p. 6; *Aux Ecoutes*, Feb. 1, 1936,

p. 6; *Marianne*, Jan. 29, 1936), and Jacques Stern, who became minister of Colonies, asserted that not only Herriot, but Léon Blum and Louis Marin as well had advised that Mandel be appointed prime minister (Jacques Stern in *France-Amérique* [New York], Oct. 1, 1944).

However, it must be recalled that animosity between the President and Mandel dated back to the world war, when Lebrun was forced to resign as Clemenceau's Minister of Liberated Regions and replaced by André Tardieu, who soon became Mandel's closest associate. In 1939 Mandel would try to defeat Lebrun's bid for reelection (see above, p. 227), and in June 1940 when Reynaud's government was collapsing and Mandel seemed the logical successor, he was convinced that Lebrun would never summon him (see above, pp. 243–44).

56. *Aux Ecoutes*, Feb. 1, 1936, p. 8.

57. *Ibid.*, pp. 7–8, 21–22; also *Le Cri du Jour*, Feb. 1, 1936, p. 6; L'Observateur, *Candide*, Feb. 6, 1936. According to Wormser (*Mandel*, pp. 202–4), Mandel did not expect the Popular Front to win the elections, but contemporary accounts of his opinion by his friends in the press indicate the contrary. See also Varenne, *Mon patron*, p. 147.

58. *Le Cri du Jour*, Nov. 16, 1935, p. 9.

59. After the elections, Mandel, Paul-Boncour and Flandin advised Sarraut to reshuffle his cabinet and to attempt to get a vote of confidence from the new Chamber. See Georges Lefranc, *Histoire du Front Populaire* (Paris, 1965), p. 132; also *Le Cri du Jour*, May 2, 1936, p. 7.

60. François Piétri, "Partis et groupes," *La Revue des Deux Mondes*, Aug. 1, 1965, pp. 364–65. In October 1935 Georges Gombault had said that the Radicals would not support a Mandel government for fear that he would try to separate them from the Socialists and Communists. See *La Lumière*, Oct. 19, 1935.

61. *La Nation*, Feb. 1, 1936, p. 75; *Le Jour*, Jan. 25, Feb. 1, 3, 8, 1936.

62. *L'Action Française*, Jan. 25, 1936. Contrary to the belief of *L'Action Française*, although anti-Semitism was a problem in Alsace, which had a greater proportion of Jews than the rest of France, Mandel's appointment was popular in the recovered provinces because he was considered to be very sympathetic to their claims for special treatment. He had always been concerned with conditions in the provinces and had sat for a number of years on the Chamber Committee for Alsace-Lorraine. See statement of Nominé, the deputy from Moselle, in *Le Temps*, Feb. 2, 1936. Also Montgomery Belgion, *News of the French* (London, 1938), pp. 320–21.

63. *Le Canard Enchaîné*, Jan. 29, 1936; *Marianne*, March 25, 1936.

64. Emmanuel Paul in *Politique*, Feb. 1936, p. 130.

65. Taittinger in *L'Ami du Peuple*, Jan. 25, 1936; Henriot in *La Liberté du Sud-Ouest*, Jan. 26, 1936; Kérillis in *L'Echo de Paris*, Feb. 2, 1936.

66. L'Observateur in *Candide*, Feb. 6, 1936.

67. Pierre Gaxotte in *Je Suis Partout*, April 20, 27, 1935; Thierry Maulnier in *1935*, April 10, 1935; Raymond Recouly in *Gringoire*, March 29, 1935. Also Weber, p. 284.

68. Micaud, pp. 67–69.

69. Dobler's testimony in *Les Evénements*, II, 480.

70. Chautemps, p. 31.

71. Zay, *Souvenirs*, p. 67.

72. Gamelin, II, 201.

73. See Jean-Baptiste Duroselle, "France and the Crisis of March 1936" with commentary by John Cairns in *French Society and Culture Since the Old Regime*, eds.

Evelyn M. Acomb and Marvin L. Brown, Jr. (New York, 1966), pp. 244–68, 284–88; John Cairns, "March 7, 1936 Again: The View from Paris," *International Journal*, XX, No. 2 (Spring 1965), pp. 230–46; R. A. C. Parker, "The First Capitulation: France and the Rhineland Crisis of 1936," *World Politics*, VIII, No. 3 (April 1956), pp. 355–73; W. F. Knapp, "The Rhineland Crisis of March 1936," in *The Decline of the Third Republic*, ed. James Joll, St. Antony's Papers, No. 5 (London, 1959), pp. 67–85; C. Waldron Bolen, "Hitler Remilitarizes the Rhineland," in *Power, Public Opinion, and Diplomacy*, eds. Lillian P. Wallace and William C. Askew (Durham, N.C., 1959), pp. 244–66.

74. Lazareff, *Deadline*, p. 117. Lazareff, who received this account from Sarraut, says it was later confirmed by Flandin and General Maurin. Emile Buré in *L'Ordre*, July 25, 1945, says Sarraut gave a similar account of the meeting to him. Geneviève Tabouis also reports Mandel's intervention in similar terms in *Chantage à la guerre* (Paris, 1938), pp. 99–100. Flandin, Sarraut, Paul-Boncour, Jean Zay, and Georges Bonnet, the ministers who have given accounts of this meeting, do not report Mandel's actual words, but all agree that he was in favor of immediate military action. (See Flandin, *Politique française*, p. 199; Sarraut in *Les Evénements*, III, 582, 622; Paul-Boncour, III, 33–34; Zay, *Souvenirs*, pp. 65–67; Bonnet, *Le Quai d'Orsay*, pp. 151–63.) General Maurin, however, claims that Mandel did not speak out at this or at any other meeting. See his testimony in *Les Evénements*, IV, 908.

75. Flandin, *Politique française*, p. 199.

76. Reynaud, *Au coeur de la mêlée*, p. 182; see also Paul-Boncour, III, 35; Zay, *Souvenirs*, pp. 65–67; Debû-Bridel, p. 351.

77. Debû-Bridel, p. 346.

78. Varenne, *Mon patron*, p. 172; see also Mandel's comments at the time in *Le Cri du Jour*, March 14, 1936, p. 5. In an interview, Madame Béatrice Bretty confirmed Varenne's account. Wormser, however (*Mandel*, pp. 198–99), reports that Mandel was surprised by the vigor of Sarraut's speech.

79. *DDF*, Second Series, I, 449, dispatch from Ambassador François-Poncet to Flandin, March 9, 1936.

80. *DGFP*, Series C, V, 131–32, report of Chargé d'Affaires in France to German Foreign Ministry. See also his reports of April 8 and 9, 1936, pp. 404–5, 421–24 and reports of Ambassador in Great Britain to German Foreign Ministry, March 13, and 21, 1936, pp. 140–41, 233–34.

81. See Sarraut's testimony in *Les Evénements*, III, 602–5.

82. Even this degree of British support was not forthcoming. See Major L. F. Ellis, *The War in France and Flanders, 1939–1940* (London, 1953), pp. 3–4. "A somewhat desultory exchange of technical information with the French General Staff had . . . been maintained since 1936, . . . but full Staff conversations had been avoided. For such Staff conversations are apt to imply a military alliance and involve definite military commitments, and at that time the Government (and their military advisers) were unwilling to proceed so far while the policy of appeasement was being pursued." Full Staff talks did not finally begin until March 1939.

83. *Le Cri du Jour*, March 21, 1936, p. 3.

84. *1935*, March 27, 1935.

85. Wormser, *Mandel*, pp. 200–201.

86. Léon Bailby in *Le Jour*, March 9, 1936; Philippe Henriot in *La Liberté du Sud-Ouest*, March 10, 1936; see also the review of the press given by Sarraut in *Les Evénements*, III, 566–69.

87. *La Lumière,* March 14, 1936; *L'Humanité,* March 12, 1936.
88. Gabriel Péri in *L'Humanité,* March 12, 1936.
89. *Politique,* April 1936, p. 343.
90. See reprints of articles from *Candide, Choc,* and *Le Canard Enchaîné* in *Le Journal du Médoc,* March 22, 1936.
91. Cited in Micaud, p. 93.
92. *Marianne,* March 25, 1936, p. 3. On March 11, however, *Marianne* had reported that Mandel wanted to recall several classes. See also *Le Cri du Jour,* April 4, 1936, p. 7 and April 11, 1936, p. 6.
93. Pierre Gaxotte in *Je Suis Partout,* Jan. 11, 1936.

Chapter 12

1. *Le Journal du Médoc,* Feb. 23, 1936.
2. *Le Démocrate et Petit Médocain, Le Journal du Médoc,* March 1, 1936.
3. *Le Journal du Médoc,* May 10, 1936.
4. *Ibid.,* April 12, 1936; also *Le Démocrate et Petit Médocain,* April 5, 1936. See also Garby's program in *Le Journal du Médoc,* April 26, 1936.
5. Louis-Georges Planes, *La Liberté du Sud-Ouest,* April 25, 1936; also Pol, pp. 154–55.
6. See Mandel's program in *L'Action Médocaine,* April 26, 1936.
7. *Paris-Soir,* April 9, 1936.
8. Louis-Georges Planes, *La Liberté du Sud-Ouest,* April 25, 1936.
9. *Gringoire,* Feb. 21, 1936.
10. Syndicat National, *M. Mandel.* See also *Le Populaire,* April 1, 2, 7, 1936.
11. *Le Journal des Débats,* June 2, 7, 1936; *L'Humanité,* June 7, 1936; *Le Cri du Jour,* June 13, 1936, p. 12; *Gringoire,* June 19, 1936; Bois, pp. 291–92; Coblentz, pp. 184–85; Senator Jean Philip in *Annales du Sénat,* Jan. 26, 1937, p. 33.
12. *Notre Temps,* May 21, 1936; *Marianne,* June 3, 1936; Gaston-Martin in *L'Entente des Gauches,* reprinted in *L'Action Médocaine,* July 26, 1936.
13. Coblentz, pp. 192–94.
14. *Ibid.,* p. 26; Lazareff, *Deadline,* p. 305.
15. Interview with Henry Lémery; also see *L'Action Française,* Jan. 26, 1939; Bardoux, p. 286; Fabre-Luce, *Vingt-cinq années,* I, 176; Tabouis, *Cassandra,* pp. 220–22; Wormser, *Mandel,* p. 204.
16. Roche, p. 156.
17. Tabouis, *Cassandra,* p. 291.
18. Wormser, *Mandel,* pp. 184, 204.
19. Zaharoff: Donald McCormick, *Pedlar of Death: The Life of Sir Basil Zaharoff* (London, 1965), pp. 230–31; Archduke Otto: Mallet, I, 59; Lloyd George: *Le Jour,* March 22, 1938; Antonesco: *L'Ami du Peuple,* Dec. 19, 1936; Titulesco: Champeaux, I, 102; King Carol: *DDF,* Second Series, I, 642; Grand Croix: *L'Avenir du Médoc,* Feb. 9, 1936.
20. American Embassy: Tabouis, *Vingt ans,* p. 317; British Embassy: André David, *Message à de jeunes anglaises* (Montreal, 1942), p. 47.
21. Russian Ambassador: *L'Action Française,* Jan. 26, 1939; Duke of Windsor: interview with Henry Lémery.
22. Varenne, *Mon patron,* p. 172.

23. *L'Echo de Paris*, Sept. 20, 1924.

24. *Le Cri du Jour*, April 10, 1937, p. 20.

25. *L'Ami du Peuple*, Oct. 19, 1936.

26. Interview with Taittinger. It seems unlikely, but Mandel's friend Georges Wormser, who is a banker and who joined the executive board of *L'Ami du Peuple*, reports (*Mandel*, p. 205) that he knows nothing about the circumstances under which Mandel gained control of the paper.

27. Interview with Lafue. According to Georges Wormser, however (*Mandel,* p. 205), they were written by Jacques Roujon.

28. For left-wing comment about Mandel and *L'Ami du Peuple,* see *La Lumière,* Sept. 19, 26, Oct. 3, Nov. 7, 1936.

29. Simon Arbellot, *J'ai vu mourir le boulevard* (Paris, 1950), pp. 129–31; Louis Truc, *Je Suis Partout*, Jan. 28, 1944. Truc, the son of the Catholic literary critic Gonzague Truc, later wrote a history of the Action Française movement.

30. *Le Canard Enchaîné*, Oct. 7, 28, 1936. According to Wormser (*Mandel,* p. 205), Jacques Roujon remained editor-in-chief, but his name is not mentioned by any of the writers for the paper.

31. Truc, *Je Suis Partout*, Jan. 28, 1944.
32. *La Lumière*, Nov. 7, 1936.

33. Truc, *Je Suis Partout*, Jan. 28, 1944.
34. Feb. 27, 1937; also Oct. 6, 1936.

35. Nov. 19, 1936.
36. April 28, May 16, 1937.

37. Oct. 22, 1936.
38. March 4, 1937.

39. April 5, 1937.
40. Oct. 9, 1936; Nov. 8, 1936.

41. Dec. 24, 1936.
42. June 25, 1937.

43. Dec. 27, 1936.
44. Nov. 26, 1936.

45. Feb. 17, 1937.
46. March 8, 1937.

47. *Le Journal du Var,* Jan. 14, 1911; also Henry Torrès, *Campaign of Treachery,* pp. 182–83.

48. Nov. 22, 1936.

49. Nov. 18, 1936.

50. Oct. 16, 17, 1936.

51. There is no record of when Mandel began to consider Soviet Russia as a necessary element in France's system of alliances, but it must have been fairly early if one can judge by a remark of Laval's in March 1935: "There is . . . the Mandel who is crazy about Great Britain and who loves Russia, and then there is the Mandel who loves war and hates Germany because Clemenceau taught him to." Maurice Martin du Gard, "Les memorables," *Revue des Deux Mondes,* Nov. 15, 1966, p. 197.

52. On Blum's attitude toward a military alliance with Soviet Russia, see Nathanael Greene, *Crisis and Decline: The French Socialist Party in the Popular Front Era* (Ithaca, N.Y., 1969), pp. 96–97.

53. The speech was printed in *Le Temps,* Nov. 12, 1936. Stalin apparently agreed. At about the same time as Mandel's speech, he also used the analogy with Turkey when he informed Ambassador Coulondre through an intermediary that he wanted France to be strong against Germany, but that "she should conduct her internal affairs as she liked, without worrying that the Soviet government might interfere." Robert Coulondre, *De Staline à Hitler* (Paris, 1950), p. 40.

54. *L'Ordre,* Nov. 12 ,1936. See also Geneviève Tabouis in *L'Oeuvre,* Nov. 12, 1936 and Louis Thomas in *Le Cri du Jour,* Nov. 14, 1936.

55. *L'Humanité,* Nov. 13, 1936.

56. *Candide,* quoted in *Le Journal du Médoc,* Dec. 5, 1936.

57. Werth, *Twilight of France*, p. 72.
58. Emile Buré in *L'Ordre*, Nov. 13, 1936.
59. *L'Action Française*, Nov. 13, 1936.
60. *Le Journal du Médoc*, Nov. 14, 1936.
61. Franz Borkenau, *European Communism* (New York, 1953), pp. 192–221; Brower, pp. 160–75.
62. On September 6 Blum declared: "I sympathize with anything that increases French solidarity in the face of a possible danger. But this stirring up of patriotic feeling, this sort of preventive mobilization for battle—that, no! I do not believe, I will never admit that war is inevitable." Quoted in Chastenet, VI, 165.
63. *La Lumière*, Dec. 12, 1936; see also Emmanuel Berl in *Les Pavés de Paris*, Aug. 12, 1938, p. 4.
64. Geoffrey Fraser and Thadée Natanson, *Léon Blum: Man and Statesman* (London, 1938), p. 291. Although Natanson was an old friend, Blum reportedly later withdrew his authorization for the book. See Colton, p. 504.
65. On Senatorial opposition to Blum's government, see the comments of Pierre Cot and Marius Moutet during the colloquium on Blum's term in office, in *Léon Blum, chef de gouvernement, 1936–1937* (Paris, 1967), pp. 166–71.
66. Wormser, *Mandel*, p. 208. Some people must have suspected that Mandel was involved, for one writer has stated that "Mandel was as much responsible as Joseph Caillaux for bringing Blum's reign to an end." See Stanton Leeds, *These Rule France* (New York, 1940), p. 69.
67. See *L'Ami du Peuple*, Nov. 9, 1936; May 24, Aug. 20, 1937.
68. *L'Alliance Démocratique*, Nov. 20, 1936.
69. Morice, vol. III, tome I, p. 154.
70. See speeches by Senators Jean Philip, Babaud-Lacroze, and Paul Laffont in *Annales du Sénat. Débats parlementaires*, Jan. 26, 1937, pp. 32–44; also debates in Senate, May 25, 1939, pp. 450–62 and June 1, 1939, pp. 469–88; *Rapport fait au nom de la Commission du Commerce, de l'Industrie, du Travail et des Postes sur les conclusions de l'enquête ordonnée le 26 janvier 1937 et relative à la gestion du ministère des postes, par M. Paul Laffont, sénateur*, in *Le Journal Officiel. Sénat*. Session ordinaire de 1938, *Documents Parlementaires*. Annexe No. 277. Session of April 13, 1938, pp. 161–67; Huc and Robin, pp. 106, 154–56.
71. *L'Ami du Peuple*, Dec. 4, 1936; *Le Temps*, Dec. 5, 6, 1936.
72. *Annales du Sénat*, Jan. 26, 1937, pp. 32–40.
73. *Ibid.*, pp. 40–44.
74. *Rapport...par M. Paul Laffont*; debates in *Annales du Sénat*, May 25, 1939, pp. 450–62; June 1, 1939, pp. 469–88.
75. *La Lumière*, July 1, 1938.
76. *Le Populaire*, June 20–July 10, 1938; *La Bourgogne Républicaine* (Dijon), June 20–Aug. 23, 1938.
77. *Parti Socialiste. 35ᵉ Congrès national, tenu à Royan les 4, 5, 6, 7 juin 1938* (Paris, 1938), pp. 526–27.

Chapter 13

1. See *Le Matin*, Jan. 17, 1938, and *L'Action Médocaine*, Jan. 30, 1938.
2. Debû-Bridel, p. 407; *Aux Ecoutes*, Jan. 22, 1938. Supported by Mandel and Reynaud, Blum made another unsuccessful attempt to form a National Union government in March. See Desgranges, pp. 198–99; *Aux Ecoutes*, March 12, 1938; Micaud, p. 146n;

Debû-Bridel, p. 424; Fabry, pp. 136–37; Colton, pp. 292–97; Werth, *France and Munich* 123–27; Greene, pp. 197–200.

3. Wormser, *Mandel*, pp. 209–10.

4. *La Nation*, April 16, 1938, p. 246.

5. Gabriel Péri in *L'Humanité*, April 24, 1938; *L'Action Française*, April 11, 1938; Montigny, *Les heures tragiques*, p. 243. An indication of Communist reconciliation with Mandel was the picture published on the front page of *L'Humanité* on April 12 showing him taking office as minister of Colonies.

6. *DBFP,* Third Series, VI, 150, Phipps to Halifax, June 22, 1939.

7. *DGFP*, Series D, I, 1073, Chargé d'Affaires in Paris to German Foreign Minstry, April 14, 1938.

8. Debû-Bridel, p. 435.

9. Suarez and Laborde, p. 83.

10. *L'Ami du Peuple*, Jan. 18, 1937; also March 4 and Aug. 7, 1937.

11. Pierre-Etienne Flandin, "Le conflit tchécoslovaque et la situation politique," *Revue de Paris*, Oct. 15, 1938, p. 732; see also the interview with Mandel in *La Tribune des Nations,* March 10, 1938.

12. Desgranges, p. 72.

13. *Ibid.*, pp. 198–99.

14. Stéphane, pp. 109–10. (Flandin later stated that Stéphane's account of the interview exactly reflected his thought. Guy Raïssac, *Un soldat dans la tourmente* [Paris, 1963], p. 387.) See also the statement by Flandin in an interview in *Le Matin*, Dec. 12, 1940: "It is certain . . . that the Jewish clique has everywhere eliminated those men who could have exercised an influence for peace. . . ."

15. *Je Suis Partout*, Jan. 23, 1937.

16. *L'Action Française*, April 11, 17, 1939; *Je Suis Partout*, Feb. 4, April 22, May 10–Sept. 16, 1938; also *Le Jour*, Jan. 8, March 22, April 11, 1938.

17. *Je Suis Partout*, July 14, Aug. 16, 1944.

18. *Le Petit Journal*, June 30, 1938.

19. *L'Epoque*, July 8, 1938.

20. *Les Pavés de Paris*, Aug. 12, 1938, pp. 1–5; Aug. 26, 1938, pp. 5–10.

21. *Nouvelle Revue Française*, December 1958, 1150.

22. *L'Ami du Peuple*, Nov. 27, 1936.

23. André Stibio in *L'Ordre*, Aug. 19, 30, 1938.

24. *DBFP*, Third Series, II, 220, Phipps to Halifax, Sept. 2, 1938.

25. *FRUS*, 1938, I, 601, Bullitt to Hull, Sept. 15, 1938.

26. *DGFP*, Series D, I, 216.

27. William Strang, *At Home and Abroad* (London, 1956), pp. 135–36; *DBFP*, Third Series, II, 510, Phipps to Halifax, Sept. 24, 1938; pp. 535–36, Halifax to Phipps, Sept. 25, 1938; pp. 543–44, Phipps to Halifax, Sept. 26, 1938.

28. *DGFP*, Series D, II, 221–23, Welczeck to German Foreign Ministry, April 8, 1938.

29. *DGFP*, Series D, II, 548, Welczeck to German Foreign Ministry, Aug. 10, 1938.

30. Zay, *Carnets secrets*, p. 17.   31. Taylor, p. 39.

32. *Ibid.*, p. 196.   33. *Politique*, Nov. 1938, p. 907.

34. Simone, p. 237.   35. Eubank, p. 50.

36. *DBFP*, Third Series, II, 309, Phipps to Halifax, Sept. 13, 1938.

37. *FRUS*, 1938, I, 601, Bullitt to Hull, Sept. 15, 1938; also Werth, *France and Munich,* p. 252.

38. *FRUS*, 1938, I, 601, Bullitt to Hull, Sept. 15, 1938.

39. *Je Suis Partout*, Sept. 23, 1938. He was reported to have said, "If any concession is made to Hitler, I will hand in my resignation, Daladier will fall, and a government of public safety will declare war."

40. *FRUS*, 1938, I, 616, Bullitt to Hull, Sept. 19, 1938.

41. Zay, *Carnets secrets*, pp. 3–7; Paul Marion in *La Liberté*, Sept. 21, 1938; Werth, *France and Munich*, p. 263; Henriot, *Comment mourut la paix*, p. 4; Fabre-Luce, *Histoire secrète*, p. 51.

42. *FRUS*, 1938, I, 620–21, Bullitt to Hull, Sept. 19, 1938.

43. According to Bonnet and his friends, while the Czech cabinet was deliberating, Mandel and Reynaud were telephoning Beneš, either directly or through intermediaries, to advise him to reject the plan and hold out until Bonnet could be replaced as minister of Foreign Affairs. (See Bonnet, *Défense de la paix* I, 250–51; Champeaux, II, 135–36.) After the war, Robert Bollack, a personal friend of Mandel, confirmed the story. He reported being present when Mandel telephoned Beneš and advised him not to let himself be dictated to by Paris or London. If Czechoslovakia were attacked, France, England, and Russia would come to his aid. "Everyone would follow you and Germany would be beaten in six months without Mussolini, and in three months with Mussolini" (*L'Intransigeant*, May 9, 1948). Georges Wormser (*Mandel*, p. 219) repeats the story without, however, indicating whether he is merely accepting Bollack's account, was present himself, or heard about it from Mandel. On the other hand, one of Mandel's associates, when discussing Bollack's account, merely smiled and said that Mandel, who always acted through intermediaries, would never have exposed himself to recriminations by calling Beneš personally (interview with Mandel's associate, who preferred to remain anonymous). What Bollack possibly overheard was a conversation between Mandel and some Czech representative in Paris. In an interview, Geneviève Tabouis said that Mandel sometimes communicated with Beneš through the British diplomat Oliver Harvey.

44. For a discussion of these conversations and communications, see Arthur Furnia, *The Diplomacy of Appeasement* (Washington, D.C., 1960), pp. 343–45; Eubank, pp. 301–3; Boris Celovsky, *Das Münchener Abkommen, 1938* (Stuttgart, 1958), pp. 356–74.

45. Churchill, I, 302.

46. Desgranges, p. 239; Zay, *Carnets secrets*, p. 9. Reynaud insists that the resignations were presented to Daladier but were withdrawn when the Prime Minister warned that the first mobilization measures were in course, that war was coming, and that to resign under such conditions would be desertion. See Reynaud, *Au coeur de la mêlée*, p. 271. The contemporary versions given by Zay and Desgranges, who received an account from Champetier de Ribes, contradict Reynaud. According to Bonnet, Daladier denied that the resignations were actually presented. Bonnet, *Défense de la paix*, I, 251–52. Daladier confirmed this in a personal interview with the author.

47. *La République*, Sept. 23, 1938.   48. *L'Humanité*, Sept. 23, 1938.

49. Zay, *Carnets secrets*, pp. 11–17.   50. Churchill, I, 309.

51. Henriot, *Comment mourut la paix*, p. 12.

52. Montigny, *Les Heures tragiques*, p. 104.

53. Werth, *France and Munich*, pp. 288–93.

54. *Le procès Flandin*, pp. 85–86.

55. Varenne, *Mon patron*, pp. 175–76. See also Blum's testimony in *Les Evénements*, I, 258: "There were at least two members of the cabinet who were dissuaded from resigning only with great difficulty, Paul Reynaud and Georges Mandel."

56. *La Liberté*, Oct. 6, 1938.

57. Paul-Boncour, III, 104. Paul Stehlin, who was at Munich, reports that immediately after the conference Daladier said, "I think that Paul Reynaud and Georges Mandel are going to resign. I will replace them." See Stehlin, *Témoignage pour l'histoire* (Paris, 1964), p. 105.

58. *L'Action Française*, Sept. 28, 1938; *Je Suis Partout*, Sept. 30, 1938.

59. "If these cannibals persist/ In making heroes of us,/ Then our first bullets/ Must be for Mandel, Blum, and Reynaud."

60. *La République*, Oct. 2, 3, 4, 1938.

61. *Je Suis Partout*, Oct. 7, 1938; *La Liberté*, Oct. 5, 6, 1938; *Le Jour*, Oct. 4, 1938; Emmanuel Berl in *Les Pavés de Paris*, Oct. 7, 1938.

62. Reynaud, *Au coeur de la mêlée*, p. 288.

63. Wormser, *Mandel*, pp. 220–21.

64. *Ibid.*, pp. 211, 216.

65. Weber, pp. 373–74.

66. Jean Touchard and Louis Bodin, "L'Etat de l'opinion au début de l'année 1936" in *Léon Blum, chef de gouvernement, 1936–1937* (Paris, 1967), p. 64.

67. Marcel Jouhandeau, "Comment je suis devenu antisémite," in *Le péril juif* (Paris, 1939), p. 12. Jouhandeau continued: "I hereby vow to call for the vengeance of my people against them [the Jews] so long as there remains a single one in France who is not subject to special laws."

68. Taylor, p. 34; Jean-Paul Sartre, *Anti-Semite and Jew* (New York, 1965), pp. 86–87; Szajkowski, pp. 19–20.

69. *Le Populaire*, Nov. 19, 1938.

70. According to Georges Wormser (*Mandel*, p. 244), Mandel regarded Nazism as "an outbreak of the anti-Semitism that has always been virulent or latent across the Rhine, . . . the resurrection in a brutal form of old feelings, which only idealists and those who delude themselves believe have disappeared. It is the eternal Germany reappearing after the failure of Weimar. . . ."

71. Interview with Pierre Lafue. At least two anti-Semitic journals that continued their policies, *Le Cri du Jour* and *Gringoire*, never dared to attack Mandel personally. By 1938 Louis Thomas' *Cri du Jour* had become one of the most anti-Semitic journals in France, but in the midst of the Czech crisis he declared (Sept. 10, 1938, p. 18): "We must have three hundred Mandels in the top posts of the government and administration so that France will be strong, prosperous and respected." See also *Gringoire*, April 15, 1938.

72. Alexander Werth reports that Pierre Mendès-France also felt "handicapped by the unfair fact that he is not considered 'entirely French.'" See Werth *Lost Statesman: The Strange Story of Pierre Mendès-France* (New York, 1958), p. 79. A public opinion poll in 1946 reported that 43% of the people did not consider Jews to be full-fledged Frenchmen. By 1966 this figure had been reduced to 19%, but 50% (45% of the Communists, 57% of the Gaullists) still would oppose having a Jew as head of state. On the basis of the 1966 poll, Roland Sadoun of the Institut Français d'Opinion Publique declared that almost 20% of the French show "serious characteristics of anti-Semitism." See the report in *Le Nouvel Adam*, Dec. 1966.

73. Wormser, *Mandel*, pp. 218–19, 224.

74. Albert Memmi has said in reference to Pierre Mendès-France, "In the opinion of all, he made the mistake of reacting like a Jew, of allowing himself to be affected by anti-Semitic accusations. But how could a politician who wishes to represent and

defend his fellow citizens, to act in their name, not consider their moods, and especially their reservations as far as he was concerned? ... The weak point of Jewish politicians is their Jewishness, even though they deny it and try to camouflage it. And in that one recognizes the fundamental irony of the Jewish fate, imposed on them and denied, heavy and yet transparent. Blum and Mendès-France did not act as Jews, but they could not prevent their actions from being hindered and thwarted in the name of their Jewishness." Memmi, p. 226.

75. *Le Populaire*, Nov. 14, 1938.

76. Debû-Bridel, p. 511.

77. See Andrê Scherer, "Les 'Mains libres' à l'Est," *Revue d'Histoire de la Deuxième Guerre Mondiale*, Oct. 1958, pp. 1–25.

78. Tabouis, *Vingt ans*, p. 380.

79. *Je Suis Partout*, May 20, 1938; Jan. 6, Feb. 24, June 16, July 28, 1939; *Candide*, Feb. 8, 22 and March 8, 1939; *L'Action Française*, Nov. 4, 5, 7, 1938; Feb. 1, 3, 1939.

80. Bührer, pp. 175–76; Catroux, p. 39. In 1952 the journalist André Simone (Otto Katz), author of a book on the fall of France, *J'Accuse* (New York, 1940), and former assistant of the German Communist leader Willi Münzenberg, was tried and executed by the Communist government of Czechoslovakia for treason. He was accused, among other things, of having been Mandel's spy. At his trial Simone testified that in September 1939 he joined Mandel's espionage service. See Peter Meyer, "Stalin Follows in Hitler's Footsteps," in *The New Red Anti-Semitism: A Symposium*, ed. Elliot E. Cohen (Boston, 1953), pp. 6–7.

81. *Je Suis Partout*, May 27, 1938; *Candide*, Feb. 8, 1939; *Le Canard Enchaîné*, April 20, 1938; *Messidor*, May 6, 1939; interview with Georges Bonnet.

82. *Le Jour*, May 16, 1938.

83. Del Vayo, p. 312.

84. Zay, *Carnets secrets*, pp. 50–54; see also *DBFP*, Third Series, V, 799–800, Phipps to Halifax, April 28, 1939.

85. Werth, *France and Munich*, p. 404.

86. *Je Suis Partout*, April 22, May 27, 1938; *Le Jour*, May 16, Dec. 30, 1938; *Le Canard Enchaîné*, April 20, 1938.

87. Torrès, *Campaign of Treachery*, pp. 182–83. Mandel's opinion of the Italians had not changed since 1911. See the *Journal du Var*, Jan. 14, 1911.

88. Note prepared for author by Max Brusset, one of Mandel's assistants. See also Bührer, pp. 94–95, and Lieutenant Colonel Yves Jouin, "La côte française des Somalis; La participation française à la résistance Ethiopienne, 1936–1940," *Revue Historique de l'Armée*, Nov. 1963, pp. 149–62.

89. Guariglia, p. 426. Guariglia was the Italian Ambassador in Paris. After September 1939, however, Mandel tried to placate the Italians. He explained to Guariglia that he was certain Mussolini would enter the war in 1940, but he wanted to prevent him from justifying his decision by any action of France's.

90. Bührer, pp. 78–90; Catroux, pp. 7–10; also Roger Lévy, "French Neutrality during the Sino-Japanese Hostilities," *Pacific Affairs*, December 1938, pp. 433–46; Andrew Roth, "French Indo-China in Translation," in Lévy *et al.*, pp. 117–48.

91. Bührer, pp. 78–90; *FRUS*, 1939, I, 271, Bullitt to Hull, June 5, 1939.

92. *L'Ordre*, May 12, 1938; also *Marianne*, July 27, 1938; *Le Temps*, Nov. 7, 1938, March 14–20, 1940; *La Tribune des Nations*, Dec. 15, 1938; *L'Illustration*, May 11, 1940 (The entire issue was devoted to the colonies); *La Revue du Parlement*, March 15,

April 20, May 15, 1939; and for a review of the press, *L'Action Médocaine*, April 24, May 1, 8, 15, 29, July 3, Sept. 4, Nov. 20, Dec. 11, 1938; July 2, 1939; Jan. 7, 1940.

93. Roques and Donnadieu, pp. 9–10. Whereas Mandel conceived of the colonies as a means of strengthening France so that she could play her traditional role in European politics, the defenders of Munich saw them as compensation for France's weakness in Europe and proposed that she turn to developing them as an alternative to the traditional role she could no longer play. See Larmour, pp. 245–46.

94. Nov. 6, 1938 and Nov. 8, 1939. See *Le Temps*, Nov. 7, 1938. The second speech was reprinted as "The French Colonial Contribution since the Beginning of the War," *The Asiatic Review*, January 1940, pp. 94–97.

95. Henry, pp. 353–55; Jean Philip, "Les idées de M. Mandel," pp. 13–26; *Le Cri du Jour*, Sept. 10, 1938, p. 18; Sept. 24, 1938, p. 22; April 30, 1938, p. 5; June 11, 1938, pp. 11, 22; Wormser, *Mandel*, p. 213.

Mandel seems to have given meticulous attention to everything, for twenty-five years later he is still fondly remembered by historians at the colonial archives in Paris for having demoted an archivist who withheld access to documents legally open to the public. (Incident related to the author by a historian who frequently uses the archives.)

96. *Je Suis Partout*, Feb. 4, 1938. On the Violette bill, see Marie-Renée Mouton, "L'Algérie devant le parlement français de 1935 à 1938," *La Revue Française de Science Politique*, March 1962, pp. 93–128.

97. Ellen J. Hammer, *The Struggle for Indochina* (Stanford, 1954), p. 15.

98. Philippe Devillers, *Histoire du Viêt-Nam de 1940 à 1952* (3d ed., Paris, 1952), p. 71; Roques and Donnadieu, p. 149; Bührer, p. 103; Roth, pp. 133, 138.

99. Varenne, *Mon patron*, pp. 158–63; Catroux, pp. 33–36; Bührer, pp. 101–5; Emile Schreiber in *L'Illustration*, May 11, 1940.

100. For the difficulties encountered by the Popular Front in bringing about colonial reforms, see Charles-André Julien, "Léon Blum et les pays d'outre-mer," and Robert Delavignette, "La politique de Marius Moutet au Ministère des colonies," in *Léon Blum, chef de gouvernement, 1936–1937* (Paris, 1967), pp. 377–94.

101. Joseph Buttinger, *Vietnam: A Dragon Embattled* (New York, 1967), I, 231.

102. *The New York Times*, July 11, 1939.

103. David Lloyd George, *The Truth about the Peace Treaties* (London, 1938), I, 546.

104. Bührer, pp. 17–36.

105. Rocques and Donnadieu, pp. 139, 157.

106. Bührer, pp. 58–71; Roques and Donnadieu, pp. 151–52.

107. Bührer, pp. 109–10.

108. *Ibid.*, pp. 67–76.

109. *The New York Times*, March 17, 19, 1940; *The Times* (London), March 18, 1940; *Le Temps*, March 14–20, 1940; Wormser, *Mandel*, p. 215.

110. Mandel's report to the Senate Commission des Colonies, Dec. 27, 1939, reported in Bardoux, *Journal d'un témoin*, p. 162.

111. Cyril Falls, *The Great War, 1914–1918* (New York, 1961), p. 14; also Shelby Davis, *Reservoirs of Men: A History of the Black Troops of French West Africa* (Chambery, 1934), pp. 156–59.

112. Bührer, p. 49n.

113. *Ibid.*, p. 14.

Chapter 14

Epigraph: Adolf Hitler, *Mein Kampf* (Boston, Houghton Mifflin, Sentry Edition, 1943), p. 668.

1. Zay, *Carnets secrets*, p. 46.
2. *Les Pavés de Paris*, March 24, 1939, pp. 4–5.
3. Emmanuel Berl in *Les Pavés de Paris*, April 21, 1939, p. 16; July 14, 1939, p. 8.
4. Berl noted that "it takes courage today to admit that one was a *Munichois* in October." *Ibid.*, April 21, 1939, p. 7.
5. Jacques Polonski, *La presse, la propagande et l'opinion publique sous l'occupation* (Paris, 1946), p. 59.
6. Maurice Renand, "Laval's Methods: The Republic—Jews—Freemasons," in *FDGO*, III, 1056.
7. Fabre-Luce, *Journal de la France*, I, 228.
8. *France-Amérique* (New York), June 13, 1943.
9. Kérillis, *Laissons-nous démembrer la France?*, pp. 249–51.
10. Beer, pp. 206–7; interviews with Albert Bayet and Georges Gombault; Wormser, *Mandel*, p. 249.
11. Varenne, *Mon patron*, pp. 198–99.
12. *Ibid.*, pp. 148–49.
13. Bleustein-Blanchet, p. 192; also Simone, p. 235.
14. Zay, *Carnets secrets*, p. 63.
15. Laubreaux, p. 76. Laubreaux received his information from Jean Mistler, President of the Chamber Foreign Affairs Committee.
16. Lazareff, *Deadline*, p. 240.
17. Interview with Bonnet; De Monzie, p. 150; Stéphane, p. 109.
18. Interview with Bonnet; Desgranges, p. 198; Montigny, *Le complot*, p. 147.
19. Desgranges, p. 199.
20. Tabouis, *Vingt ans*, p. 399. This is probably one of the most quoted phrases of the war. See Fabre-Luce, *Journal de la France*, I, 188; Stéphane, p. 109; Guerdan, p. 59; Lazareff, *Deadline*, p. 306; Emile Buré in *France-Amérique*, June 13, 1943; Gabriel Lafaye in *L'Atelier*, Sept. 5, 1942; Robert de Saint Jean, *France Speaking* (New York, 1941), p. 244; Cárcano, p. 73; Guariglia, p. 427n; Un Témoin (Robert Lazurick), p. 11.
21. Interview with Flandin in *Le Matin*, Dec. 12, 1940.
22. *L'Oeuvre*, Aug. 9, 1940.
23. Pertinax, p. 151.
24. Bleustein-Blanchet, p. 193; Zay, *Carnets secrets*, p. 88.
25. Pertinax, p. 276; Bührer, p. 184; Montigny, *Les heures tragiques*, p. 16; Fabre-Luce, *Journal de la France*, I, 125.
26. Unpublished notes of one of Mandel's associates, who preferred to remain anonymous. Also Montigny, *Les heures tragiques*, p. 16. For the rationale of an attack on Italy at this time, see Chautemps, pp. 59–60.
27. " 'Souvenirs' de Georges Mandel," in Geneviève Noel, pp. 238–39. (The "Souvenirs" are the record of conversations between Mandel and a friend.) See also Bardoux, p. 160; Un Témoin, pp. 10–11.
28. Jon Kimche, *The Unfought Battle* (London, 1968). See also Adolphe Goutard, *The Battle of France, 1940* (New York, 1959), pp. 55–72; Andre G. Prételat, *Le destin tragique de la ligne Maginot* (Paris, 1950), pp. 49–75.
29. Montigny, *Les heures tragiques*, p. 16.

30. Noel, p. 238.
31. Kérillis, *I Accuse de Gaulle*, p. 34. 32. Melville, p. 24; Jones, p. 51.
33. Interview with Daladier. 34. Pertinax, p. 276.
35. Reynaud's name was usually coupled with Mandel's. Bois, pp. 131–32; Melville, p. 24; Emrys Jones, p. 53; Taylor, p. 222.
36. Aragon, I, 65.
37. Bois, pp. 160–61.
38. Wormser, *Mandel*, pp. 227–29.
39. Henry Lémery, *D'Une république à l'autre: souvenirs de la mêlée politique, 1894–1944* (Paris, 1964), pp. 229–30.
40. Wormser, *Mandel*, p. 252.
41. *Je Suis Partout*, Feb. 23, 1940; see also *Le Temps*, Jan. 8, 1940; Raymond Recouly in *Gringoire*, Dec. 21, 1939.
42. Chautemps, p. 65.
43. Lazareff, *Deadline*, p. 271; also *Le Canard Enchaîné*, March 27, 1940; *The New York Times*, March 22, 1940. *Je Suis Partout* (March 21, 1942) reported that Mandel had told a foreign diplomat: "To me, the ministry of the Interior means just one thing: instituting a reign of terror. Right now no one is fighting, and the French people would not see the need for the terror. But when war begins in earnest, it will be a different story."
44. Buré, *Clemenceau et Mandel*, p. 51. According to Wormser (*Mandel*, p. 254), the only post for which Mandel would have given up the Colonies was the ministry of War, where he could have made a direct contribution to France's military effort. This was the post that Clemenceau took over in World War I.
45. Bois, pp. 199–201; *La Lumière*, March 29, 1940.
46. Stibio, *Indiscrétions*, pp. 126–27. Stibio was a journalist closely associated with Mandel in the years before the war.
47. Thomas Jones, *A Diary with Letters, 1931–1950* (London, 1954), p. 457.
48. Lazareff, *De Munich à Vichy*, p. 219.
49. Berl, p. 64.
50. Bührer, p. 184.
51. Mendès-France, p. 4; Spears, I, 220; Montigny, *Les heures tragiques*, p. 16; *Je Suis Partout*, May 10, 1940.
52. De Monzie, p. 231.
53. *The New York Times*, May 19; *Le Populaire*, May 20; interview with Léon Bailby in *Gringoire*, May 23; *Je Suis Partout*, May 24; see also *France-Magazine*, June 4, pp. 6–8; André Chaumeix in *Paris-Soir*, May 20; *Le Temps*, May 21; *L'Oeuvre*, May 20; *Candide*, May 22; *La Liberté*, May 24, 1940.
54. *L'Action Française*, May 21, 1940.
55. De Monzie, p. 60.
56. Letter to author, June 29, 1961; see also Gaxotte's article, "Sur Georges Mandel," *Le Figaro*, July 1, 1964.
57. De Puységur, p. 107. 58. See Rossi, p. 285.
59. Laubreaux, p. 177. 60. Rebatet, p. 363.
61. André Stibio in *L'Ordre*, June 24, 1945; Varenne, *Mon patron*, p. 199; Lazareff, *De Munich à Vichy*, p. 285; Bleustein-Blanchet, p. 194; Wormser, *Mandel*, p. 254.
62. *Le Cri du Jour*, Nov. 3, 1934, p. 14.
63. Taylor, p. 251; also *Un Témoin*, p. 17.
64. Livois, II, 538.

65. *Le Temps*, May 24, 27, 1940; *The New York Times*, May 25, 26, 1940.

66. Péladeau, p. 164; also Cardinne-Petit, p. 206.

67. Testimony of Flandin in *Le procès Flandin*, p. 118; Reynaud, *Au coeur de la mêlée*, p. 740. Weygand erroneously states that the government failed to order civil servants to remain at their posts. Weygand, pp. 129–30. In at least one case, it was the military authorities who gave orders to evacuate despite Mandel's instructions to the contrary. Jean Vidalenc tells the story of one official, dismissed by Mandel for deserting his duties, who was able to produce proof that he had been ordered to leave by the military authorities. See Vidalenc, p. 118.

68. André Stibio in *L'Ordre*, June 24, 1945.

69. Vidalenc, p. 159.

70. Cardinne-Petit, p. 214.

71. Rossi, p. 320n.

72. Jean de la Hire, *Le crime des évacuations; les horreurs que nous avons vues* (Paris, 1941), pp. 9–12.

73. Weygand, pp. 147–48.

74. On the confusion surrounding the decision not to defend Paris, see the testimony of Léon Blum in *Les Evénements*, I, 260; also John Williams, pp. 305–9.

75. Official estimates of the number of foreigners imprisoned range from 2,500 to 10,000. See Daladier's testimony in *Les Evénements*, I, 69; Rossi, pp. 147–48; and de Jong, p. 92. But these estimates would appear to be too low. On the indiscriminate arrest of foreigners and their treatment, see Arthur Koestler, *Scum of the Earth* (New York, 1941); Pol, pp. 229–74; and the bibliography listed in Szajkowski, pp. 18–19.

76. See Daladier's account of the measures he took in *Les Evénements*, I, 69.

77. Galtier-Boissière, pp. 149–51.

78. Pierre Nord, *Mes camarades sont morts* (Paris, 1947–49), II, 150.

79. Interview with Pierre Lafue.

80. Aragon, I, 244–45; IV, 273; VI, 96. See also Ehrenburg, IV, 257.

81. Ehrenburg, IV, 221, 256–58.

82. See Rossi, pp. 32, 160, 285, 295, 296, 311, 319, 327, 333, 334, 336.

83. Aragon, IV, 106, 163; VI, 91. Although the Communists accused Mandel of having arrested party members by the hundreds, Angelo Rossi has been able to find little evidence to substantiate the charge. See Rossi, p. 317n.

84. Lefranc, p. 32.

85. *Gringoire*, May 30, 1940.

86. Garçon, III, 306–16; Lefranc, pp. 32–33; also Daladier in *Les Evénements*, I, 68–69.

87. Un Témoin (Robert Lazurick), p. 17; Lazareff, *De Munich à Vichy*, p. 285. Lazurick's account has to be used with caution. He sometimes quotes "conversations" at which he was not present and which do not agree with the versions given by participants. He implies by his choice of a pseudonym that he was "a witness" of the incidents related. Yet he carries his narrative of events in France up to June 25, whereas by the twentieth he was already aboard the *Massilia* and on the twenty-fifth, was in Morocco.

88. On Mouton, see the testimony of Paul Winckler at Pétain's trial, *Le procès de Maréchal Pétain* (Paris, 1945), I, 313–14.

89. Coston, *Dans les coulisses*, p. 43.

90. Lesca, pp. 197–220.

91. See article on de Ludre in *Dictionnaire de la politique française*, published under the direction of Henry Coston (Paris, 1967), p. 652.

92. On the fate of the political prisoners, see Lesca, pp. 197–220; Louis Lecoin, *De prison en prison* (Paris, 1946); Léon Moussinac, *Le Radeau de la Méduse: journal d'un prisonnier politique, 1940–1941* (Paris, 1945).

93. See *Gringoire*, Nov. 21, 1940; Rebatet, p. 407; Coston, *Dans les coulisses*, p. 44; Xavier Vallat on the Vichy Radio, July 20, 1944, cited in *Le procès de Xavier Vallat* (Paris, 1948), p. 165. See also the macabre statement of Jean Galtier-Boissière about the guards who reportedly killed de Ludre:
"Worthy policemen, practitioners of the art of official murder, ... for the symbolism of this affair, it would have been fitting that the Nazis turned to you to carry out the execution of your former boss, Georges Mandel." "Histoire de la guerre, 1939–1945," *Crapouillot*, Nos. 1–5 (1948), p. 154.

94. *Je Suis Partout*, June 20, 1942. See also the article on de Ludre in *Dictionnaire de la politique française*, published under the direction of Henry Coston (Paris, 1967), p. 652, where Coston revises his earlier opinion. He says that it is impossible to accuse Mandel of responsibility for de Ludre's death, for no document has ever been found implicating him. Yet, Coston goes on to say, "it seems that the accusation, so often repeated between 1940–1944, was at the root (à l'origine)" of Mandel's own assassination. This is the first time that any connection, aside from Galtier-Boissière's symbolic one (see note above), has ever been made between Mandel's assassination and de Ludre's death. (For Mandel's assassination, see above, pp. 287–94.) Coston does not explain why he makes the connection, but he obviously believes that de Ludre's death had more important consequences than has generally been assumed, for in his article on Jean Zay (p. 1077), the former minister of Education, who was assassinated shortly before Mandel on June 20, 1944, Coston says: "That summary execution, really an assassination, is even more horrible because Jean Zay had no responsibility in the death of Count Thierry de Ludre.... He had never been minister of the Interior, and therefore could not have been the object of more or less justified [sic] reprisals by the *Cagoulards* imprisoned under the Third Republic."

95. Beer, p. 212.

96. Gurvitch, p. 553.

97. Brasillach, pp. 17–18; *Candide*, August 7, 1940; Saint-Paulien (Maurice Sicard), *Histoire de la collaboration* (Paris, 1964), p. 49.

98. Beer, pp. 213–14; Spears, II, 31.

99. *Candide*, Aug. 7, 1940.

100. Stibio, *Indiscrétions*, p. 84.

101. Spears, II, 29.

102. *Ibid.*, 42.

103. Interview with Chautemps in *Le Jour* (Montreal), Oct. 11, 1941, reprinted in Louis Gros, *La République toujours* (Avignon, 1945), p. 183.

104. DDI, 9th Series, IV, 52, report of conversation with Franco by Italian Ambassador Gambara to Ciano, April 13, 1940.

105. Langeron, pp. 10–11.

106. Ghilini, p. 131; also Montigny (*Le complot*, p. 148), who reports that one of Reynaud's ministers called Mandel "the brain of the team for whom Paul Reynaud is the speaker."

107. Wormser, *Mandel*, p. 261.

108. Reynaud's speech at the dedication of a monument to Mandel, July 7, 1948, printed in *Georges Mandel: Anniversaire, 1948*, pp. 4–5. See also Reynaud's statement in *La France a sauvé l'Europe* (Paris, 1947), II, 260n, where he speaks of "La parfaite communion de pensée qui existait entre Mandel et moi." In *Au coeur de la mêlée*, p. 702n, this is modified a bit: "Between Mandel and me there reigned, on this point as on so many others, a strict community of views." In *Les Evénements*, VIII, 2371,

Reynaud says: "I had complete confidence in Mandel." Yet in the latest version of his memoirs, after twenty years of reflection, Reynaud asserts that Mandel refused to accept the Interior in March 1940 because he believed that the government was bound to fail (*Mémoires*, II, 304). This is hardly an indication of reciprocal confidence or of "a perfect communion of thought."

109. Larmour, p. 241.

110. Stibio, *Indiscrétions*, pp. 125–28; on the differences between Reynaud and Mandel as "corridor" politicians, see also Debû-Bridel, p. 422.

111. *Les Evénements*, VIII, 2389.

112. Louis Marin, "Gouvernement et commandement: conflits, différends, immixtions qui ont pesé sur l'armistice de juin 1940," *Revue d'Histoire de la Deuxième Guerre Mondiale*, Oct. 1952, No. 8, pp. 6–7.

113. Zay, *Carnets secrets*, p. 88.

114. Bleustein-Blanchet, p. 193.

115. Reynaud, *Au coeur de la mêlée*, pp. 104–5. There are conflicting reports concerning Mandel's opinion of the nomination of Weygand. Reynaud states (*ibid.*, pp. 488–89) that Mandel was impressed with his fighting spirit, and Georges Wormser (*Mandel*, pp. 259–60) gives an account of a discussion in which Mandel justified the appointment. See also Spears, I, 204–5. By contrast, however, Roger Langeron (pp. 11–12) says Mandel was afraid that Weygand might turn out to be another Hindenburg.

116. The war cabinet was composed of the ministers directly concerned with the conduct of the war.

117. Reynaud, *Au coeur de la mêlée*, pp. 381, 705. For Baudoin's account of his appointment, see *The Private Diaries of Paul Baudoin* (London, 1948), pp. 1–7.

118. Lazareff, *Deadline*, p. 290; also Pertinax, p. 246; Bois, p. 295. In September 1939, a noted defeatist, Jean Mistler, president of the Foreign Affairs Committee of the Chamber, exclaimed: "We can hope for nothing so long as Léger remains in office." Laubreaux, p. 77.

119. For Reynaud's failure to consult his colleagues, see Chautemps, pp. 81, 91–92, 95, 122–23; Laurent-Eynac, minister of Aviation in Reynaud's cabinet, in *Les Evénements*, V, 1441; Alphonse Rio, minister of Merchant Marine, in Louis Noguères, p. 77.

120. Pertinax, p. 276; Lazareff, *Deadline*, p. 306; Bois, pp. 313–14; see also Mandel's earlier comments about Reynaud in de Monzie, pp. 60, 206.

121. Jean Fernet, *Aux côtés du Maréchal Pétain* (Paris, 1953) pp. 198–99.

122. Bois, p. 313; Mendès-France, p. 5.   123. Reynaud, *Mémoires*, II, 337–38.

124. Interview with Lamoureux.   125. *FRUS*, 1940, I, 92.

126. *FRUS*, 1940, I, 229, Bullitt to Hull, May 18, 1940.

127. Bleustein-Blanchet, pp. 195–96; also Bois, pp. 314–15; Révillon, pp. 20–23. Un Témoin, p. 11; Bührer, p. 148.

128. Chautemps first related this incident in his wartime *Lettre à Pertinax*, July 1943 (Typescript copy available in the Bibliothèque de Documentation Internationale Contemporaine). Reynaud called it a fantasy (*La France a sauvé l'Europe*, II, 242). Chautemps answers Reynaud and reprints the story in his *Cahiers secrets de l'armistice, 1939–1940* (Paris, 1963), pp. 100–104.

129. Baudoin, pp. 49–50; Reynaud, *Au coeur de la mêlée*, p. 687; Spears, II, 98–99.

130. Spears, I, 207.

131. Wormser, *Mandel*, p. 261.

132. *La France a sauvé l'Europe*, II, 179.

133. Bankwitz, "Maxime Weygand and the Fall of France," pp. 225–42. See also Bankwitz's longer study of the origins of civil-military discord, *Maxime Weygand and Civil-Military Relations in Modern France.*

134. Reynaud, *Mémoires,* II, 402.

135. Baudoin, pp. 105–6.

136. Noel, p. 241.

137. See Mandel's account of the incident as reported by Léon Blum in *L'Oeuvre,* V, 132–33.

138. Woodward, p. 62.

139. Reynaud, *Au coeur de la mêlée,* p. 779; testimony of Lebrun in *Les Evénements,* IV, 1008–9; Laurent-Eynac, V, 1451–52; Langeron, pp. 34–37. Weygand's own account, defending his good faith in presenting the report, is both confusing and unconvincing. See Weygand, pp. 161–62.

140. Spears, II, 223; also Reynaud, *La France a sauvé l'Europe,* II, 451.

141. Spears, II, 227–29.

142. Immediately after being imprisoned by the Vichy authorities in September 1940, Reynaud began to write a defense of his actions. An early version, a mixture of history and memoirs, circulated in manuscript copies. The first printed edition, *La France a sauvé l'Europe,* appeared in 1947 in two thick volumes. In 1953 a thoroughly revised edition appeared in one large volume under the title *Au coeur de la mêlée.* From 1960 to 1963 another revised edition appeared in two volumes under the curious title of *Mémoires.* Because of the number of corrections and additions he wanted to make, Reynaud's publishers refused to return the proofs of the 1953 edition to him. See Reynaud's testimony in *Les Evénements,* VIII, 2401. For an example of the type of analysis that must be applied to Reynaud's memoirs as well as to those of Weygand and others, see Pierre Dhers, "Le Comité de guerre du 25 mai 1940," *Revue d'Histoire de la Deuxième Guerre Mondiale,* June 1953, pp. 165–83.

143. Churchill, II, 179.

144. Alvarez del Vayo, p. 312; Kammerer, p. 33.

145. Introduction to Alexander Werth's *Twilight of France, 1933–1940* (London, 1942), pp. xvi–xvii. See also the comments of Lord Lloyd in Varenne, *Mon patron,* p. 188; Bois, p. 270; Torrès, *Campaign of Treachery,* p. 189; Anatole de Monzie in Gheusi, IV, 294; Kammerer, p. 192; Pol, p. 156; Lucien Galimand, *Vive Pétain, Vive de Gaulle* (Paris, 1948), p. 36.

146. Bois, p. 281.

147. Pertinax, p. 275.

148. Spears, II, 98. Also Alfred Duff Cooper, *Old Men Forget* (London, 1953), p. 275.

149. Unpublished notes of one of Mandel's associates who prefers to remain anonymous. Mandel told him: "You are aware of the hostility the President of the Republic has always shown me. In recent days especially, it was thought that the presence of an Israelite at the head of affairs in France would not facilitate matters, and would seem to be a provocation to Hitler."

150. Robert Vansittart, *The Mist Procession* (London, 1958), p. 210; de Saint Jean, p. 292; Beer, p. 212; W. Somerset Maugham, *Strictly Personal,* (New York, 1941), p. 212.

151. Spears, II, 230.

152. Robert Murphy, *Diplomat among Warriors* (New York, 1964), p. 37.

153. Louis-Jaray, p. 16. This book was undoubtedly seized by the censor. I have been

unable to find a copy of it in France, but one is available in the New York Public Library.

154. Torrès, *Pierre Laval*, pp. 181–82; see also Wormser, *Mandel*, pp. 221–24.

155. *FRUS*, 1940, I, 253, Biddle to Hull, June 14, 1940.

156. Spears, II, 245.

157. Baudoin, p. 113; Laurent-Eynac in *Les Evénements*, V, 1453–54.

158. Baudoin, pp. 57, 88; for Chautemps' defense, see his *Cahiers secrets*, 104n.

159. Georges Monnet in *Les Evénements*, V, 1425; Léon Blum, *L'Oeuvre*, V, 35–38.

160. Jules Moch, speech at the dedication of a monument to Mandel, July 7, 1948, in *Georges Mandel: Anniversaire 1948*, pp. 12–13; Blum, *L'Oeuvre*, V, 109.

161. Révillon, pp. 20–22.　　162. Spears, II, 271–73.

163. *Ibid.*, 260.　　164. Planes and Dufourg, p. 88.

165. Unpublished notes of one of Mandel's associates.

166. "Les carnets de L.-O. Frossard," *L'Aurore*, Feb. 16, 1949.

167. Léon Blum in *Le procès du Maréchal Pétain* (Paris, 1945), I, 234–35.

168. Léon Blum, speech at the dedication of a monument to Mandel, July 7, 1948 in *Georges Mandel: Anniversaire 1948*, p. 10.

169. Louis Lévy, pp. 154–55; Pertinax, p. 306; Kammerer, p. 192.

170. Planes and Dufourg, pp. 95–97.

171. *Ibid.*, p. 101. The conversation concerned the proposal for a political union of France and Great Britain.

172. *Ibid.*, p. 116.

173. *Ibid.*, pp. 94–95. Their account is based on information supplied by General Lafont.

174. *Ibid.*

175. Testimony of Christian Fouchet at the preliminary investigation before Weygand's trial, reproduced in Reynaud, *Mémoires*, II, 438–39. See also Kammerer, pp. 178–79.

176. *DGFP*, Series D, IX, pp. 507, 521, reports from Stohrer, Ambassador in Spain, to German Foreign Ministry, June 3, 5, 1940. See also General Bernard Serrigny, *Trente ans avec Pétain* (Paris, 1959), pp. 173–74; Henri Michel, *Vichy, année 40* (Paris, 1966), pp. 29, 33. Mandel suspected that Weygand's actions were politically motivated. See Chautemps, p. 107; also Noel, p. 236.

177. Bardoux, p. 363; Warner, pp. 170–72.

178. Cárcano, pp. 102–3. The author was the Ambassador from Argentina.

179. Noel, p. 243.

180. See Mandel's comments in Spears, II, 315.

181. Baudoin, p. 117; Marin in *Les Evénements,* IV, 1080; Reynaud, *Au coeur de la mêlée*, p. 833; Spears, II, 315–16; Frossard, *L'Aurore*, Feb. 9, 1949.

182. Reynaud, *Mémoires*, II, 432.

183. Blum and Marin in *Les Evénements*, I, 260; IV, 1080.

184. Spears, II, 301.

185. De Gaulle, I, 78; Spears, II, 297–98; report of Drexel Biddle in Langer, pp. 40–41.

186. Bankwitz, *Maxime Weygand and Civil-Military Relations in Modern France*, p. 304.

187. De Gaulle, I, 79.

188. Baudoin, p. 117.

189. Spears, II, 228; Duncan Grinnell-Milne, *The Triumph of Integrity: A Portrait*

of Charles de Gaulle (New York, 1962), p. 40; Le Provost de Launay, *Paroles Françaises,* June 27, 1947; Langer, p. 35. According to Jacques Benoist-Méchin, the antagonism between Madame de Portes and Mandel became so acute at Bordeaux that Reynaud's mistress was looking for some gunmen to assassinate Mandel. *Soixante jours qui ébranlèrent l'occident,* III, 450n. Unfortunately, Benoist-Méchin fails to give any reference for this statement.

190. De Gaulle, I, 70–71.
191. Noel, pp. 247–48.

Chapter 15
Epigraph: Georges Mandel in Noel, p. 247.
1. Wormser, *Mandel,* p. 265.
2. *FRUS,* 1940, II, 453; Gordon Wright, "Bullitt and the Fall of France," *World Politics,* Oct. 1957, pp. 85–86. Also Baudoin, p. 61; General P. A. Bourget, *De Beyrouth à Bordeaux* (Paris, 1946), pp. 58–59.
3. Spears, I, 207.
4. *Ibid.,* I, 205; Baudoin, p. 56; de Gaulle, I, 55; see also Bankwitz, pp. 318–19.
5. Planes and Dufourg, pp. 104–5.
6. Louis Rollin in *Les Evénements,* V, 1396; Bois, p. 384; Coblentz, pp. 219–20; Torrès, *Campaign of Treachery,* p. 206; Wormser, *Mandel,* p. 270.
7. Henri Becquart, *Au temps du silence; de Bordeaux à Vichy* (Paris, 1945), pp. 19–20.
8. "Une page d'histoire," *Sept Jours,* Nov. 24, 1940, p. 2.
9. Henri Amouroux, *Le 18 juin 1940* (Paris, 1964), p. 193. Amouroux's account seems to be based on information supplied by Charles Pomaret, Pétain's minister of the Interior.
10. Carlo Sforza, *L'Italie telle que je l'ai vue, 1914–1944* (Paris, 1946), p. 204.
11. Louis Rollin in *Les Evénements,* V, 1396–97.
12. Pierre Lazareff, "The Fall of France," *Life,* Aug. 26, 1940, p. 74.
13. Harry Greenwall, *Three Years of Hell* (London, 1943), p. 92.
14. The informer was the journalist Georges Roux of *Je Suis Partout.* According to Louis Rollin, Reynaud's minister of Colonies, the accusation was based on the distribution of rifles on the sixteenth to the Indochinese guards of the Ministry of Colonies. *Les Evénements,* V, 1397.
15. Bührer, pp. 196–98; Reynaud, *Au coeur de la mêlée,* pp. 967–68; Albert Lebrun, *Témoignage* (Paris, 1946), pp. 86–87; Révillon, pp. 54–57. For Lafont's part in the incident, see Planes and Dufourg, pp. 113–16.
16. Bonnet, *Le Quai d'Orsay,* p. 329.
17. Testimony of Madame Bretty in "Le procès du Général Noguès, I, 132. See also Bois, pp. 385, 391; Buré, *Clemenceau et Mandel,* p. 53; Pertinax, p. 309; André Stibio in *L'Ordre,* Feb. 7, 1945.
18. Spears, II, 314–17.
19. The Earl of Birkenhead, *Halifax: The Life of Lord Halifax* (London, 1965), p. 459. Birkenhead's account is based on Halifax's diary.
20. Unpublished notes of one of Mandel's associates.
21. Interview with Mandel's assistant Max Brusset. But according to Wormser (*Mandel,* p. 275), Mandel was firmly opposed to leaving for England. The accounts of two of Mandel's friends, one written shortly after the event and the other recounted to me

many years afterwards, indicate, however, that Mandel was anxious to get to England. Lord Lloyd's story seems to confirm this. Also see below, note 32.

22. Quoted in Langer, p. 51.

23. Daladier in *Les Evénements*, I, 79–80; also Gabriel Delattre, "Le journal de bord du *Massilia*," *L'Aurore*, Oct. 3, 1944.

24. Blum, *L'Oeuvre*, V, 43–47; Herriot, *Episodes*, p. 91.

25. Herriot, *Episodes*, pp. 96–97.

26. It is difficult to state precisely how many representatives were at Bordeaux in June 1940. The number of two hundred was first given by Jean Montigny (*Toute la vérité*, p. 24) and has been generally accepted. According to Senator Révillon, however, there were only thirty to thirty-five senators and seventy to eighty deputies. *Mes carnets*, 66n.

27. Barthe, p. 13.

28. Kammerer, p. 271.

29. Louis Marin in *Le procès du Maréchal Pétain*, I, 217–18; also Mendès-France, p. 39.

30. Bührer, p. 202.

31. Noel, p. 247.

32. Delattre in *L'Aurore*, Oct. 5, 1944. Wormser's account of Mandel's plans at this time disagrees with the reports of other observers. According to Wormser (*Mandel*, p. 273), Mandel had no intention of forming a government in North Africa. He expected that Parliament would meet in Algiers and make all the necessary decisions. Wormser adds that Duff Cooper and Lord Gort were sent to North Africa a few days later (see above, pp. 259–60) in order to coordinate military efforts, not to bring Mandel to England: "They knew he had decided to stay on French soil."

There are a number of problems with Wormser's account: 1) Louis Marin, Pierre Mendès-France and Gabriel Delattre all report that Mandel was anxious to get to North Africa even though it was probable that most members of Parliament would not be leaving; 2) According to Mandel's assistant Max Brusset, an associate who prefers to remain anonymous, and Lord Lloyd, Mandel was planning to leave for England; 3) According to British sources, the purpose of sending Duff Cooper and Gort to North Africa was to help Mandel form a resistance government, and failing that, to bring him to England. In order to accept Wormser's version, one would have to reject all of these other accounts. The discrepancy, I believe, is not one of fact, but of chronology. Wormser's account reflects Mandel's opinions on June 16–17. At first, he was opposed to leaving for England, and did not want to establish a rival government. But thereafter Mandel's views evolved rapidly. As a result of his own arrest on June 17, the pressure being exerted on many deputies by Laval and others, and the government's delay in departing, by June 18 Mandel seems to have been ready to leave for England and to lead a resistance government if necessary.

33. Weygand, pp. 186–87.

34. Montigny, *Toute la vérité*, pp. 26–27; see also Warner, pp. 180–84.

35. Bührer, pp. 198–99.

36. Kammerer, p. 270.

37. Delattre in *L'Aurore*, Oct. 5, 1944; see also Planes and Dufourg, pp. 183–202. Their account of the trip is based on Commander Ferbos' journal. Portions of his log had been published with distortions during the war; first, in an abbreviated version in *Le Matin*, Nov. 30, 1940, "Un carnet de bord accablant: Quand le *Massilia* vaguait vers la terre promise." The author was identified simply as "a passenger on the ship." A more complete though still distorted version was published in *Aujourd'hui*, July 2, 3,

4, 1941, under the title "L'Odyssée du *Massilia.*" This time the author was identified as "A witness whose position enabled him to observe all the details of the *Massilia* incident."

38. Daladier in *Le procès du Maréchal Pétain*, I, 126.

39. Mendès-France, p. 45.

40. Testimony of Noguès in "Le procès du Général Noguès," I, 45; testimony of Yvan Martin in *ibid.*, II, 38–42; J. Le Templier in *L'Ordre*, July 17, 1945. Le Templier and Martin were in the office when Mandel made the telephone calls to Noguès.

41. Truchet, p. 91.

42. Dillon, p. 139.

43. Duff Cooper, p. 282.

44. Dillon, p. 141; testimony of Noguès in "Le procès du Général Noguès," I, 46.

45. See Harcourt's notes in Planes and Dufourg, p. 197.

46. Duff Cooper, p. 283.

47. Order from Noguès to Admiral Harcourt, June 26, 1940. Photocopy in Planes and Dufourg, between pp. 196 and 197.

48. Noguès' report to the government at Bordeaux, June 26, 1940, in "Le procès du Général Noguès," VI, 10–12.

49. Testimony of Noguès in "Le procès du Général Noguès," I, 47–48, 51, 56.

50. On November 12, 1942, even though he himself at that moment was coming to terms with the Allied forces who had landed in North Africa, Noguès still refused to shake hands with General Giraud, who had earlier joined the Allies. "I don't talk to rebel generals," he exclaimed. He was finally brought to mutter an ungracious "Bonjour," to which he immediately added, however, "traitor." Albert Kammerer, *Du débarquement Africain au meurtre de Darlan* (Paris, 1949), p. 474.

51. Churchill, II, 220–21.

52. Bret, pp. 170–72.

53. Denis Saurat, *Watch Over Africa* (London, 1941), pp. 4–5.

54. Bret, pp. 172–76.

55. It was Léon Blum who called Mandel "the first resister." See Alexander Werth, *France 1940–1955* (New York, 1956), p. 134.

56. Emmanuel d'Astier de la Vigerie, *Les dieux et les hommes* (Paris, 1952), p. 37.

Chapter 16

Epigraph: Quoted in Joseph Caillaux, *Mes prisons* (Paris, 1921), p. 150.

1. Baudouin, p. 150.

2. See Laval's testimony in *Le procès du Maréchal Pétain*, I, 601; also Laval, p. 119. Concerning Mandel's arrest, Laval's friend and biographer, Alfred Mallet, says: "Laval had nothing to do with that affair, which was handled by other and higher authorities. At Casablanca Mandel told his lawyer Giovonni, who informed me of the statement: 'Pierre knows nothing of what they are doing to me.' " Mallet, I, 163n. The least of the many possible objections to this account is that Mandel never referred to anyone in this familiar manner.

3. In *Adrien Marquet devant la Haute Cour* (Paris, 1948), p. 162. Mandel's dislike of military leaders was well known. See Bührer, p. 57. During the First World War he used to refer to them as "les mutilés de cerveau." See Charles Braibant, *Un bourgeois sous trois républiques* (Paris, 1961), p. 308.

4. "Le procès du Général Noguès," I, 51, 74.

5. Blum, *L'Oeuvre,* V, 60.

6. Quoted in Maurice Ribet, *Le procès de Riom* (Paris, 1945), 291.

7. Blum, *L'Oeuvre,* V, 68.

8. Moulin de Labarthète, p. 35. According to the preliminary dossier for his trial after the war, Alibert was the most insistent in wanting to prosecute the *Massilia* passengers. See extract from the dossier at the Bibliothèque de Documentation Internationale Contemporaine (Q pièce 489 Rés.).

9. See Georges Loustaunau-Lacau's report to Pétain of his conversation with Laval in Louis Noguères, p. 633; also Wormser, *Mandel,* pp. 258–59.

10. Barthe, pp. 38, 42; André Le Troquer, *La parole est à André Le Troquer* (Paris, 1962), p. 29.

11. Delattre in *L'Aurore,* Oct. 6, 1944; Révillon, pp. 109–11.

12. Herriot, *Episodes,* pp. 142–45.

13. Quoted in "Le procès du Général Noguès," I, 53.

14. Colonel Loireau was the third judge to arrive at this conclusion. The first one, M. Goulleu, was dismissed when he stated there was no basis for trying Mandel. (Information supplied to American Embassy in France by one of Mandel's lawyers, Jan. 27, 1941. See State Department Document 851.00/2240.) The second, Major Joulin, refused to have Mandel arrested as the government wished, and merely issued an order for him to appear before the court. As a result, he too was dismissed. (Reynaud, *Au coeur de la mêlée,* pp. 1011-12.) The trial was transferred from Casablanca when someone remembered that any case in Morocco involving the external security of the state had to be tried before the Military Court at Meknes.

15. Some time later, Loireau received a great pile of documents from the Ministry of Colonies, most of which concerned "the distribution of propaganda funds for the purpose of increasing the consumption of colonial products, especially of bananas."

16. Deposition of Loireau in "Le procès du Général Noguès," V, 2–7.

17. Some of the telegrams, still in code, are reproduced in Planes and Dufourg, p. 196. These authors would have liked nothing better than to prove that Mandel had asked the British government to send representatives. Moreover, Planes had access to the government archives. Thus if the telegrams had been deciphered, he would almost certainly have published the messages.

18. Noguès' letters to Ministry of War, July 29 and Sept. 5, 1940, in "Le procès du Général Noguès," VI, 13–14.

19. Constitutional Act Number 5 as implemented by decree of Aug. 1, 1940.

20. Moulin de Labarthète, p. 370.

21. *FRUS,* 1940, II, 378–79, Murphy to Hull, July 29, 1940.

22. Charpentier, p. 136.

23. Bruckberger, p. 25.

24. Weil-Curiel, II, 99–100.

25. Barlone, p. 95.

26. Bruckberger, p. 25.

27. General Bernard Serrigny, *Trente ans avec Pétain* (Paris, 1959), p. 187.

28. For *L'Humanité,* see Rossi, *Les communistes,* pp. 333–34. For this period I consulted three national dailies, *Le Matin* (published in Paris), *Le Petit Parisien* and *Le Temps* (published in the unoccupied zone); two national weeklies from the unoccupied zone, *Candide* and *Gringoire*; and two local weeklies from Mandel's constituency, *L'Echo du Médoc* and *Le Journal du Médoc.*

29. *The New York Times,* July 24, 1940.

30. *Le Petit Parisien,* July 25, 28, 29; Aug. 4, 5, 1940. Morice's servility is particularly

striking because before the war under the editorial direction of Mandel's friend Elie-Joseph Bois and of Morice himself, *Le Petit Parisien* was considered to be a leading *belliciste* journal.

31. *Le Temps*, July 28, 1940; *Candide*, July 31; *Gringoire*, Aug. 1; Marcel Déat in *L'Oeuvre*, July 26; see also J. C. (Jacques Chastenet) in *Le Temps*, Oct. 17, 1940.

32. *The New York Times*, July 27, 1940.

33. *Le Journal du Médoc*, July 27, 1940; *Le Petit Parisien*, July 25; *Candide*, July 21; *Gringoire*, Aug. 8; *L'Oeuvre*, July 26, 1940.

34. *Le Temps*, Aug. 16, 1940.

35. *Le Journal du Médoc*, Aug. 24, 1940.

36. The story was reprinted in the following journals: *Le Journal du Médoc*, Aug. 24, 1940; *Le Petit Parisien*, Aug. 16, 1940; *L'Illustration*, Aug. 24, 1940, p. 13; and in Charles Maurras, *La seule France* (n.p., 1941), pp. 310-13. It was elaborated on in the anonymous book, *Dans les coulisses des ministères et de l'état-major, 1930-1940* (Paris, 1943), pp. 412-36, where the exact wording of Mandel's purported message was given: "In accord with our British allies, and in this hour of national distress, I have assumed power. The colonial army and the French fleet will continue the war until victory." The account has been accepted by Beau de Loménie, *La mort de la troisième république*, p. 346; Maurice Martin du Gard, *La carte impériale: histoire de la France outremer, 1940-1945* (Paris, 1949), pp. 19-20; Churchill, II, 219; Planes and Dufourg, p. 197; Benoist-Méchin, II, 489; Bonnefous, VII, 256-57; Chastenet, VII, 248. The only one to treat the account with the proper degree of skepticism is Albert Kammerer, p. 343.

37. Le Juge d'Instruction Militaire au Tribunal Militaire de Meknès, Ordonnance de non-lieu, 7 septembre 1940. I am indebted to one of Mandel's associates, who preferred to remain anonymous, for permitting me to see a copy of the Ordonnance.

38. *The New York Times*, October 4, 1940.

39. Mandel later informed Reynaud that Loireau had been instructed to issue a death sentence. Reynaud, *Au coeur de la mêlée*, p. 1012.

40. Moulin de Labarthète, p. 379.

41. *Les Evénements*, IX, 2834.

42. *Le Temps*, Oct. 20, 1940; Nov. 19, 1940; also Soupiron, pp. 41-42.

43. Soupiron, p. 41. The suspicions of the Vichy authorities were also aroused when several bars of gold bearing the stamp of the Bank of England were found in Mandel's luggage from the *Massilia*. Their hopes of discrediting Mandel, however, were destroyed by Georges Wormser, who had sold the bars to him and was able to provide receipts for the transaction. Wormser, *Mandel*, pp. 282-84.

44. Soupiron, p. 41.

45. See the account of Mandel's imprisonment in an eight-page pamphlet entitled *Documents officiels sur l'assassinat de M. Georges Mandel par le Gouvernement de Vichy*. The pamphlet was published by a Resistance group, "Tout pour la patrie," founded in the Gironde in June 1940. The Committee, which named Mandel honorary president, was headed by Emmanuel Barbe, who visited him a number of times in prison.

46. Varenne, *Mon patron*, p. 206; also Aron, *Histoire de Vichy*, p. 396; Harold Nicolson, *Diaries and Letters, 1939-1945* (London, 1967), p. 294.

47. Groussard, pp. 254-55. Groussard was imprisoned with Mandel and Reynaud. He reports that during the liberation Courrier was in fact executed by members of the Resistance movement.

48. Reynaud, *Au coeur de la mêlée*, p. 1011.

49. Undated (*ca.* Jan. 1941) draft copy of a letter from Mandel to Churchill.

50. Report of Mandel's lawyer to American Embassy at Vichy, Jan. 27, 1941. State Department Document 851.00/2240.

51. Report from the Security Police in Berlin to the German Foreign Office, Feb. 5, 1941. See Document CXXVIIa-49 at the CDJC.

52. Report from head of the German Security Police in France, Feb. 11, 1941. See Document LXXV-251, p. 10 in CDJC.

53. Moulin de Labarthète, p. 372.

54. Vallat's letter to Obersturmführer Dannecker, Aug. 1, 1941, printed in Léon Poliakov, *Le IIIe Reich et les Juifs* (Paris, 1959), p. 317.

55. G. Saint-Bonnet, *Vichy capitale: ce que j'ai vu et entendu* (Paris, 1941), pp. 49–50. Suspension points in original.

56. *Au Pilori*, Aug. 30, 1940; Jan. 3, 1941; see also his books *Les sangsues de Marianne; nos parlementaires* (Paris, 1944), p. 153; *Qu'était le juif avant la guerre? Tout. Que doit-il être? Rien.* (Paris, 1942), pp. 105–8.

57. See Henriot's article in *Gringoire*, June 5, 1942, and his book *Comment mourut la paix*, pp. 1–2. Also the articles in *Gringoire*, Aug. 1, 1940; Jan. 2, 23, 1941; Jan. 2, June 5, Aug. 7, Oct. 2, 1942.

58. *L'Atelier*, Dec. 7, 28, 1940; also Jan. 11, Feb. 8, May 10, July 26, Aug. 2, 1941.

59. *Je Suis Partout*, April 18, 1942.

60. Quoted in *Gringoire*, June 6, 1941. See also the statement of the Academician Abel Bonnard: "Contrary to what one might believe, Mandel still reigns in the heads of many who condemn him in their hearts, and when I say Mandel I am only choosing as a symbol that obscene little devil of political life, who has become the frightful Satan of the catastrophe." Quoted in *Cahiers de la Résistance*, No. 3, *La Presse dite "acquitée"* (Paris, 1950), p. 21n.

61. *Je Suis Partout*, Feb. 21, 1942.

62. *Le Cri du Peuple*, April 29, 1942 and June 25, 26, 1942; also *The New York Times*, Aug. 27, 1942.

63. *Gringoire*, May 9, 1941; also *Je Suis Partout*, Sept. 13, 20, 1941.

64. *Candide*, July 31, 1940; *Je Suis Partout*, May 19, 1941; *The New York Times*, Oct. 4, 1940; Ghilini, *A la barre de Riom*, p. 158; "Another Traitor," *The Living Age*, Nov. 1940, pp. 238–40 (article reprinted from the *Basle National-zeitung*).

65. Hermann Hönig, *So starb die Dritte Republik* (Berlin, 1942), p. 47; also "Jüdische Bildnisse," *Der Weltkampf*, March 1939, pp. 97–106; Heinz Ballensiefen, "Frankreichs Schuld," *Zeitschrift für Politik*, June–July 1940, p. 280.

66. Reynaud, *Au coeur de la mêlée*, p. 1020. During the war Mandel and Blum had been special targets of Nazi radio propaganda. See Ernst Kris and Hans Speier, *German Radio Propaganda* (London, 1944), pp. 220, 251.

67. Langeron, p. 82.

68. See report dated Oct. 13, 1940 from Neubert, Secret Police Secretary acting as liaison agent with Rosenberg's Einsatzstab (Document LXXXIX-9 in CDJC); quarterly report for period Jan. 1–March 31, 1943 from Manuscript Section of Rosenberg's staff (Document CXLI-149 in CDJC); report of Dr. Wunder, head of the analysis section of Rosenberg's staff, July 22, 1943 (Document CXLI-152 in CDJC). Most of Mandel's papers were lost during the battle for Germany in 1945. The official French commission for locating seized property found only a few bits and pieces of no value, which were returned to Madame Bretty. The last reference in German documents to Mandel's books and papers is contained in a report dated August 21, 1944 from Dora

Salamon of Rosenberg's staff at Ratibor in Silesia (now Raciborz in Poland), where the papers known as the "Westakten" were sent. Salamon reported that the papers, which had been gone over a number of times, no longer contained much of any use. "The remaining papers of Georges Mandel," she said, "consist of letters, reports and documents of a military and political nature (not from him). . . ." Document CXL-14 in CDJC.

69. Reynaud explains that neither he nor Mandel was responsible for the formation of these territorial guards, which were in any case regular military units. Reynaud, *Au coeur de la mêlée,* pp. 983–85.

70. *DGFP,* Series D, XII, 244–45; telegram from Abetz to Ribbentrop, March 8, 1941. Also in Reynaud, *Au coeur de la mêlée,* p. 987.

71. *DGFP,* Series D, XII, 245n; telegram from Ribbentrop to Abetz, March 9, 1941.

72. *DGFP,* Series D, XIII, 26–27; telegram Number 1909 from Rudolf Schleier, Counselor at the German Embassy in Paris, to Ribbentrop, June 26, 1941.

73. *DGFP,* Series D, XIII, 88–89; telegram from Ribbentrop to German Embassy, July 5, 1941 (emphasis added). In the first edition of his memoirs, Reynaud translated the key passage: "Nous sommes également disposés à renoncer à ce que Reynaud et Mandel . . . nous soient livrês *ainsi que nous le propose Darlan.*" ("We are also willing to give up the extradition of Reynaud and Mandel . . . as Darlan proposed to us.") *La France a sauvé l'Europe,* II, 9. In the second edition, in an irenic spirit, Reynaud changed the translation because "the translation of this passage, while literally exact, could be interpreted as meaning that Darlan had consented to the extradition, when the text meant to say the contrary." As re-translated the passage reads: "Désireux, d'autre part, d'acquiescer au voeu que nous a exprimé Darlan, nous sommes également disposés à nous désister *de notre demande* tendant à l'extradition de Reynaud et Mandel . . . ." ("Wanting, moreover, to agree to Darlan's request, we are also willing to give up *our demand* for the extradition of Reynaud and Mandel. . . .") *Au coeur de la mêlée,* pp. 987–88.

Reynaud seems unaware of Schleier's report of June 26 to which Ribbentrop's telegram is a direct reply. Read in conjunction with this report, the first translation, which accords better with the English translation in Series D, Volume XIII of the *DGFP,* seems to be the correct one. Schleier clearly states that Darlan offered to turn the two ministers over to the Germans.

74. *DGFP,* Series D, XIII, 88–89; telegram from Ribbentrop to German Embassy, July 5, 1941.

75. Telegrams from Abetz to Ribbentrop, Aug. 8, 18, 1941, in Reynaud, *Au coeur de la mêlée,* p. 989. A vain search was made through French archives for documents incriminating Mandel and Reynaud. As a consolation prize, Vichy offered to supply the Germans with documents concerning former Ambassador Bullitt. Letter of Dec. 22, 1941 from Dr. Albrecht of the Ministry of Foreign Affairs. Document CXXVa-19 in CDJC.

76. Reynaud, *Au coeur de la mêlée,* p. 1023n.

77. Paul Reynaud, *In the Thick of the Fight* (New York, 1955), pp. 632–33. These passages concerning the decision of the Council of Political Justice do not seem to be in any of the French editions of Reynaud's memoirs. See also Louis Noguères, pp. 336–42.

78. Soupiron, pp. 50–51.

79. Telegrams from Abetz to Ribbentrop, Oct. 17, 31, 1941, in Reynaud, *Au coeur de la mêlée,* pp. 990–91. To the Germans, Pétain's condemnation of Mandel and Reynaud

to an indefinite term at Portalet for indefinite reasons was obviously not enough. They continued to press for a formal condemnation to life imprisonment. See note of Dec. 9, 1941 from Abetz to Brinon in Louis Noguères, pp. 348–49.

80. Letter from Ministry of Foreign Affairs to German Army Commander, Dec. 22, 1941. Document Number CXXVa-19 in CDJC.

81. Pétain, *Quatre années au pouvoir*, pp. 20–21.

Chapter 17

1. Groussard, p. 283.

2. *France-Amérique* (New York), July 1, 1945. The draft copy of the letter was found on Mandel's body after his assassination.

3. Letter dated August 16, 1945, in Isorni, *C'est un péché*, p. 31. On conditions at Portalet, see also Isorni, *Souffrance et mort,* pp. 167–69; Reynaud, *Au coeur de la mêlée,* pp. 1035–37; Blum, *L'Oeuvre,* V, 201.

4. Account given to Geneviève Tabouis by Madame Bretty. In *La Victoire* (New York), Nov. 11, 1945; Aron, "L'Assassinat de Georges Mandel," p. 74.

5. Letter dated June 30, 1942.

6. Letter dated May 14, 1942.

7. Michel Clemenceau's testimony at trial of Fernand de Brinon, in *Les procès de collaboration*, p. 172; interview with Michel Clemenceau.

8. *Je Suis Partout*, Feb. 21, 1942.

9. Testimony of Michel Clemenceau in *Le procès du Maréchal Pétain*, I, 277; see also Reynaud, *Au coeur de la mêlée*, pp. 1035–37.

10. Léon Boussard, "Relations between Pierre Laval and Maréchal Pétain: De Gaulle and Mandel," *FDGO*, III, 1529.

11. Mallet, II, 276.

12. Paul Lévy, *Journal d'un exilé* (Paris, 1949), p. 118.

13. Eugène Frot, "Abetz—Georges Mandel," *FDGO*, III, 1430–31.

14. Kérillis, *I Accuse de Gaulle*, pp. 35–39. In 1949, when de Gaulle was scheduled to speak at the dedication of a monument to Mandel in Lesparre, Madame Bretty wrote to the Deputy Emile Liquard, who had arranged the ceremony: "You are disturbing the dead to make of his tomb a political springboard.... I am astonished that General de Gaulle is associated with your plans—a man who did not feel obliged to bring from England the necessary aid for Georges Mandel's escape; a man who since his return to France has never under any circumstances spoken the name of this martyr of the Republic; who never on any occasion felt it his duty to pay his respects at his tomb; who never in any fashion has interested himself in his orphan child of fourteen; in short, a man who, by his persistence in this attitude, has clearly shown a total indifference both to the life and to the memory of Georges Mandel. Besides, did he [de Gaulle] not declare in Algiers that he was not working to whiten sepulchres? Well, truly here is one that has no need of it." *Les Nouvelles de Bordeaux et du Sud Ouest*, Sept. 23, 1949. This local newspaper was the only one to print the letter in full, but a copy of it is in the archives of *Le Monde*.

15. Interview with Pierre Lafue.

16. Interview with Besselère published in *Le Populaire*, Sept. 16, 1944. See also the statement of Eugène Frot in *FDGO*, III, 1430–31. In reply to Frot's question why he did not escape, Mandel replied: "It isn't necessary and it wouldn't be of any use."

17. Reynaud, *Au coeur de la mêlée*, p. 499n.

18. Mandel was probably also in communication with the British through one of his lawyers, Goëau-Brissonière, who was a member of the Resistance and in contact with British Intelligence. See Bleustein-Blanchet, p. 215.

19. Roques was killed in February 1943 while trying to return to England. On his activities as liaison agent between the Free French in London, Mandel, and other political figures in France, see Colonel Passy (Charles A. Dewavrin), *Souvenirs* (Monte Carlo, 1947), II, 267, 318–19; André Stibio in *L'Ordre*, Feb. 7, 1945; and articles by Alain Armengaud, Demos and S. Nacht, "Nos camarades morts pour la libération: Philippe Roques," *La France Intérieure*, March 15, 1945.

20. Letter dated August 20, 1942 in Charles de Gaulle, *War Memoirs, Unity, 1942–1944. Documents* (London, 1959), pp. 40–41. Strangely enough, de Gaulle never attempted to communicate with Reynaud. See interview with Reynaud in Louis Guitard, *Lettre sans malice à François Mauriac* (Paris, 1966), pp. 296–97.

21. Wormser, *Mandel*, pp. 281–82.

22. Groussard, pp. 319–21.

23. Interviews with Varenne and Pierre Lafue.

24. Paul Reynaud, "Churchill and France," in Charles Eade, ed., *Churchill by his Contemporaries* (London, 1953), p. 323.

25. Reynaud, *Au coeur de la mêlée*, pp. 1037–38.

26. Louis Noguères, pp. 342–43.

27. Information revealed in the Acte d'accusation in "Le procès de Karl Oberg et de Helmut Knochen." A typescript of this trial can be found in the CDJC in Paris.

28. Jacques Crozat, "Une année au Portalet avec les cinq prisonniers de Vichy," *Le Figaro Littéraire*, Oct. 12, 1957.

29. Note written on margin of Mandel's telegram. See Louis Noguères, pp. 342–43. On Laniel's visit, see the account of André Thoumieux, in *FDGO*, III, 1343–44.

30. Reynaud, *Au coeur de la mêlée*, pp. 1038–39.

31. Jean Leguay, "Jewish Affairs; The German Invasion of the Free Zone; Reynaud and Mandel," *FDGO*, III, 1158–59.

32. Charpentier, p. 194. The Germans also took Raymond Amar and Baba Diallo who were deported to Germany and died in a concentration camp.

33. Reynaud, *Au coeur de la mêlée*, pp. 1042–43.

34. See Mandel's "Carnets de captivité," in *L'Ordre*, Feb. 21–March 4, 1945. The "Carnets," which were found on his body after his death, consisted of a small memo book and notes written on the margins of newspapers or on odd bits of paper. These "memoirs" were edited by Mandel's friend, André Stibio, who says that he omitted many political passages referring to other Frenchmen. See Stibio's introduction in *L'Ordre*, Feb. 21, 1945.

35. Letters of April 5, July 29, Aug. 17, Sept. 14, 17, 20, 27, Oct. 5, Dec. 6, 17, 22, 27, 1942; Jan. 3, 21, Feb. 1, April 1, 1944. I am indebted to one of Mandel's associates for allowing me to see these letters.

36. Brinon was another of Mandel's acquaintances who had already done what he could in a minor way to help him. Mandel had known Brinon at least since 1918, when he had him appointed to Clemenceau's staff in the War Department. See Brinon's testimony in *Les procès de collaboration*, p. 178. On Brinon's aid to Mandel, see *ibid.*, p. 198, and Brinon, p. 231.

37. Letter of Sept. 27, 1943.

38. "Carnets de captivité."

39. Bardoux, *La délivrance de Paris*, p. 111.

40. Léon Blum in *Georges Mandel: Anniversaire 1948*, p. 8.

41. Letter dated December 12, 1943.

42. In *Georges Mandel: Anniversaire 1948*, p. 8.

43. "Carnets de captivité."   44. *Ibid.*

45. Letter dated Dec. 6, 1943.   46. "Carnets de captivité."

47. Telegram from Abetz to Ribbentrop, May 13, 1944. Document CXXV-99 in CDJC; printed in Baraduc, pp. 220–22. See also Reynaud, *Au coeur de la mêlée*, pp. 992–97.

48. Telegram from Hilger, Ribbentrop's SS assistant, to Abetz, May 30, 1944. Document CXXV-97 in CDJC; printed in Baraduc, p. 222.

49. Abetz, *Histoire d'une politique*, p. 354; Laval, pp. 117–18.

50. On the North African trials, see Robert Aron, *Histoire de l'épuration* (Paris, 1967), I, 239–70. Aron does not mention the fact that reprieves were granted to Derrien and Magnien in order to avoid reprisals against Mandel, Reynaud, and Blum.

51. Blum, *L'Oeuvre*, V, 518.

52. *Ibid.*; see also Blum's speech in *Georges Mandel: Anniversaire 1948*, p. 9.

53. For obvious reasons, Abetz claims to have been kept in ignorance of Mandel's arrival. In an attempt to dissociate himself completely from the assassination, Abetz asserted at his trial after the war that Mandel had not been brought back in accordance with his plan— to be shot in reprisal for the execution of Colonel Magnien—but at the instigation of General Oberg, head of the German security police in France. See account of his trial in *The Times* (London), July 18, 1949. (There is no full account of Abetz's trial available. Selected passages were printed in Abetz, *D'Une prison*, and only brief résumés were published in *Le Monde*.)

The fact that only one hostage was returned seems to confirm Abetz's story, because according to his plan, all three prisoners were to be handed over to the Vichy government. His explanation also accords with the statement of one of Mandel's biographers that the former minister had been brought to France at the request of the Milice, who wanted to murder him in revenge for the assassination of Philippe Henriot. See Coblentz, p. 237. If the Milice were responsible for Mandel's return to France, it may be that their choice of him as a hostage, rather than Blum or Reynaud, was not entirely arbitrary. Since Mandel was a former colleague and associate of Henriot in the Gironde, his death may have had a symbolic significance for the Milice not possessed by the death either of Blum, who was also a Jew, or of Reynaud, who had also been one of the leading advocates of war against Germany.

Although no one else has ever suggested the connection, it is also possible, as Henry Coston has recently said (*Dictionnaire de la politique française* [Paris, 1967], p. 652), that Mandel was assassinated in retaliation for the death of Comte Armand Thierry de Ludre in 1940. See note 94 to chapter 14 above.

54. Deposition of Darnand referred to by the judge, M. Bouëssel-Dubourg, in "Le procès de Karl Oberg et de Helmut Knochen," Sept. 25, 1954. See, however, Darnand's statement in Delperrie de Bayac, pp. 506–7, where it appears that the conversation with Knochen took place before Mandel's arrival in Paris.

55. This is the conclusion of Prosecutor Flicoteaux in the Acte d'accusation in "Le procès de Karl Oberg et de Helmut Knochen." It is based in part on a message from Knipping to Darnand's *chef de cabinet* at Vichy after Mandel's assassination (see above, p. 293).

56. Testimony of Oberg at his trial, Sept. 25, 1954. Knipping states that he was unable to get in touch with Vichy (see Delperrie de Bayac, p. 508; also Brissaud, p. 434), but

it seems improbable that Knipping was unable to put a call through to Darnand or some other member of the Vichy government for a period of two or three days. Either Knipping received the approval of his superiors at Vichy, or he was carrying out a plan he had formulated with the Germans.

57. "Ministère public c/MM. Boéro, Néroni et Lambert," pp. 5–7. See also Taittinger, p. 287. Knipping, however, states that it was the Germans alone who delivered Mandel to La Santé. He says that he only agreed to take Mandel to the Château des Brosses because Baillet did not like having so eminent a prisoner and was afraid Mandel might escape. See Delperrie de Bayac, pp. 508–9.

58. Coblentz, p. 238.

59. "Ministère public c/MM. Boéro, Néroni et Lambert," p. 61.

60. *Ibid.*, pp. 10–11.

61. Interview with Besselère in *Le Populaire*, Sept. 16, 1944.

62. He reportedly left La Santé with two suitcases, but only one was brought with his body to Versailles. See *La France Intérieure*, Aug. 15, 1944, p. 26, and Bardoux, *La délivrance de Paris*, p. 312. Colonel Groussard (pp. 262–63) speculates that the missing suitcase might have contained the account of French history from 1914 to 1940 that Mandel was supposedly writing in Vals in 1941. No one else has ever mentioned this history.

63. Laval, pp. 117–19.

64. Laval claims to have learned of Mandel's arrival only after the assassination. See Laval, pp. 117–18 and his testimony in *Le procès du Maréchal Pétain*, I, 600–601. His assertion is borne out by the overwhelming testimony of all of his assistants and colleagues who describe his surprise at learning that Mandel had been brought back to France, turned over to the Milice and assassinated. See the accounts in *FDGO* by Amedée Bussière, I, 556–57; Marcel Guillaume, III, 1086; Maurice Renard, III, 1056; Roland Lapeyronnie, III, 1090–91; André Guenier, III, 1260–61; Louis-Dominique Girard, III, 1531; Paul Marion, III, 1549. Also Walter Stucki, *Von Pétain zur vierten Republik* (Berne, 1947), p. 45.

According to one of Mandel's former assistants, however, Laval had been informed of his arrival in Paris and had refused to accept responsibility for him. Instead, he told the German authorities: "The French government has rejected the proposition of the German government concerning the imprisoned French political leaders. Mandel, therefore, must be returned to the authorities who brought him to Paris. If, however, these French authorities do not want to take him back, he should be taken to the Château des Brosses near Vichy in order to be interned." Varenne, *Mon patron,* pp. 213–14. Unfortunately, no source is given for this account, but if true it would explain the delay in Paris while the Germans decided what to do and would also explain why Knochen contacted the Milice. On this point, see also Delperrie de Bayac, p. 510, who places Laval's refusal to accept Mandel a day or two before Mandel's arrival in Paris. He makes no mention of an order to take Mandel to the Château des Brosses. According to Delperrie de Bayac, Laval was playing Pontius Pilate, refusing to assume responsibility for Mandel's death, but refusing as well the opportunity to get Mandel back into French hands and assure his protection. Laval was simply attempting to establish his own innocence in case Mandel were assassinated.

65. Brinon, p. 233; also Tracou, p. 323.   66. *Je Suis Partout*, July 21, 1944.

67. Tracou, p. 331.   68. Taittinger, p. 287.

69. "Le Ministère public c/MM. Boéro, Néroni et Lambert."

70. Aron, *France Reborn*, p. 295.

71. Brissaud, p. 437. The prosecution at the trial of Boéro, Néroni and Lambert affirmed that Mansuy was definitely dead ("Le Ministère public c/MM. Boéro, Néroni et Lambert, p. 65).

72. Letter to the author from the Secretary General, La Cour d'Appel de Paris, Jan. 28, 1961 (signature illegible).

73. *Ibid.* See the brief reports in *Le Monde*, Feb. 2, 3, 4, 1947. It would seem to have been a common practice at the time not to have official stenographic reports, even when a man was on trial for his life. There is no official stenographic report, for instance, of the trial of Pierre Pucheu in Algiers in 1944. See General Schmitt, *Toute la verité sur le procès Pucheu* (Paris, 1963), p. 15. For Knipping's trial, however, there must have been some unofficial record, for André Brissaud (*Pétain à Sigmaringen, 1944–1945* [Paris, 1966], p. 565) cites a stenographic account of the trial in his bibliography. In 1961 I wrote to Maître Floriot, Knipping's lawyer, and more recently to André Brissaud for further information about a trial record, but have received no reply.

74. Brissaud, p. 437.

75. Testimony of a witness named Vernoux, quoted by Prosecutor Flicoteaux in "Le procès de Karl Oberg et de Helmut Knochen," Oct. 5, 1954.

76. *Les procès de collaboration*, p. 268.

77. *Ibid.*, p. 303.

78. See above, p. 288.

79. Testimony referred to by Maître Catrice, Oberg's defense attorney, in "Le procès de Karl Oberg et de Helmut Knochen," October 8, 1954.

80. *Ibid.* Maître Catrice, of course, was trying to prove that Oberg and Knochen had nothing to do with Mandel's murder. For Abetz's discussion of the proposal with Darnand, see his telegram to Ribbentrop, May 13, 1944, Document CXXV-99 in CDJC, printed in Baraduc, pp. 220–22. One other indication of Darnand's complicity is contained in a curious document at the CDJC (Document CCXXI-63), which seems to be a report from the rabbis of the Fédération des Sociétés Juives de France. According to this report, Darnand presided over a meeting of the Milice in Paris on July 5 in which it was decided to ask the Germans to return Mandel, who was to be executed in reprisal for the assassination of Henriot. The report also states that "Vichy, after vigorous refusals, finally accepted after it received the following order from the Gestapo:

'By order of the German government, the Jew Mandel will be turned over to the police of Marshal Pétain on July 9 . . . so that they can deliver him to the Milice, who, in accord with the occupying authorities, will begin the trial of Mandel, and fix personal responsibility for the murder of Philippe Henriot.' "

This report, however, raises more questions than it solves: (1) on July 5, Mandel was already in Paris; (2) there is no indication that Darnand was in the capital on that date; (3) no documents have ever been found confirming the request of the Milice or the order from the Gestapo. Thus, the report may simply reflect the beliefs of many people at the time, or it may be based on information not yet confirmed in other sources.

81. Abetz, *D'Une prison*, pp. 297–300. This was a rather ticklish argument for Floriot to use, for two years earlier he had defended Max Knipping of the Milice against the same charge. Unfortunately, the exact line of his defense in that trial was not revealed in the skimpy newspaper reports. In any case, in Abetz's trial, Floriot's argument was based in part on a statement by Fernand de Brinon, which he quotes: "For Abetz, turning Mandel over [to the Milice] was an order from Himmler, transmitted by

Oberg—a measure taken in reprisal for the assassination of Philippe Henriot. . . ." According to Oberg's lawyer, Maître Catrice, however, Abetz stated that "if some Germans played a part in the assassination of Georges Mandel, Oberg and Knochen certainly knew nothing about it." See "Le procès de Karl Oberg et de Helmut Knochen," Oct. 8, 1954.

82. Abetz, *Histoire d'une politique*, pp. 353–54.

83. *Le Monde*, July 24–25, 1949.

84. Quoted in *ibid.*, July 24–25, 1949.

85. *Ibid.*, July 23, 1949.

86. *Ibid.*, Feb. 25, Sept. 12–13, 1954; also *L'Humanité*, March 1–11, 1954.

87. See the Acte d'accusation in "Le procès de Karl Oberg et de Helmut Knochen." The failure to find any documents in the German files directly concerned with Mandel's assassination may mean only that the order was given verbally. In her study of the Nazi movement, Hannah Arendt quotes from a party report which stated that ". . . the active National Socialist molded in the prepower struggle takes it for granted that actions in which the party does not wish to appear in the role of organizer are not ordered with unequivocal clarity and down to the last detail. Hence he is accustomed to understand that an order may mean more than its verbal content, just as it has more or less become routine with the order giver, in the interests of the party . . . not to say everything and only to intimate what he wants to achieve by the order. . . ." *The Origins of Totalitarianism* (New York, Meridian Books, 1958), p. 399n.

88. See Jacques Delarue, *Histoire de la Gestapo* (Paris, 1962), pp. 258–317, 371–421.

89. *Le Monde*, April 23, 25, 1958.

90. At Knochen's trial, Paul Reynaud was asked to reveal what he knew about the death of Mandel. Reynaud said: "Mr. President, I was in Germany at that time. What I know is what I've learned since. I could not give the precise sources, perhaps, because all that is a little vague in my mind, and many things have happened, but the account that was given me is very clear in my memory." Reynaud then went on to reveal what he had later learned from other people about Mandel's death.

Not only was hearsay evidence admitted in these trials, but frequently important documents were not introduced into the trial record itself, but were merely cited or referred to by the prosecuting and defense attorneys. Because these statements are taken out of context, there is no way of determining the weight to be given to them.

Another unfortunate feature of these trials was the evident bias of the judges. Oberg's trial had to be postponed from February to September 1954, because the presiding judge called the Gestapo leader "a war criminal." See *Le Monde*, Feb. 26, 1954. During Abetz's trial, when his defense attorney referred to the "murder" of Philippe Henriot, a judge interrupted him: "We call the murder of Philippe Henriot an execution." See *Le Monde*, July 19, 1949.

91. Brissaud, pp. 436–38.

92. Delperrie de Bayac, p. 514.

93. *Ibid.*, p. 505.

94. *Ibid.*, pp. 513–14 and Abetz, *D'Une prison*, pp. 299–300.

95. Marius Sarraz-Bournet, *Témoignage d'un silencieux* (Paris, 1948), p. 194; see also the account of Abetz's testimony at his trial in *The Times* (London), July 18, 1949.

96. Mallet, II, 323.

97. Laval, p. 119.

98. In Louis Noguères, pp. 344–45.

Chapter 18

1. The latter was a permanent feature of his thought. As early as 1911 he had condemned "the wretched practice of blaming the institutions for the faults of the men in office who should provide direction for the state." See *Le Journal du Var*, Feb. 13, 1911.

2. In 1935 Mandel said: "To succeed in Parliament, you must not be preoccupied solely with big problems, no matter how important and pressing they may be. You must, above all, pay attention to men and enjoy influencing them; you must love politics, its intrigues and plots. Those journalists who criticize politics are a bit naive, because there will always be politics as long as there are men. Under kings, under dictators, under tyrants it takes different forms. But it is always there, and I see no way of getting rid of politics, even supposing that it might be good to do so, which seems far from proved." *Le Cri du Jour*, March 9, 1935, p. 8.

3. For a description of the psychology of the moderates, see Abel Bonnard, *Les modérés* (Paris, 1936).

4. Albert Thibaudet, *Les idées politiques de la France* (Paris, 1932), pp. 147-50. Favreau, pp. 38-39, while noting the moderate, Orleanist aspects of Mandel's thought, also places him in the authoritarian Radical tradition of Clemenceau.

5. Interview with Albert Bayet. Mandel's assistant Pierre Lafue has written of him: "Better than anyone else in our time, he embodied the double tradition of Jacobinism and of the centralizing kings, who always affirmed the primacy of politics over economics." *Sud-Ouest* (Bordeaux), July 7, 1954.

6. Quoted in Edmond Michelet, *Le gaullisme, passionnante aventure* (Paris, 1962), pp. 80-81.

7. Charles de Gaulle, *Le fil de l'épée* (Paris, 1944), p. 69.

8. Spears, II, 229-30.

9. *Ibid.*, 276.

10. Noel, pp. 244-48.

11. Roger Priouret, *La république des députés* (Paris, 1959), p. 47.

12. Bois, p. 291.

13. *L'Ordre*, March 4, 1945.

14. *Ibid.*, March 6, 1945.

15. Mandel's almost illegible handwriting and the blood stains on the sheet of paper make it extremely difficult to decipher. For a picture of the note, see Wormser, *Mandel,* photo facing p. 156, and *Point de Vue*, July 5, 1945. Part of the version above appeared in *Point de Vue*; the rest was transcribed for me from the original by Madame Bretty.

16. Speech by Blum on July 8, 1946, *L'Epoque*, July 9, 1946. In a speech on July 7, 1948 Blum said that in 1940 "all of us . . . recognized him as the leader he truly was, a leader whom circumstances prevented from showing what he was capable of. . . ." *Georges Mandel: Anniversaire 1948*, p. 10. For the opinion of former adversaries, see the remarks of Vichy Minister of Justice Maurice Gabolde, "Problems of the Judicial System," *FDGO*, II, 606, and of the right-wing journalist Louis-Georges Planes, a follower of Pétain, who devoted a chapter of his unpublished memoirs to Mandel and concluded it by asking: "In the interest of France, should it be regretted that his political career ended so prematurely? Taking everything into consideration, I believe so. . . . Mandel had a cold, lucid and vigorous political mind, which would have been of great service to liberated France." "Mes rencontres" (MS).

Bibliography

The Bibliography is divided into four parts. The first is an alphabetical list of all the important books and articles on Georges Mandel, including some of the more significant newspaper articles. The second is a list of newspapers and journals of special interest for a study of Mandel. The third is an alphabetical list of other books, articles, memoirs, reports, and theses important for a study of Mandel or frequently cited in the notes. (Full bibliographical information for works referred to only once or twice is to be found in the notes in which they occur.) The fourth part is a list of interviews.

BOOKS AND ARTICLES ON MANDEL

Aron, Robert. "Le destin tragique et l'assassinat de Georges Mandel," *Le Monde et la Vie*, Dec. 1960, pp. 60–65. Reprinted as "L'Assassinat de Georges Mandel" in *Les grands dossiers de l'histoire contemporaine*. Paris, 1964, pp. 67–92.

[Bainville, Jacques]. "Georges Mandel," *Revue Universelle*, Dec. 1, 1920, pp. 661–65. Reprinted under the same title in *Ceux qui nous mènent*. Paris, 1922.

[Bührer, Jules]. *Aux heures tragiques de l'Empire, 1938–1941*. Paris, 1947.

Buré, Emile. *Georges Clemenceau et Georges Mandel*. Conférence prononcée à New York, Philadelphia et Baltimore entre 1943 et 1944. Paris, 1946.

——. "Georges Mandel, dernier parlementaire de grand style," *Je Suis Partout*, October 21, 1933.

"Carnets de Captivité." See Stibio.

Coblentz, Paul. *Georges Mandel*. Paris, 1946.

Crozat, Jacques. "Une année au Portalet avec les cinq prisonniers de Vichy. Blum, Mandel, Daladier et Gamelin vus par le médecin qui les assista." *Le Figaro Littéraire*, October 12, 1957, pp. 1, 7.

Daudet, Léon. "Un tribun: Georges Mandel," *L'Action Française*, March 2, 1924.

Fabre-Luce, Alfred. "Conversation avec M. Georges Mandel," *Le Pamphlet*, March 17, 1933, pp. 15–16.

Favreau, B. *Georges Mandel, un Clémenciste en Gironde*. Paris, 1969.

Fayard, Jean. "Georges Mandel, le juge," *Candide*, March 8, 1934.

Fournol, Etienne. "Georges Mandel," in *Le moderne Plutarque, ou les hommes illustres de la Troisième République*. Paris, 1923, pp. 87–108. Also published in *Revue Politique et Littéraire*, April 16, 1921, pp. 244–48.

Georges Mandel: Anniversaire 1948. Paris, n.d. Speeches by Blum, Reynaud, and others at dedication of a plaque to Mandel on July 7, 1948.

Henriot, Philippe. "Mandel," *La Liberté du Sud-Ouest* (Bordeaux), May 8, 1924.

Henry, Charles. "M. Georges Mandel, homme d'état," *Correspondance d'Orient*, August 1938, pp. 353–55.

Ignotus (Georges Suarez?). "Georges Mandel," *Revue de Paris*, Feb. 1, 1936, pp. 500–514.

————. "Georges Mandel," *Revue de Paris*, Jan. 15, 1940, pp. 203–12.
Lafue, Pierre. "Le dialogue Tardieu-Mandel," *1935*, June 26, 1935.
————. "Georges Mandel," *La Tribune des Nations*, July 25, 1935.
Louis-Jaray, Gabriel. *Georges Mandel*. Paris, 1940.
"M. Mandel ou le pactole médocain," *Les Annales Politiques et Littéraires*, Sept. 8, 1933, pp. 268–69.
Martet, Jean. "Avec Georges Clemenceau," *Les Annales Politiques et Littéraires*, Dec. 15, 1929, pp. 547–55.
Noel, Geneviève. " 'Souvenirs' de Georges Mandel" in *La mort étrange de la Troisième République*. Paris, 1960, pp. 235–52. Anonymous account of conversations between Mandel and a friend in 1942.
Oulmont, Charles. "Entretiens avec M. Mandel sur la radiodiffusion," *Revue Politique et Littéraire*, Feb. 15, 1936, pp. 132–33.
Philip, Jean. "Les idées de M. Mandel," *La France Active*, May/June/July 1939, pp. 13–26.
————. "Souvenirs," *La France Active*, July/Aug. 1935, pp. 20–29; Sept./Oct. 1935, pp. 17–31.
Roques, Philippe, and Marguerite Donnadieu. *L'Empire français*. Paris, 1940.
Sanvoisin, Gaetan. "Prologue aux élections: la politique de Mandel," *Revue Hebdomadaire*, April 1932, pp. 157–70.
Sarraut, Albert. "Georges Mandel." Speech before the Société historique d'Auteuil et de Passy, March 4, 1957 (Mimeographed).
Stibio, André, ed. "Les carnets de captivité de Georges Mandel," *L'Ordre*, Feb. 21–March 4, 1945.
Syndicat national des agents des PTT. *M. Mandel, ministre de la Troisième République et des PTT*. Paris, 1936.
Truc, Louis. "Comment le juif Mandel assassina *l'Ami du Peuple*," *Je Suis Partout*, Jan. 28, 1944.
Varenne, Francis. *Mon patron, Georges Mandel*. Paris, 1948.
————. "Une célèbre collaboration: Georges Clemenceau, Georges Mandel," *Miroir de l'Histoire*. Feb. 1953, pp. 73–80.
————. "Si Georges Mandel était présent," *La Revue Politique et Parlementaire*, April 1954, pp. 16–26.
————. "Souvenirs sur Georges Mandel," *Oeuvres libres* (1945), No. 228, pp. 181–220.
Villette, Pierre. "Georges Mandel, orateur politique," *L'Opinion*, March 7, 1924.
Williams, Wythe. "The Tiger's Cub," *Europe*, March 3, 1936, pp. 10–11.
Wormser, Georges. *Georges Mandel: l'homme politique*. Paris, 1967.

NEWSPAPERS AND JOURNALS OF SPECIAL INTEREST
FOR A STUDY OF MANDEL

1. *Those for which he either wrote or helped set editorial policy*

Le Siècle	7 articles: Aug. 29, Sept. 6, Oct. 22, Dec. 11, 1902; Jan. 1, 16, June 11, 1903.
L'Aurore	162 signed articles of various length; some are mere reports, but many are long analytical pieces: from Nov. 2, 1903 to May 5, 1906.
Le Journal du Var (Toulon)	52 long analytical articles: from May 21, 1910 to March 28, 1911 and from Sept. 13 to Dec. 7, 1912.

L'Homme Libre	55 relatively brief articles: from May 7, 1913 to Aug. 24, 1914.
L'Echo National	From Jan. 10, 1922 to May 15, 1924. Mandel did not personally write for this paper, but he publicly assumed responsibility for everything which appeared in it.
Revue Hebdomadaire	"Pour sauver l'Alsace," Oct. 4, 1924, pp. 103–11. "Et les promesses électorales," Oct. 25, 1924, pp. 474–84. "Au carrefour de deux politiques," Dec. 20, 1924, pp. 344–56. "A l'instar d'Ugolin," Jan. 17, 1925, pp. 299–309. "Rappel aux principes," Feb. 21, 1925, pp. 358–68. "Le grand syndicat des mécontents," April 18, 1925, pp. 348-57. "Pour sortir du gâchis," Oct. 24, 1925, pp. 446–56. "La philosophie de Locarno," Nov. 14, 1925, pp. 202–12. "Cartel = Ignorance," Jan. 9, 1926, pp. 207–21.
Candide	20 articles: from Jan. 3 to July 18, 1929.
1933	7 articles: from Oct. to Dec. 1933.
1934	7 articles: Jan.–Feb. 1934.
L'Ami du Peuple	320 editorials, signed A.P. These were written by Pierre Lafue at Mandel's direction. From Sept. 18, 1936 to Oct. 30, 1937.

2. *Those consulted on various phases of his career*

The dates indicate the period for which the journal was consulted methodically. Weeklies were consulted almost every week of the years given; dailies were consulted for the days immediately surrounding the principal events of Mandel's career.

A. *Newspapers from the Bordeaux Region*

L'Action Médocaine	(1924–40) Mandel's local newspaper in Lesparre.
La Concentration Républicaine	(1928–32) Center weekly.
Le Cri Populaire	(1918–24) Journal d'union socialiste et ouvrière.
La France de Bordeaux et du Sud-Ouest	(1919–40) Radical-Socialist daily.
Les Girondins	(1919) Center weekly opposed to Mandel.
Le Journal du Médoc	(1919–41) Center weekly.
La Liberté du Sud-Ouest	(1919–40) Catholic daily.
La Petite Gironde	(1919–40) Center daily.
Le Petit Médocain	(1919–40) In 1927 became *Le Démocrate et Petit Médocain*. Radical-Socialist weekly.
Le Rappel Girondin	(1931–36) Center weekly.
Le Républicain	(1923–32) Center weekly.
Le Réveil Médocain	(1919–34) Mandel gained control of this newspaper in 1924. Except for the title, it was an exact reproduction of the *Action Médocaine*.

B. *Paris Newspapers*

The names are those of writers who expressed a particular interest in Mandel's career.

L'Action Française	(1919–40) Léon Daudet
L'Alliance Démocratique	(1934–39) Official organ of the Alliance Démocratique

Aux Ecoutes	(1918–40) Paul Lévy.
Le Canard Enchaîné	(1931–40)
Candide	(1928–44) Jacques Bainville
Le Courrier du Parlement	(1910)
Le Cri du Jour	(1934–39) Louis Thomas
L'Echo de Paris	(1924–38) Henri de Kérillis
Gringoire	(1928–44)
Les Hommes du Jour	(1919)
L'Humanité	(1919–39)
Je Suis Partout	(1930–44) Pierre Gaxotte
La Liberté	(1924–40)
La Lumière	(1931–40) François Albert and Georges Gombault
Marianne	(1932–40)
1933, 1934, 1935	(1933–35) Pierre Lafue
La Nation	(1928–39) Organ of the Fédération Républicaine de France (Louis Marin)
L'Oeil de Paris	(1928–32) François Albert
L'Oeuvre	(1919–40)
L'Ordre	(1929–40) Emile Buré
Les Pavés de Paris	(1938–39) Emmanuel Berl
Le Populaire	(1924–40)
Le Progrès Civique	(1919–24) François Albert
La République Démocratique	(1921–23) Official organ of Le Parti Républicain, Démocratique et Social (Alliance Démocratique)
Revue Politique et Parlementaire	(1919–24; 1928–1939)
Le Ralliement des PTT	(1934–35)
Le Temps	(1919–40)
La Tribune des Fonctionnaires	(1934–36)

3. Selected list of works consulted

Abensour, Léon. *Clemenceau intime: souvenirs de son ancien secrétaire.* Paris, 1928.

Abetz, Otto. *D'Une prison.* Paris, 1950.

———. *Histoire d'une politique Franco-Allemande, 1930–1950.* Paris, 1953.

Allard, Paul. *Les favorites de la Troisième République.* Paris, 1942.

Amouroux, Henri. *Le 18 juin 1940.* Paris, 1964.

Annales (Annales de la Chambre de Deputés). See France.

Annales du Sénat. See France.

Aragon, Louis. *Les communistes.* 6 vols. Paris, 1949–51.

Aron, Robert. *France Reborn: The History of the Liberation, June 1944–May 1945.* New York, 1964.

———. *L'Histoire de Vichy, 1940–1944.* Paris, 1954.

Aubert, Louis, et al. *André Tardieu.* Paris, 1957.

Auvade, Robert. *Bibliographie critique des oeuvres parues sur l'Indochine française.* Paris, 1965.

Bailby, Léon. *Pourquoi je me suis battu.* Paris, 1951.

Bankwitz, Philip C. F. *Maxime Weygand and Civil-Military Relations in Modern France.* Cambridge, Mass., 1967.

————. "Maxime Weygand and the Fall of France: A Study in Civil-Military Relations," *Journal of Modern History*, XXI (Sept. 1959), pp. 225–42.

Baraduc, Jacques. *Tout ce qu'on vous a caché.* Paris, 1949.

Bardoux, Jacques. *La délivrance de Paris.* Paris, 1958.

————. *Journal d'un témoin de la Troisième.* Paris, 1957.

Barlone, Daniel. *A French Officer's Diary, 23 Aug.–1 Oct. 1940.* New York, 1943.

Barthe, Edouard. *La ténébreuse affaire du "Massilia": Une page d'histoire (18 juin 1940–octobre 1940).* Paris, 1945.

Baudouin, Paul. *The Private Diaries of Paul Baudouin.* London, 1948.

Beau de Loménie, Emmanuel. *La mort de la Troisième République.* Paris, 1951.

————. *Les responsabilités des dynasties bourgeoises.* Vols. III, IV. Paris, 1954–63.

Beer, Max. *La guerre n'a pas eu lieu.* New York, 1941.

Benda, Julien. *La jeunesse d'un clerc.* Paris, 1936.

Benoist, Charles. *Souvenirs.* 3 vols. Paris, 1932–34.

Benoist-Méchin, Jacques. *Soixante jours qui ébranlèrent l'occident, 10 mai–10 juillet, 1940.* 3 vols. Paris, 1956.

Berger, Marcel, and Paul Allard. *Les secrets de la censure pendant la guerre.* Paris, 1932.

————. *Les dessous du Traité de Versailles.* Paris, 1933.

Berl, Emmanuel. *La fin de la IIIᵉ République.* Paris, 1968.

Bibliothèque du Centre de Documentation Juive Contemporaine. Catalogue No. 1. *La France de l'Affaire Dreyfus à nos jours.* Paris, 1964.

Binion, Rudolph. *Defeated Leaders: The Political Fate of Caillaux, Jouvenel and Tardieu.* New York, 1960.

Bleustein-Blanchet, Marcel. *Sur mon antenne.* Paris, 1947.

Blum, Léon. *L'Oeuvre de Léon Blum.* Vol. V. *1940–45. Mémoires. La prison et le procès. A l'échelle humaine.* Paris, 1955.

————. *Souvenirs sur l'Affaire.* Paris, 1935.

Bois, Elie J. *Truth on the Tragedy of France.* London, 1941.

Bonnefous, Georges and Edouard. *Histoire politique de la Troisième République.* 7 vols. Paris, 1956–67.

Bonnet, Georges. *Défense de la paix.* 2 vols. Geneva, 1946–48.

————. *Le Quai d'Orsay sous trois républiques, 1870–1961.* Paris, 1961.

Brasillach, Robert. *Journal d'un homme occupé.* Paris, 1955.

Bret, Paul-Louis. *Au feu des événements: mémoires d'un journaliste, Londres-Alger, 1929–1944.* Paris, 1959.

Brinon, Fernand de. *Mémoires.* Paris, 1949.

Brissaud, André. *La dernière année de Vichy, 1943–1944.* Paris, 1965.

Brower, Daniel R. *The New Jacobins: The French Communist Party and the Popular Front.* Ithaca, N.Y., 1968.

Bruckberger, Raymond. *Nous n'irons plus au bois.* Paris, 1948.

Buell, Raymond L. *Contemporary French Politics.* New York, 1920.

Byrnes, Robert F. *Antisemitism in Modern France.* New Brunswick, N.J., 1950.

Caillaux, Joseph. *Mes mémoires.* 3 vols. Paris, 1942–47.

Cambon, Paul. *Correspondance, 1870–1924.* Vol. III, Paris, 1946.

Campbell, Peter. *French Electoral Systems and Elections, 1789–1957.* London, 1958.

Cárcano, Miguel Angel. *Victoria sin alas.* Buenos Aires, 1949.

Cardinne-Petit, Roger. *Les soirées du "Continental." Ce que j'ai vu à la censure, 1939–1940.* Paris, 1942.

Catroux, Georges. *Deux actes du drame indochinois*. Paris, 1959.

Champeaux, Georges. *La croisade des démocraties*. 2 vols. Paris, 1941–44.

Chapman, Guy. *Why France Collapsed*. London, 1968.

Charpentier, Jacques. *Au service de la liberté*. Paris, 1949.

Chastenet, Jacques. *Histoire de la Troisième République*. Vols. V, VI, VII. Paris, 1960–63.

Chautemps, Camille. *Cahiers secrets de l'armistice, 1939–1940*. Paris, 1963.

Chichet, Etienne. *Feuilles volantes*. Paris, 1935.

Churchill, Winston S. *The Second World War*. Vols. I, II. Boston, 1948–49.

Colton, Joel. *Léon Blum: Humanist in Politics*. New York, 1966.

La Commission Stavisky. See *Rapport general* . . . .

Corday, Michel. *L'Envers de la guerre: journal inédit, 1914–1918*. 2 vols. Paris, 1932.

Cornilleau, Robert. *Du Bloc national au Front populaire*. Paris, 1939.

Coston, Henry. *Dans les coulisses de la République: ministres, préfets, et policiers, agents d'exécution de la dictature maçonnique*. Paris, 1944.

———, ed., *Dictionnaire de la politique française*. Paris, 1967.

———, ed., *Partis, journaux et hommes politiques d'hier et d'aujourd'hui*. Paris, 1960.

Daudet, Léon. *L'Agonie du régime*. Paris, 1925.

———. *La Chambre nationale du 16 novembre*. Paris, 1923.

———. *Député de Paris, 1919–1924*. Paris, 1933.

———. *Moloch et Minerve ou l'après-guerre*. Paris, 1924.

———. *Paris vécu: rive gauche*. Paris, 1930.

Debû-Bridel, Jacques. *L'Agonie de la Troisième République, 1929–1939*. Paris, 1949.

de Gaulle, Charles. *War Memoirs*. 5 vols. London, 1955–60.

De Jong, Louis. *The German Fifth Column in the Second World War*. London, 1956.

Delattre, Gabriel. "Le journal de bord du *Massilia*," *L'Aurore*, Oct. 3–10, 1944.

Delperrie de Bayac, Jacques. *Histoire de la Milice, 1918–1945*. Paris, 1969.

Del Vayo, Julio Alvarez. *The Last Optimist*. New York, 1950.

Desgranges, Jean. *Journal d'un prêtre député, 1936–1940*. Paris, 1960.

Dillon, Eric Fitzgerald. *Memories of Three Wars*. London, 1951.

Duff Cooper, Alfred. *Old Men Forget*. London, 1953.

Duverger, Maurice. *La démocratie sans le peuple*. Paris, 1967.

Ehrenburg, Ilya. *Men, Years, Life*. 4 vols. London, 1962–63.

Eubank, Keith. *Munich*. Norman, Okla., 1963.

Les Evénements. See France. Assemblée Nationale.

Fabre-Luce, Alfred. *Histoire de la révolution européene*. Paris, 1954.

———. *Histoire secrète de la conciliation de Munich*. Paris, 1938.

———. *Journal de la France, mars 1939–juillet 1944*. 2 vols. Geneva, 1946.

———. *Vingt-cinq années de liberté*. 3 vols. Paris, 1961–64.

Fabry, Jean. *De la Place de la Concorde au Cours de l'Intendance: février 1934–juin 1940*. Paris, 1942.

Ferry, Abel. *Les carnets secrets d'Abel Ferry (1914–1918)*. Paris, 1957.

Fischer, Jacques. *Doumergue et les politiciens*. Paris, 1935.

Flandin, Pierre-Etienne. *Politique française, 1919–1940*. Paris, 1947.

———. *Le procès Flandin devant la Haute Cour de Justice, 23–26 juillet 1946*. Paris, 1947.

France. *Annales de la Chambre des Députés. Débats parlementaires*.

France. *Annales du Sénat. Débats parlementaires*.

France. Assemblée Nationale. *Rapport fait au nom de la commission d'enquête sur les événements survenus en France de 1933 à 1945.* Par M. Charles Serre. 9 vols. Paris, 1951.

Frossard, Ludovic-Oscar. "Les carnets de L.-O. Frossard," *L'Aurore*, Feb. 4–16, 1949.

Funk, Arthur Layton. *Charles de Gaulle: The Crucial Years, 1943–1944.* Norman, Okla., 1959.

Galtier-Boissière, Jean. "Histoire de la guerre, 1939–1945," *Crapouillot*, Nos. 1–5 (1948).

Gamelin, Maurice. *Servir.* 3 vols. Paris, 1946–47.

Garçon, Maurice. *Histoire de la justice sous la Troisième République.* 3 vols. Paris, 1957.

Gatineau-Clemenceau, Georges. *Des pattes du Tigre aux griffes du destin.* Paris, 1961.

Gheusi, Pierre B. *Cinquante ans de Paris.* 4 vols. Paris, 1939–42.

Ghilini, Hector. *A la barre de Riom.* Paris, 1942.

Gicquel, Jean, and Lucien Sfez. *Problèmes de la réforme de l'état en France depuis 1934.* Paris, 1965.

Goguel, François. "L'Influence des systèmes électoraux sur la vie politique d'après l'expérience française," in *L'Influence des systèmes électoraux sur la vie politique.* Paris, 1950.

———. *La politique des partis sous la Troisième République,* 3d ed. Paris, 1958.

Graux, Lucien. *Les fausses nouvelles de la grande guerre.* 7 vols. Paris, 1916–20.

Greene, Nathanael. *Crisis and Decline: The French Socialist Party in the Popular Front Era.* Ithaca, N.Y., 1969.

Groussard, Georges A. *Service secret, 1940–1945.* Paris, 1964.

Guariglia, Raffaele. *Ricordi.* Naples, 1950.

Guerdan, Léon. *Je les ai tous connus.* New York, 1942.

Guérin, Jean and Bernard, eds. *Des hommes et des activités autour d'un demi-siècle (à Bordeaux).* Bordeaux, 1957.

Gurvitch, Georges. "Social Structure of Pre-War France," *The American Journal of Sociology*, Vol. XLVIII (March 1943), pp. 535–54.

Henriot, Philippe. *Comment mourut la paix: le procès des responsables.* Paris, 1941.

Herriot, Edouard. *Episodes, 1940–1944.* Paris, 1950.

———. *Jadis:* Vol. II, *D'une guerre à l'autre, 1914–1936.* Paris, 1952.

Hilberg, Raul. *The Destruction of the European Jews.* Chicago, 1961.

Horne, Alistair. *To Lose a Battle: France, 1940.* London, 1969.

Huc, Benjamin, and François Robin. *Histoire et dessous de la radio en France et dans le monde.* Paris, 1938.

Hytier, Adrienne Doris. *Two Years of French Foreign Policy: Vichy, 1940–1942.* Geneva, 1958.

Isorni, Jacques. *C'est un péché de la France.* Paris, 1962.

———. *Souffrance et mort du Maréchal.* Paris, 1951.

Jardillier, Robert. "Mes crimes," *La Bourgogne Républicaine* (Dijon), June 20–Aug. 23, 1938.

Jones, Emrys. *The Shame of Vichy.* London, 1941.

Jouhandeau, Marcel. *Le péril juif.* Paris, 1939.

Kammerer, Albert. *La vérité sur l'armistice.* Paris, 2d ed., 1945.

Kérillis, Henri de. *Français, voici la vérité!* New York, 1942.

———. *I Accuse de Gaulle.* New York, 1946.

———. *Laisserons-nous démembrer la France?* Paris, 1939.

———, and Raymond Cartier. *Faisons le point.* Paris, 1931.

Lachapelle, Georges. *Elections législatives du 16 novembre 1919.* Paris, 1920.

372   *Bibliography*

———. *Elections législatives du 11 mai 1924*. Paris, 1924.
Lacotte, Eugène. *Dessous des cartes*. Paris, 1929.
Lamoureux, Lucien. "Mémoires," *Le Bourbonnais Républicain* (Allier), 1952–56.
Langer, William L. *Our Vichy Gamble*. New York, 1947.
Langeron, Roger. *Paris, juin 40*. Paris, 1946.
Larmour, Peter J. *The French Radical Party in the 1930's*. Stanford, 1964.
Laubreaux, Alain. *Ecrit pendant la guerre*. Paris, 1944.
Laval, Pierre. *The Unpublished Diary of Pierre Laval*. London, 1948.
Lazareff, Pierre. *Deadline*. New York, 1942.
———. *De Munich à Vichy*. New York, 1944.
Lebrun, Albert. *Témoignage*. Paris, 1946.
Lefranc, Georges. *Les expériences syndicales en France de 1939 à 1950*. Paris, 1950.
———. *Histoire du Front populaire, 1934–1938*. Paris, 1965.
Lesca, Charles. *Quand Israël se venge*. Paris, 1941.
Lévy, Louis. *The Truth about France*. Harmondsworth, Middlesex, 1941.
Lévy, Roger, ed. *French Interests and Policies in the Far East*. New York, 1941.
Livois, René de. *Histoire de la presse française*. 2 vols. Lausanne, 1965.
Mallet, Alfred. *Pierre Laval*. 2 vols. Paris, 1954.
Marcellin, Louis. *Politique et politiciens*. 4 vols. Paris, n.d.
Marrus, Michael R. "The Politics of Assimilation: A Study of the French Jewish Community at the Time of the Dreyfus Affair." Unpublished doctoral dissertation, University of California, Berkeley, 1968.
Martet, Jean. *Georges Clemenceau*. New York, 1930.
Maurras, Charles. *La seule France*. N.p., 1941.
Mayer, Arno. *Politics and Diplomacy of Peacemaking: Containment and Counterrevolution at Versailles, 1918–1919*. New York, 1967.
Melville, Cecil F. *Guilty Frenchmen*. London, 1940.
Memmi, Albert. *Portrait of a Jew*. New York, 1962.
Mendès-France, Pierre. *The Pursuit of Freedom*. London, 1956.
Micaud, Charles A. *The French Right and Nazi Germany, 1933–1939: A Study of Public Opinion*. New York, 1943.
Michel, Henri. *Bibliographie critique de la résistance*. Paris, 1964.
Michon, Georges. *Clemenceau*. Paris, 1931.
"Ministère public c/MM. Boéro, Néroni et Lambert (Assassins de M. Georges Mandel). Cour de justice. Audience du 25 octobre 1944. Débats complets." Lyon-Paris: R. Bluet, 1945. A typescript of this trial can be found at the Bibliothèque de Documentation Internationale Contemporaine (Q 182 Rés.).
Miquel, Pierre. *Poincaré*. Paris, 1961.
Montigny, Jean. *Le complot contre la paix, 1935–1939*. Paris, 1966.
———. *Les heures tragiques de 1940*. Paris, 1941.
———. *Toute la vérité sur un mois dramatique de notre histoire: ... 15 juin–15 juillet 1940*. Clermont-Ferrand, 1940.
Monzie, Anatole de. *Ci-devant*. Paris, 1941.
Mordacq. Jean J. H. *Clemenceau au soir de sa vie, 1920–1929*. 2 vols. Paris, 1933.
———. *Le ministère Clemenceau: journal d'un temoin*. 4 vols. Paris, 1930.
Morice, Charles. "Quarante ans de journalisme: presse et parlement, souvenirs et anecdotes." 4 vols. MS memoirs in Bibliothèque Nationale.
Moulin de Labarthète, Henri du. *Le temps des illusions*. Geneva, 1946.
Noguères, Henri. *Munich or the Phoney Peace*. London, 1965.

Noguères, Louis. *Le véritable procès du Maréchal Pétain.* Paris, 1955.

Noguès, Auguste. "Le procès du Général Noguès, 23-26 octobre 1956." Typescript copy.

Oberg, Karl. "Le procès de Karl Oberg et de Helmut Knochen devant le Tribunal Militaire de Paris." Sept.–Oct. 1954. Typescript copy available at the Centre de Documentation Juive Contemporaine.

Pannetier, Odette. *Quand j'étais Candide.* Paris, 1948.

Paul-Boncour, Joseph. *Entre deux guerres.* 3 vols. Paris, 1946.

Péladeau, Paul. *On disait en France.* Montreal, 1941.

Pertinax (André Géraud). *The Gravediggers of France.* New York, 1944.

Pétain, Philippe. *Le procès du Maréchal Pétain.* 2 vols. Paris, 1945.

———. *Quatre années au pouvoir.* Paris, 1949.

Pierrefeux, Guy de. *Le revenant: propos et anecdotes autour de Caillaux.* Strasbourg, 1925.

Planes, Louis-Georges. "Mes rencontres." MS memoirs.

———, and Robert Dufourg. *Bordeaux, capitale tragique et la base navale de Bordeaux–Le Verdon, mai–juin 1940* (Paris, 1956).

Poincaré, Raymond. *Au service de la France.* 10 vols. Paris, 1926–1933.

Pol, Heinz. *Suicide of a Democracy.* New York, 1940.

Prévost, Jean. *Histoire de France depuis la guerre.* Paris, 1932.

Privat, Maurice. *La commission d'enquête.* Paris, 1931.

———. *Les heures d'André Tardieu et la crise des partis.* Paris, 1930.

———. *Oustric et cie.* Paris, 1931.

———. *Pierre Laval.* Paris, n.d.

———. *Pierre Laval, cet inconnu.* Paris, 1948.

"Le procès de Boéro, Nèroni et Lambert." See "Ministère Public . . . ."

Le procès Flandin. See Flandin.

"Le procès du Général Noguès." See Noguès.

"Le procès de Karl Oberg et de Helmut Knochen." See Oberg.

Le procès du Maréchal Pétain. See Pétain; see also Louis Noguères.

Le procès de Riom. See Ribet.

Le procès de Xavier Vallat. See Vallat.

Les procès de collaboration (Brinon, Darnand, Luchaire). Paris, 1948.

Puységur, Armand de. *Qu'était le juif avant la guerre? Tout. Que doit-il être? Rien.* Paris, 1942.

Rapport général fait au nom de la commission d'enquête chargée de rechercher toutes les responsabilités encourues depuis l'origine des affaires Stavisky, par Ernest Lafont. *Annexes (dépositions).* 6 vols. Paris, 1935.

Rebatet, Lucien. *Les décombres.* Paris, 1942.

Révillon, Tony. *Mes carnets, juin–octobre 1940.* Paris, 1945.

Reynaud, Paul. *Au coeur de la mêlée.* Paris, 1951.

———. *La France a sauvé l'Europe.* 2 vols. Paris, 1947.

———. *In the Thick of the Fight.* New York, 1955.

———. *Mémoires.* 2 vols. Paris, 1960–1963.

Ribet, Maurice. *Le procès de Riom.* Paris, 1945.

Ribot, Alexandre. *Journal d'Alexandre Ribot et correspondances inédites, 1914–22.* Paris, 1936.

Robinson, Jacob, and Philip Friedman. *Guide to Jewish History under Nazi Impact.* New York, 1960.

Roche, Emile. *Caillaux que j'ai connu.* Paris, 1949.

Rossi, Angelo. *Les communistes français pendant la drôle de guerre: une page d'histoire.* Paris, 1951.

Saint Jean, Robert de. *France Speaking.* New York, 1941.

Schlesinger, Mildred S. "The French Radical Party: Its Organization and Parliamentary Politics, 1914–1932." Unpublished doctoral dissertation, Yale University, 1961.

Shirer, William L. *The Collapse of the Third Republic: An Inquiry into the Fall of France in 1940.* New York, 1969.

Simone, André (Otto Katz). *J'Accuse.* New York, 1940.

Soulié, Michel. *La vie politique d'Edouard Herriot.* Paris, 1962.

Soulier, Edouard. *Le Bloc national républicain.* Paris, 1924.

Soupiron, Paul. *Bazaine contre Gambetta, ou le procès de Riom.* Lyons, 1944.

Spears, Edward L. *Assignment to Catastrophe.* 2 vols. London, 1954.

Stavisky Commission. See *Rapport general* ....

Stéphane, Roger. *Chaque homme est lié au monde.* Paris, 1946.

Stibio, André. *Indiscrétions.* Paris, 1951.

Suarez, Georges. *Briand.* 6 vols. Paris, 1938–1952.

———. *Nos seigneurs et maîtres.* Paris, 1937.

———, and Guy Laborde. *L'Agonie de la paix, 1935–1939.* Paris, 1942.

Szajkowski, Zosa. *Analytical Franco-Jewish Gazetteer, 1939–1945.* New York, 1966.

Tabouis, Geneviève. *They Called Me Cassandra.* New York, 1942.

———. *Vingt ans de "suspense" diplomatique.* Paris, 1958.

Taittinger, Pierre. *Et Paris ne fut pas détruit.* Paris, 1948.

Taylor, Edmond. *Strategy of Terror.* Boston, 1942.

Un Témoin (Robert Lazurick). *Les dessous de l'armistice.* Paris, 1944.

Thomas, Louis. *Histoire d'un jour.* Paris, 1939.

———, ed. *Documents sur la guerre de 1939–40.* 2 vols. Paris, 1941.

Torrès, Henry. *Pierre Laval.* New York, 1941.

———. *Campaign of Treachery.* New York, 1942.

Tracou, Jean. *Le Maréchal aux liens.* Paris, 1949.

Truchet, André. *L'Armistice de 1940 et l'Afrique du Nord.* Paris, 1955.

Vallat, Xavier. *Le nez de Cléopâtre: souvenirs d'un homme de droite, 1919–1944.* Paris, 1957.

———. *Le procès de Xavier Vallat.* Paris, 1948.

Vidalenc, Jean. *L'Exode de mai–juin 1940.* Paris, 1957.

Warner, Geoffrey. *Pierre Laval and the Eclipse of France.* London, 1968.

Weber, Eugen. *Action Française: Royalism and Reaction in Twentieth Century France.* Stanford, 1962.

Weil-Curiel, André. *Le temps de la honte.* 3 vols. Paris, 1945–1947.

Werth, Alexander. *France and Munich.* London, 1939.

———. *France in Ferment.* London, 1934.

———. *France, 1940–1955.* New York, 1956.

———. *Twilight of France.* New York, 1942.

———. *Which Way France?* New York, 1937.

Weygand, Maxime. *Recalled to Service.* New York, 1952.

Williams, John. *The Ides of May: The Defeat of France, May–June 1940.* London, 1968.

Wohl, Robert. *French Communism in the Making, 1914–1924.* Stanford, 1966.

Woodward, Sir Llewellyn. *British Foreign Policy in the Second World War.* London, 1962.

Wormser, Georges. *La république de Clemenceau.* Paris, 1961.
Wurzburg, Frederick. "The Politics of the Bloc National." Unpublished doctoral dissertation, Columbia University, 1961.
Zay, Jean. *Carnets secrets de Jean Zay.* Paris, 1942.
————. *Souvenirs et solitude.* Paris, 1945.

4. *Interviews*

These interviews were conducted between September 1959 and July 1961.

Albert Bayet
Georges Bonnet
Madame Michèle Bordenave
Madame Béatrice Bretty
Max Brusset
Général Jules Bührer
Madame Emile Buré
Julien Cain
R. P. Robert Carré
Louis Castex
General Georges Catroux
Richard Chapon
Jacques Chastenet
Edmond Claris
Michel Clemenceau
Paul Coblentz
André Coudy
Edouard Daladier
Lucien Dazat
Jacques Debû Bridel
Pierre Dignac
Jean Fayard
Emile Gellie
Roger Giron
Georges Gombault
Madame Philippe Henriot
Charles Henry
Jacques Kayser
Pierre Lafue

Lucien Lamoureux
André Laurent-Eynac
Robert Lazurick
Henri Lémery
Martial Massiani
Henri Massis
Martial Michel
Jacques Millerand
Jacques Miqueau
Jean Odin
Stefan Osusky
Joseph Paul-Boncour
Marcel Pellenc
Louis-Georges Planes
Georges Portmann
Paul Reynaud
Emile Roche
Adrien Rothschild
Albert Sarraut
André Stibio
Madame Geneviève Tabouis
Pierre Taittinger
René-William Thorp
Henry Torrès
Xavier Vallat
Francis Varenne
Paul Vigneau
Georges Wormser

Index